Christina Stead

Born in London, Hazel Rowley took an honours degree at
the University of Adelaide in French and German, and wrote
her doctoral thesis on the portrayal of self in the autobiographies of Simone de Beauvoir and Violette Leduc. She
has lived several years in France and Germany, and has been
a Visiting Scholar at Columbia University, New York, the
Sir Robert Menzies Centre for Australian Studies, London,
the Humanities Research Centre, Australian National University and the Edward A. Clark Center for Australian Studies
at the University of Texas at Austin. She now lives in
Melbourne and teaches at Deakin University.

CHRISTINA STEAD

a Biography

Hazel Rowley

Secker & Warburg
London

First published 1993
by William Heinemann Australia
First published in Great Britain 1995
by Martin Secker & Warburg Limited,
an imprint of Reed Consumer Books Limited,
Michelin House, 81 Fulham Road, London SW3 6RB
and Auckland, Melbourne, Singapore and Toronto

Copyright © 1993 by Hazel Rowley

The author has asserted her moral rights

A CIP catalogue record for this book
is available from the British Library

ISBN 0 436 20298 0

Printed and bound in Great Britain by Clays Ltd, St Ives, plc

Contents

Prologue

IT WAS THE interviews Christina Stead gave late in life that first aroused my curiosity. 'I'm a good-natured person,' she would insist. 'I don't expect anything, because I don't care. I take everything as it comes.' The façade she displays is brusque and pragmatic. ('Most children live through great tragedies and they grow up and they're just normal and ordinary, and it's good for them.') Her rhetoric is scientific—influenced, she would always say, by her naturalist father. ('When you're a little girl and you look in an aquarium and you see fish doing this and that . . . you don't criticize and say they should do something else. And that's the way in which I was brought up.')

This detached persona seems scarcely reconcilable with Stead's fiction, repeatedly described by critics as 'savage' and 'furious'. In her two autobiographical novels, *The Man Who Loved Children* and *For Love Alone*, Stead's fictional counterparts plan murder and suicide. And Stead often said she invented nothing in her fiction— neither characters nor plots. I found myself wondering about the person behind the mask.

Christina Stead left Sydney as a young woman of 26; she returned aged 72, a figure of international repute, rivalling Patrick White as the finest writer Australia has produced. Though her

Australian years were a wellspring from which she drew repeatedly, virtually the whole of Stead's writing life—46 years in all—was spent in the northern hemisphere.

No major writer of any nationality has been more truly cosmopolitan than Christina Stead, with her genius for portraying disparate locales, voices and expressions. Joyce in exile remained quintessentially Irish; D. H. Lawrence abroad, grumble as he might about his homeland, remained unmistakeably English. Stead was Australian in the sense that restlessness and travel are an Australian tradition. And yet, as an Australian expatriate who set her novels in Europe, New York and the north of England, she was rejected by her compatriots as 'un-Australian'—a parochial defensiveness that endured until the late sixties.

Culturally, Christina Stead was as adaptable as a chameleon. Perhaps it is no coincidence that her generation witnessed dramatic change. She was a child of the Edwardian era and came to maturity during that period of cataclysmic change straight after the Great War, before radio and jet travel transformed communications. Like other progressives in her generation, she firmly believed that the sexual liberation of women would bring about major social transformation, and that revolutionary Russia was the world's great hope.

She arrived in England in 1928. Wall Street crashed the following year. The movements of Stead and her companion Bill Blake would reflect those of a tide of expatriates. They were in Paris at the same time as James Joyce and Gertrude Stein, the doyens of 'modernism'. They were in the United States when John Steinbeck's *The Grapes of Wrath* was celebrated as the great proletarian novel. When leftwing solidarity gave way to the Second World War and its tragic aftermath, the Cold War, Stead and Blake fled McCarthyist America for Europe. But the atmosphere there had changed too: the ideals of a generation had been shattered. Stead's fiction, set in three continents, expresses and takes issue with the cultural and political values of the times.

Wherever she was, Stead's internal baggage went with her, but its dead weight was something she hid from others. 'Why does anyone want to know about the life of a writer?' she once asked defensively. 'The writer is usually engaged in telling the story of other people's lives.'[1] Her curiosity about other people was unquenchable. She was fascinated by ordinary lives and the extraordinary passions that propelled them along. But she was the least reliable of sources when it came to her own life. She avoided introspection and detested self-revelation. In later life, she destroyed all the drafts of her manuscripts and most of her private papers, diaries and intimate correspondence. She hated being photographed; the few photographs that exist convey a mask-like inscrutability. Her clothes, adorned as they were with frills and ruffles, were a kind of disguise, an attempt to hide her inner self. Even passages in her private diaries are written in code.

Stead would sometimes say that she had no need to write an autobiography; she had already written it in her books. But her fiction is transmuted reality. Her obvious *alter egos*, Louisa, Teresa, Lydia, Persia, Laura—all with names ending in *a*, like Christina—are idealised Christinas. None of *them* is hanging in Stead's notorious gallery of fictional monsters. Those all have other models, but just like Victor Frankenstein's creation, Stead's monsters partly represent her own shadow side.

Nabokov once commented: 'Literature is invention. Fiction is fiction. To call a story a true story is an insult to both art and truth. Every great writer is a great deceiver.'[2]

A biography is not a life; lives cannot be recovered. No one knew better than Stead that life itself is a narrative. We are continually revising our memories and hopes, rationalising disappointments, modifying the way we present ourselves to ourselves and others. Everything we do has a hidden aspect; every incident has several versions; each moment of our lives is invisibly shaped by our unpruned, tangled past.

Turning life into story is one of humanity's enduring pleasures. Stead may not even have been aware of the paradox when she wrote: 'The true portrait of a person should be built up as a painter builds it, with hints from everyone, brush-strokes, thousands of little touches.'[3]

1

Ocean of Story

JULY 1902–AUGUST 1917

In Christina Stead's memory, her mother was a dim vision of pale skin, dark eyes, and long dark hair lying across a pillow on a high brass and lacquer bed.[1] She herself, dressed in a red twill dress, was swinging on the bedpost, singing to her mother, who had always liked her singing. It must have been morning, for the sunlight filtered through the front window of their white-washed cottage. Suddenly the nurse, an ugly old woman, told her to go away and stop annoying her mother. The little girl looked at her mother, confidently. 'Yes, go, Chrissie.'[2]

Filled with a sense of betrayal, the child left the room. She was fingering the panelling of the door, not knowing why she had been sent out, when her aunt came along: 'What are you doing there—spying?' Although she was only 2½, the child knew what was meant. Her aunt shooed her away. Seventy-seven years later, Christina Stead was still angry.[3]

But had she imagined it all? Later, the sick young woman became blurred in Stead's mind with Emma Bovary on her deathbed, where she too was visited by a frightened small daughter.[4] Did Stead really recall Sydney in the summer of 1904? Or was that darkened room actually in Yonville-L'Abbaye, a provincial town in Normandy?

Christina Stead never made much consciously of the loss of her mother, though she did once say, comparing herself to a guttercat, that she had not trusted anyone since she was about 2.[5]

After her mother's death, she became her father's special girl. 'My mother died—he mothered me.' David George Stead was a 'lively young scientist', a zoologist, brimming with stories about the marvels of the natural world and its strange inhabitants. In the evenings, with the light falling from the streetlamp through the open slats of the venetian blind and his foot on the packing-case on which his daughter slept, he would tell his tales. 'And it went on and on, night after night, for more than two years.'[6]

Among the last things Stead wrote were two tender pieces reconciling her to the 'unusually gifted man' whom she had reviled in her most famous novel, *The Man Who Loved Children*. It was her father, she acknowledged, who had taught her to swim in the 'ocean of story'.[7]

★   ★   ★

Christina Ellen Stead was third-generation Australian. She liked to think her family history was shaped by literature. In *Great Expectations*, published in 1861, the convict Magwitch is transported to Australia, where he makes his fortune in sheep. In 1862, Stead's paternal grandfather (an avid reader of Dickens) packed his bags, farewelled his family in Kent and boarded the *Hotspur* for the three-and-a-half-month voyage to Sydney. He was 16 years old.[8] Whether or not fiction played so decisive a role in Samuel Stead's destiny, Australia did offer an opportunity for hard-working tradesmen to break out of the English class system. By the time Samuel Stead came to Sydney, gold had paved the way for a boom in the Australian economy that was to last for thirty years. Samuel did not make his fortune, but he was enterprising and found employment with a firm of building contractors, later setting up his own business in North Sydney. His last family house was named after Dickens' house, Gad's Hill. Late in life he joined the Dickens Society, and as a child, Christina was occasionally taken to see her grandfather perform at socials, where he would recite from the novels, joyfully impersonating Scrooge, Nicholas Nickleby, Quilp and Fagin.

At the age of 22, in 1868, Samuel Stead married 19-year-old Christina McLaren. Scottish born, she had come to Australia as a baby with her newly widowed mother.[9] Samuel purchased a small plot of land on Walker Street, a winding street not far from the harbour in St Leonards (now North Sydney), where he built a modest two-storey weatherboard house. There Christina produced seven children by the time she was 32. One daughter, May, died in infancy, leaving three boys and three girls: Sydney, Samuel, Christina, Jessie, David and Florence.[10]

Grandfather Samuel—with twinkling eyes, moustache and a dashing dark red handkerchief—was a 'freethinker', as atheists were then called, who occasionally took snuff and enjoyed a glass of port.[11] He belonged to the Order of Odd Fellows, the oldest of the several orders of British lodges transplanted to Australia,[12] committed to ideals of brotherhood, democratic sharing of responsibility and mutual financial assistance. Modestly imitating the ritual and symbolism of Freemasonry, the Odd Fellows appealed largely to tradesmen and skilled artisans. In time, Stead took his turn for a year as Grand Noble of his local Lodge.

His wife Christina, by contrast, was a kind-faced but plain woman, with an austere, world-renouncing piety. As a member of the Plymouth Brethren, a nonconformist Protestant sect, she regarded smoking, alcohol, dancing, gambling and the theatre as vices.[13] But like the Odd Fellows, the Brethren were strongly democratic, rejecting ecclesiastical organisation on the grounds that it was a denial of the spiritual equality of all (male) believers. The younger Stead children, David and Florence, occasionally accompanied their mother to meetings. David's strong individualism may well have reflected his mother's anti-hierarchical tradition.

David George was born on 6 March 1877. He was a handsome boy, with thick yellow hair, tender blue eyes and a happy nature. According to his daughter Christina he actually shone: his 'pale blaze' came from more than just his fairness; it was a sign, she believed, of his 'vitality' and 'self-trust'. It dazzled people. If his older siblings had 'some sentimental and quite uninformed views of England', David responded to the country of his birth like Adam in Eden. 'Australia was his prolific and innocent garden.'[14]

Despite their mother's cultural sobriety, the Stead household was cheerful and musical, with frequent family singsongs around the piano. When they sang in the evenings in the front room with the lights on and the blinds up—tunes from operas and rousing old favourites like 'The Battle Cry of Freedom', 'When Johnny Comes Marching Home' and 'John Brown's Body'—passers-by would stop in the street to listen.[15]

One terrible night in the winter of 1893, their mother died of an angina attack.[16] She was 44. Only 16 years old and particularly close to his mother, David was devastated. He vowed to keep her rules of life. Christina Stead, her grandmother's namesake, recalls:

He never went to the theatre or to concerts; he abhorred
dancing, because of the contact of bodies; he did not allow
kissing or embracing in the home, nor endearments, nor
cajoling, which he thought led to degrading habits of mind . . .
He whistled very tunefully, and usually tunes from operas, but
only moral operas—*Martha, William Tell, Maritana* . . . He was
shocked that the arts so often dealt with what seemed to a pure
man, unsavoury subjects.[17]

Indeed, David George held a strange mixture of both parents'
views, and with passionate fervour. He was an atheist, like his
father, and so committed to atheism that he refused to enter a
church. Yet he was a puritan, like his mother, and just as firm about
never letting a drop of alcohol pass his lips. He had his father's good
looks and liveliness, and his mother's sureness of purpose.

All three boys left school at the age of 12. Sydney and Samuel
became painters and signwriters; David was apprenticed to the
Sydney rubber-stamp maker Karl Faulk, where he learnt to pride
himself on his decorative lettering.[18] But Nature had always been
his passion. In his late teens he attended a zoology course at Sydney
Technical College, where he boiled down and mounted a cat and a
dog that would stare at his children from glass cases. And he
became an active member of the New South Wales Naturalists'
Society, a group of committed amateurs. In 1898, at 21, he joined
the Linnean Society of New South Wales, the professional naturalists' body. By 1900 he had several short articles published by the
prestigious British Linnean Society.

* * *

David's lively younger sister Florence—who had her father's beautiful voice and taste for acting—went to work at 14 as a seamstress
in the workrooms of David Jones, the fashionable department
store. It was through Florence that David met Ellen Butters, an
embroideress, whom he married on 17 August 1901, the year
Australia was formally declared an independent nation. It was a
nation of divided loyalties—the fierce nationalism of the 1890s was
countered by cultural ties to the British Empire and Mother England. The Federal Parliament had been opened in Melbourne by the
Duke of York (later King George V), and Australian volunteers
were fighting for the Empire in the Boer War.

Twenty-five-year-old Ellen Stead, pretty, gentle and pious, also
found her loyalties divided that year. Though she came from an
ardently devout family, her wedding was not a religious service: the

24-year-old groom was adamant about that. It is thought that he even tried to forbid his wife to pray. Ellen's father, equally head-strong, banished his daughter and her new husband from the family home. Ellen's brother Duncan later claimed that she visited her mother and siblings secretly,[19] and was bewildered by the strange world into which she had married: 'snakes in the copper and creatures everywhere and she not allowed to pray'.[20]

Two months after her marriage Ellen was pregnant, and it was in their modest two-roomed cabin on Kimpton Street, Rockdale, south of the city, that Christina Ellen Stead was born on 17 July 1902, the year that Australian women gained the right to vote in federal elections. Grandfather Butters refused to speak to his daughter or look at his grandchild.[21]

In the next year or so, the family moved to Oakleigh Villa, a whitewashed house with a stone verandah and picket fence, standing alone on a rutty road leading to Rockdale station.[22] David Stead set up his menagerie in the back garden. He kept venomous black snakes, and a diamond snake, whose erratic eating habits he noted with interest.[23] However, his special interest was not snakes but fish. David Stead's expertise in this area was acknowledged by the NSW Fisheries Commission, who employed him in May 1902, although he had no formal qualifications. He was made a scientific assistant under Harold Dannevig, Director of Fisheries for the Commonwealth. That year the government printer published his article on the Murray cod.

Christina Stead liked to think she looked like her mother, but the one surviving photograph of Ellen Butters reveals little resemblance. In the solemn studio photograph, Ellen is in her early teens: a comely adolescent with docile brown eyes, full lips and a long dark plait. She is wearing a prim dress with a high neck, leg-of-mutton sleeves, and a fur collar clasped by a large, ornate brooch. A lace kerchief is tucked into her belted waist and she has a white communion book in her lap. She looks timid, submissive—the daughter of an authoritarian Victorian father.

As a child, Christina was very fair and had several of her father's features, though in her, unfortunately, they did not form the same harmonious blend. Her father was tall and strongly built. In photographs he has the air of a man who knows he is handsome. His large forehead, prominent nose and resolute chin give him a proud, self-confident bearing. His daughter had the same imperious presence.

In the family it was said that Christina looked like her father's sister Jessica—something she hated to hear, not because Jessica's appearance was unpleasing, but because she had remained an 'old maid', a fate Christina regarded with horror.

*   *   *

Ellen Butters' parents, Christina Stead's maternal grandparents, were also from the British Isles. Richard Cameron Butters, born in Ireland of Scottish parents in 1832, was an adventurer who left Ireland with his brother in the aftermath of the Great Famine for the gold diggings of California. From there, hearing about the discovery of gold in Australia, they came to New South Wales. Richard Butters was 27 when he married Mary Boote at the Scots Church in Jamison Street, Sydney on 25 April 1859.[24] The clergyman who officiated was John Dunmore Lang, the first Presbyterian minister in Australia and well known in Sydney society as a republican and polemicist. Straight after marriage, Mary, 21 and fresh from Birmingham, found herself plunged into the rigours of rural life. The couple travelled by bullock dray to Wattle Flat, near Sofala, in the heart of the western goldfields of New South Wales, and settled in a wattle-and-daub hut where Mary gave birth to ten children. Ellen, born in 1876, was the ninth.[25]

Since activity on the goldfields had waned, Richard Butters became a road contractor.[26] And in time, a warden of the church and the first Stipendiary Magistrate for the district. His downfall was his fiery temper and obstinacy. When his daughter Ellen was 4, he left the Bathurst region to fight a business legal battle in Sydney. He lost the court case, and it was in straitened circumstances that the family settled in the harbour-side district of Woolloomooloo. The Butters' children were talented, articulate and deeply religious, active in debating clubs and in the church.[27] One can imagine their consternation when Ellen married an atheist.

*   *   *

Like the rest of the Butters family, Ellen had a gift for words—her brother William became a distinguished poet[28]—but she had little opportunity to exert any influence over her daughter. Christina was 2½ when Ellen was rushed to Prince Alfred Hospital, Camperdown, with acute appendicitis. It is likely, given Stead's vague picture of her mother ill in the front bedroom, that Ellen had been ill for some time. Was Ellen pregnant again? Did she wonder whether she was being punished for ceasing to pray? After eighteen days in hospital, Ellen Stead died on 9 December 1904. At the age of 28, she was buried in the General Cemetery at Rookwood. No minister was present. The official witness of burial was her father-in-law, Samuel Stead.[29]

Ironically, some time after Ellen's death, her own father became an agnostic, moving among 'disbelievers' in Sydney's philosophical circles.[30]

Would Christina Stead have become a writer had her mother lived? In later life, she would trace her facility with language to her mother's side of the family, but this was doubtless more from a wish to deny her father's influence than from any real conviction. Had her mother survived, Christina would have been spared the trauma of early abandonment. Equally, she would have escaped the trial, occasioned by her father's remarriage, of living with a stepmother who disliked her. It seems beyond doubt that a sense of abandonment and rejection, accompanied by anger and self-loathing, were factors in her impulse to write, though one cannot know how much weight to assign them. As Freud observed, 'Before the problem of the creative artist analysis must, alas, lay down its arms.'[31]

> When my mother died I was so young that I did not miss her;
> I lived with a sprightly goodlooking pair of young people,
> a loving brother and sister, my father David and my aunt Flo,
> and I had a little girl to play with, my aunt's baby daughter.
> The house was gay and full of music. My father whistled,
> imitated birds, hammered, sawed and took photographs; my
> aunt sang, ran the sewing machine; they told us innumerable
> stories about real and imaginary people.[32]

After Ellen's death, David's younger sister Florence had moved into Oakleigh Villa with her 18-month-old daughter Gwendolin. Christina Stead's idealised portrait of the brother-sister ménage is striking, and repeatedly carries over into her writing. While her fiction affords scarcely a glimpse of cosy intimacy between husbands and wives, it contains several brother-sister relationships that verge on the incestuous.[33] This 'loving brother and sister' clearly served as the unconscious model of a happy sibling couple.

The arrangement suited everyone. The previous year Florence had married a doctor, Hugh Walker-Smith, whom she had met in an amateur repertory company, but it was a paper marriage only.[34] For the time being, she was only too pleased to be housekeeper to the brother she so admired. David Stead provided the financial support, enabling Florence to stay at home and look after the two girls, who each thus gained both a sister and a surrogate parent. Years later, Christina Stead would fondly inscribe books to her 'sister-cousin'.

In Stead's overtly autobiographical novel *The Man Who Loved Children*, good-hearted Aunt Bonnie, stage-struck and always bursting into song as she goes about her housework, creates a scandal within the self-righteous Pollit family by becoming pregnant outside marriage. Florence Walker-Smith, despite her liberal-mindedness, is likely to have been pained by these revelations.

Each morning when David Stead left for work at the Fisheries Commission, Florence set about amusing the girls. She kept a theatre scrapbook and read the *Green Room*, Australia's sixpenny theatre monthly. Though they rarely, if ever, were taken to the theatre in their childhood, Christina and Gwen 'were full of stage lore, knew all about divas, prima donnas, jeune premiers, entrances, exits'.[35] David tolerated his sister's theatre talk, but did not approve, and was always admonishing her to read proper newspapers and books instead.

Christina was to have a lifelong respect for kind, open-minded 'Auntie Florrie', who knew 'it took all sorts to make a world'. Her talents as a mimic, pianist and singer brought her occasional small parts in musicals, but she had no opportunity to develop her gifts and, as a deserted wife, she was to lead a life of drudgery as a seamstress and domestic servant. But she cultivated a certain sweet fortitude: 'Well, it is Kismet, isn't it? A merry heart goes all the way.'[36]

As a father, David Stead was in his element. He saw himself as an educator of the masses, particularly children. Before breakfast, he would carry his daughter around his study and ask her to name in turn the various solemn faces whose photographs hung around the room: James Cook, Cuvier, Buffon, Darwin, Huxley. After this came the photographs of fish. Christina was even expected to know the Latin names for their body parts and the botanical names of plants. Later, she would find foreign languages comparatively easy. And her memory was always exceptionally good.

It was a lively existence. The menagerie in the backyard grew and grew: the tortoise was often obliged to bear the weight of small passengers; there were guinea-pigs, mice, rabbits, a duck, an echidna, and, of course, the snakes. David and Florence read the girls the children's classics: *Alice in Wonderland*, *The Water Babies*, Hawthorne's *Tanglewood Tales*. The supreme moment for Christina was bed time, when she had her father all to herself. Gwen had a cot in her mother's room; Christina slept in her father's room on a packing case containing treasures, real and imagined, that he had collected: a 'crocodile head with a bullet hole over the left eye', an ivory whale tooth, a giant Japanese spider-crab, dried human heads, a snake's skeleton and 'the kneecap of some monster extinct millions of years before'.[37]

Her father told her stories of the outback, about the first Australians and their corroborees, about 'brave canoe-sailors, men washed away by wind and current'. Tales of Krakatoa and Mauna Loa, volcanoes which blew people's heads off, convict ships, Captain Cook's travels, Charles Darwin's voyages in the *Beagle*, and extinct monsters—the triceratops, mastodons and giant kangaroos—that used to roam the mud swamps among the cycads.[38] The stories went 'on and on, night after night'. They left her with a feeling of wonder and excitement, a curiosity about 'men and nature', and a sense of the equality of all creatures—black people, white people and coral insects alike. Infused with her father's passion for the Australian continent, she was filled with a 'curious feeling . . . of terrestrial eternity, a sun that never set'. Although her mother was dead, she did not think of death as a horrible personal doom. She knew it was necessary 'for evolution to take place'.[39] The stories of those many nights filled the child with a sense of the infinite: even death, necessary for the evolution of the spècies, had its magic. 'I rejoiced in it,' Stead would write. 'It was like a grand cloak covering me, and allowing me to see unseen; "the cloak of darkness".'[40]

Even after her father left the room to talk to his sister in the kitchen, it was still alive with voices. The little girl's head was filled with a clamour of 'interminable, stupid conversations'.[41] The pieces of furniture—her father's double bed, the rug, the fireplace—talked to each other. The chest of drawers would say: 'I am so heavy, full of old clothes, the drawers squeak in and out', and the floorboards would chime in: 'What about us? We have your weight, you're crushing us.'[42] She went to sleep amid these dialogues, the seeds perhaps of her own story-making.

Stead later thought it strange that the pieces of furniture were so 'morose' and 'grumpy'.[43] Looking back, she could not remember her father or her aunt ever voicing discontent, though both had their sorrows. She surmised that the complaints of the furniture reflected her own dissatisfactions.

★   ★   ★

All was not quite idyllic. An unpublished draft by Christina Stead describes a little boy who in every way resembles her, confronting a recurring drama over the morning porridge. The little boy is placed on a high chair in front of the plate of lumpy oatmeal which he stubbornly refuses to eat.

"He must sit there till it's eaten," his father would say gaily
but firmly as he ran for the tram ... In the evening, an
enquiry was made. "If he won't eat it for breakfast it must
be given to him for lunch. We must break his will."[44]

Already Christina was conscious that she was not a pretty girl,
unlike her cousin Gwen. Children used to pass by Oakleigh Villa
on their way to and from school. Untidy, 'monstrous' children,
squawking and yelling. Among them was a gentle, goodlooking
little boy in a hat, sailor blouse and boots. Pressing his face against
the picket fence, Dickie would call out to 'G'ennie'. He was not at
all interested in Gwennie's cousin. In another unpublished draft,
Dickie is asking for 'Dulcie':

"I'm here," said Laurel. "I want Dussie!" Dulcie climbed down
the steps and put her face to the fence, a soft murmuring and
little cries of joy occurred. Laurel felt a sort of painful
resignation: she knew already that she was not pretty and
sweet like "Mother's darling," Dulcie.[45]

Christina called out to passing boys, but they did not answer, and
Florence scolded her. That these incidents shaped her sense of
identity is clear from a brief note in Stead's papers, possibly dating
from the late 1930s when she was writing *The Man Who Loved
Children* in a state of considerable anguish. Unusually, the note is
directly self-analytical and not given a fictional guise.

The injustice re G [Gwen], I noted but I never felt any resentment
against AF [Aunt Florence] or G. What remained was the boys
who did not answer ... I still remember all these things clearly
and they made up the "calendar" of my earliest memories ...
(I am trying to cure a serious feeling of rejection and discomfort,
which is a nuisance to me, affects my relations with people; and it
is obvious it is "my fault" because if I can ever get out of it, their
behaviour is different, friendlier, stronger, etc. I must absolutely
over-come this "rejection fear" now.)[46]

Christina Stead's early memories were all associated with a sense of
rejection, which she attributed to her physical unattractiveness. In
all her stories about her childhood, she is acutely conscious of
personal appearance. Her father, she writes, was an 'extremely
handsome man'. Her mother, her Aunt Florence and Gwen were
pretty. She was not.

This burning sense of her own plainness was reinforced by her
father. That his eldest daughter was not endowed with good looks
was a source of chagrin he made no attempt to conceal. He was
obsessed with appearance himself. Worse, he expounded the theory, flattering to himself, that appearance reflected character: his own

handsomeness and fairness were the outward signs of his goodness and innocence.[47]

In *The Man Who Loved Children*, Stead says of Sam Pollit: 'Like many a handsome body, Sam was not only revolted by deformity and plainness but actually saw essential evil in it.'[48] To David Stead, plainness was a kind of deformity.

★   ★   ★

Then came the catastrophe that was permanently to undermine Christina's security. By 1906, her father was becoming well known in scientific circles. An extraordinarily energetic man, he gave lectures, wrote scientific articles and newspaper columns on a vast number of nature subjects: emus, snakes, crabs, spiders, mosquitoes, amphibians, and monotremes.[49] He had published two monographs, *Crustaceans, Ancient, Modern and Mythical* and *Fishes of Australia*, each with splendid photographs, and was already at work on a third, *Edible Fishes of New South Wales*.[50] While involved in numerous nature societies, he was also a member of International Conciliation, one of the world's first peace bodies, based in New York.[51] His work entailed quite a bit of travelling: he was often away for a few days, inspecting oyster leases and the stocking of rivers and dams, checking the position of sewage farms. But then he took to being away on Saturday afternoons and not coming home until long after Christina had gone to bed. He was paying his respects to a lady.

David Stead met Ada Gibbins through her father. Frederick John Gibbins was known as 'the Oyster King' of the northern rivers, where he owned dozens of leases. He also owned pearling luggers in Torres Strait, timber mills at Terrigal and a wharf at the foot of Market Street, where the timber from the family mills was shipped for storage in his Sussex Street warehouse.[52] Gibbins clearly warmed to David Stead and invited him to meet the family. While Stead had no personal fortune, his future did seem promising. Whether or not Frederick Gibbins encouraged the unlikely courtship between David Stead and his youngest daughter (known in the family as 'Tott'), he did nothing to deter it.

One Friday evening, when Christina was 4, her long fair hair was put in rag curls which she had to sleep on all night. The next afternoon, wearing her best dress and hat, she went with her father by tram to the neighbouring district of Arncliffe, from where they took a pony trap along the old, convict-built Wollongong Road to a handsome two-storey mansion on the hill. They were visiting a lady whom Christina was told to call 'Aunty Tott'.[53]

The lady had black hair, olive skin, dark eyes and long fingers. Her skirt was very full, her waist quite tiny. Next to the house was a small orchard. 'You can run about and stay here till I call you,' her father told Christina.[54] Later, they had tea and cakes in the house, served by the maid. French windows opened onto the tessellated verandah, where an ancient Mexican parrot sat on its perch and shrieked.

★　　★　　★

Ada Gibbins, the youngest of eight surviving children, had been born in 1879 at the family home in Kent Street in the heart of the city.[55] Six years later, the family had moved to Dappeto, the mansion on the hill, named after the area south of Wollongong where Frederick Gibbins spent his childhood.

Frederick Gibbins, born in 1841, was the only son of Ann Meredith and a convict called John Gibbins, who arrived from England in 1829, sentenced to fourteen years' transportation for theft.[56] He was 18 years old. It was John Gibbins, more than anyone in Christina Stead's own family, who, like Magwitch, transformed himself from felon to successful businessman.[57] His son Frederick had further increased the family fortune.

Ada was greatly attached to her indulgent father. 'Old Dad', as his numerous grandchildren were to call him, was a handsome, lively man, very much in the Edwardian mould. Ada's mother, Catherine ('Old Mum'), had been born into the landed Pickett family from the Brisbane Water area: a strongly built woman with snowy hair pulled tightly back. Her blunt, no-nonsense speech shocked Christina when she was a little girl; later, she thought her remarkably like the raunchy old women in Shakespeare's plays. 'Old Mum', a country girl at heart, still liked to collect honey from the bee-hives and to milk the family cow.[58]

Ada had her mother's fine eyes but none of her practicality. No doubt because of her fragile health, she had been sent to the Blue Mountains to a small private finishing school, Hurtlands, at Springwood.[59] There she had learnt the ladylike accomplishments she would need in a world of visiting cards and 'At Homes'. Ada painted water-colours, sang in a thin quavery voice,[60] played the piano weakly and prided herself on delicate embroidery—something she was to teach Christina.

By 1906, the year she met David Stead, Ada was 27. She had finished school ten years before and now found herself stuck at home with her parents and an older brother who drank too much. All her siblings except the dissolute Ernie had married; their bedrooms were closed up. There was nothing to do: housework and cooking were done by servants.

David Stead wanted to re-marry. And, by the time she met David, Ada must have been seriously worried about her marriage prospects. It seems, from the beginning, to have been a marriage more of convenience than of love. David Stead was probably charmed, initially, by Ada's dark eyes and society girl coquetry;[61] he certainly liked and admired her father. Ada was doubtless attracted by David's looks; perhaps his energy and enthusiasm seemed to offer a remedy for her own boredom.

In an unpublished sketch based on her stepmother, Christina Stead refers to an earlier engagement which had been broken off, leaving 'Pitti' heartbroken and close to a nervous breakdown. When 'Ewan', a young naturalist, proposes to her, she is at first relieved. She accompanies him on several naturalists' expeditions and although too prettily dressed for that group, she charms people. Ewan, however, is astonished by her ignorance: she does not even know what stamens and pistils are. Quite soon Pitti begins to find Ewan's unbending ways oppressive: he disapproves of the novels she devours, disapproves of alcohol, disapproves of God himself. She runs away to relatives. When she tells her aunt she does not love her fiancé, the aunt retorts: 'Do you want to be left on the shelf?'[62] Christina would always claim that her stepmother was married off by her father, Frederick Gibbins, against her will.[63]

The wedding was held on New Year's Day, 1907. The Gibbins family would have liked a large church wedding. This time, David Stead was prepared to compromise to the extent of agreeing to a religious service—but no church. The Anglican rites were performed in the drawing room at Dappeto.[64] It was pouring with rain. Christina sat near the temporary altar in a Swiss muslin dress and a large white hat. On that summer day, according to Stead's fictional notes, the little girl felt beautiful.[65] Her father wore a new suit and the bride a dress of cream brocaded satin, with a veil of Brussels lace.[66] After the ceremony they adjourned to the dining room, where a feast was spread out on the long oak table. That afternoon, Christina acquired her third mother in four and a half years.

*　　*　　*

David Stead's second marriage brought about a dramatic change in his circumstances. The benevolent Frederick Gibbins made available to the couple a substantial colonial mansion, a mile away from Dappeto, which he had bought in 1890 and rented out. For the next ten years, David and Ada Stead were to live there rent free, with their ever-expanding family. Florence and Gwen Walker-Smith lived with them at first, Florence acting as an unpaid maid about the house, but after a time she found work as a domestic servant elsewhere.

The Bexley-Arncliffe district was still almost rural. Lydham Hill, as the Steads called their home on the knoll, was one of the original houses, dating from the 1850s.[67] Built of local sandstone, it comprised four large rooms, each with pink and black Italian marble fireplaces, and two sloping attic rooms upstairs. The kitchen and washrooms lay across a flag-stoned yard. The front of the house looked out to the Pacific through the headlands of Botany Bay, Cape Banks and Cape Solander. From the attic windows they could see the monument to Captain Cook's landing. In April 1770 when the *Endeavour* had anchored in these waters, Cook and the naturalists Joseph Banks and Daniel Solander—the first white men to land on the east coast of Australia—had seen natives on the coastal plain. The hills beyond, on which Lydham Hill now stood, were then covered in rugged vegetation. The crew had netted vast quantities of fish and plucked large oysters off the rocks. The botanists made note of the brightly coloured birds, a strange hopping animal, and scraggly trees with thin, strongly-scented leaves. David Stead was to follow in their footsteps, with camera as well as notebook.

It was a fine life for children. In the mornings, the front windows of Lydham Hill were generally drenched in sunlight; in the evenings, playing at the back of the house, the children would watch the sun disappear behind the Blue Mountains in a crimson and orange blaze. Cool sea breezes tempered the humidity of summer, though in winter the coal fires never quite warmed the large rooms.

The house was on three-and-a-half acres of land, which comprised two paddocks, an old orchard and a belt of pines and camphor laurels. It was 'a marvellous playground' for children,[68] and the outbuildings—the former stables, coach house and servants' quarters—were ideal for David Stead's collection of stuffed animals, bones and artefacts. Two large Japanese turtles lived in a well in the courtyard; cages contained snakes, possums and injured birds; a tall aviary housed a boobook owl and kookaburra, finches and budgerigars. Two emus, Dinnawan and Mundoey, acquired as striped chicks, ran around in one of the paddocks. Occasionally they would escape, stalk along the gravel drive and swallow whatever lay on the kitchen windowsill.[69]

In later years, in Paris, London and New York, some small thing would trigger Christina Stead's memory of this house and the 'whole landscape of childhood' would rise up before her, leaving her almost breathless with nostalgia. She would 'hear the eucalypts rustling at old Lydham' and smell the pungent smell of 'the cockchafer beetles, burnished gold, falling from the boughs'.[70] From Paris she told a friend:

> You know those nights when for some reason all you did when a little child rushes back over you: I did not get a wink of sleep, thinking of the time we built nests in the pine-needles and flapped round pretending to be starlings . . . or hid in the kangaroo grass pretending to be prince and princess.[71]

★　　★　　★

'My stepmother was kind to me until her first child was born, and then I was the outsider.'[72] Christina was always acutely conscious that she was different from the other children, a semi-orphan. Within ten years Ada had six of her own children. The four boys were named after famous scientists; the girls, more modestly, after the women in the family. David Darwin arrived on 4 October 1907, Catherine Ada on Christmas day 1908, Frederick Huxley in June 1911, Doris Weeta (an aboriginal name for a spotted bower-bird) in October 1913, Samuel Kelvin in February 1915 and Gilbert Jordan in October 1917.

Christina now called Ada 'mother', but Ada never let her forget that she was 'another woman's girl'.[73] Gwen Walker-Smith remembers her cousin as a difficult, stubborn child, often sullen; Ada tried to impose her ideas, and Christina resented her from the beginning. Ada was short-tempered, often sarcastic, with a dry sense of humour and a tendency to exaggerate. Although she could be very amusing when she was relaxed, Ada was anything but easy-going.[74] Caught in the crossfire of allegiances, David Stead found it more comfortable to appease his wife. (In *The Man Who Loved Children* Sam Pollit tells Henny, Louisa's stepmother, reproachfully: 'I taught her not to coax me or kiss me, or climb on my lap as the others do because in the beginning it made you so angry.'[75])

Christina thought it 'very natural' that her stepmother did not like her—let alone love her.

> My stepmother did not like me, very natural, as I was the kind of child only a mother could love and then probably with doubts: her treatment of me was dubious. Sometimes servants thought I was my father's illegitimate child, at other times, they fancied I was an orphan on my stepmother's side: friends who came to the house took me aside and told me what I owed the kind people who had taken me in. I myself with dark, thunderous looks, frowns and portentous behaviour did nothing to discourage the idea I was something the gipsies had left behind.[76]

Christina saw the fault as her own: even a real mother would find it hard to love *her*. Unconsciously she may have believed that her own mother had left her because she was bad: such feelings are not unusual in children whose parents have died. At another level, she was angry about being deserted. It is a small step from being unloved to believing oneself unlovable. And those who feel rejected have an uncomfortable way of making sure they really are. Christina was to become, as a writer, an observer, a professional outsider.

★　★　★

Stead had a vague memory of Ada as she was one year after her marriage: 'a beautiful dark, thin young lady in a ruffled silk dressing gown, mother of a very large red infant in a ruffled bassinet, receiving in state a company of very beautiful young ladies, all in their best dresses'.[77] But Ada Stead's pampered upbringing in no way equipped her for the life she would lead. She was pregnant, on average, every second year, and although in the Lydham Hill years they usually had a servant to help, there was too much for one servant to do. There were clothes and sheets to be turned in the copper and squeezed through the mangle. There was ironing, done with heavy flat-irons; there was mopping and sweeping, polishing and darning. There were beds to make, the wood stove to stoke, meals to cook.

Florence Walker-Smith lived with them on and off, between paid domestic positions, and she and Gwen visited often. If she was able to, Florence would come and help when Ada was ill or about to give birth. The other helper was Christina, whom everyone called 'Peg'. Her father, who gave all children nicknames, had decided that his ruddy-skinned daughter was 'Pig Face' or 'Piggy'. Kindly Aunt Florence, horrified, had insisted on changing this to 'Peg' or 'Peggy'.[78]

Since her father saw no need for it, Peg did not make an appearance at school until the unusually late age of 7. At Bexley Public School the teachers were shocked to discover that Christina, a big girl for her age, was still 'unlettered'.[79]

The dilapidated primary schoolhouse, down the hill from the Steads' house, gathered in boys and girls from dwellings scattered around the district. Looking back, it pained Stead to remember how the poorer children were ostracised and humiliated.[80]

Blucher boots were stiff work-boots with heavy soles, cheap and long wearing. It was accepted that children who came to school in blucher boots would leave school early and do rough work. They might even work on the road alongside their fathers, who, too, wore blucher boots. The very word was

socially significant: "he's wearing blucher boots!" The nice girls looked down and away in shame, the dirty girls grinned.[81]
After school, Peg would be sent to fetch milk from Dappeto. This meant crossing pastures, jumping over foul gutters, trying not to slip on the muddy, unpaved streets. She was terrified by a boy from one of the farmhouses who often waylaid her, and she dreaded spilling the milk on the way back. In the family she already had a reputation for being clumsy—'always in the wars'.[82]

Once she learnt to read, Christina could escape alone into another world. Every Saturday, she walked a mile and a half into Bexley and spent her pocket money on books by her namesake, W. T. Stead, or books of fairy tales, which cost a penny each.[83] Her favourites were the Brothers Grimm and Hans Christian Andersen. Later, she would read these to the children at bed time.

★   ★   ★

David Stead liked nothing better than to entertain young children. His own favourite book as a child had been Joel Chandler Harris' tales of Uncle Remus, Tar-Baby and Br'er Rabbit, and he was an adept at Uncle Remus-speak. A letter he wrote to his children in 1922 ended: 'Luv to evryboddie and all be goode. Thoes who duz thare dutie ar luvly wuns thay will get some frottie and some kurren bunz. From DadPad the Boald.'[84] David Stead's other linguistic model was the American comic writer Artemus Ward. Though this endless wordplay could be tiresome at times,[85] it was at least an imaginative lexical system which David Stead taught his children to explore.

Sunday, he decreed, was 'Funday'. (Study on that day was outlawed, to the bitter resentment of his eldest son, David Darwin.[86]) 'Funday' was organised by David Stead, King of the Kids. For his own children, and any of the neighbourhood children he could enlist, David Stead invented stories, thought up exuberant games, initiated magnificent adventures.

He was a great walker, and liked to take Christina on long walks, saying it would make her grow. She would always remember and resent her father for one fifteen-mile walk along the coast from Rockdale to Cronulla—'nearly killing me'.[87]

At Christmas the family usually went to Woy Woy, in rugged sandstone country north of the Hawkesbury River, where Ada's mother's cousin, Rachel Davis, had a boarding house. While her other siblings were still too small to play with her, Christina would wander off alone, through scrub dwarfed by sea-winds to the sand dunes, from where she looked down on mangrove swamps and the sweep of ocean beaches.[88]

At weekends, there were visits to Dappeto. Stead, who would read 'shoals of detective novels' in her life, was grateful when these authors left the scene of the crime to the reader's imagination, for Dappeto would always be the setting she imagined. The house had all the appurtenances of a detective novel: French windows giving on lawns, flowerbeds, windows with drainpipes, numerous stairs, rooms contiguous and adjoining, balconies.[89] A spiral staircase led up to a belvedere where they would stand between 'stiff blue waves of slate' and survey the surrounding cow paddocks.[90]

She would spend hours examining the bibelots and pictures at Dappeto. Over the chimney, opposite her place at the table, was an oil painting in a heavy gilt frame. It showed a table on which were arranged 'globulous heavy grapes', fruits and flowers, and plumy, bloody, disembowelled birds and fish with a knife stuck in them. Even its name was mysterious: did *Still Life* mean there was still life in the fish and birds?[91]

*   *   *

David Stead saw himself as a natural leader. A dominating character, charming, energetic and imaginative, he was the major influence in Christina's life. He was her father, her own blood; unlike Ada, he loved her. Indeed, he talked a great deal about love, in an abstract sort of way. At times they were close companions: both were bursting with ambition, both shared a lively curiosity about the world, a vivid imagination, an interest in language, a love of story and jokes. By the time she was in her early teens, it was his daughter who was David Stead's confidante, not his wife.

Committed to imparting to the community a love of nature and through that, a belief in goodness and justice, David Stead's substitute for religion was Nature. He saw himself as an apostle of 'Right, Justice and Truth' (his words) and he wanted his children to follow in his path. He was always saying that he loved 'humanity and the mass more than anything else'. People were fundamentally good; the wicked were merely insufficiently educated.[92] As an adult, Christina Stead realised he would have made a good minister among puritanical, earnest New World dissenters.[93]

David Stead shared the optimism of his idealistic generation. He was convinced he was right because he believed himself somehow chosen. For him, 'Fate' had replaced the notion of God. Christina Stead explains:

He believed in himself so strongly that, sure of his innocence, pure intentions, he felt he was a favored son of Fate (which to

him was progress, and therefore good), that he was Good, and he could not do anything but good. Those who opposed him, a simple reasoning, were evil.[94]

He was an impressive character. One of the early and most outspoken conservationists in the country, in 1909 he co-founded the Wildlife Preservation Society of Australia—the precursor of the Australian Conservation Foundation. In 1910, on the strength of his books and articles, he became one of the youngest Fellows ever elected to the British Linnean Society. The same year, at 33, he was promoted within the Board of Fisheries to Superintendent of Fishery Investigation—all without high school education.

A born teacher, he was a willing and popular speaker, illustrating his talks with lantern slides. A favourite with audiences, one which Christina came to know well, was 'Giants and Pygmies of the Deep'. He often took her to lectures and naturalist expeditions, hoping to encourage her interest in science. She would meet entomologists, geologists, botanists. 'They bored me to death,' she said later. 'Unbearably prosy' characters, they were 'always correcting each other about some trivial matter, like the name of a beetle'.[95]

         *   *   *

Though he gave so much time and energy to children, David Stead was not a loving or supportive father. He would romp and tease and call the children affectionate names, but they could never quite please him. When David Darwin came second in French one year, his father's only comment was, 'Why not first?' The following year, when he did come first, his father merely shrugged and said, 'Of course, from a son of mine!'[96]

What 'the man who loved children' really loved—more than the children as individuals—was the power to form young minds. He was against compulsory schooling: he would have preferred to educate his children himself. He had very definite ideas, on which his children endured endless diatribes. There was no God. Cats and dogs carried disease. Alcohol was evil. Doctors were fools. Makeup was vulgar. Ada accepted the taboo on alcohol, keeping only a bottle of medicinal brandy in the house.[97] Doctors came to the house for births, and Ada called the doctor when the children were seriously ill, but sometimes at the cost of a domestic row. If the children ventured a different viewpoint, their father would retort, 'Under my roof you do as I say.'[98] The children made a joke of his horror of hydatids (larval tapeworms) which he told them were carried by cats and dogs. It became a 'comic danger cry' in their games: 'Watch out, hydatids!'[99]

In Christina Stead's ironic terms, her father was 'part of the Huxley-Darwin reasonable-rational nature-agnostic mother-of-all-things-fresh-air-panacea eclectic-socialist universal-peace-manhood-suffrage-and-vegetarianism of the English breed, inheriting from the eighteenth century age of light and Jean-Jacques . . .'[100]

But all this was based on prejudice as much as reason. He objected to his Australian-born children learning subjects like French and history, steeped as it was in the dubious legends, class divisions and 'bloodstained scroll' of 'wicked old Europe'.[101] He proclaimed the equality of all peoples, but disliked Jews (whom he called money-lenders) and did not think much of the French, despite the benefits of the Enlightenment. Publicly, he espoused the rights of women, but his letters to the family were spiked with misogynist remarks. (Women, he believed, should be pretty, wholesome and domesticated; too often they were conniving and manipulative.[102]) He wanted his children to do well at school, yet he was jealous when they did. 'He was conscious of the fact that he didn't have any academic qualifications whatsoever,' said Thistle Harris, his third wife, 'and it acted as a frustration to him all his life. I think it affected his whole personality.'[103]

Conflict between David Stead and his children began when the children reached the age of dissent, and Christina was the first to do so. During her adolescence, alongside her love and admiration for her father went an anger that verged on hatred.[104] It would not have helped, her brother David comments, that her father regularly called her 'a lazy fat lump'.[105] (She was big-boned, but never fat.) In *The Man Who Loved Children*, Louisa Pollit, a young adolescent, has to endure constant jibes about her size. 'When she walks she wobbles,' says her father observing her.[106] 'Take your fat belly out of the sink,' says her stepmother, seeing Louisa slop dishes about, wetting her dress.[107] Whether or not everyone called Christina a 'barrel of lard'[108] as they do Louisa, Stead once wrote to friends: 'Always I felt like a cripple. Do we all? Why is it? I have never been a cripple—and I thought it was because my father thought I was ugly.'[109]

The David Stead counterparts in Christina Stead's fiction have a sadistic streak. In the short story 'Uncle Morgan at the Nats', Uncle Morgan, Chairman of the Naturalists, goads his 3-year-old niece to put her hand in the fire. He is 'training the child to obey'. The story was essentially true: David Stead had apparently tried to persuade 3-year-old Gwen to do just that.[110] In *The Man Who Loved Children*,

Louisa Pollit, at 11, has started to have doubts about her father and to resist him. Sam Pollit is bewildered and disturbed by this new turn of events: 'I'll break that miserable dogged spirit of yours,' he tells her.[111] He boasts that he knows her inside out: 'You are myself.'[112] In fact, though he pries into his daughter's private diary and tries to prod her inner thoughts, he is far from understanding her. In his frustration, he attempts to colonise not only her mind but her body. Playing with the children one day, he joins mouths with his baby son and pushes chewed food into his mouth, explaining to the others that parent birds do this to their nestlings. He then calls over his adolescent daughter.

> She got up and came to his side, rather shyly. "Right here!" Surprised, she came closer. Mottled with contained laughter, he stretched his mouth to hers, trying to force the banana into her mouth with his tongue, but she broke away, scattering the food on the floor and down the front of her much spotted smock, while everyone clamoured and laughed. Sam himself let out a bellow of laughter, but managed to say, "Get a floor cloth, Looloo-girl: you ought to do what I say!"[113]

Christina Stead claimed this was also based on fact.[114]

The Stead children learnt from an early age that their father was not someone you could absolutely trust. With him you had to be on your guard: he set you up, challenged you, humiliated you when you least expected it. Games often ended in tears.

★　★　★

When Christina was 12 years old, her father submitted a scheme for a deep-sea trawling industry to be run by the State Government. There was a severe shortage of fish in the Sydney shops, and David Stead drew the government's attention to the huge variety of edible fish in the coastal waters off New South Wales.[115]

Trawling at that time was virtually unknown in New South Wales. Labor Premier William Arthur Holman was enthusiastic: he was eager to establish government-owned industries.[116] In June 1914, David Stead was sent by the Department of Fisheries to Britain, Europe and the United States to purchase and equip three modern steam trawlers and to enquire into methods of fish distribution and canning. He took with him a collection of 131 specimens of New South Wales fish as a present to the British Museum.[117]

He sailed at the end of June 1914, and was in France when war broke out in August. Surviving letters from France and Norway reveal the extent of his obsession with standards of female beauty— a preoccupation which affected his eldest daughter painfully.

The Parisienne is splendid—she is lithe, she is supple, most graceful and beautifully formed. If a man never noticed women anywhere else he would notice them in France and specially in Paris . . . So many of the faces are so beautiful too—without make-up, of course—and, in very many cases, even where there is make-up, in the fashionably dressed women, it is done so artistically, as to reduce its offensiveness to a minimum.[118]

In Stavanger, David Stead was arrested by the beauty of Norwegian women:

Many of the girls are so pretty, with lovely flaxen hair (the real thing) and blue eyes and loveliest of complexions, with mostly "peach" and, sometimes, "apple" cheeks. And *this is very wonderful*: there are hardly any really plain girls in Bergen, Hangesund or Stavanger. I could not say that of any village, town or city I have ever seen before in my life . . . Sunny dispositions are everywhere apparent in nice clean honest faces of both sexes . . . I hope our Australian governments will do all they can to attract suitable people from among these splendid industrious coastal Scandinavians to our continent . . . The infusion of such splendid blood into Australia can only bring benefit to our posterity and present population.[119]

Not only did David Stead worship beauty: he would have liked to rid the world of ugliness. How could he expect his eugenic enthusiasms to be shared by his 12-year-old daughter, to whom this letter was principally addressed, painfully conscious as she was of her plainness?

David Stead had several books on eugenics.[120] His attitude reflected the period, in which there was much theorising about the 'racial' superiority of the Nordic peoples. A personal friend and self-made man whom he greatly admired was David Starr Jordan (1851–1931), the world's leading ichthyologist, the first President of Stanford University, and a scientist who openly advocated eugenic practices. Starr Jordan, like David Stead, championed progressive reform and world federalism. As Director of the World Peace Organisation, he was the foremost exponent of the dysgenic significance of the Great War: it violated the process of natural selection by killing vast numbers of the able-bodied male population, leaving the physically or mentally unfit at home to perpetuate the race. His ideas were elaborated in his book *The Blood of the Nation, A Study of the Decay of Races through the Survival of the Unfit*.[121]

Starr Jordan visited Sydney a couple of times. Christina remembered him well, as one of the few visitors to the house at Bexley—'a tall imposing man with a broadbrimmed hat and dark clothes.'[122] He was, like David Stead, a passionate believer in the good of nature, fresh air and exercise, education and democracy. Though both men shared an optimistic progressivism which harked back to the Garden of Eden, Starr Jordan was more hardheaded than Stead, and nothing of a socialist. He was impatient with sentimental charity, which encouraged the survival of the unfit. Like Stead, he had humble beginnings and believed that his own example proved that the strong naturally rose to the top. In David Stead's autograph book, he wrote a maxim from Emerson that impressed Christina: 'The world stands aside to let pass the man who knows whither he is going.'[123]

David Stead was away from Sydney for almost the whole duration of his wife's fifth pregnancy. One postcard to Ada has survived.[124] Written in late February 1915 from Boston, the message was a few dull lines about the picture on the other side; there was no 'dear Ada' and no 'love David', no concern about her health. Yet earlier that same month she had given birth to Samuel Kelvin.

★   ★   ★

The Man Who Loved Children contains a short but passionate melodrama written by 13-year-old Louisa for the occasion of her father's fortieth birthday. In this violent Oedipal drama, called *Tragedy of the Snake-Man*, there are just two characters: Anteios and his young daughter, Megara.[125]

Megara tells her father that in his company she feels guilty, yet she knows she is innocent. He, with his 'rascally wiles', ravishes her peace of mind, her solitude. Now she shares her solitude with a stranger called hate. 'If I could, I would hunt you out like the daughters of King Lear.'

'Horrible,' cries Anteios. 'What a she-devil!'

The daughter begins to choke; she feels herself being strangled. The stranger is a snake and he has turned, she realises, not on her father but on her.

MEGARA: (Shrieking) I am dying. You are the stranger. You are killing me. Murderer! Murderer! Mother!

ANTEIOS: I am only embracing you. My beloved daughter. (But he hisses.)

MEGARA: Mother, father is strangling me. Murderer! (She dies.)[126]

Christina Stead created Louisa who creates Megara. The further one dives into the textual vortex, the purer is the daughter's hatred for her father. Stead was 36 when she wrote this little melodrama in her dingy New York apartment, and though it is presented as a piece of Louisa's juvenilia, Stead knew she was plunging into her own unconscious.

* * *

In *The Man Who Loved Children*, Henrietta Pollit screams that she has had enough of having babies, scrubbing floors, putting up with her husband's 'vile animals' and his 'everlasting talk, talk, talk, talk, talk'.[127] On another occasion, Sam Pollit, expatiating upon love and goodness, tells Louie that he has sacrificed his whole life to nature and mankind. She starts to scribble something down, and he imagines she is taking notes. When he bends over her shoulder to look, he reads: 'Shut up, shut up, shut up, shut up, shut up. I can't stand your gassing, oh, what a windbag, what will shut you up, shut up, shut up.'

Sam Pollit, of course, is 'terribly hurt', and instead of reflecting even for a moment on his own behaviour, the all-loving Sam flings at her:

> What is the matter with you? You're mean and full of hate ...
> I think of love and you are all hate. Sitting there you look like
> some mean cur in the street, whining and snivelling ... What
> can I do with a girl like you? You have no looks ... I don't
> understand you.[128]

The Man Who Loved Children recreates the fierce tension in Christina Stead's relationship with her father: the admiration, disappointment and anger on her side; the double binds and contradictions on his. With her stepmother it was easier: Christina never expected anything from her, and was surprised by their brief interludes of mutual sympathy. 'They ... made an etching out of me,' she wrote later, explaining the bitterness that marks the novel. 'I am deep-bitten.'[129]

* * *

Brolga, *Kooraga* and *Gunundaal*, the three trawlers that David Stead had bought in Hull and christened with aboriginal names, arrived at Port Jackson in April and May 1915.[130] The State Trawling Industry was officially established in June, with David Stead as General Manager. 'For five lively years,' writes his daughter, 'we had nothing but trawling and fishing talk.'[131]

For David Stead, who called himself 'a state socialist', this was the ideal opportunity to bring together his scientific expertise and his social idealism. Brandishing the slogan 'Fresh food for the people', he set out to provide cheap and wholesome food for the less wealthy. His was a grandiose vision: he assured the government of a regular, cheap fish supply and a profit within the first twelve months. The Municipal Fish Market and the state-owned fish shops would eradicate the 'grasping middlemen', he claimed. His lack of diplomacy soon created enemies.

But his dream was quite realistic. Wartime Australia suffered from low wages and a high cost of living, and the waters off Botany Heads were in fact an untapped source of nourishing food. He was right: the coast of NSW proved to be among the best fishing grounds in the world. Out of the trawling nets came John Dory, snapper, whiting, flathead, leather-jackets, barracouta, ling, silver dory, skate—many of which the public had never seen.[132] Premier Holman recalled later: 'The newly obtained catches appealed to the public imagination like miraculous draughts, and people came literally in their thousands.'[133] By 1917, four more trawlers, built in the Sydney dockyards, were added to the fleet.

But trouble brewed. The fishermen, out for days at a time, went on strike for Sundays in port. David Stead was caught between being a strike-breaker and supplying fish for the people. Stead wrote:

> My father, a staunch Labour man, who believed in the people, in the good of man, attempted to break the strike by getting helpers from the office and shops, from our family and among friends, to scale and gut, to save the fish which lay then at the docks. There was great enthusiasm I remember: he was satisfied with this activity and everyone "pitching in", "lending a hand" (one of his favourite jolly ideas).[134]

There were worse difficulties. War conditions made it difficult to import machinery: the launching of the other trawlers was delayed and the Australian-built vessels ended up costing far more than the imported ones. But the fundamental problem was political: the State Trawling Industry posed a threat to private interests. Although David Stead argued that a young socialist industry was not supposed to make a profit, that it was for the people, his enemies made much of the alleged financial losses, using them as an excuse for what Christina Stead later described as 'shocking crass attacks, both on the government, its ministers and on him personally'.[135]

*   *   *

By her early adolescence, Christina knew she was going to be a writer. Writing was something she was good at, something she loved to do; it was a means of shining, of feeling good about herself. When she was 11, she won the district essay competition for a piece on the life-cycle of a frog,[136] thus spawning her writing career very much in the shadow of her father.

At 12½, she had been sent to Kogarah Intermediate School, something between a vocational school and an academic high school for girls. She was there only a year before St George Girls' High was opened, in February 1916, and the girls were transferred to the new school, a rambling old villa beside an orchard. The institution's small size made it seem like a private school. Nine teachers, all with university degrees, taught 143 students.

Christina liked to stand out, and just as she enjoyed the shock it always caused when she announced her religion as 'atheist',[137] she now made an ostentatious display of her writing. In a world in which David Stead made everyone into his satellite, it was a useful defence to act the same way by writing fiction, playing God in creation. She achieved notoriety with a poem called 'Green Apricots', which made mock of a new teacher who rebuked the girls for eating unripe apricots from the orchard. The final stanza read:

> Who is it, on the hanging bough
> Green apricots once saw, and now
> Finds them scattered, lying low,
> And goes at once, to make a row?
> > Green apricots!
> The puny fruit that has no care
> And to bright yellow will come ne'er
> Got somehow tangled in her hair,
> > Oh, *"ces cheveux!"*[138]

In later years, Christina Stead greatly regretted her 'malicious poem'. She would never forget that the teacher was almost driven from the school by the hostility of the girls, without anyone quite knowing why she was so disliked.[139]

By contrast, the poems she wrote to her English teacher were without the cruelty—though just as public. Everyone in the class knew that Peggy Stead had a crush on Miss Paradise, and was writing what she grandiosely referred to as her 'Paradise Cycle'. Wildly ambitious, she intended the cycle to comprise hundreds of poems in every conceivable form and metre. It reached thirty-four.[140] Angela Carter was later to comment that Stead 'was, from the very beginning . . . a writer of almost megalomaniac ambition'.[141]

Writing had become a means of attaining power over others, and resisting their power over her. By writing—and showing her writing to others—Christina could reduce people by ridicule or raise them to great heights. It was an important and lasting discovery.

*   *   *

Within the ten years they lived at Lydham Hill, Ada Stead was transformed from an elegant young spitfire into a querulous, frazzled and embittered shrew, who took out her frustration on the children—particularly her stepdaughter. Her fictional counterpart Henrietta Pollit ('Henny') undergoes the same drastic metamorphosis:

> The dark lady of the ruffles had disappeared and in her place was a grubby, angry Henny, who, after screeching, and crying at them all, would fall in a faint on the floor.[142]

Gwen Walker-Smith and David Darwin well remember the fainting fits. Without any warning, Ada would fall straight down in a rather shocking way—on her face, side or back. Somehow, miraculously, she never broke a bone. Christina, horrified at first, gradually became used to it and would run for a pillow and let her stepmother lie there, very pale, until she came to herself.[143]

Ada had had these momentary seizures since childhood: she may well have suffered from *petit mal* epilepsy, which was hard to diagnose. But over the years, David Stead came to regard her fainting spells, fairly or not, as a spoiled woman's trick. The rest of the family also came to suspect they were at least partly self-induced. 'Sometimes she would get into a state and throw herself on the floor,' says Gwen Walker-Smith, who conjectures that it was probably her aunt's way of 'getting away from things'.[144] (Ada used to say as much herself.) 'She was an emotional woman, very unhappy, and under great strain with all those kids.'

As a child, Gwen Walker-Smith was aware of the 'feeling of tension in the air when David and Ada were together'. Her aunt, she recalls, 'had no idea how to manage on a limited budget. To get away from the children she would go to town and buy things the family could ill afford'.[145] David Stead's Public Service income did not go far among six children, and they relied on 'Old Dad' not only for the free house, but also for extras, such as wages for the servant. Ada's visits home—she found gracious Dappeto and conversations with her earthy mother a welcome retreat these days— invariably resulted in a small handout. Back at Lydham Hill, looking tired and worn, she would console herself with endless cups of tea and games of patience. The piano was rarely touched, except when Florence Walker-Smith came to stay.

Later in life Christina Stead was not without sympathy for her stepmother. 'She married the wrong man, that's all,' she would say, 'and that's extraordinarily difficult.'[146] In *The Man Who Loved Children*, Henny, mad with frustration, talks of going back to her family and taking the children with her. Ada Gibbins no doubt made the same threats. But the reality was that a wife's situation completely lacked legal protection. A husband was not legally

bound to provide for her future or for their children's; wives had no rights either in the guardianship of the children or in the distribution of the family's accumulated wealth. Ada was virtually a prisoner in her own house—a situation her stepdaughter saw very clearly in later years: 'Cells are covered with the rhymes of the condemned, so was this house with Henny's life sentence, invisible but thick as woven fabric.'[147]

*   *   *

David Stead's scientific ambitions for Christina were more typical of a father's for a son; he certainly did not have the same aspirations for his other daughters. She was good at science at school, eager to impress her father. But since she was a daughter and not a son, David Stead was dismayed that she was not prettier. His deep ambivalence, transmitted to Christina, meant that the scientific meetings did not at all achieve the desired effect.

> What repelled me, it's shameful of me, but it's true, is the women used to dress very plain: long plain skirts, hair way back, in a bun, and I couldn't stand it. Not for me![148]

> I made up my mind at the very earliest age that I would not be a scientist: I intended to have nice dresses and to get married, and I very soon observed that these earnest women were either not married, or were married to men that seemed to me very old and very homely.[149]

'If women are to cultivate the sciences they must remain celibates for life,' opined the *Bulletin*, the radical, republican journal, in 1888.[150] This view of professional women was just as prevalent two decades later, and the social stigma attached to unmarried women was as strong in the Stead household as anywhere else. David Stead's sister Jessica—the aunt whom Christina was said to resemble—was an unmarried 'pupil teacher' (as infant teachers without formal training were called), and an object of pity and disdain within the family.[151] Older schoolmistresses belonged in a grievous category of 'old maids' and 'dessicated virgins'—for those who married were obliged to leave the service. It did not warm Christina to the teaching profession, for if there was one thing she determined early not to be, it was that object of derision: an old maid.

*   *   *

> INTERVIEWER: 'It has been said that [*The Man Who Loved Children*] is perhaps the greatest book about family life that's ever been written. It is certainly the most powerful evocation of what it's like to live in a family that I've ever read.'

CHRISTINA STEAD: 'That's a terrible criticism, isn't it?'
INTERVIEWER: 'Terrible criticism?'
STEAD: 'Of family life.'[152]

Written in New York when Christina was in her thirties, the novel for which she is now best known was no hymn to her father, nor to family life. On the latter, Stead agreed wholeheartedly with the pessimistic Strindberg. In later life, she freely acknowledged the fact that the Pollit family was based on her own family. She even admitted—though she was always cagey about her feelings—that writing the book caused her intense emotional distress. She would then revert quickly to a pragmatic stance which disclaimed the singularity of her own case: 'Most children live through great tragedies and they grow up and they're just normal and ordinary ... It strengthens their character.'[153]

Stead's public matter-of-factness contrasts starkly with the cauldron of seething emotions in the novel itself. At the time of its publication, in 1940, critics would complain that the novel was overwhelming. Mary McCarthy protested: 'The reader is put in the position of the awestruck children listening in their beds to a night-long family quarrel.'[154] Clifton Fadiman found Sam Pollit nerve-shattering: 'You're ready to scream at him as if he were not a character in a book but a man in your living room.'[155] *New York Times* critic Charles Poore exclaimed: 'In the end one is not so much inclined to ask mercy for the family but mercy for the reader.'[156]

Randall Jarrell was one of the few to find the novel's overbearing quality a strength:

> *The Man Who Loved Children* makes you a part of one family's immediate existence as no other book quite does. When you have read it you have been, for a few hours, a Pollit; it will take you many years to get the sound of the Pollits out of your ears, the sight of the Pollits out of your eyes, the smell of the Pollits out of your nostrils.[157]

★   ★   ★

At the time of writing, Stead commented that the novel had 'a plot derived from, although not exactly mirroring, our home in the early days, not the *procès-verbal*, but the dramatic truth'.[158] In other words, it represented the emotional truth—her own. She was conscious then that her novel was both 'true to life' and an artistic construction, that it was not just a matter of what she put in: it was also a matter of what she left out.

In later life, Stead would deny the gap between the 'dramatic truth' and reality. 'I was brought up by a naturalist, and I *am* a naturalist,' she would say,[159] implying (in the tradition of nineteenth-century realist writers) that hers was the impartial, objective gaze of the empirical scientist. For her, she made clear, there was no difference between snakes and people: she observed life, she took notes, and she wrote about what she saw. She went so far as to insist that she had recreated her family life exactly, once claiming she had written the truth 'word for word'.[160] It was a bizarre stance for a creative writer to take, one which disowned the complex process of fictional transformation.

What her claim does indicate is a desire for control altogether reminiscent of her father's. David Stead was always saying that he worshipped 'truth'. He meant *his* truth: he interpreted the world largely according to his own needs. His daughter made the same claim about *The Man Who Loved Children*: it told the truth. 'They were so much alike,' says Gwen Walker-Smith of Christina and her father. 'That was the clash.'[161]

★   ★   ★

Like the fictional *alter egos* she would later create (Louisa in *The Man Who Loved Children* and Teresa in *For Love Alone*), Christina as an adolescent was full of passionate, romantic yearnings intensified by a sense of outrage. Books were her solace, her refuge and her companions. They nourished a sense of self-worth that her daily existence could not provide. As a reader she could identify with both the heroes in fiction and the writers who created them. She read voraciously, re-reading favourite authors constantly and learning lengthy passages by heart.

She had a marked penchant for the fantastic, the ghostly, gothic and grotesque. The sumptuous and erotic mediaeval world of *Arabian Nights*, which she read in Richard Burton's famous translation, coloured her imagination for life. In her own fiction, she would not be able to resist occasional images of genies bowing their way out of snuff jars in smoky spirals.[162]

She liked old tales and legends. The stories in her mother's King James Bible (which her father had kept, despite his hostility to religion) were wonderful. And the scientific books in her father's library were full of true adventure. She would always admire the writing in Darwin's *Origin of the Species* and *Voyage of HMS Beagle*.[163] And she was fascinated by George Cuvier's *Animal Kingdom* and Heinrich Schliemann's *Troy and its Remains*. One book that particularly haunted her was on venereal disease, with poems by the insane and stories about nuns who dreamt that the Devil jumped over the wall into the convent.[164] She also read the bush ballads and stories of Henry Lawson, Banjo Paterson, Steele Rudd, members of the 1890s 'stockwhip and wattle-blossom school'.[165]

The family was 'full of Dickens',[166] and Christina read every one of his novels, even though for the most part her own father disapproved of novels. When she changed the children's sheets, Christina would find concealed in the linen cupboard romantic novels from the local library.[167] They did not interest her, but she was amused that Ada took no more notice of David's puritanical prejudices than she did. Books, in his view, should not treat 'unsavoury subjects', and if there had to be wrongdoers, they should be chastened in such a way as to discourage others.[168] He would have thoroughly disapproved of Strindberg's bitter short stories about marriage, yet they enthralled his daughter, who saw Strindberg as the only writer to tell the truth about families.[169] In time, her filial revolt would go much further. Not only did she read novels with 'bad subjects': she was to spend her life writing them.

She treasured *Peer Gynt*, Ibsen's drama about a dreamer and wanderer, and learnt long passages from the William Archer translation by heart. And it was with something akin to rapture that she discovered Milton, Byron, Tennyson and Keats: her early poetry shows the influence of English Romanticism. For her fifteenth birthday her father gave her the complete works of Shelley. She loved *The Cenci*, and her character Louisa vigorously identified with Beatrice:

> . . . I, alas!
> Have lived but on this earth a few sad years,
> And so my lot was ordered, that a father
> First turned the moments of awakening life
> To drops, each poisoning youth's sweet hope.[170]

But her great love was Shakespeare. Later she would claim (doubt-less an exaggeration) that as an adolescent she read the family's battered tome of his *Complete Works* from beginning to end every year.[171]

By this time the family assumed that their dreamer would be a writer, though they were too preoccupied with their own struggles to pay her scribblings much attention. As an adult, Christina Stead was grateful that she had been left alone to develop in her own way. When she saw precocious American children being 'prodded and puffed' by their parents, she thought the result disastrous.[172]

At school Christina was not an outstanding student. Her ambi-tion lay elsewhere. In the NSW Intermediate Certificate examina-tion for which students sat after two years of high school, her results were an A for art and Bs for English, history, French, botany and maths. It was November 1916; she was 14½, the legal age for entering the work force, and the age at which most pupils, especially girls, left school.

That summer, in January 1917, 'Old Dad' died. The Gibbins family vaguely knew that Frederick Gibbins' investments in the Lake George Gold Mine had failed, but only now did they learn of the extent of his debts. Dappeto and Lydham Hill, the genteel family homes, would have to go under the hammer.[173] It was a shattering blow to David and Ada Stead. The last thread to fine bourgeois living had snapped. Ada had not only lost the father she loved; she had lost all connection to the life for which she had been brought up.

It was probably their bleak financial prospects that made David Stead suggest to Christina that she take up an apprenticeship in journalism. She was aghast: she wanted to be a writer, not a journalist—especially not a woman journalist, confined to the women's pages. Her father must have been halfhearted about the idea himself, for he soon agreed to her staying on for the two years it would take to finish school.[174]

Within the family, things were at a low ebb. To her dismay, Ada found herself pregnant once again. David Stead had to look for a new house at the same time as an embarrassing public inquiry was being held into the State Trawling Industry. Premier Holman supported him, but Holman too was under a political cloud, and partly for the same reasons: he was a threat to private industry. According to H. V. Evatt, Holman's biographer in 1942, Holman was principally destroyed by a 'systematic campaign of political vilification'.[175] This was to apply equally to the State Trawling venture.

David Stead found a house at Watson's Bay.[176] Today the Watson's Bay area is prime Sydney real-estate; in 1917, it was a sleepy little village with fishermen's shanties, boatsheds and fish nets drying in the sun. Still surrounded by large areas of bushland, it was a favourite Sunday picnic spot for city dwellers. Not until the 1920s, with the advent of the family car, did the farther eastern suburbs become popular residential districts.

The weatherboard house at No. 10 Pacific Street, one of the few two-storey houses in the area, was dilapidated. In parts its external walls and wooden floors were quite rotten. It had been built by 'Captain Jack', a retired master mariner, in the mid 1880s.[177] David Stead, a good handyman, would be fixing it up, with the help of his boys, for years to come.[178] They moved on 31 August 1917, just six weeks before Gilbert Jordan (named after Starr Jordan) came into the world.

The children loved the sprawling ramshackle house that fronted straight on to the harbour and was within a short walk of the Heads. Standing on the sandstone boulders at the edge of the natural swimming pool at the end of the garden, they saw fish glide past. Looking up, they saw a wooden jetty, yachts, a dredge, motorboats. They were in their element. So was their father. For Ada, who disliked the sea and detested the smell of fish and seaweed, it was a terrible wrench. From elegant Lydham Hill to this unpretentious, reeking bay!

Christina had just turned 15. When she was not reading or writing, she was composing in her head. Wonderful, solitary hours were spent describing things to herself, and improving upon the description.[179] She was training herself to see small details, to hear the exact rhythm and cadence of dialogue, to observe the external world, to be aware of internal conflict. 'How blunt our senses are,' one of her characters would exclaim, 'how many thick veils hang between us and the world. How will we ever refine our eyes to see atoms and our ears to hear the messages of ants?'[180]

Twenty-one years later, in *The Man Who Loved Children*, Christina Stead would re-create the atmosphere of the day they moved to Watson's Bay:

Henny heard the men moving in some heavy thing, and heard her husband say wearily, "Looloo-dirl, make some cawf!" The reek of weeds forever damp and of the brackish water came up to her and the smell of the ground under the veranda. It had rained slightly in the night. Louie, who pretended not to hear Sam's call, came in a dawdle round the house and leaned against the veranda post behind the vines, chewing a grass stalk. She was droning to herself and presently she droned clearly, "Oh the waterskin crawls shorewards; and the leprous sky scales earthwards, from the musical moaning channel, to the dirty margin. It was halfwater; the surface was dull, and the sky was windy."

At that particular moment, Henny awoke from a sort of sullen absence and knew what was happening; her heart was breaking. That moment, it broke for good and all.

"Stop that rot," she cried madly to Louie, startling her out of her wits, "I never heard such damnfool tommyrot. Go and get the coffee. A big lumbering sheep, and on a day like this, she holds up the veranda post." Louie, with tactful soft-footing, disappeared from behind the vines, and presently Henny heard her saying,

"I say, Dad, this gas won't turn on; it's jammed."

The men trundled backwards and forward and puffed. Louie soon came to the veranda with a cup of tea for her mother (Henny's heart would not stand coffee), "Mother, Daddy says, Where do you want things put?"

"What the devil do I care? Put them on the orchard and make a bonfire of them. Put them where you like," she ended, less ungraciously. "Is it my home? It's your father's idea. Do what you like; all I want is a place to lie down, and get me a bed for Baby. Tell him I am not going to lift a finger to fix up his stinking tenement: the animals have better cages. Go on now, don't stand there staring."

Louie, not at all offended, and now observing more closely the many defects of the old house, the hanging window cords, unlatchable latches, and sunken floors, went in to say, "Mother says put everything where you like."

Sam, only too pleased, at once hallooed and whistled for the gang of children and consulted their tastes. It was not hard to suit most of them.[181]

Calling her fiction the 'truth' was the adult Christina Stead's way of controlling her universe, then and there as well as for posterity. After she had written *The Man Who Loved Children*, either out of revenge or through a fusion in her imagination, she used to refer to her father in letters and conversation as 'Sam'.

When she sat at her typewriter at the age of 36 to write about her family, it was she at last—not her father—who had the whip hand over her childhood.

2
Embarkation for Cythera

SEPTEMBER 1917–APRIL 1928

A FEW METRES from their tall, weatherboard house, which David Stead named Boongarre, after an aboriginal chief who had lived in the area,[1] ocean liners from all over the world—Shanghai, Naples, San Francisco, London—anchored in the harbour awaiting quarantine inspection. Christina's bedroom was upstairs at the back of the house; from her window she could see the ships sliding past the lighthouse and signal station at South Head. She loved to stand there late at night and look out at the ships in the harbour 'lighted like a Christmas tree', and the 'great subtropical moon' hung over the water like a lantern.[2] The children knew the tides, the signals from the clifftop about ships and storms, the movements of the pilot boat, the *Captain Cook*. In later years, Stead would maintain that it was living by the water, with the international shipping activity before her eyes, that made boarding a ship in her mid-twenties and going abroad herself seem the natural thing to do.[3] Australia was 'a sparkling land',[4] but like so many of her talented contemporaries, she would feel herself beckoned by the cultural centres of the Old World.

★   ★   ★

Watson's Bay was a windy part of the world: soon the family was experiencing the battering of October gales. Christina liked to lie in bed listening to the boom of ocean rollers against the cliffs. Even though Boongarre was protected under the hill, the spray from the surf would reach their roof.[5]

The children swam for nine months of the year. To Ada's dismay, the house was always full of sand brought in by the children. There were mice too, and occasionally rats would come up from the waterfront. On summer evenings, large black cockroaches scurried along the footpaths and the kitchen benches. In front of the house, the garden ran down to the harbour; at the water's edge, several sandstone boulders formed a natural pool. When the young children were playing in the water, someone would always have to stand on 'Pegler Rock'—the biggest of the boulders—and watch out for sharks.[6] As young boys, David and Fred scoured the rockpools for crabs and little oysters, which their father made them boil because of typhoid.[7] In the early years, they paddled around in an old rowboat; when they were older, they would sometimes go out with the fishermen, coming back with fish that Ada then had to cook, though the smell made her feel queasy. Once they caught a twelve-foot blue pointer shark, lurking in shallow water within fifty feet of the house. This caused considerable excitement, and their father, enthusiastically discoursing on the many virtues of fish oil,[8] got them to boil down its liver in the laundry copper. It was one of his madcap ideas: after several hours, the shark's liver had yielded four gallons of oil, but the terrible stench pervaded the whole neighbourhood and the copper would never be the same again.[9]

* * *

Christina had lost her childhood fairness: her long hair was light brown now, and usually worn tied back in a ribbon. A tall, big-boned adolescent, with keen grey-blue eyes, she had developed womanly curves early. But she had a rather ruddy complexion, a stubborn-looking jaw and buck teeth. She was definitely no beauty.

She was happiest in her own world, where her imagination had free rein. She liked to walk up the hill and sit among the boulders and pines at the cliff top, describing to herself a view that never failed to delight her—a scene she would later portray lyrically in her two Australian novels, *Seven Poor Men of Sydney* and *For Love Alone*. Her first publication, a sonnet called 'The Hill', appeared in the school magazine when she was 16, and begins:

> I stand upon a hill—on either hand
>   Lie darkening waters. At my feet, the sea
> Clothed with faint mists that steal upon the land,
>   E're yet the moon has risen, roars sullenly.[10]

The heavy influence of the English nineteenth-century poets is clear from the poem as a whole.

Along the clifftops, the place known as 'The Gap', an indentation in the cliffs where the sea pounds the rocks with hellish ferocity, was the city's favoured suicide spot.[11] Christina used to contemplate the desperation of those who threw themselves over the cliff and worry that the bodies would be dashed open on the shale platform below instead of finding a more gentle death in the foaming ocean.[12] Michael Bagenault, in *Seven Poor Men of Sydney*, taking a last determined step towards the edge of the cliff, is stricken (too late) by the same thought: 'What if I should fall upon a rock?'[13]

Christina knew that women threw themselves over The Gap because they were pregnant outside wedlock. On summer evenings, when she walked home down the hill and through the park, she would hear groans and strange cries emanating from the bushes and tangled scrub. She was fascinated, curious, and vaguely repelled. Her fictional counterpart Teresa, in *For Love Alone*, imagines herself walking through 'a strange battlefield . . . with sounds of the dying under the fierce high moon'.[14]

★   ★   ★

Despite the beauty of the bay, life at home had become 'atrociously wretched'.[15] They were poor these days: it was a struggle to clothe the family and maintain the house at a respectable standard—a struggle Ada to a certain extent gave up. At 38, she had six children under 10 and a difficult adolescent stepdaughter. There was no question of domestic help any more. And Florence Walker-Smith had found domestic work in a country home, which to her dismay, meant that Gwen had had to be sent to relatives.

Ada, bitter about the wretchedness of her situation, rarely even spoke to her husband. When they did speak, there were sharp words, and sometimes dramatic rows. David Darwin recalls his mother hitting his father with rage on more than one occasion; he never saw his father hit back.[16]

David Stead had no idea how to deal with wilful adolescents. Christina was 15 now, and seeing his authority slipping, David resorted to taunting and belittling her, making invidious comparisons with other girls, pretty girls, *nice* young ladies. Gwen Walker-Smith remembers her cousin's frequent 'withdrawn almost sullen silence'. According to Stead later, most days saw her in tears of rage and frustration.[17]

But there were good moments, happy times, and these made Christina feel guilty for feeling so often resentful and angry. She was at her best with the younger children, inventing stories and games, taking them on walks, mothering them. At Christmas time, she put 'hours of loving ingenuity' into making presents and preparing surprises for them.[18] Over sixty years later, her sister Weeta, recalling this distant past, declared Christina 'the most wonderful sister any young girl could have wished for'.[19]

*   *   *

Three days after moving to Watson's Bay, Christina began at Sydney Girls' High School on 3 September 1917.[20] It was a little awkward joining her second year class in third term, but she soon loved the school. The soothing forty-five-minute ferry-steamer trip via Parsley Bay, Neilsen Park and Garden Island, past hills covered in red roofs, past sloping gardens with 'walls loaded with creepers' and the grey towers of the Rose Bay convent in the distance delighted her. On summer mornings, she would gaze across the glaze of the water and imagine the heat smoking on the distant hills. The task she had set herself as a future writer was to describe the smallest details 'with the accuracy of a miniature painter'.[21] Observation was a challenge she took seriously.

From Circular Quay, she walked past the shipping offices and warehouses, up a mild incline, past the dignified colonial government buildings on Macquarie Street, to the red brick school on the corner of Elizabeth and Market Streets. A teacher stood guard at the iron gate, checking that the girls were walking sedately, wearing their hats and gloves.

Sydney Girls' High, the oldest state girls' high school in New South Wales, was known for the number of students who won bursaries to the university.[22] Two 'Old Girls' of Christina's parents' generation, both former editors of the *High School Magazine*, had become well-known local authors. Ethel Turner's children's novel, *Seven Little Australians*, was published in 1894, when she was 21; and Louise Mack, who had left for Europe at the age of 27, had written a number of light romances, several of them (*Teens, Girls Together* and *Teens Triumphant*) based on her school experiences. A recent Old Scholar, Marjorie Barnard, was excelling in history at Sydney University; later, she would make her name as a distinguished fiction writer and literary critic, often writing in collaboration with Flora Eldershaw as 'M. Barnard Eldershaw'.

The austere schoolhouse, previously St James's School, had been designed by the famous convict architect Francis Greenway and built by convicts in the 1820s. A dingy and cramped two-storey building, with a small asphalted yard shaded by two large Moreton

Bay fig trees, it was enclosed by a high stone wall that added to the impression of a prison; but the girls developed a strong affection for the old building, in which lessons were punctuated by the clattering of trams and honking of motorcars.

Christina Stead was one of the first pupils at Sydney Girls' High School to record 'no church' under 'Religion' in the Admissions Register.[23] She liked to be different. Kathleen Grieves, one of her classmates, recalls an incident that occurred the following year, in November 1918, when the girls were about to attend thanksgiving services for the end of the war:

> We stood in groups according to denominations and the
> Church of England group was nearest the foot of the stairs.
> We were waiting for Miss Garvin to lead us over to St James.
> She came down the old stairs, ... buttoning her gloves, passed
> a severely scrutinising glance over us and finally to the tall girl
> standing aside said, "Why are you not with one of the
> groups?" In a deep hoarse voice Peggy Stead answered, "I am
> an atheist." Miss Garvin looked at her for two seconds and
> then said, "Oh? Well, just get over here with the Church of
> England group and come along."[24]

*   *   *

The atheism came, of course, from David Stead; so did Christina's socialist sympathies. With a father who called himself a 'state socialist', Christina had grown up proud of Australia's working-class heritage and labour tradition. ('We're the seed of rebellious men,' boasts one of the working men in *Seven Poor Men of Sydney*— 'the martyrs of the nineteenth century Trades Union England, all the men who stole bread rather than see their wives and children starve.'[25]) Australia, with its old-age and invalid pensions, maternity allowances and female suffrage, enjoyed an international reputation for social reform. However, the Great War was producing a new conservatism. The tide of loyalty to the Empire meant that labour organisations, which opposed conscription, were regarded as traitors. The Bolshevik Revolution in 1917 would further polarise Left and Right: it gave conservative newspapers a new menace: the Reds. (Indeed, the Communist Party of Australia would be formed in 1920.) Christina Stead had great respect for her progressive history teacher, Miss Barnes, who had the girls discussing the *Communist Manifesto*.[26]

It was the era of patriotism. At the cinema, silent newsreels of 'battleships loaded to the gunwales with cheering soldiers dipping victoriously through freshening seas' were accompanied by rousing nationalist music.[27] 'Anzac' and 'Gallipoli' had become emotionally charged additions to every Australian schoolchild's vocabulary. At Sydney Girls' High, the girls knitted socks for the men fighting on the Belgian front and filled boxes with Christmas comforts for 'our men in France'. They brought things from home and set up stalls in town to raise money. The school magazines of 1917 and 1918 were filled with rhetoric about the 'noble deeds' of the 'glorious Allies', and included a Roll of Honour—names of fathers, brothers and sons who were serving the Empire.

Christina Stead was sub-editor, then editor, of those patriotic issues of the school magazine, yet she herself was no war patriot. Her father was a committed pacifist: so was she. Thirty-seven when war broke out, David Stead condemned it as mass murder: he was hardly likely to join the forty per cent of Australian males aged between 17 and 40 who volunteered for the Imperial Forces. To the family's horror, his sister Jessica would sometimes stand on Macquarie Street handing out white feathers to able-bodied men passing by.

In *Seven Poor Men of Sydney*, 20-year-old Michael Bagenault does not at first enlist in the war overseas. 'The bosoms of the nice ladies his mother knew swelled with righteous venom',[28] and he receives a white feather in the post. The social pressure is so intense that he eventually signs up. He is one of the fortunate ones who returns, but he is a different man, with broken spirit and shattered nerves— 'one of the derelicts left by the flood-tide of war'.[29]

More than 60 000 Australians died in the war. No army in the Empire suffered losses in greater proportion. War memorials commemorating the dead sprang up in every small town. Christina's age-group was too young to lose fiancés, but the girls were well aware that the pool of potential husbands had shrunk.

★   ★   ★

Christina was in the third-year tug-of-war team in 1918, but she was not much interested in sport, absorbed as she was by her studies, her reading and writing. She enjoyed all her classes, and did well. English, with Miss Ethel Gretton, was her favourite subject. She prided herself on being good at French, too, and she would be grateful for those school *dictées* when called upon, as a secretary in London and Paris in the late 1920s, to write letters in French. Later she claimed that her 'whole view of life' was formed by Guy de Maupassant, the profoundly pessimistic nineteenth-century naturalist writer whom they studied at school.[30] Inspired by the sobriety and simplicity of Maupassant's writing, Christina borrowed all the

French books she could lay her hands on from the Sydney Municipal Library: from Rabelais to Chateaubriand, Hugo and Zola.[31]
Zola's naturalist doctrine, which claimed that writers should develop
the meticulous observation of scientists, would be an important
influence on her own writing. She 'fell overboard' for Balzac, a
lifelong passion.[32] His extraordinary powers of observation seemed
to encompass the whole world, and yet the strength of his imagination liberated him from the constraints of the real world. Zola and
Balzac had scientific principles and a breadth of curiosity to which
Stead herself aspired.

George Henry Lewes' two-volume biography of Goethe affected
her profoundly. Goethe, like Balzac, was more than a literary
genius: his wide-ranging interests included morphology, genetics
and foreign languages. Lewes' biography gave rise to a new dream:
she too would one day attend an old European university and
consort with 'free, delightful, intellectual young spirits'.[33] The
wartime mood was venomously anti-German, and German was
not taught at her school; nevertheless, Teutonic culture, with its
Sturm und Drang and High Romanticism, had great appeal for a
passionate, rebellious adolescent.

Since the school did not have its own library, the girls were
regularly issued with two library tickets from the Sydney Municipal Library. Christina collected them from girls who did not want
theirs and would call in at the library after school with ten or more
tickets.[34] Classmates remember her as 'literature mad'.[35] In the
evenings, she would sit in her room with a pile of books on each
side of her: to the right the books to be read, to the left those already
consumed. As an adult she boasted: 'Not only did I swallow them
alive, but I remembered them too.'[36] Her brother David recalls her
reciting lengthy tracts of Byron's 'Battle of Waterloo'.[37]

Christina was intensely interested in the major and minor passions 'running in the undergrowth of poor lives'.[38] While still at
school, she decided that her first book would be called something
like *The Lives of Obscure Men*.[39] The idea would grow on her: the
title of her first novel would be *Seven Poor Men of Sydney*. In the late
1940s, she briefly toyed with the idea of compiling an Encyclopaedia of Obscure People, a subversive *Who's Who*.[40]

Stead's last year at school, 1919, was one her generation would
never forget: the terrible Spanish influenza, which raged world-
wide, took 10 000 Australian lives in eight months—a death rate as
high as for an equal period in the war. New South Wales schools
closed for several weeks.

That year, Peggy Stead was sole editor of the school magazine (though modesty, it seems, prevented her from including any of her own writing) and one of seven senior prefects elected by the staff. She was happy at Sydney Girls' High, and developed a certain confidence, though she did not have a close friend and ate lunch by herself. But there were two girls at the school whom she ardently admired.

Clare Tarrant and her three sisters were orphans and lived with their aunt in considerable poverty.[41] To Christina, Clare was an *alter ego*, someone else who was eccentric, talented and on the outside. In class they would pass each other 'girlish joky letters'. Years later, Stead recalled:

> Clare, who was subtle, witty, merry, very able, did nothing much in class. She left it to the two weeks before Finals, to cram; and she was an expert crammer. She could have topped almost every class, but she had a reckless attitude, a sort of humane scorn for achievement . . . She came to school in rags . . . and her shoes were torn to bits. Once in desperate (though laughing) revolt, she tossed her ragged shoe over the girls' outhouse, then had to climb on the roof to get it down.[42]

Christina Stead was always drawn to reckless, high-spirited, talented people, who did not take themselves too seriously. But she and Clare were no more than acquaintances.

Tempe Datson was altogether different. Blonde and blue-eyed, outstanding at schoolwork and athletics, she was extremely popular. Tempe became Christina's new crush. Everybody in the class knew about it: Peggy was always scribbling sonnets for Tempe. At the time, Tempe laughed at them and privately tore them up, embarrassed. It was something she would come to regret.

Tempe remembers Peggy as 'plain looking', with no interest in clothes. 'Peggy was rather odd. You wouldn't want to make friends with her.' Because Tempe lived nearby, in Double Bay, she was sometimes invited to Boongarre for a meal, but her relationship with Christina remained quite distant. Tempe's impression was that the Steads had a 'happy home life', though Peggy did not seem to like her stepmother much. To Tempe, Mrs Stead seemed 'pleasant' and Mr Stead 'an interesting man, with a fine build'. Peggy was evidently very proud of him.[43]

David Stead, for his part, was charmed by the polite and smiling Tempe Datson. When she left on a trip for Europe in 1935, aged 33, he was at the quay to see her off.

It was less easy to be proud of his own plain and sullen daughter who somehow had a knack of arousing hostility in people. Was it the strong jaw and contemptuous air? Was it the clumsy, attention-seeking behaviour? Or her literary pretensions? Phyllis McEwan describes the adolescent Peg as 'terribly plain', 'self-opinionated' and 'strange'.[44]

The poet and community activist Mary Gilmore met Christina through David Stead when Christina was in her late teens, and would remember her later as a 'lank-haired pallid-faced anyhow-dressed girl'. In 1936, when Gilmore read *The Salzburg Tales* and was struck by its 'genius', she mused that she would never have thought that 'that girl' would have attained such heights.[45]

There were only four years of high school in those days with the Leaving Certificate, a state examination, at the end. Stead sat the exam in November 1919 and did well: Honours in English, A for Botany, and Bs in French, Maths I and II and Modern History. Her results won her an Exhibition to the university, a scholarship which paid her fees and an allowance for books, but Stead was not eligible to take an arts degree. Latin was a pre-requisite for a Bachelor of Arts, so in the Faculty's view, Stead was officially 'unmatriculated'. Kogarah High had probably not offered Latin, but it is surprising that she was not encouraged to take it up at Sydney Girls' High. It seems that Stead had not thought of going to university until her third year of high school: she took Latin in her last year, hoping to pass the supplementary examination early in 1920. But despite the encouraging quotation from Horace that Miss Gladys Edgington had written in the front of her book—*'Contra audentior ite qua tua te fortuna sinet'*[46]—Christina was unable to catch up four years' work in one. She would have been accepted for a science degree, but she had no desire to become one of those dreaded creatures with a long black serge skirt and bun.[47] There were two options left to her: a year's scholarship for secretarial training at a business college, or a two-year Teachers' Training Scholarship. She opted for Teachers' College. She hated the idea of being any kind of schoolmistress, but teachers' training at least meant she would be paid £50 a year to study for two more years—though afterwards she would be bonded to the Education Department for a minimum of five years. The year Stead began at Teachers' College, 1920, the pay for women teachers was increased to four-fifths of the male salary.

Along with the other young female teachers-to-be, Christina Stead, at 17, had to sign a contract with the Department of Education, stating that she had no intention of marrying until her bond was either paid back or worked off. Although it would not become law in New South Wales until 1932 (with the introduction of the 'Married Women (Lecturers and Teachers) Act'), it was expected that women would resign when they married, thereby creating positions for single women dependent on the income. No wonder the teaching profession was irrevocably connected in Christina Stead's mind with being *unmarried*. 'It was a rather terrible prospect,' she admitted. [48]

★   ★   ★

> Naked, except for a white towel rolled into a loincloth, he stood in the door-way, laughing and shouting, a tall man with powerful chest and thick hair of burning gold and a skin still pale under many summers' tan. He seemed to thrust back the walls with his muscular arms; thick tufts of red hair stood out from his armpits.

The striking figure—half Jesus, half Samson—who straddles the opening of *For Love Alone* is Andrew Hawkins, modelled (once again) on David Stead. Casting the seeds of his daughter Teresa's worst fears, he is complacently boasting to his two adolescent daughters that his beauty has attracted many a woman. 'Inward and outward beauty,' he explains, 'strike one chord.' Looking at them, he muses aloud: 'What a strange thing that I didn't have lovely daughters. I who worship beauty so much!' When, after more of this, 19-year-old Teresa explodes with anger, his taunts ring out:

> Look at her! Pale, haggard, a regular witch. She looks like a beggar. Who would want her! What pride! Pride in rags! Plain Jane on the high horse! When she is an old maid, she'll still be proud, and noble. No one else will count! [49]

Such taunts were a constant refrain in Christina Stead's own adolescence. Like Teresa, she appeared cold and indifferent, but in fact her father's poisoned arrows hit their mark.

> There was a glass pane in the breast of each girl; there every other girl could see the rat gnawing at her, the fear of being on the shelf. Beside the solitary girl, three hooded madmen walk, desire, fear, ridicule. [50]

She was made to understand that finding a man was something to which she could scarcely hope to aspire. As Stead said later: 'We were brought up to be pretty and catch men. I wasn't pretty and they didn't think I'd catch one.' [51]

David Stead's taunts made Christina mad with anger. She would explode, make threats, brood. When her fury eventually subsided, she would nurse her misery and hate herself. It was an exhausting, demonic cycle, and it left her over-sensitive. Her characters Michael Bagenault and Teresa Hawkins have the same defensiveness. 'When anyone twits me or insults me, I can't stand it,' says Bagenault, who detests his father. 'I want to cry or kill them, or commit suicide ... I go on thinking over the insult for weeks and crying inwardly.' [52]

Stead's relationship with her disapproving, coaxing father ebbed and flowed. She hated him, she loved him; she resented him, she pitied him. For years she was his confidante. The Oedipal tensions were further intensified when David Stead told her, in 1919, that he had fallen in love with a schoolgirl her own age.

Sixteen-year-old Thistle Harris had recently joined the New South Wales Naturalists. Thistle was beautiful, passionate about botany, sweet-natured and full of admiration for David Stead, who at 42 was in his prime. Christina, who often went on the Naturalists' excursions and knew Thistle, was shocked. It seems that David Stead decided the romance was too outrageous to pursue, though he continued to hanker after his young friend. The following year, Thistle Harris, who was studying botany and zoology, bumped into Christina in the university grounds. Thistle said 'Hello Peg'. The response (she recalls) was a frosty 'Good afternoon, Miss Harris'.[53]

Christina's feelings toward her father were further complicated when he lost his job early in 1920. For several years, as Manager of the State Trawling Industry, he had been the target of calumnious attacks by the conservative Opposition in Parliament. He was accused, quite unfairly, of 'fishing out' the waters, of gross mismanagement. There were vicious notices in the newspapers, blackmail, public and private pressure. It was to Christina, not his wife, that David Stead spoke of these troubles. She would say later, 'I can never forget his expression, in misery, at the numerous unfair and even rascally charges voiced in parliament and carried in the newspapers.'[54]

David Stead was thoroughly naive when it came to politics, as Christina Stead later recalled. 'He knew of course that private enterprise wanted the ships either with them or at the bottom of the sea; but he did not believe that "evil men" were either in the majority or could rally so much strength.'[55]

> He would sit at the table when the morning papers came containing attacks upon him and he would in detail explain what was wrong, what the lies and fables were . . . "Write to them," we would cry, the young ones, too, "write to the papers, tell them." . . . Then he would sit back, saying nothing, looking exhausted and defeated.[56]

'Dare to be a Daniel', he would say, and 'Truth crushed to the earth shall rise again'. But it did not. Eventually, 'driven wild by constant attacks, and conscious of his own integrity, he hotheadedly did a rash and dangerous thing'. He told only Christina of this 'irreparable mistake', which provided the ammunition the Opposition needed. Whatever it was—it is not clear—it ruined him.

Early in 1920, the Royal Commission into the State Trawling Industry praised David Stead's hard work, scientific knowledge and enthusiasm, but came up with the verdict that David Stead was 'first and foremost a scientific man', not a business manager.[57] He was relieved of his post. The project that had been his conception and his pride and joy acquired a new general manager; David Stead was merely retained as a consultant to the Minister's advisory board. In time it was even decided that he would lose all claims to superannuation. This was a bitter turning point in his life.[58]

He was not to have regular work for almost two years. In September 1921, under the pseudonym 'Dinnawan, the emu, the king of the plains', he began a weekly series called 'The Great Outdoors' for the children's section of the *Sunday Times*. The jauntily written articles—featuring Nundaba the Snake and Mi' Poo' Yoo the mullet—were addressed to a character called Everyboy. In David Stead's universe, girls had a secondary place.[59]

* * *

Christina Stead started at Sydney Teachers' College in February 1920. The new red-brick building had been opened that very month in the grounds of Sydney University, but the two institutions were quite separate (though the college Principal, Alexander Mackie, was also Professor of Education at the university), and quite different worlds. The 850 trainee teachers at the college were mostly women, and the lecturers mostly men. Stead would later speak of Sydney Girls' High with enthusiasm, but the Teachers' College was not a place that aroused any loyalty. In university circles it was generally accepted that Teachers' College Scholarship holders were a class below university Exhibition holders, and that primary school teachers, like Stead, were inferior to secondary school teachers.

Dymphna Cusack, a contemporary of Stead's and later a friend, attended the college three years after Stead: she took the year-long Diploma of Education course after her university degree. Cusack loathed its drab 'reformatory school ugliness' and the dull, hidebound lecturers who 'had inherited the Empire, the glory of World War One, the sanctity of sex'. 'This was a time,' she writes, 'when the theories of the great post-war educationalists were inspiring a new direction. We were never made aware of it, except in our private reading.'[60]

The subjects considered suitable for teachers of primary children were language, education, history, drawing, gardening and nature study. Language was concerned with phonetics, writing and diction. The history course Cusack found lamentably uninspired after studying under genuinely progressive history professors at the university.[61] Education was the history and theory of method,[62] but (according to Bernard Smith, who was a student at the college a decade later) there was little critical engagement with the subject.[63] In her first year, Stead got a distinction for education, and credits for other subjects.

For those truly interested in the practice of teaching (Stead was not), Professor Alexander Mackie, a small and cheerful Scot, gave a useful course. Mackie, then 44, had come from Edinburgh fourteen years before to establish the college, and he prided himself on an interest in pedagogic experimentation.[64] He at least made reference to the new Montessori method of teaching, founded in Italy, which stressed pupil self-reliance. The year Stead began studies at the college, a 'lady teacher' was sent to Harvard University to study the education of subnormal children—an area of expertise the college hoped to develop, and which would have some bearing on Christina's own path.[65]

In her second year, 1921, Stead scored distinctions in two subjects, Education & Logic, and Ethics Psychology, and credits or passes for the rest. Her execrable handwriting was considered a problem for a teacher. Another was her weak speaking voice, and the following year she would be given special tuition in voice production.[66] Her final mark, at the end of the two-year primary teaching diploma, was a 2A.

In 1921, Stead co-edited the college magazine, *The Kookaburra*, and a poem of hers, 'The Gentle Supervisor', published in the college magazine of 1921,[67] shows that she had not given up the habit of adulatory poems. This one was humorous and aimed at a male lecturer: it is not clear whom. The same issue contained a second poem by Christina E. Stead, as she now signed herself, various humorous columns which suggest that she projected herself as something of a college wit, and a four-page short story, 'The Key of the House of Shadows'. Evidently she no longer suffered from undue modesty as an editor.

Only the story, 'The Key of the House of Shadows', indicates unusual talent. Set in an old French town, it is told by a first-person narrator in a confidential, anecdotal style reminiscent of Edgar Allan Poe. Like his stories, the narrative moves quickly from the everyday world into the realm of the fantastic and horrific, juxtaposing naturalistic and supernatural elements.

It was possibly after reading this story that Stead's art teacher, a young woman engaged to be married, suggested that Stead write a book of short stories which she would then illustrate. Stead was enthusiastic, and took the idea seriously. She rose at dawn to write, before leaving for college on the ferry.

The following year (she was still attached to the Teachers' College), she won a small Teachers' College prize for her poem 'In the Great Hall', which paid lyrical tribute to the university's 'hushed hall' with its 'tendrilled arches'.[68]

* * *

At the end of Stead's second year at Teachers' College, on 31 December 1921, David Stead left for Singapore to take up a year's appointment as Special Fisheries Commissioner in British Malaya.[69] He needed the salary badly, but he also liked to think he would be contributing to 'the great international work' which was 'some day, going to make all men brothers'.[70] His unfair treatment over the State Trawling Industry had not destroyed his idealism.

He wrote to the family once every month or two, whenever a boat was about to depart for Australia, and several of his letters have survived. They give an interesting insight into his relationship with Christina at the time—a relationship that was likely to have been improved by distance. It was to 'Pegler', now 19, that David Stead wrote more fulsomely, and it was *her* letters to which he most looked forward.

David Stead's health suffered from the tropical climate.[71] Normally such an energetic man, in Asia he struggled with headaches, insomnia, fever and terrible lethargy. At times he felt close to physical breakdown. Unlike his white associates, he never allowed himself the relief of alcohol. He wrote to Christina:

You see a lovely vista of palms and wonderful trees—and it is too hot to go for a walk. . . . Then you see a lovely sheet of water; but it is too hot to go out on it. Because it is TOO HOT everywhere. The heat wilts you like a soft leaf—just like a pumpkin leaf goes in our place on a very hot day in Sydney.[72]

He liked his gifted Chinese secretary and interpreter, Tan Guan Hoe. Once he visited Abishegenedan, a Tamil engineering friend, in a quarter of Singapore never frequented by white men. ('He pictured himself to us, a tall fair man, all in white, trading cheerily down the dark streets in the evening, a smile for all along the crowded noisy pavement and littered road.')[73] But he was lonely and homesick.

In *The Man Who Loved Children*, two letters from Sam Pollit in Malaya are taken almost word for word from a long, humorous letter that David Stead wrote to Christina from Singapore in July 1922. He had just visited a Chinese Buddhist Temple. The 'burning of joss sticks and firing off of crackers' was 'a great way of worshipping', he told her with joyful irreverence. 'You get something for your money.'[74] He described the torture scenes on the walls of the temple ('terrible pictures showing what will befall the unbeliever who flouts the gods') with great relish, admitting that he had originally intended the letter for Weeṭa, but 'I know you love blood-and-thunder'.

Other letters reveal David Stead's hortatory, messianic side. In one, he lectured Christina about the need to be always curious and alert.

> Most . . . people are extraordinarily unobservant. It is the same in Australia, and it is the same everywhere in the world that I have travelled in. Is it any wonder then that I am solitary. I do all my rambles in the cities of the world exactly as I did my rambles up and down the coast and in the fastnesses of mountains and gullies in my beloved Australia—alone.[75]

His homilies had a tendency to circle back to himself, as another letter to Pedler—his childlike distortion of Pegler—shows even more clearly.

> So, Pedler dear, I suppose Fate sent me here after all to do something more to make the idea of justice for the helpless a living one. But I couldn't have those ideas without having built myself up in the study of social and international economics.
> I get on splendidly with all these villages and villagers. They say I am *good* and *just*. I am *not*; but I think they are good and must be helped and *shall* be helped, by me and by my men . . .[76]

David Stead believed passionately in social justice and rights for native peoples (he felt especially strongly about Australian aborigines): in Singapore he once refused to sit on an official platform where there were no native representatives (only British).[77] But there was considerable self-congratulation in the image of himself as the shining prophet of justice sent to help the oppressed dark races. It is striking that he teased the natives in the same paternalistic sort of way that he teased his own children. From Pagi Pagi he wrote to 'Pedler':

> You should see my Indian stenographer laugh when I joke about his 'color'. Sometimes I tell him I can't see him he's too dark. The other day I stopt [sic] suddenly in the middle of dictation to say that I thought I saw his soul, notwithstanding the pigmentation (rather 'heavy') of his skin. And yet he says that my presence ennobles him & has given him a new view of honor and right. They are not used to human feeling from 'superiors'.[78]

The 'man who loved children' was equally the 'man who loved the natives'.

For all his 'Pedler dear', there is, in David Stead's letters, a peculiar lack of tenderness and empathy. In his solipsistic world, his dreams for his children were mere extensions of his dreams for himself. He seemed to have no sense of his eldest daughter as a *different* person, with her own anxieties, emotional needs and torments. This made it very difficult for her (especially as she had no recourse to a loving mother or even close friends) to establish a healthy sense of her own, separate identity.

When Sam Pollit, in *The Man Who Loved Children*, outlines to the children his hopes for the unity of mankind, a system which he says could be called 'Monoman' or 'Manunity', Louisa says drily, 'You mean Monomania'.[79]

* * *

Christina's letters *to* Malaya have not survived, but it is clear that she had her own excitements and turmoils that year. She was to have gone out teaching, but was saved from this dreadful prospect by 'dear Dr. Phillips'.[80] Gilbert Phillips had observed her interest in psychology: in 1922 he arranged for her to be given a Teachers' College scholarship to be his research assistant in psychology.

It is unlikely that the research interested Stead a great deal. Intelligence testing was then attracting intense interest in the domains of education and psychology and was being used internationally to determine differences between the sexes, whites and negroes, and social classes. French psychologists Binet and Simon had devised tests intended to single out 'dull' children. The 1916 Stanford revision of the Binet-Simon test had extended its application. Stead's job was to go round to various government schools testing children individually. She had to present them with a set of problems, verbal and pictorial, and determine their intelligence quotient by calculating their alleged mental age against their actual age. One schoolboy appeared to have the remarkable IQ of 182 (the Binet-Simon average was 100), and the report she wrote does not suggest that she questioned the test's reliability.[81]

Several years later, Stead would have a character in *Seven Poor Men of Sydney* criticise the Binet-Simon tests on the grounds that they appeared to demonstrate that poor children were 'ten per cent. below the average, middle-class children at par, and rich children ten per cent. above the average'.[82]

Christina had enrolled for Psychology II at the university that year, as a non-matriculated student, taking it as a non-degree subject. This course in experimental and abnormal psychology complemented her research. Professor Tasman Lovell even gave lectures on Freud, which were very popular with the students.[83]

Stead scored a bare pass, but it at least afforded her the opportunity to mix with university students.

Lucy Firth also studied Psychology II that year, and by September Christina was occasionally staying over at her house—presumably to save herself the trip to Watson's Bay after lectures or union debates in the evening. Lucy was 29, almost a decade older than her fellow students. Coming from a poor background, she had worked for some years before enrolling at the university. Christina was embarrassed by Lucy's primly-dressed, old-maidish style,[84] but Lucy was a serious student and an interesting woman. She was taking history, philosophy and psychology, and nearly every year she would come equal first. That year, once again, she shared the Psychology II prize with her friend Walter George Keith Duncan.

Lucy Firth would be 'Miss Haviland' in *For Love Alone*, an admirable but pitiful figure: a young old-maid. Even her name has cruel resonances of Miss Havisham in *Great Expectations*. Keith Duncan (as he called himself) was to be the model for Jonathan Crow, the young man in *For Love Alone* with whom Teresa believed she was in love.

Keith Duncan (whom his friends, with the Australian passion for abbreviation, called 'Dunc') was 19, a year younger than Christina, when she first set eyes on him in 1922. Goodlooking in an intense, nervous sort of way, he was dark-haired and lean, with a narrow face, a broad, agile mouth and brown eyes that would flash behind his glasses with righteous conviction.[85] Yet photographs from the time betray an uneasy, anxious look behind his casual boyish poses.

As a second-year undergraduate, Duncan was just beginning to take part in the university debates which—along with his consistently outstanding marks—would make him a well-known campus figure. The university newspaper, the *Union Recorder*, frequently refers to his eloquent, melodramatic rhetoric. But the debates' secretary was not uncritical. After one performance came this note on Duncan: 'The speaker should try to overcome his incoherency of thought, and also realise that sarcasm is a dangerous weapon, which needs skilful handling.'

* * *

For Love Alone, which depicts this period in Stead's life, is a powerful evocation of a young woman in a permanent state of sexual desire. It is made to seem only too natural in this 'fruitful island of the sea-world';[87] everyone suffers 'the torments of the southern sun'.[88] Girls ripen early in the Antipodes. The sun, violent and relentless, has a sexual force. Teresa, half-maddened by the noon heat, would experience a 'torment of desire ... as the sun mounted'.[89]

The novel conveys a lasting impression of the sheer sensuality of summer in Sydney. Nature dominates; the physical aspect of life cannot quite be contained. In the scorching heat, people smell like foxes; young women's new-washed hair gives off a 'scent of little woodland beasts'. When Teresa, 'a powerful, full-blooded young woman', walks home late one evening, past the murmurs of lovers in the park, it is full moon and high tide, the sound of cicadas fills the bay, and people are sitting 'in their moist warm gardens, talking and hitting out at the mosquitoes'.[90] At the house, Teresa drags on a black bathing-suit she has grown out of ('sleek and fishy to swim in') and splashes around in the water ('on her front ... like a young prawn'), dreaming about gently drowning.[91]

This is no fog-bound London adolescence, yet this upside-down society ('winter is in July, spring brides marry in September, and Christmas is consummated with roast beef, suckling pig, and brandy-laced plum pudding at 100 degrees in the shade') had adopted the straitlaced Victorian morality of the Old Country. Australian schoolgirls had to wear thick cotton stockings and gloves even in blistering heat. And though it was tacitly acknowledged that young men experience sexual desires, a nice young lady was not supposed to feel lust as long as she remained unmarried.

The young women in Stead's fiction toss in bed from the age of 14. In *The Beauties and Furies*, Oliver calculates how many 'loving-nights' Elvira, married at 21, missed out on from the age of 14. One senses that it was a calculation Stead had made about herself. Fourteen when she first experienced the 'torment of desire', Stead had to wait until she was 26 before she gratefully surrendered the burden of her virginity. It meant that she had twelve and a half years in which to imagine, fantasise and fear the 'night of the senses'. 'Hunger of the stomach can be confessed,' she would write later, 'but not sexual hunger.' The need to conceal it made it 'fiercer, madder'.[92]

Stead's wide reading gave her insights, albeit confused, into the ways of the flesh; as a young girl she had been aroused by the enchantments of *Arabian Nights*; at school her imagination was further piqued by Zola, Swinburne, Thomas Hardy, Stendhal's essay *On Love*. Like the fictional Teresa, Christina knew 'the disorderly loves of Ovid, the cruel luxury of Petronius, the exorbitance of Aretino, the meaning of the witches' Sabbaths, the experiments of Sade, the unimaginable horrors of the Inquisition, the bestiality in the Bible, the bitter jokes of Aristophanes and what the sex-psychologists had written'.[93] At university, she read Havelock Ellis, Adler, Freud, Krafft-Ebing. All this produced a potent mix in her imagination. Jottings Stead made when she was planning *For Love Alone* in the early 1940s describe the febrile, masochistic fantasies of a young woman:

> Virgin after being excited is torn by bayonets in her womb: animals trained to flesh-eating, but only the lower parts: woman exposed to lusts of deer, horse, bull, and thus torn to pieces . . . women in gaol visited foully by gaoler and greatest criminals . . . wasteful man keeps beautiful girl for year or more, letting her see all obscene plays and his acts with other slaves, but she must not taste it, he likes to see her suffer . . . girl is tormented by men who do the act coitus interruptus, until she is so wild that she flings herself at their feet, is trampled on, begging for love.[94]

All her life, Stead firmly believed in a link between sexual deprivation and madness: in those virginal years she sometimes feared she was going mad. But it was not just the seemingly interminable period of sexual frustration: there was also the dreadful marriage panic. Young women lived with fear and ridicule. What if they were not married at 25 or 30?

> Teresa suffered for herself and the other girls; each year now counted against them; nineteen, and has she a boy-friend? Twenty, and does she like anyone particularly? Twenty-one, now she has the key of the door; she ought to be looking round! Twenty-two already! Twenty-three and not engaged yet? Twenty-four and not even a nibble?[95]

The unmarried woman stood to miss out on everything: sex, love, motherhood, and social respectability. For many—certainly for Christina Stead—it seemed a fate far worse than death.

★ ★ ★

In January 1923, Christina Stead could put it off no longer: she was obliged to take up her first teaching appointment. She was 20 when she began her teaching career at Darlinghurst Girls' School, in the middle of Sydney's inner city slums, on a salary of £143 per year. (The Public Service Basic Wage for males was set at £193 per annum in September 1923.[96]) After one week teaching a large class, her voice gave way. The headmistress expressed concern about the progress of the class. Christina consulted a doctor, who diagnosed chronic pharyngitis and recommended having her tonsils out. At the end of February, tonsils still intact, she wrote to the Education Department asking to be transferred to a position that would relieve the strain on her voice, suggesting 'work with small groups of

subnormals, or experimental work in psychology'.[97] She was granted
a week's sick leave without pay,[98] and then transferred to Blackfriars Correspondence School, in the hope that the largely clerical
work associated with teaching children in the outback would suit
her better. She remained at Blackfriars until the end of the year, but
her voice was only a symptom of the real problem, which was that
she detested teaching.

The following year, 1924, Gilbert Phillips came to the rescue
again, and employed Christina at the Teachers' College as a Junior
Lecturer in Psychology, on a salary of £175 per annum.

In July and August 1924, her father was in Honolulu, as part of a
New South Wales Government delegation attending the Pan-
Pacific Food Preservation Conference. He came back very excited.
After the conference, he had been in an aeroplane for the first
time—US airmen had flown him right into the crater of the Kilauea
volcano. His scientific and eugenicist friend David Starr Jordan had
been at the conference and the two men had talked about international progress, the future of the Pacific area and brotherhood
between America and Australia.[99] It must have made Christina
more determined than ever to travel herself.

★   ★   ★

The crisis came in 1925. The Junior Lectureship at the Teachers'
College had been for one year only, and in January 1925 Christina
Stead had to return to primary teaching. She spent part of the week
at Glenmore Road Public School and part of the week at Darlinghurst Public School. By February, her voice had given out again
and she was back at the Correspondence School. In May, the
Education Department established a 'Special Class' at William
Street Public School: a class of 'feeble-minded' children who had
been culled out of nearby schools. It was thought that this work
might interest Miss Stead, who had previously expressed interest in
subnormal children and had special training in intelligence testing
and abnormal psychology.

She lasted scarcely five weeks at William Street. It was not that
she did not like the children; she did. Two of them, born to
syphilitic parents, were deaf and dumb; she thought them 'utterly
sweet'. There was a 'wild boy', with whom she tried the standard
ploys she had learnt in educational psychology, and a nice adolescent boy who tried terribly hard ('like the clerk in Russian literature') but was no good at anything and he knew it. And there was a
beautifully dressed little girl ('like something from a German
opera') who looked 'absolutely pure and sweet' but had no brain at

all. There was nothing Stead could do to help them; they never made any progress, and she found it depressing. In truth, she found teaching—any sort of teaching—so depressing that she was close to a nervous breakdown. Years later, she would say, 'I didn't have the nervous strength. I have plenty of nervous strength for books. But all those little shrimps, no . . . I couldn't do it'.[100]

The problem was not the demands on her time, the preparation, the unruly children or her weak voice. It was more that she had a complete psychological block. From the day she had signed up with the Education Department and assured the administrator that she was not thinking of getting married, Christina had been terrified by the spectre of becoming 'an old maid of a school-ma'am'.[101] As she walked through the school gates in the mornings, every fibre in her body rebelled. She had taught for only eighteen months but she had 'reached breaking point'.[102]

In *For Love Alone*, the female teaching 'treadmill' appalls Teresa, who can only see women teachers in terms of 'being condemned to servitude for life'. The unmarried ones, she observes, seemed to 'go queer'.[103] Her own panic and desperation have become physical nausea.

> As soon as she caught sight of the school buildings in the morning, their dirty yellow, and heard the bell, the shrieks, the boots rushing across the asphalt; as soon as she smelled that thick oily and dusty scent which school buildings alone give out, human grease and neglected corners, old varnish and urinals in the heat, the little oils from lunches in paper and boot polish, old stuffs ironed at home with the soap still in them, the dirty heads; that huge, fat, sickening smell that poured down the street, on every side, and seeped from outside into the purer dust of the closed schoolroom—as soon as she saw it and smelled it, that illness to which she was condemned for life, until she was sixty, when a woman is not a woman, she began to float in her misery, not to walk. She forgot her feet and yielded herself to a kind of delirium of horror.[104]

That year Christina, determined to get out of teaching as soon as she could, had been going to an evening class in stenography. She was quite serious now about her plan to travel abroad, and she had been told that a secretary could find work overseas, whereas a teacher could not. To be a secretary in the city, in an office surrounded by men doing business, seemed bliss compared with being stuck in a classroom surrounded by women teachers jaded with 'kid-whacking'. But she was trapped—under bond to remain in the teaching service until 31 December 1927.[105]

By mid June 1925, Christina could take it no more. She had had enough of being 'Miss Stead' at the front of the room, chalk in hand. On the morning of Thursday 18 June, instead of going to William Street, she went to Central Station and took a train to Gosford. She was fleeing to her kindly Aunt Eva and Uncle Charles, her dead mother's relatives who had a citrus orchard in Narara.

Teresa does the same in *For Love Alone*. She flees to Narara. And in the train she feels a surge of elation: she has broken away from the treadmill, done something for herself, something daring and courageous, for the first time. 'She had never felt so well in her life. She could hear laughter, from the hills shouldering off their forests, from the rivers slipping away down.'[106] She tells herself this is only the first stage of a larger, grander, more perilous journey.[107]

A few days later, David Stead took the train to Narara and persuaded Christina to come home.[108] But Christina had at least made her point: by running away, risking a humiliating dismissal from the Education Department, she had made her father and stepmother understand that her antipathy to teaching was serious, that her mental health was in jeopardy. On 25 June 1925 she applied for two weeks' sick leave. On the medical certificate her doctor wrote that she was suffering from neurasthenia.[109] In a memorandum accompanying it, Gilbert Phillips, her official teaching supervisor, commented 'Miss Stead is at present quite unable to continue teaching. In my opinion she is temperamentally unfitted for ordinary class teaching.'[110] As a result, the Education Department granted her a whole month's leave without pay.

No longer was Stead's voice the problem; now it was her 'temperament'. On 13 July, with only four days of her sick leave remaining, Christina, unable to face the prospect of returning to the classroom, applied for a month's extension. This time, her doctor wrote on the medical certificate that he was strongly urging Miss Stead to give up teaching altogether, that she was 'temperamentally quite unfitted for such an occupation'.[111] Gilbert Phillips used the same phrase: 'temperamentally unfitted for teaching'.

But the leave was not extended, and Stead's time off expired on Friday 17 July. It was her birthday, the day she turned 23. She had fulfilled only two and a half years of her five-year bonded service, and was liable to pay back £68. But that day she made a momentous decision. Never again would she stand in front of a class. Never again would she pace the playground on supervision duty; never again would she stand in a teachers' room that smelt of 'hot face powder and sweet tea'.[112]

That very day she wrote to the Director of Education—in

scarcely legible handwriting that suggested (whether deliberately or not) a degree of mental derangement—that the Registrar had recommended that she ask for permission to resign from the service. Gilbert Phillips, a loyal mentor to the end, supported this: 'In my opinion Miss Stead has genuinely tried to serve the Dept. but her temperament is such that she will never be of use as a class teacher.'[113]

Having faced the ignominy of being seen to have failed, there was the bond to pay back: a debt that would have delayed her travel plans by at least two years. (The third class boat fare to England was about £45.) That she was prepared to do this shows the measure of her desperation.

Christina's bond guarantors were Ada Stead and Emma Pattison, Ada's older sister. On 7 October, Ada Stead wrote to the Department, in her elegant, rounded hand: 'As bondsman in the case of Miss Christina Stead, I beg to apply for release from payment of my obligation in view of the fact that Miss Stead resigned solely on account of ill health. A Medical Certificate to that effect is enclosed.'[114] This time the accompanying medical certificate claimed that Christina's neurasthenia made her 'permanently incapacitated' for teaching.[115]

Within a week, the Director of Education, Mr S. H. Smith, wrote back. In view of the evidence of the medical certificates, the resignation of Miss Stead would be accepted without the enforcement of the conditions of her bond.[116]

Christina was extraordinarily fortunate.

*   *   *

Christina was not the only member of the family to act impetuously that year. Her father, now 48, had been approached by the New South Wales government to investigate methods of controlling and exterminating the rabbits that were ravaging the New South Wales countryside. Soon after he had been appointed Rabbit Menace Enquiry Commissioner for New South Wales, work took him to Brisbane. On the Friday evening he boarded the train south to visit a 23-year-old friend who was teaching botany (her first appointment) at a high school in Murwillumbah, near the border of New South Wales and Queensland.

Thistle Harris was at home that evening, miserable because it was a long weekend and her fellow teachers had left town, when her landlady came to tell her there was a man to see her. David Stead took her to the pictures. The next day they went camping with friends. It poured with rain and she slept in his arms. On Monday he returned to Brisbane. On Tuesday afternoon, one of the children in Miss Harris' class glanced through the window and said, 'There's a man out there'. He had a big grin on his face.

When Thistle returned to Sydney for the September vacation, the romance became an affair. Her parents were about to separate and she was staying with friends, in freer circumstances than usual. But her father somehow got wind of his daughter's affair with a married man his own age, and before Thistle returned to the north, he 'gave David an earful'. And Ada Stead wrote a couple of letters to Thistle, pointing out 'a few things'.[117] Thistle was persuaded she must have nothing more to do with a married man whose eldest child was her own age, and whose youngest was only 8. She was quite miserable about the decision, but when David sent her letters and parcels she resolutely sent them back. The romance was called off a second time.

David Stead, also much in love, told Christina everything. Some vaguely fictionalised drafts, perhaps intended for a story, suggest that Christina reacted calmly this time.[118] She may have secretly admired her father for throwing himself into his passion, just as she would have liked to do.

*   *   *

By the middle of that year, Christina had a passion of her own to occupy her thoughts. From June 1925, she attended an extramural tutorial class in psychology, held on Monday evenings at the university.[119] The tutor was Keith Duncan. Known for his controversial and outspoken ideas, he had attracted an interesting group of people. Lucy Firth went along. Herman Black, an economics student (later Chancellor of Sydney University) was there. Marie Byles had graduated in law the previous year and was the first woman to be registered as a solicitor in New South Wales. Florence James was a vivacious New Zealander who had come to Sydney five years before and studied at the Conservatorium of Music for two years before deciding to take an arts degree instead. The same age as Christina, she was in her final undergraduate year and active in the Sydney University Drama Society.

Class discussions ranged widely over social and philosophical questions.[120] The object, Herman Black recalls, was nothing less than 'the Reform of the Universe'.[121] At 23, Duncan had the brash confidence of a postgraduate who had topped virtually every subject in his first degree. The previous year he had graduated with First Class Honours and the University Medals in History and Philosophy and now he was doing an MA in philosophy, hoping to win a scholarship to London to do his doctorate there. Stead was very impressed. From a working-class family, brought up in the slums, Duncan's success was due to his own hard work and determination. She felt lazy and undeserving by contrast.

An eloquent lecturer, Duncan liked nothing better than to challenge accepted beliefs and stir up a good argument. He saw himself as a leftwing liberal, not a communist; but like most of the group, he believed at that time that Russia was the hope of the world.[122] In cavalier fashion he blamed imperialism and capitalism for most of the world's ills: the modern wage slave was in a far worse position than the ordinary slave, he would claim.[123] Religion and morality were merely repressive impediments to clear thought. The world's only chance of salvation lay in eugenics, education[124] and 'the scientific spirit'.[125] Unrestricted migration of white races to Australia 'would militate against the solidarity of labour'.[126]

Dora Russell's controversial book *Hypatia*, published that year, proclaimed women's right to sexual freedom and pleasure, attacked marriage and advocated 'free love'. Duncan approved of these ideas, which the group discussed with vigour. Dora Russell's basic tenet was that the true force of creation was love between men and women. Stead wholeheartedly agreed.

Herman Black would later recall Christina Stead in that group as 'a striking, not-very-communicative young girl'.[127] Florence James' first impression was of a 'rather beaky profile and prominent upper teeth, and her characteristic way of speaking—airing strong opinions, yet speaking with diffidence'.[128]

In *For Love Alone*, Teresa goes to Jonathan Crow's discussion group and finds his 'hunger for learning' and world-weary cynicism immensely appealing. She is not the only young woman to find him attractive. His provocative manner, his slum background and academic successes make him 'the gadfly of desire'.[129] Keith Duncan, too, was popular with women: this doubtless became part of his appeal for Christina. In later life, however, she would make caustic comments about this aspect of his personality:

> He had a certain number of girls he kept on a string. Quite
> different types too . . . And he led off with this "Pity me" routine.
> You know, "I come from the slums" and all that kind of thing,
> and "I had to struggle hard to get here" . . . He was very rich in
> detail of his struggles. Motherly hearted women—which I regret
> to say . . . we all are—naturally bleed for this kind of struggle.[130]

Apart from Stead's occasional comments, which all reinforce the picture of the tortured relationship painted in *For Love Alone*, we have to rely on the novel for any real insight into the nature of

Stead's relationship with Keith Duncan. What is clear is that her passion for Duncan was, from the very beginning, as frustrating as it was nourishing.

Duncan provided a model of a determined and hardworking young man who had expanded his own horizons. He consumed books as avidly as she did; he cared about ideas; he intended to see something of the world. It may well have been Duncan who invited Stead to hear Christopher Brennan lecture in the Men's Union. Associate Professor in Comparative Literature, poet and German scholar, Brennan was original and brilliant, though an alcoholic, and his lectures attracted many students not enrolled in his subject. Stead was excited by one he gave on Greek tragedy, which seemed to open doors to new worlds.[131]

In *For Love Alone*, Teresa Hawkins and Jonathan Crow sometimes walk part of the way home together. They arrange occasional outings, and both hope that the other will make some sort of physical move, but Teresa is shy and awkward, and Crow is passive, wary of emotional involvement. His brief moments of warmth are followed by long stretches of coolness. Teresa's emotions are tossed hither and thither, and she believes herself in love.

★　　★　　★

Around the time that she resigned from the teaching service, July 1925, Stead finished the book of children's stories she had been writing for the last four years. Several were elaborations of stories she had invented as bedtime stories for her siblings—exotic fantasies, probably inspired by the *Arabian Nights*. Her art teacher at the Teachers' College had produced half a dozen illustrations, as promised.

Strangely, Christina was not particularly ambitious about publication; it was her father who submitted the manuscript to George Robertson of the firm Angus & Robertson, Publishers. The reply came on 21 July 1925:

Dear Mr. Stead,

I read and enjoyed Peg's stories. They are remarkable for their language and imagery—in fact they are charming. The trouble is that poetical fantasies like these are too old for young children, and older boys and girls who could, and ought to, appreciate them mostly prefer books of adventure, stories of school life, and so on. I am writing as a Sydney publisher; a London publisher with forty million constituents—or, better still, a New York one with a hundred million—might be glad to have them. Besides, they would have no difficulty in finding an illustrator capable of drawing beautiful princesses, etc.

From your letter, I gather that Peg is quite young, and have no hesitation in saying that she will be heard of in the world of letters one day.[132]

The letter contained some encouragement, and David Stead had determination. He called in several times to Angus & Robertson's offices seeking further advice, but the publisher was always busy. In October 1925, David Stead wrote again, asking if Robertson would suggest some publishing houses in New York or London. He explained that he was 'the more keen on this because it seems to be really the only thing (this story writing) that Peg is thoroughly interested in'.

The curious thing is that she does not seem to value very highly the actual publication of them; yet I feel sure that if some of her stories were published it would give her a tremendously added interest—not only in such work, but in life generally.[133]

David Stead had every reason to feel concerned about his daughter at that time. It is clear that he *did* care about her and tried to be encouraging in his way, for he seemed to be doing all this unasked. And it is not as if he did not have distractions of his own at the time.

In his reply, Robertson merely suggested asking a friend in London or New York to run the gauntlet of publishers, adding that Angus & Robertson would take 200 copies if the book was published in England at six shillings or under.

Angus & Robertson were not interested in budding new writers nor in any Australian fiction, however good, unless it was commercially viable. They were cutting down their local publications during the 1920s, preferring to reprint English or American bestsellers instead. Four years later (in 1929), they would reject the joint winners of the *Bulletin* prize: Katharine Susannah Prichard's *Coonardoo* and M. Barnard Eldershaw's *A House is Built*. Fortunate authors found an English publisher, which as least guaranteed distribution in England, for English and American publishers did not republish books published first in Australia. But Australian authors were paid lower royalties for the 'colonial edition', which was subject to heavy English income tax.

Angus & Robertson, Australia's only major publishing house, would not publish Christina Stead until 1966—over thirty years after she had made her name abroad. It was, she would tell Nettie Palmer in 1951, 'disgraceful'.[134] Her first volume of stories was destined never to be published. Several years later, the manuscript was lost in France.

★   ★   ★

Soon after giving up teaching, Stead landed her first secretarial job, with the Sydney architect Mr Weeks. Later she would reflect how kind he was to her, considering the poor standard of her typing.

She had lunch sometimes with Marie Byles and Florence James in the Botanical Gardens, close to their various offices. All three women had a fierce determination to travel, and would spur each other on with their talk of 'getting away'. Each of them had studied the shipping schedules and worked out when she would be able to afford to sail. The venturesome Byles, one of the first women to walk the city streets in trousers,[135] was a keen bushwalker and camper, and had exotic plans to climb mountains in Asia and Europe and to see the world on freighters and cattle-boats.[136] (Later she would write books about these experiences.) Florence James had graduated and was working as a secretary in her father's engineering firm. Not obliged to pay board at home, she was saving money fast and intended to sail in 1927. She was engaged to a Dutchman from Java, a lawyer, but intended to travel around Europe and see something of the world before she settled down. Beautiful and theatrical, Florence could hardly have been more different from Christina, yet they were destined to become the closest of friends.

In May 1926, Keith Duncan, who had just been awarded a Master of Arts degree and the University Medal for Philosophy, was one of four Sydney graduates to win a travelling scholarship to Europe.[137] It paid the first-class return steamship passage and a living allowance of £200 per annum for two years. Duncan was going to study political science at the London School of Economics.

He left Sydney aboard the *Osterley* on 26 August 1926. With him were Ian Henning, a French and German scholar heading for the Sorbonne, Raymond McGrath, an architect proceeding to Oxford to study fine arts, and John Beaglehole, an historian from Wellington, New Zealand. They played quoit tennis, enjoyed the first-class food and occasionally treated themselves to a liqueur at sixpence a head. Four days after leaving Sydney, Beaglehole wrote to his parents: 'We do a good deal of arguing . . . The Sydney lads are right willing controversialists.'[138] He added that Keith Duncan knew 'a whole lot about social problems' and had a good sense of humour.

He is mad on Bertrand Russell at present. Henning says one day "Who is this Bertrand Russell, anyhow?" Duncan looks at him wonderingly for a moment & then bursts out "Good God, have you ever heard of Jesus Christ?" He is going to London too which is cheerful.[139]

By the time the young men disembarked, Duncan and Beaglehole had arranged to room together in London and had plans to visit their friends in Paris and Oxford. They had read each other's theses and assorted writings. McGrath, who had illustrated a collection of his own poems with woodcuts, promised to illustrate Beaglehole's book of poems when it was finished. There was a fine future for a talented young man on a travelling scholarship.

Christina had to go abroad the hard way—with neither a scholarship nor help from her parents. She told herself reproachfully that she had been lazy at university: as a consequence, she would have to save up and offer herself her own travelling scholarship.[140]

Florence James sailed in August 1927. Shortly beforehand, Marie Byles invited a group of young women friends, including Christina Stead, for a weekend at her parents' cottage at Palm Beach, north of Sydney. Florence James, in high spirits, sprawled on the kitchen table and sang 'O, Shenandoah, I love your daughter'. That weekend would be the inspiration for the opening scene of *Miss Herbert*, written some thirty years later.

*   *   *

Once in England, Keith Duncan wrote to Christina, and for twenty-one months, until Stead's own arrival in London, they corresponded. It is likely that Duncan's letters reflected his behaviour in person: certainly, in *For Love Alone*, Crow's letters contain occasional bursts of warmth which build up Teresa's hopes, followed by messages designed to hurt or humiliate.[141] The fact that letters took six weeks to arrive by boat further added to the ambiguity of their relationship.

The family noticed the blue envelopes on the mantelpiece, waiting for her when she got home late in the evening; they were vaguely aware that there was a young man in her life who had gone to England. Christina talked about Duncan a great deal to her cousin Gwen;[142] at weekends they sometimes went on long walks together and Christina would stride along, 'shaking back her unruly hair' and talking in 'high pitched nervous tones' about getting away.[143]

Duncan had headed for the cultural centre of the English-speaking world. To be educated at the London School of Economics by the best minds in England was the aspiration of every budding political economist in Australia. But why did Christina Stead feel she had to leave Australia? She had no place awaiting her in a famous institution. Was it really because of Duncan that she was so obsessed with getting to Europe?

In later life Stead would vehemently protest if anyone suggested she had left Australia because of its cultural inferiority. When the term 'cultural cringe' (meaning Australia's obsequious attitude to England's cultural heritage) was introduced by A. A. Phillips in the 1950s, Stead would insist that the phenomenon had not existed in her day. But it did, and she must have known it. She had already experienced it at the hands of the publishers Angus & Robertson.

The 'colonial attitude', as Nettie Palmer observed in 1930, was marked by a 'rawness of judgement' and 'timidity of thought'.

> Waves of uncertainty sweep over us. Is this continent really
> our home, or are we just migrants from another civilization,
> growing wool and piercing the ground for metals, doomed to
> be dependent for our intellectual and aesthetic nourishment . . .
> on what is brought to us by every mail from overseas?[144]

It took over three months for return mail or for a book order to be filled from Europe. In 1920 an Australian crew had broken all records by flying from England to Australia in less than thirty days (without radio or weather reports), but regular commercial flights were still decades off. In 1928 the population of Australia was a mere six million and fragmented by the distance and rivalry between the major cities. Australian writers were isolated from one another, as well as from the rest of the world.

Australian literary culture was still far too dependent. Nearly all books and magazines were from England; even American books arrived in English editions—usually several years later. The few good Australian novels were usually out of print in Australia. The only magazine with literary interests, the *Bulletin*, had lost its influence.[145]

Ambitious Australian artists (in whatever sphere) knew that they had to leave the country to give their career a chance. The greatest Australian writer at the time, 58-year-old Henry Handel Richardson, had been living in Europe since 1887: her 1908 novel *Maurice Guest* was set in Leipzig. Few in Australia had even heard of the first two volumes of her Australian trilogy (*The Fortunes of Richard Mahony*), which would make her name when published complete, in 1930.

Stead would have heard that Miles Franklin, author of *My Brilliant Career* (1901) had gone to America in 1906 and was still away, and that Katharine Susannah Prichard (now 45), author of *The Pioneers*, *Black Opal* and *Working Bullocks*, had left for London at 25 and spent several years in England before returning to Australia.

Christina Stead did not know what to expect abroad; she scarcely knew enough about the world to articulate her fuzzy ambitions.

But Duncan had left for London; the brilliant students all headed for Europe. With a vague but powerful belief that she had a great destiny, she knew she had to go to see for herself.[146]

It was not 'for love alone' that Christina wanted to follow Duncan to England: she was far more in love with what he represented: wider horizons, the experience of European culture, the flight from a world she instinctively knew to be narrow and parochial. She did want love—she wanted it desperately—but if it was only love she was after, she could have found it at home. The proof? Colin Lawson.

She was now working as a secretary in a large hat factory, Henderson's, just behind Central Railway Station. The hats were made on the premises: there were showrooms and an office in which Christina worked. One of the salesmen, Colin Lawson,[147] a lively young man who was passionate about music and opera, was intrigued by the romantically thin and pale new secretary, and he began to pay her court. She seemed to care only about literature and love: he nicknamed her Tosca. On Fridays he sometimes brought her flowers.[148] Christina found his attentions a great solace, but resisted his overtures. In *For Love Alone*, the young salesman Erskine calls Teresa 'La Traviata' and she, parched as she is for affection, is dangerously drawn to this man who seems genuinely to desire her. But Teresa tells herself:

She did not want to love anyone here just when she was going.
If she loved him, she might stay here—for ever, anchored in the little harbour where she was born, like a rowboat whose owner had died and which had never been taken off the slips.[149]

*   *   *

From 1927, David Stead was out of work again. He had written a five-volume report on the rabbit menace and was writing a monograph on whales and whaling, and now that radio had become the new state-of-the-art medium, he was giving some of the first school broadcasts on nature subjects. Though he kept tirelessly busy, the man who used to leave for work in the mornings whistling and get off the ferry in the evenings full of tales about his day now found himself pottering about the house, with no regular income. His rigid principles remained unbending, even with a household of adolescents.

Christina would have liked to leave home, and she sometimes toyed with the idea of taking a room in town closer to the hat factory, but it was cheaper to stay at Boongarre, even though she paid board and the season ticket on the ferry was expensive. She stayed out till late most evenings and after stepping past the motorcycles that were invariably being cleaned or repaired by David and Fred, she would find her dinner kept warm. Kate, now 19, mostly did the cooking. The boys were earning: Fred was an apprentice motor mechanic; David was working by day and studying metallurgy in the evenings at Sydney Technical College. At 20, he was an angry young man who had not spoken to his father for a whole year. These days, the older members of the family kept more or less to themselves.

No-one took much notice of Christina and her strange moods. She looked shabby and neglected, for she did not want to spend her money on clothes: her dresses and stockings were patched. She slept badly and ate badly. The small degree of confidence she had enjoyed in her school years was gone: no longer did her grand future seem at all assured. She was desperate and frightened, afraid of failure. (In *Letty Fox*, the young female protagonist remarks, 'What a beautiful girl says can never really be stupid, whereas with a plain girl one always feels that what she is really saying is, "I am a failure".'[150])

Christina had become quite obsessive. So determined was she to save money that she had adopted a severe asceticism which bordered on masochism. It was a long walk from Circular Quay to the hat factory, but she walked summer and winter, morning and evening, intent on saving the tram fare.[151] In *For Love Alone*, Teresa is the same: she walks everywhere—to the point of utter exhaustion.

> The tram ride only cost twopence, so that it might seem folly to wear oneself out in this way, but she was afraid to give in on any count and in some way the endless walking, walking, meant England. She was walking her way to England.[152]

Teresa's walking is also a means of 'outstripping . . . failure'.[153] She tells herself that if she walked the extra way, if she could overcome this small hurdle, then she would triumph over larger ones.

Each day, Christina rose early and spent an hour or more writing before catching the ferry to work. 'Day of Wrath' was a story she wrote after the *Greycliffe* disaster.[154] In the late afternoon of 3 November 1927, the ferry-steamer SS *Greycliffe*, bound from Circular Quay to Watson's Bay with 125 passengers on board, many of them schoolchildren, collided with a passenger liner bound for San Francisco. The ferry sank immediately—the worst shipping disaster ever to occur inside Sydney Harbour.[155] Divers were recovering bodies for days afterwards. It was a shock to Christina, who imagined the bodies below, 'with a glow on their cheeks still through the green gloom of the deep-water channel'.[156]

On a hot summer day in February 1928, Christina's cousin Ettie,

Uncle Sam's daughter, was married at Bellevue Hill—a wedding which caused some family trauma, for the bride was pregnant.[157] Christina was there, and to all the world she looked aloof and contemptuous. Only her fiction (*For Love Alone*) betrays the anguish she was really suffering in a world where everyone talked of 'hope chests' and 'Mr. Right' and girls being 'on the shelf'. Christina did not want to marry the 'neighbour's son'.[158] She wanted a love that did not shackle her: spiritual companionship, passion, equality, creativity. It was to find this sort of love, she believed, that she had to leave Australia. But she was already 26 that year. And going to a new city where she knew no-one but Keith Duncan was a risk. What if Duncan rejected her? What if she missed out altogether? As she wrote later:

> There's a glamour of a diabolic, miserable sort attached to wandering, unhappy, uneasy, unkind rebel sons; but what about daughters—daughters who will not conform have no glamour, respect or love: what they have in mind interests no-one. They have no position in society—and what man will ever marry them?[159]

★　★　★

After work in the evenings, Christina was in no hurry to go home, and would usually go to the Public Library on the corner of Bent Street and Macquarie Street for several hours. She filled her letters to Duncan with discussion of her eclectic reading: Nietzsche, Freud, John Stuart Mill, Edmund Burke's speeches, Frazer's *The Golden Bough*.[160]

For a time she attended evening classes in life-drawing at Julian Ashton's Sydney Art School, but eventually decided she had no real talent for drawing. She was interested in art—particularly the work of contemporary Australian painters: Hans Heysen, Norman Lindsay, Elioth Gruner, Julian Ashton[161]—and made regular pilgrimages to the New South Wales Art Gallery in the Domain. One old-fashioned painting in the European collection haunted her with its sense of entrapment, and she went back and back to gaze at it.[162] *The Sons of Clovis* portrayed two brothers, 'hamstrung, deathly pale, floating bound on a barge down a ghastly grey river'.[163]

Stead's first novel, *Seven Poor Men of Sydney*, would reflect her own desperation in her twenties in Sydney: all the characters are constrained—physically, psychologically or economically. All, without exception, suffer from a 'vermicular pain' in their head and bowels—the pain of intense loneliness.

★　★　★

'One must have chaos in one, to give birth to a dancing star.'[164] Stead delighted in the poetry of Nietzsche's aphorisms and learnt substantial passages of *Thus Spake Zarathustra* by heart. In Nietzsche, the philosopher who claimed that God was dead and that conventional morality stultified and repressed the individual, and that 'noble-minded and aspiring people' often 'undergo their severest trials in their childhood',[165] Stead found consolation and inspiration. Would she be one of the *Übermenschen*, with the courage to rise above the general 'herd' and bear the burden of her freedom in a joyful, Dionysian affirmation of life?

Nietzsche's 'free spirit' (an individual 'beyond good and evil' and responsible to himself) is a 'youthful soul' who repudiates his fetters and chains, experiencing a 'rebellious, arbitrary, volcanically erupting desire for travel, strange places, estrangements'.

A will and desire awakens to go off, anywhere, at any cost;
a vehement dangerous curiosity for an undiscovered world flames
and flickers in all its senses. "Better to die than to go on living *here*."

To Christina Stead this must almost have seemed a personal message. Once the 'free spirit' had broken away, Nietzsche promised, his creativity would bloom.

It seems to him as if his eyes are only now open to what is *close at
hand* . . . What a good thing he had not always stayed "at home",
stayed "under his own roof" like a delicate apathetic loafer![166]

Just as Nietzsche condemned the 'loafer' who stayed at home, so did Stead. Although she would always describe herself as a writer who observed without judging, in her early fiction there is a clear sense of *winning* or *failing* in the game of life—and an implicit moral judgement. As critic Diana Brydon points out, Stead's 'fictional characters divide themselves between those who embark on the voyage and those who refuse the voyage to remain on the shore'.[167] In an interview for the *Australian Women's Weekly* in 1935, seven years after leaving Australia, Stead would claim that whereas some people become 'wanderers', others 'stew all their lives in their own juice and ferments'.[168]

Women who find Nietzsche's philosophy an inspiration for their own lives are to some extent obliged to read him against the grain. His wanderers are unequivocally male and his opinion of women unapologetically low. Nietzsche was the inspiration behind the avant-garde Sydney magazine *Vision*, which so excited Stead when it appeared in 1923 and 1924.[169] *Vision*'s celebration of passion and sexual freedom liberated her turgid imagination.[170] Edited by Jack Lindsay, Kenneth Slessor and Frank C. Johnson, and influenced by the artist Norman Lindsay, Jack's father, it was Dionysian in its bohemian intoxication with life and love, post-Romantic in its literary tradition, and close to Dadaism and early Surrealism in its youthful rebelliousness.[171] But this rebelliousness was decidedly male.

Vision poets Kenneth Slessor and Christopher Brennan perpetuated the misogynist tradition of the peregrinating male hero who needed to flee the domestic hearth. In Brennan's poem 'The Wanderer' (not published in *Vision*, but which Stead certainly would have read),[172] the hero, 'driven everywhere from a clinging home' is eager to 'spread the sail to any wandering wind of the air'.

But it was also in *Vision* that Stead met a powerful counter-myth, which offered her sustenance as a woman. Kenneth Slessor's poem called 'The Embarkation for Cythera' (after Watteau's painting) was published in the February 1924 issue, and the idea of the journey to Cythera, 'that port of love' where 'lovers twine/ darkly with naked thighs', would become a key 'animating myth' in Stead's life and work.[173] Cythera, mentioned in no less than four of her novels,[174] symbolised a place where she could fulfil her 'secret desires',[175] a place where the expression of love was not taboo and where women's talents, unregimented and unconstrained, could burst forth with a 'primeval force'.[176]

Christina Stead well knew that the stakes were far higher for the free spirit who was female. Among her unpublished papers are notes, probably dating from when she was writing *For Love Alone* in the early 1940s, which spell this out explicitly:

Everyone knows to what conformity, cowardice and submission girls are trained: most families still ardently believe that a pretty face is worth more than wit, health, genius and ambition: ardour and curiosity is detested in a girl, passion is a shame to a family.

Yet, despite this training in docile femininity, there would always be 'coldhearted or flamehearted girls' who are rebels and wanderers.

Although there isn't a woman alive who . . . is not perfectly aware of the ignominy, detestation, and social death that awaits her if she does not conform, there are a lot of women who cannot conform. The refractory spirit is in them.[177]

The female rebel, 'inspired secretly or openly by her own glory or strength', will throw off her 'miserable training'. But left to her own resources, with no-one to guide her, the female rebel acts awkwardly. 'It takes years before she knows what kind of human being she is: in the meantime she acts roughly and clumsily, like a young bird in which the nest-building instinct is not yet shaped.'[178]

* * *

It was 28 March 1928, a cool Wednesday morning in late summer. The *Oronsay*, a Royal Mail Steamer of the British Orient Line, was preparing for departure at No. 7 wharf, Woolloomooloo Bay.

The whole family had gathered there to see Christina off. She was travelling to London, third class. As one of the 'steerage' passengers, her name was not among the passengers listed in the _Sydney Morning Herald_ that day.

Weeta sobbed as they said their final farewells. Christina, dressed in a summer dress and broad-brimmed hat, had dry eyes.[179] When the ship pulled out and the streamers eventually snapped, Uncle Sam drove the children round to South Head, near Watson's Bay, where they excitedly held up a large white sheet.

It did not occur to Christina until they had passed through the Heads and were sailing along the coast, that she might never see Australia again. She already sensed that she would be nostalgic for the fresh sunrises, the red-hot January days, the hills outlined with bushfires.[180]

Standing on deck, scanning the coast, she was awed by what she knew to be a momentous moment in her life. She did not know that she would never see her father or her stepmother again. Nor her brother Fred. And that she would eventually return to Australia as a grey-haired, famous writer. But she sensed that her own life—her _creative_ life—was only just beginning. She might not be happy in her future life, but she had done what she had to do.[181]

3

Port of Registry: London

MAY 1928–JANUARY 1929

IT WAS AN unusual voyage. Unlike Keith Duncan, Christina Stead did not play quoits in the fresh sea air. Nor did she enjoy a shipboard romance, as Florence James had done. Her only friend was a nightwatchman. In the daytime, she slept.

The *Oronsay* had just left Perth when a young alcoholic heiress tried to throw herself overboard, delirious with drink. The ship's doctor, anxious to avoid a recurrence, asked for volunteers from third class to look after his first class patient. The job entailed preventing the stewards from supplying the woman with gin.

Stead came forward. She told herself she would fatten up on the rich first class breakfasts she was given at the end of her shift — a great improvement on the steerage fare of stewed apricots and tea. She would describe the furtive cabin-visiting and petty dramas of the A- and B-deck microcosm in her autobiographical short story 'A Night in the Indian Ocean', written in Paris a year or two later. In this, Stella, the young volunteer nurse, is shocked by, but feels sympathy for the pitiful woman lying in bed in diaphanous chiffon, craving alcohol (which she had been given by her mother to keep her quiet as a child) and the embraces of a man — any man. When Stella confides that she has a male friend in Europe, the heiress advises her bitterly: 'If you get a chance, marry him. Take my tip.

Don't wait and don't you live with him without marrying him. It doesn't pay. I know men.'[1]

Stead's nights were spent fetching the heiress water, rubbing her feet and keeping her amused. When her patient was asleep, she would go on deck and sit with the old watchman, who would bring them coffee 'from the bridge'. It was his last trip; he was about to retire. He told his young friend that she would have to work for six months in England before becoming eligible for the £1 a week dole, and if she could not find work in London, she would be welcome to stay with him and his wife in their cottage on the coast while she looked around there. His words made Stead anxious: she had never even considered that she might not be able to find work.[2]

*   *   *

Colombo and Aden were a glimpse of Asia, the rugged mountains of Calabria Stead's first view of Europe. As the ship emerged from the Straits of Messina around midnight early in May 1928, she was on deck to see Stromboli's fiery fountain erupt into the moonlight.[3] There were brief calls in Naples, Toulon and Gibraltar—then the last leg northwards.

Stead's youthful imagination had been inflamed by the Continent, not England, that 'cloud-sunk . . . adamantine island chained to the shifting bank of the Channel'.[4] Yet she must have been moved by the first view of the country her grandparents had left. For young colonials, the chalky cliffs of Dover symbolised much more than the excitement of arrival, the culmination of six weeks on the water. At school they had studied Shakespeare, Dickens, Keats; most were more familiar with British than Australian history and better acquainted with the names of English plants and trees than with indigenous flora. To the inhabitants of the great Southern Continent, England and London were 'familiar yet unfamiliar, in a dreamlike, paradoxical mix'.[5]

But a great weight hung on Stead's shoulders. This voyage was also symbolic, and spelt success or failure. It was only partly about escape, flight from her family: it was also a quest, a quest for love. As the ship chugged into Tilbury, Stead probably felt too numb with anxiety to be excited.

*   *   *

Disembarking from the *Oronsay* into the bustle and noise of Tilbury docks on 5 May 1928, the new arrivals were faced with a depressed economy. After ten years, England had still not recovered from the First World War. Unemployment was above 10 per cent. The industries on which the nation had relied before 1918—coal, iron and steel, shipbuilding and textiles—were precisely those now in decline, and exports were down. The nine-day general strike in May 1926 had polarised the country and left the working class bitter—a bitterness exacerbated by legislation in which Baldwin's Tory government attempted to clamp down on compulsory trade-unionism and strikes.

The population of Greater London had increased almost 10 per cent during the Twenties, as country people drifted to the city looking for work. Inner city boarding-house districts were congested, and there was chronic overcrowding and poverty in the East End. Already in 1919 a Select Committee on London Traffic had declared conditions intolerable. Before the war, motor cars had been the privilege of the rich; now the middle class aspired to a family car. Traffic lights had not yet been introduced in London, nor had driving tests: fatal accidents were legion. Pollution from cars added to the dismal effect of grime and smut from coal-burning domestic chimneys.[6]

May 1928 saw the female voting age in England lowered from 30 to 21. Women were breaking out—Christina would have her hair bobbed that year. *Lady Chatterley's Lover* and Radclyffe Hall's novel about Sapphic love, *The Well of Loneliness*, were published, and both were banned immediately in England. Virginia Woolf's 1928 essay, *A Room of One's Own*, discussed the plight of the woman writer in a country where women earned less than men and still lacked anything like the educational opportunities.

★   ★   ★

Australian writers have frequently described how the surge of intoxication they experienced on first seeing Dover was superseded, at least initially, by numb shock. When 18-year-old Ethel Richardson—the future Henry Handel Richardson—arrived from Melbourne with her mother and sister in 1888, she was dismayed by the ugliness and filth of Tilbury and 'the miles on miles of dismal slums' through which the train travelled to the sooty terminus.[7] Katharine Susannah Prichard, arriving twenty years later, was equally horrified.[8] When Jack Lindsay arrived from Sydney in 1926, he was hardly able to believe that people 'could live in such a dwarfed and sootied world'. He felt betrayed. 'To have come so far for this.'[9]

There is no record of Stead's first impression of England. Her first letter to her cousin Gwen, dated 12 June 1928, after five weeks in England, conveyed neither awe nor horror. London was 'something like Sydney', she remarked dully. 'I have to pinch myself so that I won't take everything for granted.' By July she was admitting that traffic-infested London would be 'unbearable' were it not for the many little squares 'with millions of light fluttering leaves'.[10] It was as well that she arrived in the spring: Stead would always detest the bleak northern hemisphere winters. And when she left London for Paris, after nine months, she would describe London as 'crooked, narrow, mean, dirty and ill-conceived'.[11]

There is little information available about Stead's first few months in the northern hemisphere. Although she wrote to her family, the letters have not survived. Only the sporadic letters she sent to Gwen and Florence Walker-Smith were lovingly preserved. Armed with these, as well as various comments Stead made later in life, we are obliged to speculate.

In *For Love Alone*, Christina Stead's fictional counterpart, Teresa, met from the boat by Jonathan Crow, quickly sees that the gap between them has widened. After twenty months in England, Crow is more worldly and self-assured. His voice is 'firmer, more melodious' (though his 'rasping, assertive, complaining tones were there, as before'). Handsome in his fine clothes, 'he could have any woman for the asking', Teresa thinks to herself. She, on the other hand, is a 'friendless girl', too thinly clad for the cold English spring. Aware how thin and worn she looks, she shrinks from Jonathan's gaze.

Keith Duncan was acutely conscious that the English looked down on colonials, and his friends were mostly Australians, New Zealanders and Boers;[12] nevertheless, being a postgraduate at the London School of Economics lent him a certain status. He was hearing lectures by the great minds of the day: Arnold Toynbee, Sydney Webb, George Bernard Shaw, Bertrand Russell. The latter was his idol: Beaglehole, his room-mate, wrote home that Duncan followed Bertrand Russell round 'like a dog'.[13]

Duncan was fortunate to have Professor Harold Laski as his doctoral supervisor. The newly appointed Professor of Political Science was in his mid thirties, a brilliant, witty speaker, and a prominent figure in the British Labour movement. He blended certain Marxist views with his Labour sympathies, but his traditions were firmly Benthamite and Liberal, and his influence on Duncan, whose thesis was on the evolution of the philosophy of Liberalism in England, was profound.[14] Open house was held at the Laskis' on Sunday afternoons. There his postgraduates would meet anyone from cabinet ministers, trade union leaders and Indian nationalists to American playwrights. Duncan and his friends declared Laski 'friendly and companionable enough to be a colonial'.[15] As a Jew and a leftwing radical, Laski knew what it was to be an outsider.[16]

Though this stimulating cultural environment gave Duncan a new air of confidence, he was still the angry young man he had always been. Christina, sounding distinctly sceptical, described him in her first letter to Gwen:

> He has a thorough-going indignation for (what he conceives to be) all forms of oppression, depression, impression, repression, suppression, compression and (irrational self-) expression, in short for all forms of everything which does not represent (what he conceives to be) Liberty and Justice.[17]

★　　★　　★

Keith Duncan shared a large room at 21 Brunswick Square in Bloomsbury with the historian John Beaglehole. Stead found a room ten minutes away, in a working women's clubhouse at Cartwright Gardens, a *demi-lune* of boarding houses[18] overlooking one of London's 'providential squares'.

Anxious not to deplete her savings, Stead did not even give herself a few days to look at London's landmarks before she set about finding work. At the first employment agency she was told of a position at Strauss & Company, a grain exchange business requiring a secretary with a good knowledge of French. She was put off by the pay: £2 10s a week—less than she had been earning in Australia.[19] (Duncan and Beaglehole's scholarship money was £4 a week, and they considered themselves 'poor students'.[20]) Moreover, when she heard that the agency claimed the first week's pay, she left the office in disgust.

By the end of that day, she had traipsed all over town and discovered that all agencies charged the first week's wage, and that the wages offered by Strauss & Co. were higher than anywhere else. She had also realised the extent of unemployment in London and that secretaries who knew French were alarmingly plentiful. Feeling foolish, she presented herself again at the first agency at opening hour the next day. Miraculously, the job had still not been filled: two applicants had been turned down. She took a bus to the City and hurried nervously through the maze of narrow streets clutching a map and a book.

Strauss & Co.'s office was in St Mary Axe, not far from London Bridge and the Tower of London. The Associate Manager who interviewed her was a short, genial New Yorker in his early thirties, who had only just arrived in London himself. Years later, Stead recalled her first impression of Mr William Blech: 'I thought he looked nice . . . Very nice. I thought he looked marvellous. So pure. What girls think! But I wasn't wrong, really.'

She got the job. All her life, she remained dumbfounded by this piece of luck. 'I must have looked like a dead duck. But I think the clincher was—Bill told me years afterwards—that I looked so shy and at the same time serious. I was carrying a book of Bertrand Russell. And I think that got him. So he engaged me.'[21]

William Blech, who disliked the English and their condescending manner towards Americans, was pleased to be employing an Australian. This particular colonial (he told her afterwards) seemed to have something about her.[22]

* * *

By mid-June, after six weeks in London, Stead was able to tell her Aunt Florence that Piccadilly, Pall Mall, St Martin-in-the-Fields, St Paul's now seemed like her 'own backyard'. 'Tired of hearing all the great monuments of London lauded indiscriminately,' she had 'approached them with a gauche irreverence,' she admitted, but found St Paul's 'glorious and august', even with its coating of filth. Her domicile at No. 33 Cartwright Gardens was just 'five minutes from where Carlyle used to live and seven minutes from where the Protector's daughter is buried'.[23]

Nevertheless, her daily life was 'not intensely exciting', she told Florence Walker-Smith. In truth, her relationship with Duncan was tense and upsetting, but this was not something she chose to divulge to any members of her family.

She wrote that she had spent 'a thoroughly delightful evening' at Keith Duncan's, with John Beaglehole and a visiting New Zealand woman. They had listened to Duncan's assortment of new gramophone records—from Wilhelm Backhaus and Fritz Kreisler to *The Mikado* and *Lilac Time*—and had passionate discussions. 'However,' she allowed herself to add dolefully, 'all the jollifications are spread out evenly over quite a long period.' Duncan was going to rumbustious postgraduate orgies at which his friends dressed up, danced around lamp-posts and gave mock speeches. She was not invited.[24]

One Sunday afternoon, she found her way through the 'subterranean tubes, corridors, lanes, subways, arteries' of the Underground and spent three hours at the National Art Gallery, emerging 'with a head full of Venuses of dubious virtue'. But sightseeing on her own made her feel rather forlorn. 'At one moment you feel grand to be there on your own and seeing the sights and treading historic grounds

and smelling historic smells and the next you feel like some small sort of insect crawling about miserably waving its antennae . . .'[25]
She remained the daughter of a naturalist.

Her new job was 'really delightful', and she was using her school French.

> Yesterday I had to write my two very firstest letters in French
> and of course I was positive they would both be wrong and
> would have "de" and "pour" in the wrong places, etc.
> I positively blushed from timidity—but no! they were both
> right. Wonderful luck. I was quite pleased, but I am feeling
> rather shaky now in case I can't keep up my reputation.[26]

William Blech, her immediate boss, was unlike anyone she had ever met.

> I have a boss who knows (the names of, at least) Europe's
> uncrowned heads and obliges me with discourses on every
> subject under the sun at a moment's notice and even in the
> middle of dictation, and is not too proud to give me
> 1. all the bibliographies I require for
>   a) music
>   b) economics
>   c) literary criticism
> 2. his assistance when the Managing Director goes too fast or
> too Roumanian.
> 3. his blessing when I have an appointment (early) at the
> hairdressers.
>   ! ! ! ! ! ! !

The incredulous exclamation marks are hers. Mr Blech seemed to her extraordinarily brilliant, erudite and compassionate. Not at all the typical investments manager, he was a Marxist. Short and rotund, he had the energy and vitality of a 'small Vesuvius'.[27]

The Managing Director was also an astounding character. Alfred Hurst, born Avrom Hersovici, even managed to surpass Blech's energy. A Sephardic Jew from Romania, Hurst had come to England as a boy, gone to school in London's East End, begun his career as a runner for a grain company, and now possessed a substantial fortune.[28] A 'short giant' with 'a great skull, bull neck, prizefighter's shoulders, gorilla's chest, thick waist and fleshy limbs',[29] he, like Blech, was to thread his way through Christina Stead's future and into her fiction.

Eager to improve her French systematically, Stead responded to a newspaper advertisement by a private tutor. She paid the young Frenchman for several sessions in advance and met him in the visitors' room of his Bloomsbury boarding house. At the third meeting he suggested they go dancing at the Russell Hotel. She refused; her interest in him was confined to learning French. He did not turn up for the next lesson and soon afterwards she received a postcard from Switzerland. She never heard from him again.[30] After that, she enrolled in a French class at Hugo's, the language institute, and enjoyed the lessons immensely.

She was lonely, but she was not bereft of company. Her elderly cousins lived at Streatham Common, on the southern outskirts of the city. Great Aunt Emma, Uncle Cecil and their two unmarried daughters, Winnie and Jessie, were old-fashioned but welcoming and kind. Emma Martin was the sister of Samuel Stead, Christina's paternal grandfather, who had died seven years before, in Sydney. David Stead had written to his aunt, asking her to keep an eye on Christina.

Aunt Emma had kept contact with the Australian family she had never met and she was overjoyed to receive one of its members after all these years. She brought out the family album and showed Christina a photograph of Samuel and Christina Stead and their six children. David George, a young boy in a sailor suit, was sitting next to his mother. 'Look at him,' Christina pointed eagerly. 'A white blaze on the plate, taking up more space than the others even at five!' Her cousins protested. 'How can you say that of a little boy?' She insisted it was true. No one blazed like he did.[31]

Soon Christina made a friend her own age. They possibly met while sightseeing. Francette Hubert, from Asnières-sur-Seine, near Paris, was in London to learn English, and worked as a secretary in a shipping office in the City. It was with Francette, full of enthusiasm for sightseeing, that Christina visited the London landmarks. Beside her French friend, who knew far more about European art and history, Christina felt ignorant and naive. '*Vous êtes une poire, une poire,*' Francette would say, shaking her head in disbelief.[32]

They taught each other French and English idiomatic expressions. It was decided that Christina should speak French and Francette English, and they would correct each other. Christina told Gwen:

Francette has taught me quite a lot of infamous expressions which I must never use outside of Montmartre and then only when disguised. And I have taught her that she must never say "My God" which is innocent in French but scandalous in English: ... that one must not say "at thirty, one is blown-up" when one means "one is in full bloom."[33]

Over the next few months, she grew very fond of Francette's 'yellow head, her artistically painted little Mongol face ... her little temper, her great kindness, her sunny wit and enormous under-standing of the heart'.[34] It was agreed they should meet in France the following spring.

Francette had come to London on a romantic 'wild goose chase'. Christina was beginning to think she had too. Their favourite subject was the ways of the heart, a subject about which the French woman could talk with considerably more experience than Christina. It was probably Francette who recommended *De L'Amour*, Stendhal's meditations on the perversities of love, infatuation, jealousy and feminine pride which so delighted Christina. And when Francette went home, just before Christmas, she sent Christina the illustrated edition of Pierre Louÿs' erotic novella *Aphrodite*. Re-issued that year in a new underground edition, it contained a chapter censored from the 1896 original, and the frontispiece was a series of bold engravings of organs in highly explicit amorous postures,[35] which Stead declared 'finely vignetted'.[36] Stendhal and Louÿs were both mentioned in the novel she had just started to write.[37]

Francette Hubert would be the inspiration for Francesca in *The Beauties and Furies*, who proclaims: 'One should do anything for love.'[38]

★   ★   ★

At the end of *For Love Alone*, Teresa, having just seen Jonathan Crow, that teaser of women's hearts, pass her in the street, sighs bitterly: 'It's dreadful to think that it will go on being repeated for ever, he—and me! What's there to stop it?'

For Love Alone, written in 1942–3, is fiction, though autobiographical. However, Stead would always talk as if the novel were a sequel to *The Man Who Loved Children*, with Teresa an unproblematic representation of herself as a young woman and 'Jonathan Crow' merely a pseudonym for the man himself. Crow was easily identifiable by those who knew Keith Duncan.[39] His appearance, working-class background, manner of speaking: these details were deliberately true to life—and this gave an illicit punch to the bits Stead made up. The fictionalisation of her past gave her real power: the power to re-cast reality.

By insisting that her autobiographical novels, *The Man Who Loved Children* and *For Love Alone*, were 'the truth', Stead tried to have things both ways: she wanted the liberty of invention and the authority of non-fiction. The temptation, of course, was to make herself look better and Keith Duncan worse—if not for her own satisfaction and revenge, then for the sake of the story: a young woman finding love and independence against the odds. A good story was always more important to Stead than the facts: even within the novel, James Quick, the New Yorker based on William Blech, enjoys tossing his conversation with Jonathan Crow about in his mind afterwards, 'improving and depraving it' to tell Teresa.[40] As the contemporary American writer Nora Ephron puts it:

Fiction at the very least . . . is a chance to rework the events of your life so that you give the illusion of being the intelligence at the center of it, simultaneously managing to slip in all the lines that occurred to you later.[41]

Some details in the novel are invented; others are 'improved and depraved'. One obvious change is that Stead has Teresa Hawkins arriving in London in 1936, not 1928, as she herself had—a change she made in order to bring in events surrounding the Spanish Civil War at the end of the novel. To collapse together events which in reality occurred years apart seems a small thing, but it necessarily entailed fracturing the novel's autobiographical truth: Teresa's psychological state at the end of the novel does not reflect Christina's after the same period of time in London.

However, even if details are invented or distorted, scattered clues extraneous to the novel suggest that it gives a good impression of the sort of torment Stead suffered in her first few months in London. Unfortunately, nothing more than scattered clues is available.[42]

* * *

For Love Alone is a brilliant study of thwarted sexual desire. Teresa's attraction to Jonathan Crow, unrequited, is dangerously close to a 'mortal fascination'.[43] 'Do any of us know what we are doing in sex?' muses the sapient James Quick at one point.[44] Great emphasis is placed on Jonathan Crow's seductive appeal. A whole array of women in Sydney and London fall for him. With his dark looks and his 'strange dark eyes' (a Lawrentian touch), Crow appears to Teresa 'very virile'.[45] She is attracted by his long mobile mouth, his capacious hands. Above all, she is captivated by the sound of his voice, which 'altered all the time and was full of natural devices, slurring, drawling or sharp, keen notes, an irresistible burring of affection, soft laughs and pauses of self-blame'.[46] Her first impression of him as 'a dark axe-faced man' had long since faded.[47]

Teresa is never able to predict Crow's mood; he is 'sardonic and naive, cruel and gay, tender and cold' in one breath.[48] One minute he stirs her by the depth of his feeling for suffering humanity; the next he talks flippantly about his friends' sordid sexual abuse of a housemaid. He presents himself as a passionate advocate of women's rights, and at the same time he vilifies women incessantly, denouncing them as parasites hellbent on luring a male to the altar. His talk of sexual equality—though Teresa does not yet see this—is entirely self-interested: 'modern women' are supposed to practise 'sexual freedom' without ensnaring their men.

He wants to take her to bed—or rather, he wants her to take him to bed—but without emotional ties. Teresa misses the implications of the hints he drops and believes he is still a virgin suffering from the same physical torment as herself. She can see that he desires her at times, but he also seems as timid and awkward as she when it comes to making overt advances. So far is she from understanding the real nature of this power struggle with a misogynist that when Crow kisses her on the lips, soon after her arrival in London, she takes this for a declaration of love.

> His lips were warm. She had always heard, on the ferry going to work, that the proof of real love was the kiss, that a man who received a kiss with cold lips from his wife began to think of divorce. A little smattering of ferry-lore, garbled like this, was all she knew of love in practice. Therefore, her first thought was, on receiving this extraordinary kiss, "He loves me after all."[49]

Jonathan's rare embraces are clumsy and rough; mostly he refrains from touching Teresa altogether. Sexually passive, he is also wary—understandably so—of her romantic expectations. His secret affair with the servant-girl in his house (which the reader sees; Teresa doesn't) is altogether less loaded, for she cannot exert any rights nor entertain the slightest expectations of any future with her 'gentleman'.

★   ★   ★

Keith Duncan had a summer job as a tutorial class lecturer in the university extension program in Oxford. He talked of having an early joint-birthday celebration before he left: his birthday was 11 July and Christina's just six days later. Stead told her Aunt Florence:

> We are going to have a cake with 51 candles. It is all arranged —you see, he is 25 and I am 26, so *we* are really 51! Creeping old age doth grasp us![50]

The party was not mentioned in her next letter, written on Keith Duncan's birthday, and perhaps it had never taken place. Stead merely remarked, 'Keith is tutoring at Oxford and having a gloriously lazy time in dazzling sun, he says—which makes me painfully envious.'[51]

One week later, Christina told Gwen, 'It makes me feel wicked that I am not always as happy as a lark with all your kind thoughts.' Gwen had sent her a pretty double-silk brassière (unfortunately a little small); a Watson's Bay acquaintance, Nellie Molyneux, had sent her a handkerchief embroidered with blue birds for happiness. Christina, who had opened the parcels at her Aunt Emma's, had enjoyed shocking her staid cousin Jessie by insisting that she try on the brassière in the garden.

She was writing to Gwen from the office. Mr Blech had 'tootled off to Paris' for five days, 'partly on business', and there was not much work for her to do. She did not mention the other reason for her boss' visit to Paris: his wife and 8-year-old daughter were living there, and he crossed the Channel as often as possible to see them. The letter continued:

> Heaven! I am tired, I could sleep for a week ... I get tireder and tireder, although I have not much office work to do. But the fact is that it is the sitting still and the waiting and the doing-nothing that knocks one out, *if* all the time one is sitting still, etc. one's head goes running on and running on about nothing in particular ... When I get near bedtime, I am consumed with a desire as bad as any described in the most harrowing novel by the most able author, but it is only to go to sleep. I don't think I shall ever get up off this chair, for instance: I think it would be charming to go on for ever, dreaming ... and get deeper and deeper in the flood of oblivion until saturated, when I should like to go to sleep, like mad Ophelia, singing silly songs.

Stead was easily carried away by words, and the allusion to able authors indicates her self-consciousness in regard to her art. But there was surely more to this than the literary pleasure of describing a near-trance. It is a curious cry in the dark from someone who normally took great care to appear cheerful. She knew that her words were likely to cause concern, for she added, by way of feeble reassurance: 'Don't get alarmed: I went to bed late last night, that's all.'[52]

It was auto-hypnosis that Stead was describing—a state, Breuer claims, that occurs in people prone to habitual reveries if they have suffered protracted anxiety.[53] An all-pervasive desire to sleep, to blot out the world, is also a common symptom of depression.

Stead is likely to have been musing on the parallels between the scorned Ophelia and herself. Keith Duncan had rejected her. It must have seemed to the 26-year-old Stead that the three hooded madmen—desire, fear, ridicule—were crowding in on her.

The degree of Stead's desperation can be gauged from her apparent conviction that she was going to die. Later in life, she readily alluded to this romantic notion, without ever elaborating. She recalled that she occupied the long, lonely summer evenings of 1928 writing a novel—'under such stress' that she 'never expected to write another book'.[54] But she had resolved to leave something behind her.[55]

At first she had hammered away on an old Corona borrowed from Duncan, but she soon bought her own typewriter with her savings. The title of her novel was *Death in the Antipodes*. Later—with Dickens' *Seven Poor Travellers* in mind[56]—she would call it *Seven Poor Men of Sydney*.

During the summer and autumn of 1928, Stead reached a nadir of self-loathing. In Sydney, she had eaten little and walked to the point of exhaustion; now she resumed her old habits. When Florence James saw her early in November for the first time in eighteen months, she was shocked at how thin she was.[57] Every morning Stead walked from Bloomsbury to St Mary Axe; every evening—until she became 'too feeble for it'—she walked home. Later, she would comment: 'I didn't realise the connection between my walking and this continued privation and my feelings.'[58]

Christina Stead, wary and self-contained, very rarely discussed her emotions in letters. It is to her fiction that we must turn for clues about her inner life.

In both *For Love Alone* (written *about* this time) and *Seven Poor Men of Sydney* (written *at* this time), Teresa and Catherine eat badly—mainly buns with cups of tea. Both are virgins, lonely and desperate, physically fidgety and verging on manic.

In the avowedly autobiographical novel *For Love Alone*, written fourteen years later, Teresa is jilted by Jonathan Crow. She is close to a nervous break-down: when she climbs into bed, 'the strange orchestra with fifes and tympani' begins to beat and gets 'louder and more furious each night'. Rejected by the man for whom she crossed the world, her voyage to England now strikes her as 'a buffoon Odyssey'.[59] She is, she tells herself, 'a detestable thing, an ugly, rejected woman'.[60] Crow's rejection of her is perfectly understandable: 'Who could love me? Do I love myself? Then why should he?'[61]

She resolves to die, but is not quite ready to kill herself. 'Impulsive bloody suicide is a coward's death,' she tells herself. A more 'honorable suicide' would be to work herself to death. That way, she would have time to finish her 'testament'.

An extraordinary piece of writing—especially for its layers of self-reflexivity—is Teresa's Introduction to her novel. Here she describes herself spending those 'long pale evenings of the northern twilight' writing. Her testament, *The Seven Houses of Love*, depicts 'the ages, a sacred seven, through which abandoned, unloved women passed before life was torn out of their clenched, ringless work-worn fists'.

Teresa has also written some notes: 'A System by which the Chaste can Know Love'. These notes portray in a tone of feverish lyricism a woman's life as a metaphor for sexual intercourse. In the first house, the word 'love' carries 'floating ideas' that will cause the young girl 'physical warmth, a naive joy'. In the second, the adolescent girl imagines 'scenes of festive and dark violence'. In the third, she experiences 'yearning lust'. And so on. The sixth house, 'Heaven and Hell', is her experience of love as tyranny and humiliation. The seventh house is 'the last star'.

> To die by the last effort of the will and body. To will, the consuming and consummation. To force the end. It must be dark; then an extraordinary clutching of reality.[62]

The Seven Houses of Love is the fiction within the fiction. In reality, Christina Stead was writing *Seven Poor Men of Sydney*, which contains the very same themes. Catherine and her half-brother Michael each contain something of Stead herself: each grapples with madness and suicide.[63] Certain passages in the novel come close to being paeans to death.

Catherine, who describes herself as 'insupportably lonely', romanticises madness: 'I am terribly unhappy: my heart is bursting, that is why I have to go mad.'[64] Michael struggles against madness: 'Am I going cuckoo? Is this how it starts? No wonder they shriek out, madmen, if it feels like this.'[65]

Brother and sister are obsessed with suicide. Walking by the harbour one stormy evening, Catherine calls out, half to herself, half to her companion:

> "Come, sweet sea!" She added: "Come sweet death, I mean." She lay back on the grassy slope, sopping wet. "That is the sort of death I would like, to go down in the swilling storm-waters, ough, guff, gubble, gup, and you're drowned: that death I could die a thousand times."[66]

This is, once again, death as orgasmic dissolution. Michael thinks of suicide, but decides 'he could not let the waters close over him without first knowing the sweet profound experience of cleaving to a loving woman's flesh and sinking into oblivion with her'.[67] In the end (having experienced sexual rapture), he leaps over the notorious 'Gap' and sinks into oblivion in the sea.[68] The imagery of abysses, drowning, sleeping and leaping is consistently sexual.

Madness; suicide. Why does Stead impose such a tragic quietus on her shadow selves? In a novel about pent-up sexual desire, cruel loneliness and frustrated aspirations, madness and suicide are seen as a means of regaining lost power and reasserting selfhood. By *writing* about madness and suicide, Stead could assert herself vicariously, through her characters. Ironically, by writing the novel, she was working herself not to death, but back to life.

*   *   *

William Blech was curious about the young man his secretary mentioned from time to time. He found himself wondering what kind of
man attracted her. Keith Duncan, who knew how much Christina
was impressed by her boss, the Marxist investments manager who
seemed to know something about everything, was equally intrigued. Duncan was planning to go to the United States to pursue
postdoctoral research, and he welcomed the opportunity to meet a
New York intellectual. Some time in the autumn, when he returned
from Oxford, a meeting was arranged—without Christina.

'Bill came back with very negative opinions,' Stead recalled later.
He apparently probed Duncan about his feelings for Christina, and
the disdainful Duncan had let drop that Christina thought herself a
writer. Back at the office, Blech asked his secretary whether he
might see something she had written. One Friday, she handed him
her work in progress, *Death in the Antipodes*.

> He took it away one weekend. We weren't friendly—well, we
> were friendly, but we weren't close. And he brought it back
> and he looked at me, he had beautiful brown eyes, ... and he
> looked at me with absolute astonishment when he sat at the
> desk opposite me. He called me in from my little typist den
> and he said: "It has mountain peaks."[69]

Whenever she told people that she met William Blech within a
week of arriving in London, Christina Stead would say she had
won the great prize in the lottery.[70] She had a keen sense of the
guiding hand of Fate, and she always believed their meeting to be
pure serendipity.

When she wrote to Gwen Walker-Smith early in September
1928, though Stead did not mention Blech, his presence loomed
large between the lines. It was his opinions she was airing, and the
letter was suffused with a new joy and confidence.

> I understand the only place to live on the Continent (of great
> towns) is Bruges, which is all 16th century horsefairs, great
> patron bourgeois merchants, religious processions and steeples.
> I don't like London: I have a good mind to try Bruges,
> therefore: but how! I feel like a bird which has just learned
> to fly. I wish to explore the universe of stars![71]

The next letter to her cousin, four closely typed pages, was written
in mid October: the beech trees in Cartwright Gardens were
shedding their leaves. Once again, the letter spoke of everything
but the man who was rapidly becoming the focus of Christina's
attention. She had been to concerts conducted by Sir Thomas

Beecham and Sir Henry Wood. (She does not say with whom she went.) Beecham impressed her with his 'charming manners' towards the musicians: 'he beckons them up like lambs and brushes them back like daisies and smiles ineffably in the soft sweet passages'. At the Proms, Sir Henry Wood was 'woolly and playful'.[72]

Several characters in the novel she was writing were printers, Stead told Gwen, and so she was studying the history and mechanics of printing. She was also musing on spiritual matters. She had just read *Apologia pro Vita sua*, Cardinal Newman's account of his spiritual development; *Commonsense Theology* by the agnostic rationalist C. E. M. Joad and A. N. Whitehead's philosophical treatise on symbolism. Moreover, she was still persevering with Bertrand Russell's *The Analysis of Mind*, the book she carried at her job interview.

'I live a very circumscribed life,' she told Gwen, 'so that I am ashamed to write about it.'

* * *

In *For Love Alone*, Teresa finds herself tripping into work with new enthusiasm for life. She tells her boss: 'You light up everything when you explain it. The world has changed for me since I knew you.'[73]

Christina told Mr Blech: 'I love to hear you talk. It helps me forget.'[74] Blech too found himself curiously drawn to his secretary. He was probably inviting her to concerts with him. And on two or three occasions in October he arranged to meet her at Lyons Corner House in Tottenham Court Road, to talk after work.[75]

* * *

For Love Alone was written more than a decade after the failed romance with Duncan. Though she believed she had worked herself into a state of sympathy with her character Jonathan Crow —several passages are narrated from his point of view—Stead's anger was intact. Indeed, if the second half of the novel is weaker than the first, it is because Stead had an overriding ulterior motive: to take revenge.

A brief glimpse at the imagery used to portray Crow reveals the degree to which the portrait was artistically heightened. His very name betrays the author's hostility.[76] But it is in the final chapters of the novel that his come-uppance is delivered. His condemnation not just by Teresa but also by the affable James Quick intensifies the force of the authorial axe.

Before he meets Crow, Quick reads an essay by him on the biological and social differences between the sexes and races. Appalled by its racism and misogyny, Quick surmises that Crow is 'a dim-witted, dim-faced, bobbing pedant'.[77] In a subsequent chapter, Quick sits in the Tottenham Court Road Corner House, waiting to meet Crow for the first time:

> He had not been watching long before he noticed a shrewd and unscrupulous-looking man in his thirties, who strolled round the stands and looked sharply at him, perhaps a private dick, he thought. The man was swarthy, oak-complexioned, with a hammered-out distorted and evil face and a syncopated rolling walk which looked like the business stroll of the second-rate spottable spy.[78]

This is the stuff of detective fiction, negative to the point of caricature. The two men find a table and talk. Quick, true to his name, gets the measure of his rival within minutes. He is struck by Crow's 'shrewd, hard look and twisted, canny smile'. Further conversation confirms his hunch:

> ... an ambitious small-town man, sly, ignorant but a cudgeller of faculty cabals, a wit-picker, a notion-thief, a man bound to get on, a paste-and-scissors scholar, of the kind that often makes a name for himself by writing forewords to great works.[79]

Our final glimpse of Jonathan Crow comes at the end of the novel. It is dusk. Teresa, out walking with James Quick, sees a 'peculiar, sliding, fumbling figure' go by. They pass under a streetlamp; in this light, the figure has the bluish tinge and unshaven lantern jaw of expressionist caricature. Then Teresa recognises him. She feels 'a pang as if faced by a murderer. The vile-faced man, the bent-backed man, walking crowded with all the apparatus of melodrama was Jonathan Crow!'[80] He is every bit the exaggerated villain of Victorian melodrama whom audiences love to hiss.

★   ★   ★

In 1987, aged 83 and terminally ill with cancer, Professor W. G. K. Duncan, very bitter about Christina Stead, recalls the rapidity with which she transferred her affections from him to *Mr Blech*, as he calls him, with mocking emphasis. 'Frailty, thy name is woman!' he mutters drily, unwittingly echoing Stead's own many borrowings from *Hamlet*. He himself could never have done that, he says.

'Christina must have been very lonely,' I say.

'That's no excuse. Loneliness is no excuse. It was so quick.'

'But you were probably quite cold towards her,' I suggest.

'That's true.' He nods.

It is February 1987, mid morning. The air has the desert dryness of Adelaide summers. We are in the Helping Hand Home, in the leafy tranquillity of North Adelaide, the gracious old district favoured by the university establishment. Professor Duncan and his wife Dorothy have recently moved in here, to rooms on separate floors.

He is sitting at a table by the window, in baggy flannel trousers and a waistcoat—as if he had walked out of a photograph from the 1920s. Were it not for the heat we could almost have been sitting in his student room in Bloomsbury. He is a little deaf. I have to raise my voice.

He has silver hair, a narrow face, and behind his heavy glasses, large brown eyes which fix me intently. He has no intention, he says, of talking about 'that woman Christina Stead'. His eyes flash over the top of his glasses. He tells me she is guilty of 'gross mis-representation', that in her books she says things about people that are not even erased by that person's death, things that will never be forgotten.

And then we talk about Christina transferring her affections with undue haste. He pauses, looks out at the garden, and mutters: 'If that's what women are like, God preserve me from them!'[81]

*   *   *

Was Stead guilty of 'gross mis-representation'? Literary critics today argue that writing can never be a representation, a mirror to life; realist literature is merely a set of literary conventions to which we have become so accustomed that we are no longer aware of the immense gap between writing about life and life itself. Though it is by writing oneself that one becomes acutely conscious of this gap, in interviews Stead regularly made the opposite claim: her fiction reflected reality almost exactly. This claim would have been even more offensive to Keith Duncan than the novel itself. Though there is considerable sympathy for Crow in Part One of *For Love Alone*, Stead's portrait of Jonathan Crow is ultimately not generous; but this really matters only when art claims to be life.

Duncan's outrage is understandable. Take Jonathan Crow's affair with the London housemaid. If Stead invented these details, Duncan was made to look guilty by association; if the story was true, he would have been horrified to see it in print. Either way, he lost.

If Duncan chose never to say anything about the novel, it was no doubt because he preferred not to draw attention to a portrait which was both false and uncomfortably accurate. Paradoxically, the fiction became even 'truer' than it intended. In the novel, published in 1944, Crow is described as 'the sort that climbs slowly but successfully on his undangerous stupidity . . . to be head of his department'. Had the novel been published seven years later, this sentence would have been defamatory, for in 1951 Duncan was appointed Professor of History and Political Science at the University of Adelaide.

Dr Hugh Stretton, Duncan's colleague at the University of Adelaide, and someone who knew him well in his last thirty years, comments:

Duncan was an odd, interesting man, cold but very strongly committed to unexceptionable good causes (civil liberties, lifelong education for everyone, good public libraries). He was a total chauvinist husband, but capable of very hard-working, self-effacing kindnesses to a few friends and favourite students ... I could see plenty of psychological truth in the Crow portrait. But it is vengeful, without much compassion for his internal emptiness or respect for (what turned out eventually to be) the very active, genuine reformer that he became.[82]

★ ★ ★

Several months passed before Stead contacted Florence James, whom she had first met at Sydney University, and who was now living in London, working as a freelance journalist. Christina would not have wanted to share her misery over Keith Duncan with her, especially as they had other friends from the university in common. Florence James had no difficulty attracting men (she had already broken off her engagement to the Dutch lawyer from Java), and would only have inflamed Christina's burning sense of failure.

But by late October, Christina's life had taken a turn for the better, and she dispatched a note to Florence proposing lunch and a Saturday afternoon concert at Queen's Hall, where Elizabeth Schumann was singing. A few days later, James wrote to her mother:

The concert was delightful, mostly German lieder, and she has an exquisite voice. Afterwards we met Chris's chief who was also there and he bore us off to tea, which incidentally took about two hours. Mr. Blech is a German Jew and what he hasn't read or doesn't know about in art, literature and music seems almost negligible—not that he's a particularly discerning critic although a very opinionated one—but marvellously stimulating company. Christina and I walked back here afterwards and cooked supper on my gas ring: she's a very nice girl and I'm hoping to see more of her.[83]

Stead enjoyed the evening too, for five weeks later, in early December, she wrote to Florence James with another proposition. She was renting a large room at the corner of Cartwright Gardens and Marchmont Street for six months, while the owner, an artist, was in South America. Would Florence like to share it with her?

It was 'very superior accommodation', James recalls.[84] The doors and windows were painted black with scarlet knobs; cushions of every shade were strewn around. A china cupboard contained fine willowpattern dishes; there was even a disappearing washstand.[85] Florence told her mother:

I'm thinking seriously about it. Christina would be an ideal companion, except that one would have to keep one's eye on her, she's the least businesslike of mortals, and is always trying to take more than her fair share of any burden. In the first place she says 10/- a week for me. Now I know she's paying 28/- and as she's out from 8 to 6 every day when I have the room to myself, half shares is the least I could contemplate ...

Christina, by the way, is in the midst of writing a novel.[86]

The room was expensive for one person; by comparison, Keith Duncan and John Beaglehole were paying 17s 6d a week each for their shared room in Brunswick Square.

The following Sunday, 16 December, Florence packed up and took the first instalment of her belongings round to Marchmont Street, where she found Christina and Francette Hubert cosily drinking tea in front of the fire. Francette was shortly to return to France.

The three went to the Cartwright Gardens clubhouse for lunch, then Christina accompanied Florence to her old room in Chelsea and they transported a large chest to Bloomsbury by threading a walking stick through the handles and taking one end each.[87]

Now that she was happier, Christina was consciously trying to fatten herself up. Whereas Florence saved money by cooking on their gas ring, Christina paid 15s a week for breakfast and dinner at the clubhouse. Florence explained to her mother, 'Christina is a slim creature and needs feeding.'[88]

Florence James and her friends were lively, interesting women, whose company did Christina good. Margaret Dunbar-Smith— 'Madge'—was adopted; her foster father was an architect of some standing, and they lived in a beautifully restored house in Queen Square, Bloomsbury. Stead found her 'precious in an A. E. Coppard sort of way'.[89] A slight figure with auburn hair and a bouncy walk,[90] Madge worked in Bumpus', the bookshop in Oxford Street, and was in love with H. E. Bates, whose first novel, *The Two Sisters*, was published when he was only 19. They seemed to Christina to enjoy 'a kind friendship'.[91]

Iris Fischer, redhaired, musical and highly adventurous, was from a Tyne-Tees working-class family, and a teacher. Stead found it reassuring that though 'not beautiful or dashing', Iris was much loved by her boyfriend. She wrote to Gwen:

Fisch is ... a magnificent girl, smiles like the sun—composes fugues, tramps all over Iceland alone, prances through Europe with a tent and a young man, who is now in the sulks because she won't marry him.

She added:

Florence is a Sydney girl whom I met once or twice before coming over, but I never thought I should be sharing my dearest secrets with her in a Bloomsbury square, and my Jewish buns and my Yiddish godfather.[92]

They shared clothes as well as secrets. That is, Christina borrowed from Florence, who had brought some smart clothes from Sydney. Florence recalls Christina trying on one of her evening dresses. It was a perfect fit, but Christina had only walking shoes to wear with it.

Christina liked domestic elegance. She was very proud of a lace tablecloth she had bought, and whenever they had guests she would bring out pretty napkins and dishes. Florence liked to drink her tea, bohemian-style, out of a mug; Christina would fuss with cups and saucers. They were, James points out, rebelling against very different family backgrounds: she had had fine china at home; Christina had not.[93]

★ ★ ★

'I am atrociously tired, I know not why.' It was early January 1929. Dense 'pea-soupers' regularly cast London in 'a graveyard gloom'.[94] But Stead's fatigue was no longer due to depression. She told her aunt that the sleeping arrangements were to blame. There was only one bed in their new room, and she and Florence were taking it in turns, week about, to imitate 'St Simeon Stylites and Other Celebrated Martyrs' by sleeping on a wooden trunk with a chair at one end and a suitcase at the other. She joked: 'I am further guided along the path of godliness ... by the landlady never having found it necessary to instal a bath.'[95] For their ablutions, performed behind a screen (Florence was amused by Christina's extreme modesty), there was a basin with a pull-down lid and a bucket beneath. Fetching water involved a trip downstairs.

In fact, the cause of Stead's exhaustion was not the bed; nor was it work on her novel, which had slowed down in recent weeks. It was simply that her life was in utter turmoil. That morning, 9 January 1929, only seven months after she had stepped ashore in England, a telephone call had come from Mr Blech, who was in Paris for a few days. He was making arrangements to return to work in Paris in a few weeks' time. Would she join him as his secretary? When she wrote to Gwen that afternoon, Stead was dancing on a highwire:

'I have been shouting Banzai, Halleluia and other Hebrew sounds ever since, because he is a very nice fellow and Paris sounds fine to me.'

Her family must have been very curious by now about the 'very nice fellow' to whom Christina only ever referred in her letters as 'Mr. Blech' or 'my employer'. The many typing mistakes in her letters did not suggest top secretarial skills: was it purely for business reasons that Blech wanted her in Paris? Though Christina remained non-committal, near the end of her letter came this astonishing morsel:

My employer tells me that I have no idea how to dress and I will look a different woman when properly dressed (frankness is charming), so I have a soft anticipatory thrill and feel those voluptuous stirrings and those plenitudes we all feel when we consider the sort of woman we could be if we had the right climate and care.

*   *   *

At first, Christina herself did not know what to make of this sudden and dramatic turn of events. Among her unpublished papers are notes about this period that reveal her complete lack of confidence in her own charms:

Because Bill though separated from his wife was not divorced, when he asked me out, he also asked my room-mate, a splendidly built handsome girl . . . so that for some time I thought he had fallen in love with her, until one concert conducted by the then young and promising conductor John (later Sir John) Barbirellis [sic], when he sparkled and I felt dreary and let down and upon returning home my room-mate said: "If you ever treat him that way again, I shall refuse to go with you. In any case it's no fun playing gooseberry." I thought her modest and shy, that she was wrong; but she was right.

William Blech, a tornado of energy, was swirling both women off their feet. He would turn up with a friend and they would go as a foursome to the theatre, concerts and restaurants. For Christina and Florence it was an introduction to an entirely new world. One evening they would go to a seedy-looking little Soho restaurant known only to the *cognoscenti*; the next they would be ushered inside the plush Café Royal on Regent Street. Florence James well remembers the animated conversation and laughter. The men chose the food, and the men paid.

Sometimes it was Stead's Managing Director, Alfred Hurst, who made up the foursome. A married man with children, he was an inveterate Don Juan: he had a luxurious bachelor flat at No. 14 Park

Lane, Mayfair, for romantic assignations. For the time being, however, William Blech was living there, and all parties were back in their own rooms at the end of the evening.[96]

Christina must have been rather shocked by the libertine world in which she found herself, but she was also dazzled by Bill's worldliness. Her notes continue:

Bill, though not much older than me, behaved like a father to me: to him, coming from the brilliant city of New York, I was an apt and interesting but almost ignorant outlander, almost a child, almost a savage, and he eagerly, with sparkling, continuous wit and information, did his best to educate me . . . He loved to impart, and he did it gaily, affectionately, without pedantry . . .[97]

With her avid curiosity, sense of fun and love of language, Christina Stead must have been an exciting and appreciative companion for William Blech. Finding herself with two Jewish bosses, she had already plunged into a study of Jewish culture. With her Christmas bonus from the office she bought an English-Yiddish grammar and taught herself smatterings of Yiddish.[98] In her lunch hour she liked to walk to Whitechapel, the Jewish East End area, and wander around the vast network of lanes trying to decipher the Yiddish signs. On wet days she would sit in the library in the Mile End Road and read about Jewish legend in the *Encyclopaedia Judaica*—material which she later worked into *The Salzburg Tales*. Blech was proud of his Jewishness; so was Stead.[99]

★   ★   ★

'You will of course have sized up the situation,' Florence James told her mother in a long and colourful letter dated 23 January 1929, 'I'm basking in reflected glory from Christina as far as Mr. Blech is concerned.' She added: 'It's really a delightful situation for she's such a modest soul, quite unused to being made a great deal of fuss of.'

The previous fortnight, Florence explained, had been a frenzy of social activity. One evening, Christina had come home from work 'with dancing eyes' and told her to get dressed quickly as Mr Blech had managed to get tickets for Artur Schnabel's piano concert and they were going to dinner first. The evening was concluded at Verrey's in Regent Street, 'a very elegant café'. The following Tuesday, Blech took them to the Pro Arte String Quartet; on Thursday, he and a friend, Mr Kempner, came round to the flat; on Saturday, they saw *Thérèse Raquin* at the Q Theatre. On Sunday, Blech took Christina to Cambridge for the day. On Monday morning, Christina and Florence, exhausted, vowed they would go to bed straight after the delivery of the Australian mail in the evening.

Behold, we'd finished reading it when the bell rang. Two gentlemen to see us. Mr. Blech and Mr. Kempner in full evening dress. "How long will it take you two girls to change, and we'll do a night club!" Well, the two girls didn't take long to change! We disported ourselves in the Piccadilly Hotel ...

We really had a delightful evening, and thoroughly interesting. On Friday they were to have dinner at Mr Blech's flat in Park Lane, followed by a string quartet, then a nightclub. When the time came, Mr Kempner was in bed with flu, so the nightclub had to be cancelled. Florence told her mother: 'Mr. Blech's so thoroughly smitten himself he's anxious to wish the rest of the world into a state of similar beatitude.'[100]

*　　*　　*

In mid January, in Cambridge, at the lectern of a famous church, William and Christina exchanged their first kiss. The following Sunday, they made an excursion to Canterbury, through countryside white with snow.[101]

In *For Love Alone*, Stead has Teresa and James Quick spend a day in Canterbury. Coming back on the evening train, through countryside 'white with young moonlight', Teresa is 'miserable and maddened' by Quick's frenzied passion. Quick, holding 'the near-fainting Teresa in his arms', talks blithely about their 'union'. He tells her, more dramatically than sensitively, that he wants them to become lovers, continuing:

"If the law says I am married, I will make you my back-street wife." Yes, even if she would not live with him as his wife but was afraid of public opinion "as so many nice girls are" he would take care of her, get her a room somewhere, furnish it, and come to see her.[102]

Quick eagerly rushes on:

He would bring her books, music, take her to concerts, theatres, if she wished, send her to the university—make a woman of her, make a brilliant woman of her, the sort of woman who in all ages had charmed men, the Montespan of the age ... He was a stepping-stone, he told her; she would be a Staël, a Récamier, a Catherine II. He would take her to Paris, and elsewhere, no one who knew her now would know her then; he would make her over entirely.

Faced with this awesome prospect, Teresa, understandably, feels overwhelmed, no longer quite her own person. Moreover, she has serious misgivings:

In all this storm of words he had only mentioned marriage once and then in a dubious way. She wanted to go to the

Sorbonne—but to be a back-street wife, to give with one
hand and take with the other—not that![103]

Christina Stead would have been every bit as loath as Teresa to
become a 'back-street wife', a mistress. She did not want a lover to
be a stepping-stone; she wanted a husband. Yet it is likely that
William Blech's initial propositions did not include actual marriage.
Though he seems to have blurred this point when talking to
Christina, he was not formally separated from his wife. He was a
proud father; his wife was Jewish and beautiful, and though their
relationship was not fulfilling, they had reached some sort of *modus
vivendi*. His mother, who was also financially dependent on him,
thought the world of Mollie, his wife. He knew the havoc it would
cause if he divorced and broke up the family. His daughter Ruth
was the age his elder sister had been when their own father had
abandoned them: he well remembered the misery that ensued.
Blech was a progressive, a feminist even, but in his world wealthy
financier friends kept mistresses. The wives, provided they were
adequately cared for financially, accepted the situation.

Years later, Stead told a friend: 'Dear Bill said once to me in the
beginning of things that he would like to be to me what G. H.
Lewes was to George Eliot.' She joked: 'I was not very pleased,
because G.E. was not a pretty girl.'[104]

* * *

FEDERAL BUREAU OF INVESTIGATION
This case originated at New York City.
Date when made: 2/2/44.
Character of Case: Internal Security.
Title: WILLIAM JAMES BLECH, with aliases: William Blake,
William J. Blake, William James Blake, George B. Collingwood,
George S. Kent.
SYNOPSIS OF FACTS:
Subject was a Single Taxer at the age of 15 and acted in
Democratic Party at 18. Protested America's entry into First
World War. From 1919 to 1926 he was connected with private
banking in Wall Street and wrote for the 'Magazine of Wall
Street'. From 1926 to 1934 he engaged in banking activities in
Paris and London.
. . . Friends and associates of subject label him 'intellectual
Communist', 'a fellow traveller', and 'cynical capitalist' but
all maintain he is not dangerous. Subject reported to have
profound admiration of and respect for Russia and is great
student of Communist theory.[105]

Born in St Louis on 28 July 1894, William James Blech was the second child of German parents, who were among the two million Jews to migrate to the United States between 1870 and 1914. His father, Gustavus Maximilian Blech, a doctor, was born in Strasburg in 1867; his mother, Rosa Sachs, was born in the Baltic seaport of Riga in 1869. When she was young, her family, well-to-do and liberal German Jews, had moved to St Petersburg then Königsberg, where, family legend has it, one of the four brothers was physician to the Tsar.[106] Certainly, the family belonged to the small minority of privileged Jews in tsarist Russia. But during the 1880s and 1890s new laws prohibited Jews from owning or renting land outside towns or cities; quotas restricted their entrance into the *gymnasia* and the universities. Pogroms—organised massacres of Jews— were deliberately provoked by the tsarist government, in some 600 villages and cities, to divert the discontent of the Russian peasants into racial hatred and religious bigotry.

Rosa Sachs was 18 when she sailed past the Statue of Liberty in 1887, joining two of her brothers in New York. Small and squat, with large brown eyes, she read and spoke five languages fluently and played the piano well. She soon married Dr Gustavus Blech, another recent immigrant. But the marriage was a bitter disappointment: they were not well off and Gus was an incurable womaniser.[107] In 1891 Rosa gave birth to a sickly girl, Jenny. Three years later, she bore their only son, named after the influential American philosopher and psychologist William James.

William's first five years were spent in St Louis, Missouri. An industrial city on the west bank of the Mississippi, it contained a large German community that had left Europe after the failure of the 1848 revolution. The community was active and enterprising, boasting four daily German newspapers and several German 'Kindergartens'. Jenny and William did not learn English until they started school.

When William was 5, the family moved to Chicago, and it was in that port and railway city that Gustavus abandoned them. Rosa, who clung ferociously to bourgeois respectability, found herself tarnished with the disgrace of divorce. Gustavus remarried; before long his cheques stopped coming. In desperate straits, Rosa decided to move with her children to New York, close to her brothers.

They settled in the slums of lower east Manhattan, and Rosa told people she was widowed. The Lower East Side, the area south of Houston and east of the Bowery, was, at the turn of the century, an impoverished ghetto of European Jewish immigrants, where Jews from all the Yiddish-speaking centres of Europe lived in clusters according to their nationality. Henry Roth, in his novel *Call It*

Sleep, paints a memorable picture of this tumultuous corner of Manhattan, with its 'avalanche of sound' in which the screams of babies, bickerings of mothers, bawling cries of hucksters and yowling of cats blended with the clattering of horse-cars, honking of automobiles, banging of garbage cans, the cacophony of small industries and the boat horns on the East River.[108]

Because of the heavy Jewish migration of the early 1890s, the dark tenement houses were dangerously overcrowded and sanitation was wretched. In the stifling summer months, roofs, fire escapes and side-walks were converted into sleeping quarters. In 1899 the Board of Health noted the mounting incidence of tuberculosis, the 'White Plague', in the city.[109] In 1903, at the age of 12, Jenny Blech died of tuberculosis. William was only 8 at the time, and his sister's death marked him deeply—both his character and his politics.

In *The World is Mine*, the first novel of William Blake (as Blech would later call himself) a young Spanish boy, Cristóbal, sees his older sister Carmen die of tuberculosis.

All night long her hacking cough, her constant hemorrhages, and pathetic cries rang in Cristóbal's ears, and blinded his eyes . . . He held the hand of his courtyard companion and comrade of long tales, that her courage might be fortified by his steadiness.

He sneaked beside fruit stalls to steal oranges for her; he even did three hours of errands every afternoon for the apothecary so that he could earn a small bottle of cod-liver oil. All the feeble arms of the poor were employed against the inflexible enemy, death. They lost.[110]

In the hurly-burly of the New York slums, William became his mother's protector and adviser. They were not religious; unlike most of his schoolfriends, William was not sent to the *Cheder* to learn Hebrew. Rosa, coming from a privileged Russian family, did not speak Yiddish at home. She was also unusual in that she had something close to a profession: she could teach the piano. Her pupils were wealthy daughters from the neighbouring affluent areas where her brothers lived. While his mother gave piano lessons, William, left in the home of one or other of his uncles, would amuse himself by reading whatever was around: encyclopaedias, medical and legal books, dictionaries. One of his teachers, amazed by the boy's extraordinary wealth of information, cited Oliver Goldsmith's lines to describe him:

And still they gazed, and still the wonder grew,
That one small head could carry all he knew.[111]

The communist writer Mike Gold, the same age as Blech and in the late 1930s a close friend, also wrote about growing up on the East Side in his 1930 bestseller *Jews Without Money*.[112] For the young Yiddish-speaking boys of the tenement houses life comprised constant gang warfare. Yet if the ghetto was squalid and tough, there was also a hunger for learning in the Mosaic tradition, and a closeness of family life. William Blech was in class with some rough young hoodlums: one was to be Gyp the Blood, a famous gangster. But fortunately, the young thugs left 'the professor' to his books; 'Will' was a non-combatant even in those days.

His mother's piano lessons did not bring in much money and although he was something of a prodigy at school, William had to go to work at 14. A benevolent family friend, John T. McRoy, a Scottish engineer who had amassed a fortune through various inventions, employed him as his runner and secretary. McRoy, a socialist and philanthropist, helped establish several talented boys on Wall Street.[113]

In a 1941 article for the American communist newspaper *New Masses*, William Blake would paint a tongue-in-cheek picture of Wall Street in 1908:

> The street, unlike its present resemblance to a sylvan glade, was animated. The rank and file of Americans held it in abhorence as a seat of iniquity and therefore of prosperity. It contained 10,000 "runners" or messenger boys, who, in the pre-gangster era, ambled along gently, $100,000 in United States twos sticking out of their back pockets, whistling the latest Eva Tanguay or Irene Franklin song, and deep in the lore of *Nick Carter, Buffalo Bill, Young Wild West, Pluck and Luck* . . . Boys got $5 a week, $5 at Christmas, and were allowed to hear overtly private conversations between Burnside-bearded partners whispering about a hot tip from George Gould on reorganized Missouri Pacific. The proud messenger boy then ran home to Uncle Schultz, who took his life savings, $300, out of the German Savings Bank and bought Missouri Pacific from the secretive tipsters. Thus the messenger boy's salary was paid for a year and so Wall Street justified its old maxim that its employees cost nothing, because their relatives paid for their salaries by listening to inside information.[114]

From being a Wall Street runner, 19-year-old William Blech moved into an office on Wall Street—a spectacular but not altogether rare transition for bright working-class boys at the time.

The overthrow of the Tsar in February 1917 was greeted with loud rejoicing in immigrant families and in the American press, both Left and Right. (The conservatives preferred a government run by businessmen to the feudal Romanovs, and rightly assumed that the new government would pursue the war against Germany more vigorously.)

Colonel Gustavus M. Blech, surgeon-general in the Medical Reserve Corps of the US Army, was horrified when his son, who was called to serve the forces in August 1917, declared himself a conscientious objector to the war. (They saw each other briefly then, for the first time since Gustavus left the family, and would not meet again until the Thirties, in Chicago.[115]) Young Blech was influenced by the radical socialists who denounced it as a capitalist war that espoused national patriotism rather than international working-class solidarity.

Blech was among the many idealistic young Americans who became communists as a result of the Bolshevik Revolution of October 1917. John Reed, with his impassioned speeches and revolutionary writings in defence of the Revolution, became a hero in communist circles, and Blech heard him speak before he left for Russia. He was to die there in the autumn of 1920, buried with other revolutionary heroes under the Kremlin wall.

Twenty-three-year-old William Blech went underground in Boston. Most Americans regarded conscientious objectors as traitors, but his girlfriend, Mollie Grossman, a progressive and a suffragette, worked as a secretary to keep them both. The two had known each other since childhood when they had attended the same public school and William had sometimes gone to Mollie's in the afternoon. Mollie, from a well-off Russian-Polish Jewish family, had completed high school and proceeded to study French and German at Hunter College. The young pair eventually gave in to family pressure and married in New York on 13 October 1918.[116]

During the 1920s, Blech worked on Wall Street—some of the time employed by Alf Hurst, who came briefly to New York from Scotland to set up a grain business. Blech attended extramural evening courses in history and economics at Columbia University, and wrote articles on stocks and bonds for *The Magazine of Wall Street*.

Their daughter Ruth was born on 30 April 1921. Six years later Mollie Blech, who had long harboured a dream to go to France, chaperoned a niece across the Atlantic to seek medical treatment. She took Ruth with her. When William joined them, after seven months, his talkative little daughter greeted him in French.

Throughout the Twenties Americans, taking advantage of the favourable exchange rate and lower steamship fares, had flooded into the artistic capital of Europe. In 1927, William Blech, who had developed transatlantic financial contacts, worked in a private

American bank, the Travelers' Bank, on the fashionable Place Vendôme. Like his wife and daughter, he loved Paris. In the evenings, after dinner, the family would stroll to a nearby café. Ruth, who could rarely be persuaded to go to bed before 11 pm, would drink sweet pomegranate *grenadines* and enjoy the attention of the people around, while her parents drank cup after cup of coffee. She remembers a world of talk and music. Her father had built up an impressive record collection and friends would come to the apartment to listen to music. Ruth was very proud of her papa. And he was a devoted father.

William and Mollie had drifted into an affectionate but distant relationship. They had been married for nine years now, and were accustomed to spending time apart. Mollie, a modern woman, used to say that marriage stifled individuality. In the States, she had sometimes taken Ruth and gone for several weeks to the luxurious kosher hotel her mother ran in the country, leaving William to his long hours of work and his political meetings in the evenings.[117] And she and Ruth had packed up and left for France without him. So it did not seem strange that William, eager to spend time in Europe's financial capital, should go to London early in 1928 to work in Alf Hurst's London and Scottish grain exchange business. It was a temporary arrangement and he promised the family he would make regular trips across the Channel to see them.

And then, one day in May, when spring was in the air, a young Australian woman walked into the office clutching a book by Bertrand Russell, and applied for a job.

4

La Parisienne

FEBRUARY 1929–JUNE 1931

LONDON WAS BITTERLY cold that year. Household pipes were frozen. In the icy streets a constant procession of muffled people carried jugs of water. By the time the milk was plucked from the doorstep in the morning, it had turned into ice-cream.[1]

On a Friday afternoon in that bleak February of 1929, Christina Stead scrolled the office notepaper into her typewriter. It was her last complete week at the St Mary Axe office: the following Friday she would be leaving England. At the top of the letter she typed her new address.

> Care Travelers' Bank,
> 20 Place Vendôme,
> PARIS, France.
> 8.2.29

Dear Gwenyth,

The above address will be mine next week, so will you please address your letters as above in the future? . . .

I have been wondering if you have been feeling much better since your holiday and have not been troubled any more by the weakness, and headaches you last wrote me about. What you want is a long holiday say six weeks in duration, a sea-voyage, a voyage to Paris, a voyage to see your cousin. I want to see you: can't you come over here to see me? I don't see why my entire family should desert me and go and live in the Antipodes. Please let me have a short note, in any case, and let me know how you are.

This is only to be a short note, too, because I am getting ready to go to Paris, where I will work with my present manager, Mr. Blech, in a new banking office associated with the Travelers' Bank, which is a very flourishing association, an American bank under a most able American, a friend of Mr. Blech. You may have heard by this time that I am going to marry Mr. Blech (his name is William James Blech, and I call him Wilhelm). Wilhelm is a German Jew of American upbringing, small, very loquacious, very astute in business and literary affairs and art, highly educated and original: he is 35, has a white skin with black hair and beautiful brown eyes, has small, delicate hands: a small head square-set like a Teuton as to the back, with a curious Mongolian forehead and high cheek-bones, the lower face, Teutonic. He is a South German, his family coming from Karlsruhe. The family is intellectually distinguished and his cousin is Dr. Leo Blech, Director of the Berlin State Orchestra. His father is a distinguished surgeon in the U.S. His chief characteristics are his marvellous humanity which melts stones and metals, and his brilliant eyes which shine out of his face, sometimes in a startling way, when his skin is looking particularly white.

Wilhelm and I are going to Fontainebleau for a short vacation before we start work in Paris, as we are both weary of the dirt and cold here, and we both have warm blood in our veins. Wilhelm's previous marriage is not yet dissolved, but as he has actually separated from his wife I am going to live with him in the meantime. I love him dearly and he loves me very dearly, which is a strange thing to me, but which is sincere. He wins the heart of every one of my friends, so that I would have you believe too in the essential firmness and sincerity of our relation. You will perhaps be offended by the fact that I will live with him before we are married, but I hope you will not. I do not even wish him to marry again at all, if it is better for his career not to do so, but he loves a home and he loves children, so that he is very anxious to marry me as soon as possible. We will not have any children for a couple of years, according to our present feelings, not because we don't want them but because we want to become firmly established in Paris, and have a good financial background first. Also, I am thinking, I should like to go about Europe a bit and there are various things I should like to work at first. However, I am looking forward to some hopeful future when my little Gwen will come and visit Wilhelm and me in Paris, and I hope it is not a very distant future. I want to import quite a few of my relatives and it means that Wilhelm and I will have to work our fingers to the bone. Wilhelm is thoroughly Hebraically tribal in the matter of relatives.

I am throwing away all my clothes as not being good enough for Wilhelm, bless his heart, and I am very nigh naked. My friend Florence James has gone out today to get me some lawn underlinen and some lawn for a nightdress she is going to make me. We go to Fontainebleau (it may be Montingy-sur-Loing or Barbizon, which are just outside Fontainebleau) on Friday morning next, by the "Golden Arrow" express and arrive at Fontainebleau about 6.30. My beloved Wilhelm has all sorts of crazy notions about what he is going to do to my appearance when we get to Paris—such and such a wave, and such and such an eyebrow shave, and such and such a rouge and this perfume. I ask him if he expects me to cook his omelettes aux fines herbes if I have to get myself up to this extent, but his one object in life is to see what sort of a Parisienne he can make of me. I tell him I will be a perfect "sight" but he says ... he will then take me out to Australia to see what the relatives think of his highly polished Christina. He is planning a trip to Australia with me in about five years: it *may* come off. Isn't it delightful though? You don't know how happy I am—I am only lacking in one thing, my Gilbert and the rest, my Gwen and the rest.

    With much love,

    Peg

    (or as some people like to say Christina Blech)

Things had moved extraordinarily fast in recent weeks. It was only a month ago that her boss had rung from Paris inviting her to work there as his secretary and it had only become clear around that time that he had a romantic interest in her. Now the talk was of marriage. Christina could at last tell her family about her relationship with Mr Blech.

She had been cautious at first, not accustomed to being loved. It was not something she could trust easily, and she was well aware that to William Blech, with his European-American heritage, effusive, passionate words came easily. But she was at last convinced of his sincerity. He wanted to marry her, he talked about children, he wanted to meet her family.

She embroidered a bit in her letter to Gwen. This was perfectly understandable, given what she was announcing: that she was about to move in with a married man. She polished up Blech's credentials and made the romance appear less flurried and the divorce more imminent than they really were. It is likely that Blech had touched up the facts when he told them to *her*. In reality, he was not formally separated: his wife and daughter (Stead had not mentioned the daughter in her letters home) were expecting him home again soon. It is true that Gustavus Blech was a distinguished surgeon in the States, but he was an absolute stranger to his son. William *was* 'highly educated', but he was an autodidact, like David Stead, with neither secondary nor tertiary qualifications. (Blech often fudged this point.) Stead—revealing her own prejudices— liked to portray her future husband as more German than American; however, Blech had not set foot in Europe until the previous year. Like many immigrant children born in the New Country, his German, though more or less fluent, was full of grammatical mistakes. For a year Stead persisted in calling him 'Wilhelm', but she would eventually stop trying to deny his American side. All his American friends called him Bill, and so, in the end, did she.

Despite her libertarian protestations that she did not mind whether she married her 'beloved Wilhelm' or not, Stead was actually dreading the family's reaction. She fully expected them to be 'troubled if not outraged'. When their letters arrived twelve weeks later, she was taken aback. 'I did not trust them enough,' she told Gwen. 'As it is Mother has been very kind indeed and Dad also, and also the family in England.'[2] Since her father had always expressed the standard prejudices about Jews, Christina particularly appreciated Ada's encouraging comment that Jews were reputed to be good to their wives.[3] The only sour note came from Aunt Jessica, Stead's maiden aunt in Sydney, who declared that she was ashamed that any woman in the family could conceive of living with a married man.[4]

William Blech certainly led Christina to understand that she would be 'Madame Blech' before the end of the year. When they left England, Florence James told her mother: 'They are hoping to be married quite shortly.'[5] In truth, Stead was far more sensitive about her marital status than she made out to Gwen. She badly wanted to be married. She was no Dora Russell, who disapproved of conventional legal marriage and upheld free love (though even Russell ruled out 'poaching on another's preserves'.)[6] Neither was she a Simone de Beauvoir who was just then joyfully entering into a *union libre* with Jean-Paul Sartre (though she too would have preferred to marry him). Stead was not a 'New Woman'. To her, it was not marriage that represented a form of female bondage; it was spinsterhood. And rationally, she was quite right: the 'free woman' risked a great deal. Rebecca West, who had had an affair with the already-married H. G. Wells and became pregnant by him, had learned the hard way that an unmarried mother was 'the most outcast thing on earth'.[7] Christina Stead would always firmly hold the view that committed love (ideally marriage) was a wonderful liberation for women.

Marriage is an all-important goal for Stead's young women. Near the end of *For Love Alone*, Teresa, now living with James Quick, looks out of the train window (a classic female metaphor) and realises that her struggles have ended, that she has 'reached the gates of the world', and that 'the first day lay before her'. And at the end of *Letty Fox*, Letty, who has finally found a husband, declares:

It's a question of getting through life which is quite a siege, with some self-respect. Before I was married I had none; now, I respect not only my present position, but also all the efforts I made, in every direction, to get here . . . The principal thing is, I got a start in life; and it's from now on. I have a freight.
I cast off, the journey has begun.

*   *   *

Before the happy couple left London, Blech took Stead's women friends to a final celebratory dinner in Soho and Madge Dunbar-Smith threw a small farewell party. Stead finished up at the office on Wednesday, 13 February, with one day to shop and pack. She and Florence made a brisk excursion through the snow to buy her an evening dress, and Madge and Florence were still sewing their contributions to Christina's trousseau on the eve of her departure. On Friday, 15 February, at 11 am, the honeymooners left London on the luxurious *Golden Arrow*.

They stayed at the Hôtel de l'Aigle Noir in Fontainebleau, a former private residence with a grand entrance court. It was across the road from the palace, the country residence of the kings of France and Napoleon's favourite domicile. From there the Black Eagle had set off, incognito, for the island of Elba.

Mid February. Fontainebleau was covered in snow, under a radiant sun. The forest was half hidden in a ghostly mist and the palace fountains had snap-frozen in mid fall. The 'ice world' was like a fairytale stage décor;[8] it left a powerful impression on Stead, who made it the setting for a passionate episode in *The Beauties and Furies*. Her fictional honeymooners take a room in the Hotel of the Black Eagle and walk in the palace grounds.

In the freezing sunshine they went through the bare grounds where the blue and sepia forest, tall, thick and old, melted into

the luminous alleys and at hand a white swan swam half
congealed by the high clipped birches, and the falling fountain,
suddenly frozen, glittered with its stalactites over the great frozen
central basin. Not a blade of grass moved and not a bird flew
down the perspective of the great water, but under thickety trees,
officers and children skated with coloured cloaks and gloves over
a pond. Beyond, dazzling and enchanted, lay the leafless forest.[9]
It was probably on Sunday that Blech and Stead took a bus through
the forest to the mediaeval town of Moret. Like the fictional
honeymooners, Oliver and Elvira, they wandered past the ruined
abbey and 'improbably romantic houses' arm in arm, smiling into
each other's eyes. 'They were so in love that afternoon that they
returned from Moret by taxi and pulled down the blinds to stop
even the winter sun from coming into their room.'[10]

'This is your feast of life beginning, your new adolescence,'
Oliver tells Elvira, in *The Beauties*. 'You will not miss any nights
now: every one will be gemmy with bright lights and loving eyes
and stars and kisses.'[11] Autobiography has crept into the fiction
where it does not belong: the fictional Elvira Western, married for
the last seven years, has not been deprived of loving eyes and kisses.
It was Stead herself who had been missing out on these; and
although Oliver is modelled partly on Keith Duncan, in this scene
he sounds very like the exuberant William Blech.

Christina Stead had had to wait until she was 26½ before she
finally experienced 'the night of the senses'.[12] *Her* imprisonment (as
she saw it) had lasted twelve and a half years.

Fontainebleau marked the end of a long and tortured period of
loneliness in which Stead's virginity had become an intolerable
inhibition. Few women writers, even in recent times, have written
as candidly about the young woman's 'torment of desire' as Stead
would do in *For Love Alone* in 1944.

Stead had imagined her first night of love often enough, but it
was something 'that no one could build up out of lonely flesh'.[13]
Her advantage was that she was deeply in love with William Blech;
but she was sleeping with another woman's husband, and the risk
she ran should not be underestimated.

Later, Christina would say that their 'anniversary' was 17 February
(though since she and William liked to combine it with a Valentine's
Party, it came to be 14 February).[14] This must mean that though
they arrived in Fontainebleau on the Friday evening, they did not
actually make love until Sunday, 17 February.

Emotions probably ran high. And if Blech had not fully realised
the enormity of his responsibility before, he must have realised it
then. He must have dreaded the anguish ahead, the inevitable

confrontations with Mollie. In *For Love Alone*, when the married James Quick eventually has his precious Teresa in his arms all night, he moans in his sleep and weeps, foreseeing that 'there was no solution but a bitter one'.[15]

★   ★   ★

Christina Stead had expected to love Paris. She did. Snow lay piled under the trees and blocks of ice floated on the Seine, but the city was wealthier, more beautiful and far more animated than London. 'The cafés were full, their terraces, glassed-in against the cold, were planted with clients, like conservatories with pot-plants, the stoves burned bright.'[16] She loved the old apartment houses, with their ornamentation in stone and iron, and the grand and imposing boulevards. The people all seemed chic. Stead would capture her poetic first impressions of Paris in *The Beauties and Furies*, which pays tribute to that 'garden of lovers, joy of youth, nest of revolution, city of the thrice-fired blood!'[17]

Paris seemed to her a wonderful place to be a woman. On her first morning there, she and Blech were having breakfast at the Lutétia in the Latin Quarter when three men and a woman came in. The woman was plain and spinsterish, but Stead was struck by the gallant way the men behaved towards her and by the woman's grace and confidence.[18] She concluded that French males seemed to know how to bring out the charm in every woman, however lacking she might be in conventional beauty. This, for the daughter of David Stead, was a revelation.

Wilhelm treated her with great chivalry: she found herself being 'fed, sunned, dressed in grand chic, petted, educated, loved, indulged, taken (intelligently) all over Paris, musiced, champagned, cabareted, zooed'.[19]

'My beloved is coming back from London tomorrow evening,' she wrote to a Watson's Bay acquaintance, Nellie Molyneux, at the end of her first week in Paris. 'I must go and have my hair waved, or else buy some flowers to put in the salle à manger.' She was revelling in being the wife—a role she had feared she might never have the opportunity to play.

He is a ridiculous person, but how lovely!—He would first of all go to London for a week, for he has a lot of business to transact; then he decided he could do it in four days, then in three, then he said he would return to me on Sunday, but now he rings me this morning that he will come back tomorrow at midday, and he only left yesterday at midday! He is most kind to me, and loves me very much: it is surprising to me and I am not used to such a romance, but I am really very happy.[20]

Stead, who would never regard herself as worthy of love, looked upon her happiness with grateful wonder. In early April, she wrote to Nellie again, and this time she pretended to be complaining about her lot:

I never get any opportunity to do any exploring by myself—
I have seen some parts of Paris inside-out, but always under the
wing of Mr. Blech, who is a marvellous raconteur, rapporteur
—a great memory and ingenuity and enthusiasm—and who
will not leave my side for even two hours. I was never so lived
with in my life: the result is that everything rushes past me in a
dream—anecdotes, histories, tableaux, epigrams, dramas,
obscenities: I see nothing with my own eyes. Mr. Blech also
cannot stand still: he is the prince of intermittent vulcans: the
only way I can appreciate a thing . . . is to hang over it for an
hour, mope, mingle and maunder in an epileptic state which
would give him the yellow jaunder if such should be his fate . . .
Well, it is only by appealing to his most powerful emotions that
I can get him to stand still for one minute to look at the Sainte-
Chapelle, the Bridge of St. Geneviève, the Sacré Coeur or the
river Seine as it softly floweth. After one minute of standing
stock still in the name of love, fatherhood and Paradise, he bears
me onward, while I am left with one-sixtieth of a vision.

She added happily: 'You hear the lover's complaint; the troubles of a person too happily husbanded, garnered, threshed out and shot into a sack in the best season of twenty-six years.'[21] She was jubilating in her metamorphosis from the raw Australian-grown product into a highly polished 'Parisienne'. And if we stretch the metaphor a little (as she probably intended), it seems she was enjoying her sex life.

But her complaints were not entirely ironical. She *was* feeling rather overwhelmed by her new life. Two of the young women in her fiction, Teresa in *For Love Alone* and Emily Wilkes, in *I'm Dying Laughing*, have whirlwind courtships, and both are slightly uneasy about their new happiness. Emily tries to explain this to her husband Stephen:

"I guess I'm not happy living the perfect romance," she said to
him; "it's my training; it's too good; I'm an unbeliever; how can
it happen to Emily the Dope?"

"But it can. You'll get used to it. You'll learn."

He began to talk about their future—we'll do this, we'll
try that, we won't have any children at first; I have a daughter
and that's enough. I'll take you to the best hairdressers and
couturières, we'll get rid of your freckles, if you like. On the way
back to the hotel, he bought her a large box of chocolates.

He did everything with such gaiety, such inner and outward grace, she felt like a pleased child and yet she did not quite like it.

"It's because I'm used to the battle of life," she said to herself.[22] In those first years in Paris, very much in love, Christina Stead was the happiest she would ever be. But she knew better than most people that happiness is a highly precarious state. The shadow side of love is fear of its loss; she would always feel the tug of these tensions.

★   ★   ★

At first they rented a small apartment in the rue Mesnil, near the Place Victor Hugo, a fifteen-minute walk from the Champs-Elysées and a short bus trip to the office at No. 9, Boulevard Haussmann. The American & Foreign Discount Corporation, as it was called, was associated with the Travelers' Bank, but ten minutes away by foot. And the bank itself had moved from the Place Vendôme (where Blech had worked briefly before going to London) to No. 18 rue de la Paix, which runs between the Place de l'Opéra and the Place Vendôme. Stead enjoyed walking in this sector, past the exclusive fashion houses—Cartier, Worth, Paquin, Houbigant.

The Travelers' Bank, a private American bank, speculated on the foreign exchange market and dealt in securities on the stock and commodities markets. Patronised by wealthy South Americans, English and French aristocracy, and playboys and gamblers from around the world, its greatest asset was its Managing Director, Bertrand Coles Neidecker, known to his friends as Peter Neidecker. A handsome man, with irresistible charm, he was 'a free and easy, devil-may-care chap', a gambler by nature, who revelled in risk and adventure. Yet somehow people instinctively trusted him. During the war, when he was in the American Air Force in France, he made money by selling American telephone books to Germans wanting to know the addresses of relatives in New York so they could write to them for money.[23] In 1923, knowing nothing about banking, he had opened the bank in Paris, initially getting it off the ground by giving exceptionally good rates of exchange to American soldiers. Now it was a thriving family business, with Peter's two brothers, Aubrey and George, as nominal co-directors.[24]

The working day began for Blech and Stead at 10 am and ended soon after 8 pm when the New York Stock Exchange closed (at 3 pm New York time). Lunch was usually a leisurely two hours; occasionally, in the late afternoon, they would go out again for a hot chocolate or a glass of port. Stead, as secretary, typed letters in

French and English and sometimes worked at the cable switch-board, telegraphing transfers to New York. Unlike Blech's, her workload was light, and after the first few days, when she conscientiously looked around for more work, she used her free time for personal letters, making notes and writing. Peter Neidecker, aware that she was using bank time in this way, appears to have been quite lenient. His attitude is likely to have been that of Jules Bertillon, his fictional counterpart in *House of All Nations*, who admires successful writers just as he admires successful bankers—as talented con people. For Bertillon, art, like banking, is a comfortable way to get oneself fed by the rest of humanity: 'a rather delicate little trick for getting jam'.[25] The price of Neidecker's indulgence towards Stead was the hard work he extracted from Blech.

In the evenings they frequented the artist-and-expatriate cafés on the Left Bank: the Dôme, the Coupole or the Select on the Boulevard du Montparnasse—or the more expensive Café de Flore or Deux Magots in Saint-Germain-des-Prés. After some months they moved to the Left Bank themselves, renting a flat near the Panthéon. Stead loved the French cafés with their shining nickel and brass bars and cheery waiters. They were, she quickly realised, ideal loitering places for a writer wanting to know more about the lives of Parisians. She was convinced that it was no coincidence that in Germany, France and Austria, all famed for their culture, the café was a central focus of artistic and literary life.[26]

They rapidly got to know people: Blech was infinitely gregarious. Despite their admiration for the French, most of their friends were Americans—often of European descent. In their two worlds, financial and cultural, they straddled the Atlantic.

Many of their friends eventually would work their way into Stead's fiction. Samuel Putnam lived just near the Dôme and supported his wife and 3-year-old son by translating from French, Portuguese, Italian and Spanish for a Chicago publisher.[27] With Ezra Pound (whose views were becoming uncomfortably 'prefascist'), Putnam edited the *New Review*, a quarterly published in Paris and distributed in New York, which reported on European and American literature, arts, radio, cinema and photography. Cocteau, Ford Madox Ford, James Farrell, Boris Pasternak, Beckett and Henry Miller all appeared in the magazine.[28] Sam Putnam was more immersed in Parisian bohemia than most of their friends and Stead enjoyed the stories he told. One evening, a year or two previously, Sam and Riva Putnam had given a party for Jean Cocteau and Ezra Pound at the Café de l'Odéon; a fight broke out in the homosexual contingent; one hit another with his stiletto heel;

another American friend (Eric Townsend) intervened, braining the aggressor with a carafe.[29] Stead noted the details in her diary.

It was Putnam who introduced Stead to Louis Guilloux, whose proletarian novel *Le Sang Noir* influenced her early writing.[30] A page of notes survives, in which Stead forms comparisons between Guilloux and Joyce: both write cinematic scenes; both see their role as active, explanatory and sometimes philosophical (as opposed to Flaubert, who believed the writer should be entirely off-stage); both use two characters as mirror or shadow selves[31]—all techniques Stead was to try out in her early writing.

Eric Townsend was a wealthy loafer from Baltimore in his early forties, who spent his days drinking on the *terrasse* of the Deux Magots and lived off cheques sent from home. While other Americans were talking about the stock exchange, the daily *Herald-Tribune* crossword puzzle or places to eat, the inebriated Townsend would tell Stead wonderful stories, most of them risqué. (She often missed the point.) Slightly deaf, he spoke in a low 'threadbare voice' she called 'Prospero's whisper' and paused only to dip his moustache into his Pernod.[32] Stead was to model several minor characters in her fiction on Townsend.[33]

Another eccentric friend, who lived partly in Paris and partly in New York and worked at times for the Travelers' Bank, was Frederick Sard, a brilliant, unstable character, 'a great show off'. He would make vast quantities of money and live the 'high life like a sheik', then lose it all.[34] A Marxist, he believed, like Blech, that Russia offered the salvation of the world. Like Marpurgo, his fictional counterpart in *The Beauties and Furies*, he was a lover of music and widely read, expressing himself in tortuous phrases. His wife, Manya, was a large, bighearted Slav, but her high, scratchy voice irritated Stead, who attributed it to sexual deprivation.

Surrounded by voluble people, Stead prided herself on being 'that precious thing; a good listener'.[36] One of her café acquaintances, she told Gwen, was a handsome Jewish woman of Spanish origin, Rhoda de Pinto.

> She spends the hours telling me all about her lovers, of which there has been a large number: as I cannot riposte with tales about mine, I simply listen and acquire an enormous stock of information about other people's history: which is a talent one polishes to a high degree in Paris.

But there was an art to drawing people out.

> Don't think it is easy to be a good listener: if you let the person spill the beans too early, she will have a grudge against you for a few days, feeling that you encouraged her to give

herself away. Don't imagine I try to be a clever kid, but the fact is something takes people here: they will divulge their life histories within half an hour of meeting a person: a café has an "Open Sesame" effect.[37]

Stead was always making notes: she wrote down striking anecdotes, jokes, snatches of dialogue in French or English; she copied out phrases from political screeds that appeared on the hoardings. Letters from friends and family were chronologically filed in manila folders (a different dossier on each person); she cut out interesting newspaper items. The stuff of fiction was life itself. Like her character Marpurgo, she sniffed up details 'with the animal delight of a dog reconnoitring fenceposts'.

One evening, she was sitting alone in the Dôme—Blech was in London—and she was joined by Polianski, a Serbian symbolist painter, who had grumbled to her and Blech about the hard life of an expatriate artist until they had felt compelled to buy two small, colourful washes. As he sat down, chatting in French, Stead noticed that he was unshaven and thin. He started on his usual theme: painting was an expensive *métier*, Paris was full of talented artists, and his exuberant style did not sell. 'All Slavs are *démesurés* and they are not understood here.' Did she think Mr Blech might like to buy more of his gouaches? The next day Stead drafted a story based on their exchange.[38] Later, Polianski would be woven, in embellished form, into *The Salzburg Tales* and *House of All Nations*.[39]

On another occasion, they met an oil magnate from Baghdad. With childlike delight, Stead told Gwen (who as a child had shared her passion for *Arabian Nights*):

Son Altesse Sérène the Emir Mahmed a Rachide . . . went to Oxford and writes English and Arabic verse: you can imagine what a mood I was in! I went cautiously and looked out of the window to see if he departed on a magic carpet. To hear Wilhelm and Haroun discourse on ancient Arabian and Jewish history, not to mention Feisul and the moderns was enough to turn your hair: it took me fourteen hours of sunlight to return to normal.[40]

Stead, who saw herself as a word-stringer only on paper, was hugely impressed by the verbal skills of the French. In this country, conversation was an art form.

Whether the French discovered long ago, like the Jews, that conversation is the cheapest of entertainments, or whether their love for it springs from their natural witty and analytical minds, no one can say . . . In the cultured French circles, the ability to spin words, to reverse, invert, pervert and controvert ideas and to divine character makes every foreigner sit back in surprised (and often ashamed) silence.[41]

Not every foreigner sat back in silence. Not William Blech. At first, Stead herself was held back, if the conversation was in French, by her self-consciousness about her accent and grammar. 'Willy, on the other hand, blunders gaily ahead, raises and lowers his voice dramatically, smiles seraphically, and is radiantly successful, sans grammar, sans accent—but with a genius for expression which is his very particular talent.'[42] She was unduly shy about her own French: she wrote French well from schooldays and soon spoke it fluently, with only a light accent.[43] She had a talent for languages: over the years she would learn quite good German and an impressive smattering of Russian, Italian and Yiddish.

★ ★ ★

Expatriate artists, particularly Americans and white Russians, formed a large and visible presence in Paris in the Twenties. The city was rivalled only by Berlin as the literary and artistic capital of Europe. In the autumn 1928 issue of *Transition*, displayed in the bookshops when Stead and Blech arrived, various American expatriates explained why they chose to live in Europe. They spoke of American puritanism, the repressive work ethic, the tastelessness of American mass culture, subservience to the god–dollar and indifference to the spirit and intellect. Gertrude Stein declared:

America is now early Victorian very early Victorian, she is a rich and well nourished home but not a place to work. Your parents' home is never a place to work it is a nice place to be brought up in.[44]

Stead was even more emphatic in a letter to Gwen:

Paris is the refuge of most Anglo-Saxon artistic gentry with free minds, who have not been able to support the stupidity and intellectual self-deceit of their countries. England is of course worse off than any: New York produces some good work, but the futurists work over here. What is there in Paris? ... It is more than economic, more than traditional: it lies in the fact that in this "Police State" (as they call it) there is a free commune of the mind and senses ... It is partly also, I think ... the suavity, intelligence and amiability of the French people.[45]

The anti-realism, irrationalism and experimentation which had been sweeping Europe since the war were now finding their expression in English language and literature. In Paris, James Joyce and Gertrude Stein were the doyens of modernism: Joyce's 'Work in Progress' regularly appeared in *Transition*. His friend and fellow countryman, Samuel Beckett, was in his early twenties and just starting out as a writer in Paris.

By the time Stead and Blech arrived, at the tail end of the period of expatriate euphoria, Ezra Pound, Hemingway and F. Scott

Fitzgerald had left and Gertrude Stein no longer held her salon, though she and Alice B. Toklas still lived in the rue de Fleurus. But the poet Natalie Barney still held a Friday afternoon salon in her rue Jacob apartment, where French and American writers could meet over tea and cakes. Samuel Putnam, a regular visitor, relished the heady atmosphere of wit and abandon there. (William Carlos Williams was amazed by the sight of Barney and her lesbian friends dancing by moonlight around the temple of Eros she had erected in the garden.[46]) Janet Flanner continued to link New York and Paris with her fortnightly 'Letters from Paris', published in the *New Yorker*.

The many 'little magazines', which published experimental work that would not normally find an outlet elsewhere, were badly affected by the devaluation of the dollar later that year. In most cases they folded. The most important, *Transition*, survived for another decade. Proclaiming the 'Revolution of the Word', it promoted all that was new in the arts. Founded in 1926 by Eugène Jolas, an American citizen brought up in France, the quarterly was filled with discussion of the current 'isms': German Expressionism, Dadaism, Surrealism, Vorticism, Futurism. Joyce and Stein featured regularly, alongside translations of André Breton, Thomas Mann and Kafka. Stead and Blech followed the *Transition* debates with interest.[47]

An important focal point for expatriate writers was Odéonia, as Adrienne Monnier called the bookshop-lending libraries she and Sylvia Beach had established at No. 7 and No. 12 rue de l'Odéon, in the sixth *arrondissement*. Monnier, a large, monk-like figure with her cropped hair, long skirts and cape, presided at the Maison des Amis des Livres, and would often be seen talking to Gide, Valéry, Cocteau, Barrès or James Joyce in the front room. Photographs of writers covered the walls; the kettle was always at the ready.

Just down the street, her companion Sylvia Beach ran Shakespeare & Company, an equally famous landmark—for French and expatriates alike. Beach, neat and girlish-looking in her severely tailored suits, was a modest, helpful presence. On the shelves were English-language writers: Joyce, Yeats, Pound, T. S. Eliot, Virginia Woolf, Theodore Dreiser, Whitman, Sinclair Lewis, Sean O'Casey and books brought out by small local presses. On the magazine racks were the latest issues of European and American cultural and political magazines, including *Nation*, *Dial*, the *New Masses* and the *New Republic*.

Beach's greatest claim to fame was to have published *Ulysses*, in 1922, after it had been refused by English and American publishers. The book was still banned in English-speaking countries, so that tourists and expatriates thronged to buy it, hoping to smuggle it back past Dover and New York customs officials. The Continent was less censorious: a German translation had appeared in 1927 and the French translation, *Ulysse*, appeared in February 1929, the month Blech and Stead arrived in Paris. Because other books banned in English-speaking countries were available at Shakespeare & Company—the unexpurgated Florence edition of *Lady Chatterley's Lover*, for example, and Radclyffe Hall's 1929 lesbian novel *Well of Loneliness*—Sylvia Beach had developed a reputation she did not care for, as a promoter of eroticism. In fact, her bookshop merely reflected the greater liberalism of French culture.

Monnier and Beach promoted literary experiment and encouraged new writers. It would be Sylvia Beach to whom William Blech turned early in 1930, asking for her opinion on another decidedly experimental novel by an expatriate Anglo-Saxon—Christina Stead's *Seven Poor Men of Sydney*.

*   *   *

The sheltered expatriate women from puritanical English-speaking cultures were often unprepared for the openness about sex which they found in Paris. (Henry Miller, who arrived in Paris in 1930, insisted, as he turned out his first stories, that it was not pornography that was obscene, but inertia.) When Anais Nin arrived in the mid Twenties, she was deeply shocked by the open talk about sex—though six years later she had written a tribute to the controversial D. H. Lawrence and plunged into an affair with Henry Miller.

Christina Stead prided herself on casting off the vestiges of her repressive upbringing as rapidly as possible. She appears not to have flinched at the obscenity in *Ulysses*, and was contemptuous of the 'erudite customs officials' in Britain, America and Australia who placed the book on the censored list. When Malila Slade, an Australian friend of Florence James, contacted her in Paris in May 1930, Stead took her to the Casino de Paris in Montmartre (where the black dancer and singer Josephine Baker used to perform), and though her companion was unable to understand the French jokes, Stead found the 'obscene wit' and the spectacle of naked dancing girls 'really very gratifying'.[48] From an early age Stead saw herself as a sexual libertarian.

*   *   *

Coming from a Sydney not yet transformed by European immigration, Stead had never seen anything like the range of foods available in Paris. She loved to go shopping, filling her canvas bag with a *baguette*, Russian herrings, halva and exotic salads. She and Blech bought cheap, sweet white Burgundy from a dark cellar in their street. Her teetotalling upbringing was now the distant past.

Encouraged by Blech, she was trying to put on weight—hardly a chore in a place where for a mere Fr.1.60 she could have a coffee and a large slice of *tarte aux pommes*. She was drinking abundant quantities of sterilised milk, and eating bananas, cakes and cream. Eric Townsend recommended a 'disgusting drink' guaranteed to fatten her up at the rate of four pounds a week: a bar of chocolate, a glass of milk and one raw egg, mixed together.[49]

Blech, only 5'3½" and inclined to put on weight, had to watch his diet. He was a very moderate drinker, but he did love food. His real foible was 'cawfee', as he called it: as many as thirty cups a day.

★   ★   ★

William Blech could not have expected his wife or mother, now living in Paris too, to welcome Christina Stead's presence in that city—and they did not. Mollie Blech's wrath was directed less at her unfaithful husband than at the 'other woman'. As a little girl of 8, Ruth Blech learnt never to utter Christina's name in front of her mother. And the situation never changed. When Ruth married, in 1953, her husband was warned never to refer to a certain person in Mollie's presence.[50]

Nobody could have anticipated the tragic impasse. Who would have imagined that for twenty-three years Mollie Blech would refuse to grant a divorce? Happiness had come Stead's way at last, but it had a sting in its tail. Occasionally she had the nagging and dismal feeling that she had still not quite managed to secure a husband.

Within their first few weeks in Paris, William Blech introduced Stead to his mother. It was to be anticipated that Rosa Blech, who was very fond of her daughter-in-law and grand-daughter, would not warm to this plain and awkward outsider, this *shiksa* from Australia. Her son ignored the undercurrent of hostility: by early June he was making arrangements for his mother to live in the room next to their apartment and to share meals. Stead, aware of his strong sense of family loyalty, did not feel she could object, but she commented warily to Gwen Walker-Smith:

> Mrs. Blech is a tiny worrying little body, who knows three or four languages (like every blessed Jew I ever met) and is unhappy when she cannot live on the fat and heavy Jewish fare.[51]

She was painfully conscious that Rosa Blech thought her plain, and she suffered from comparison with Mollie. Once, after she had had her hair set badly, she hung back from visiting Rosa, telling Gwen:

> I feel an oddity and I have to go and see Bill's mother who is a
> charming little person, but has a small head full of private
> comment, so that I dress up for her while appearing nonchalant.[52]

This was a rare admission: Stead's letters home rarely so much as
hinted at the domestic tensions in her life.

Fortunately for Stead, Blech's plan to have his mother live next
door fell through on this occasion. Rosa, only 60, plainly preferred
her independence. She thought she might settle in the spa town of
Baden Baden in south-west Germany, not far from the French
border. In the meantime, she travelled to Riga, her city of birth, to
visit relatives.

Letty Fox, written some thirteen years later, gives a good impression of the tensions between the women in William Blech's entourage.
Grandmother Fox, closely drawn from Rosa Blech, calls Persia (her
son's companion) *die Konkubine*. Whether or not Mrs Blech senior
ever applied this unpleasant epithet to Christina, she certainly spoke
of her to Mollie and Ruth as *die Schöne* (the beauty), in a tone of
lacerating irony.[53]

In late June there was a family crisis when Mollie Blech, dismayed by the turn of events, talked of returning to the States with
Ruth. Stead wrote to Gwen Walker-Smith:

> As things are now, it looks as though we must think of going to
> the States as soon as it can be managed. Wilhelm's little girl is
> going there with her mother, and Wilhelm is very devoted to
> her. She is a beautiful and charming little girl, very intelligent
> with good manners, gay and spoilt in the best way, that is, she is
> not cranky, but she is uninjured by hardship or bad manners. Her
> mother is a beautiful woman and has excellent manners, and a
> very good intelligence: Ruth has the same characters [sic].[54]

Only to Florence James did Christina confide her anxiety and
resentment. She had no desire to go to the States quite yet; she
wanted to immerse herself in French life. But she was not in a
position to protest. She felt sure that Mollie Blech, knowing that
William would want to be near his daughter, hoped to shake off his
Australian mistress by returning to New York. As it happened,
Mollie changed her mind and she and Ruth stayed on in Paris.

Stead was very good with young children, but she wisely stayed
in the background where Ruth was concerned. William would visit
Ruth at Mollie's flat or he would call and take her out—to the zoo,
the cinema, a museum. Sometimes he took along 10-year-old Nadine
Lewin, the daughter of their Russian-born American friend Lina
Lewin, a widow. Nadine recalls that as a young girl she found
Christina quite delightful: amusingly eccentric, generous to a fault
and a wonderful storyteller.[55]

★   ★   ★

I see lots of things through being with Wilhelm who is so
ardent and intelligent, and in every respect it is the happiest
period of my life: I did not have such good luck before; by
pure chance I have become very happy: I never expected it.[56]
Stead had fulfilled both her youthful dreams: to be in Europe and to
have a loving companion. If ever she had hesitated, that year in
Paris, she fell deeply in love with William Blech. There was so
much she admired about him: his energy and curiosity, wide-
ranging culture and flow of words, his affectionate sociability, his
cosmopolitanism, his political commitment.

Heavens, what a Niagara of energy from morning till night:
he gets up at eight in the morning, he works, discourses, reads,
finds situations for his friends, writes, attends to everything
with vivid interest, gets home at midnight, refuses to go to bed
until 1.30 or 2.00 because he must read (I generally give up the
ghost at 1.30 or thereabouts)—seven days he does this, the
eighth day he perishes in his tracks, and we go to bed at 9 p.m.
and I heave a great sigh and fall straight asleep (as you can
guess). Girl, what a life! But what fun![57]
His friends all use the same expression: Blech's knowledge was
'encyclopaedic'. He was one of those truly rare human beings with
an almost comprehensive culture.[58] Nothing was too obscure or
trivial for his lively curiosity. Stead was moved to discover that he
remembered every detail she ever told him about her family and
friends in Australia.

And Christina loved Blech's sense of fun. He had a beautiful
voice, resonant and modulated. A skilled mimic, he would always
be performing 'private theatricals'—impersonating, 'in far-reaching tones', characters like Stonewall Jackson, Abraham Lincoln,
Alexander Hamilton or Benjamin Disraeli. Stead sometimes worried about what the neighbours might think, but it was 'very good
fun'. The element of inventive play, the laughter that she had
enjoyed as a child, had come back into her life. She and Bill shared a
keen sense of the absurd; they took delight in jokes, silly stories and
word games. Each knew how to make the other laugh.

Stead was fiercely proud of her 'small Vesuvius', but there was
something else too—something to which she was not at all accustomed. Bill, that soft-eyed, pale-faced man, brought out an
extraordinary tenderness in her. There was something childlike and
vulnerable about Blech's appearance. No beauty, he was short and
plump, with podgy hands. His large brown eyes were set in an
unusually white, translucent face; when he was tired he looked

green. His dark brown hair was already thinning; his round head sat sturdily on his square shoulders. When he was speaking seriously, his expression was 'earnest, devoted and saddened', leading Stead to remark in her diary: 'Due to his having no hard lines, Bill can look extremely piteous and sorrowful.'[59] Because he did not like spending money on himself, his clothes often looked shabby, frayed, slightly ill-fitting. Whenever he lost weight, his suits became too big for him, accentuating his smallness. When he was anxious or excited, he would pace up and down, twisting his handkerchief into knots and talking to himself.[60]

At weekends, they would take a tram to the countrified outer suburbs and go for long walks. Blech loved to walk, and Stead was also a good walker. Sometimes they took a train out of Paris—to Chartres, Nancy, Burgundy, the Loire Valley. If they were lucky enough to find some 'true sun' (rather than 'the pallid silvery northern variety'), the Australian was delighted.[61] In July, on a brief trip to Bordeaux and Tours, 'Wilhelm's thick white skin' turned light brown. Stead thought this wonderful.[62]

French courses were either during the day when Stead was at work, or too expensive. Instead, she took up bookbinding. Madame Ingeborg Birgesen ran a course in a dilapidated building in the rue des Grands Augustins near the river, and the workshop hummed 'with talk, hammer-taps, the creaking of presses and the roaring of flames in the stove'. The teacher shared with her Australian pupil a great appetite for improbable tales. Birgesen's fictional counterpart, the Danish bookbinder in *The Salzburg Tales*, 'talked all day and recounted hundreds of tales, mostly improbable, like a female Munchhausen'.[63]

Blech was passionate about music, but now he and Stead found themselves going more to the cinema than to concerts: they saw all the new French films as they appeared. The 'talkies' were the new art form, and French cinema—with Jean Renoir, Marcel Carné and René Clair as directors—was impressive. Stead was particularly interested in the use of dream technique and the presentation of the unconscious. Always partial to horror stories, she savoured every minute of *Caligari* and *The Fall of the House of Usher*.

'We are a model ménage,' she told Gwen. 'We live in each other's company from 12 midnight to 12 midnight . . . The funny thing is, I am getting more and more used to it: it is always a deeper pleasure—and of course, when he has to go away for a couple of days, and he comes back, we feel as if we had really been separated for months.'[64]

Blech often went on business trips to Rouen, London, Antwerp, Bruges, Ghent. In September, when he went to Germany to meet his mother in Berlin and help her settle into Baden Baden, Stead was truly envious. She had steeped herself, during her adolescence, in translations of Goethe, Schiller, Theodor Storm and Nietzsche; now she was impatient to experience the culture across the Rhine for herself. Berlin, famous for its opera (Brecht and Kurt Weill had just written *The Threepenny Opera*), avant-garde theatre, jazz cabarets and beer Kneipen, was particularly enticing.

Yet the Germans brought out Blech's penchant for caricature. Berlin, he wrote to her, was 'the elephant's testicles'. In Berlin, 'endless shaved heads and 3-ply necks ogle in heavy jazz rhythms at blonde girls'.[65] The descriptions in his letters and the 'recitals' on his return were so colourful that Stead was able to describe Germany to Gwen as if she had been there herself:

Berlin is the centre of glass-buildings, futurismus, post-futurismus, music, gaiety, night-life, brilliance, heavy philosophy, Jewish genius, strange finance, revolving post-Reinhardt theatres, passionate ideations, heavy Teutonic fantasy, goose-step culture, reverberate beliefs, negations, assertions—of Nature, Sex and Freudianism, Jungism, Adlerism, of Sex, Pollution and Nature, of Sunlight Cures, Heavy Affirmations, the Cult of Cults. It is the hot potatoes. It is Sin: it is the Gaiety. It is the elephant's pyjamas . . . Nevertheless everyone agrees there is one drawback to Germany—the Germans: the hard-headed cultivator of Modernismus wears a shaved head, glasses, a 3-ply neck and a tremendous belly.[66]

We recognise the future author of *The Salzburg Tales*—the delight in irony, the heaping up of detail and imagery, the exorbitant lists, the love of parody. The letter also shows how much Stead was influenced by her companion. His humour and ability to bring a scene or a person to life in an avalanche of vivid and inspired images were equal to Stead's own.[67] She would always be a scavenger. If she liked something someone had written or said, she would somehow work it into her own writing.

Later in September, Blech was in London at the time of a sterling scare. He had seen it coming and sold a group of shares short, but London brokers were not keen to do business just then and he decided to leave early. He just had time to take Florence James to *Juno & the Paycock*, Sean O'Casey's play at the Abbey Theatre. He gave her the tickets he had booked for *The Apple Cart*, Shaw's satire on the monarchy, currently causing a sensation in London.[68] Blech's visits were 'bright spots', Florence told her mother.[69]

Blech always made time to visit the London bookshops, and he would return to Paris with a pile of novels and books on economics. Alf Hurst had commissioned him to write a book on grain markets in Britain, which Blech was working on in the evenings. In September, Blech brought Stead *A House is Built*, a novel by two Australians writing in collaboration: Marjorie Barnard and Flora Eldershaw. Stead already knew of Marjorie Barnard, who had attended Sydney Girls' High five years before her, and the novel's success in Australia and England must have acted as a spur.

While Blech was away, Stead saw *Tosca*, *Cavalleria Rusticana* and *The Barber of Seville* at the Opéra Comique, which seemed to her to have perfected traditional stagecraft. 'I only go to the theatre when he is away,' she told Gwen, 'for we have plenty to do when he is here.'[70] On other evenings she would stay in the office and work on her novel *Seven Poor Men* until late, or go home, cook supper and read. She was reading the latest Soviet novels, which Blech and his friends admired. 'Watch and work with Russia!' Frederick Sard admonished *Transition* readers. He added: 'Whether or not one is a communist, or believes in the materialistic conception of history or in applied Marxism, in Russia the material exists for a new social synthesis.'[71] At the bar of the Coupole, Ilya Ehrenburg, the Bolshevik writer who had fled to Paris disillusioned with the excesses of the revolution, was always ready to discuss Soviet literature.

Stead would maintain an interest in Russian literature throughout her life. But at that time she was far more excited by modernist writing. She liked the experimentation with language and form, and the complex relation between waking life, dreams and the unconscious in contemporary writing. She was very impressed with Mann's *The Magic Mountain*, which she read in September 1929, while Blech was in Germany. In December that year Mann was awarded the Nobel Prize for Literature. 'The whole takes some reading and brave men have died under the strain,' Stead told Gwen, 'but if you really want to make life insipid, destroy modern literature, and crack your brain, and enjoy it violently into the bargain, read *The Magic Mountain*.' The character Settembrini reminded her of her father, she told Gwen.[72]

She read D. H. Lawrence for the first time that year, and thought him 'a marvellous man'.[73] *Sons and Lovers*, Lawrence's autobiographical novel which portrayed his Oedipal relationship with his mother, would no doubt have made her reflect on her relationship with her father. In *For Love Alone*, the portrait of her own sexually-charged adolescence bears unmistakable traces of Lawrence in vocabulary and imagery.

For Stead the greatest contemporary writer was James Joyce: his flamboyant gift of language was 'the most extraordinary imaginable'. Like Lawrence, Joyce had written an autobiographical novel about a difficult childhood and adolescence from which he emerged as an artist: these would be useful models when Stead came to writing *The Man Who Loved Children* a decade later. But it was *Ulysses* that impressed her most. She re-read it carefully, with the help of 'learned commentary', and appreciated its genius more than ever. Joyce's work-in-progress, published in *Transition*, needed to be read 'with a rhyming dictionary, an encyclopaedia, the grammars of ten languages, and an annotated "crib"', she told Gwen, adding that the effort was well worth it.[74] In 1932, when she was polishing *Seven Poor Men of Sydney*, she made the bold comment that there was 'no living writer in English ... not indebted to [Joyce's] methods and his vocabulary'.[75]

Not everyone shared her enthusiasm. D. H. Lawrence thought *Ulysses* obscene. Virginia Woolf described it as 'the scratching of pimples on the body of the bootboy at Claridge's'. (She and Leonard Woolf, who ran the Hogarth Press, were among those who declined to publish it.) Some Leftists, such as Blech, regarded *Ulysses* as an admirable mirror of the decay of capitalist civilisation; others condemned it as decadent and counter-revolutionary. Frederick Sard wrote to *Transition* editors Eugène and Maria Jolas, Joyce's loyal partisans, decrying 'the bankruptcy of art as form ... evidenced in the latest work of Joyce'.[76]

Stead's early fiction is influenced by contemporary modernist writing, particularly Joyce. *Seven Poor Men of Sydney* and *The Beauties and Furies* make sudden shifts in tone and register. They also contain the modernist interest in dream and fantasy, references to Freudian psychoanalysis, frequent allusions to other literary works, and speculation about the nature of narrative itself. Critics of Stead's early work often felt compelled to make comparisons with Joyce.[77] Stead had taken a very different path from those writers who stayed in Australia in the Twenties and Thirties, where 'dun-coloured' realism still reigned supreme.[78]

*   *   *

Then came 'Black Thursday', 24 October 1929, the Wall Street crash. It marked the beginning of a world economic crisis which first reached the banking centre of New York, then London, Vienna and Berlin, and was to last over a decade. Many small investors lost everything; there were suicides among speculators. At first France, with its heavy stocks of gold, was not affected like Britain and America, though the crash immediately hit the Americans in France, whose dollars were devalued. The next few months saw many of these reluctantly head home. Others moved to the south, where prices were lower. Paris would be a less lively place for Stead and Blech in the years ahead.

★   ★   ★

On a business visit to London in mid November 1929, between the first and second act of *The Three Sisters*, William Blech pressed Florence James to return with him to Paris the following evening. Christina was going through a difficult patch, and she would appreciate having her closest friend with her just now.

For Florence, it meant throwing in her secretarial job at the ANZ Bank in London, but it seemed a good time for a holiday. She had just completed a shorthand course, her boyfriend was causing her anguish, and Christina needed her.[79]

The Channel crossing was unusually rough. William, a terrible traveller, could not wait to see the lights of Boulogne. He and Florence had dinner on the train and arrived at the Gare du Nord at 9 pm.

Florence had last seen Christina in February: a blissfully happy woman waving from the window of the *Golden Arrow*. She was nonplussed to find her 'shockingly thin'. In a letter from Paris, she told her mother that Christina had been 'really ill', with an 'inward chill'. She added: 'There have been more complications than I can recount in Wilhelm's domestic affairs—not in his and Christina's love for one another, I have never seen a more beautiful relation.'[80]

The truth was that Christina had just terminated a pregnancy. It had come at a bad time: she and Blech had had to move apart, since any hope of an equitable divorce arrangement was jeopardised by the prospect of Blech being charged with adultery. In the last weeks she had been living by herself, in delicate health and melancholy mood, in a modest hotel in the seventh *arrondissement*.

'I never felt the abortion was traumatic for Chris,' Florence James recalls, 'only a necessity, which she put behind her as quickly as possible.'[81] For Stead, the worst trauma was the domestic situation. She was beginning to wonder whether William really wanted a divorce. Pained by Mollie's unalleviated distress, he had told Mollie that Christina was about to take up a job in Geneva and disappear. Whatever the reason for the lie, it naturally rekindled Mollie's hopes. Christina was now terrified that William would decide to return to his family. Would he think that he had purchased her love too dearly, that it had been paid for with too much cruelty? Would he now be cruel to *her*?[82]

Later in life, she would recall with gratitude Eric Townsend's friendship during these forlorn weeks: he had visited her, brought her food and stayed to talk.[83]

Florence could see that William was everything to Christina: 'her friends, her experiences came through him'. Nevertheless, she was

surprised to discover the extent of Christina's insecurity. She saw
that Blech had 'not painted the real picture' to Christina: he did not
seem nearly as determined to divorce as he had originally made out.
Not wanting to hurt either woman, he was stringing both along.
'His vacillation was something we couldn't have anticipated,' says
Florence.[84]

The two friends shared a tiny double room in the Hôtel Royal
Park—which, Florence told her mother, sounded much grander than
it was. They ate in a nearby *brasserie*. For the first few days they
mostly slept, talked and ate, with Christina working at the office
for a few hours each afternoon. After some days, she had regained
sufficient energy to take Florence to the Louvre, followed by lunch
at the Dôme. They went to the *coiffeur* for a shampoo and set each.
And on two or three evenings they went to the cinema.

Christina found the precariousness of her situation intensely
painful, but she was not bitter. Among her papers are two unusually intimate diary entries, from 9 and 15 December 1929, which
provide a revealing glimpse of her feelings at this time.[85]

Monday, December 9.
Saw Eric yesterday, talked about Wilh. and meant to rise early
this morning to go early to the office to see Wilh. but could
not sleep—angry because Eric said Wilh. would die a beggar
and a failure ... Got up, sat with quilt round me near
window, saw dark clear sky, stars, suggestive closed facades
of French houses, ashamed of fretting ... Fl. sympathetic,
don't know why I am so wretchedly badhumored.

William had spent the weekend with Mollie and Ruth, and Christina, dreadfully afraid that he might be enjoying his weekend, had
hardly slept. On Sunday, Eric Townsend had invited her to lunch
and they had discussed William's personality. The conversation had
left her very upset.

Eric said to me:
I understand Will, better than you because Will is like me,
he will always be a good henchman, he needs someone to
make him work: you are different ...
I was indignant, but I could not be angry, what is the use,
I was his guest, also prejudiced, also Eric is unsympathetic, I
feel a conscious maleness. I said:
It is not so, Wilh. is a brilliant man ... If he hears people
saying what you say ... it depresses him, it does him no
good. On the other hand, if he is praised and encouraged, he
becomes very gay, exaggerated, but he does very good work.[86]

Townsend retorted that she got on with Bill because she did not ask
for much. The whole exchange had got under Stead's skin. On

Monday morning, she felt terribly frustrated with herself and her
situation.

> Miss Wilh. at night with every kind of tenderness and lack ...
> Encouraged myself in case I should find Wilh. not unhappy
> over his weekend (as it proved); recalled Tchechov's women
> who lose their lovers through empty lives, resolved to work,
> great energy to "work," but the usual lack.

When she arrived at the office, she found Blech working happily,
enthusiastic about writing another book on economics—this time
for Peter Neidecker. She herself was a tangle of conflicting emotions:

> Told Wilh. about Eric's treachery and detraction, flushed with
> emotion, only letting off steam. Wilh. content with Mollie at
> present—a terrible pain to know it, I only hope for them to be
> unhappy whatever I say; as a result pained and upset. Wilh.
> started to sketch his book for Pete. We did 4 or 5 pages, Wilh.
> dictating at top speed, very facile and well-phrased, me
> making mistakes as usual, Wilh. putting in information which
> he learned when we were in Bordeaux, and so on—said:
> "Wouldn't you wonder where I learned it all, you would never
> think I would remember all that!"
> I said: "No, you are a wonder, you are like a silkworm that
> keeps on spinning silk out of its inside." He kissed me warmly.

She reassured him that those people who judged him had not 'one
quarter of his passion, enthusiasm, talent or knowledge'.

William left the office pleased with the pages he had written. Left
alone, Stead thought about Mollie and wept. At home, she asked
herself: 'Why am I so hideous? I would prefer she should be
unhappy and lonely than that I should be.' She cried again. The day
before, Florence had wept about *her* love life, and said that perhaps
if she had an 'inner life' and her 'own work', she would not mind so
much. To comfort her, but inwardly convinced she herself was
different, Christina had said, 'No. It is the same with all women'.
Now, 'ashamed', she realised she was really no more independent.

The picture of Catherine, in *Seven Poor Men of Sydney*, sheds
some light on Stead's own inner dialogue. Catherine in some
respects represents Stead's shadow self. In the novel, Baruch Mendelssohn (Blech's counterpart) asks her incredulously: 'Do you
want to be happy as women are, bound to one spot of earth by the
delightful chains of ceramics, carpets, cobwebby laces, a marriage
ring?' She laughs and answers, 'If the truth were told, yes; although
I would fret against them.'

Baruch shakes his head, and tells the passionate Catherine:

> You can't get that, you're not the sort ... I knew a girl who
> learned eight European languages perfectly from her eight

lovers ... You should give your magnificent passion exercise, since it is your sole and jealous interest. It is your way of living: exacerbate existence![87]

★   ★   ★

By 15 December, the time of the second diary entry, Florence James had returned to London and Stead had moved to the Hôtel du Danemark, close to the Jardin du Luxembourg. Blech had suggested the hotel so that he could see her when he visited his mother, who lived nearby. Rosa Blech had not stayed long in Baden Baden.

The hotel was old, run down and not very clean. The concierge, curious about Christina and her regular male visitor, called her alternately Madame and Mademoiselle. Christina was now sometimes calling Wilhelm 'Bill'.

Feel much more cheerful as if Bill and I had somehow set up house again. B. says M. cannot sleep at night and I wonder if it is because I delay going to "Geneva": nobody can be happy: I am just about as happy as possible at present, as I see Bill and have free time. The Montparnasse quarter suits me, not so lonely: had breakfast at Dôme, jam omelette and coffee: interesting rugged and sharp faces.

She notes that she dreamt of three coffins stacked on top of each other: one contained a man, another a woman and the other twins. All had been buried alive.

Out of the top one a man got, hale, and a woman out of the second or middle one: they unlidded the bottom and on top was the live twin, who scarcely was awake, and underneath the dead twin with half his face putrified and mossy and all falling into dissolution.

Stead often imagined herself as a twin: the wanderer and her wraith. Did she conclude that the figures were Bill, Mollie and herself? If so, her fears would seem to be transparent: at the bottom of the pile, closest to death (one half is already dead) lies Christina.

That day, a Sunday, Stead walked through the Montparnasse cemetery in thoughtful mood. It was 'cold and weepy' weather; the leafless trees were blowing gently. She stood and watched adults and children, dressed in black, praying in front of the small family chapels. In her general disarray and to her regret, she forgot to sit down at the gate before she left. ('On leaving a cemetery, you must sit down for a time at the gate, so that the ghosts who are following you, will become discouraged and return to their own dwelling-places.'[88])

Threatened by the loss of Bill's love, she was conscious of being powerfully in love with him. Her diary is full of admiration for him. When Eric Townsend ('anti-semitic at heart, partly out of a shadowy kind of jealousy of Bill') provocatively suggested in conversation with Bill that Germany could do without its Jews, Bill argued 'with splendid and creative rage'. She added, frustrated with her part in the discussion: 'I lose the meat of what he says: I can only get it by studiously cultivating the memory, but I am so anxious to answer him, or stand on his side that I forget.'

That evening Bill 'came home', and they had supper at an American bar near her hotel. He reminded the waiter of something he had forgotten to charge them for and Stead, 'very sentimental', almost cried at the 'perfect goodness of his heart'.

*   *   *

Stead's fiction, written later, suggests that she came to see all this in a different light. In *The Beauties and Furies* (1936) and *Letty Fox* (1946) Elvira and Persia both miscarry with intent; and both find themselves lying alone and in pain in a hotel room, while their lover is elsewhere, preoccupied with another woman. Elvira develops metritis. Feverish and unable to sleep, she tells Oliver reproachfully: 'You were away when I was in trouble.'[89] In *Letty Fox*, Persia, Solander's mistress, is left to recover in an Antwerp hotel while Solander Fox is in Paris fussing over his wife. Oliver and Solander are both portrayed as chronic ditherers.

*   *   *

'On the female side, I am a little lonely,' Stead admitted.[90] She missed Florence. In Sydney she had hankered after male company; now she moved in a world of men: bankers, businessmen, artists— primarily friends of Bill. Her banking novel, *House of All Nations*, set in Paris in 1931–2, portrays this man's world: there is not one significant female character in its 800 pages. The women are shadowy background figures—wives, mistresses, daughters.

At Christmas the fountains were again frozen over. Stead found the general mood of gaiety, the millions of lights, the snow and rain exhilarating. Eric Townsend and his French girlfriend Suzanne invited them for a traditional turkey dinner.

Townsend aroused ambivalent emotions in Stead: she liked him and disliked him. He made her angry, yet she sought out his company. She rationalised this apparent contradiction to herself by saying that the 'study of personality' was her 'private passion',[91] and that as a writer, she needed to enter into the mind of people unlike herself. But there was clearly something else too. The diary entry of 9 December 1929, outlining her conversation with Town-send, indicates a rivalrous sparring (each professing to know Bill better than the other) reminiscent of David Stead's claims to omniscience. In *The Man Who Loved Children*, Sam Pollit maddens his daughter Louisa by claiming that he always knows what she is thinking, or that they are one person:

> "You will be all right, Looloo," concluded Sam, kissing her good night. "You are myself; I know you cannot go astray."
> "I won't be like you, Dad."
> He laughed, "You can't help it: you are myself."

David Stead shared Pollit's inability to recognise other people as separate entities, with minds of their own. And it may well have been this colonising tendency that caused his eldest daughter to become so self-contained, secretive and private. It also left her with the desire to do to others what was done to herself: to try to clamber inside their skin, to control them by taking over their very voice. Fiction provided the perfect justification for what was basi-cally an obsession with control. As one critic puts it:

> Here is, perhaps, the satirist who loves her objects, not in the Christian way of loving the sinner while hating the sin, but in something like the naturalist–observer's desire to possess her objects through knowledge.[92]

★   ★   ★

Stead projected herself as a serious and ambitious writer. In Sep-tember 1929, after eight months in France, she told Gwen Walker-Smith, 'I am still struggling with a novel. If it comes through satisfactorily it ought to be saleable in Australia and I hope will make me a little money.'[93] Yet interviewed in her old age, Stead would vehemently deny that she was ever ambitious. She even claimed that the entire impetus to publish *Seven Poor Men of Sydney* came from Bill, who allegedly took the manuscript to Sylvia Beach without her knowledge.[94]

It is unlikely that Blech showed the manuscript to Sylvia Beach without telling Stead. He gave it to Beach early in 1930, several months before Stead left for Salzburg; Beach was encouraging and urged Stead to find an agent in London. Margaret Dunbar-Smith, the friend who had helped promote H. E. Bates, took on the job of hawking the manuscript round London. But publishers were not willing to risk such an unconventional first novel. In May 1930, one publisher rejected it on the grounds that it was 'fantastic and digressive', but said he would consider a revised version. Stead was bitterly disappointed (she did not have the heart to tell her stepmother when she wrote to her that morning), but she was uncompromising at that stage, believing it 'impossible to revise it, and artistically a mistake to attempt it'. Blech did persuade her to revise 'several very clotted pages' before submitting it to a second publisher.[95] This was probably the Hogarth Press, for in late June Florence James wrote to her mother:

> I have been reading Christina's manuscript. It came back from the Hogarth Press with a little note that it was not their type of book. I doubt if she will get it published in London, it is so amazingly original and outspoken that only a very courageous firm could touch it. The ms. as it stands has a number of faults, but the thought behind and the prose are so uncommon and beautiful that I think Christina's literary gift one of the most amazing I have met.[96]

By the time Stead returned from Salzburg in September, the manuscript was with a fourth publisher. She reported to Gwen that all were in agreement: 'it has power but is not very easily read'.[97] American friends suggested she send them a copy of the manuscript so they could try New York publishers as well, but this would have involved typing the whole manuscript out again. Understandably, Stead hesitated.

Since no early draft of the novel survives, we do not know how different it was from the published version.[98] The novel, depicting the struggles of young city workers in the depressed Sydney of the 1920s, has an overtly socialist underpinning, but it is not likely to have been considered too outspoken. Florence James thinks that the Sydney setting was considered 'of too narrow an interest'.[99] The unorthodox treatment of the subject was more likely to be the main problem. The way the novel juxtaposes conventional realism with the poetic and hallucinatory has always disconcerted readers. There is no linear plot, no obvious authorial message; the characters are not yet the rounded portraits they would become in Stead's later fiction. She was a word-drunk young writer, and the novel contains some indulgent over-writing.

But it has a peculiar brilliance. The poetic exuberance of *Seven Poor Men*'s style has a James Joyce quality. Its description of stormy, moonlit Sydney nights and tormented, restless characters has something of Emily Brontë or Dostoevski. And certain haunted passages call to mind Poe or Baudelaire. In later years, the Australian critic Dorothy Green would comment that this first novel of Christina Stead's was a path-breaker in terms of Australian literature: 'It was *Seven Poor Men of Sydney*, rather than any early Patrick White novel, which broke free from kitchen-sink realism into the world of poetry, without losing touch with the ground.'[100] At the time of its publication, Australian critics were too intimidated by its eccentricity to realise the significance of its innovations.

There is little doubt that Stead was consciously influenced by Joyce. Like him, she was writing about the modern city. Like him, she lived in exile and wrote from memory about her city of birth. As in *Ulysses*, the characters in *Seven Poor Men* are at times almost disembodied voices. In a 1935 interview, Stead would explain that the dynamic of the conversation had been more important to her than the characters as rounded individuals. 'Conversation is diffuse, disjointed, full of popular sayings and banalities local in time and place which do not express character at all, or very little.'

She added:

My purpose, in making characters eloquent, is the expression of two psychological truths; first, that everyone has a wit superior to his everyday wit, when discussing his personal problems, and the most depressed housewife, for example, can talk like Medea about her troubles; second, that everyone, to a greater or lesser extent, is a fountain of passion, which is turned by circumstances of birth or upbringing into conventional channels.[101]

With this first novel, Stead insisted that the characters were 'not actually drawn from life'; they were 'like most characters, crystallisations of various types of men and women'. In fact, there are aspects of herself in both Catherine and Michael. Catherine was also loosely modelled on Esther Wait, the elder sister of Mildred Wait, a friend of Christina's at Teacher's College. Stead was fascinated by the stories she heard of this wild young woman who once went so far as to commit herself to a mental asylum. Tom Withers was inspired by Eric Townsend, her Paris friend. The only truly admirable character was Baruch Mendelssohn, modelled on Bill Blech.

*   ★   ★   ★*

'I'm blessed if I can get down to another piece of work: I have half a dozen themes but no backbone.'[102] By the summer of 1930, Stead was feeling tired and demoralised. Her domestic situation was as difficult and unresolved as ever: she was still living by herself in a hotel, with visits from Bill. Publishers had not shown much interest in her novel. At the Travelers' Bank, she had accumulated two years' worth of holiday, six weeks in all, and she was keen to go away somewhere. Sadly, it would have to be on her own. In August, Mollie Blech's mother was due to visit from the States, and Bill felt he had to be around. He had built up Mère Grossman as a powerful Jewish matriarch, who was crossing the Atlantic 'to fortify a wronged offspring'.[103] He persuaded Stead that it would be better if she left Paris while his mother-in-law was in town and suggested she go to the Salzburg Festival—a chance for her to experience Germanic culture at first hand.

Stead arrived in mid July[104] and found Salzburg and its surroundings 'indescribably romantic'.[105] In a rare handwritten letter (when she had a typewriter, she even typed postcards), she drew ornate little sketches of the local costume for Gwen, pointing out the lace, embroidery and colours.

The festival began on 1 August, with Hugo von Hofmannsthal's *Jedermann*, a modern re-working of the mediaeval English miracle play *Everyman*. Directed by Max Reinhardt, it was an open-air performance in front of the Cathedral. Stead took careful notes. She went on long walks by herself and on organised excursions to the surrounding lakes and border towns; she enjoyed the little puppet theatre in Salzburg (the first time she saw puppets), but she was lonely and anxious. It was the longest period she and Bill had been apart and his letters—brief, jovial and hastily penned—did not do much for her tranquillity of mind. 'Enjoy yourself without regard to money,' he told her paternally, 'and see if you can get in with a good crowd at the centre of Salzburg's life.'[106] Another begins: 'Chris dear, pardon for a *very* hurried note. (Oh dear I will be late for the Duchess.)'[107] Stead had found the Alice in Wonderland joke amusing on previous occasions, but this time she must have wondered whether the Duchess was Bill's wife or his mother-in-law.

On 5 August, she told Gwen she was 'badly missing Wilhelm' and had almost decided to go home early, on 21 August—after Gluck's *Iphigenia in Aulis*. She said 'almost' because the decision was not entirely in her hands. Indeed, Blech wrote entreating her to keep to the original plan: she should leave Salzburg on 20 August, spend a week in Munich and arrive in Paris at the end of the month. 'Do please follow any dates as they will be the best all around.'[108] She wrote that she was fed up with the constant rain and wet feet, but her hint fell upon deaf ears: 'Leave me to grapple with actions and obligations while you meditate the humid eternities in excelsis.'[109]

Mollie, he wrote, was reproaching him for his 'hard' and 'inflexible' attitudes. He added: 'If she knew what my marriage to you will mean to me, she would be in a different state, so I treat her with jocular silence.'[110] This was probably not entirely reassuring to Stead.

Evidently she was trying to sound cheerful, for in his letter of 19 August, Blech wrote:

'Awfully glad to hear that your many, many qualms have disappeared in Salzburg. Mountain air and absence from me is in all ways gut.'

Mollie and Ruth now planned to leave for the States in late October. This time, Bill was not intending to follow—at least not immediately. 'I have begun a gentle search for lodgings for your good self pending lodgings for our good selves,' he told Stead,[111] who had given up her hotel room to save money.

Blech's letters were bantering and loving, but they were neither intimate nor passionate. In his large, round, sloping hand full of emphatic underlinings, he joked that he wanted her happy and fat: 'Are you, or are you not spending the last fortnight in an orgy of fattening. Remember a skinny girl means <u>divorce</u>, a fat girl <u>perpetual love</u>.' The letter was signed: 'Heavy affection, Wilhelm.'[112] In another, signed 'William James Cook', he declared: 'I love you, dirty little merino, and Watson's Bay waste wool refuse.'[113]

*   *   *

Soon after her return to Paris, Stead went away again—possibly once more to remove herself from the scene of domestic crisis. This time—a rather surprising arrangement—she met Bill's mother at Aix-les-Bains and they spent a week on the Riviera. To Gwen she wrote warmly of the 'unmoderated colors and dazzling days'[114] in Nice and Monte Carlo. The Mediterranean coast reminded her of Australia, but it did not suffer from Australia's insularity. She would have liked to live there permanently—a view shared by many expatriates.

In November Stead went away yet again by herself—this time returning to Fontainebleau and the Hôtel de l'Aigle Noir. She was thinking of setting a romantic scene in this place and wanted to make notes, but it was a sad place to be—full of poignant memories. The town and forest were desolate under a heavy grey winter sky: it rained incessantly, the trees were naked and it was dark by 4 pm. There were no tourists—just soldiers from the artillery school. It was almost two years since their honeymoon sojourn there and Stead was still not married to the man who had first made love to her in that very hotel.

After attempting a walk through the forest early in the week and sitting for several hours on a wet tree trunk to read, she went back to the hotel and put herself to bed. She had caught a cold. Her mood was bleak.

*   *   *

'Fontainebleau is the only argument against communism,' she wrote to Gwen. 'It seems unlikely that anyone but a lord glutted with pride and riches would spend the money to build a thing so exquisite and ornate.' She added that it was a poor argument nonetheless—'a drop of grease in a fire'.[115]

In Bill Blech's company, she had come to see herself as a communist sympathiser, and her letter to Gwen shows that she tended to parrot his views.

> Wilhelm believes . . . that next year the first serious blows will be
> felt by the capitalism of the world arrayed seriously for the first
> time against the successful communistic state of Russia which is
> determined to wreck the capitalistic world. It is marvellous that
> Soviet Russia has put itself into a position to frighten the whole
> of Europe in so short a time since the revolution, especially since
> it is still fighting in the interior, with its own misery and lack
> of production. Nobody likes to look forward to revolution, even
> when they are workers and revolution is for the good of the
> workers . . . however capitalism, in producing more unemployed
> than the police can cope with and more fear for tomorrow's
> bread than the heart can bear, is failing in every country.

It was Blech's view that Australia, wracked with unemployment, should repudiate her debt from the Great War, and Stead tried to persuade her cousin of this:

> Australia got hooked into a war she didn't want and had
> nothing to do with: she lost a lot of youth and much money,
> and now when she has difficulty in paying her "debt" she gets
> no thanks but hard words from the old country. Maybe you
> think it unpatriotic, but actually that is how most foreigners
> regard it: they regard the Empire as a sell, especially for the
> colonies which are sold.[116]

Three years later, when it came to revising *Seven Poor Men of Sydney* for publication, she was no longer the parrot; she had intelligently absorbed Blech's Marxist framework and made it her own. 'How does a small minority oppress a large majority?' asks Baruch in the novel, and both *Seven Poor Men* and *House of All Nations* go some way towards answering his question. Stead's first novel also dramatically takes up the torch for Australian independence from Britain. Just as young people need to be freed from parental bonds, so, the novel implies, Australians need to work out their own destiny without the interference of the old country.

At the same time, the creative characters in *Seven Poor Men* know they must break away from Australia and become 'wanderers'. They need to breathe a different air. Now that she was ensconced in the heart of Europe, Stead was more aware than ever of Australia's parochialism. She told her cousin, somewhat tactlessly, that a Sydney woman she met in Paris was 'all that there is of Australian, plus a strong accent, simple, colonial, unsophisticated'.[117] And when Gwen sent her a book called *Australia Beautiful* for Christmas 1930, Christina told her that she found herself nostalgic only for the sun and the bush.

It is awfully interesting for me to see the Hans Heysens, Lindsays, Gruners, Ashtons and others reproduced in this book: I remembered the solemnly virtuous pilgrimages I used to make to the Art Gallery to study these lads: now they seem to have an awful similarity, as if they have nobody but each other to inspire each other: I was really fascinated to see how they have changed, or how I have, after having become complaisant of the wildest and purest fantasies of genius and emulation over here. It is striking how we suffer from humbleness, obtuseness and timidity, in a superb climate for artists, simply because we are out of touch with the hot springs and fountains of Europe.[118]

In 1935, in an interview with the *Australian Women's Weekly* soon after the publication of *Seven Poor Men,* Stead's ambivalent attitude towards Australia, both nostalgic and patronising, is striking:

It is perhaps obvious that I have not forgotten Sydney during my absence—the climate, the importance of the Labor Movement in everyone's daily life; the type of society which is near to being a one-class society, the importations into social and national life from England.

To me, of course, this Australian society, even as it stands, is much preferable to English society, hideous with its class divisions, evident even in the Labor Movement here.

Australia's "robust and selfish Labor Party," as Haldane says, despite its corruption, makes men livelier and manners freer out there . . .

I may not return to Australia, but I am glad I sprang from that raw, fresh and unhistorical society.[119]

Leaving Australia and leaving her family had been the same thing, and there is a sense in which she conflated the two. *Seven Poor Men* depicts parents in an extremely negative light: Michael Bagenault is overjoyed when he discovers that the father whom he has often wished dead is *not* his father, and that he is illegitimate, gloriously fatherless.

Stead may well have thought that by travelling across the world, she too had cut the ties with her father. However, while her first novel must have hurt David Stead, it also owed him a considerable debt. Near the end of the narrative is an extraordinary speech by Koḷ Blount, a long monologue about the 'continent of mystery' they inhabit. A lyrical description of Australia in the dim ante-glacial past, Australia as the undiscovered Terra Australis, Australia as the unconquered land of aborigines, then Australia after white settlement, it brings to mind the enthusiastic David Stead and his stories about the country he loved.

That was the trouble: she still loved David Stead. His occasional letters, with their wonderful descriptions of nature, were a living reminder to Christina of her father's unusual powers of observation and talent for expression—gifts he had generously showered upon her in childhood. At some stage, she destroyed her father's letters. Two short extracts are all that remain. These she had cut out and pasted onto a sheet of paper, with other notes for an unpublished novel, *The Wraith and the Wanderer*. The first extract she used almost verbatim in the draft of her novel.

Thursday mg.
This morning before breakfast while clearing up the front path,
I came across a most lovely example of the St. Andrew's Cross
yeepi. It looked most beautiful. Do you remember it? A beautiful
symmetrical concentric lined web, on a small scale, with the
misty pearly cross on it, the spider splayed on the cross. The
early mg. sun was shining through the dark meerschaum legs and
the beaut. banded body—the web dotted with little beads of dew
and tiny beads of insect stickfast. Dadpad.

The second extract, from the same or another letter, is interesting for other reasons:

Grand easterly gale blowing this morning. I have just been up
to the Gap, but could not stop long because of the glare on the
surf (I have dreadful trouble with the glare—much worse than
it used to be. With thick, lowering conditions, such as to-day,
the glare is much worse than in bright sunlight). It is a
magnificent sight, looking out to sea—as far as one can see.
I was thinking of you and wished so much that you could see
it again, instead of being stuck in that stuffy rue Jean Bart,
among those more than stuffy people.[120]

Was David Stead serious about 'stuffy rue Jean Bart'? Sixteen years before (when his family was stuck in stuffy Sydney), the same man had written ecstatic letters from Paris, full of the glories of the French capital. It was precisely this egotism—in the guise of concern—that Stead would depict in *The Man Who Loved Children*. Somehow, her father's experience was always more valid, more precious, than anyone else's.

David Stead was 52 now, and his eyes were troubling him. However, from all that distance, he still had the power to upset and irritate Christina, filling her with resentment and compassion.

'Overcote', in *The Salzburg Tales*, is a story by a 50-year-old public stenographer about her father—an atheist and a sentimental but mocking man. During the narrator's childhood, he took up with another woman, who was 15 at the time. Now, as an older man, her father remains manipulative:

> We never go near our father . . . You can't forgive the things he
> does . . . He can write a good letter, too: but I can't read his letters
> any more, they are so touching, you almost begin to be sorry for
> him, and they are so insincere: he is all the time laughing up his
> sleeve at you if you come; and he cries if you stay away . . . [121]

After two and a half years away, Stead was beginning to feel a stranger to the family. Her father's romance with Thistle Harris had resumed around the time Christina left Australia. Thistle, missing him badly, had written to David. This third time, they were not going to be put off. In 1930, Ada had moved out of Boongarre and gone to live with her cousin Rachel Davis, at The Entrance. She wrote to Christina less these days. David Stead and the girls wrote occasionally, but everyone was so 'ridiculously discreet' that Christina never had much real sense of what was going on.[122] She worried about her stepmother. And she was conscious that the younger children had acquired quite different personalities by now: she no longer knew them.

Interestingly, she cared a great deal about her image in the family's eyes. Christina admitted to her Aunt Florence her great propensity for tearing up letters. She told Gwen that she had written her Aunt Florence 'a very rubbishy letter from Bordeaux' which she hoped would go astray. 'I was hot, blinded, newly and very badly coiffed, tormented by peanutsellers and rugsellers.'[123]

Far more upsetting than a plague of peanutsellers was to have her hair badly set. Though she believed that in Paris she had learnt to dress in a way which suited her build, and that this gave her new confidence, she was as painfully self-conscious as ever. In this respect too, David Stead's influence was not eradicated by mere distance.

* * *

At the beginning of 1931, Blech had found a pleasant modern apartment on the rue Jean Bart, near the Luxembourg Gardens and the Montparnasse cafés. After having lived apart for over a year, he and Stead moved in together again. Christina was intensely relieved. Mollie and Ruth had made a temporary trip to the States and were now living in the South of France.

With *Seven Poor Men of Sydney* doing the rounds of publishers, Stead had begun a novel loosely based on Keith Duncan. As indicated by its rather shrill title, *The Young Man Will Go Far*, she had lost nothing of her hostility. (Later, scarcely less sarcastic, it became *The Travelling Scholar*, then *The Beauties and Furies*.) Blech had seen Duncan on one of his trips to London, and Christina was able to report to her cousin: 'Keith Duncan . . . is still hanging on to various scholarships in London and expects to get others to take him to the States.'[124]

The novel was abandoned, but remnants reveal it to be an early working of the material in *For Love Alone*.[125] Oliver Gillybrand, a precursor to Jonathan Crow, is 23, dark, poor and a 'new-minted bachelor of arts' at Sydney University. He goes for long walks with Sara, a young writer. Then he wins a travelling scholarship to England. They write to one another.

★   ★   ★

Early in 1931, *Seven Poor Men of Sydney* was conditionally accepted by Peter Davies, a 34-year-old London publisher. Having had a burst of success the previous year with Frederic Manning's novel *Her Privates We*, set on the Somme Front, Davies was partial to Australians. But his conditions were stringent: not only did he want Stead to revise the novel but he also wanted another novel from her *before* he published *Seven Poor Men*. The idea was to attract readers to the new author with a less unconventional book.

On a visit to Paris in March 1931, Davies arranged to meet Stead and Blech for lunch at Philippe's, an exclusive restaurant near their office. Davies and his assistant James Grant were already there when the two arrived. On the table in front of them was the manuscript Stead had proudly bound in Moroccan leather. The long lunch was very pleasant: Stead would remember that first meeting fondly. It was a moment for celebration: she had been writing with publication in mind since the age of 21—eight years. She had been quietly determined, not impatient, but now she was anxious to be published. Stead would always be grateful to Peter Davies for taking her on as a young and unknown writer.

Davies struck her as extremely English, cultivated and kind: 'I am sure he has never offended anyone in the whole of his life.' His passion for literature was such that he appeared to be in the business more for love than money. His catalogue was 'a record of his personal tastes and fancies . . . almost a profession of faith'.[126] She had vaguely heard of his connection with Peter Pan, but timidly refrained from broaching the subject at their first meeting.[127]

Peter Llewellyn Davies, she would discover later, had had a tragic life and loathed his association with the boy who never grew up. Ever since J. M. Barrie's play had opened in London in 1904 and Barrie had claimed that all five Llewellyn Davies boys were models for his young hero, they had been a target of public curiosity. But it was the third son, Peter Pan's namesake, who was assumed to be the real model. At Eton he was teased incessantly about it. Fiction and fact had merged in a sinister way when their father and mother died in 1907 and 1910, leaving behind five young boys—now truly 'the lost boys'.

The eldest son, George, was killed in Flanders in 1915. Peter fought at the Somme and won the Military Cross in 1918, but came home with emphysema and severe depression. In 1921, the youngest brother, Michael, was drowned. When Peter Llewellyn Davies established his publishing house in 1926, it was under the less conspicuous name of 'Peter Davies Ltd', but the English newspapers had duly announced: 'Peter Pan Becomes Publisher'. And when, on 5 April 1960, Peter Davies would end his life by throwing himself under a train in the London Underground, the event made headlines in English and American newspapers: 'The Boy Who Never Grew Up is Dead'.[128]

Davies' assistant, James Grant, struck Stead as 'a perfect stage Englishman—a brilliant classical scholar, an Eton boy, who pretends all the time that all he knows about is racing and grass'.[129] Two years later, when he read the manuscript of *The Salzburg Tales*, Grant recognised himself as the tweedsuited 'English Gentleman' who carried a cane and winked at ladies and whose 'intelligence was only occasionally allowed to gleam through a moving cloud of flippancies and racing metaphors'. In feigned wrath, Grant sent the author the message that he did not possess a walking cane (let alone of fine snakewood) and he *never* winked (or pulled his moustache) at ladies.[130]

In Philippe's that day, it was decided that Stead should aim to complete another book by the end of August—six months hence. Back in London, Peter Davies wrote to confirm the terms of the contract. He enclosed a £50 advance and a friendly note to Blech asking him to make sure that Miss Stead did not overwork.

When Gwen also admonished her cousin not to work too hard, Christina, touched, wrote a frivolous reply—on Café de Flore writing paper to emphasise her point:

I really never do a stroke of work and Paris is a holiday . . .
Bill read your kindly adjuration to me, not to overwork
myself, and he is busy laffing and holding his sides at the idea.
He is more than rude!

Bill Blech added his round handwriting to the bottom of the letter:
I note in your letter a touching solicitude for your poor Peg,
with counsel for her not to overwork herself. Allow me,
politely but firmly, to indicate that labour has been alien to
her experience for three years. Piracy and not labour is the
mechanism by which she extracts hard French cash. W.J.B.

'So Wilhelm says!' Christina scribbled in the margin.[131]

Neither of them was exactly slothful. That particular Monday
evening, they had arranged to meet after work, at 8 pm, at the
Régence, a chess café opposite the Louvre. Blech, coming from the
bank, got there late; the stock market was more than usually bearish
that day. Stead, who had been writing in the office and forgotten
the time, arrived later still. They lingered there a while listening to
the classical quartet playing in the corner, observing the scene and
making up stories about their fellow drinkers. Then they walked
home in the rain, past the beds of red, white and blue hyacinths in
the Tuileries gardens, across the Seine with its shimmering lights,
to the rue Jean Bart, where 'Bill discoursed for about an hour and a
half, as usual on everything under the sun'. Then they 'sallied forth
again' and sat in the Flore until well past midnight. It was there that
they wrote to Gwen.[132]

★　★　★

After signing the contract with Peter Davies in April 1931, Stead set
herself a punishing writing schedule of 4000 words a day, determined to finish the next novel by the end of August.[133] She gave it
the Nietzschean title of *The Wraith and the Wanderer*,[134] and remaining fragments reveal it to be autobiographical material—material
which Stead would re-work in later novels. Sally, the protagonist,
sees herself as a 'clumsy ugly duckling'. As an adolescent, made
restless by the sultry Sydney nights, she falls in love first with her
English teacher then with a girl in her class and composes sonnets
for both. Richard Lovelace is an early portrait of Oliver Fenton and
Jonathan Crow.[135]

'I am not a born writer,' she told Gwen, meaning that she was
indolent. 'But I must say that when I have actually launched myself,
I get the profoundest and most passionate satisfaction from writ-

ing.' Life outside fiction never quite lived up to her expectations and made her 'fretful', she admitted.[136]

The problem with life outside fiction was that it was beyond her control. There were frustrations, domestic worries. In March 1931 she made a business trip to London for the Travelers' Bank and stayed with Florence James, who wrote home: 'It has been a sheer delight having her here, I wish she could stay and we could set up house together again—she is the one out of all my friends that I know nothing can change.'[137] But on Sunday night, the eve of her departure, Christina suffered what she thought was an appendix attack. On Monday morning, she looked ill and was nervous about making the Channel crossing. Florence persuaded her to see a doctor, who told her that she could manage the trip back, but that she should have her appendix removed as soon as possible.

On a second business trip in June, she lunched with Peter Davies in Soho and handed him four chapters of *The Wraith and the Wanderer*. And she had another attack. This time, the doctor thought the problem was probably 'nervous' and that the operation could wait. Stead notes in her diary around this time:

> Bill goes south next week and will return with family: says Mollie is becoming even softer and more dependent: find the situation distracting and will endeavour to make trip to Chartres for purposes of novel during their sojourn in Paris.
>
> Feel complete happiness with Bill and cannot understand (temperamentally) all these hitches, although endeavour to understand all for sake of not questioning Bill. Have moments of acute despair remembering past and Mollie's refusal to free us.[138]

It was not just the deadline for her novel that was causing her anxiety.

5

In the Phantom Buggy

JUNE 1931–JULY 1935

SOME TIME IN 1931, Blech and Stead moved from their office in the Boulevard Haussmann to the Travelers' Bank at No. 18 rue de la Paix, where Stead, to her delight, was given a plushly furnished office all to herself. Even here, she was fortunate to be able to devote time to her own writing. And from this vantage point she made notes on characters and conversations within the bank.

Our best insight into the Travelers' Bank comes from *House of All Nations*, Stead's fourth book, begun in 1935, after she had left Paris. The novel, set in 1931–2, has as its background the terrifying rise of Hitler, the Japanese attack on Manchuria, the demise of Ramsay MacDonald's Labour Government in England, and Hoover's overthrow by Roosevelt in the United States. The financial world is in a state of alarm. Austria's largest bank, the Creditanstalt, has collapsed; Germany is in severe economic trouble; and in September 1931 England goes off the gold standard.

Later in life, Stead freely admitted that she had based the fictional Banque Mercure on the Travelers' Bank, adding that it was as close a picture as she could paint without running into libel problems.[1] It was in 1931, during those difficult times, that Peter Neidecker, the director, began to lose his nerve. ('I want to scram,' says Jules Bertillon, his fictional counterpart. 'Now is the time to shut up

shop.'[2]) But the bank was saved by a sudden windfall and Neidecker, the passionate gambler, was able to pride himself on
making money in a dissolving world. Somehow his bank managed
to stay afloat when all around the financial titans—Kreuger, Loew-
enstein and Insull—were crashing. As Michel Alphendéry (the
character based on Bill Blech) puts it nervously:

> We're in the phantom buggy with him. We're riders of the storm:
> all of us together with him in this phantom bank, built on misery,
> shining out of mire, solid in an earthquake, soundproof in thunder,
> a living lightning conductor: an accident in capitalism.[3]

In the novel, the Banque Mercure collapses at the end of 1932; the
Travelers' Bank would manage to keep going until July 1935.

*   *   *

Peter Neidecker's charming, roguish ways fascinated Stead. He
would appear in three of her early works, and Jules Bertillon, the
director of the bank in *House of All Nations*, is the most seductive
character in her gallery of rogues.[4] All three fictional portraits of
Neidecker are fundamentally warm, and yet morally and politically
Neidecker stood for everything Stead allegedly despised. What she
and Blech admired were his bursts of generosity, his boyish enthusiasm, his inventive mind and humorous American language, his
sheer recklessness. He was a man who would be sure to 'go out
looping the loop'.[5]

Throughout her life Stead would find herself haunted and obsessed by certain individuals, who attracted and angered her at the
same time. They were the people on whom she based her major
fictional characters, and they were, without exception, charming
and manipulative, highly articulate, energetic, humorous. Indeed,
ambivalence was the motor behind Stead's most powerful writing.

Her liking for such characters was reinforced by Bill Blech, who,
by his own admission, had a tendency to have 'crushes' on men.[6]
From 1929, for six years, Blech too fell under Neidecker's spell.

*   *   *

Stead went to London on two more business trips, in January and
June 1932. There may have been other trips as well. Florence James,
writing about her friend six years later, described Stead's banking
experience in very rosy terms:

> At first she was regarded with astonishment and admitted with
> politeness but reluctance. London is very conservative and
> whoever before had heard of a woman representative dealing
> in such business? But it was not long before Christina Stead

visited brokers and bankers on the same terms as any man and became an accepted member of the elusive financial fraternity whose business is international.[7]

We get another picture altogether if we read between the lines in *House of All Nations*. Here it is Adam Constant who is sent to London as a representative of the bank. Constant, a minor but significant character in the novel, is a 24-year-old bank clerk, a committed Marxist who plans to leave soon for Red China.[8] Jules Bertillon and his brother William do not inform him properly about the business he is to do, but he knows it is probably shady. In London, as he visits brokers, bankers and financial journalists, he feels foolish.

> He bit his lip and set out once more on the weary lope, upstairs and downstairs, into all sorts of little offices, and grand upper storeys of banks, to face surprised kindly little men, who treated him with a coddling air as if he were a rather advanced five-year-old and they had to amuse him till the policeman arrived to take him home.[9]

This is far more likely to resemble Stead's own experience as a woman in the banking world.

In the novel, Constant finds himself promoted and moved to a luxurious office of his own, with considerable spare time on his hands, in which he writes poetry. When his book of poems is accepted by a publisher, Michel Alphendéry almost dances with pleasure and says, 'Wouldn't it be too funny if your book of poems proved to be the only constructive thing this bank ever produced?'[10] Stead herself had always hoped to recuperate her time in the bank, transforming the experience into art.

Adam Constant also plans to write a novel about the bank, and his words can be read as an encoded statement of Stead's own intention:

> There are no men in this bank . . . only an infection of monsters with purses at their waists that we wait upon and serve . . . My dream is that one day I will get them all down, I will leave them on record. I want to show the waste, the insane freaks of these money men, the cynicism and egotism of their life . . . Although, of course, there are plenty of living intelligences among them, sidetracked talents, even warm breasts, perspicacious men amongst them, but all, all compliant and prostituted.[11]

What is striking is that the moral message, even here, is highly ambiguous. Are these men 'monsters' or 'warm breasts'—pimps or prostitutes? (The whorehouse analogy is reinforced by the title, *House of All Nations*, which refers to an exclusive Parisian brothel patronised by the international élite.[12]) Despite his forceful statements, for a Marxist, Adam Constant is strangely attracted to these 'perspicacious men' and 'sidetracked talents'.

Constant's ambivalence reflects the equivocation within the narrative itself. Readers are ultimately uncertain as to whether the novel is a hard-hitting exposure of international stock manipulation or a playful and indulgent satire. But no wonder Stead equivocated: Bill Blech was one of the pimps.

Another was Alfred Hurst—Henri Léon in *House of All Nations*. Hurst the wealthy wheat broker, the 'Grand Jew', as Stead called him, would occasionally come over from London or Antwerp and treat Bill and Christina to expensive dinners, shows and cabarets.[13] At the end of 1931, he was courting Florence James and trying, unsuccessfully, to persuade her to accompany him to Paris for Christmas with Christina and Bill.[14] No-one could have been more committed to the game of profit making than Hurst. Bill Blech once commented: 'The best you can make of a bargain with him is the worst of it.'[15] Yet Hurst liked to call himself a socialist, and he was friendly with Labour ministers in high places. The Jewish socialist M.P. Emanuel Shinwell was his friend from Glasgow days in the early Twenties, and Prime Minister Ramsay Macdonald had even written a preface to Hurst's book on the grain trade in Great Britain, *Bread of Britain*, published in 1930. Entirely written by the unacknowledged Bill Blech, it was a thoughtful exposition of the farm relief question and policies of price-fixing, and a sustained plea for state control of the British grain trade. It had been widely praised by reviewers for its 'clearness and impartiality'.[16]

*　　*　　*

On the basis of the four chapters Stead had handed him in June 1931, Peter Davies announced *The Wraith and the Wanderer* among the forthcoming books in his Autumn and Christmas catalogue, giving the publication date, a little optimistically, as November 1931. He heralded it with exceptional trumpeting.

THE WRAITH AND THE WANDERER
by Christina Stead

Miss Stead is an Australian by birth; she is still in her early twenties; [sic] she lives in Paris; and she has written a first novel to which it seems quite impossible to deny the quality of genius. It is an altogether extraordinary book, displaying the *macabre* imagination of an Edgar Allan Poe, the descriptive fervour of a Herman Melville, the loftiness of vision, in certain passages, of a Dante. Yet so far from being in any sense imitative, it is a highly original and extremely modern story. To describe it is almost an impossibility. It is a book to be read and read again with increasing admiration.[17]

But the August deadline went by and *The Wraith and the Wanderer* was not finished. Stead had struck problems: it is likely that she still lacked the requisite emotional distance from her own childhood to be able to write fiction about it. And that winter her progress was further delayed by illness.

On a business trip to London in January 1932—this time staying at the prestigious Grosvenor, her expenses paid by the bank—she once again became 'very sick', and decided it must be the poisonous smog and dismal atmosphere of London.[18] But the London doctor had been right in the first place, and her troublesome appendix was removed some time in the spring of 1932.

It was around that time that she decided to abandon the novel, which was not going anywhere. This decision would not have been made lightly. She was very aware of time passing. In July she would turn 30, and she had made no progress since she signed the contract with Davies a year ago. Her first book, contingent upon a non-existent second book, still awaited revision.

She needed to produce something fast, and for some time she had been thinking she would like to write more short stories. She loved bizarre tales, fairy tales, folklore and legend, the *Arabian Nights*, the stories of Poe, Hawthorne, E. T. A. Hoffmann. Her plan was extremely ambitious: she would attempt a tale cycle in the variegated manner of Boccaccio's *Decameron* and Chaucer's *Canterbury Tales*. Her group of characters, Stead decided, would meet in the Capuchin woods overlooking Salzburg and entertain one another with strange stories from all over the world. To have diverse characters telling stories would allow her to experiment with all kinds of narrative modes.

She began with a brief prologue—a description of the town of Salzburg and its imposing mountainous surrounds. The narrator is on the scene, awaiting the beginning of the Festival, observing the actions like a reporter.

A stage has been put up in the Cathedral Place for the Miracle Play of "Jedermann," German bands are playing Mozart and Wagner in all the cafés, the Residenz Platz is packed with visitors awaiting to hear the Glockenspiel at six o'clock ring out its antique elfin tunes, tourists pop in and out of the house at number nine, Getreide-gasse, where Mozart was born, musicians and actors are walking and talking under the thick trees on the river-bank . . .

Opposite the fortress, across the river, is the yellow-walled
Capuchin convent in its tall wood. One has to pay a few
groschen each day at the Convent Gate to enter the wood.
Within the gate, transported there from Vienna, stands the
little wooden hut in which Mozart wrote "The Magic Flute."

Even in her apparently naturalist mode, Stead the symbolist was
never far away. These are real details, but standing as they do in the
prologue to Stead's tales, the cultural icons are also keys to the
narrative. We readers are about to 'enter the wood', in which we will
be told stories, embedded in the ancient and rich European tradition
of story-telling. Like *Jedermann*, they will often be re-tellings of old
stories. Readers, like the tourists of Salzburg, will travel to a variety
of places—the stories are set in nineteenth-century Russia, in England,
France, Austria, Italy, Spain, Australia—and meet people from all
over the world. Just as *The Magic Flute* draws on every kind of
music and ranges widely in tone, these tales will draw from the
broadest possible spectrum of story-telling (anecdotes, jokes, legends,
ancient folklore, horror stories and church-inspired moralities).

Stead wrote the first draft of *The Salzburg Tales* at great speed,
working on it during the day at the bank and in the evenings at
home on the kitchen table. The stories she liked best were those
inspired by Jewish folklore—dangerous subject matter in those
anti-semitic times, she joked.[19] Surrounded as she was by Jewish
friends and their self-deprecating humour, she allowed herself the
indulgence of ironic stereotypes: the 'Centenarist' (so-called because
he organises centenary festivals to commemorate the births and
deaths of great composers of music), the only Jewish storyteller,
has 'a dark craft profile, like an ancient Venetian, with a long,
pointed nose and thin lips'.[20] But all the characters in *The Salzburg
Tales* are caricatures, and the Centenarist, a mystic and learned soul,
has the great virtue of being 'as full of tales as the poets of Persia'.

One or two of the four stories set in Australia had been written in
Sydney almost a decade before.[21] Now Stead reconstructed them
from memory, the early manuscript having been lost in Paris.[22]

The first draft of *The Salzburg Tales* was written in a state of high
creative excitement. Stead raked up her acquaintances from all over
the world and ransacked her 'unforgotten lore for tales, analogies
and arguments'.[23] She was revelling in her talents, writing with a
new buoyancy and confidence, allowing her wit and imagination
full play. In terms of technical and imaginative brilliance she would
never surpass this early book.[24]

The revision was painful: she cursed her 'constipated meticulousness'[25] and 'terrible vice' of correction, which would often involve six or seven re-typings. After a day of hammering at the typewriter, she felt 'dead to the imaginative world'.[26] In all, it took her just over a year to write the book. She sent off a first batch of stories to Peter Davies in March 1933 and the rest of the manuscript in August that year.

★　★　★

'Bill and I are wondering where we can fly to,' Stead told Florence James anxiously in April 1933. They were frightening times. In January, a beer-hall agitator—Adolf Hitler—had been named Chancellor of the Third Reich. Late in February came the Reichstag fire. Hitler, declaring it a communist plot, had dissolved Parliament, arrested thousands of communists and socialists, suspended civil liberties, and silenced opposition parties and trade unions. In March, the Reich had established a concentration camp at Dachau. April saw a national boycott of all businesses owned by Jews, and draconian measures announced against Jewish men living with Aryan women.[27]

In May the books were burning. Works by Heine, Marx, Freud, Einstein and Stefan Zweig were thrown into the flames, along with the works of non-Jewish radicals—Brecht, Heinrich Mann, Erich Maria Remarque. Leftwing intellectuals and prescient Jews were beginning to flee the country; many headed for Paris. The world was beginning 'to believe the unbelievable', as Zweig would write in 1942.[28]

The literary world now talked about 'revolutionary literature'. In this threatening atmosphere, many writers—Stead included—believed they had a moral responsibility. In December 1933 she noted, 'Gide and all the writers of merit and intelligence have gone into the revolutionary camp'.[29] André Gide, a patrician figure in French literature, had surprised everyone when he embraced Soviet communism in the struggle against fascism.[30]

Another celebrated extra-Party 'fellow-traveller' was the brilliant André Malraux, the same age as Stead, who won the prestigious Goncourt prize that year for his novel *La Condition humaine*, set in revolutionary China. Stead admired its passion, drama and psychological acuity. Third prize went to Party member Paul Nizan for *Antoine Bloyé*, the story of a peasant boy who won a scholarship and found himself divided in his class interests. Stead was impressed by its sincerity and simplicity: 'There is no drama, no emphasis; it is as plain as a working man's life.'[31]

By the end of 1933, business friends were returning from Germany with sinister reports of massive re-armament. In France too, Stead observed, there was 'naked preparation for war'. She was horrified to learn that French armament makers were selling huge supplies of armaments to Germany. It was a cynical world they inhabited.[32]

* * *

The Travelers' Bank was a cynical microcosm in a cynical world and by 1933, when they and their contemporaries were preoccupied by questions of moral and political responsibility, Stead and Blech felt increasingly uncomfortable about working there. The bank had somehow continued to totter along with remarkable success, despite regular crises. Neidecker, of course, was not alone in his corrupt approach to banking in those years, when anything that made a profit was considered good business. Tax avoidance, managerial secretiveness, lax accounting and bogus companies were standard practices.

Operating in a depressed world economy, the Neidecker brothers and Bill Blech performed as stockmarket bears, gambling on a falling market. Blech was one of the Paris bears who helped to ruin the swindler Ivar Kreuger by driving down the prices on Kreuger's securities, and forcing him to go deeper into debt to support his own stocks and bonds.[33] The Swedish Match King shot himself in September 1932. Blech's strategy brought the bank a major windfall, allowing it to continue to operate with the appearance of solvency.[34] Blech, who himself did very well out of the venture, took the view that Kreuger ('a poor smelly vulture pierced by the arrow of deflation'[35]) deserved all he got. The fact is, however, that pierced tycoons drag innocents down with them.

In *House of All Nations* too, the Kreuger windfall saves the bank. Alphendéry's action is depicted by the narrator as selfless, if not exactly heroic.

> Alphendéry was again whispered about as the power behind the throne . . . But Alphendéry had not sold short either Insull or Kreuger for his own account! "I am small time and I remain it," he said. Jules, floating on a cloud of glory, made Alphendéry a present of half a million francs; Alphendéry sagely put them in a safety deposit and went on living in the Place du Panthéon.[36]

Apart from lucky speculation within the law, the Travelers' Bank kept afloat by means of highly illegal balancing—or *contre-partie*—operations. Much of its business was not genuine: the transactions were simply book entries resolving themselves into what were in fact bets on the stock market against the bank's clients. In short, the bank was a 'bucket house': the bucketeers financed their transactions with outlays from clients.

For tax evasion and to cover transactions carried out by the bank against the operations of some of its clients, Neidecker had set up various branches abroad—on the Riviera, in Brussels, Amsterdam, London and New York.[37] He also floated a number of bogus companies, such as the London Reserve Insurance Co. Ltd, in which Bill Blech employed Florence James Heyting for a few hours each week. (In September 1932, Florence had married her original fiancé, Pym Heyting, the Dutch lawyer.) Operating from a splendid office in Bush House at the top of Fleet Street, Florence was paid a nominal wage to forward mail. Christina explained in a letter: 'The idea is that the L.R.I. is a concern doing business in London and which has just started business with the Bank.' She added: 'Please destroy this letter.'[38] It is plain that she was perfectly aware of the illegality of the proceedings.

Shortly after her marriage—possibly prompted by her husband, who disliked Bill Blech—Florence James became uncomfortable about 'the cloak and dagger style' of business proceedings. One letter from the Travelers' Bank instructed her to forward any messages in a sealed, blank envelope to Miss Stead and to place this envelope inside another addressed to Mr Blech at No. 10 rue Jean Bart, with no reference to Miss Stead on the outside envelope.[39] When Florence expressed disquiet to Christina, Stead told her it was because of her unmarried status that she had instructed the bankers to leave her name off correspondence: '... their sense of propriety alone, suggested the ridiculous plan of the inner envelope.'[40]

By 1933, Bill Blech had lost his taste for wild-cat schemes of speculative investment which, as a Marxist, he could only view as 'pure theft' and 'titanic pickpocketing'.[41] He often talked of leaving the bank and 'going bolshevik'.[42]

Stead's fiction gives a clear enough indication of her doubts and private fears about Bill Blech. In her very first novel, *Seven Poor Men of Sydney*, Joseph, the simple, good-hearted printer and Tom Withers (modelled on Eric Townsend) discuss Baruch Mendelssohn (modelled on Blech). We recognise the upsetting conversation Stead had with Townsend back in 1929, when Bill was spending the weekend with Mollie.

In the novel, Joseph claims that Baruch is brilliant. Tom Withers replies:

"I'm not saying he's not brilliant, I know he's brilliant: but brilliance doesn't get you anywhere. It's character, it's will.

And then you have to be a bit of a fanatic; not to see too many sides of a question."

"He takes sides," Joseph said.

"Of course. Because he can talk like a Burke, and grin like a Chinese idol so that, whatever happened, he could make . himself a place; he's brilliant. But it's not conviction, it's just involuntary. It's not heroism, it's not foresight. He knows the coming world of demagogues is made for tikes like him."

"You're jealous."

"I'm not jealous: listen, you've just met the smartest man you ever met. You're bowled over. I've had experience: he won't go far; he's a weakling."[43]

The most detailed picture of Blech in the whole of Christina Stead's fiction is the portrait of Michel Alphendéry in *House of All Nations*. A warm portrait, it is by no means idealised. Alphendéry has sold his soul—at least for a time. His colleague Aristide Raccamond (the blackmailer) reflects:

Alphendéry was a valuable man—personal charm, living wit kneaded into him . . . with something feminine, compliant, winning, responsive that attracted men—old, Jewish, Central European blood? A man who loved men's company and knew how to bring out the best in them and who suggested ideas to them, so that they felt richer through him; he got a lot of affection and a lot of business, purely through his affectionate behaviour and encyclopaedic information but rather a light intellect, a pessimistic, cynical, skating, skimming, inverted, scholar's intelligence, due entirely to the lack of a great urge in him.[44]

Why does Alphendéry remain in a job he detests? Partly out of fear of poverty: he has an 'army of dependants'.[45]

He also stayed partly out of misguided loyalty to his employer. And partly out of inertia. In a terrible state of paralysis, Michel Alphendéry oscillates between despair and exuberance. Even Jules Bertillon, observing his frequent fits of gloom, asks him why he does not go and join the communists if that is what he wants to do.

He felt unspeakably melancholy. Jules had recommended him to give up this mad and detested life and join his real friends. But Michel could not contemplate leaving Jules yet . . . He went to a workers' meeting that evening and gave one hundred francs to the collection, immediately after felt extremely gay and lighthearted, and came back to the bank the next day without a thought of leaving and everything went on as before.[46]

Alphendéry—like every other character in the book, including the narrator—is in the sway of Jules Bertillon, a princely figure, 'fragile, tall, elegantly dressed'. Lighthearted, debonair and daredevil, he runs the bank 'like a booth in a bazaar'. 'It's easy to make money,' he says. 'You put up the sign BANK and someone walks in and hands you money. The façade is everything.' Portrayed as an avatar of Mercury (the god of trade and commerce), Bertillon is not only full of cunning, he also seems blessed with Mercury's winged sandals. ('I'm just a gilded pickpocket and, believe me, a pickpocket has to have twinkling ankles.')

Bertillon respects his brilliant investments manager, Michel Alphendéry, the mastermind behind many of the bank's most successful ventures, yet he exploits him and makes no bones about it. He tells Alphendéry that his preferred employees would be either dopes or communists.

Dopes are grateful to you for keeping them because they're dopes and communists because you know they're communists ... Look where you stand with me, Michel. You are a sort of limited power of attorney; you have the right, also, to buy and sell stocks, bonds, gold, commodities, transfer them in or out as you wish; you sign checks, you accept accounts, you make decisions. But you're not a director, you haven't got a contract, and I could turn you out tomorrow if I wanted to ... Why is it you're not ambitious and you don't try to steal my job? Because you're a communist. You despise me. You wouldn't let your friends see you standing in my shoes.[47]

★ ★ ★

Throughout 1933, Stead was revising her short stories and driving herself hard, typing until late at night. She was tired and thin again. Blech, suffering the effects of 'constant stock exchange attendance',[48] lay awake till the early hours and groaned in his sleep. He was expected to manage the bank by himself for up to a month at a time while Peter Neidecker went to the States on business or took off with his family on their yacht, *Etoile Filante*, to sun himself in the Balearic Islands.[49] Because Blech's financial know-how and flashes of brilliance had more than once saved the bank from ruin, he could rarely be spared. Stead was incensed that Neidecker, 'the idlest fellow of an idle world', could not see that Blech needed a holiday. In November 1933, she wrote to Florence James:

I was so mad this morning thinking of the miserable twelve days taken last year—our only vacation, that I started to rouse on Bill, for I remembered that it was only by staging a scene last year that I got him to move. He promised to talk the whole business over tomorrow afternoon with Pete.[50]

Three months later they had still not had a holiday.
There is now no chance of our getting away for some time.
An unexpected happening on Saturday leaves Bill with a great
deal of responsibility for at least a month, if not much longer.
It is horrid and I nearly cried with mortification and anxiety
about Bill's health.[51]

        ★   ★   ★

In March 1933, when Peter Davies set eyes on the first half of *Tales
in the Capuchin Wood*,[52] as Stead called her book of short stories at
that time, he was dismayed. He had already announced *The Wraith
and the Wanderer* in his catalogue and now, in its place, he was
confronted with short stories every bit as unconventional as *Seven
Poor Men of Sydney*. Considering this too great a business risk, he
again asked Stead to write something else. But now she put her foot
down, and insisted that she would produce nothing else before
Seven Poor Men of Sydney was published. Peter Davies agreed to
go ahead.

The publication date for *The Salzburg Tales*, as they became, was
January 1934. Peter Davies arranged American publication with
D. Appleton-Century later that year. During the waiting period,
Stead began to lose confidence. She declared herself 'quite dissatisfied with the kindergarten style of *The Salzburg Tales*' and told
Florence James that she wanted to write about something 'richer
and stronger' than 'this old backwoods stuff'.[53] She had several
projects in mind: a love story set in Paris, a novel about the bank,
and a novel about the passions of women, their 'struggles for
domestic and economic position' and 'the distortions imposed by
society and physical inferiority'.[54] The seeds of *The Beauties and
Furies*, *House of All Nations* and *For Love Alone* were already planted
in her mind.

        ★   ★   ★

'Her ladyship decided not to "free" us after all! What a training in
patience!'[55] Mollie Blech had appeared to be on the brink of con-
senting to divorce, and then she changed her mind. For Christina it
was a cruel blow. She wrote the bitter news to the newly married
Florence James in March 1933:
Mollie is still on the theme, "though you don't love me, you
owe it to the child to live with me, especially now that your
salary may be cut down" so you see a divorce is not in the air
with that lady. Bill is extremely tired of the ridiculous
discussion and either wants to get her off to America finally,

or to go to England himself. He even spoke of going to
Australia, this week, or South Africa, but it is all nebulous,
till we know what is going to be done.[56]
More than half of Bill Blech's earnings were going to his wife,
daughter and mother. From September 1931 10-year-old Ruth
Blech had boarded at Beacon Hill School, Bertrand and Dora
Russell's very expensive experimental school in England. It suited
Mollie's progressive, anti-authoritarian ideas, and Ruth had loved it
there,[57] but after a year Bill could no longer meet the exorbitant
expenses involved. He and Mollie had talked of sending her to
school in Germany for a year to learn the language, but by 1932 it
was no longer a suitable place to send a little Jewish girl.[58] Instead,
she was sent to a boarding school on the outskirts of Paris—chosen
because it appeared to be the only one in the whole of France where
the children could have regular baths.[59] Despite their passion for
France, Bill and Mollie remained very American.

Bill's mother had been living with her kind, rather slow-witted
niece Jenka, in a small apartment near the Buttes-Chaumont park.[60]
At the end of the year, to save Bill's money, she moved into a hotel
in the rue Jean Bart, and spent most of the day in their crowded
apartment, eating with Bill and Christina, and not retiring to her
own quarters until the late evening. 'It is not a very satisfactory
arrangement either for her or us,' Stead told Florence James, 'but
the best we can do until we know what we are going to do.'

She is a very sweet person, has no faults at all, except that she
has a permanent weakness for describing potato pancakes,
meatballs, stuffed salmon etc. at all hours of the day and year.[61]

Christina was taking German lessons in secret to surprise Bill at
Christmas, and for practice, she was laboriously translating a 1929
communist book, *Illustrierte Geschichte des Bürgerkriegs in Russland*.[62]
Her long-term aim, perhaps inspired by their translator friend Sam
Putnam, was to get a firm grip on German and Russian, in addition
to French, in the hope of earning money as a translator of fiction.

The other motive for learning German was to understand Rosa
Blech better. The old lady spoke a patois peculiar to herself:
German broken down to something resembling Yiddish—a language she had developed to communicate with the old ladies she
met in the park, where she would sit and talk for hours. She
resorted to this language whenever she wanted to say something to
Bill that she did not want Christina to understand. To add to the
difficulty of communication, Rosa Blech had trouble understanding
Christina's soft voice and non-American accent. Christina complained to Florence:

I am almost hoarse, for I have to repeat everything I say three or four times. You may think I have a colonial accent, but to her it's pure glottal abstraction: I am trying to learn American for moments of urgency, but I am not too good at it.[63]

One of the stories in *The Salzburg Tales*, 'The Little Old Lady', portrays the tension between a querulous old German-speaking woman and her son Paul's female companion. At the Opéra Comique together, the old lady tells her about Paul's ex-wife:

"I never saw such a pretty little girl. Twenty years they knew each other, and loved each other, before they were married: it was a real romansch. They were little playmates together."

Paul's betrothed was silent.[64]

*   *   *

In letters Stead regularly complained of fatigue—insomnia was to be a problem all her life. A tense, restless person, plagued by anger and self-recrimination, she was what she called a 'waker and dreamer'.

She would often lie awake and think about her family in Australia, her childhood. Sometimes these were nostalgic memories of 'the old, old days' when she played with her cousin in the kangaroo grass and pine needles of Lydham Hill.[65] More often, they were painful memories.

These days, letters from home arrived at intervals of three months or so. From her father came the usual 'rhetoric about the sun, the sea, prosperity, the light of human progress and other dreamy notions'.[66] From the others came letters about 'fishing and swimming and taking in the washing', depending on the writer.[67] (The domestic letters were from Percia Stead, her brother David's wife, whom she had never met.) Ada, now living with her son Fred and his wife Mavis in the Blue Mountains, now wrote only rarely. Thistle Harris had moved into Boongarre, and because she was living with a married man, the Watson's Bay locals tended to shun her. (Harris, recalling this period later in life, says she minded less than David did.) Sixteen-year-old Gilbert had run away from home, stowing away on a ship, and nothing had been heard of him since August 1933.

*   *   *

When they stayed too long in Paris without a break, Stead became decidedly 'tetchy'.[68] As a girl, she was used to long walks in the fresh breezes of Sydney Harbour or excursions to the country with her father; now, too, she was happiest when she and Blech were able to get away to the country for a few days. In the spring of 1933, they paid a brief visit to Montpellier, Aigues-Mortes and

Nimes, where they watched six bulls being slain by toreadors 'in Carmen costume'.

> The heat poured down and fried our wits, and we lusted for blood like the most Mediterranean desperadoes surrounding us . . . You know how mild Bill is: well, he clapped enthusiastically for every bull weltering in its gore, and almost threw his hat (the proper sign of admiration) to the torero![69]

One of the stories in *The Salzburg Tales*, 'Don Juan in the Arena', would be a satiric re-enactment of a Spanish bullfight.

At Easter, they made a brief reconnoitring trip to Antwerp: Blech was thinking of moving there for a time to work with Alf Hurst, though the proximity to Germany was a deterrent. In summer they spent a weekend in Mont St Michel with Frederick and Manya Sard. In September, Aubrey Neidecker, the Bank's Associate Manager, rang from Hendaye and insisted that Christina and Bill join him for the weekend, all expenses paid. He drove them along the coast from St Jean de Luz into Spain. 'It was fine but not restful,' was Stead's cursory comment.[70]

In December 1933, Alfred Hurst visited Paris, and over a luxurious meal at Prunier's, tried to persuade them to join him in Antwerp. For the first time since Stead had known him, this restless woman-iser seemed to be in love. In Brussels he was living with Mitzi (he called her Mary), a German woman, pretty and smart, who had divorced her husband for him. Were it not for his family commitments in England, he told everyone, he would marry her. From his house in Brussels, he motored to work each day in Antwerp, his grain business was flourishing, and he had a hotel-flat in Antwerp where Bill and Christina could live free of charge.[71] Blech thought the offer tempting for a year or so, but Stead wanted to move back to London—smog or no smog.

She had had enough of being on the periphery of the English-speaking world: her English syntax was beginning to sound French. Much as she loved France, Stead felt a foreigner there. 'You can't write about foreigners,' she asserted. 'They write better about themselves.'[72] The English were less foreign to her, though she needed to become better acquainted with contemporary British literature and politics.[73] In London, she hoped to be able to earn money by freelance journalism.

Heavy snow fell in Paris just before Christmas and the bitter cold was 'like a slug on the head'. Blech, who hated the cold and felt 'villainously fatigued', wanted to head south for Christmas. Stead wanted to stay put and work.

*   *   *

The Salzburg Tales were published in England on 18 January 1934 to considerable acclaim. Unlike most first books by young writers, it was given lengthy reviews in all the prestigious papers, sometimes by well-known reviewers. The collection was generally deemed remarkable, auguring a dazzling future for this 31-year-old Australian writer with her startling imagination and cosmopolitan sophistication. The *Times* called her 'a writer of many gifts', with 'an altogether admirable command of the fantastic'.[74] The *Times Literary Supplement*, lavish in its praise for this 'ingenious and rollicking fantasy', concluded: 'It is difficult to decide which are the best of these stories. Their wide curiosity, their emotional detachment, their artistry and felicity of expression make Miss Stead a writer of unusual interest.'[75] Rebecca West commented: '*The Salzburg Tales* is the most delightful miscellany I have read for a long time. It has the charm of Heine's *Florentine Nights*: it is a little like Hans Andersen's *What the Moon Saw*; but it has its own wild charm, and obviously it is a work of a strong and idiosyncratic talent.'[76]

In Australia, with its almost wholly naturalistic short-story tradition,[77] the collection seemed highly eccentric, yet when the British edition arrived in Australia, reviewers were enthusiastic. The first copies sold out rapidly and interested readers had to wait weeks for additional supplies to arrive from England. Stead's family, who had been forwarded advance copies, sent congratulations. ('They are all a little *cagey* in their criticisms,' Stead told Florence James. 'I think they are waiting to see what the critics say before they commit themselves.'[78])

In the United States, where the book was published by D. Appleton-Century in September 1934, the reviews were almost all positive. The *New York Times* declared many of the stories 'insubstantial stuff, though undeniably clever'. The most outspoken in his praise was the up-and-coming Clifton Fadiman, who announced in the *New Yorker* that Miss Stead's tales were 'far better than the *Decameron*'.[79]

It might be better, and less misleading, to call Miss Stead an astringent De la Mare, a humorous Poe. But these comparisons are treacherous, too, for she can do things, with a flick of the wrist, that are quite beyond Poe and De la Mare: tell Chassidic legends more tenderly than Martin Buber himself; impale literary butterflies on the needles of malicious paragraphs; weave medieval legends that sound as if you had looked in upon them years ago through the dim pages of the *Creta Romanorum*; relate funny stories about goldfish that predict the fluctuations of the stock market . . .[80]

Stead had based a number of the characters in her tales, and the storytellers themselves, on people she knew. She wondered what their reactions would be. She told Gwen that several stories were about Bill's mother, and that 'The Mirror' was a depiction of Bill. Most of the personages were friends of theirs: 'and they are like I have tried to describe them'.[81] The Centenarist was based on Frederick Sard, the Banker on Peter Neidecker, the Doctor from New York on Harry Bakwin. Though the portraits were embellished, with many details wholly invented, the individuals concerned had no trouble recognising themselves, and their reactions were mixed. Stead was a little concerned as to what Margaret Dunbar-Smith would think about the story 'A Colin, A Chloe', alluding to Madge's literary friendship with H. E. Bates, which had ended in bitterness when he married someone else.[82] Stead's story, a mixture of the real and the fantastic, would in no way have consoled her friend. Stead sent Madge a copy of the book—a gesture greeted with silence. When Florence James told Stead that Madge was upset, Stead replied:

> I read over the short story under discussion, this morning, on receipt of your letter, and admit that the likeness is rather striking —but it isn't vicious, so if she recognises it, perhaps she will forgive, especially since the bloke-hero is out of favour definitely.[83]

Frederick Sard was none too pleased, Stead told Gwen.

> I have just had a port wine with The Centenarist. He arrived from New York two days ago ... He is not very pleased to be "The Centenarist" I think ... On the other hand, other "characters" (The English Gentleman, the New York Doctor of Medicine) were very pleased, and even flattered, even though the portraits are not wholly complimentary.[84]

Stead's portraits would never be 'wholly complimentary': that was the problem. And already with her first publication, she was referring to real people by their fictional names, blurring the boundaries between fiction and reality. Stead lived out the same paradox as the Philosopher in *The Salzburg Tales*, who says, 'I only tell fairy tales, for I would rather be seen in their sober vestments than in the prismatic unlikelihood of reality'.

*   *   *

'I sit here,' Stead grumbled, 'and hear nothing on earth but Nazis, stockmarket, and stockmarket, Nazis, Stavisky and the air units, air units and Stavisky.'[85] She and Blech had been alarmed by the outbreak of violence in Paris in February 1934. The Stavisky crisis, the biggest of a succession of scandalous frauds involving corrupt politicians, brought to a head public disgust with the failure of the Radical Socialist Party to cope with severe economic deterioration and rising unemployment. Alexandre Stavisky, a stockbroker of Russian Jewish origin, had engaged in large-scale international operations, selling worthless bonds. During investigations, Stavisky was found dead, and it was discovered that his activities were known to certain Government ministers. Rightwing extremist groups—the *Action Française* and the *Croix de Feu*—registered their discontent with the Government, trade unions and the Communist Party in three days of rightwing riots. On 6 February, which came to be known as 'bloody Tuesday', there was a mass demonstration with all political factions in the Place de la Concorde. Police fired on the angry mob, killing seventeen and injuring hundreds in the bloodiest street battles since the Paris Commune of 1871. After this, Edouard Daladier's Radical Socialist government resigned.

Fear of a rightwing *coup d'état* and the prospect of France succumbing to the fascist madness that was gripping Italy and Germany brought the left factions together. A 24-hour general strike was held on 12 February, called by the non-communist trade unions. A United Front meeting against fascism was planned for 27 May. These events would form the background of *The Beauties and Furies*, set in Paris in 1934.

Stead wrote to Florence James on 16 May: 'The cops have been ordered to "observe order", that is, use their batons with great severity. The city has been over-garrisoned and over-policed for months. We are quite miserable here.'[86] Blech, like many others, believed civil war could well break out within six months. It forced a decision: they resolved to leave Paris and the bank in June.

Most of their American friends had gone home. Those who had clung on after the dollar fell were now fleeing before the war clouds burst, and Sylvia Beach's English language bookshop was struggling to survive the exodus. The Sards had left, and Lina and Nadine Lewin. Samuel Putnam had returned to the States in 1933— the Depression having put an end both to little magazines and to translation opportunities. In his memoirs, Putnam would recall that Blech and another friend saw him onto the train for Le Havre. Putnam, loath to leave Paris, was in an alcoholic daze.[87]

These days it was German more than Russian that one heard in the Dôme: Paris had become like 'a suburb of Berlin'. Stead had the impression that the entire German exile community turned out to the Max Reinhardt production of *Fledermaus*.[88]

★　　★　　★

Stead was hard at work again, this time revising *Seven Poor Men of Sydney*; Peter Davies wanted the completed manuscript by May 1934. A demanding task, it meant going back to a manuscript begun five and a half years earlier, in a quite different frame of mind. In bleak moments she felt the manuscript was a 'frost' and unworkable, but Blech kept her to her task. Both Davies and James Grant had given some editorial guidance: they wanted cuts and some elaboration; she was to try to flesh out the characters and improve some of the speeches. (Stead told Florence James she was to 'whip up the drama and tone down a certain larrikin which my love of local colour laid on rather thick'.[89]) To capture the characters' Marxist rhetoric, she was reading Marxist theory and questioning Blech about political economy. Several of the characters were printers: on a trip to London in March 1934, she visited a printing works and took detailed notes.

At the beginning of May, Stead stopped work at the bank to devote herself to finishing the book. She was now aiming to complete it by mid-June 1934, before they left Paris. It would not have helped her tranquillity to discover that she was once again in a state she wryly described to Florence James as 'a Malthusian sickness to which I have been susceptible in my time'.[90] Her letter revealed neither regret, self-reproach nor self-pity: she merely wrote that she had been 'rather sick for some days'. Bill took her to Reims for the weekend to recover. She thought it quite the 'airiest and prettiest town in France'.[91]

Beyond coy allusions to a 'little operation', Stead wrote nothing about her terminations—neither in letters nor her fiction.

Did she really want a child?

Early in 1934, Florence James Heyting, who was thinking about children herself, had asked Christina about her plans in this regard. Christina had just become a highly successful published author, and was beginning to envisage a future without children.

> I seem to be too tired to think of them at present: they may
> eventuate this year, but I must admit the truth, I do not yearn for
> them: my ideas have turned to other channels, or else I am so
> used to the present family regime that I think it well enough.[92]

However, three months later, after the abortion, she told Florence that children were on the cards: 'We are waiting for England or some other semi-permanent settlement, but we won't wait long, only a few months.'[93] And six months later again, she told Florence (now pregnant) that Bill was talking of a child after she finished *The Beauties and Furies*. 'Bill says when *this* is done we will have a baby: you know I hae ma doots.'[94] When Florence gave birth to a daughter (christened Julie Christina) on 16 July 1935, Christina wrote that she felt 'fearfully jealous'.[95] But in the next few years, when Florence was absorbed with her two young daughters, Christina would privately disparage her as a suburban wife and mother.

The Beauties and Furies, written the following year, in 1935, does not suggest maternal longing. The pregnant Elvira cannot decide whether to keep the baby she has conceived by her lover Oliver, but it is striking that Elvira never sees motherhood as creative, though she has no other interests in life. She envies her husband and lover their work, their 'self-expression', and tells Oliver:

"Since I bore life in me I feel a will growing in me. But the will is the infant. When he is born, he will just leave me like an old skin. I shall be the same as before, limp, aimless."[96]

Oliver, for his part, muses:

"A woman is the least individual of creatures ... To think, in the winter I shall have a child!" He smiled to himself at the idea that if he took a boat then and there, and skipped to any South American port, to Canada or the South Seas, to Majorca or Egypt, he was free to go.

One afternoon, Elvira, feeling sick, suddenly decides she 'can't go through with it', and a woman friend takes her to the *sage-femme*. Afterwards, she is in pain for several days, but feels no regret. Nowhere in Stead's fiction is there a joyous picture of maternity.

In letters from this period, Stead implied that she and Blech were equally ambivalent. Later in life, she would say that *his* unwillingness was the obstacle, telling a friend that Bill had decreed they would not have children even before he declared his love for her.

"We won't have any children! You might love them more than me." (Imagine! He had been thinking it over the weekend, for it was a Monday morning. He had not even proposed a life together; but in his innocence he had forgotten that.)[97]

She explained that Bill, having been brought up almost as an only child, found small children noisy and repulsive.

Blech did talk from time to time about having children, though this might have been to please Christina. They told themselves they were waiting for the divorce to come through; they were waiting to be settled somewhere; they were waiting for Stead to finish her next novel.

The issue of children—like the issue of the divorce or where they would live—would remain unresolved until Christina's age put an end to their vacillations.

*　　*　　*

Having given notice on their apartment at No. 10, rue Jean Bart, they were due to leave Paris on 15 June 1934. The large electric gramophone, the 700 or so records and books were packed up and dispatched by a supplier, to be stored by Florence and Pym Heyting in their large new house in Belsize Park, until Blech and Stead found a flat in London. To Stead's immense relief, she was able to send *Seven Poor Men of Sydney* ahead of them to England. She was 'horribly dissatisfied' with it and anticipated still more revision. 'Bill says he will brain me: if I live to the age of Methuselah I would still be revising *The Seven Poor Men*.'[98]

The novel appeared in October 1934, just ten months after *The Salzburg Tales*, and Stead had her first experience of an avalanche of negative criticism. Reviewers tended to compare it with the short stories, always to the detriment of the novel. Everyone was in awe of its brilliance and 'originality', but to many, the novel lacked depth and coherence. 'There is madness here, and astonishing violence of imagination,' the *Saturday Review of Literature* proclaimed.[99] But there was praise from some quarters. Edwin Muir, in the *Listener*, considered the book, despite its 'brilliant faults', a 'work of genius'.[100] And William Plomer (the *Spectator*) asserted that Stead had 'more talent, more passion and more imagination than nine novelists out of ten'.[101] In Australia, the *Bulletin* announced a 'dazzling book by a Sydney girl'; the reviewer, Montague Grover, thought it 'diabolically clever', but rambling.[102] The novel appeared in the States in December 1934 to similarly mixed reviews. In the *New York Times*, J. S. Southron, referring to Kol Blount's 'In Memoriam' speech, made the interesting observation that 'Miss Stead's love for her country, nowhere explicit, is implied in every word'.[103]

Stead found the reception very disappointing, but tried not to care too much.

> Nobody likes it very much: no doubt they will like the
> following ones in a harmonious crescendo of dubiety and
> slam: can't be helped. As long as Davies or some other keeps
> publishing I can hope to strike it lucky one day.[104]

To add to her glory in that year of publications, a fairy story of hers, 'O, If I Could But Shiver!', was one of fifteen to appear in November in *The Fairies Return*, a collection of traditional fairy stories recast in a modern setting, edited by Peter Davies.[105] Stead's story would take up Grimms' tale, 'The Story of the Youth Who Went Forth to Learn What Fear Was'. As Stead has the Philosopher say in *The Salzburg Tales*: 'every fairy-tale has a modern instance'.[106]

*   *   *

Stead and Blech left Paris in June 1934. By October they had installed themselves, their furniture and possessions at No. 78 Chiltern Court, Baker Street, on the seventh floor of a modern block of flats, with spectacular views of Westminster, Regent's Park and the city spires. This time, Rosa Blech was living with them.

Stead had wanted to be back in London, but had not reckoned with Mollie and Ruth, who had made a second brief trip back to the States and also arrived in London that June. The situation was as distressing as ever. Florence James recalls that Christina was tense whenever Bill went to visit Mollie, and would go to the cinema for diversion, sometimes asking Florence James' German au-pair girl, a Heidelberg graduate, to accompany her. One evening, the girl rang Florence saying she would be staying out later than expected because Christina was in a terrible state.

The domestic turmoil was probably the reason for Blech and Stead's decision to return to Paris. Blech had not yet formally severed his connection with the Travelers' Bank, and so they went back to Paris and to the bank, leaving Rosa Blech and most of their worldly possessions in the London flat.

It suited Stead for the time being, since she was setting her work in progress, *The Travelling Scholar* (later *The Beauties and Furies*), in Paris. She was working hard, hoping to finish the novel by early the following year. As a pick-up, she was 'scoffing arsenic'. A Swiss doctor in Paris had prescribed 'arsenyl', along with tincture of belladonna, a herbal mixture, for stomach troubles which she had feared might be an ulcer. She liked the taste of the belladonna, which calmed her nerves and helped her sleep. The doctor told her no-one of nervous temperament should be without it. From now on, she made sure she was not.[107]

That she was completely immersed in the writing of *The Beauties and Furies* is evident from her letters during this period, which have the same lightly decadent atmosphere, visionary images and playful humour. She wrote to Florence James:

Imagine what I did yesterday evening: waiting for Bill in one of the grander rooms of the Bank (I have my own little one but it is rather cold) I discovered the box of cigars of some friend of Pete's and in an access of boyish immorality began to smoke one: after not more than eight puffs I began to float, my head began to spin, my throat to have a sort of convulsion and my eyelids to flutter down. With due haste I opened the window: below, the corner of the rue de la Paix and the rue Daunou and a young gent of Argentine aspect in an automobile: the young man signals and I though groggy, close the window and think —"*that's* how one sin leads to another and souls are eventually lost, or, how puffing leads to necking." . . . What ogres men are though: the way they drink, smoke cigars and sink in debauch and still come up fresh and smiling![108]

(In the novel, Marpurgo, an inveterate cigar smoker, declares cigars very important for spiritual adventures.)

To Stead's dismay, Bill Blech spent Christmas 1934 in London with Ruth and Mollie, who were shortly to return to New York. Stead tried to console herself, and with the £15 received for *The Fairies Return* and her half-advance from the American edition of *Seven Poor Men*, she took a friend out to dinner, gave some money to the red press, and bought 'two slap-up hats' and a grape purple dinner dress.[109] But none of this could make up for being left alone in Paris during the festive season. On Boxing Day, she wrote to Florence James, 'I haven't heard from Bill, and neither has anyone here, but I suppose he is surrounded by multitudinous Grossmans.' She added, fervently: 'I hope (against hope) that we will set our house in order this coming year.'[110]

She and Bill had been together five years now, and in some respects nothing much had changed.

*   *   *

Stead had returned to a half-written manuscript, begun in 1930. Then called *The Young Man Will Go Far*, it was a portrait of Keith Duncan, but set in Paris. Now she called the novel *The Travelling Scholar*, and with the aim of making the portrait kinder, she was making the fictional character Oliver Fenton an amalgam of Keith Duncan and Frank Manuel. Both were bright young scholars who considered themselves leftwing radicals.

Dr Frank Manuel, a historian, was in Paris on a post-doctoral scholarship to work in the archives. He became a friend. One evening Stead accompanied him to a meeting of revolutionary writers—probably the Association des Ecrivains et Artistes Révolutionnaires.[111] He asked Stead to collaborate with him on a project on the Saint-Simonian period in France, 1836–48, when the peasants felt threatened by the introduction of threshing machines. The project was dropped, presumably because Stead soon left again for London, but it may have given her the idea of exploring the effect on artisans of the mechanisation of the lace industry for *The Travelling Scholar*. To find out more about lace-making—the machines and cartons used, the designing of lace, lace-dyeing—she made an excursion to the lace museum in Calais.[112]

The political situation in Paris was still fraught with tension: police stood four or five deep at some street corners. Stead and Blech were relieved to have their flat in London so that they could 'jump over the channel at a moment's notice'.[113]

*   *   *

Stead described her new novel, later called *The Beauties and Furies*, as a 'sexual drama'. In it, Oedipus runs riot. The entire narrative is spun around three Oedipal triangles which overlap and interconnect in a pattern worthy of an old Jacquard lace-machine. 'All middle-class novels,' declares Oliver, 'are about the trials of three.'[114]

The novel is set in Paris in the first few months of 1934, during the 'tempest of political troubles'.[115] Mrs Elvira Western has been swayed by the ardent entreaties of her young lover Oliver to leave her respectable, eminently sensible doctor husband in London and join Oliver in Paris; he is there to write a doctoral thesis on the French workers' movement from 1871 to 1904. Dark, melancholy Elvira is a sort of sleeping beauty whom Oliver fancies he has woken just as the thorns were closing in on her. Her only rival as beauty and muse is Paris itself.

The Beauties and Furies reveals Stead's obsession with beauty. She admired beauty. She envied beauty. An underlying moral message in the novel is that women are easily destroyed by their beauty. Merely by languidly displaying her charms ('putting out her flowers'[116]) Elvira becomes an enchantress. She is intelligent, but her energy goes into ensnaring men. Although she likes to blame her husband for making her into a useless and idle 'cabbage wife',[117] her complicity in her fate is clear.[118]

The image of life as a cyclic journey, which recurs in Stead's fiction, provides the novel's frame. It opens as it closes: on the train between Paris and London. At the beginning of the novel, when Elvira leaves for Paris, adventure is in the air: she is leaving for Paris, the 'garden of lovers'. The novel closes with Oliver on the train going back to England. (Elvira has already gone back to her husband.) Oliver is reading his poems to a silken-legged girl opposite him, who is as captivated by him as Elvira once was.

The novel has come full circle. It is winter again; the Paris 'spring' is over; Elvira and Oliver are back in the 'frozen grey suburbs' of England. For all their halfhearted attempts, neither Elvira nor Oliver (their names suggest mirror-images) are real 'wanderers'. They remain 'becalmed off Cythera'.

The only positive character is Coromandel Paindebled, daughter of antiquarians who live in the rue Jacob, in Saint-Germain— a precious enclave of artisans whose values are out of joint in the modern world of commercially-minded entrepreneurs and vandals. Passionate about her work as a book designer, Coromandel commands a fertile, chaotic inner world. An independent woman sexually and economically, she sleeps with Oliver, whom she at first finds charming. (He has not told her about Elvira.) When she realises, before long, that he has a 'flabby soul', she brushes some earth from her hands, literally, and with this gesture metaphorically brushes Oliver from her life.

★   ★   ★

In the spring of 1935, Blech and Stead returned to the Chiltern Court flat in London. Mollie and Ruth had returned to New York. Blech was still involved with the Travelers' Bank, but from a distance, which he preferred. Stead was trying to finish *The Beauties and Furies*.

In April, Peter Neidecker was summonsed to court and accused by a half-commission man of fiscal fraud and breach of trust. The bank records were investigated. Neidecker's passport was confiscated, but he was released on bail.[119]

A few weeks later, early in May, Peter Neidecker urgently summoned Bill Blech to Paris. From Paris, Blech wrote to Stead, explaining that a 'fanatical blackmailer' was laying charges against the bank. He was 'not even moved by bribery'. He added anxiously: 'I really think that his price is the bank as a solvent and going institution.'[120] Blech was loyal to Neidecker to the end.

It seems certain that Neidecker did not give Blech exact information about the bank's reserves—or lack thereof—but Blech had always known that the bank was operating in quicksand, and he was certainly implicated in the bank's shady transactions over the years. Jacques Coe, a well-known New York broker and friend of Blech's from the late 1930s onward, comments that Bill Blech never mentioned the Paris bank fiasco afterwards—though Coe and his banker friends all knew about it. 'He would have been ashamed of it.'[121]

After four days of 'sheer horror' in Paris, Blech, exhausted by the bank's recent dramas, went south, as planned, for a few days in Barcelona, followed by a health cure in Madrid. From the Hotel Colon in Barcelona he wrote that he was 'much too worried about dear old Pete to be in the frame of mind to appreciate the city'.[122] But he was still able to appreciate the 'madly beautiful' Spanish women.

From Chiltern Court, where she was cooped up with Bill's mother, Christina wrote Bill loving letters.

> It was beautiful today outside. I made a solemn resolution to join the "Proletarian Club of Round-Walkers" or "The Promenaders of the Hammer and Sickle" or whatever there is that enables me to go into the country walking on Sundays in summer.

She finished, teasingly: 'How am I going to get through the night with no Bill? A lot you care, with your madly-beautiful.'[123]

A week later: 'How I miss you: it is wretched being separated from you so very much: when will it end? I do not mind this time though, if you get better and are smiling and strong again.'

She was feeling wistful:

I hope that when you're quite well, strong and fit again that we can have a more united life . . . It would be pleasant if we had a real home where we knew we would stay for five or ten years, where we could have some ground and a large library.[124]

After two weeks, Christina, with only one letter from Bill, was feeling even more forlorn. (Due to the mule-speed of the Spanish mail, his letters would arrive after his return.)

Dear wee, hurry up and write, or I will be forced to begin to look hungrily at London's toiling millions of ginks, which I should be loath to do, but my breast is as empty as a turned-out tin of peaches: you are not domestic, you never turned out a tin of peaches, so you don't know the feeling.

Mo. That is all I have to say. Wow! I aint got a guy, I aint got a letter. I aint got nuffin. Mo and wow.

Chris xxx.[125]

★ ★ ★

In London, Blech rapidly made new friends—mostly communist journalists associated with the *Daily Worker* and the *Left Review*, established in 1934 and already the most influential of the Left magazines.[126] These friends would call in to discuss politics with Blech, filling the flat with all sorts of American and English regional accents—and plenty of smoke. After the relative isolation of their last years in Paris, Blech and Stead rejoiced in the company of these 'drifting talents', mostly men—unaffected, easy-going and adventurous.[127]

The last chapters of *For Love Alone* describe the atmosphere at the Chiltern Court flat in that spring of 1935:

Many men came to see them in the little flat in the court off Fleet Street, more men than women, many unmarried or libertine, picaresque, amiable, floating men. They came first to see James Quick who had the American's political fervour and the Marxist's political sophistication, who saw Whitehall from the American viewpoint and the White House as from the State House of some Middle-Western State. These men first loved the man and then his woman.[128]

Patrick and Anne Dooley wrote for the London *Daily Worker*. Patrick, an Irishman and a union organiser, regularly spoke at communist rallies;[129] Anne was a thin, nervous Tynesider, whose accent was a source of endless fascination to Stead. Eamon McAlpine, an ex-IRA man, now worked for the Consolidated Press in London. Under the byline Frank Pitcairn, Claud Cockburn wrote for the *Daily Worker* in London, the *New Masses* in New York, and *Pravda* in Moscow. And for the past two years he had been editing an influential mimeographed newsletter, *The Week*. Produced on a shoestring, run off in brown type on a duplicator, by 1935 *The Week* had become famous throughout Europe for printing well-founded rumours and news items which larger papers were not prepared to risk—at least not until they could quote *The Week* as the source. The paper, which regularly uncovered Nazi atrocities, was vehemently disliked by the government of the Third Reich.[130] Another frequent visitor to the flat was Ralph Fox, who discussed political and economic questions with Blech for hours at a time.

By now, Stead had decided that she was very partial to the company of men. (She complained to Bill that her women friends in London were 'such desperately married women'.[131]) After five and a half years in Paris in Blech's company, she had acquired a greater ease with people and a certain cosmopolitan refinement. The previous year, she had published two books, and she was generally considered to be a rising literary star. She spoke French fluently and had a good smattering of German. In London, she and Blech moved among writers and journalists on the Left. In 1935, at 32, she felt better about herself than she had ever done in the past.

A contemporary photograph shows her with bobbed hair parted in the middle. The eyebrows are arched, the eyes sharp and observant, the lips full; she looks challenging, somewhat defiant. When Nettie Palmer, the Australian writer, met Stead on the train to Paris in June that year, she was quite discomfited by the younger woman's elegance and worldly air. Palmer could detect no trace of Australian accent in Stead's 'nodding sing-song' voice.[132]

Always restless, always passionate, Stead now began to flaunt her interest in men. If anything, Blech seems to have encouraged her. Perhaps he understood that her need for men's affirmation was an almost desperate need to be found physically desirable. Certainly he prided himself on a free-thinking liberalism which encompassed open marriages. He himself does not appear ever to have dallied with other women—apart from Mollie. But his fierce and affectionate brotherly relationships with men may well have reinforced Christina's own preference for men.

In *For Love Alone*, one man stands out among the cluster of characters who would come to the flat to talk to James Quick. Harry Girton is 'an Oxford graduate, a radical pamphleteer who lived in a distant seedy suburb with his swarthy-browed and sullen mistress-wife'.[133] A shabbily dressed man with 'dark gold hair', his 'easygoing smile' and lingering gaze appeal to many women: he 'had loved much'. Girton is one of Stead's archetypal wanderers:

At the back of his mind was the firm intention of getting away, wandering out, and amusing the soul of his soul by picking his way through a very alien land, like Hudson, like Lawrence, like Burton.[134]

Teresa and James Quick are drawn to Harry Girton 'as driftwood is sucked in by waters rushing downwards round a hidden reef'. Teresa is fascinated by the stories that circulate about Girton's wild and dissolute personal life. His image begins 'to lure her, growing on her in her sleep'.[135] The attraction she feels for this man—over six feet tall, broad, with 'shapely limbs' and 'splendid oval blue eyes'[136]—is strongly physical. 'Differently from any other man till then, it was of his body that she dreamed.'[137]

He looked at her and a storm of the uplands blew round her ears, she reeled and felt half-mad with love, and kept thinking to herself: "It comes again, it does not die with marriage, it is not over once for all ..." Now she really felt a woman.[138]

Harry Girton is based on Ralph Fox, a handsome, restless Halifax man, with a pale face, fine nose and gentle grey eyes.[139] Two years older than Stead, he was a passionate political activist, a committed writer and journalist, and a restless wanderer. In Fox's novel, *Storming Heaven*, his hero describes his strange thirst: 'I feel I must wear my feet out seeing this world, finding out why people do what they do, why they are what they are.'[140]

Fox was the black sheep in his conservative, middle-class family. At Oxford, his studies ranged from the French Encyclopaedists to Oriental Languages. In 1920, at the age of 20, he had helped establish the Oxford branch of the Communist Party of Great Britain.[141] That same year, he travelled to the south-east of the Soviet Union, a region ravaged by famine in the wake of the White Russian armies, and was impressed by what he saw of the Soviet system. His first book, *People of the Steppes* (1925), and his only novel, *Storming Heaven* (1928), were based on his experience in Russia.

In 1925 Fox went to Moscow and worked for the Communist International, where he met an English woman, Madge Palmer, a fellow activist, whom he later married. He was back in England for the General Strike of 1926, but returned to Russia in 1929 and spent three years as librarian at the Marx-Engels Institute in Moscow, active in the Russian Communist Party. While in Moscow, he worked through vast amounts of archival material for a biography of Lenin, published in 1933. Since being back in England, he had written short books on the British class struggle and on British imperialism, and regular articles for the *Daily Worker*, the *Sunday Worker*, *New Writing* and *Left Review*, which he co-founded.

Fox read widely in English, French and Russian literature, and was currently writing a book on Marxism and literature, *The Novel and the People*. A non-sectarian Marxist, he was intolerant of easy terms of denigration such as 'bourgeois propaganda' or 'counter-revolutionary' literature.[142]

The Indian novelist Mulk Raj Anand described Fox as one of the most versatile men he had ever met:

> ... a person who could talk about the bronzes of the Tang dynasty and of Kuo-min-tang politics, of Spanish conquistadors and of the origins of the caste system, of contemporary English poetry, of the Chinese novel and of the new novel in Europe, all in one afternoon.[143]

Stead could hardly fail to be impressed.

★   ★   ★

The year 1935, in which the Nuremberg laws stripped German Jews of their citizenship and rights and Mussolini invaded Ethiopia, was a year of solidarity for the literary Left. The Popular Front was officially launched by the Comintern (the Communist International) in Moscow, which urgently argued that all Left factions must unite to form a solid block against fascism. With the aim of forming a broad Left alliance, communist parties throughout the Western world organised writers' leagues and writers' congresses. From now on, 'fellow travellers' and even liberals (previously regarded with contempt) were encouraged to participate.

The First International Congress of Writers for the Defense of Culture, a mass meeting of intellectuals against fascism, was held at the Salle de la Mutualité in Paris from 21 to 25 June. It was attended by an imposing collection of literary luminaries. Among the large French contingent were Aragon, Gide and Malraux; the Germans, now living in exile, included Brecht, Heinrich Mann, Anna Seghers, Alfred Döblin, Robert Musil, Johannes Becher and Egon Kisch. It was a gathering of people 'for whom fascism was a personal insult', as Maxim Gorki wrote from Russia, in a telegram excusing his absence.[144]

There were few radicals among prestigious British writers. In the spirit of the Popular Front, the congress organisers invited liberals Virginia Woolf, Rebecca West, E. M. Forster and Aldous Huxley. The two women did not attend. Afterwards Huxley would privately complain that it was five days of 'endless Communist demagogy'.[145]

The English delegation largely comprised associates of the *Left Review*. Christina Stead's invitation to join the British delegation as their secretary probably came from Ralph Fox, who was on the organising executive. After all, *Seven Poor Men of Sydney*, her novel about struggling workers strangled by their material circumstances, contained solid Marxist dialogue.

John Strachey, a Marxist theorist of international stature, was another delegate. He had just returned from a political lecture-tour in the United States which the American government had done its best to prevent.[146] (The following year, John Strachey and publisher Victor Gollancz would establish the Left Book Club, with the aid of Harold Laski.) Amabel Williams-Ellis (Strachey's sister), and playwright Montagu Slater were editors of *Left Review*. James Hanley, a former seaman, was generally considered Britain's best proletarian novelist. He was the controversial author of *Boy*, a novel just banned in England about a working-class boy who catches syphilis and commits suicide. Pearl Binder was a journalist and artist for *Left Review*; Shelley Wang was a revolutionary Chinese poet living in England, and Herbert Read, the future art critic, had just written the novel *The Green Child*. Travelling with the group, but representing Australia, were Nettie Palmer[147] and an unknown, John Fisher.

Nettie Palmer, 50 that year, was a significant figure on the Australian literary scene. She was energetically trying to promote interest in national writing at a time when poor publishing conditions and a lack of cultural journals meant that Australian literature was at a low ebb. Her broad reading in European and American literature gave her an assured and independent voice in Australian letters: her 1924 book *Modern Australian Literature 1900–1923* had been the first systematic critical study of its kind.

Palmer had found *Seven Poor Men of Sydney* singularly haunting. Earlier that year she had commented: 'To read [Stead's] book is to spend your time in the company of an exhilarating author, who is probably a genius ... Whatever road she may take, we shall never be willing to lose sight of her.'[148] In Paris, in April, she had been to Sylvia Beach's bookshop and seen in the window—alongside Shakespeare, Hemingway, Gertrude Stein, Whitman and Thackeray—Christina Stead's *Salzburg Tales* and *Seven Poor Men*. She was curious to meet the author in person.

While she was in London, Palmer was making the most of the opportunity to meet other expatriate Australian writers: Jack Lindsay, Brian Penton and Henry Handel Richardson. Richardson's trilogy *The Fortunes of Richard Mahony*, published as one volume for the first time in 1930, made her Australia's foremost woman writer.

Some of the English contingent had arranged to travel to Paris together on the boat-train on Friday 21 June: the congress was to open that evening. In her diary Nettie Palmer recorded her first impression of her 32-year-old compatriot:

> Christina Stead came in light-foot and assured, perfectly dressed, tailored and supple, gloves-bag-hat, shoes, all dark blue. She carried nothing superfluous, except perhaps the newspaper her husband handed in to her at the last moment. — "Hm-m. Bill's idea of a newspaper," she said to me as the train began to move: she smiled, half-guilty, but I felt as if it were her idea of a newspaper too. It had some name like *The Economist*.[149]

Nettie Palmer jotted other impressions in her notebooks. As the train was about to leave, she noticed 'a middle-sized youngish man planting his typewriter and his casual suit-case in the rack'. When he spoke to his fellow passengers, she observed 'a hint of Yorkshire in his accent'. This, Stead proudly informed her, was Ralph Fox, who had written a novel about his travels over ground trodden by Genghis Khan, and as a reporter for the communist press, made regular trips between London and Paris. Palmer learnt that he was 35 and a talented linguist—'probably the best French speaker of us all'.[150]

The Australian women sat opposite John Fisher who appeared to Nettie Palmer 'eager' and 'hungry-looking' and to Stead (she confided to Nettie later) 'a real Australian bush boy'. As the train 'glided through early summer landscape down to Newhaven', Palmer asked Stead about her work, and the three Australians discussed 'the urgent objectives of the congress'.

At Newhaven they joined the boat and went down to the saloon for a meal described by Nettie as 'a last, stern specimen of England'. From Dieppe, they travelled by train, third class, to Paris.

> Summer had suddenly appeared in full strength—there were poppies all through the wheat and dazzling sun. Christina said we'd never have enough frocks in our own suitcases, lucky we'd arrived just in time for the midsummer sales. But where were we going to stay in Paris for the six days?

Nettie Palmer was at a complete loss to know what to make of the 'elegant' and 'poised' Christina Stead. She could not match the author of *Seven Poor Men of Sydney*, that novel full of wild poetry and potency, with this sophisticated woman who seemed so concerned about clothes. How could this 'secure woman of the world' have written about the 'smells of Woolloomooloo' and 'the breakers of the Pacific against the Gap'? Did she really care about political causes? The bits of the puzzle simply did not seem to fit.

Stead's question about accommodation must have been addressed to the group generally, for she very much hoped to stay in the same hotel as Ralph Fox and his friends James Hanley and John Strachey; she was devastated when Nettie Palmer knew of a hotel where the landlady had been very pleasant on her previous visit. Stead and Shelley Wang found themselves bustled into a taxi which Nettie Palmer directed to the Hôtel des Grands Hommes in the Place du Panthéon.[151]

That evening Nettie Palmer steered the little group to the Foyer des Etudiants for a cheap but hearty dinner. Although Stead had already decided that Palmer was bossy, meddlesome and interfering, she was in better humour; perhaps it was the prospect of meeting up with the others at the evening session. She told Nettie she was ravenous and explained that she had been taking medicine with arsenic in it, which sharpened her appetite. Nettie Palmer reflected in her journal:

I don't know what anyone takes arsenic for, but Christina
Stead strikes me as one who has known T.B. — at any rate in
the past. She's not so much restless, or fatigued, as insatiable.
I notice she often refers to T.B. as a probable element in
someone *else*'s motives or plan of living: it's nothing rare or
abnormal to her. Her face is thin, with high cheek bones, but
looks as if it has been thinner. High colour close to the eyes.[152]

That evening, on the platform of the Mutualité, Gide, Malraux, Aragon and Nizan stood in front of the bright red presidential table and raised their right fists to the first bars of the Internationale. André Gide, 'Dean of French letters', gave the opening oration, receiving a rousing storm of applause.[153] The next speakers were E. M. Forster and Julien Benda. Nettie Palmer approved of these two 'liberal quietists' who questioned 'the tendencies of Communism as well as of fascism'.[154] Stead, in an article she wrote for the July issue of *Left Review*, was contemptuous of their 'genial, gentle speeches'.

Some four thousand students, workers and intellectuals were gathered together in that 'hothouse atmosphere'; among them liberals, Marxists, Christians, surrealists. All were passionately against fascism, but many found the communist rhetoric offputting. In her article, Christina Stead positioned herself wholeheartedly with the communists, and noted that the only disruptions were occasional 'rather acid passage-at-arms between Trotskyists and those whom they call Stalinists'. But her impassioned rhetoric probably appealed to her communist readers rather than reflecting deeply felt convictions.

Stead's report on the congress in the July issue of *Left Review* is the most emphatic printed statement she would ever make about the political responsibility of writers. She asserted that writers in the contemporary 'embroiled world' (the USSR was excluded from this) were witnessing 'the last corruptions of capitalist decay' and *had* to be concerned with politics. There was no place any more for 'denizens of the ivory tower'. The duty of younger writers was to:

... give up their poetic solitudes and soft self-probings to study worldly subjects, enter the political arena, take lessons from workmen and use their pen as a scalpel for lifting up the living tissues, cutting through the morbid tissues, of the social anatomy.

This was no easy task, she admitted, for 'the disruption of the bourgeois world, its disorders and anomalies, the frightful insistence of economic questions leaves the writer, whatever his origin, quite at sea'.

Certain ideas and phrases in Stead's nine-page piece sound like Bill Blech; he probably helped her with the article. Other passages of whimsical caricature are pure Stead:

Malraux, youthful, fatigued, indefatigable, bowed, gets admirers with the whites of his eyes; Barbusse calls up romance with his coiffe of Cochin-China cock; Waldo Frank takes the shine out of them all with his plump, new-world shine; E. E. Kisch with his stick, thick-set, sunburnt, pungent, limps about smouldering with silenced oratory; Feuchtwanger, little, tanned, bowed, mild, with thick shoulders and a head like a grapeseed; Huxley, one would say an emanation in a test-tube, elongating indefinitely like the filaments of Bacillus Vulgaris.

Egon Kisch, the Czech author, had recently returned from Australia where he had gone for an anti-war congress. The government had used every possible method to stop this communist from disembarking. Finally he had jumped eighteen feet onto the Melbourne wharf and broken his leg. The affair had precipitated an explosion of international publicity.

Delegates from all thirty-five nations present were asked to give a brief report on cultural censorship in their country. The Australian presentation was duly noted in the Australian press. On 27 June, the Melbourne *Argus* reported:

Miss Christina Stead and Mrs. Nettie Palmer, members of the Australian delegation to the Congress of Writers for the Defence of Culture, have presented a report strongly protesting against the Australian book censorship, declaring that taking advantage of the distance of Australia from Europe, a reactionary government is banning books that would keep Australians in touch with progressive English and European thought.

"Obscure Customs officials," says the report, "are empowered to ban such books as they choose. Moreover, apart from the banning of hundreds of books freely circulating in England, over 70 left-wing political books were banned last year. The censorship is in the hands of the Minister for Customs, a military gentleman who is not in the front rank of literary men. We demand that the worth and legality of the books should be judged by Australian literary leaders, not as at present by politicians."[155]

The Hobart *Mercury* commented: 'It is regrettable that we should thus be forced to wash our soiled linen in the European public wash-house in order to redress a domestic grievance.'[156]

* * *

Living on the same floor of the same hotel, Christina Stead and Nettie Palmer saw quite a bit of each other during their time in Paris. They did not warm to each other. It was not the most opportune time for them to meet: if Stead had 'high colour close to the eyes', it was probably because proximity to Ralph Fox and other impressive young revolutionaries made her quite heady. Having just emerged from a long period of solitude and hard work, she was feeling a little giddy with it all. Palmer does not seem to have guessed these undercurrents in Stead's life.

Both women could be dogmatic and their views diverged significantly. Though Nettie Palmer read French, German and Greek and believed it essential for Australian writers to keep in touch with the larger world, she and Vance Palmer passionately championed a distinctive Australian national culture, one that was no longer passively responsive to British and European influences. Stead's own literary influences were European, not Australian (she had not even read Henry Handel Richardson) and from her internationalist perspective, Palmer's attitude seemed narrow and provincial.

Nettie Palmer insisted that the Australians should sit together in conference sessions; Stead—for reasons the least of which was national identity—wanted to sit with the English contingent. It remained a rankling point throughout the five days of the congress.

Politically, the women were at different ends of the liberal spectrum. Both were inspired by the broad Left alliance, but Stead strongly identified with the communist element that perturbed Palmer.

Six months after the congress, Stead would write to Florence James, who had just met Nettie Palmer in London: 'She is a typical Australian isn't she . . . but she's such a good soul, kind, busy, tireless, courageous.'[157] In later years, she declared Palmer a 'good-natured, school-teacherish woman, totally without flair or imagination'.[158]

On the Sunday, yet another glaring hot day, the two Australian women set out after breakfast for a walk to the Luxembourg Gardens. Stead, Palmer noted in her diary, looked 'lightly elegant'. On their way, they passed masses of police militia in trucks and Stead mused aloud:

> Now *why* are all these gendarmes being sent out in lorries from the barracks to-day? What meeting of the people are they going to break up? Would it be that big communal picnic at St. Cloud? Look, there's another lorry being loaded with them. Who's going to be crushed?

Palmer's diary recounts the conversation in the Luxembourg Gardens. With her customary indifference to tact, Stead apparently told Palmer, who had always felt herself to be rather a plain woman:

> My father wanted me to be a scientist like himself. When I was very tiny he used to tell me the names of what interested him most—fishes with frightening faces. It was all right, but when he saw I learnt easily he took me to science meetings. I suppose I was about ten by then. I wasn't frightened of fish with ugly faces, but those science women who didn't know how to do their hair or put their clothes on! I ran away from science forever.[159]

The monologue in Palmer's diary—supposedly Stead's voice—continues in the same vein:

> I was determined to make enough money some day to have the right clothes. I must admit that I've got rather a weakness for shoes. And gloves. Yes, and hats. I buy my hats in London, but it does seem a pity not to be able to take one back from Paris now. It's not the best part of the season, though; it's too late.

Nettie Palmer, an astute observer of her fellow-beings, kept a journal throughout her life. In her portraits of people, she liked to cite dialogue, and would write whole slabs of speech in inverted commas, as if she had a tape recorder.[160] But there was an element of deception in this technique.

Fourteen Years, Palmer's published journal, is unfair to herself as well as to Stead, since it omits comments in the unpublished notebooks which portray Stead far more warmly. The conversation about hats is placed in a quite different light by these two qualifying sentences, omitted later:

> C.S. is a woman who has read enormously, studied by-ways of mathematics, histories of sorcery or period costume, always consuming them whole. These subjects leak in—so does her economics, her finance.

Also omitted from the published diary are details which show that Palmer reflected—and not ungenerously—on the contradictions she found in Christina Stead:

When she came to England, she carried her few banknotes
sewn into her corset. She now has a sense of security with her
husband (not wealthy, I gather, but security and a little more),
and her books have brought in something—as well as sudden,
dramatic fame, in a heady draught.

The fact is, Christina Stead, a magpie in her eclecticism, was as
interested in hats as in international finance. She made the mistake,
perhaps, of imagining that Nettie Palmer was equally diverse in her
interests. The other factor at play is Stead's self-image. It was certainly
important to her to be seen as an elegant, fashionable woman, who
had been influenced by her years in Paris, and she would have liked
Nettie Palmer to carry this image of her, Christina Stead, back
to Australia.

Stead's excitement was neither snobbery nor feminine silliness.
The truth, which Palmer seems not to have guessed, was that Stead
felt terribly insecure about her appearance, and that French clothes
had liberated her in some small way. Fifteen years later, Stead
would tell her sister Kate that in Paris, for the first time, she had
found clothing which suited her. She added: 'I am as plain as before
but it doesn't worry me now as I have slowly learned over a long
course of years how to behave in company and so I have a general
interior happiness which prevents me from worrying about these
things. I do not intend to be a nasty old woman.'[161]

Palmer does not seem to have realised that Christina Stead's was
the grab-bag mind of an imaginative writer rather than an intellectual—the kind of mind Patrick White describes as *his*, and for
which he, too, was criticised. His defence, in his autobiography,
could equally well have been Stead's:

I knew I hadn't a scholar's mind. Such as I had was more like
the calico bag hanging from the sewing-room door-knob,
stuffed with snippets of material of contrasting textures and
clashing colours, which might at some future date be put to
some practical, aesthetic, or even poetic use.

Patrick White adds—and Stead could not have put it better:

I believe it is this rag-bag of a disorderly mind which has
more than anything offended some of my Australian academic
critics. For them the controlled monochrome of reason, for me
the omnium gatherum of instinctual colour which illuminates
the more often than not irrational behaviour of sensual man.[162]

*   *   *

It was a sociable week. The French writers entertained the delegates
to lunch at a restaurant on the Champs-Elysées; there was tea at the

Soviet Embassy on the last day. And there were private get-togethers and late 'evening sit-ups'. For Stead the social highlight was the last evening, Wednesday 26 June, when a small group of friends celebrated the sixty-fifth birthday of Danish writer Martin Andersen Nexoe. They sat on the terrace of a restaurant in the balmy evening air and toasted him with champagne while Nexoe and American radical Mike Gold shared a veal cutlet and the older man regaled the group with stories. After Nexoe retired to bed, Ralph Fox, Mike Gold, James Hanley, Pearl Binder, Stead and Palmer stayed on drinking. In her *Left Review* article, Stead chose to focus on Mike Gold:

Michael Gold, with small, swarthy, Finnish face and turbulent hair, irresistible Mike sings the songs of the negroes converted to Lenin in the southern swamps, fields and forests, wrings his hands because we have not bought Nexoe a nosegay on his birthday, is straight-forward, gay, simple, regrets that politics takes away the time he should spend on books.[163]

The fiery André Malraux, ridden with nervous facial tics, brought the congress to a close with a tribute to their Soviet comrades. There was a final standing ovation.

Christina Stead would remember this conference as 'those amazing five days'. Ralph Fox, in the *Daily Worker*, proclaimed it 'one of the most remarkable meetings in the history of the world'.[164]

The return trip to London on Thursday 27 June was a lively affair. Stead, Fox, Amabel Williams-Ellis, Pearl Binder and Nettie Palmer travelled back together, full of the congress. On arrival in London, they discussed sharing a taxi to Hampstead, but Stead pressed them to drop in at her flat, to tell Bill Blech about the congress.[165] Two weeks later, Nettie Palmer visited the flat again:

July 12th, 1935.

Another hot July afternoon. London people, plunging into shorts, seem to feel the pressure of it. I had to go up and see Christina Stead with a message. Up . . . A huge building of flats, and hers on the seventh storey—a long corridor from the lift. Lightness, modernity. One room given up to a gramophone with masses of records on shelves, and to a typewriter, with masses of files in pigeon-holes. (Files of *Humanité*, for instance, on account of its *faits divers*, Christina surprisingly said.)

She looked flushed, emaciated, romantic. She had been writing a long, elaborate account of the Paris Writers' Congress, as well as her usual work, and taking it out of herself. Her husband, William Blake, came in, a powerful, rather nuggety dark man, and his mother, a little lonely expatriate from Germany . . .

Christina would make tea for me, gracefully whisking out pink serviettes, but adventurously, as if making *maté* in honour of a Uruguayan; and offering me some wine as if for relief.

From one window there was a view of Westminster, not only the spires but the parks. A sense of rolling carriages in golden afternoon dust (motors, I suppose). The London season in flower . . . They were speaking of Ralph Fox, who comes regularly to read economics with W.B., and what a serious, versatile fellow Fox is. And what a linguist; they declare he can talk Russian with peasants in their villages, and of course he's in Paris every few months making speeches at workers' meetings in the suburbs.

W.B. had a bit of a hangover from too many cocktails somewhere yesterday evening. I happened to mention being to dinner at the fantastic-serious Boulestin's . . . 'Boulestin,' said Blake with heavy caution, 'Boulestin's not entirely trustworthy with his *plat du jour*; that can be commonplace. But with someone who knows how to order, as I gather your host did . . .'

He's like that—a connoisseur in all the arts, an epicure to whom even Boulestin's is not the last word in cookery. When we moved back to the next room, Christina put on a special recording of 'The Sunken Cathedral'.

★   ★   ★

Years later, Stead would tell a friend that on the train to Paris, speeding through Normandy on the way to the congress, she was standing in the corridor watching the countryside when Ralph Fox came up to her and said, 'Let's get out at the next station and walk through Normandy. I don't want to go to this conference.' She felt a stab of excitement, thoughts flew through her head, and she did not answer. Two minutes later, another delegate joined them and the moment passed.[166]

If, throughout the congress and the following weeks, Nettie Palmer was struck by Stead's feverish look, it was the look of a woman flushed with love.

★   ★   ★

But then in mid July 1935, just as Stead and Blech were establishing a circle of friends in London and beginning to warm to a city neither had ever much liked, the phantom buggy crashed and the storm cloud that had darkened their existence for some time burst.

The Travelers' Bank had been in trouble for a long time now, with heavy withdrawals and bad speculations. Bill Blech had officially resigned on 3 May 1935.[167]

On Thursday 19 July, the bank in rue de la Paix did not open its doors. A notice informed clients that it would re-open the next day. But the next day the doors remained closed. The French police searched Peter Neidecker's luxury apartment on the Avenue Foch to no avail. Neidecker, his wife Sybil, his three children and his two brothers had disappeared without trace. On Saturday, the police entered the bank, placed it under seal, seized the account books and correspondence and issued warrants for the arrest of the two brothers most involved, Bertrand Coles (Peter) and Aubrey Neidecker. On 22 July, the London *Daily Telegraph* reported:

> The whereabouts of Mr. Coles Neidecker are uncertain. His yacht, the *Etoile Filante*, left Marseilles some days ago, but it is not known whether he was on board.
>
> The bank has associated institutions in France, Brussels, Amsterdam and London. It is reported to have gold reserves in London.
>
> A financial expert has been instructed to search the bank's premises and the residences of the brother. It is said that Mr. B. Coles Neidecker lost heavily in speculation in the franc. Among the charges to be brought against him is one by a depositor, Mr. Marcel Charles Reinmann, who alleges that a sum of about £6,500 was improperly employed by the bank on Stock Exchange speculations.
>
> The names of the banker's wife, Mrs. Sybil Neidecker, and their three children, appeared in the passenger list of a liner that left Havre for the United States last month.

French and English newspapers offered daily bulletins on the mystery. Police searched for the American Scarlet Pimpernel in Paris, London, Brussels, the Riviera and on the high seas. Overseas branches of the bank had also closed.[168] Sir Duncan Orr Lewis, Director of the London branch on Old Broad Street, affirmed that liabilities from the Travelers' Bank (estimated at something in the vicinity of £1 300 000) would affect its clients.[169] Frederick Sard, Director of the New York branch, claimed he had had no news of Neidecker and presumed he must be on his yacht.[170]

As a senior employee in the bank until May 1935, Bill Blech was heavily implicated. Fellow bankers in London advised him to leave Europe without delay.[171] He and Christina took two or three days to pack and make passport and visa arrangements. Their friend Jean MacAlpine (little realising what a chore she was taking on) kindly offered to see to the sub-letting of their flat. Bill Blech, his mother and Christina Stead walked out of the Baker Street flat, leaving behind furniture, books and records, not knowing if or when they would be back.

The *Daily Mail*, 24 July 1935:

New York, Tuesday.

While the police throughout Europe were searching for Mr. B. Coles Neidecker, founder and head of the Travellers' Bank of Paris which closed its doors on Thursday last, he was staying at the palatial Waldorf Astoria Hotel in New York. He has now been arrested.

The Sûreté Générale in Paris, the French Scotland Yard, has requested that he and his two brothers, Mr. George William Neidecker (a sleeping partner in the bank) and Mr. Aubrey Neidecker (manager of the Paris office), should be detained as fugitives on charges of grand larceny, state the New York police . . .

Mr. B. Coles Neidecker arrived here under his own name in the Cunard-White Star liner Britannic on Sunday and informed the authorities that he would stay at the Waldorf Astoria.

But when reporters called him on the telephone a pleasant resonant voice gaily replied, "I'm Peter Neidecker."

His questioners persisted, only to elicit the repeated assurance: "I'm not B. Coles Neidecker. I've not seen him."

At the hotel clerks replied to all inquiries with the monotonous declaration: "All we are authorised to say is that Mr. Peter Neidecker stays here."

At the office of the Travellers' Bank in Wall-Street those in charge were equally mystifying.

They vouchsafed the information, "We would much like to know where Mr. Neidecker is. We feel like fools here and cannot tell you a thing."

"All we know is that Mr. Neidecker is a very charming man, that he has nothing to hide, and that if he is in town we shall hear from him very soon."[172]

On 24 July, B. Coles Neidecker was arrested when he tried to withdraw $50000 from a frozen account in a New York bank. He was released on bail, pending trial. The same day, Aubrey and George Neidecker were provisionally detained when they arrived in Norfolk, Virginia, on a liner which had left France from Le Havre. With them were their mother, Peter's wife Sybil Neidecker and the three children. The French Embassy put extradition orders in to Washington.[173]

Christina, Bill and Rosa Blech fled London, then 'streaked through Ireland' from Dublin to Galway, catching glimpses of peatbogs and 'stormbitten isles'. Without delay, they boarded a boat for the New World.[174]

6

Manhattan Peaks

JULY 1935–APRIL 1936

THE TRIO DISEMBARKED in Boston, among boisterous Irish families emigrating to the New World. After eight years in Europe, Rosa Blech was pleased to be returning to America, which she considered home, having lived there for some thirty-three years. It was where she wanted to die, she told her son.

'After an extensive night-course on American society under C. B. De Mille and Sam Goldwyn', Christina Stead fully expected all Americans to be 'incurably tough, cruel wisecrackers, snipers of the gibe that kills, machine gunners of quickfire backchat'. In notes entitled 'America', in which she describes her first impressions of that country for American readers, she writes that she was quickly disabused. The Americans she met were 'slow and genial'. Though they could be funny, they were far from quick-witted. And after Europe, the prevailing 'flatfoot commonsense' of Americans irritated her.[1]

She could see why Boston was the 'immigrant's dream'. She loved the old brownstone districts, with their reminders of the War of Independence and the birth of the Union. The tree-lined streets had carts bursting with summer fruit, flowers and vegetables, in an abundance she had not seen since leaving Australia. The democratic atmosphere also reminded her of Sydney.

The first day in Boston I thought I was in a sort of socialist commonwealth, the policeman in his white shirt-sleeves called my taxi-driver "buddy," the postman in his blue shirt, the officials of all sorts, amiable and not obsequious: what a change from the brass hats and brass buttons of Europe, I thought.

Having heard reports of race-conflict in America, she was pleased to see negroes lunching in a low-priced coffee-bar with whites.

Though this was the depth of the Depression, America seemed to gleam with a sense of the future, like a 'skyrocket waiting to be let off'. It was the sort of place, Stead mused, that made one wish to live for 200 years to see what would happen next.[2] It struck her as the ideal place to bring up children. And yet the middle classes looked exceedingly glum. Years later she recalled:

When Bill and I first landed with his old mother in Boston, ... he took us for lunch to some big Boston hotel and, waiting for our food, I looked around and said to Bill in an undertone (not to worry the old lady): "Bill, has there been a national disaster today? Has the President died? Or what?" But nothing had happened: it was the way the faces of the public struck me—not down-and-outers—but Bostonians having a good lunch.[3]

It did not take long for her to discover the sinister underside to the richest country in the world. Beside Boston's fine bay was the 'rottenest slum' she had ever seen. And on 23 August, when she and Bill stopped to watch a demonstration to commemorate the execution of anarchists Sacco and Vanzetti eight years before, she was shocked by the extreme hostility the police showed the pickets. Was this the Land of Freedom?

They stayed a fortnight in Boston, long enough for Stead to finish revising *The Beauties and Furies* and post it off to Peter Davies. She was not pleased with 'her badly mauled manuscript': she believed that Davies' suggested revisions had ruined its coherence.[4]

They took a circuitous route, through Washington and Baltimore, to New York, and arrived in August, that notoriously sweaty month, which Stead would portray so vividly in *The People with the Dogs*. It was dawn and still fresh on the water when they approached Manhattan under Brooklyn Bridge. Stead found the sight of the 'Wall Street main ranges' and the uptown peaks (those 'miles of vertical glass') beautiful beyond expectation.[5]

* * *

She and Blech had smiles 'like sunflowers' when they emerged from the offices of her American publishers, D. Appleton-Century. They had called in to collect their mail and found themselves ushered with great conviviality into the presence of high-powered publishers, who instantly swung into gear and discussed marketing strategies. The manager, John L. B. Williams, wanted Stead to see reporters and give interviews, write an article on her first impressions of America and produce more of her highly successful short stories. Stead came out calling it 'the land of boundless importunity'.[6]

They learnt later that D. Appleton-Century was practically run by Wall Street; the heads of the firm were financial rather than literary men. 'The firm is liberal-conservative,' Stead wrote to Florence James, 'and I believe more or less strictly Gentile. (You may laugh, but anti-semitism is a very active yeast in this Germanic country. There are plenty of large banking and commercial firms who will not employ a Jew in any position.)'[7]

'Upon my honour,' Stead told Florence James, 'I think about making money here . . . financial opportunity is in the air.'[8] Within the first month, Radio of America had asked her for a copy of her forthcoming novel for a possible radio script. A friend had offered to talk to another friend about a possible scriptwriting job for her in Hollywood. A businessman in insurance, a multi-millionaire with a reputation for toughness, offered Blech work on a commission basis. Blech was sick at the thought of it, and told Stead he would create a better impression by not jumping at the first offers made.[9] He calculated that he had just enough savings to keep them for twelve months, if necessary. Stead rather hoped he would take some time off: the traumas of the last years had taken their toll. 'He is not at all strong yet,' she told Florence James; 'he has that tired little face that I hate to see.' On a strict diet to lose weight, he occasionally looked quite thin and haggard. 'I feel cheated as if somebody had stolen fifty pounds of Bill away. I like as much Bill as possible.'[10]

★   ★   ★

There was, Stead observed, a fundamental contradiction in the American philosophy of life. In *I'm Dying Laughing*, mostly written in the Fifties, Emily Wilkes probably reflects Stead's own view of the 'American dilemma'.

> You want to be free and break new ground, speak your mind,
> fear no man, have the neighbours acknowledge that you're a
> good man; and at the same time you want to be a success,
> make money, join the country club, get the votes and kick the
> other man in the teeth and off the ladder. You believe sincerely
> in Washington, Jefferson, Lincoln; and also know that you'll
> get your nose bloodied if not worse, if you don't believe in
> Rockefeller, Mellon, General Motors and Sears Roebuck.

Everything in America seemed to be expressed in terms of money. The snatches of conversation Stead heard in the street were usually

about 'bucks' and 'dollars'. In the women's magazines, marriage
and divorce were discussed in monetary terms: young women were
advised to weigh up the security value of suitors; older women
were given advice on coercing ex-husbands for alimony. 'This is
horrible, revolting,' Stead groaned. 'Nowhere else is human love
discussed in terms of the stock market.'[11]

In *Letty Fox*, a novel set largely in New York in the Thirties and
Forties, Stead would be scathing about the mercenary attitude
towards marriage inculcated in American women. A friend writes
to Mathilde Fox (modelled on Mollie Blech):

> Nothing is too good for you. You are a wife and a mother.
> You have given life ... We must protect our young. Your
> husband is obliged to keep you, and if he will not, go to a
> lawyer, and the lawyer will see to it that he pays, and if he
> will not, don't be soft, Mathilde, clap him into jail![12]

In the novel it is a Canadian woman (Pauline) who expresses Stead's
own view:

> What luck you have, you American women! Men who pay for
> everything and don't ask for accounts. Yes, it's Protestantism.
> The men believe they've done their wives insult and injury by
> sleeping with them. They must pay forever! ... As for the
> women ... they want to get married, naturally. But they
> behave as if they are disabled for life as soon as they're
> married. They go in for man-sweating.

After her experience of Mollie Blech's emotional manipulations,
Stead was not predisposed to like American women. And after
France, she was dismayed by the polarisation of the sexes in
America. The worship of the 'baby-face girl' in American films
seemed to her to reflect psychological immaturity. In mixed groups,
American men tended to exhibit a 'weariness or sense of superior-
ity' towards women, and either talked business or told 'pointless
schoolboy antiquated dirty stories'. After a few weeks in the States,
Stead told Florence James that she would have to take up tatting or
crochet.

> The long hours sitting round listening to the dispersed but
> emphatic New York prattle, Bill's disquisitions and general
> vocal thunder will drive me batty or badtempered if I don't
> have something to fill in the time ... My (universally) clever
> comments and the studied cunning of my jokes are passed over
> like sandgrains in the surf ... The result is I get into a state of
> mute rage, passive murder or heavy sleep. No woman is
> listened to in New York.[13]

*   *   *

Despite the energetic money-talk encountered in business circles, America in 1935 was a 'stricken nation', as Franklin D. Roosevelt put it. In no other country had expansion been so rapid up till 1929, and in no other country had the economic collapse been so great. When Roosevelt became President in March 1933, during yet another panic in the American banks, he had promised the people a 'New Deal'. In a series of radio addresses—his famous 'fireside chats'—he had outlined his strategy: Relief, Recovery and Reform. His Social Security Act, introduced in August 1935, provided financial aid for the unemployed and aged and made provisions for maternal and child health services and public health care, representing a radical break with the traditional American emphasis on self-reliance. The most important part of his program was work relief, which promoted the principle of relief for work done rather than a dole. Vast programs had been set up. The most extensive and controversial was the Works Progress Administration, in which up to three million unemployed men and women were hired at 'security wages' to work on jobs related to their skills, from constructing highways, buildings, schools and parks to writing books, plays and music.

The money to fund the New Deal program was raised by increased taxes. Predictably, it attracted hostility from the very quarters that had protested most loudly against a 'dole'. Stead, extremely impressed by Roosevelt's achievements, was taken aback by what she saw as a peculiarly American hostility towards social welfare recipients. In her article 'America' she remarked: 'In England the workers are regarded by the upper classes as necessary vermin or good imbeciles ... but here your successful middle classes display a great hatred of the workers, a strange burning bitterness.'

Perhaps, she mused, the emphasis on civilised behaviour in Britain served merely to conceal the class war there.

> In England the upper classes try to prevent the workers from
> wanting food, clothing and warmth by praising fortitude, by
> teaching that money is the root of all evil, by teaching that
> it is wrong to speak ill of your neighbour or think ill
> (advantageous for politicians and persons coated with scandal
> in high places), and by pretending to worship the classics,
> good form, delicacy, retirement, pastoral poetry and gardens.
> But here where the love of money is brutally outspoken and
> crassly advertised, no illusions are offered to the workers: they
> see quite plainly, through numerous scandals ... that it is all a
> scramble for boodle and nothing else.

In *I'm Dying Laughing*, Emily Wilkes points out that the virtue Americans made of success had left them psychologically unprepared for the terrible Depression in their country. They had learnt to regard themselves as winners: how could they be losers?

We're Americans, we can't fail, some sort of covered wagon will get us through; yet we see lean and tattered misery, the banks failed ... dust-storms which used to be farms bowling along the roads covering the corpses of crows and men; and we despair, despair. ... We came over in rowboats and founded the USA, we beat the old inhabitants into the dust, we won the West, and now we starve. It isn't right.[14]

★   ★   ★

Stead had not been excited about coming to New York. They had left behind a pleasant flat, with some fine possessions assembled over the last six years, and good friends. Worst of all, it had been a traumatic and ignominious departure.

At first, she found the city streets ugly; she missed the old buildings of Europe. But it took only three weeks for her to acknowledge that Manhattan had charm. 'There are hundreds of quiet spots, plenty of streets, dark, sweet, romantic, with their own atmospheres, streets like the quiet alleys of Mayfair, like old Paris, like Naples.'[15]

To her relief, Bill managed to organise accommodation for his mother with old German relatives. The arrangement was inexpensive, and Rosa Blech was happy. She was only 66, but had become quite weak. She would soon have her beautiful long white hair cut short, because her arms were too weak to plait and pin it up every morning. And her mind was wandering badly. 'She has completely forgotten the modern world,' Stead told Florence James, 'and has retreated some thirty-five years into the old days. She doesn't even want to live with Bill now, completely cheerful and rejuvenated in a circle of kaffee-klatsch old girls. This has also made us both more cheerful.'[16]

After installing Rosa, they spent a week with old friends, Sam and Riva Putnam, in their dilapidated timber house near Lambertville, New Jersey. Sam Putnam, their translator friend from Paris days, had been back in the States for two years. He too was shocked to see America in depression, and had become a stalwart communist.[17] For Stead, the brief stay in the countryside was just what she needed after the tension of the previous weeks.

I was a different person out there, mad with energy from morning to night. We came straight back to mad Manhattan and I was dazed the first day and ill for two days after with the nervous shock.[18]

To her, humans were basically animals: they had a natural habitat and suffered when they were removed from it. She considered that her body responded badly to cold northern hemisphere winters and that she was happiest when she spent time in the country. Until the visit to Lambertville she had prided herself on adapting rapidly to new cities; now it seemed that the adjustment had been only superficial.

They found a two-room flat in an old stone house on a quiet street downtown. It was cheap because the street contained factories and warehouses; they were the only residents. Stead liked the large airy rooms, the French windows and the fancy plaster ceilings. Not until darkness descended did they discover the other reason for the low rent: it swarmed with cockroaches.

In the evenings, Stead and Blech went on long walks, observing the ethnic mixes and the street life. One evening, walking along 18th Street, Stead was attracted to a neon sign hanging outside an apartment building which advertised toy and puppet makers. Fascinated, she thought she would like to write a story about puppets. But this meant knowing more about the art of puppetry. She and Blech knocked on the door and introduced themselves to puppeteer Kunz and his wife. From Kunz, Stead learnt the principles of marionetting, staging, lighting and stringing.[19] The son of a toymaker, Kunz looked a bit like a woodcut puppet himself, Stead fancied. He told them how he had fled from Nazi Germany with his large family of puppets after the burning of the Reichstag.[20]

He made them several string puppets. Their favourite was Nello the clown: a little wooden man, thirteen and a half inches high, dressed in a yellow silk pantaloon dress, whom they named after the trapezist Gianello, in Edmund de Goncourt's *Les Frères Zemganno*. Their other favourite was lisping Lucy, who called herself 'Loothy'. The puppets would remain a hobby for the next twenty years. Stead became quite skilled at working Nello's eleven strings, and was delighted when children almost believed Nello was real, without her attempting to hide his strings behind curtains. She and Bill would write each other absurd notes from or about Nello:

> Nello the Famous Clown is the author of a novel *Don't Spit on the Old Ladies*, which he describes as six characters in search of a hand-out. "It had a succès de steam," says the author, "and sold at least five copies, including the six I sent to my friends."[21]

The Kunzes and their workshop-apartment, bursting with puppets and toys, would be the inspiration for Waldemar and Dorothea Block in *The People with the Dogs*.

★　★　★

Blech and Stead had fled to New York with a couple of suitcases, no more. Their living conditions were stark. Having left all their possessions behind in London, they had no heart for acquiring new things, and they did not intend to settle in New York. For the time being they were making do with one plate, a double saucepan, a milk-measure-plus-lemon-squeezer, a coffee jar and two cups with saucers —all from Woolworth.

At first, because of the bank scandal, Bill insisted that they should keep a low profile. They hardly saw a soul during their first month in New York, and their home address was kept secret from all except a couple of trusted friends. The need for secrecy effectively put an end to any plans on the part of D. Appleton-Century to promote their new author with interviews. 'The three most intimate things have taboo written on them,' Stead told Florence James. 'The dear old Bank which went kerflooey and can't . . . be dragged into reminiscences, my family situation and my politics.'[22] Communists were not published by D. Appleton-Century; nor was America as broadminded as Europe about unmarried couples.

Stead could have done with some publicity: Americans believed in self-promotion. But she was shy, as usual, and felt scarcely presentable. American middle-class women surprised her by their smartness; there was even more good-quality clothing in New York than in Paris. And this business-oriented environment meant that one had to look well dressed to be taken seriously. She and Blech decided it was worth the investment for her to go out and 'splurge' on a smart coat and shoes. The purchases made her feel guilty but better equipped to 'fool the world'.[23]

It was worrying to have no income. Stead's last two royalty cheques had gone on London rent and the boat fare to America. Peter Davies, though he now insisted on first names, had not paid an advance for *The Beauties and Furies*. Stead was bitter about this, but too shy to raise the subject.

Since Davies was so casual about payment, Stead was extremely grateful, she told Florence, that she had a 'bozo' to keep her. 'As it is, a shred of honor keeps me from getting any clothes out of Bill's bank account and thus keeps me out at elbow.'[24] Apart from the small and irregular income from royalties, she had not earned any money since the end of 1934, when she stopped working at the bank for good.

Blech did not find work. Business was slow, the stockmarket depressed. After the Travelers' Bank disaster, he was more disillusioned than ever by the world of finance. But he still had a mild interest in the wheat business, and one option was to resort to his old backstop. Alf Hurst was wanting to set up an arbitraging business in Canada; for a while it looked as if they might be leaving for there any day. Blech longed to be back in Europe, but until they heard the outcome of the court case in France, they could not contemplate returning; and with war threatening in Europe and the Pacific, the couple were better off where they were. Bill even talked about Australia. But the trip was prohibitively expensive, Bill hated travelling, and Christina was sure he would not be happy so far from Ruth, his mother and friends.

Mollie and Ruth were also back in New York. Bill kept his address secret from them at first, telling them he was mostly in Washington and Philadelphia, looking for work.

Mollie told Blech she was thinking of a separation. Ironically, Stead felt ambivalent about divorce just then. She was afraid that her resident's status as well as her literary reputation might be affected if she were named in a divorce suit. America was far more puritanical than Europe and her tourist visa, valid for only six months at a time, was somewhat precarious. She told Florence James, her one confidante:

> It's my private belief that Bill and Mollie have arranged not to divorce so as not to give Ruth anxiety while she is growing up and at high-school. I only assume this, but it seems the most logical answer to all the paradoxes of the affair. But I am not discussing anything of this sort with Bill—at least not at present, while he is out of a job and my literary success is not yet established.[25]

Christina had lost the faith in Bill she had enjoyed in the early days of their relationship. Now, in her insecurity and frustration, she told Florence, 'When I am established, I can think of my independence—it will be too late, but I haven't much to grumble about in this life: I had a great streak of luck.'

Mollie's talk of separation turned out to be as hollow as ever. Two months later, Stead reported wearily:

> The lethargic lady makes no move towards divorce. Bill sees the little girl every few days, takes her to the pictures and so forth but does not go up to the apartment and doesn't meet the lady: it seems my coming to the land of the free and the home of the brave was a great surprise to her. I don't know exactly what she's waiting for ...[26]

*   *   *

Bill was now 41, and he longed to spend his days doing something that really interested him. His private desire was to write—historical books, fiction or non-fiction, that required the research he so loved—but he lacked confidence. He wrote easily, but suspected that good talkers made bad writers.[27] Christina may have pointed out that this was not so of her father; she certainly encouraged Bill to follow his yearnings. The problem was income.

Stead felt that their unsettled existence made it difficult for her to write anything sustained, and she toyed with the idea of a play. She read about a playwriting course, but it was too expensive. ('We couldn't bring ourselves to peel $10 off the pile.'[28]) She thought of writing more short stories, and asked Florence James to forward a book left behind in London. Stead had found Georges Polti's *Thirty-Six Dramatic Situations*, in which he outlined the thirty-six plots on which he claimed all literature was based, a great inspiration.[29]

She briefly thought of going back to Paris manuscripts originally intended to form part of a trilogy with *The Beauties and Furies*.[30] She had written four or five chapters of *The Student of Naples*, and thought it could be 'worked up into a really fine story'. But she was bored by these old manuscripts.[31]

By November, Stead was making notes for a project that filled her with enthusiasm: a novel about the Paris bank. She had been thinking of this for years and making notes; now she had time. It was by far her most ambitious project to date. From the beginning, she had high hopes for this novel.

★   ★   ★

Blech was sending testimonies about his role in the bank to his lawyer in France. What saved him was that he had rented the London flat in his name. This was taken as evidence that he was officially domiciled in England and therefore not closely associated with the bank at the time of its collapse. It was a fortunate twist of fate, for he had wanted to put the flat in Stead's name for income-tax purposes.

At the end of September Stead and Blech spent an evening with the Neideckers, who were still in New York. 'It was quite a reunion after all these months,' Christina told Florence. 'However, it was purely a friendly call: Bill does not intend to go into business with or through them.' The letter indicated no hint of resentment or anger; she and Bill found Neidecker as charming as ever. He told them that the court proceedings were expected to take some time.

> Pete has acted with real gallantry towards everyone ever connected with him, including his two brothers, despite their official positions. As to Bill, he has only been mentioned on a par with the rest of the office-staff, which is perfectly correct as he held no position. In any case, Pete has stated in his

evidence that Bill knew nothing of the bank's condition and "began going away from them from June 1934." This is a fact and makes things easier for Bill.[32]

According to Peter Neidecker, after Blech's resignation in May 1935, he and his brothers had struggled on a few more weeks, then paid the employees a month's salary and taken flight. Neidecker claimed that he himself had not been aware how little cash was left in the bank, and that his brother Aubrey had not known about certain losses. The books were 'in a perfectly fantastic state'.

In October, when they saw the Neideckers again, Stead asked Peter Neidecker if he would mind her writing a novel set in the Paris bank. He apparently gave her his 'full and glad permission' to write everything she knew.[33] He probably never imagined that she knew as much as she did.

★   ★   ★

At the same time, Stead was collecting material about her present life for a possible future novel set in the States. She was fascinated by American social relations, and though she did not know it then, this would be the subject of *Letty Fox*, a novel published in 1946, which explores and satirises American ruthlessness and conformism, sexual conventions and so-called radicalism.

American society was utterly different from English. Social divisions were 'harder, crueller and there is no joking about them'. She was shocked to learn that Paul Robeson, who was feted in London's social circles, was shunned in New York by all except bohemian and communist society.[34]

Middle-class New York seemed obsessed with social correctness. When Stead first read the newspaper advertisements, she giggled admiringly, presuming that 'the advertisers were kidding the world', but she soon realised that the message was serious enough. She cut out and filed examples of mindless advertisements and letters in women's magazines.

Though Blech assured her it was an awesomely complex business, Stead insisted that she could boil down 'social correctness' to four basic principles: '1. Be Anglo-Saxon. 2. Be hideously rich. 3. Buy and dress with a superfluity unknown to European women. 4. Go to the places mentioned, like the Gold Room at the Gotham.[35]

★   ★   ★

Their first foray into New York 'society' was a large fundraising banquet for the Communist Party held in early October. That evening, Stead and Blech met two genial and passionate men who would become lifelong friends. One was Mike Gold; the other Harry Bloom.

Mike Gold, just back from a holiday in France after the Paris Writers' Congress, greeted Stead enthusiastically. (He had read her *Left Review* article, in which she had written about 'irresistible Mike'.) He was in good spirits: on the boat going to the Congress he had met the woman he was to marry, a French woman living in America. Years later, Stead would work the shipboard romance into *I'm Dying Laughing*.[36]

In the heady, politicised atmosphere of the mid Thirties, Gold was widely regarded as the embodiment of the Proletarian Hero. Stead described him to her brother as 'the Yankee "tribune of the people", a local Maxim Gorki, known from coast to coast by lumberjacks and dockhands'.[37] His 1930 bestseller, *Jews Without Money*, a thinly fictionalised portrayal of his childhood in the Jewish immigrant Lower East Side, was generally hailed as a model of proletarian literature.[38]

Mike Gold, born Iztok Isaac Granich, was 42 that year. The eldest son of a Romanian father and a Hungarian mother, he had changed his name, unofficially, to Mike Gold, after an old man who had fought in the Civil War on the Union side. Like Bill Blech, Gold was obliged to leave school in his early teens. A few years later, influenced by the Bolshevik Revolution, his hero John Reed and the journal the *Masses*, he became a communist radical. In 1921 he had joined the editorial staff of the *Liberator*, the sequel to the *Masses*, suppressed by the government because of its anti-First-World-War stance. In 1926 he became a founding editor of the *New Masses*.

He was the type of man women found extremely appealing: a politically committed writer, a man of action, handsome in an unkempt sort of way, and with considerable personal charm. Joseph Freeman, fellow *Liberator* editor, paints this portrait of the younger Gold:

> To us Mike Gold appeared to be the outstanding "proletarian"
> of the group. He affected dirty shirts, a big, black, uncleaned
> Stetson with the brim of a sombrero; smoked stinking,
> twisted, Italian three-cent cigars, and spat frequently on the
> floor ... These "proletarian" props were as much a costume
> as the bohemian's sideburns and opera cape ... His assumed
> *naiveté*, dark, animated face and deep laughter, and his ironic
> mode of speech won people easily.[39]

Mike Gold married soon after Stead met him, and became (according to a close friend) 'an exemplary paterfamilias'.[40] The transformed Gold would be the model for Jean Frère, the brotherly comrade in *House of All Nations*. His physical description is completely Mike Gold:

> His variable, unaffected voice had the low-pitched rich, somber, or sentimental tones of an old-fashioned oboe, or became fresh and hopeful as a schoolboy's. He had a dark broad face . . . a dark, rosy skin, shining dark eyes and a rather large, but well-formed mouth, with the lower lip pouting often . . . He had extremely thick long curly coarse brown hair, growing low and irregularly on the broad forehead. When he smiled his eyes went into slits the shape of snowshoes and his mouth elongated like a longbow over his regular white teeth. He was thickset with a short thick neck, a large widespread nose, with a faintly Negroid air.[41]

We detect the narrator's warmth. Elisabeth, who became Mrs Granich, recalls that in the early days of her marriage Christina seemed 'more than keen on Mike', such that she wondered whether they had once been lovers.[42] Her conjecture is revealing: though probably unfounded, it points to an aspect of Stead's behaviour which was becoming increasingly evident—her flirtatiousness.

Mike Gold introduced Blech and Stead to his friend Harry Bloom, a tall, kind-looking man with small blue eyes and a hearty laugh. Thirty-five that year, Harry (actually Aaron) was born in New York to Lithuanian parents. As a youth, he had been active in the Industrial Workers of the World, the IWW (popularly known as the Wobblies), an exuberant and lawless section of the socialist Left whose ideology rested almost exclusively on the notion of 'sabotage'. A pharmacist, Bloom ran a drugstore at Brighton Beach, just east of Coney Island, which had a large Russian Jewish community. Because he always seemed to be patching up members of Brighton's warring gangs, his friends called him 'the Doc' or 'the Fixer'.

Observing him that first evening, Stead imagined, in her fanciful way, that he saw himself as Mike Gold's protector, his 'fidus Achates'.[43] Bloom was hearty and strong, whereas Gold, a diabetic and epileptic, was often ill—though he did not allow this to curtail his activities. Harry Bloom's brotherly loyalty towards men he loved—Mike Gold and later Bill Blech—strongly appealed to Stead. Ever since adolescence she had tended to idealise male friendship: to her, Harry Bloom would always be the 'treue Heinrich', after the faithful servant of the 'Frog Prince' in the Grimms' story by that name.

Stead flirted with both Gold and Bloom. Harry Bloom, a married man with two children, responded equally flirtatiously when his wife was not around.[44] As much as she admired fraternal loyalty, Stead had little sense of loyalty to other women.

In *The People with the Dogs*, Al Burrows is a pharmacist with a 'great joyous melodious laugh', nicknamed 'Al-the-Fixer'. His wife is jealous, and with good reason.[45]

* * *

They were sociable times, those Popular Front years, from May 1935 to the outbreak of the Second World War—and the sense of solidarity was greatly reinforced by the Spanish Civil War. Writers, generally isolated, had never seen the like and never would again. Until the war brought it all to a standstill, there were innumerable fundraising gatherings—rallies, public banquets, parties in people's homes.

The notion of a broad leftwing Popular Front was energetically promoted by communist parties around the world. Just before the Paris Writers' Congress, the American Communist Party had held the First American Writers' Congress in New York. It saw the establishment of the League of American Writers, which was broader and less sectarian in scope than the John Reed Clubs, founded in 1929 expressly to encourage proletarian writers. Stead and Blech would become League members in June 1937.

Soon after the October banquet, Mike Gold took Blech and Stead to the office of the *New Masses*, at No. 31 East 27th Street, to meet the editors: Joseph North, Joshua Kunitz, Herman Michelson and Stanley Burnshaw. Mike Gold was a committed associate, but fully occupied with his 'Change the World' column for the *Daily Worker*, the communist daily.

The name, the *New Masses*, implied a continuity with the old *Masses*, founded in 1911. In fact, its editorial direction had veered away from that of its predecessor. The *Masses* editors—Max Eastman, John Reed and Floyd Dell—had been lofty romantics, literary radicals who, although socialists, were not prepared to subordinate art to politics. Now Reed was dead, Dell was a disillusioned bohemian; and Max Eastman had become disenchanted with Stalinism and deplored the way the *New Masses* swam 'in the stream of pro-Soviet fanaticism'.[46]

Though it was not officially the organ of the Communist Party, the *New Masses* was the principal communist weekly in America, and most of its associates were Party members. The magazine's business manager was William Browder, brother of Earl Browder, who was General Secretary of the CPUSA. By the mid Thirties, the *New Masses* had become less sectarian, in the spirit of the Popular Front. Hoping to promote proletarian literature, it had recently published a number of distinguished non-Party writers: Theodore Dreiser, Sherwood Anderson, John Dos Passos, Edmund

Wilson, Erskine Caldwell, James Farrell and Ernest Hemingway.

One of the editors whom Blech and Stead met for the first time that day was to become another lifelong friend. The 'neat, limber young man with clear large appraising eyes' they first saw quietly working at his desk in the corner was Stanley Burnshaw, 30 that year and a talented poet and literary critic.[47]

Burnshaw's association with the *New Masses* was comparatively recent and not without ambivalence. He and Michelson were the only editors at that time who were not Party members, and he was often embarrassed by the dogmatism of the *New Masses* and the in-fighting. He was uneasy about the magazine's 'narrow, mechanical approach' to literature.[48] And 'secretly bored by events in the Soviet Fatherland', he was more interested in the effects of the Roosevelt work relief and distress relief programs at home. The *New Masses* had been critical of Roosevelt's reformism, which it saw as a last-ditch attempt to save the free enterprise system and stave off the inevitable and pressing economic revolution.

★   ★   ★

Proletarian literature dominated the literary scene in the mid to late Thirties. It was partly for this reason that Stead was so excited about her Paris bank novel. This novel would be ideologically correct: it would expose the sordid machinations of fraudulent capitalists. Later, she would realise that it was perhaps 'revolutionary' literature, but it was not 'proletarian' literature. From London, she would write to Stanley Burnshaw in October 1936, tongue in cheek:

> Everyone is still waiting with baited breath for *the* left novel. It can't be mine, as there is no member of the lower classes in my bank novel and even—I think this shows the highest moral courage—one of my chief moral heroes is a blueblooded *Count*.

What exactly was proletarian literature? It was a popular term, not confined to the extreme Left, though in the States its main champion was the *New Masses*. In 1935, Clifford Odets' one-act strike play *Waiting for Lefty* was a Broadway hit and considered good proletarian literature. That same year, Mike Gold and five comrades brought out an anthology, *Proletarian Literature in the United States*,[49] with fiction, drama, poetry and literary criticism. The writers of the future were workers, they declared. In the transition period, de-gentrified middle-class sympathisers were needed to show the workers the way. As subject matter, it was assumed that proletarian writers would certainly be 'more interested in unemployment, strikes, the fight against war and fascism, revolution and counter-revolution than in nightingales, the stream of the middle-class unconscious, or love in Greenwich Village'. (This last was a dig at editor Floyd Dell, who had always maintained that Freudian science and psychosexual themes were as important as the class struggle.)

There were endless battles over critical tenets and judgements. Mike Gold's views were among the more dogmatic. According to him, writers should not invent 'precious silly little agonies': there was drama enough in the 'suffering of the hungry, persecuted and heroic millions'. The new literature must be 'functional' and 'eschew verbal acrobatics'. Condemned were writers of the ilk of Proust and Dostoevski; indeed, Proust was scornfully designated the 'master-masturbator of the bourgeois literature'.[50] He did not fit the ideal of the proletarian writer: a smoking, drinking. robust man who slashed out his sentences with a salty disregard for the niceties of style.

> He writes in jets of exasperated feeling and has no time to polish
> his work. He is violent and sentimental by turns ... He is a
> Red but has few theories. It is all instinct with him ... His
> "spiritual" attitudes are all mixed up with tenements, factories,
> lumber camps and steel mills, because that is his "life".[51]

Modernist experimentation, interior monologue, exploration of the unconscious were well buried in the leftwing rhetoric of the Thirties. It is probably no coincidence that *House of All Nations*, written in this atmosphere, is Stead's most 'male' book: there is no sense of a woman's world behind the scenes or a female writer behind the narrative. In the Thirties, successful women writers wrote like men. Among the women associated with the *New Masses* was Josephine Herbst, an intrepid reporter (she was to report from Spain during the Civil War), whose novels were praised by Hemingway. Genevieve Taggard's poetry spoke of the necessity for self-discipline, the need to master the passions. Ruth McKenney, who was nine years younger than Stead and later became a close friend, would be ashamed of her popular stories about her family, such as *My Sister Eileen*, published in 1938, but proud of the nonfictional *Industrial Valley* (1939), about the struggles of the Akron rubber workers. Stead would admire her proletarian epic *Jake Home* (1943), about a communist labour organiser who tours the country to campaign on behalf of Sacco and Vanzetti.[52]

The standard proletarian novel formula was a conflict between capitalists and workers, which nearly always ended in defeat for the workers, but brought about the politicisation of several worthy characters. The 1935 *New Masses* prize for the best proletarian novel went to Clara Weatherwax for her sentimental and clichéd novel *Marching! Marching!* about a sawmill strike. By 1936, the *New Masses* was publishing occasional essays critical of such restrictive formulae.

Neither John Dos Passos' *USA* trilogy, which showed the degradation of character in modern materialistic America, nor Theodore Dreiser's *Tragic America*, with its hopeful belief in socialism, was considered a model of revolutionary or proletarian literature. The *New Masses* had to wait until 1939 in order to be able to cite a major novel to illustrate their literary creed. *The Grapes of Wrath* would not only win Steinbeck the Pulitzer Prize; according to the *New Masses*, it possessed all the qualities of good proletarian literature. Steinbeck had personally experienced 'duststorms and tenant farmers and tractors and automobiles and hoovervilles and cotton picking and fruit picking', and he wrote with an understanding of economic forces.[53] The book even had the unusual virtue of optimism; Marxist critics were continually bemoaning the pessimism of most proletarian novels.

Christina Stead's own writing scarcely exemplified swift action, clear form, and the eschewal of verbal acrobatics, yet she spoke up for the vigour and ideology of proletarian literature. Like the indomitable Blech, like most of their friends, she was quite persuaded that good writing went together with socialism. In her article 'America', she commented: 'Art should flourish here when a labour or socialist party gains ground. Corruption can't produce good literature.'

To some extent it was more a matter of peer pressure than personal conviction. Privately she told Stanley Burnshaw that 'party politics cramps a poetic mind'.[54] But in the Thirties, whenever she wrote for a communist readership, Stead used the standard rhetoric. In her notes 'America'—possibly intended for the *New Masses*—she declared that new founts in American writing and intellectual life would certainly come from the working classes and their sympathisers, because they were dynamic and vigorous, whereas the middle classes (with their 'habits of babbits')[55] were defeated, class-bound and stale. She speculated that this was because the working classes, living in ghettoes, had not intermingled, whereas 'in the middle-classes races have been absorbed to their undoing'—a dubious theory which reflected contemporary eugenicist arguments.

In notes entitled 'Workers and Writers', which seem to be notes for a talk that she gave at a Party function in London in late 1936, Stead reasoned that workers needed education, leisure and an income in order to write. In Soviet Russia, where the workers were given payment and recognition and an education 'surpassing the education of our own middle-class', there was a great flowering of proletarian talent. In America, she told her English audience, Roosevelt had introduced the Works Progress Administration, which gave workers the basic wage in order to build roads, bridges and public gardens or write historical records, novels and plays. Having seen several of these plays, she could 'say faithfully that nothing so splendid has been seen on the English stage for a hundred years and more'.

> The American stage and fiction and memorial writing is now witnessing a renaissance seen nowhere else in the world, not even in France. Moreover, the workers on this basic wage have suddenly forgotten all ideas that they are aesthetes, amateurs, delicate, sensitive plants: they realise they are workers and they march in processions, with placards, union by union, trade by trade, art by art, with the furworkers, the builders, the carpenters. [56]

From today's perspective, the communist rhetoric of the Thirties may seem extraordinarily naive. But as it was the prevailing discourse among Stead's friends and associates, she found it almost impossible to stand aside from it. 'Proletarian literature', very much a Thirties' product, would virtually die with the advent of World War II.

* * *

At the beginning of November 1935, Stead and Blech moved to a large, handsomely furnished room, upstairs, in a brownstone house in Brooklyn. Quiet, dignified Remsen Street ended on the Esplanade, from where there was a glorious view of the Wall Street pinnacles across the East River. The French owner of No. 34 was choosy about her tenants, several of whom were young Princeton graduates, but was very welcoming when Blech (always the house-hunter) told her that his wife was an 'English writer'. Stead would always speak French with the landlady. [57]

She was busy making notes on her banking novel, then called *A Man With No Luck*. The blackmailer, the man who brought the bank down, was intended to be the main character. ('A stupid blackmailer, an unconscious hypocrite, who fancying he is motivated by virtue, is in reality activated by fear and envy.'[58]) Later, Jules Bertillon (Peter Neidecker) became the central character, and the blackmailer quite a minor one. When Florence James wrote that the title was too gloomy in that period of crisis, Blech suggested *The Blackmailer*. Then the novel would briefly be called *The Revolving Hive*. At the last moment, delighted with the whorehouse analogy, Stead would call the novel *House of All Nations*.

She later destroyed the notes and early drafts of *House*—just as she did with her other novels—but a brief record of the preparatory stages of writing has survived. [59] In 'Journal of *The Blackmailer*', written in June 1936, Stead described the immense amount of work she undertook before beginning the novel proper. First she wrote character sketches of all seventy-two characters. She wrote a detailed portrait of Peter Neidecker and, with Bill's help, made notes on Neidecker's characteristic remarks. She sketched the different intrigues to be woven into the narrative, several of which would be dropped in the course of writing and revision. Based on its actual counterpart, she drew up an intricate plan of the structure of the fictional bank, its branches and associated companies. All these notes were written in French, with the idea that it would help her recapture the atmosphere of Paris. This might explain the occasional lapses into French syntax, which several critics would observe.

At first she intended to set the story in 1934–5, the last few months of the Travelers' Bank, and she spent days in the New York public library reading French newspapers from the period. Several months later, at Bill's suggestion, she put the action back to 1931–2, the period that saw Hitler's rise to power and general international financial collapse. This involved further research.

★   ★   ★

At weekends, they saw friends. Once they visited Harry and Ruth Bakwin, wealthy friends from their Paris days, who had a large country estate with a private lake at Kitchawan, up the Hudson River. Harry Bakwin (the 'Doctor from New York' in *The Salzburg Tales*) was the Chief Pediatrician at New York's Bellevue hospital; he and his wife were art connoisseurs and had a private gallery in their New York home.

Another time they took the bus to Lambertville and stayed again with the Putnams. This time, the atmosphere was tense: Sam Putnam was showing the effects of a 'recent burst of drink'[60] and Riva was upset. The couple invested all their hopes in their son, now 10. Stead would describe the domestic situation, the alcoholism and the prodding of the child, something she vehemently disliked, in her story 'The Right-Angled Creek'.

By December, they knew enough people to host a large party on Christmas Eve. Stead bought more glasses from Woolworth and their landlady lent them jugs and bowls, but they could not bring themselves to skimp on their Christmas tree. The Norwegian spruce tree touched the thirteen-foot ceiling and they decorated it with childlike zest. They concocted a heady punch: egg-nog and cognac with whisky. They told themselves it would be 'no end economical', because no-one would be able to drink much of it. However their guests knocked it back, and 'in between times, these hard-boiled gentry drank the whisky neat'.[61]

Christmas in New York was splendid. It had snowed and the white streets were aglow with lights and Christmas trees. Fifth Avenue was 'like a Hans Christian Andersen fairy-tale'. Sixty thousand destitutes were given a Christmas dinner at the city's expense. In stark contrast was the conduct on Wall Street. Bill, who was perhaps briefly employed on contract work, came home and told Christina all about it. Christina, much amused, passed the details on to Florence James:

> On Christmas Eve, all is blue in Wall Street. Every house offers "wassail" (it is called) to its customers and friends and "all bets are off"—the telephonist sits on the boss's knee and drinks from his private flask, as it were. In fact, Bill said the girls were all horribly drunk and frankly obscene: New York girls are none too reticent even on water! It is your duty to go round and drink the wassail of the houses you know: otherwise they think (after being serious as stone images all the year) that you aren't a right guy. Dear little Bill had about eleven whiskies in the course of the day, but his hard-drinking friends (they finish off every afternoon with highballs) had notched up about 47 apiece when he left. Bill arrived home precisely at five (his appointed hour), ineffably gay, twinkling, seraphic, but perfectly steady, knowing what time it was, and with a load of goods for the party. I realised he had character![62]

They spent Christmas Day with the Bakwins, at Kitchawan. The lake had frozen over and Harry gave Stead her first lesson in ice-skating: 'I looked nice enough in borrowed gear, but did I bump!' She walked in the snow and amused herself with jigsaws and patience, while the others endlessly played bridge. Harry Bakwin drove them home in a snowstorm—'a ghostly ride at midnight'.

* * *

Life in New York frustrated them both. Blech's old friends now seemed like 'stick-in-the-muds' to him after his years in Paris, and the Wall Street world no longer held the least attraction. Stead felt isolated among people who seemed to talk about nothing but business or politics.

In the New Year, she felt thoroughly depressed when she received the proofs of *The Beauties and Furies* from London. Even at this late stage, Peter Davies was wanting major changes. To Stead's horror, he was suggesting that she 'cut out all the sections relating in any way to ordinary life and make it an "idyll"'.[63] She was heartily tired of the novel: it had originally been intended as part of a trilogy and now she wondered whether it really stood on its own. On the other hand, she rationalised, Davies had reservations about everything she had ever written. With every manuscript, his 'little fake compliments' had been accompanied by a 'library of objections'. She now believed he had made her re-write far too much: not only had it set her progress back at least eighteen months; it had also made her books mere 'rehashes'.[64]

There was still no publication date for *The Beauties and Furies*, and no advance. When Florence James had commented, six months earlier, that Davies lacked business acumen, Stead had defended him loyally: he had picked her 'out of the gutter'; he had arranged the contract with D. Appleton-Century.[65] But now she complained bitterly.

Stead was greatly cheered by a letter from Nettie Palmer, who mentioned that Rebecca West had publicly praised her originality as a writer. This provoked in Stead a rare admission of her ambition.

> Rebecca West has been very generous to me, so have others:
> ... but although I am very sensible of the approval of Rebecca
> West and the others, I hope it means nothing yet: I hope to do
> very much better than anything I have yet done, I am very
> simple-minded, I only want one thing, I thirst to do something
> so good that there will be no denying it on anyone's part.

Further on in the same letter to Nettie Palmer, Stead allowed herself an equally rare outburst of frustration and bitterness:

> I'm very grateful to you for sometimes passing on remarks like
> that of Rebecca West: although I hope to do better, it
> encourages me a bit, for I really put some gristle into the "Seven
> Poor Men" and my New York friends haven't even read it: they
> are mostly fairly well off—and they have enough anyhow to
> invest in Robert Briffault's "Europa", Thomas Wolfe's "Of
> Time and the River" and other best-sellers—but they expect
> me, out of love and friendship, to give them my books! And I
> don't. I can't. So they pass the fact that I write up in silence,
> perhaps feeling slightly injured even that I haven't sent them my
> books, and sit and talk the whole evening about the stock-
> market or whatnot. It makes me simply furious: not that I
> expect to be an object of interest, but not ever to be able to talk
> about literature, or characterisation or any of the purely
> professional subjects that absorb a writer![66]

Later that month, Stead was asked whether she would act as first reader of unsolicited manuscripts for the *New Masses*. There was no payment, but Stead was curious to see behind the scenes at the magazine, and willingly agreed. Editor Stanley Burnshaw remembers her sitting quietly at her desk reading manuscripts several days a week. She kept it up for a couple of months.[67]

Unused to the sort of manuscripts she encountered, Stead at first thought she had discovered a 'nest of geniuses' of the Upton Sinclair-Emile Zola variety. By the third week she was bored by the same re-hashed themes: boss-exposures, unemployment-suicide thrillers, hunger stories.[68]

The winter was fierce that year, the coldest Stead had ever experienced. It gave her 'sleeping sickness'; Blech, thinner now, looked blue, moped and coughed. Stead insisted that there was 'no question of his traipsing through the snow and mud of the streets looking for business'.[69] He suggested they pack up and head south.

They spent five weeks in February and March in South Carolina and Alabama. The South, too, was wet and cold. Under grey, lugubrious skies, 'fearful dismal swamps' stretched for hundreds of miles, crossed by swollen, muddy rivers. But there was occasional sunshine—one day they even went without coats—and Blech's health began to improve.

Stead loved the first buds of spring, the magnolias in bloom, the scarlet-crested birds. But she was horrified by the 'race-hatred' which hung 'like a black pestilential cloud over the whole south'. While the negroes dressed in rags and suffered from skin diseases and bone deformations from malnutrition, the whites looked corrupt and decadent. A once-off splurge, a meal at Henry's, the most exclusive restaurant in Charleston, South Carolina, allowed Stead to observe the behaviour of the white élite, and she was repelled by the plantation owners, with their large 'whisky-drinking, lynch faces' and 'clear rockcrystal blue eyes'. The negro waiters had 'a polish and respectful ease of manner unequalled in any but the finest restaurants of Paris'.

> When speaking to the waiters these plantation-owners look sullenly at the table cloth and deliver themselves of their orders as if they had suddenly fallen into a trance. The women, all of the same breed, Anglo-saxon blue-eyed, painted like streetwalkers, with bad skins (the heat and strong drink) and empty clipped speech, behave in the same manner. The men behave towards the women with that caddish caressing regimental style which gives the bystander the notion that the woman concerned is their light o'love, and for all other (white) women they have a cold insulting calculating glance.[70]

It may have been while she was in the South that Stead read *Gone with the Wind*. Set in Georgia during the Civil War, a celebration of the white middle class, the novel—to Stead's disgust—won the Pulitzer Prize that year. It was to be the fastest-selling novel yet published in the United States, with a record of 50000 copies sold in one day.

D. Appleton-Century suggested to Stead she should aim more for the female market and include some sex in her next novel.

★   ★   ★

Back in New York in March, Stead reviewed William Saroyan's stories *Inhale and Exhale* for the *New Masses*. She ridiculed Saroyan's 'ludicrous philosophical pretensions' but added that when he wrote about what he knew best—'the foreign-born populations of America, and the pool parlours, barber shops, hobo young men'—he was 'the best of his generation'.[71] Her critical voice was becoming more assured.

She was proud to hear Blech deliver a fine speech to the Industrial Workers Organisation (IWO) in April, but her pleasure turned to dismay when she was pressed to say a few words herself. She protested vehemently, but ended up being 'led on to the platform like a lamb to the slaughter', whereupon she greeted the audience, unofficially, on behalf of socialist writers in Australia.[72] She was a poor speaker and knew it: she was much more comfortable to have Bill do the performing.

★   ★   ★

The most vigorous promoter of Christina Stead in America was Clifton Fadiman. An editor at Simon & Schuster, he was the *New Yorker*'s regular book critic, and at the age of 30, already well known for his wit and incisive criticism. Early in the spring of 1936, Blech arranged a meeting. Fadiman suggested drinks at the Lafayette, a popular watering-hole for intellectuals.

They got on extremely well. Blond and softspoken, Fadiman was mature for his age and confident in his judgements. In passing, he told them that he considered Malraux the best of the younger French writers. He asked them if they knew Ralph Fox: 'a born tale-teller with a great future in novels'. Christina Stead he called a 'genius', but predicted she would need four more books to make her name.[73]

In his eighties, Clifton Fadiman could still recall their meeting clearly:

Bill had, over the phone, asked me to look out for a short
Jewish man who would never win a beauty prize (or words to
that effect). The description was accurate enough. But it did not
prepare me for his non-stop and brilliant talk, his iconoclasm,
and a kind of aggressive charm. It did not take him long to tell
me about himself—that he was a cosmopolitan, a Marxist, and

that his father was the only Jewish general (could it have been
colonel?) in the United States army. At that time (I was young
and innocent) I thought him a genius, for he dominated—and
coruscatingly—the conversation, whereas Christina seemed
passive and mouselike, though only by comparison. In
retrospect, Bill seems to me now, though a remarkable man of
high energy and trenchant wit, to have been cast in a pattern
one met frequently in the Thirties. Horace Liveright, Maxwell
Bodenheim, Ben Hecht and many others typified it: lively
minds flawed by a vein of exhibitionism that verged on
charlatanism—though Bill was not guilty of the latter.

Christina was tall (though perhaps only so in contrast to Bill,
who was shorter than I, and I am only 5'8"), bony, with a worn,
somehow sad face. She looked older than her years ... But
—and this is pure subjective conjecture and you need not take it
seriously—the most salient fact about her was that her face and
figure (she was simply *not* a handsome or pretty woman) were
at war with what I really believe was her deepest wish—to be
loved romantically, almost in the nineteenth century tradition.
I know nothing about women's clothes but during the few times
we met, surely no more than 5 or 6 in all, I noticed that her
costume had something overdone and baroque about it, trailing
laces, fichus, *extras* of one sort or another, as if she were using
decoration to compensate for the plainness of her face.
Somehow I think of her colors as purple and yellowish white.

I do not remember our conversation but I suppose it revolved
around the two matters that engrossed many literary folk in the
Thirties—sex and political radicalism. Christina and Bill were
clearly free spirits on both counts. Their views (mainly voiced
by Bill, a professional talker) influenced and tempered my own
comparative innocence.

They made it clear that they were Balzacian heroes, ready like
Rastignac to conquer the world of thought, perhaps of action.
Of Christina Bill remarked, quite casually, "She hopes to be the
greatest of modern novelists." (These may not have been his
exact words.) Christina, whose manners were perfect (Bill's
were not) nevertheless did not dissent.[74]

It was an important meeting for all three; for Bill Blech it was a
turning point. Fadiman listened with rapt attention to his stories
and admonished him to write them down. He told Blech that one
of the directors of Simon & Schuster had a blueprint for a modern
Monte Cristo novel and was looking for someone to write it—
someone unusually erudite, with a firm grasp of modern finance.

Fadiman was convinced that Blech was the man. He invited them to his apartment to meet M. Lincoln Schuster.

He was right. Max Schuster *was* impressed. A note in Schuster's publishing files states that Blake (as Americans all called him) seemed to be the 'man of destiny' for the book.[75] He asked for an outline of the projected novel.

It was probably on the same occasion that Schuster, who had liked *The Salzburg Tales*, offered Stead a contract for her next three books. She felt honoured and excited. Rumour had it that Simon & Schuster never put out a book which sold less than 10 000 copies.

What followed was sweet indeed. D. Appleton-Century, on being told of the Simon & Schuster proposal, offered Stead unusually high rates to renew her contract with them. Simon & Schuster then matched the Appleton offer: $500. Stead did not hesitate. Appleton wrote asking her to reconsider. It was all very satisfying, and Stead was pleased to be less dependent on the 'slopoke in England'. In case Davies did not want to renew her three-book contract with him, Simon & Schuster offered to arrange something with the left-wing London publisher, Victor Gollancz.

A royalty cheque for *The Salzburg Tales* arrived from England: Stead gaily blew it all—£1.15s—on a dinner with Bill, Stanley Burnshaw and his wife Madeline. Hard up though they were, she and Bill, generous by nature, loved nothing better than a good meal with friends. Peter Davies renewed his contract, sending a cheque for $250, which mostly went on clothes for both of them.

'All things considered,' wrote Stead to Florence James, 'it is just as well I have moved about the way I have done.'

> An Australian writer has little chance of making any hit in
> London and New York, if writing from Australia. At the same
> time, when I have a sort of reputation and have published
> enough to have a little income on resales and short stories,
> I very much want to go back and write a novel of Australia
> —say Broken Hill, or Queensland, not the cities.[76]

Stead was beginning to feel optimistic about the future.

★   ★   ★

The Beauties and Furies came out in America in late April 1936, one week before its English launch. Reviewers were nonplussed. Some were put off by its 'verbal showiness', others by the strange mixture of the real and the fantastic, others by its lack of an obvious message. Harold Strauss commented in the *New York Times Book Review*: 'We are forced to praise in Miss Stead's work everything that we would ridicule as stilted, overambitious and pretentious in a less gifted writer.' The erudite allusions and love of words reminded him of Joyce.[77]

In the *New Masses*, Stanley Burnshaw reviewed the novel under the pseudonym J. G. Conant. He praised it as 'an intellectually lusty book' and 'a gorgeous reading experience', but added that the novel was certainly 'a fugitive from ready interpretation'.[78] What did it signify that Marpurgo, 'self-styled Trotskyite', and Oliver Fenton, 'avowed friend of the working class', are exposed at the end as counterfeits?

It was Clifton Fadiman, more than anyone either side of the Atlantic, who praised *The Beauties and Furies*, pronouncing it Stead's 'finest book to date'. It was flawed, he averred, like all her books.

Yet it discloses such streaming imagination, such tireless wit, such intellectual virtuosity that I cannot see how anyone who reads it carefully—and there is no other way to read it—can deny Miss Stead's position as the most extraordinary woman novelist produced by the English-speaking race since Virginia Woolf.[79]

7

'A Harmless Affair'

JUNE 1936–AUGUST 1937

THE TRAIN TRACKS out of Algeciras run perpendicular to the coast. In the distance, across the Strait of Gibraltar, are the ashy mountains of Morocco. It is early June 1936: the heat is already gathering for the day. At the dilapidated railway station, hammers and sickles decorate the doors and shutters. A tall fair rather red-faced woman and a short dark olive-skinned man struggle onto the railway platform, hot, flustered, with too many bags over their shoulders. Foreigners. The porter with them has several large trunks on his cart. Altogether there are thirteen pieces of luggage. 'Millionaires,' mutters the banana-seller looking on.[1]

Stead and Blech had left New York at the end of May, taken a ship to Gibraltar, and had just crossed the small bay to Algeciras, on the Spanish mainland. From there they travelled north to Ronda in a light antique train.

The ancient town of Ronda was perched on a narrow rock plateau in the Sierras. Between the craggy cliffs was a gorge a thousand feet deep, etched by the river Guadalevin and crossed, at different heights, by a graceful Moorish bridge and a sturdy Roman one. Stead was delighted by the views, the mountain weather ('cool in the shade, sunstroke out of it'), the peasant women in their black shawls, the laden donkeys plodding up and down the precipitous

207

trails.[2] Late afternoon thunderstorms would bring a burst of rain—
brief relief from the hot, dry weather.

*   *   *

Stead had had little more than a month to enjoy *The Beauties and
Furies* in the New York bookshops. Then she and Blech had left for
Spain. Despite the threat of war, they planned to stay in Europe.
Blech had not found work in New York; in Spain he was to set up a
business for Alf Hurst.

That political 'troubles' were expected soon had been obvious
even in Gibraltar, already a refuge for land-owning families in
flight. Ronda, Stead observed, looked 'ripe for a second Red
October'.[3] In the past, the town had been run by the landlords and
was known as 'the little Vatican': now it had a communist mayor
and the *ayuntamiento* (the local council chambers) buzzed with
political discussions among workers and peasants. White walls
were daubed with slogans painted in large red letters: '*Viva la
Revolución!*' '*Viva la Republica*', 'Who does not work, he shall not
eat', and 'Death to the priests and the friars!' The local churches,
monasteries and convents were covered with atheist insults; many
had been destroyed—either by pro-republican anarchists who saw
them as symbols of tyranny and superstition, or by anti-republican
agents provocateurs paid to intensify the crisis.[4] Stead had no sympathy with the priests who hurried by nervously, looking 'ugly,
bloated, out of countenance'.[5]

General elections in February 1936 had brought the republican
People's Front into power; since then Spain had been in turmoil.
The socialists and communists hoped for far-reaching social change,
but the government was weakened by concerted opposition from
landowners, monarchists, the Catholic middle class and the military. For months, the country had been paralysed by strikes and
intimidated by a wave of political murders.

On their walks in the cool of the evening, Blech and Stead
observed workers congregating in the fields for political meetings.
Others walked along the rooftops, ostensibly cleaning and weeding, but more likely, looking for positions to site machine guns.
Stead was reminded of *La Condition humaine*, in which Malraux
described the days before the Chinese revolution, when militia men
were pacing the roofs to keep watch.[6]

Spain was still quite feudal. The large rural estates were owned
by wealthy aristocracy, often absentee landlords, who treated their
labourers like slaves. In the face of the current sweeping agricultural
reform these landlords were abandoning their estates and emigrat-

ing to Portugal and France. This explained Alf Hurst's plan for Blech to buy an abandoned olive estate while they were cheap and to set up a business. He also thought of importing North African perfumes to Gibraltar, since that free port had become a landing place for rich Andalusians and Sevilleans.[7]

In *House of All Nations*, the novel Stead would draft in Spain, Henri Léon (modelled on Hurst) talks enthusiastically to Michel Alphendéry (Bill Blech) of his plans for investment in Spain:

"I'm for the people. If they look like putting any sort of order down there, I'm going down. I'm going to buy an estate there. Not too big. And I'll go to the government and I'll say, 'Friends, I'm friendly to your cause, I believe in you: I want to put my money in your country. It's a grand country, and I like the women.' (That'll move a Spaniard's heart!)" The genial gust blew round them. "How would you like to be in olives, Alphen? I'll buy a small olive plantation down near Malaga. And I've been looking into the perfume business ..."[8]

Alphendéry, a man who regularly spoke at workers' meetings and gave money to the French Communist Party, is not at all shocked by his friend's unseemly opportunism. On the contrary. He is excited by the prospect of following the bullfights. There are certainly no heroes in Stead's fiction.

Bill Blech too liked Spain and bullfights, and Ronda's Plaza de Toros was world famous. Did Blech worry about reconciling Alf Hurst's latest money-making venture with the aspirations of the struggling Spanish people's *Frente Popular*? The new Republican government, striving to bring about agrarian reform in a country racked with poverty and under-nourishment, did not need the incursion of foreign capital, with profits going out of the country.

Blech was running out of money. He had several dependants—including Stead now, who could not live off her small royalties. He urgently needed an income.

His poor health had been a refrain in Stead's letters for years, and like many of their contemporaries, they set great store by a 'change of air'. The five weeks in the American South apparently had not been enough of a break, for on their return Stead told Florence James: 'We are wondering if Bill, for the good of his soul, oughtn't to take a whole year off in a hot climate—provided that I sell anything at all on this new novel and that my new contract turns out as expected.'[9]

Why was Blech so 'exhausted'? Stead used the word often, about both of them. In all probability, Blech's problem was mild depression. For years he had felt frustrated and handicapped by the need to provide for three dependants, and limited by his lack of formal education. If he had hung on at the Travelers' Bank for six and a half years, it was due partly to inertia, but mostly to a lack of real options. In New York, he could not bring himself to return full-time to the cut-and-thrust world of finance. His friends considered him 'brilliant', and when he was interested in something he had quite extraordinary reserves of energy. But at present he was suffering from an unusual torpidity. Long ago—as a roly-poly impoverished Jewish son of immigrants in a ruthlessly capitalist, anti-semitic America—he had learnt to protect himself by cultivating a high degree of self-irony: laughing at himself, parodying himself. It was a trait that concealed his vulnerability, but tended to paralyse him for action.

In *House of All Nations*, Alphendéry is torn between his humiliating financial dependence on self-interested capitalists and the communist ideals exemplified by his friend Jean Frère. At one point in the novel, his turmoil is such that he is scarcely coherent, but characteristically he deals with his despair by viewing his situation in an ironic light.

He sat down in his room and knotted his handkerchief. "Which is better, the quicksands or the . . . volcano? Jules is the quicksands, Léon the volcano. Can I stand—why don't I strike out for myself—Jean said . . . "It's time you cut the painter and . . . cast off and—joined us. Too much wedded to luxury." And what luxury? The luxury of being hounded to death by madmen. Mad egotists . . . My life's a ghost life. My tombstone. Here lies Heinrich Heine, poet and freeman. Here lies Michel Alphendéry, twenty-five per cent capital levy. R.I.P. Or, Michel Alphendéry: he sold short. R.I.P. Unwept, unhonored, and unsung . . . I must have peace before I die.[10]

By the time Stead wrote this in 1936–7, Blech had freed himself from the quicksands of the Travelers' Bank only to become dependent once more on the goodwill of Alf Hurst, 'the volcano'. His situation was profoundly humiliating, and Stead felt it keenly.

At the end of *House of All Nations*, after the bank's collapse, Alphendéry tells a friend: 'I've given my whole life to this sterile business. I'm not a boy any longer . . . Maybe I'll get out of it some day.'[11] This was certainly Blech's own fervent hope. He wanted to get on with his Monte Cristo novel, to try his hand at writing. Many an author has dreamt of making a fortune, then retiring somewhere idyllic to write. For Blech, Alfred Hurst's wildcat schemes still seemed to offer this faint hope. That was why he and Stead were in Spain.

⋆ ⋆ ⋆

The Travelers' Bank court case was under way in Paris, which meant that Blech ran a degree of risk being back in Europe. As a precaution, he had changed his name, unofficially, to Will Blake. His mother, daughter and friends had been asked to write to him under that name, at Florence James' address in London. The only people to be told their Spanish address were James, who was forwarding their mail, and Alf Hursι. Before he left New York, Bill had told Mollie that he and Christina were sailing to Europe via Mexico in order to procure a divorce. (Mexican divorces, though not cheap, were notoriously easy to obtain.) Bill was hoping to discourage Mollie from following them to Europe.

Once again, they were involving Florence James in cloak-and-dagger games. Christina asked her to forward all letters addressed to Will Blake to 53 Calle de Espinel, where they were living, and all letters addressed to Christina Stead or William J. Blech to the Ronda Poste Restante. And would Florence herself please address all future letters to Mr and Mrs W. Blake? In the envelope, Christina enclosed letters from Bill to his mother and daughter, to be posted from England. She and Bill seemed to delight in intrigue and mystery.

⋆ ⋆ ⋆

It was soon clear that there was no question of doing business in Spain. Fortunately, their circumstances were eased by cheques from America. Stead was sent $250 by D. Appleton-Century as royalties from previous books and $500 by Simon & Schuster as an advance for her next three books. On the strength of this, she and Blech decided to spend the summer in Ronda, writing.

Once established in their comfortable lodgings, Stead plunged into her banking novel. She had been mulling it over for years and making notes for months: now she was ready to write. Conscious that in New York she had done no serious writing for almost a year, she worked at a furious pace. She had great hopes for this novel, to be published by New York's most enterprising publishing house. 'It looks exciting enough in its rough state,' she wrote to Florence James in mid July, 'and I hope Simon & Schuster will make a hit with it.'[12] She was enjoying writing 'off the bat'.[13] This time, she resolved, she would forgo the agony of endless revision.

In Ronda, Blake (as he would call himself from now on) made a start on his Monte Cristo novel. Inspired by that magnificent setting, he made the hero of *The World is Mine* a Spaniard: Don

Cristóbal Pinzón becomes the richest man in the world, yet he is determined to destroy the capitalist system. The story ends in 1936 with the ignominious death of the hero in Ronda: his remains are thrown into the Guadalevin, at the bottom of the gorge. This melodrama mixed financial intrigues and spirited adventures with high philosophy and Marxist economic theory. The first chapters were largely written in cafés, where Blake could observe the life around him. For him there was no beginner's block; he wrote as easily as he talked. Stead, quite envious, told Stanley Burnshaw, 'Bill is a born novelist: he dashes ahead, no going back, no scratching out. It's a gift.'[14]

They were living in a tailor's house in the Calle de Espinel, a narrow, lively street in the ancient merchant quarter. Their two rooms overlooked an inner courtyard where young women sat sewing by hand, singing as they worked. The day began with a breakfast of *churros*, *bunuelos*, oranges and roasted coffee. Between mid morning and early evening it was too hot to venture out. Stead closed the long shutters and typed. The lack of distractions was ideal: it reminded Stead of a Spanish convent (before the political troubles).

On 17 June, Stead noted in the diary she was keeping at the time that the 'blackmailer', her main character, was 'taking on rolls of flesh'. She was plunged in the world of her characters. 'To me they certainly now exist and converse with each other inaudibly, in my mind, even when I am thinking of something else,' she wrote in her diary.[15] In the evenings, she and Bill would discuss the personalities who had worked in the bank. Bill also wrote her out a summary of the relevant political and financial events between May 1931 and July 1932.

Years later, Stead would claim that she wrote *House of All Nations*—800 pages in all—in six weeks in Spain. Ronda, she would say by way of explanation, was her ideal habitat: a dry climate, on a rock base. In fact, though she certainly worked furiously at the first draft in the Calle de Espinel, the novel was not finally completed until the following summer—a year later.

House of All Nations was an extraordinarily ambitious novel. Stead's fourth book was far more realist than anything she had yet written; this time, she was determined to curb her excursions into the fantastic. She wanted it to be a revolutionary novel, a novel that exposed the paltry schemes of capitalist rascals. It was a world she knew well: just as Steinbeck had lived with the 'oakies', she had lived among bankers.

Her inspirations were Dickens' *Oliver Twist*, Thackeray's *Vanity Fair*, Tolstoy's *War and Peace*, Balzac's *Comédie humaine*, Malraux's

Les Conquérants—panoramic novels loaded with characters and fast changes from one scene to another. And, as usual, Stead turned to Shakespeare for guidance. 'One could suggest that the original English novel is *Hamlet*,' she noted in a paper she would deliver in 1939 on the 'many-charactered novel'.[16] She was also interested in contemporary novels that had been influenced by cinematic techniques. (*House of All Nations* has 'scenes' rather than chapters.) For good cinematographic writing, she turned once again to *Ulysses*; another important model in this respect was Louis Guilloux's sprawling, revolutionary novel, *Le Sang Noir*, published in France the previous year.

The realist writers whom Stead read for inspiration worked meticulously from life, from historical material, such that their novels were also sociological documents. Dos Passos' *42nd Parallel*, which she admired, was only semi-fictional—the sort of novel, Stead wrote, 'which seems to arise from the fright the novelist gets when he looks at the "New York Times" and feels he is a poor second to it'.[17] There was, in the mid 1930s, an emphasis on documentary writing: in April 1937 a new London journal called *Fact* claimed that the immediate task of socialist writers was to observe and record the facts, the ground of reality.[18] Influenced by the prevailing atmosphere, Stead wanted not only political events but also characters and conversations to be based on documents, letters and scrupulous observation.

Nevertheless, *House of All Nations* goes beyond conventional realism. For Stead, the extraordinary always lurked behind the ordinary. She even managed to weave her magical threads, her Arabian Nights flights of fancy, into the tough tapestry of international finance. Her characters engage in sparkling dialogues, gags and aphorisms, and our lasting impression of the bank is as a 'palace of illusion'. As Harold Strauss was to put it, in the *New York Times*:

> One should not suppose that Miss Stead has turned her back on fantasy. If the elements here are realistic, their assemblage is a crazy-quilt of impressions and associations ... If her knowledge of private banking, of bucketeering and grain options, of foreign-exchange speculation and account gathering, of stock manipulation and politico-financial intrigue is little short of miraculous, she scatters the bright fragments of her information across the skies of her novel in the disorder of star dust.[19]

* * *

Stead liked the heat and the deep retreat: in Spain there were no distractions, no friends, no telephone calls. The only problem for her, as a light sleeper, was that the Andalusians came to life at night.

Eventually she fell asleep, her head full of the Paris bank, but she would be woken at 6 am, when the animated political discussions finally ended and the apprentices left for their Maestro's atelier.[20] Blake found the heat trying, and the concentrated protein diet of southern Spain—mainly 'ironclad' chickpeas—did not agree with his stomach. After three weeks he fell sick and when he improved, they decided to head north.

They spent two days in Madrid. Stead disliked the city, but appreciated the Prado museum. From there they spent four or five days in San Sebastian, a Basque fishing port on the Bay of Biscay, at the foot of the Pyrenees. To their astonishment, though it was early July and the middle of the tourist season, most of the hotels were firmly shuttered. The locals advised them to move on to Fuenterrabia, between Spanish Irun and France. Once there, they put up at the Hôtel de France, which sheltered a number of wealthy Spaniards who felt safer close to the border.

The day before Christina's birthday, 16 July, there was a rather sinister incident. Bill had gone out to buy Christina perfume, when Republican police flagged down the bus in which he was travelling. The passengers were told to alight. Bill was singled out and made to stand apart from the others. Eventually, after some interrogation, they let him go. Only afterwards did he realise that he resembled José Maria Gil Robles, the rightwing leader of the Spanish Catholic Party whom the police were after.[21] (Robles in fact had fled to Biarritz the day before.)

On 17 July, a military uprising led by General Francisco Franco broke out in Spanish Morocco. It was not announced on Madrid Radio until 18 July, by which time the revolt had spread to the mainland. Within forty-eight hours the whole country was involved in civil war.

There is no mention of a political crisis in Stead's letter to Florence James on 18 July: although the government announced insurrections in many of the provinces, it claimed to have the situation well in hand. The north coast was firmly in the hands of the Republicans. Red republican flags flew from the houses and cars; hammers and sickles were daubed over walls and the voice of Madrid radio loudly crackled: '*Viva el Frente Popular.*' Young Republican males, dressed in overalls or ragged corduroy trousers, raced around in highpowered cars requisitioned from the wealthy, their hunting rifles propped on the back seat. Raised clenched fists had become the universal salute. One French-speaking Republican told Stead and Blake: 'Maybe we'll lose this time: what does it matter if we do? . . . We'll always rise again in a few months, no matter what happens.'[22]

By the end of July, the bucolic summer sojourn was over.

Fuenterrabia was darkened at night to avoid air raids, and a 9 pm curfew put an end to evening strolls. Swimming and fishing were prohibited in the resort town. With the fishermen no longer going out, Stead and Blake were embarrassed to be eating precious food supplies. And it had become clear to them that the Hôtel de France was run by monarchist conspirators.

They no longer enjoyed their retreat. There was no news about the reception of *The Beauties and Furies* in England, and Bill had not heard from his mother. At the end of July, they asked the Republicans at the *ayuntamiento* for safe-conducts to cross into France. Since they had not been required to register their foreign money in Gibraltar, they decided to hide it in a toothpaste tube to secrete it across the border. Soon afterwards, Stead told Florence James:

> The morning we left, under the aegis of the United Front
> Committee, with the red flag proudly waving on our taxi, the
> priest staying in the hotel was arrested and the poor silly old
> Catholic proprietress nearly went out of her mind with
> superstitious fear, alternately clasping the prayer-book and
> expecting the "communists" to set fire to her house. The
> communists hadn't set fire to anyone's house in the district
> but that made no difference.[23]

They were rowed across the Bidassoa River, the border between France and Spain, in a dinghy called *Lulu*. In France, they were detained for several hours, along with other refugees. Eventually they were released. Stead opened the toothpaste tube once more. All was well.

They took a bus to St Jean-de-Luz, where a bank teller told them Fuenterrabia was 'thick with corpses'. 'E.A. Poe couldn't do so well,' Bill commented to Christina.[24] They plainly had no inkling of the seriousness of the situation. Just days after their departure, the Andalusian poet Garcia Lorca would be executed by Franco's insurgents. Six weeks later, San Sebastian would fall to the fascists.

*   *   *

He was not Gil Robles, certainly, but Bill Blake had his own reasons for wanting to travel incognito through France. In St Jean-de-Luz they obtained visas for Belgium, and Blake worried that the police might be at the Gare d'Orléans to greet them. It was a nervous trip from St Jean-de-Luz to Paris. At the station Stead rang Blake's lawyer, who was able to tell them that Blake had not been mentioned in any plaint. They felt 'a flush of relief'.[25] When they arrived in Belgium on 30 July, with their thirteen pieces of luggage (including linen, books, manuscripts, marionettes and a coffee pot), they felt fatigued but 'honeymoonish' with relief.[26]

The Spanish Civil War soon took a frightening turn for the worse. On 1 October 1936, Franco was declared chief of the Spanish state by his followers; he was soon to be recognised as such by fascist Germany and Italy, who gave extensive support to the military insurgents. Young German pilots bombed Spanish civilians from brand new Junkers and Heinkels. With limited backing from the Soviet Union, the Spanish Popular Front government relied on untrained international volunteers and outdated armaments.

In early August, when Stead received a letter asking for her time and money in the struggle against fascism, she was worried that the inspiration for *House of All Nations* might not survive the dislocations of her wandering life, and told Florence James, 'I feel it is my duty not to do my duty'.[27]

Back in Melbourne in October 1936, Nettie Palmer, who had also been in Spain that summer, was horrified by the developments. She set about giving broadcasts, writing articles and addressing meetings to raise money for the Spanish Relief Committee. Fascism, she told her fellow Australians, had become an international issue.[28]

★　★　★

In Antwerp, Stead and Blake moved into Alf Hurst's suite in the large, ultra-modern Century Hotel. Since Alf was shortly due to arrive from London, Blake tried to find them a flat. One landlord looked him up and down and remarked that he hoped '*Monsieur*' was not '*Israélite*'.[29] Others implied it. Fortunately, when Alf arrived, he moved into his small Flemish-style house in nearby Brussels, and they were able to stay on at the Century.

Hamburg, located in Nazi Germany, had lost business to Antwerp: the Belgian free port was flourishing. Alfred Hurst's grain business, at No. 9 rue des Douze Mois, was thriving. When Hurst was in Antwerp, he performed wonders with his 'magic voice' and the five telephones on his desk. When he was away, approximately one week in two, business would drop dramatically and Blake could catch his breath.[30] 'Alf is full of life and business,' Stead told Florence James, 'and if he did not occasionally take trips to England and elsewhere would prostrate Bill. Himself too! After a day's Napoleoning, he has to sink into bed at 9 p.m.'[31]

Bill Blake was underpaid: he and Stead had no illusions about that. Jacques Coe, a New York financier who knew him and Hurst well, is convinced that this was always the case when Blake worked for Hurst. 'Bill got a salary from Alf, but there is no doubt he was worth ten times this to Alf.'[32]

All too easily, Stead would also find herself caught up in Hurst's exploitative 'little schemes'. He expected her to do small typing and translation jobs as tokens of friendship, she told Florence.

> He is really a darling fellow in intimacy, full of charm, although a rogue in the way he tries to steal from my writing-time to get all his odd jobs done, to avoid paying a salary to another typiste. (He thinks to work a little blackmail, quite innocent blackmail; he employs Bill—at a stenographer's salary—and he thinks that to keep Bill's job, I will do a lot of little friendly jobs on the side! What a transparent little scheme: you really can't dislike him for it.)[33]

Could she not? Her anger was scarcely concealed beneath the coy display of affection. The problem was that she and Blake were too dependent on Hurst's goodwill to complain.

Naively, Stead seemed to think she could outwit Hurst. He talked of her accompanying him on a trip to Romania, the land of his boyhood, so that she could acquire the insight to ghost his autobiography.

> When I bring up the subject of what he is going to *pay* me for the proposed "ghosting", he gets sentimental about the dear old days and the dreams of his boyhood. However, I am very anxious to get a trip through the Balkans if it is possible; I have already plans for writing a wheat-novel myself and I hope it eventuates. I tell him plainly I won't write it under his name and he doesn't believe it: he has the impression all merchants have, that scribes are people who will do anything if you throw them a crust, so we are each biding our time.[34]

The trip through the Balkans went the way of many of Alf Hurst's wild schemes. However, a decade later, Stead did write her 'wheat novel', *A Little Tea, A Little Chat*, in which Robbie Grant is an extremely *angry* portrait of Alf Hurst.[35] For the moment, though, Hurst was Henri Léon in her Paris banking novel. Léon has a smile like a 'sudden sunrise' and a 'beautiful husky voice', and though he employs his friend Michel Alphendéry 'at as low a salary as possible', he is also capable of occasional acts of generosity—'almost unprecedented in the business world'.

Though she knew Alf Hurst could be a 'mean bastard',[36] Stead remained loyal to him until the late Forties, when she wrote *A Little Tea*. In 1941, Blake would give Hurst a copy of his American civil war novel *The Copperheads*, writing on the flyleaf: 'To my best friend and true brother, Alfred H. Hurst.' And in 1944, Christina Stead would inscribe a copy of *For Love Alone*: 'To Alfred H. Hurst —our lifelong friend and one brother.'[37]

*   *   *

Stead was not enthusiastic about Antwerp. The autumn sky was as 'blue as skimmed milk'. She thought the Belgians ugly and over-weight. ('I feel practically a beauty, but I prefer to be among beauties.'[38]) At least Antwerp was largely French-speaking. And in the cafés, women enjoyed an even greater freedom to sit alone than in Paris. The town was also only fifteen minutes from the Dutch border, in case of a German invasion.

Stead plunged straight back to work, regretting that their moves had caused her to lose time and momentum. Their only friends were Alf Hurst, his Austrian lady-love Mitzi Ender, and his office-manager, Edgar Lallemand, half Walloon and half Flemish. Lallemand was Jewish, an active communist and interested in a wide range of literature. Stead was delighted to discover that he had not only read Joyce and D. H. Lawrence but that he had even heard of her American poet friend Stanley Burnshaw.

Stead and Blake could not make any definite plans. Their future depended largely on Hurst, who was waiting for the outcome of a court case in Liverpool before deciding what to do with his London and Antwerp businesses. He still intended to open a business in Spain, provided the revolution went to the government. That plan also involved waiting. He talked, too, of buying several small self-supporting estates in England or France, one of which Blake and Stead could make their home. Blake liked the idea of a cottage on an acre or so of land near Ely, in England, or perhaps in Normandy or the Dordogne.

Stead said nothing when Blake talked of living in France again: she now wanted to settle in an English-speaking environment. She had become heartily tired of their wanderings and Bill's confusion. He disliked dull Antwerp; at times he voiced a regret that they had not gone to New Mexico with Mike Gold, or back to the Putnams' country place near Lambertville in New Jersey. At other times he regretted that they had gone to America at all: it had been a waste of money and time. 'Poor fellow,' Stead wrote in her diary. 'Our life is madly disordered; I feel he is beating his wings in a dark room.'[39]

Privately she was pinning considerable hope on her new novel, fervently hoping it would bring in the money they needed, that it would be a turning point in her literary career. The bank was a 'wonderful subject' and she was excited to be writing in a 'new mode'. She told Florence James a second time that she had 'the comfort of knowing that S. & S. really push a book when they bring it out.'[40] At the very least, she trusted the novel would have a '*succès de scandale*'.[41]

She was not consistently optimistic. In bleaker moments, she told herself that her new book would be bound to be criticised, even if it were good. Perhaps, she told herself, her troubles with critics were only just beginning.[42] One day, Blake came across a June copy of *Nation* in the office, with a review by Dorothy Van Doren of *The Beauties and Furies*. Van Doren disliked the book's 'garrulous pretentiousness', but its 'more serious defect' in her view was that it was 'without virtue, seriousness, morality'.[43] The criticism kept Stead awake that night. She too believed in the importance of a moral message, yet somehow *House of All Nations* was one more novel full of 'scallywag characters'. Here, too, there was no 'moral hero'. Should she introduce one, she wondered? A kind of folk hero, perhaps? Someone like Mike Gold? But how would such a character fit in to her novel? Finally, she decided to insert two or three episodes near the beginning of the novel in which she would introduce Jean Frère and Adam Constant, friends of Michel Alphendéry, who eat and drink together in the little bar near the offices of *L'Humanité*. Frère is outside the world of the bank; Adam Constant, 24 and a poet, is a bank teller who talks of going to join the Red Army against Chiang Kai-shek. The novel now had three positive Marxist characters: Alphendéry, Constant and Frère—modelled (at least partly) on Bill Blake, Ralph Fox and Mike Gold.

She was reading Diderot, whom Blake greatly admired, and was inspired by the picture of the eighteenth-century Enlightenment, that 'age of delightful, unembarrassed reason'. Her new novel was given an epigraph from *Le Neveu de Rameau*: 'You are compensated for the loss of innocence by loss of prejudices. In the company of wicked people, where vice throws off the mask, you learn to recognize them.'[44] Perhaps she felt this to be her own compensation for her life among the financiers. But there were times when she was so sick of 'the bunch of thieves' that she wished herself in Walden, Thoreau's solitary retreat.[45]

Blake, always eager to explore new surroundings, organised excursions to the country on Saturdays and Sundays. But Stead was not feeling at all receptive to the charms of Belgium. She felt terribly restless, unusually sexually skittish. Was it the diet, she wondered? The grey skies? The 'nervous indoor life'? Was it because nearly all the characters in her current novel were men? (She had been rather shocked to realise this.) In her solitude, she was keeping a diary, which she intended to destroy later. In mid August 1936, she noted: 'Pepper in entrails, heart beating, small appetite and general wretchedness and no relief to date.' In late August she and Bill spent a weekend at Liers, a 'delightful town' with a 'Hans Andersen clock tower'. But Sunday was a disaster: 'Walked much, I unbearably irritable and Bill very angelic.'[46] In early September, the monotony of the endless business talk around her was temporarily relieved by a visit from Ann and Patrick Dooley, communist friends from London. Stead found it 'a breath of salt air' to talk to people interested in books.

By day, Blake was selling guilders, buying Belgian francs, buying Winnipeg wheat and selling it in Liverpool; in his spare time he worked on his Monte Cristo novel. In September, when Hurst spent a week with his family in London for Yom Kippur, Blake had a week off to work on his book. He was, Stead noted, 'excited and entirely rejuvenated'. In the Rocher de Cancale, a Spanish café in the old quarter, he read her the first three chapters. Stead pronounced them a 'sort of cross between Shakespeare's worst moments, Coningsby, Laurence Sterne, and what you will: in other words, pretty good'.

But Blake, working intensely, was constantly tired, and Stead did not find this easy to accept. In her diary, she alluded cryptically to her sexual frustration. Though she had intended to destroy it later, thirteen close-typed pages have survived. Sixteen lines of it are written in an elaborate mono-substitution code. A second version of the diary also survives, in which all the intimate details have been suppressed, the code passages have disappeared and some names are disguised: Alf Hurst has become Jack Brame; Edgar Lallemand is called Wallon.[47] The new version is 'artful', somewhere between reality and fiction. It even has a title referring, obliquely, to Bill: 'First Days of a Modern Monte Cristo'.

The two different versions indicate not only that the original was meant to be destroyed, but also the trouble Stead took to cover up certain truths and to create personal myths. Nobody, not even Bill, was to have access to her inner self, since her childhood her one sacred place. In her fiction, reality was transformed into something she could control.

Significantly, Teresa, Stead's fictional counterpart, also resolves, early in her relationship with James Quick, to keep her thoughts to herself. In a delightful moment of 'unchecked intimacy', she had once tried to explain to him her complicated feelings about their relationship. For Quick this truth-telling was terribly threatening. He went 'so cold, that she felt the warmth dying out of his breast'.

She realized her mistake, with a pinching of the heart, and at once abandoned the thought of telling him the truth about her love . . .

She resigned herself now to playing a part with him, because she loved him, and in order to give him happiness. She felt the fatigue of life, believing like so many young women that she had found out the truth, which was that man and woman cannot be true companions for each other. But she did not

wish to confide in a woman. What woman knew more than
she did? . . . She thought that each day would be a step farther
into the labyrinth of concealment and loving mendacity.[48]

Reality and fiction merged in Stead's 'labyrinth of concealment'.
Her study of cryptography and use of code, her constant use of
initials or fictional names in her diary and even in letters, the
wholesale destruction of her papers in later years: all this shows
how she protected her privacy with a desperate ferocity. When she
talked about her life to friends or in interviews, it would be in the
form of *story*, a refracted reality, a kind of legend.

The accidental survival of Stead's original diary allows us a rare
glimpse of her private thoughts. Seven years into her relationship
with Bill, she had become quite impatient. She was angry about
Mollie, angry about Bill's interminable waverings and frustrated by
their wandering life style.

All these years wandering chiefly due to fear [of] her
retributive raids, search for work which will allow us luxury
of keeping her to annoy us, etc. We waste his money, lose
homes, books, split friendships, have no circle: everything I
write is in vacuum, he continues to work at worthless jobs.
Yet will not make up his mind to cut the painter . . . Even the
experiences we have are no good to us: no time to consolidate
them, no place of repose and the ridiculous perennial question
of M. He has illusion that M will "try to get a job" while
money is still coming to her easily . . . "If Mollie comes over
here, we will leave for a few weeks"!!!! M knows very well the
power of a tenacious attitude towards this conciliation and
retreat, and there we stand where we were five years ago.

She reflected that they could have been leading 'a happy and useful
life' and Bill would not have aged so fast. As it was, at 44 he was
easily fatigued and his face was lined—'with hollows whenever
weary'. When she tried to discuss Mollie with him, he would say:
'Oh, C, let's discuss it another time' or 'Are you going to start
bothering me too? I'm going to get rid of you!' ('Tired joke', she
noted in brackets.)

The diary sections written in code are flawed, with numerous
mistakes, but so is her normal typing. Only able to be deciphered
by decoding experts, the code passages express frustration about
her lack of sexual activity, to which she attributes her 'severe
headaches'.[49] 'CWU WIJKWFWAT BNLDU JU LRBC MQKL
ACWU BFWLJAD; KSQ VWTWVDV KDVU FJQEDFY
QDUGNIUJKFD.' ('His inability comes as much from this climate; our divided beds largely responsible.') In code, she mentions
her 'passion for Ralph Fox'.

A brief passage not in code indicates that her anger was also (as usual) anger with herself, mixed with self-pity.

> In general am complicated ass ... yell mighty loud when my
> feelings are hurt, otherwise do what tractor could do better.
> The whole summer gone—Spain, Antwerp—while I twiddle
> indoors on typewriter—gone mad. Result, my skin is dry,
> I am thin and a virtual misery: I haven't as much voice as a
> new shoe and my dreams are puerile ... Charming outcome
> of the sturm-und-drang of 17.

Perhaps Stead had received a letter from Ralph Fox on 17 July or 17 August. Elsewhere she notes, in her usual cryptic style, 'Can't keep wolf from door: two or three days post and there he is, upsets me.' In mid September, she writes:

> In evening wanted to go on a bust, but how, where: don't
> know how to bust, understand Ralph Fox's occasional bust,
> poor varmint; my life too regular for an artist.

The lament was modified in the revised version: 'My life is too regular for an artist; Peter Davies is right, I should at least take snuff.'

One week Stead suffered a 'terrible depression' and could not work at all. She wept and raged, threatened to throw in her writing, and told Bill that six years of her life had been 'a martyrdom to arbitrage'. As a result, he agreed they should move to London as soon as possible.

*   *   *

It was autumn and the light in their room at the Century Hotel was becoming too weak to type by.[50] Stead was greatly relieved when they left for England in mid October, though the duration of their stay depended on Alf Hurst's court case. It turned out well: he won it. This meant that he could keep up the London business and employ Blake there.

House-hunting began again. At the end of the first day they went to sleep exhausted in their own downy bed at the MacAlpines. (The 'Macs' and Florence James had been storing their furniture ever since they had fled to the States over a year ago.) They had a pub dinner in Swiss Cottage with Florence James and Pym Heyting, her solicitor husband, but the Heytings had moved house that day and were tired. The dinner was not a success.

The next day, Mac took them round in his car looking at flats. Soon they were ensconced in a 'postage-stamp flat'—one room with an alcove off the living room as a bedroom—at Red Lion Court, off Fleet Street.[51] (This is the flat Teresa and James Quick share in the last chapters of *For Love Alone*.)

One of Stead's primary reasons for wanting to return to London was Ralph Fox. When she had left London in July 1935, she was very much in love with him, and her passion had not dissipated. Whether she and Blake had heard from him in the intervening fifteen months is not known, but she had certainly heard *about* him from their mutual friends. She and Blake had been back in London only a few days when they bumped into Fox. It was a Sunday. They were coming out of Lyons Corner House in Tottenham Court Road, their old haunt, when they saw him crossing the street with a pretty young woman. He seemed embarrassed when they greeted him. It was obvious to Stead that the pair were lovers. Not revealing her feelings this time, she noted in her diary: 'R. tired, hair greying, slight paunch, badly dressed, talking of "getting old" but this is no doubt merely to excuse his slight bulge. Tendency to make satirical remarks about everybody, due no doubt to fatigue.'

Ralph Fox was just back from Portugal, where he had been investigating the full extent of Prime Minister Salazar's aid to Franco.[52] Fox told them he was planning to leave for Spain in a few weeks—to fight in the International Brigade.

The Spanish Civil War had become the focus of a world in crisis. A crusade in which the issues were unambiguous, this war against fascism encapsulated the hopes, fears and theories of all liberal-minded people. Blake's friend Claud Cockburn was in Madrid, reporting for the *Daily Worker* under the name Frank Pitcairn. In London, there were pro-Republican rallies, pro-Republican manifestoes, and pro-Republican cultural events. Jack Lindsay's play *On Guard for Spain* was playing at the recently formed Unity Theatre, along with Randall Swingler's poem for voices, *Spain*. In their first week in London, Pat Dooley rang to invite Blake and Stead to a fundraising meeting for Spain at which he was speaking.

The fight against evil was temporarily focused on Spain, yet fascism was also stirring in London. Early in October, Sir Oswald Mosley and thousands of his blackshirted, jackbooted supporters had smashed windows, looted shops and assaulted Jews in London's East End.

One Thursday evening in late October, Eamon MacAlpine was visiting Stead and Blake when Ralph Fox phoned to say he was on his way round. 'Mac', a brash Irishman, ex-IRA, and now (Stead noted in her diary) 'a decayed revolutionist', disliked Fox and said, 'I'm blowin',' but he stayed another hour, vigorously running down Fox and his Stalinist politics. Mac was critical of the current purges in Moscow and Stalin's refusal to send adequate troops and munitions to Spain. He had not liked the way Fox had gloated over the execution of one-time leading Bolshevik Zinoviev, shot in August 1936 (along with fifteen others) by Stalin's firing squad. During this tirade from Mac, Stead shut the door and window, afraid that Fox would arrive and overhear him. When Fox arrived, with his girlfriend in tow, Mac brushed past them in the hall with such an air that Fox remarked to Stead: 'I don't think he likes me.' The notes in Stead's diary continue with false ingenuousness:

Lousy evng. No milk, kitchen in mess, two men talk war all time and leave girl and me on side. Myself feeling nervous and unstable, don't know why. Fox a slightly unstable type himself, voice changes considerably, demeanour, criticisms of men and women, as his confidence rises and falls. He has great charm, despite this instability which is suspected by all and disconcerts some.

Fox's girlfriend was Ann Dubrowski, a militant union organiser in the needle-trade. The details of that disturbing evening would be worked into *For Love Alone*, with more openness than in Stead's diary.

Fox called several times at the flat after that. He would sit and talk to Bill; Christina would listen, make coffee, observe and admire. Fox's biography of Genghis Khan had appeared that spring, widely praised for the thoroughness of its research into Mongolian history as well as for its colourful writing.[53] He was currently writing a book on Marxism and literature, *The Novel and the People*.[54] Like his American counterparts at the *New Masses*, he advocated socialist realism and a simple prose style, but he was less doctrinaire. Fox believed in heroes—'the heroic must come back to the novel'—and cited Dimitrov, the Bulgarian communist falsely accused by the Nazis of complicity in the burning of the Reichstag, as an example of 'moral grandeur and courage'. According to Fox, Marxists should be writing epic stories: 'In our modern life there are extraordinary subjects crying out for imaginative treatment.' On the other hand (Stead, immersed in the revision of *House of All Nations*, would have been consoled by this), he did not believe that revolutionary novelists should restrict themselves to portraying heroic characters. Why not villains? He would like to see a modern novel with a great business man, a Rockefeller or Krupp, as its focus. 'Renaissance adventurers ... were violent, bloody and cruel in the open, [modern capitalists] are so in the dark,' he declared.

Stead was amazed to learn, one evening, that Bill and Ralph Fox had both enjoyed the autobiography of Lady Margot Asquith, the upper-class wife of the former Prime Minister. Traditionally, the Left found personal writing self-indulgent: in February 1936, Charles

Madge had complained in the *Left Review* that 'all bourgeois poems now begin with "I"' and that too many contemporary novels were autobiographies.[55] Yet to Stead's astonishment, Ralph Fox told her he had been wanting to write his autobiography and the history of his native town Halifax for years; he had simply not yet decided how to cast it. Excited by this talk of autobiography which liberated an impulse she had so far dutifully repressed, Stead hardly slept. The day after that conversation, 25 October, she noted in her diary:

> Sunday. Mac arrived before we were up (11.15 a.m.). I had been restless, inspired by Margot's auto[biography]. Thought of a novel of child-psychology & autobiog for some time at night ... Mac [&] Bill talked Neid[ecker], Alf, Trotsky, Russia, Spain while I made coffee, made bed, dressed and after an hour I was énervée, due to Mac arriving before I had my dream out, a thing that puts me out for the day.[56]

Though she did not know it yet, the conversation with Fox had planted the seeds of her next novel, in which she would plunge back into her own childhood.

Fox himself was planning a novel on the civil war in Central Asia. Stead told Stanley Burnshaw (who was trying his hand at a novel), 'Everyone is still waiting with bated breath for *the* left novel and much as I love Ralph Fox, I hope it will be yours.'[57] In the encoded way she liked to convey her emotions, she was telling Burnshaw more than he guessed. She had written the magic words, 'I love Ralph Fox'.

★   ★   ★

Christina Stead would remain obsessed with Ralph Fox for the rest of her life. Over the next decade, she portrayed him, always in shadowy form, in three novels and a short story. His fictional counterparts, paradigms of the Nietzschean 'free spirit', are figures of exceptional physical magnetism—and all are burdened with an ugly, jealous wife. The very names of two characters—Adam Constant (in *House of All Nations*) and Luke Adams (in *Letty Fox*)—suggest that for Stead, Fox represented 'the eternal Adam'—the original man.[58] Letty Fox's surname was also a tribute to him.

Stead's posthumously published short story 'A Harmless Affair' closely resembles the Harry Girton episode in the last chapters of *For Love Alone*. In both narratives, a passionate woman (Lydia/Teresa) enjoys a cordial married existence, but marriage has awakened in her a potent awareness of her own sexuality. She develops an overwhelming passion for a virile writer and man of action (Paul Charteris/Harry Girton) who is about to go away and fight in

China/Spain. Attracted by his melting smile and shabby clothes (a sign that he is 'revolutionary' and 'honest'), she is even excited by the rumour that he is a heartbreaker. He visits the house often and talks politics with her husband. When once they find themselves alone, they are self-conscious, nervous. She sees him to the door and suddenly tells him that she will go away with him. He smiles at her with his knowing smile.

In *For Love Alone* the two spent a night together and shortly afterwards, Harry Girton leaves for Spain. As he bid farewell Teresa, he says: 'If I don't come back, remember me. Do my work for me, fill my place, be me.'

'A Harmless Affair' is closer to actuality. Lydia falls in love with the handsome Charteris, but then she and her husband Tom go away for two years. When they return they meet him unexpectedly. He is with a young woman (Rosetta), an activist, and is embarrassed to see them. He looks untidy and pale. Lydia thinks to herself: 'This is the man I nearly lost my head over.' But he starts to drop in at their flat again and her obsession mounts once more. The romance is not consummated; it remains 'a kind of dream'. He returns to his jealous wife, but this relationship is tormented and he tells people he is off to China: 'What have I to stay here for?' Eventually he goes away and is killed.

One of Stead's most sensual pieces of writing, 'A Harmless Affair' is about *desire*. The affair remains 'harmless'. (The irony of the title is powerful, for her longing for this man has taken over Lydia's whole existence.) When he comes to the flat, she is almost in a trance:

> He seemed so potent, full of manly strength that she felt like fainting: she seemed to get a little delirious although she had not drunk very much, and began to think that he was all honey, all roses, and so on. She found that she had moments of absence, when she heard nothing of what was going on, but only heard beautiful words about him, "His limbs gather passion as the bees honey and I am the hive . . ." Her feeling this evening was so powerful that she could not believe he did not feel it, that Tom did not feel it, it seemed to have thickened and made fluid the air.[59]

Lydia tells herself (just as Teresa does) that this man resembles her temperamentally and physically, though he is a male and 'rather handsomer and sweeter'.

When he leaves for the front, Lydia regrets 'that she had not known Paul's love' and bitterly regrets 'not having in her body a child of this dear and intimate man'.[60] When, some months later, he is killed in action, she is devastated.

For quite a long time, perhaps two years or three, she knew that if the choice had been lying in his Chinese grave with Paul or living her happy, unclouded and fertile life with Tom, she would have taken a long time to choose and what would have been the choice?[61]

★   ★   ★

Bill Blake's daughter Ruth believes that Stead and Fox did spend a night together; she seems to remember her father telling her, years later, that the two had gone away together for a weekend and that it had been a difficult time for him.[62] On the other hand, it is possible that Ruth Blake, who typed the final manuscript of *For Love Alone*, was confusing fact and fiction. With Christina Stead, this was easy to do.

When she was writing the last chapters of *For Love Alone* (in 1942), Stead wrote to Bill Blake:

I believe last night I dreamed about every eligible man I have ever known—when I woke up I could remember clearly—Ralph Fox, Jack Goodman, (you of course)—all very nice, affectionate, friendly to me, no sex.[63]

If there *had* been any sort of affair with Fox in 1936, Bill Blake had not been told about it.

Almost forty years later, Stead told Ron Geering, her literary executor, that she regretted the episode with Harry Girton at the end of *For Love Alone*. 'It was silly of me—but I went ahead and put in that Harry Girton thing—which I should not have—it didn't happen and probably hurt Bill terribly—you can't believe it—but I didn't think of that!'[64]

In her old age, she would often feel guilty about Bill, but there would have been no reason to lie to Ron Geering about Ralph Fox. Stead liked to project an image as a woman with a certain past, a woman who had been much loved. She was unlikely to deny an affair with Fox had she had one.

All we know for certain is that Ralph Fox was the passion of her life. And his premature and heroic death in Spain allowed her to transport this passion into the realm of myth. Ralph Fox was someone who never disappointed her. He never grew old. With him she was free of the ambivalences and anger that characterised her relations with others. With him transmuted into a passionate memory, she could turn reality into fantasy without any uncomfortable hiatus.

★   ★   ★

For an author who wrote so lyrically about the anguish and joy, pain and ecstacy of sexual desire and sexual frustration, Stead was exceptionally reticent when it came to writing about the raptures of physical love itself.

The power of 'A Harmless Affair' comes from the portrayal of 'cruel desire', and in the last chapters of *For Love Alone*, Teresa's desire for Harry Girton similarly builds to a crescendo. For weeks he has been teasing her with his surprise visits and lengthy absences. How does Stead portray the eventual consummation of their passion?

Teresa and Harry manage to get away in a train together, heading for different destinations via Oxford. Once there, the pair spend the afternoon lamely sightseeing—too inhibited to do anything else. Finally, they go to a seedy tavern in the suburbs (*his* suggestion) and sit downstairs in the bar, listening to the radio with workers from the town. At long last, they timidly announce to one another that they are tired.

> They went upstairs with a candle to a small back bedroom with raftered ceiling and an extraordinarily thick mattress, made of lumps of various materials and without buttons. There was a painted wooden washstand with floral china and the privy was a shanty in the yard; but the room, the halls, and the stairs, as they saw when they walked out in the moonlight across the flagged yard, were wide, bare and clean. Though they were tired, each did his best to please the other and Teresa strove to prove that she was no child at love. At first they wanted to go to sleep but the whole night passed before they slept and for hours they were as close as creatures can be. The sun rose in a clear morning and the light fell on the bare boards through the thickly curtained windows. Teresa got up quickly and dressed. The business of the night was over and she had never stayed late in bed in her life. She had a feeling of order and modesty in rising early and making everything tidy.[65]

The climax of the novel's last two chapters is summed up in two sentences. The passage is starkly unromantic, with the lovemaking reduced to 'the business of the night'. The surroundings are tawdry. We are conscious that these lovers are merely doing what scores of others have done before them, in the same shabby room. Even the moonlight is glimpsed only as the characters make their way to the privy.

It is interesting that although she has tried to seem sexually experienced, Teresa is actually quite repressed. The passage is focalised through her: it is she who thinks of their lovemaking as 'the business of the night' and who needs to re-establish her feeling of 'order and modesty' by rising early, dressing and 'making everything tidy'. Throughout the whole episode, she behaves as if she were wishing to prove something—to herself, to Girton, to Quick. The sexual desire that overwhelms her like 'a blow' comes when she *thinks about* Girton (beforehand and afterwards)—not when she is actually with him.

★   ★   ★

On 28 November 1936, Ralph Fox wrote his will, leaving his personal belongings and any monies accruing from his books to his wife, Madge Elizabeth Palmer.[66] The war in Spain was dangerous: Franco was intent on capturing Madrid. There had been fierce fighting and terrible massacres. Churches had been turned into prisons and there were air raids daily. On 1 December, 5000 Germans would land at Cadiz to join Franco.

Two other young combatants from the Communist Party who left at the same time were poet John Cornford and novelist and Marxist literary critic Christopher Caudwell. Both would be dead within two months.[67] Caudwell's last book, *Illusion and Reality*, published posthumously, was a sophisticated theoretical indictment of the contemporary 'Agitprop' mentality, which espoused communist agitation and propaganda.

From Albacete—the town between Madrid and Valencia where the new recruits received what little training was available—Ralph Fox wrote to his friend Harry Pollitt, General Secretary of the British Communist Party. They urgently needed more recruits, he told him. He himself was anxious to stop cooling his heels in that dull place and get to the front line. 'What is happening here is really the greatest thing since 1917. Victory means the end of Fascism everywhere sooner or later, and most likely sooner.' A letter to his wife, Madge Palmer, was optimistic:

> I don't know when the stalemate will break, but it should not be long. I am sure it is still true that one severe defeat for the Fascists would win the war. Not at once of course, but their morale, already weakened, won't stand defeat.[68]

Fox left Albacete, with 150 or so other Britons, in late December 1936. Part of a French battalion, they were all shockingly unprepared. Their guns were nineteenth-century German revolvers; they did not even have tin hats for protection. The battalion headed south-west, where a critical situation had developed near Cordova in Andalusia: Franco's Nationalists were attempting to cut the road to Madrid. Major Gaston Delasalle, who headed their Marseillaise batallion, planned to create a diversion by taking the village of

Lopera, held by Nationalist forces. (For his incompetence, he was later accused of being a coward, a fool and even a fascist spy.) On the night of 3 January 1937—a freezing winter night—he gave the order to attack. Total confusion reigned. His men found themselves running into a wall of fire. Ralph Fox and John Cornford were both killed.[69] Stead and Blake were told the news by a journalist friend at 11.30 pm on 4 January 1937. The news was in the British papers the next day.

Inevitably, Fox was compared with Byron, who had also died at 36 among craggy hills and shattered olive trees—in Byron's case, fighting for the liberty of the Greeks. Spain was a hero's war: one of Fox's comrades-in-arms described him later as 'very dashing' in his black beret, black leather coat and large revolver.[70] Valentine Cunningham points out the romantic mythologising of fighting writers like Fox and Cornford by the Left:

> It has been estimated that over 80 per cent of the 2,762 Britons in the International Brigades were working-class. One of the cruellest injustices to their memory and bravery has been literary people's readiness at losing sight of them in the "poet's war" legend.[71]

Tributes to Fox flooded in to the *Daily Worker*.[72] A memorial meeting was held in the Friends' Hall on 13 January. *Ralph Fox. A Writer in Arms*, a book written that year in his memory, contains glowing comments from friends all over the world.

Along with Amabel Williams-Ellis and Montagu Slater, the editors of *Left Review*, Christina Stead wrote a memorial letter. As good communists, they strove to justify Ralph Fox's death in terms of the ends for which he fought, and they took up Fox's own call to arms in inflated revolutionary rhetoric:

> We write this letter in the belief that such sacrifices, although almost unspeakably tragic, are not vain, and that the writers of England, writers and citizens, must step in and try to fill the places of these men, both by serving, themselves, in the cause of political and intellectual liberty, and by making known the careers and purposes of the dead. Ralph Fox spent his manhood and talents in the love and service of liberty: the gift of this rich life and the sacrifice of a prolific talent can only be fully justified if it is used consciously by them and by us to rouse his countrymen to an intense understanding of the evils of reaction and an intense will to combat and crush them.[73]

Mike Gold's message had the same stiff-upper-lip tone:

> We grieve for dear Ralph Fox, good friend, good soldier. But many more of us mean to fight and even die like him before

this thing is finished ... He was only doing his proletarian
duty; his job.[74]

It was the first war Stead had ever supported, and her attitude
contrasted sharply with Virginia Woolf's after she lost her nephew,
Julian Bell, in the same war. A generation older, Woolf simply saw
it as a crying waste.[75]

In the autumn of 1937, the *Left Review* conducted a poll in which
148 British writers were asked to take sides on the Spanish war.
Ninety per cent of those approached were opposed to Franco. T. S.
Eliot, Ezra Pound, H. G. Wells, Vera Brittain and Vita Sackville-
West declared themselves neutral; Evelyn Waugh, cousin of the
radical Claud Cockburn, claimed: 'If I were a Spaniard I should be
fighting for General Franco.' In the pamphlet published afterwards,
Authors Take Sides on the Spanish War, Christina Stead's statement
was more optimistic than many of the others:

> Franco, the traitor, image of his caste, with eighty per cent of the
> army and desperate foreign allies expected to win back Spain for
> the landlords in three days. The resistance of Spain's Republican
> Government is a guarantee of the eventual victory of the common
> people against these sterile powers: but to shorten their struggle,
> we must expose the Fascists' allies at home and abroad.[76]

She was wrong. A Republican victory was not guaranteed. The
Spanish Civil War would rage for a further two and a half years,
costing over a million lives. And in the end Franco was victorious.
Evil triumphed after all. It made Ralph Fox's death more 'unspeakably tragic' than ever.

★　★　★

In striking contrast to Stead's stolidly revolutionary public response
to Fox's death was her semi-mystical private one. For her, the
Supernatural always hovered in the shadow of the material world.
She firmly believed in the hand of Destiny. In later life Stead would
say that when she first travelled to England, she was—unbeknown
to either of them—travelling to William Blake. In the same way, it
was her absolute conviction that she was *fated* to cross paths with
Ralph Fox. It was with a 'singular feeling of destiny' that she
believed his physical and spiritual restlessness mirrored her own
temperament, that they were twin souls.[77]

At the time of Fox's death, she experienced a telepathic connection with him. In the mid 1940s, sitting in a restaurant in Gramercy
Square, New York, Stead would tell her friend Edith Anderson about
a sequence of prophetic dreams she had around the time of Ralph
Fox's death. (Edith understood them to have been lovers.) On two

nights she dreamt that Ralph Fox was standing on the far side of an open trench, staring at her. On the third night the open trench was there but Ralph Fox was not. Anderson, young and extremely impressed by Stead, was convinced by the story: 'I no more doubted her psychic powers than I doubted she was the greatest living writer in English.'[78] Stead attributed great fatidic significance to dreams; it took her some time, in the mornings, to shake off their shadow. And she strongly believed in telepathic communication at the hour of death. In *Seven Poor Men of Sydney*, written several years before Fox's death, Kol Blount has a series of visionary dreams at the very time his friend Michael plunges over a cliff.

As well as her three dreams about Ralph Fox, Stead would tell friends how she lost consciousness at the time of Fox's death. Among her unpublished papers is a stilted love poem (vaguely derivative of Donne in its conceits), almost certainly written soon after Fox's death.[79] The names are the same as those in *House of All Nations*; in the novel, Adam Constant is more or less an amalgam of Ralph Fox and herself; Judith is a shadowy image of herself. In the passionate poem 'Judith's Sorrows for Adam Constant', Judith, addressing her dead lover Adam, explains that she fainted at the moment of his death. The first stanza reads:

> One day of pain I lay down on the ground
> Drunken with fever: dreams and senses left
> Me sightless, fainting: when I woke, some sound
> Or pain or fancy had my forehead cleft
> But yet I shook no more. The sun had shone
> On all the towns of the world and then come back
> Half-hearted and upon his rounds had gone
> Once more, when I learned what poor sun did lack.
> The selfsame hour I slept, your head was split.
> Your warm blood fed the earth, your gentle breath
> Cried to its sister air: I would be quit
> To darken with your dark and make one death.
> Life have I still and life to death life gives,
> I do not know which one of us most lives.

In a video-interview when Stead was 78, she would again allude to the incident described in the poem. She tells the camera with obvious emotion that a friend with whom she had 'a curious connection' had gone to the Spanish Civil War. She and Bill were living at the time in a little flat near Fleet Street.

Bill and some journalist were chatting. I had a shower and sat down on the floor. For some reason I fell asleep, dead asleep, for two to three hours. I passed out really, and I never do.

And it was at this very hour that this man was killed in Spain. She concluded mysteriously: 'There are plenty of stories in life you can't tell—and that's one.'[80]

Stead's passion for Fox brought back the mystical intensity of her youth. Another poem, likely also to have been written around this time, contains two stanzas vaguely reminiscent of Emily Dickinson, in which the narrator decides she needs anguish in her life.

> I love to live with discontent
> And doubt; long days of slothful quiet
> Give me no joy. I would be rent
> With passion, for passion keeps joy nigh it.
>
> Sorrow, he is a friend of mine
> And in my bosom finds he ease;
> Around his dark my limbs all twine,
> Long years we did each other please.[81]

Sorrow has become her lover. It is a dramatic idea. Despite her admiration for reason and the Enlightenment, Christina Stead was a convinced Romantic, who prided herself on her sixth sense. Her mystic leanings disconcerted Bill Blake, a die-hard rationalist, but he recognised it as part of her creative imagination.

★   ★   ★

Soon after they had arrived in London, at the end of October 1936, Stead had sent *House of All Nations* off to Simon & Schuster in New York. That winter, Clifton Fadiman, her editor, came on a business trip to London and discussed the manuscript with her. To Stead's despair, he wanted major revision. It was the very thing she had dreaded and she resented Fadiman's suggestions as much as she had resented Peter Davies'. One page of Fadiman's editorial notes survives, written in his assured, breezy style. The notes are extremely detailed and also encouraging: he praises the 'stuffed carp scene' as 'one of the great comic scenes in English literature'. (Stead makes food a metaphor for wealth: the 'fat people', the Hallers, stuff their guests, the Raccamonds, to bursting point.) But Fadiman adds: 'You overwhelm the reader, just as the Hallers overwhelm poor Rac[camond]. Condense.'[82] His message, repeated several times on that one page alone, was to cut and condense. Stead agreed to some cuts. Privately, she was convinced that Fadiman was speaking from ignorance: he knew nothing about banking.[83]

She had lost her momentum completely. Everything seemed pointless. She wrote to her brother Gilbert, now aged 19:

Why are we here? We really don't know. We went to Spain and we got here. First, the rebellion broke out; then Bill was offered a sort of trinkgeld job in Antwerp, then we couldn't stick that city of the marshes and the only other thing to do was to come to London. We don't like it and we don't want to be here.[84]

It was an age of heroes—and Stead greatly admired people like Ralph Fox and André Malraux. Yet her new novel still had none. Somehow, the three Marxists in *House of All Nations* had turned out to be floundering characters, compared with the energetic money-makers. Stead had wanted it to be a revolutionary novel, and now she felt a little besmirched by its cynicism. She told Gilbert:

My new novel is ... about banking and full of crooks. I hope to wash my soul white as snow after this dousing in soot, by writing an innocent book about something or other, but I haven't yet thought up a pure subject ... I would like to go out to grass, like Nebuchadnezzar ... If Bill didn't want to run from England so fast, I might tackle an English working class town (or Welsh), but I'm afraid I won't have the time to do it. There's very little else to my life ... I'm still like a typist. I type from foggy morn till sooty eve, year in, year out ... One of these days I'll be a bright baby instead of a dull dodo and go and spend a year in the country, and associate with cows, dandelions and all those other sedative efforts of Nature.

Stead was definitely out of sorts with the world.

★   ★   ★

Questionnaires were fashionable in the Thirties. In 1934, the communist Louis Aragon had sent a questionnaire asking other leading French writers: '*Pourquoi écrivez-vous?*' The responses, published in the French communist review *Commune* in April that year, had initiated a lively debate about the responsibility of the contemporary writer. On 11 January 1937, Christina Stead, still Secretary of the British Section of the International Association of Writers for the Defence of Culture, sent out three questions to major British writers.

1. For whom do you write? 2. Does the writer suffer as an artist when he becomes active in politics? 3. Does any social setting appear ideal for literary creation, as, Athenian, monastic, Medicean, contemporary English, collectivist, anarchical or another?

The questions were badly formulated by the *Left Review* associates, and the writers' replies were often curt.[85] George Bernard Shaw wrote that whether the writer suffered from politics depended on the time he gave to politics and whether it was party politics or 'real politics'. He added that a writer who could not write anywhere had mistaken his profession. Havelock Ellis, David Garnett, Naomi Mitchison and Ethel Mannin wrote brief replies, liberal in tone. Only Jack Lindsay, the expatriate Australian recently converted to communism by events in Spain, made an emphatic political statement. (He later recalled meeting Stead around this time in the *Left Review* offices.[86]) He replied that he cared only for readers who were part of the movement towards a classless society. As for the writer and politics: 'In the present world I fail to see how anyone could be an artist at all unless in some form or other he took a part in politics.' The setting? 'Any period seems to me equally of use as a setting, if one has control of the marxist dialectic.'[87] Stead and Blake were to become close friends of Jack Lindsay in the early 1950s.

Though Christina Stead could not help admiring uncompromising revolutionary statements such as Jack Lindsay's, she herself was closer to writers like Gide and Malraux, who at that time were trying to straddle liberalism and orthodox Marxism. In a recent interview in *L'Humanité*, Malraux had stated that a novelist must not neglect individual psychological portrayal. Gide's view, published in *Commune*, was that 'all literature is in grave danger as soon as writers feel obliged to obey an order from above'.[88]

Stead was at a loss to know what she would write next. Amabel Williams-Ellis suggested she write something for the newly formed Left Book Club. Isidor Schneider asked her to write something on the cultural tradition in Australia for the *New Masses*. She said she would, but the idea did not inspire her.

She was interested, too, in writing a novel about a 'revolutionary type', but it was the *psychology* of a revolutionary that interested her more than his actual deeds. What made someone into a political revolutionary? What sort of psychological impulses were at stake? She tended to think of people as *types*: Alf Hurst was the 'Don Juan type' or the 'Napoleon type'; Keith Duncan was the 'bachelor type'. (She did not know that in 1934, back in Sydney, Duncan had married Dorothy Anderson, an English woman he had met while teaching in the extramural summer program in Kent in the 1920s.[89]) In her liking for taxonomy, Stead was as much a naturalist as her father.

Stead's curiosity about revolutionaries had been a motive for working at the *New Masses*. She had made notes about Mike Gold and would continue to do so over the next few years.[90] When Stanley Burnshaw wrote from New York describing the bitter factionalism among the *New Masses* associates, Stead answered that this was typical of the Left. She added dutifully, 'And I say this as a good stalinist.'

Would he please tell her more? she asked him. 'I have an insatiable thirst for rounding out the details, also the fulfilment of personality.'[91]

In January 1937 she briefly played with the idea of a novel based on the Radek trial. Karl Radek, editor of the Soviet newspaper, *Izvestia*, was one of seventeen currently being tried in Moscow, and Stead, assuming their guilt, was interested in 'the madly complex characters of the accused'.[92] Their communist friend, barrister Dudley Collard (who spoke some Russian) was attending the trial, and she could question him for background colour.[93] But the thought of the enormous research the project would entail put Stead off. Moreover—though she nowhere stated this—it was far too explosive an issue. The few on the Left, such as Stephen Spender, who cast doubt on the authenticity of the 'confessions' from Lenin's formerly trusted colleagues, were treated with contempt.[94] It was not possible to conjecture that an exemplary social system did not possess an exemplary judicial system.[95]

If ever Stead's faith in Stalinism were to be seriously shaken, it would have created tension under her own roof. When Christian Rakovsky came before his prosecutors in the show trial of March 1938, he 'confessed' ten years of treachery to the revolution and named his old friend, the American Max Eastman (ex-editor of the *Masses* and now a well-known critic of Stalinism) as an accomplice.[96] Bill Blake, who clearly harboured no doubts about the authenticity of the evidence, wrote to Mike Gold:

> It would be a pleasure to trounce the cocky "authority" who attempts to vindicate that synthesist of garbage-cans, Max Eastman. Poor Rakovsky is the boy to stand on the other side—he fell into treason by the idealist route and was always a little (not much) less dirty than the others. But for Eastman—the chain![97]

*   *   *

Blake wanted to spend spring and summer in Normandy, or else go to Hollywood to look for work. In the end, they went to Montpellier. In this romantic old Mediterranean town surrounded by vineyards, both finished revising the novels they had begun with such zeal a year earlier in Spain.

Stead signed her novel with an uncharacteristic little flourish: 'Montpellier, France 1937'. In early June, Blake proudly wrote to Mike Gold: 'The strangest thing has happened, Mike. I have written a book, lazy, spouting Bill Blech.'

> It is so charlatan, lousy, fako, that at night, when I sleep I expect the Heeby-Jeebies on horses to tweak my nose above my pillow to punish me for my crimes. But who knows. John Dumm Public may like it, and I be able to buy Clam chowders for friends.[98]

By the summer of 1937, the mass exodus from Europe had already begun. It was clear that war was coming. Hitler constantly reiterated Germany's need for more territory—*Lebensraum*. Himmler, head of the SS, had established a new concentration camp at Buchenwald for enemies of the state. Franco was tightening his grip on Spain.

Blake had sworn he would rather live in Patagonia than go back to New York. And Stead, having written almost nothing during their year there, declared that 'the whole spirit of New York is opposed to the creative mind'.[99] Yet in July 1937, they left Cherbourg on the SS *Aquitania* bound for New York City.

8

The Battleground of Life

AT THE BEGINNING of September, Stead and Blake were installed in an apartment at No. 403 W. 115th Street, at Morningside Heights, the Columbia University district. 'It is on a narrow ridge between Harlem and the Hudson and is full of churches, belfries, parks and of course the Campus, so there is plenty of air and not too many barrack-apartment-houses,' Stead told Florence James.[1] She felt reasonably positive now about being back in the States. It was at least an English-speaking environment, and unlike England, it was removed from the arena of war. They had friends in New York. It was full of European refugees, many of them well-known intellectuals and literary figures. And there were things she wanted to write about American society, which still managed to amaze her. 'Everyone in the USA is tough as steel,' she wrote to her brother Gilbert. 'There is no getting away from it: whether it's with razors, sabotage, State Police or social ostracism, everyone here is "plenty toff": that's the outstanding characteristic.'[2]

Rosa Blech was living with them again. Quite weak by now, she never ventured beyond the local block and seldom played her small upright piano.[3] To Stead, Rosa was 'still the kobold she always was, asking her million questions a day about the minutiae of life and uttering the inevitable wise-saws'.[4] But Rosa liked New York, and Stead hoped she might be better humoured than she had been in Paris and London.

But things were worse. Christina alluded to the household tension in a letter to her sister Kate, though she described it, in the vaguest possible terms, as a structural problem. 'The couple situation is a very odd one and the mother-son relation is a very odd one, and they simply don't mix.'[5]

In fact, Rosa's wandering mind had become quite paranoid, and many of her private terrors were associated with her son's de facto companion. Above all, she would tell people that the 'shiksa' was starving her, hoping to finish her off.[6] Stanley Burnshaw remembers Stead telling him the hurtful things Rosa Blech would say. She pretended to shrug at them, but Burnshaw sensed her pain.

Not only did Rosa talk about Christina behind her back: she would do so in front of her too—in her German-Yiddish mishmash.

> She used to hold conversations with Bill at breakfast, say, and when it came to concern me, she would break into this *mysterious* language (and the shiksa has a good many amusing conversations written down, from this source). She also spoke that way when irritated, as when "Jenka" (her niece) did not work. When Jenka was temporarily out of work because of a factory strike, Mrs. Blech, though in principle a socialist, chided her: "A arb't'r muss arb't." [*Ein arbeiter muss arbeiten*: a worker must work.][7]

Stead, who understood German by now, never let on that she could follow the conversation. She wrote down several exchanges between Rosa and 'Vill' (as Rosa called William) and between Rosa and her goodnatured young niece, Jenka, Rosa's favourite companion.[8] In Stead's thinly fictionalised notes, 'Mrs. Segal' speaks a jumble of German, Yiddish and English—a language sprinkled with clichés and muddled references to literature, particularly Shakespeare. ('Nu, what is life? A dream, hat Shakespeare ... geschrieben. Der war ein kopf!')

A difficult and cantankerous old woman, 'Mrs Segal' is relentless in her pursuit of trite details. Her main preoccupation is food: what others eat, how things are cooked, where things were bought. She complains about a lack of food in the house. Her life is empty and unhappy: 'Ich get up early. Ich get up at 7.30. Then I go to bed again. Was ist das für a life: immer in Bett ... Old is no joke.'[9] Her self-pitying refrain is that she has not long to live: 'Nu, what can I do? I am almost to the last chapter. Man muss "Finis" schreiben.' Similar conversations appear in *Letty Fox*, although for the sake of comprehensibility, Grandma Fox speaks a jumbled English, not German.[10]

Forlorn, manipulative characters based on Rosa Blech had already worked their way into *The Salzburg Tales* and *House of All Nations*. The portrait in *Letty Fox*, which Stead would write after Rosa Blech's death, is rounder and more sympathetic. Grandma Fox is a 'queer little thing, sharp, angry, and disappointed'.[11] Frightened of death, lonely and unhappy, she is sure that her friends and neighbours think of her as 'a rag of flesh, carrion, on the dump heap'.[12] To raise herself in their eyes, she boasts about her glamorous European past, inventing stories about her rich daughter-in-law and her talented grand-daughter. But the details are not consistent. Her companions laugh behind her back. By the end of her life she has 'entered that region of personal misery and isolation which seems like madness to others'.[13]

When Bill visited Mollie and Ruth, whom he had not seen for over a year, he was amazed to learn that Mollie had thought they were no longer married. (He had told her that he and Stead were going to Europe via Mexico for a divorce.) Encouraged perhaps by this strange turn of events, Blake did some contract work for his stockbroker friend, Jacques Coe, specifically to make the $500 for a Mexican divorce. According to Coe, in just one week, Blake wrote a 'brilliant' and meticulous report on Mexican Eagle oil shares, enabling Coe to pull off a major deal with a previously sceptical client and make a spectacular profit.[14] Blake made his $500, but though a Mexican divorce took only about twenty-four hours, and could even be done by proxy, Blake did not go through with it.

Over the next nine years in the States, Blake would do intermittent bursts of contract work for financiers. Alf Hurst was also in New York, and would remain there for the duration of the war. Blake worked on and off at Hurst's Grain Union Corporation, advising Hurst on straddles, arbitrage opportunities and foreign exchange trends. Hurst also did business in Canada, which involved Blake in occasional trips north.

Ruth Blech, now 16, was short and pretty, with her father's lively brown eyes and vivacity and the restlessness of both her parents. Her libertarian and unsettled transatlantic upbringing had made her precocious—in fact, quite a handful. As a fresher at Cornell University in upstate New York, she was finding the remote campus exceedingly dull. She wanted to study in Radcliffe, Cambridge, a college affiliated with Harvard, where a particular young man—a student communist leader and son of a wealthy rabbi—was studying. Stead told Florence James:

> She is kicking about being in a small town (after spending
> her life in the metropopolishes [sic] of this earth), but Bill
> is anxious for her to lose momentum during the next three

years, while she is working hard: the New Yorkers are such
a nervous, high-strung and soon-pessimistic and Mammon-
worshipping breed and he doesn't want her to be like them.[15]
But Bill had limited authority when it came to Ruth. On a wintery
afternoon in early January, she turned up at the 115th Street apartment
and regaled Bill, his mother and Christina with stories about the
New Year's Eve 'bacchanalia' at her grandmother Grossman's country hotel. Her grandfather had recently died and his wife was
evidently feeling liberated. Stead noted various details in her diary.
Everyone was 'wild' to get to the 'great Grossman saturnal'. The
family hotel was packed and the servants turned out of their rooms.
'All bets were off': the rooms were filled with drunken couples
'sleeping heartily with other husbands and wives'. For the first time
in their lives, the Grossmans danced on the sabbath night. The old
lady, her daughter Mollie and grand-daughter Ruth were all drunk.
No guests went home before dawn. ('Even "nice pure" young girls
of nice pure parents and nothing much said.') Ruth had a 'splendid
time'.[16] In *Letty Fox*, Letty delights in shocking her paternal
grandmother with the same story.[17]

Stead would see quite a bit of Ruth during the New York years,
giving her the opportunity to observe Ruth's evolution between the
ages of 16 and 25. The two women never really warmed to each
other; their relationship was always awkward. But there were
moments of relative closeness. Stead was curious about the aspirations and experience of the younger generation of women. She had
emerged from her own repressed adolescence convinced that sexual
freedom for women would have a revolutionary effect on the
relationship between the sexes. Yet when she talked to Ruth and
her teenage friends, she saw that nothing had changed fundamentally. There was far more sexual freedom, but the young women
still seemed pathetically eager to please men, and just as hellbent on
finding a husband. This was a subject Stead would explore in *For
Love Alone* and *Letty Fox*, begun a few years later.

★ ★ ★

Stead was 'fooshing about', undecided about what to write next. At
first she thought of working up the trilogy begun years earlier in
Paris, and when Blake invited Clifton Fadiman to the apartment, in
December 1937, she asked him to give his opinion of the two
unpublished manuscripts. Fadiman, after all, had greatly admired
The Beauties and Furies, part of this trilogy. However, he did not
think the other manuscripts showed much potential. Stead was still
hurt and annoyed when she wrote a note to Stanley Burnshaw,

inviting him and his wife Madeline to call in for an 'eggnog' on Christmas day.

Fadiman took the stuffing out of me, with some quite idiotic criticisms of a bundle of unfinished MSS. (Bill inveigled him up here and I broke my good rule, never to show critics and "impeded creators" unfinished work.) His criticisms, "confused", "too intellectual", "too romantic", "faded like Ibsen", "unnatural", "nineteenth century", "too elliptical, too oblique", "true but uninteresting", (all under the guise of compliment, strange as it seems) made me decide to go in for selling hats.[18]

Temporarily bereft of creative ideas, and in need of money as usual, it seemed a good idea to find temporary work. Peter Neidecker's wife, Sybil, who was working as a fashion consultant in a large Fifth Avenue store, suggested a series of fashion articles, on the basis of Stead's long years in Paris. Stead favoured translating for a publishing house, an idea she had nursed for years, and with this in mind, she was doing translation exercises with Elisabeth, Mike Gold's French wife. Mike and Elisabeth, who now had a son, lived a block away, in W. 116th Street. They saw a lot of each other.

Bill Blake did not share Stead's disorientation. No sooner had he finished *The World is Mine* than he started work on an under-graduate textbook on Marxist economic theory, and another historical novel. Stead quite envied his flow of ideas, and admired the liveliness of his writing. 'He has ten times the novelist in him that I have.'[19]

Blake was impatient to see his first book in print. Stead made out that she was 'grey, old and wise' after years of 'long fangdangling' by Peter Davies,[20] but this time, she too was nervously awaiting publication. She was burning with ambition. Her father's pre-publication copy of *House of All Nations*, sent to him in May 1938, was inscribed:

For my father—
nearly 350,000 words—
104 scenes—
a book written in the sweat of my brow—
a hope to do better in the future—
an unsatisfied ambition—
all these—
affectionately, in one binding—
Pegler. Christina E. Stead.[21]

Clearly, it remained her all-consuming wish to impress her father.

Their books were due out in the spring, then postponed to the summer of 1938. In the meantime, Stead and Blake made plans for the future. He would go to Reno, in Nevada, and get a divorce. They would go to live in a smaller city—Boston perhaps, or even a country town. They would at last make a trip to Australia. Christina's family was pressing them to visit: 1938 was the tenth anniversary of Christina's departure as well as the 150th anniversary of white settlement in Australia. They would perhaps have a child—though Stead, unconvinced, told Florence James:

> Bill is very anxious for a "Benjamin" but ever since my appendix operation I have had nothing that carried through the first month; I have never been to a doctor since, I am supposed to go now, but I keep putting it off.[22]

Plans were all prefaced by 'If money is to hand', or 'If we make a million'. But Stead and Blake pinned great hopes on 'S & S', as Simon & Schuster was called locally. 'They are the liveliest outfit I ever struck,' Stead told Florence James. 'Something of the Travelers' Bank in them ... everyone worked to death and everyone with figures in their mind's eye.'[23] The comparatively young firm had a dazzling record of best-sellers: they knew how to promote books and it was rumoured that their average sales were 20 000 per book. Their current winner was Dale Carnegie's *How to Win Friends and Influence People*: over 600 000 copies had been sold in 1937 alone. Privately, Stead was horrified by the moneymakers and 'success-cynics' in the publishing game. She was aghast when Bill's first manuscript came back from Simon & Schuster's literary editor ('a really charming and decent young man') covered with 'vile' margin comments such as: 'What we want here is some really luscious screwing.' By contrast with the commercial American hype, Peter Davies, with his genuine love of literature and naivety with money, suddenly seemed an 'Olympian character'.[24]

But Stead and Blake, like their other leftist friends, were personally divided when it came to commercialism.

> It is no good throwing up my hands in despair because they are simply moneymakers: they are also very anxious to help you make money and get your name about in other fields (it all helps their game) and so, one way or another, short stories or articles and so forth, they will help us out.

When Stanley Burnshaw was sent an advance copy of Blake's novel, he pointed out many defects, but said he thought the book would sell well. It took Bill some time to recover from this 'carper's field day' (as he called it),[25] but Christina thanked Burnshaw warmly: 'I simply rejoice in your affirmations about the book ... I think Bill has the wisdom and affirmation and humanity of a great writer, and all he needs is to take himself seriously.'[26]

★   ★   ★

Although they hoped for good publicity, Stead and Blake preferred to be out of town for summer, when their books were to be launched. In May 1938, they went to live in the vacant stone-and-weatherboard cottage near Lambertville, New Jersey, temporarily vacated by the Putnams. For Stead, the dry heat in Lambertville was 'like wine'.[27] And Lambertville was close enough for them to make occasional day trips to New York City. She spent her time dreaming, weeding, watching birds, going for walks and reading Tolstoy and 'the old masters'.

The land was originally a berry farm. Now it was overrun and untended. At the bottom of the property, a wooden bridge crossed a trout brook covered with tiger lilies and banks of poison ivy. Stead wrote enthusiastically to Kate about the native birds and plants. One of the great charms of the American countryside for an Australian who had never seen them before were the flashing fireflies.

> The first time I saw them, I held my breath and it was a very tangible enchantment, it was the Midsummer Night's Dream: each spark shot up through the air, or wound about so much like a fairy, and in so many lovely spots—in thick fields of daisies and wind-breaks of pine-trees, through tall weeds and on the tips of tall trees ... that I for the very first time knew that there could be a real emotion and a real marvel behind the idea of fairies. The beavers, squirrels and all the peeping things give rise to the idea of elves and dwarves and now I see the natural origin of the fairies.[28]

These fertile surroundings, Stead was convinced, were infusing her with new vitality. On 7 June, the day before *House of All Nations* was due out in New York, she wrote to Stanley Burnshaw, entreating him to bring Madeline, who was pregnant and ill.

> ... here Nature is in tune with her, titmice, catbirds, flycatchers, wrens, robins, cows, hens, dogs and poison-ivies, are all in maternal mood, and if she isn't subject to hay-fever, the country air will probably make her feel splendid. We'd love to have her ... Now that I think of it, we miss you both, an awful lot.[29]

She wrote a review of a Russian novel, Pozner's *Bloody Baron*, for the *New Masses*.[30] And inspired by the brooding wilderness around her, she began a ghost story, 'The Right-Angled Creek'.[31] It has all the gothic trappings she relished in Edgar Allan Poe: nature is all-powerful and out of control; the Lambertville house is haunted by the ghost of an Indian princess (Pocahontas—Poky for short);[32] there is a mad woman, and a sinister death from poison ivy. The suspense builds up. The summer heat builds up. The narrative, lush as the wilderness in which it is set, resembles a Brueghel painting. With her usual delight in self-reflexive literary allusions, Stead mentions Poe and Brueghel in the story.

Clare and Sam Parsons come to spend summer in their friends' country house, which they soon call 'Poky's Place'. Clare, a nature-lover, delights in the 'rioting insanity' of the place; Sam, a city boy ('a stubby dark man' with a 'resonant Mid-Western voice') tramps up and down the tracks talking to himself, musing on his 'past business relations' and the books he intends to write.

Nature is out of control; so is Laban Davies—'a pathological drunk like Poe', who struggles in vain against his addiction. Davies, a writer and translator, is modelled on Samuel Putnam.[33] That summer, Stead read books on alcoholism, including Luther Benson's *Fifteen Years in Hell*, and books about the district, its natural resources and social fabric. Her background research was always thorough.[34]

The setting allowed Stead to indulge her 'premonitions' and 'grisly fancies'.[35] She told Stanley Burnshaw, after his weekend visit with Madeline:

> Poky is lying low, but we have discovered a large number of fat green freshwater eels in the brook; or rather, I have, Bill won't so much as glance at eels and the like and I believe it's because he won't face the primitive evil in Nature. However, he has glanced at snakes this summer, and probably in a month or two he will come round to the eels too.[36]

Years later, she would tell her editor that the story was 'all true' ('well most of it')—especially the ghost, 'the only one I ever ran into'.[37]

★   ★   ★

House of All Nations was launched in New York on Wednesday 8 June 1938. It was attractively presented, with a dust-jacket and title page designed by their friend Philip Van Doren Stern, who was head of the S & S manufacturing department and a novelist himself. The publicity was good. Stead's photograph was even on the cover of that week's *Saturday Review of Literature*, beaming at her from all the news-stands. A flattering picture, taken around the time she left Australia, ten years before, her long hair is knotted in the nape of her neck, she is wearing a smart tailored jacket, and looks serious, full-lipped, bright-eyed and intelligent. Inside the magazine, the novelist Elliot Paul declared that he was held by the book 'to the highest pitch of excitement'.[38]

Reviewers were impressed that this Australian woman writer had

managed to familiarise herself with the intricacies of European financial intrigue. Once again, many used the word 'genius'. Everyone
admired the book's vitality and energy, although the praise was
often qualified. Alfred Kazin commended 'its enviable critical intelligence, its dexterity and thought-driven vigour'. ('What you feel
throughout is that Miss Stead is much bigger than her novel, that
she will need a stream of novels to shelter her fully, for no one
novel can hold her at this point.')[39] In the *New York Times Book
Review*, Harold Strauss wrote of Stead's 'miraculous' knowledge of
international finance, her 'pyrotechnic imagination' and the 'star
dust' effect of her writing, but complained that it was 'loaded down
with a vast amount of documentary material'.[40] Clifton Fadiman
wrote in the *New Yorker* that the novel was 'full of rich comedy,
crowded with Balzacian characters, and, despite certain flaws and a
tendency to congested detail . . . a work of extraordinary talent'.[41]

The communist press was divided. The *New Masses* saw it as
'evidence of the trend in contemporary fiction away from spiritual
autobiography and toward an objective account of the social forces
that work through the conflict of human wills'.[42] However, Henry
Hart's review in *Direction*, the magazine of the League of American
Writers, was damning: '. . . it is too long and too difficult for most
of the critics to assimilate. In such circumstances, it is always safer
to praise.'[43]

Peter Davies had bought the shoots for the book straight from
Simon & Schuster, and the novel appeared simultaneously in England. Less widely reviewed in that country, its reception was also
less generous. The novel was considered excessive, too detailed,
too long.

*   *   *

Stead had been 'quite, quite sure' that *House of All Nations* would
sell 10 000 copies—'even if the publishers lay down on it'.[44] She
was in for one of the most bitter disappointments of her life. Simon
& Schuster, that sparkling firm of literary capitalists, were as dubious
as Peter Davies had always been about the selling power of her work.

Stead had never dreamt that Simon & Schuster's commercialism
might go *against* her. Indeed, it is extraordinary how much faith she
and Blake had pinned on the capitalist machinery. Six months after
publication, she still felt thoroughly betrayed by her publishers. She
wrote to Florence James.

> The publishers . . . thought it was just another "lady's"
> maundering novel and only printed 3,000. The superb reception
> it had here took them by surprise and their first action was to
> write to me asking me to reduce my royalty because they were

losing money, and making a vague threat—otherwise they wouldn't reprint. I fought tooth and nail and found the financial disappointment unpleasant because I had thought I could visit Sydney out of the "House." They refuse to reprint more than 6,000 and now have dropped it. I thought of breaking contract— but who is better? Look at my experience with Peter![45]

It seems that 9000 copies were printed in the end.

In a state of bitter frustration, Stead confronted Peter Davies. She had always been impeccably polite to him; now she told him how disappointed she was with her publishers on both sides of the Atlantic. It would not have helped her case, she told him, that he had told Simon & Schuster he did not much like the novel. Caught out, Davies was obliged to confess—in that Etonian style that Stead had once found charming.

It was very naughty of Simon, that astute man, to say I told him
I didn't like the *House of All Nations*. I can't imagine myself ever
saying of any book of yours that I didn't like it, just like that.
There are thousands of words in it I love, and all of it I greatly
and enthusiastically admire, and none of it do I take to my soul as
I do certain passages in *The Salzburg Tales* and *The Beauties and
Furies*. And I do not think it a book, or perhaps even the sort of
book, which you ought to write if you desire either fame or
success. You are certainly the only writer I have ever published to
whom the attribute of genius can be applied, so I may very well
be wrong in all this, but I can't help thinking it.

He concluded:

I am truly sorry you aren't happy with S. and S., the more
so as I don't know how you are to get away unless there is
a loophole in your contract. Perhaps there is? On the other
hand, aside from your personal feelings, I don't think it
necessarily follows that anyone else would sell you better.
They are generally regarded as first rate "stunt" publishers.[46]

Stead had grudgingly admired Peter Davies' lack of interest in marketing strategies, but now his words had the same ring as her American publishers.

★   ★   ★

Blake was equally angry about Stead's treatment by her publishers. Almost twenty years later, in 1959, Simon & Schuster in New York and Gollancz in London accepted William Blake's novel, *We are the Makers of Dreams*. Blake had written the novel years earlier—in 1942, four years after the debacle of *House of All Nations*. At the time no publisher had been interested.

The English and American editions of Blake's novel have significant variations. One particular scene has been omitted from the Simon & Schuster edition.[47] Peggy Gordon, a British writer now in New York, is clearly modelled on Christina Stead.

Peggy Gordon, writer, cook, and bottle-washer for her eloquent but clumsy husband, had finished a novel, a picture of *The Age of Brass*, one in which love relations did not provide the pretext for the development of character. Not that Peggy was opposed to passion, but she was anxious to write a novel, and that she had done. There covetousness and malice, generosity and devotion, fantasy and ambition, were as powerful actors as in a labelled morality play.

Timidly, she took it to a publisher's. In London she was used to the publishers' offices, dusty places near Covent Garden, small by American standards, overlooking old burying grounds and fruit stalls, in which esteem for letters persisted even under the rumble of profits. But Peggy, waiting in the anteroom of a publisher's, in the heart of concrete and steel, with the paraphernalia of switchboards and luxury offices and a snappy air of modernity, thought, "Here, at least, they are of the tempo of this age."

So *The Age of Brass* went into the editorial hopper and came out tagged with reports. Editorial Department had many recommendations to make, but "first we must hear from the Sales Department."

The Sales Department chiefs came in, two young men in mortal fear of dismissal, whose high salaries had got them so involved that their neuroses actually interfered with their business . . . The assistant burgeoned with objections: "You see, Peggy, 85 per cent of fiction is bought by women, who can afford the price. Nearly all of them live in metropolitan areas, urban, comfortably off, so that fiction is a product destined for a special market. Now, does your book appeal to them?"

"Does that explain *The Grapes of Wrath*?" she asked impatiently.

"There are exceptions. But basically you have to consider one market. Now the women want to read about their interests, which are either getting married, staying married, or, if they lose the gentleman, acquiring another . . . Now a compelling love story, like the musky Rhett Butler and Scarlett O . . ."

The scene continues for several pages in the same vein. Peggy is so upset that shortly thereafter she suffers a miscarriage. ('The shock brought about by the slick characterization of her novel, her life work, had been the cause, just as the enthusiasm for the manuscript had given her the vitality to conceive.')

No evidence suggests that the disappointment had this effect on Stead,[48] but the image of miscarriage is a potent one, and it reveals how hurt Blake was on Stead's behalf. As he perceived it, her vitality, her very ability to produce, were at stake.

★ ★ ★

William Blake's *The World is Mine* was published by Simon & Schuster on 4 August 1938—two months after *House of All Nations*. It was promoted as a best-seller: less than two weeks after publication, sales had reached 6000 copies, and the novel was rated ninth on the *New York Times Book Review* best-seller list. By mid August it was on its fourth printing;[49] by early December it had sold 10 000 copies. Blake was told that it narrowly missed out on a Book of the Month Club nomination: the novel exposes the Church's dubious financial procedures, and the Catholic Church exerted pressure against it.[50]

A flurry of extravagantly positive reviews appeared. Clifton Fadiman paved the way: 'Mr. Blake has certainly ripped off something to make your eyes bug out.' In the *Daily Worker*, Mike Gold called William Blake 'a new proletarian Dumas'.[51] Poet and critic Louis Untermeyer confessed the book had made him 'grin, goggle, check the references, admire, swear softly, gasp and keep on reading'.[52]

A more sober response came from the poet Stephen Vincent Benét, who regretted that Mr Blake had 'larded his melodramatic story with quite so much portentous philosophizing'.[53]

Since *The World is Mine* and *House of All Nations* were about the bankruptcy of capitalism and from the same publisher, comparisons were inevitable. Harold Strauss, in the *New York Times*, compared Blake's coldly rational prose to a ledger page. He was not really enamoured with Stead's novel either: 'The great novel about modern financial manipulations is still to be written.'[54] But many critics preferred Blake's book. And in the short run, Blake's racy novel fared far better than Stead's.

It was rumoured that the novel's larger-than-life capitalist-cum-anarchist hero, Cristóbal, resembled the author, and Blake was not averse to fostering this image himself. Edd Johnson's interview with Blake for the *New York World-Telegram*, on 31 August 1938, is revealing:

> [Mr. Blake] was interviewed this morning over a cup of coffee in a drug store at 116th St and Broadway after mysterious arrangements had been made with his publisher to produce him.
>
> He would not divulge his true name, his address or his marital status, although he mentioned that he has a daughter in

Cornell, "who is also a chatterbox," and referred in passing to "an interrupted first marriage."

He appeared at the appointed time and immediately began to talk in rapid sentences. He stirred his coffee furiously as he talked, overturned a pitcher of cream in the midst of a discussion of the 6% of women who are prostitutes and the 27% of men who are loafers.

He was born, he said, of German-Jewish parents in Chicago. His father was an army surgeon, "a terrible patriot, a regular Prussian." His mother was a musician. Both were atheists ...

His mother and father were divorced and he came to New York with his mother. At 14 he quit high school and got a job as secretary to a wealthy man who liked radicals.

"I was the oratory type," Mr. Blake said.

At 15 he got a job as statistician in a brokerage company. He spoke German and French fluently, was a mathematical prodigy and an authority on European history before he left school.

He worked in private banks, analyzing earning reports, mapping out financial strategy, advising boards of directors and writing prospectuses for stock and bond flotations ...

In the early years of the World War he made his first fortune on borrowed money in commodities, but when President Wilson broke off diplomatic relations with Germany he became "active with the opposition." He was not in sympathy with Germany, but violently opposed to the war—a conscientious objector.

"Some of those prison scenes in my book may not have been imagined," he said, and then quickly changed the subject and refused to be lured back.

His fortune disappeared during the war. At its conclusion he went back into Wall Street, "working for people who wanted my brains and weren't interested in my politics."

. . .

I am more European than American," he said. "I like the European respect for privacy. That is one of the reasons I won't talk about my private life."

. . .

He started to write *The World is Mine* while sitting in a café in Andalusia, where the story opens, and drinking sweet wine. He drank sweet wine while writing the 741 pages of the entire novel.

When the Spanish war broke out he was in Irun, in Northern Spain, and for several weeks was under the siege by General Franco's forces. The siege, although laid in Andalusia, is described in the concluding chapters of the book.

Politically, Mr. Blake is an anarchist turned Marxist. Personally, he is a gourmand. Professionally, he is a successful capitalist.

So is. his book's hero.

"But it is not a portrait of me," Mr. Blake hastened to explain. "The man is a billionaire, the richest man in the world, the symbol of all capitalism. I am not that type."

He says he is described — "a horrible picture, but an accurate picture" — in *House of All Nations*, by Christina Stead, "referred to in one clipping as my wife."[55]

Sipping his sweet Spanish wine as he worked, Mr. Blake splashed out his prodigious story of gold and passion, of intrigue and torture and blood, on a canvas so broad that critics expressed amazement that any man could know so much. Mr. Blake does not share their amazement. He is accustomed to doing amazing things.

"I am a terrific worker," he said. "I write 10,000 words a day, and ninety-nine per cent of it stands without revision. I work all the time — twelve or fourteen hours a day."

Mr. Blake said he did not believe an author's personal life belongs to his public before he has written at least four books. *The World is Mine* has been on the stands less than a month. Already Mr. Blake has written a second novel. That leaves him two to go.[56]

Bill Blake, like many autodidacts, compensated for his lack of formal education by a tendency to boast, as well as a greed for knowledge. His success may have gone temporarily to his head, but the need to impress was always there.

With *The World is Mine*, William Blake's writing career was launched to a spectacular start. He passionately hoped that he had found an alternative to working in finance.

* * *

Stead and Blake left Lambertville in the autumn of 1938, and briefly sublet the Burnshaws' house at Croton-on-Hudson, on the outskirts of New York City. (The Burnshaws' baby was due in December, and they preferred to live near a hospital.) Stead was feeling depressed. As well as the bitter disappointment of *House of All Nations*, there had been tragic news from Australia that summer. In August, her brother Fred had been killed by a truck while riding his motor-bike.[57] Just 27, he left behind a wife and two children. No record survives of Stead's response to the news, but the depiction of Leo, Teresa's younger brother in *For Love Alone*, is an unusually tender portrait. Leo, like the characters based on the dead Ralph Fox, is one of Stead's idealised male figures. She makes him that combination she always found so seductive: a revolutionary (he leads a strike at his factory) and a gentle romantic, who plays the guitar and has a soft spot for women.[58] Interestingly, Leo is also inordinately proud of his sister Teresa.

*   *   *

Before his novel appeared, Bill officially changed his name to William Blake. The choice had nothing to do with the famous poet: he had never liked the way English-speaking people pronounced his surname—something like 'Bletch'—and he had been using the name Blake for years.[59] Most people already called him Bill Blake. Perhaps he also wanted to dissociate himself formally both from the father who had never done anything for him and from the *Vaterland* which was vigorously disowning its Jewish citizens.

In August, Stead announced the name change to her brother Gilbert, adding, tongue-in-cheek: 'I don't have to change mine: mine happens to be the world's best literary name, everyone seems to have heard it and no-one forgets it.'[60] She was feeling disillusioned that summer.

The name 'Stead' had its own problems, she told Gilbert. Middle-class Jews often took it for a Danish or Swedish name, whereupon they assumed she was anti-semitic.

I never heard any such nonsense from working-class Jews, as
they're not interested in the trash of "semitism" but in their work,
their union, or whatever it is. You get so tired of this race stuff in
crazy Europe, that the only resort is to believe there are no races
at all worth mentioning, which is pretty much the truth anyhow.

By June 1942, when a report from Poland revealed that the Nazis had killed over a million Jews, Stead saw things very differently, and planned to write a novel about the Jews, that 'martyred people'.[61] But in 1938 her impatience had to do with her general attitude to cultural difference. While she had an expatriate Australian's fascination with foreignness and exoticism, she and Blake were too genuinely cosmopolitan to see cultural difference as something that separated people from one another. She was to be equally impatient with the Women's Movement in the 1970s which—as she saw it—polarised the sexes, emphasising their differences. Stead wanted a world in which cultural and biological differences were neither apologetically concealed nor aggressively proclaimed.

Her attitude towards Jewishness reflected that of most leftwing Jews in the Thirties. More concerned to be world citizens than to be regarded as Jews, they advocated assimilation. At the same time, they continued to differentiate between Jews and Gentiles, often at their own expense. In Michael Gold's *Jews Without Money*, the Rabbi, landlord and pawnbroker are treated as egregious villains. In *House of All Nations*, Stead has the Jewish Marxist Alphendéry tell his colleague, 'What is it the Jew doesn't want to lose? Not Judaism, dear Herr Rosenkrantz, but the bourgeoisie, of which he is the archetype, the most concentrated example.'[62] Bill Blake had in his first novel a caricature of a 'Dr. Isaiah Gladsteyn', a psychoanalyst who 'smoothed out the neurotic troubles of middle-class Israelites'.[63] His second novel, *The Painter and The Lady*, satirises an old Jewish money-lender.

Ultimately, Bill Blake's anti-Jewish jokes and stories were simply another facet of his self-irony. He and his friends were proud of their Jewishness, just as Stead was proud to have a Jewish partner. According to Stanley Burnshaw, himself a Jew, Bill if anything deliberately cultivated a Jewish style, and most of their friends were Jewish.[64] He and Christina liberally used Yiddish expressions.[65]

★　★　★

Although it officially promoted a Popular Front consisting of most shades of leftwingers, the *New Masses* certainly implied that the true revolutionary was a member of the Party. In January 1938, Bill Blake had officially joined the Party, proposed by Mike Gold. But his membership was short lived. He did not have the temperament for party politics at cell-meeting level; his mind was too theoretical. When, having just joined the Upper Broadway branch, Blake received a letter requesting that he attend a New Member Class the following Monday, he told Stead he would try to get out of it. She protested: 'Not the *first* meeting.' But she could not resist teasing him: 'They'll be sitting you down and teaching you the ABC of bundism.' (The Bund was a Jewish Workers' Union in Russia, Lithuania and Poland.) Blake bridled at the thought: 'I know more about it than they do.'[66]

Before long, they had left for Lambertville, then Croton, which made attendance at meetings impossible, unless Blake stayed overnight with a friend in New York. He attended meetings intermittently for the rest of that year and eventually stopped paying his dues. His membership officially lapsed in April 1939.[67] As a 'member at large', he continued to be in great demand as a speaker at political meetings and rallies.[68] Reports of the sensational Moscow trials in the American press did not sway his loyalty to Stalinism.

As a foreign resident in the United States, Christina Stead could not join the Party. She regretted this for one reason only: it would have provided material for the novel she wanted to write about communist radicals.[69] Her commitment was to her writing, not politics. She disliked political meetings, with their endless rhetoric in smoke-filled rooms. However, she did join the League of American Writers, which united writers against fascism, with regular readings, discussion panels and fundraising activities.

Though she rarely dared to say so, Stead took a whimsical view of unyielding allegiance to an ideological line. Having offered to review for the *New Masses* André Malraux's Spanish Civil War novel, *L'Espoir*, which had received mixed reactions from the Left, she turned to Stanley Burnshaw, another 'fellow traveller', for a second opinion.

> I have a very serious question to ask you: have you read André Malraux's "L'Espoir" and if so what . . .? I can lend you a French copy if you want to read it: you're an intellectual, you have the afflatus, you're not in, but alongside the Party (capital p shows good faith), and I should very much value your opinion on his latest book. Of course, Bill doesn't think much of the calibre of a guy who is not in, but alongside the Party, and so it's no good my breaking up the happy home discussing it with him. I think I understand Malraux: I like him, anyhow; and I think the Party-ites misjudge him.[70]

To many, Malraux seemed to care more about the revolutionary struggle, the violence and heroic *camaraderie*, than about socialism as a goal. Undoubtedly, Stead was attracted precisely to this hero quality. Malraux, who had led an air squadron for the Republican forces in Spain, had written his novel 'on the field of action, after work, in the evening'. Though she admired his 'descriptive genius' and considered that he had achieved 'that perfect synthesis and simulacrum of life of which the novel alone is capable', most of all, she admired Colonel Malraux himself: 'He is a man with an extremely austere sense of duty towards his fellow man and towards his art.'[71]

Stead was convinced that writers had a political responsibility, but like a good many other fellow-travellers, she was impatient with simplistic notions of proletarian literature, and she was courageous enough to say so in the *New Masses*. Her review of the Finnish novel, *Meek Heritage*, praised its revolutionary content and contrasted it with sentimental proletarian writing. 'It is a sort of counterblast to those writers who seek "folk-poems" from the horny-handed farmboy who has come to beg for bread, those who wish to set up falsely colored proletarian ideals in idle, romantic narratives.'[72]

Her courage had been fortified by Ralph Fox's widely praised posthumous book *The Novel and the People*, of which extracts appeared in the *New Masses* shortly after his death.[73] Fox was scornful of the 'hardboiled school' of proletarian literature, which made fiction into a 'scarcely disguised political tract'. He argued that it was 'completely foreign to the spirit of Marxism to neglect the formal side of art'.[74] And he supported Engels' view that 'the more the opinions of the author remain hidden, the better for the work of art'.[75]

To Fox, celebrating the workers was not as important as depicting characters against their social background, showing them to be determined partly by social forces. 'There is no human character, no emotion, no conflict of personalities outside the scope of the revolutionary novelist.'[76] His conclusion was as Nietzschean as it was Marxist: 'The one concern of the novelist is, or should be, this question of the individual will in its conflict with other wills on the battleground of life.'[77]

These were views congenial to Stead. In her fiction, personal relations were always grounded in the social and economic world. But she did not care to voice her own opinions or take a moral stance. Nor was she interested in presenting heroes and happy endings where there were none. Hers was a universe of contradictions, incongruity and strife. Indeed, the charges of energy in Christina Stead's fiction are generated precisely by the *unreconciled* elements, by individual wills 'in conflict with other wills on the battleground of life'.

* * *

Towards the end of the year, Stead was surprised to see an Australian envelope with Florence James' handwriting among a pile of letters forwarded to Croton-on-Hudson. With the threat of war in Europe, Florence had gone back to Australia with her two girls: her husband was joining them later. After ten years in England, Florence's reaction gave Stead 'a palpable notion' of what Australia was like these days. 'Perhaps I shouldn't like it any better than I did before.'[78]

Like most expatriates, Stead's attitude to Australia was extremely ambivalent. She missed the climate and the bush, but shuddered when she thought of Australia's provincialism and isolation. She felt resentful when she considered how little Australians fostered artistic talent, and that, even so, expatriate artists were treated like deserters. In 1938, for the first time, she was featured next to her father in Australia's *Who's Who*, but her talent and contribution to Australian literature had never been celebrated by Australian critics. Entrenched in the realist tradition, they disliked the 'over-luxuriance' of her writing and its elements of modernist experimentation.[79]

In his 1936 book *The Foundations of Culture in Australia*, P. R. Stephensen, who had recently returned to Australia after several years in England, attacked the colony of Australian émigré-writers in London: Jack Lindsay, Henry Handel Richardson, Christina Stead, Frederic Manning and others.

> Had these people remained here, and dealt with the realities of Australia, instead of with the fantasies of European glamour and European antiquity, they would with ease have created a body of Australian literature which, added to that we already possess, would by now have been enough to make Australia's name and quality resound as one of the most highly cultivated and civilised nations upon the earth. But no; the shirkers, they have cleared out, funked their job.[80]

His language is jocular, but the message was serious.

In Australia, critics were obsessed by the need to determine whether books were *Australian* or *Un-Australian*. Of Stead's four novels so far, only *Seven Poor Men of Sydney*, set in her home city, qualified as 'Australian'. Reflecting on the exceptional 1938 harvest in Australian literature, the foremost Australian critic, H. M. Green, paid Christina Stead only grudging tribute.

> The year produced three novels that are outstanding: Christina Stead's *House of All Nations*, Xavier Herbert's *Capricornia*, and Seaforth Mackenzie's *Chosen People*. The first does not really concern us, for its author left Australia ten years ago and settled abroad, and the book is cosmopolitan in tone and subject. But it is difficult to pass it over entirely. Huge, packed, amorphous, it is neither a popular nor an artistic success, but it shows its author to possess a combination of qualities such as I have found in no other writer to-day.[81]

Nettie Palmer tried to retrieve *House of All Nations* for Australian literature by arguing that Stead had written 'an Australian novel of a new genre', pointing out that Stead used occasional Australian phrases and imagery—about gold diggers and surfing. But then Palmer was obliged to admit that Stead used images 'from every-where else too'.[82]

This pointless debate about 'Australianness' continued until the late Sixties. In the name of cultural nationalism, the debate merely proved the parochialism and defensiveness of Australian culture at the time.

* * *

By the beginning of 1939, it was eighteen months since Christina Stead had finished *House of All Nations*, and she had only just decided on the subject for her next novel. Almost three years earlier in New York, reading about state socialism, she had suddenly thought she would like to write about her father's life—his upbringing, beliefs and character—but for that project she needed to be in Australia to research the social background.[83] She was also very excited when Ralph Fox confessed his liking for autobiography. Now she decided to write about her own childhood. She would still be writing about her father, but her father as an adult. And for that she could work from memory and personal correspondence.

To avoid the New York winter, she and Blake went to St Augustine, Florida, in January 1939, where Blake researched his novel on the American Civil War, *The Copperheads*, and Stead started to plan *The Man Who Loved Children*. In May, back in New York, they moved into a six-room apartment at No. 152 E. 22nd Street, in the Gramercy Park area. The apartment was large so that 70-year-old Rosa Blech, now in poor condition, could live with them. So could Bill's cousin Jenka, as Rosa's companion.[84]

It was a big step for Stead to decide to write autobiographical fiction. Earlier autobiographical attempts had been discarded in 1932, and she had written *The Salzburg Tales* instead. Not only the Left, but Anglo-Saxons generally, tended to deem it 'priggish and conceited' to write about one's childhood: as critic Fay Zwicky points out, it was made to seem 'a luxury and an indulgence inimical to material progress and utilitarian survival'. In the English-speaking world, there was not the same interest in the *Bildungsroman* (a novel portraying the formation and development of an individual) as in France and Germany. Two of Stead's literary models, D. H. Lawrence's *Sons and Lovers* and Joyce's *Portrait of the Artist as a Young Man* were received more sympathetically in Europe than in Britain.[85]

Brought up in the stoic Anglo-Saxon tradition, Stead rarely allowed herself to explore her own emotions. She had majored in psychology and made no bones about being fascinated by the psychology of others, but she was uncomfortable with self-revelation. And she and Blake were both fiercely impatient with what they regarded as the self-indulgence of popular psychology. In both *The Beauties and Furies* and *Letty Fox*, Stead ridicules the way psycho-analytic jargon reduces everything to an Oedipus complex or a 'father fixation'. Yet, even if she disliked the Freudian vocabulary, she must have recognised in her struggle with the shadow of her father a classic Freudian scenario.

When she had left Australia a decade earlier, Stead had resolutely left her past behind. Once in the northern hemisphere, she had adopted new ideas, other cultures. Her father was prejudiced against Jews, businessmen and the French; he abstained from alcohol and never went to the theatre or cinema. Christina Stead enthusiastically embraced all these aspects of her new existence. But she had not managed to exorcise the ghost of her father.

Relations with her family in the last ten years had been amicable but distant. In 1938 there had been a flurried exchange of books. Christina sent her father *House of All Nations*. His de-facto wife, Thistle Harris, a botanist, sent Christina and Bill a copy of her *Wildflowers of Australia*. Bill posted off *The World is Mine*, with the inscription:

To David G. Stead, father of a miraculous daughter and
himself highly esteemed by long and indirect knowledge
by "William Blake." Wm. J. Blech.[86]

The picture Christina painted of her father was plainly not wholly negative, yet she was painfully aware that her childhood had left her emotionally scarred. Now, just like Virginia Woolf at a similar age, she felt compelled to write about the figures who had loomed so large in her early years.[87] Six months into writing *The Man Who Loved Children*, she told Thistle Harris: 'I have left it all these years, not able to touch such an autobiographical subject, but last winter I decided to get it off my chest once and for all.'[88] In an interview when she was 75, Stead would say that the novel 'demanded to be written':

I was quite solitary, although I was very happy with Bill,
my husband . . . But I was crying every two months and just
couldn't stop. I didn't know it then, but it was because of
my terrible experiences as a child.

Then one day I wrote down everything to clarify my feelings.[89] Christina Stead was 36 when she began *The Man Who Loved Children* in the winter of 1938–9. Virginia Woolf, at 44, had found that writing *To The Lighthouse* went some way towards dispelling her parental ghosts. Stead too would say, just two years later: 'It was a great weight off my mind, I ought really to say my soul, writing *The Man Who*—it was as if I escaped from jail, although it may seem savage and mean to others.'[90] At the time, however, plunging into the past brought violent emotions to the surface and caused her extreme emotional distress. The E. 22nd Street apartment was dark and dreary, overshadowed by high rises with factories on the ground floor. Stead felt oppressed by the stonework and brickwork around her.[91] Her internal world—far more oppressive—was overshadowed by her father. The memories came flooding back. She slept badly. She raged. She wept. Among all that masonry, she was effectively undertaking her own psychoanalysis.

Could she exorcise the pain of her past by writing about it?

As the novel was being typeset, she told Florence James that writing it had given her 'the jitters'. ('Part of it is taken from my homelife and not very amiable.') She had been 'too down' all these months to write to the family. She still could not write home. It was 'a snake's life', she considered, to shed one's skin as she had done.[92] The choice of image—more evocative of her Sydney childhood than her life in urban New York—suggests she had not shed her skin completely.

Writing about her past made her examine her childhood clinically, from the outside. It crystallised the misery of it all: her father's failure to put himself in her place, his fundamental indifference—an indifference that was part of his charm. As she was writing it, Stead told Thistle Harris that it was one of her aims in life never to see her father again.

It has been a grand thing for me to get this plucked out of the back of my mind. But, a thing David could not realise, that home was so atrociously wretched and I was so ill at ease as a result that I do not want to see Australia, except on some gilded visit, if I ever get the gilding. Yes, I could live in Victoria, or Queensland, or go out back, say to Broken Hill, that is something I should like to do for a while—but I do not want to see Sydney, nor my family, nor anyone connected with the old days.

She added, 'I'm not unforgiving—how could it be so when no-one is to blame?—they just made an etching out of me, I am deep-bitten.'[93]

Why did Stead write these things to Thistle Harris, whom she scarcely knew? Her long letter to Thistle in July 1939, which reduced David Stead to a case study of egotism, could hardly have been more hurtful about the man Thistle loved. Christina well knew that Thistle might show the letter to David. By aiming her missile indirectly in this way, Christina was hurting both her father and Thistle Harris in one deft move.

Christina had clearly not come to terms with Thistle, who seems to have brought out her sense of rivalry. While writing *The Man Who Loved Children*, she told Thistle she had three more novels brewing.

I hope I get some backbone and go at it a bit faster than usual, for time draws on and I have only turned out *four* books. It's frightful to think of.

Are you working on another plant book? I hear that this one was written some years ago, but publication was held up.[94]

* * *

Novels do not linger on the lulls between storms; the 'domestic agony' and 'shrieks of madness' Christina Stead experienced throughout her adolescence and early womanhood are condensed into two years in the fiction.[95] She invented some incidents completely: David Stead never gathered the older children together at the bottom of the stairs to listen to the shrieks of their mother in labour; nor did Christina write a play for her father's fortieth birthday. The Pollit children are hybrid versions of their real-life models. And unlike Louisa, Christina never gave her stepmother poison—though she fantasised about it.[96]

Samuel Pollit, at 38, tall, yellow-haired and ruddy-skinned, with 'sparkling, self-satisfied eyes', is a naturalist who left school at 12 and now works for a government department. Henrietta, his highly-strung second wife from a wealthy Baltimore family, has black hair and olive skin, and looks like a 'thin, dark scarecrow'. Her sixth child is born in the course of the novel, and 'Henny' excels in bitter diatribes against her lot. Louisa, Sam's daughter by his previous marriage, is a young adolescent, awkward and heavy. Books give her access to a fertile private world.

How true to life are Sam and Henny? Like all fictional characters, they distil and reassign aspects of the people on whom they are modelled. Sam Pollit lacks David Stead's broad erudition, so important a dimension of the real man. And while Henny is Ada Stead at her most wretched and worn, she is also more glorious than her real-life counterpart. Henny's verbal fluency and flights of imagination are not Ada's: these belonged to the stepdaughter herself. Most of Christina Stead's fictional characters are capable of brilliant verbal pyrotechnics; it is not always an accurate reflection of their models.

David Stead's language, on the other hand, did not have to be whipped into thicker cream. Nor was there any need for Stead to exaggerate her father's portrait for fictional purposes. When writing *The Man Who Loved Children*, she was plainly driven by unresolved rage and resentment, but David Stead's real-life character was sufficiently extravagant and infuriating to need no further embellishment. In her old age, Thistle Harris commented that she saw *The Man Who Loved Children* as 'substantially true'.[97]

The writing and revision of *The Man* took Stead a year and a half. No drafts have survived, but a few straggling notes indicate that she prepared for writing with her habitual thoroughness. One page, entitled 'Aunt Josephine', is a character sketch of her dreaded maiden aunt Jessica, noting her expressions, opinions and prejudices.[98] Stead must have typed pages and pages of similar character sketches—always concentrating on the character's voice.

Considerable research was involved in transposing the novel's location from Sydney to Baltimore. Stead and Blake spent time in the genteel districts of Georgetown, Washington. Tohoga House, the Pollits' first grand home, is based on an actual house in the area. (Since David Stead gave things Aboriginal names, Sam Pollit gives his house the Indian name for Georgetown: Tohoga.[99]) Together Stead and Blake explored the shabbier parts of Baltimore, at the head of the Chesapeake Bay, in order to find an equivalent for the house at Watson's Bay. Stead studied local government booklets on trees, subsoil, salinity and the condition of the water in the estuary. It was typical of her ambivalence towards her father that at the very moment when she was writing about the tyrannical upbringing she had endured at his hands, she prided herself on getting the naturalist details right. She also studied local Maryland and Virginia folklore: the story Louisa tells the children, 'Hawkins the North Wind', is based on a Maryland legend.

Why did Stead bother to change the location, which entailed significant alterations in the characters' speech and preoccupations? The explanation Stead gave later, that it was to shield the family, was not the reason.[100] Already with *House of All Nations*, she had been faced with problems of discretion and libel, yet she had made very little attempt at disguise.[101] She was not at all keen to transfer the setting to America; it was Simon & Schuster who insisted on it, persuading her that it would make the book more marketable for an American readership. Indeed, Stead was so loath to make it an American novel that at first she even contemplated re-writing *The Man Who Loved Children* for Australia afterwards, with Australian settings.[102]

And why did she change the novel's time-frame from the 1910s, when she was an adolescent, to the late 1930s? Critic Jose Yglesias suggests that Stead's intention was to give the book contemporary political relevance.[103] But the real reason was linked to the change in location: the America Stead knew was contemporary America— the Thirties; unlike Bill Blake, she was no historical novelist. It was her good fortune that the Franklin Roosevelt government of the Thirties in many ways resembled the progressive New South Wales government earlier in the century. David Stead had admired that Labor Government and its policy of state socialism which enabled him to establish the State Trawling Industry; similarly, Sam Pollit is a 'great partisan of the Roosevelt work plans'—largely 'because of the work done in fish and forestry conservation by the W.P.A. and C.C.C. workers'.[104]

But the spatial and temporal dislocations provided a thorny challenge, to which, several critics maintained, Stead was unable to rise.[105] Mary McCarthy was to comment:

Though there is a compulsive circumstantiality of detail in
the book, the sense of reality is feeble. The action takes place
during the Roosevelt administration, when Samuel Pollit is
supposed to be between thirty-eight and forty years old; yet all
his taste, his slang, and his opinions date from twenty or thirty
years earlier; no young New Dealer, for example, would talk
about "Teddy" Roosevelt, or display such a close acquaintance
with the works of Artemus Ward ... Some of Miss Stead's
most strikingly squalid effects are got from the use of slang
that is surely not American but British.[106]

If *The Man Who Loved Children* had been the Australian book Stead
wanted to write, it would not have had these flaws. Nevertheless,
after ten years away, and living among Americans, it would also
have presented a challenge to recreate the nuances of Australian
speech.

Stead found the revision as tiresome as always. 'Bill had to drag
me through the last revision by the hair of my head, I couldn't bear
it any more.'[107] Not only was the subject harrowing, but the
daunting mass of 'surplus material' and 'surplus drama' kept getting
in the way.[108]

According to Randall Jarrell, who twenty-five years later would
do more than anyone else to promote the novel, it contained
passages that ought not to be there—passages that looked to him
like an 'intrusion of raw reality into the imagined reality of the
book'. He pointed out that 'one of the most puzzling things about a
novel is that "the way it really was" half the time is, and half the
time isn't, the way it ought to be in the novel'.[109]

Piled up on her work table, as Stead was drafting the novel in
their dingy apartment, were her father's writings. David Stead had
sent her his small monographs, *Giants and Pigmies of the Deep*, *The
Tree Book* and *The Rabbit in Australia* when they were published in
the early to mid Thirties. She probably asked him for copies of his
newspaper columns and radio broadcasts for schoolchildren about
the 'great outdoors' and his travels in Malaya. Presented in the
chatty, didactic style he had used with his own children, they were
a living reminder of her father's voice. The most important source
for Stead were the letters her father had written from Malaya in
1922–3. It seems that she wrote home asking for these, for at the
top of a letter from Singapore, written on 20 January 1923, David
Stead typed a note dated Nov. 1941: 'Have just re-read this befr
sndg [before sending]. Don't be too hard on poor Dad. Remember
tht he was sick, tired and nostalgic. Love Dad.'[110] Her father's
colourful letters enabled Stead to portray Sam Pollit in Malaya,
a place she had never seen.

The surviving letters from Malaya reveal the extent to which Christina Stead used real-life letters in her fiction.[111] Chapter 6 of *The Man Who Loved Children* contains one of David Stead's original letters virtually verbatim.[112] It poses an interesting question: when does 'naturalism' become 'plagiarism'?[113]

In his letters from Malaya, Sam Pollit coincides perfectly with David Stead: the convergence is quite remarkable. By placing her father's letter within *her* novel, Christina Stead had annexed and asserted power over her father's creative product.

Or so it seemed. How must Stead have felt when Clifton Fadiman commented, in his review of *The Man Who Loved Children*, that the novel as a whole did not come off, but that Sam's letters from Malaya were astounding—'extraordinary writing'?[114] It must have seemed to her that she had not, after all, managed to subjugate the shadow of her father. In the very domain in which she struggled to break free from him—her writing—he maintained his power.

In the novel, young Louisa Pollit struggles with the same dilemma. As an apprentice writer Louisa wants both to impress *her father* and to express *herself*. This is her bind.

Though Stead 'captured' her father in her novel, she would always remain ligated—even at the other side of the world. Perhaps this explains the strange attraction she had felt as a young woman to a painting in the New South Wales Art Gallery, an old-fashioned picture of the sons of Clovis on a barge and bound, by their father, so that they would not inherit his kingdom. Later in life, she recalled: 'I used to look and look at those two boys . . . going down the river . . . Tied. Hamstrung.'[115]

★   ★   ★

While she was writing *The Man Who Loved Children*, Stead could not have been easy to live with. Nor was Rosa Blech. The situation at home was 'very painful, almost impossible'. Just one month after they had moved into the large apartment near Gramercy Park, Rosa Blech became ill and was taken to hospital. On 21 June 1939, she died. It was sudden, 'but not too soon'.[116] Stead told Thistle Harris:

> She did not have any particular illness, just fell to pieces, wore out, and died of uremia at the end, a very common end for aged persons. She had little pain, just general weakness and a little confusion for about a month and unconsciousness at the end. She spoke all sorts of languages picked up in Europe at the end and her last words were—"A quoi bon?" (What's the use? a very common saying of hers—she was a pessimist, I'm afraid.) The nurse attending her said she said "Aqua bon" but we knew what she had really said. At first we couldn't get

used to the strangeness of not having her to consider. In everything we did, we would say to each other, "What will she think? What will she say? Will she like it?" or "She's sure to say so-and-so," or when we were out we used to say, "If Mother saw us going to have a cocktail now, she'd say we were tramps," etc. It's like getting yourself free of a whole suit of clothing of cobwebs. But her quick and relatively easy death, and the fact that she was cremated without any religious ceremony or even music (her own idea) makes the idea of death pagan and you are not visited by remorse, horror or even much sorrow. It is a wonderful way to come to an end.[117]

In *Letty Fox*, old Grandma Fox is tormented by persecution fantasies. Near the end, she even begins to have suspicions about her beloved son Solander and grand-daughter Letty. But it is her son's companion whom she dreads. Persia, she imagines, is starving her, hitting her, poisoning her, waiting for her money. Grandma Fox's last words are also: 'But what is the use?'[118]

In deference to Mollie Blech, Christina Stead did not attend the funeral.[119] In the novel, Persia does. She is escorted by a family friend, and stands in the back row among strangers, unacknowledged by members of the Fox family (even Solander). That *Letty Fox* contains these painful little details about Persia's humiliating situation as Solander Fox's mistress—even if they were not always true of Stead's actual life—is revealing. Though the story is told from egocentric Letty's point of view, Persia's pain is tangible.

Only after Rosa's death did Bill learn that his mother had had a twin sister, who ran off at 21 with a Russian officer.[120] Just as Rosa, in her obsession with social respectability, told everyone she was a widow rather than a divorcee, she told no-one about her wayward twin. Stead would work these details into *Letty Fox*, and Solander Fox's reaction was probably close to Bill's own:

"My heavens," said Solander, with tears in his eyes, "don't tell me that my poor little mother concealed all this from me? Poor, poor little thing! What she carried in that little head— what troubles, what disgraces—life is hard!"[121]

Rosa Blech had managed to save $3000, a considerable sum. But though she had lived largely at Bill's expense, she left all her money to her grand-daughter Ruth.[122] As Stead saw it, Rosa's final gesture from beyond the grave demonstrated her hostility towards the 'shiksa'.[123]

'It is odd to see a man of Bill's age suddenly afloat on the ocean of life,' Stead told Florence James.[124] Two weeks after his mother died, Bill lost his earliest protector on Wall Street, John McRoy, the wealthy inventor for whom Bill had first worked as a boy of 14.

A few months later, Jenka got married. Stead and Blake were at last on their own again—'after years of un-ease'. Having leased the large dark apartment for a year, they were obliged to remain there that summer, and felt restless and depressed. Stead agonised over her novel, which seemed to progress 'at a snail's pace'. In addition to her sinus headaches, her regular New York ailment, she suffered from mysterious 'collywobbles'.[125]

*　　*　　*

Political events reinforced Stead's gloom. September 1938 had Prime Minister Chamberlain signing the Munich Pact, which gave Sudetenland, a region of Czechoslovakia, over to Nazi Germany—a step widely seen as a cowardly appeasement of Hitler. In November 1938, 'Kristallnacht' heralded a new phase of terrorism against Jews throughout Germany. Shops were looted, Jews were murdered and Jewish property henceforth belonged to the Reich. In Spain, during the severe winter of 1938–9, Franco's Nationalists swept to victory. In March 1939, the Germans invaded Prague. In May, Hitler and Mussolini signed a ten-year military alliance, their 'Pact of Steel'. War was imminent.

It was against this frightening backdrop that the League of American Writers held the Third American Writers' Congress in June 1939, a three-day meeting at the New School for Social Research. Shattered by the Republican defeat in Spain and wary of the temporary peace brought about by the Munich Pact, more than 500 delegates attended. At the opening session on Saturday, 3 June, League President Donald Ogden Stewart challenged authors to fight with pen and typewriter for the defence of civil and cultural liberties in the United States. Thomas Mann, Honorary President, spoke to a capacity audience about the barbarism of the Nazis.

In the fiction session the next day, five writers, all committed communists, presented brief papers. Louis Aragon spoke about the social character of the novel; Richard Wright talked about the short novel; Sylvia Townsend Warner discussed historical fiction; Dashiell Hammett spoke about tempo in fiction. Christina Stead spoke about the many-charactered novel.

As author of the many-charactered *House of All Nations*, Stead suggested that this was the ideal form of novel for a world in chaos in which the individual felt small. No writer could take sides when dealing with such a large array of characters: the writer 'is in the position of an impartial, disabused and merry god' and the reader has to 'draw his own conclusions from the diverse material, as from life itself'.

Stead's paper celebrated multiplicity and impartiality. But this was scarcely the stuff of revolutionary literature, and she felt obliged to make an awkward genuflection to communism at its conclusion by suggesting that a truly revolutionary novel would have a hero who stands out from the mass. 'The great story, the writer may think, would be this—a sea of many lives, the world of today, from which rises a greater life, drawing sustenance from them, acting, sinking back to them—Dimitrov, Lenin, the section organiser.'[126]

Just as she had done in her *Left Review* article four years earlier, Stead asserted that people 'feel flustered and do not know where they stand'. Comments such as this reflected her own bewilderment in the face of menacing political events on the one hand and ideological constraints on the other which, try as she might to parrot them, simply did not suit her as a writer.

★　★　★

Blake and Stead were among 400 American intellectuals to sign an Open Letter addressed to 'All Active Supporters of Democracy and Peace'. A declaration of faith in Stalinist communism, it denounced the 'fantastic falsehood' promoted by Trotskyist writers associated with *Partisan Review* that Soviet socialism was no different from totalitarian fascism. The Open Letter, dated 14 August 1939, insisted: 'The U.S.S.R. was and continues to be "a bulwark against war and aggression".'[127]

Just one week later, on 23 August, came the announcement of a Non-Aggression pact between Russia and Germany. Soviet Russia had become Adolf Hitler's ally. The shocking news caused a spate of resignations from the Communist Party and the League—including Thomas Mann. The anti-fascist platform to which they had all committed themselves for the last six years had collapsed. Western communists were faced with their greatest test of loyalty yet.

Blake and Stead rallied staunchly to Party policy, and remained active in the much depleted League of American Writers.[128] Their friends Ruth McKenny and Richard Bransten defended the Russo-German pact in the *New Masses*: it was necessary both to save Russia from invasion and to protect Soviet socialism.[129]

In September 1939, the English language acquired a new word from German—to *blitz*. Before dawn on 1 September, the Nazi *Luftwaffe* prepared the way, with massive aerial bombardment, for German tanks to cross into Polish territory. On 3 September, Britain's ultimatum to Germany expired and Prime Minister Chamberlain declared war on Hitler's Reich. France, Australia and New Zealand rallied to Britain's side. The war had begun.

9

Dearest Munx

JUNE 1940–JUNE 1942

'PARIS HAS FALLEN! We never thought to see that.' It was 15 June 1940. Denmark and Norway, Belgium and Holland had surrendered to the Nazis and now the swastika was flying on the Arc de Triomphe. Earlier that month there had been the Dunkirk evacuation. Stead was horrified: the war was looking grim for Britain and Australia. Nevertheless, she followed the Comintern line that it was an 'imperialist war' managed by international capitalists and that America should keep out. The growing 'martial fever' among Americans dismayed her. 'Dissenters are few. Nothing like the last war.'[1]

The Man Who Loved Children was in the hands of the publishers, Simon & Schuster. It had taken Stead almost eighteen months— a tumultuous time emotionally. Next time she would take a different tack, she told herself, 'less personal, more story and humanity, a broader canvas'.[2]

She and Blake escaped the New York summer in an old cottage at Cape Cod, 'that seahorse of land' on the blustery Atlantic coast. 'Dirt, sand, winds, insufficient bedcovers, kerosene stove falling to pieces, you know the seaside summer holiday,' she told Florence James. She liked the gales and the Moby-Dick atmosphere; Bill did not.[3]

In early October, back in New York, they moved into a brownstone house in the Old Bowery area, just off Stuyvesant Park.

A graceful staircase, illuminated by the natural light of an *oeil-de-boeuf* in the roof, led to their sunny apartment on the fourth floor, which looked over Chinese plantains to the backs of houses and their iron fire escapes. The best feature was the large, airy living room with an open fireplace. The kitchen and bathroom were modest, and then there were two small rooms, a bedroom, and a study where Blake would work when he was home. (He generally preferred the New York Public Library.) Alone in the apartment most of the day, Stead worked in the living room, and sometimes, when Blake was talking politics, in the bedroom.

> The whole scene was that of an unpretentious suburb and had
> an air of sunny quiet and no struggle, even though the trains
> ground and shrieked a few yards away, and in the high sky
> Consolidated Edison's tower rose immediately to the right.[4]

The drawback of living near Third Avenue was the noise of the El, the elevated railway, which clattered and screeched on high metal girders from one end of the city to the other. 'El-Hel' was the Rabbinical name for New York, Stead decided.[5]

They would spend the best part of two years at No. 212 E. 16th Street, and despite the noise, Stead was introduced in that house to the real charm of Manhattan life. New York would become one of her favourite cities, along with Paris. It was partly the house, which had a friendly, communal atmosphere. And it was partly the 'people with the dogs', their landlord's extended Russian-American family of dog-lovers.

Their landlord, Asa Zatz, was in his mid twenties. He lived, with his kern terrier, in a large chaotic room on the second floor. He and his mother, a medical practitioner, had bought the house when his father died in 1935. Dr Zatz had her practice on the ground floor. She died in the spring of 1941, while Stead and Blake were residents. Other rooms were rented out, and there was a communal kitchen in the basement.

Asa Zatz, his communal household and 'Cherry Orchard' family[6] would inspire *The People with the Dogs*, planned in the early to mid Forties and written in the early Fifties. In contrast to *Letty Fox* and *A Little Tea, A Little Chat*, Stead's other American novels, *The People with the Dogs* breathes a deep affection for New York. Just as *The Beauties and Furies* is romantic Paris, *The People with the Dogs* is romantic lower Manhattan, 'the last of gaslight New York'.[7]

Manhattan is not wholly idealised in the novel. A murder takes place in the first few pages—though it is a strangely surrealistic incident: most striking is the girl's orange lipstick as she falls, knifed, to the ground. In this city, ambulances squeal past, trains pass by with a 'crashing roar', desperate people roam the sidewalks at all hours. At the same time, the city is a friendly urban village. The characters walk everywhere, their dogs trotting along beside them; they drop in on friends and 'flop' at each other's places. They eat bagels and *salzstengels*, chicken fat on radish slices, herrings in sour cream, smoked oysters, sweet pickles and cinnamon cakes. They are always on the phone to each other. When Oneida's beloved bull terrier is to undergo an operation, her sisters and brothers and their spouses turn up at the vet's to commiserate.

According to Asa Zatz, Stead invented and embellished characters and exaggerated the extent of the house's communality, but much of the detail in *The People with the Dogs* is astoundingly true to life. He found his own fictional portrait as Edward Massine 'amazing'; Stead had quite brilliantly captured the way he talked. For him, the experience of reading the novel when it was published in 1952 was 'like being in analysis'. Yet he had no idea, when Stead was living upstairs, that she was even thinking of writing a novel about his family; he merely noticed that she asked a lot of questions.

Zatz's father had written plays. Asa had attended the Yale Drama School, intending to become a director; but, indolent by nature, he found himself drifting into technical jobs like lighting and staging. When the theatre was out, he would visit his actress girlfriend, Florence, and at 2 am or so, he would walk his dog Jock over to Stuyvesant Park.[8]

He would regularly sleep till noon. Almost daily visits were made to his favourite aunt and her husband, Aida and Max Kotlarsky, whose cavern-like apartment was on nearby W. 12th Street. Max, a tall, quiet, witty man, was a concert pianist, who had studied with Artur Schnabel. Tiny Aida, who looked like a 'wide-eyed elfin child',[9] was also a talented pianist, though she did not perform. She loved exotic, oriental furnishings and colourful theatrical costume. She loved their country house, deep in the Catskill mountains. Above all, she loved her dogs. Nip and Tuck, pedigree bull terriers, were her surrogate children. She and Max Kotlarsky were to be the models for Oneida and Lou Solway in *The People with the Dogs*.[10]

There was something Chekhovian about the Dolinskis, as Asa's maternal family were called. The title of Stead's novel evokes Chekhov's 'Lady with the Lapdog'. In the nineteenth century, Asa's grandfather, a Russian Jewish émigré, had bought several acres of land near Hunter, in the Catskills. Vaguely inspired by the radical ideals of the Oneida community in upstate New York, he had various cottages built on the estate for his nine children, of whom Aida was the youngest. Family and friends, he declared, would always be welcome there.

At the beginning of summer, when the concert season was in

recess, Aida and Max would retreat to this country house. Aida's siblings and their families would move into their cottages. Friends would come to stay—artists, actors, musicians. On occasion, everyone would come together for a meal, with spouses, children, cats and dogs. Stead and Blake would visit several times over the years.

★   ★   ★

The Man Who Loved Children was published in New York on 11 October 1940. Stead must have been nervous. It was her most intimate and revealing book ever, and certainly the book that had caused her the most pain. She did not hesitate to call it her 'best book to date'.[11] How would the critics react? She had complied with Simon & Schuster by making it an American novel: would they promote it properly this time?

Simon & Schuster published it with very little fanfare. Four weeks later, Stead told a friend bitterly, 'S & S are disgusted with the book and are doing nothing for it. I should have called it *How to Have Children and Generate People* ... I am quitting them.'[12] The book sold slowly at $2.75. Later, when the price was reduced to $1.75, some 5000 copies sold quite quickly.

It was destined to be one of those highly original novels that do not take off at first. Faulkner's *The Sound and Fury* (1929), Nathanael West's *Miss Lonelyhearts* (1933), and Djuna Barnes' *Nightwood* (1936) had suffered the same fate. The moment was unpropitious: people were anxious about the war in Europe and less willing than they might otherwise have been to immerse themselves in a thick novel about the idiosyncratic Pollit family. Publishers and readers were wanting morale building stories, not tales about flawed characters. By the end of the war, the book would be out of print, along with *House of All Nations*, which Clifton Fadiman now praised retrospectively as 'the best novel of finance to be found in English'.[13]

The critics, once again, were impressed—with reservations. It was compelling, they said. Miss Stead had 'a theatrical sense of action'. The characters were wonderfully real. But they were 'blighted'.[14] And the novel, they nearly all agreed, was 'remorselessly overblown'.[15]

One of the most positive reviews was Isidor Schneider's in the *New Masses*, which probably did Stead a considerable disservice in non-communist circles.[16] Schneider considered the novel an excellent illustration of Engels' *Origin of the Family*. ('The downfall of the Pollit family was to be attributed to its 'insecure and inelastic economy'.[17]) So great was his enthusiasm that he sent his review copy to the Moscow Comintern. Critic Pearl Bell would point out years later, 'With the Marxist imprimatur affixed to Miss Stead's work, no one bothered to investigate the grubby, exhilarating and overpowering reality of *The Man Who Loved Children*.'[18]

One of the few negative reviews was Mary McCarthy's, in *New Republic*. She thought it a 'peculiar, breathless, overwritten, incoherent novel'—much of it 'like an hysterical tirade'. The 'fearful, disordered vindictiveness' in the writing repelled her.[19]

Other critics were also disturbed by the anger ('shrillness') in the novel. Clifton Fadiman, trying to explain the lack of enthusiasm for Stead among some critics, commented that 'women reviewers in particular find her hard to take'. He recognised this prejudice as a double standard on the part of women as well as men.

Eventually, Christina Stead will impose herself upon the literature of the English-speaking countries. I say "impose herself" because her qualities are not apt to win her an immediate, warm acceptance. She may have to fight as long and as hard as did Joyce before gaining the suffrage of the majority. Her prose is difficult, often unnecessarily so. Her characters are like so many fiends. Her books are long, perhaps too long. They do not develop one out of the other but are massively solitary. Her humor is savage, her learning hard to cope with, her fancies too furious. Like Emily Brontë, she has none of the proper bearing, the reassuring domestic countenance of a "lady author."

But Fadiman's own reaction to the novel also disappointed Stead. Once again, he predicted that her genius ('the sheer originality, weight, and conscientiousness of her talent') would one day be acknowledged, but he was less impressed with *The Man Who Loved Children* than with *House of All Nations*—and he had been less impressed with *that* novel than with *The Salzburg Tales*. It was extraordinarily discouraging for Stead always to have her past novels celebrated as her 'peaks of achievement'.[20]

Nervous about their reaction, Stead put off sending the family a copy of the novel. She waited two months after its publication in England in June 1941 before sending a copy of the English wartime edition to Australia. And even then, she sent it to Thistle Harris— whom she scarcely knew.[21] On the frontispiece she wrote: 'To dear Thistle. A Strindberg Family Robinson. In some respects might be considered a private letter to Thistle from Christina Stead.'[22]

How was Thistle to take this? She read the novel. It certainly was not a flattering portrait of the man she loved, but it seems she graciously congratulated Stead on the likeness—adding that she loved David Stead, flaws and all.[23] Christina, who must have wondered sometimes whether she had exaggerated her father's portrait, was jubilant. To Bill, away in Canada on business, she wrote:

Had a letter from Thistle. She read *TMWLC* and says it is *exact*—my memory is faultless ... "A monster, an undeveloped personality and a lovable child," says she. So I hope you now believe your own woman and realise she is *not* crazy.

To Thistle, she wrote back:

Yes, I feel the characters in *TMWLC* are very, very real: recreated, but real. I am always surprised at my memory for detail ... Sam did really boil a fish for oil (a shark, not a tetrapturus, but I had to make it North American) and Henny really did play cards out of desperation and so on, so on: it did not happen exactly all on one day but what I did is a very real representation of life as it was then. As to the details: I am very happy to hear you say that you recognise them. I did not invent, naturally ... I am opposed to inventing in *life*. Life is so strange and we know it so little, that nothing is needed in that direction: we need only study: but real invention is needed in placing, and re-arranging, and re-creating.[24]

Thistle Harris, though she did not say so to Christina, was terribly hurt by the portrait of David Stead. In later years she would admit that she thought the novel 'tremendously cruel'. Strangely, she claims not to know whether David Stead ever read it: 'It's not the sort of thing I could have asked him.' She presumes—since she left it lying round the house quite openly—that he did. But, according to her, they never discussed it.[25] Gilbert Stead insists that his father did read the novel, for they talked about it, and he recalls that his father was shocked that Christina saw things in so black a light.[26]

Kate Stead and Gwen Walker-Smith were dismayed by the novel's indiscreet revelations. (Kate thinks that Ada probably never read the book.) David Darwin Stead considered the portraits of his parents 'caricatures', and several scenes 'greatly exaggerated'.[27]

The brief review of the novel in the *Sydney Morning Herald* in September 1941 would have made it clear to anyone who knew the Stead family that the novel was autobiographical.[28] Considering how American reviewers damned Sam Pollit, David Stead was fortunate that the anonymous Sydney reviewer was so mild.[29] 'At a casual glance,' wrote the reviewer, 'no one could fault Samuel Pollit. His devotion to his family is striking. He is patient with poor Henrietta ... and yet, one feels all the time that one must reserve judgement.'

The most striking feature of the *Sydney Morning Herald* review is its schoolmasterly condescension—a familiar tone in Stead's Australian reviews.

Hitherto Miss Stead has scorned to tread the path of the conventional novelist. In this latest book, however, she has decided, at last, to adopt an orthodox novel form, to modify her "rich and strange" mode of expression, and to deal with men and women with whom the average reader might easily be acquainted.

The character studies are excellent: both psychologically and emotionally they react in logical and convincing fashion. And there is, in spite of the normality of its appearance, a suggestion of originality in both outlook and expression about the novel which gives promises of future high achievement.

Reviewers tended to write as if Stead were just a beginner, yet this was her fifth published book in six years. And just how arbitrary their judgements were would become clear twenty-five years later when *The Man Who Loved Children* was re-issued by Holt, Rinehart & Winston, and hailed by critics as a 'marvellous neglected novel',[30] a 'long-neglected masterpiece',[31] a 'big black diamond of a book'[32] and 'one of the superb novels of the 20th century'.[33]

★ ★ ★

Asa Zatz, Stead and Blake's landlord, quickly became a friend. He enjoyed calling in upstairs from time to time for a chat, and Stead and Blake always seemed pleased to see him and would bring out their gallon container of cheap red wine.

> Visiting them was always a treat for me. Can you imagine the conversations one had with them? For some reason they liked me. I suppose I was learning, I was young. That such a young man was their landlord must have been interesting for them.
> I was crazy about both of them, especially Bill, because of his brilliance. He was the most incredibly brilliant yet unpedantic man you could imagine. It was always worth asking him: "Hey Bill, what do you think of so and so?"[34]

Zatz found Christina rather forbidding. He remembers her as 'fair, spare and lanky', with 'keen eyes, a jutting jaw and prominent front teeth'. To him, her clothes were drab and oldfashioned—mostly brown skirts and frilly blouses. But she was lively, with a wonderful sense of humour and a 'pleasant giggle'. She loved to hear his jokes and Yiddish stories. (The males in *The People with the Dogs* tell each other jokes almost as a form of greeting.) And she was, he recalls, very interested in a course he attended on cryptography.

Asa was particularly impressed by Blake's vast erudition and extraordinary memory. He remembers one occasion at the house in Hunter when Bill pulled a volume out of the bookcase and challenged him to test his memory.

> [Bill] once told me to give him fifteen or twenty minutes to memorise the details of Gibbon's *Decline and Fall of the Roman*

Empire. He really *had* taken in the details! Maybe it was only half the book—I can't remember—but I was amazed! . . . You'd ask him something and he didn't just give a quick answer. . . . He told me he hadn't forgotten anything he'd read since the age of eight or something, and I believed him.[35]

In 1940, at 46, Bill was well known in the States as a Marxian political economist and historical novelist. His book *Elements of Marxian Economic Theory and its Criticism* had appeared the previous year, re-issued shortly afterwards under the title *An American Looks at Karl Marx*.[36] It was lucid, entertaining, and selling well as an undergraduate textbook. During 1939, Simon & Schuster had published his second novel, *The Painter and the Lady*, dedicated to the memory of Ralph Fox.[37] Though the novel raised serious questions about the political function of art, it was as 'wildly playful' as the first. By his own admission, Blake tended to view the universe as 'a melodramatic joke of some sixty-legged Brahmin God'.[38]

Asa recalls that Bill, shocked to find him so 'politically illiterate', got him reading Marx, starting him off on *Value, Price and Profit*. When Asa complained that it was difficult, Bill retorted that it was the ABC of Marxism, written for workers.[39]

His political curiosity aroused, Asa sometimes went along to hear Bill speak at Party social functions. 'Bill was always the star. There was no stumping him.'[40] Bill was also a skilled fundraiser. 'He'd collect money after the meetings, bully people into forking out.' Among Stead's papers is an admiring note to Blake from the *New Masses* treasurer: 'No one has ever come near you in collection eloquence at an NM meeting.'[41]

* * *

A decade later, Stead would write wistfully from Holland: 'I feel such affection thinking back to New York. . . . I don't grow much attached to anywhere, but I think the New York people were my closest.'[42]

Regular visitors to the flat, Zatz recalls, were Ruth Blech, who 'chatted nineteen to the dozen', Stanley Burnshaw, whom Zatz thought 'a crusty fellow', and Harry Bloom, with his 'wonderful laugh'.[43] Alf Hurst (whom Stead called 'the Great Noise') was often there, but Zatz did not warm to him.[44] Mike Gold and Elisabeth would sometimes drop in: they now had two sons and were living on a single-tax commune, the 'Freeacres Community', in New Jersey.

Around this time, Stead and Blake met Ettore and Jessie Rella. Tall, lanky Ettore struggled to make a living from his poetry and poetic dramas; for the most part Jessie, talented with needlework, supported them.[45] Stead told Stanley Burnshaw that Rella's poetry had 'a free, colourful, intense, masculine style', adding: 'He is a man, as mountain men and mining men and poet men are men.'[46] Rella's exotic background appealed to her; born in Telluride, a silver-mining town high up in Colorado, he had an Albanian father and an Italian mother. To Stead, partial as she was to the exotic, he would always be her 'Albanian friend'.

Another frequent visitor was a man Bill Blake liked to call his brother: 60-year-old Henryk Grossmann. Originally from an afflu-ent Jewish family in Cracow, Grossmann had been Professor of Economics at Warsaw, where he had written a learned treatise on the collapse of capitalism, before leaving in the mid Twenties to work at the Institute of Social Research in Frankfurt. Like most of his colleagues there, he had fled to the States in 1937.

Grossmann's views on political and economic questions were close to Blake's, and the two men would talk until late into the night. Blake had great respect for Grossmann's work, but among his exiled Frankfurt colleagues, now re-grouped at Columbia Uni-versity, Grossmann was out on a limb. Whereas the Moscow purge trials had left the others thoroughly disenchanted with the Soviet Union, Grossmann remained a committed Stalinist. And theo-retically Grossmann was a stalwart of the Old Guard which stressed the economic base, whereas Theodor Adorno, Max Horkheimer, Leo Lowenthal and Herbert Marcuse had become more interested in questions of ideology and culture.[47]

Grossmann never talked about his personal life, and only after the war would Stead and Blake discover that he had left an ex-wife and son behind in Poland. Stead pitied Grossmann in his extreme loneliness. And she enjoyed his old-fashioned Central European gallantry: the hand kissing and bowing. Later she would describe him as 'one of the men who meant something to me'.[48]

Asa Zatz remembers the 'wonderful parties' Stead and Blake used to throw. The small upstairs apartment would be crowded with people eating, drinking and talking. Stead was gracious and smiling, obviously enjoying the role of hostess. She had always prepared marvellous food: curried eggs, Hungarian and German sausage meats with pumpernickel, fresh green salads and potato salads with chives, mixed sour pickles, smoked cheeses. Bill would be some-where in the room talking and laughing, surrounded by admiring friends. At Christmas, he would dress up as Santa Claus, make speeches and hand out presents to the children.

Stead sometimes saw Lina Lewin, their Russian friend from Paris days, now in her late fifties. And she was friendly with Pilar

Libenson, a Spanish communist who had been in the Spanish Civil War, then concentration camp, before emigrating to the States. Ten years younger than Christina, highly educated and darkly beautiful, Pilar was married to Leon, a biochemist from Argentina; they had two young children. Stead was interested to hear about Pilar's frustrations as a wife and mother, and in 1942, while she was writing *For Love Alone*, she wrote to Blake:

> Pilar ... anxious to free herself as a woman, not satisfied to be a mother: says it is not creative ... Women of all kinds are intimately, personally, conscious of their remaining social disabilities. The example of women in Russia of course has stirred them up. "It doesn't *have* to be this way."[49]

From Pilar Libenson Stead learnt a smattering of Spanish. 'It gave me a false sense of accomplishment,' Libenson recalls. 'Chris was very good at languages.'[50]

The woman who made the greatest impact on Stead during the American years was Ruth McKenney. They were never close friends—Stead did not allow people access to her vulnerable inner self—but she certainly admired this strange, ebullient woman, extroverted and articulate like Bill Blake. McKenney too was a popular speaker at communist functions. She and her husband Richard Bransten would be immortalised in Stead's novel about revolutionaries, *I'm Dying Laughing*.

Nine years younger than Stead, Ruth McKenney was already an established writer. Her autobiographical novel *My Sister Eileen* had been a fantastic success in 1938, and Ruth and Eileen McKenney had become part of American legend: Ruth, the bright, lively but unattractive aspiring writer; Eileen, her younger sister, a Celtic beauty who was always falling unhappily in love.

Born in Indiana in 1911 into a working-class Irish-American family, Ruth McKenney had studied at Ohio State University, while her younger sister Eileen married and had a son. By the time Ruth graduated, Eileen's marriage had broken up. The two women had come to New York with baby Patrick, and shared a studio apartment in Gay Street, Greenwich Village. Ruth supported them by selling humorous stories to the *New Yorker*. At the same time she wrote a monograph on the United Rubber Workers of America, *Industrial Valley*. They were happy years—idealised in her autobiographical writings. Her sister, she would write, was the love of her life. 'For ourselves, we just loved each other, fiercely, firm in the conviction that every man's hand was against us.'[51]

McKenney met Richard Bransten in August 1937 and they married, with characteristic impetuousness, just twelve days later.

'It is a good thing we married so suddenly on the first fine tide of joy,' McKenney was to remark, 'for if we had waited around, in some mealy-mouthed way, we should have discovered our contradictions, battled furiously, and probably parted.'[52]

Richard Bransten came from a wealthy, conservative California family that disapproved of his radicalism. To placate the family, he used the pen-name 'Bruce Minton' for his political activities.

They made a strange couple. Bransten (his friend Stanley Burnshaw recalls) was 'spectacularly thin' and 'unathletic-looking, with a tension in his expression that could be gloriously dissolved when he laughed'.[53] He suffered deeply from lack of self-esteem. McKenney, short and overweight, completely lacked Bransten's grace. But she did not lack confidence in her own talents.

From the beginning, McKenney and Bransten argued ferociously —usually about money. Though McKenney had always been poor, money, like food and drink, was something over which she had very little control. Bransten, though he despaired about their debts, also lived in a mythological world when it came to money. Their spendthrift ways would horrify Stead and Blake over the years.

Most of the couple's wealth came from Ruth McKenney's highly successful comic writings. In 1940, as sales of *The Man Who Loved Children* limped along, *The McKenneys Carry On* went through several reprintings. (That year, too, *My Sister Eileen* became a Broadway hit, and two years later, it was made into a popular film.) Over the years, Ruth McKenney continued to churn out best-selling stories about her eccentric family. But she never valued this 'cornmeal mush' read by 'full-bellied Bible belters';[54] her ambition was to write serious revolutionary novels. Once asked in an interview if the stories about her family were true, she replied: 'Pretty much, only I left out all the real catastrophes. As a matter of fact I had a perfectly horrid childhood.'[55] She and Stead had a number of things in common.

Ruth McKenney's worst tragedy occurred four days before *My Sister Eileen* opened on Broadway. McKenney and Bransten were living in Connecticut. Eileen McKenney had been married for seven months to the writer Nathanael West, author of *Miss Lonelyhearts*, and they were living in Hollywood. The sisters were running up huge telephone bills talking to one another. Then, on 22 December 1940, Eileen and Nathanael West were killed in a car accident, travelling back from a duck shooting weekend in Mexico. Eileen was 27, Nathanael West 37.

It was the tragi-comic duality in Ruth McKenney's life that Stead wanted to reflect with the title *I'm Dying Laughing*.

★　★　★

The *New Masses* congratulated itself on being the only newspaper in the country to have 'unequivocally opposed two imperialist wars'. It argued that it was the speculators who wanted war, not the workers.[56] In May 1941, Stead and Blake were among 119 writers to sign the Call to the Fourth American Writers' Congress, a gathering of writers for peace. A strong anti-war statement, it denounced the Roosevelt administration for its warmongering. Among the better-known signatories were Theodore Dreiser, Dashiell Hammett, Lillian Hellman and Orson Welles.[57]

Then came a cataclysmic about-turn. On 22 June 1941, Germany invaded Russia, breaking the Nazi-Soviet Pact. The CPUSA now called for immediate measures to aid the Soviet Union and its allies against the fascist aggressors.[58] The communist front organisation, the American Peace Mobilization, of which Stead and Blake were members,[59] changed its name to the American People's Mobilization. When the Japanese attack on Pearl Harbor eventually brought America into the war in December, the League urgently called 'on all American writers to put their training, talent, and devotion to the service of our country'.[60]

★　★　★

Stead liked the title *Letty Fox: Her Luck*, one of the few titles she did not change during the writing process. Letty, obsessed with hunting down a husband, is predatory, like a fox. Friends comment that Stead liked the hint of bawdiness in the combination 'fox' and 'luck'.

Though *Letty Fox* was not published until after *For Love Alone*, Stead first began it early in 1941. The two novels overlap to some degree. In each, minor characters are based on Stead's father and Aunt Florence. The few remaining pages of an early draft of *Letty Fox* contain characters called Teresa and Jonathan Crow—eventually to be the central protagonists in *For Love Alone*. At this early stage, Stead thought of making Teresa and Letty sisters; she liked the polarity: saintly Teresa and libertine Letty.[61] But she soon realised that the two were products of such different times and upbringings that they could not be brought together in one novel.

They became two novels, which British writer and critic Angela Carter would describe as 'thesis and antithesis'.[62] The 'thesis' of *For Love Alone*, set against the background of a Victorian and provincial Sydney, is summed up by Teresa:

Women had a power to achieve happiness as well—but in what way? Only by having the right to love ... It was easy to

see how upsetting it would be if women began to love freely
where love came to them. An abyss would open in the
principal shopping street of every town.[63]

In *Letty Fox*, set largely in New York in the Twenties and Thirties,
the abyss *has* opened, and the shopping metaphor has a sinister
appropriateness. Young women born in the early Twenties, like
Letty, learn to see themselves as marketable products. Told in the
first person from Letty's viewpoint, with Letty herself as one of its
main objects of satire, *Letty Fox* is a deeply ironic novel about a
society that treats sex and love as commodities.

Letty has the misfortune to reach sexual maturity just before the
Second World War. The eligible men are soon being conscripted. In
the race for males, all women are each other's rivals. The cut-
throat, dirty tactics Letty uses to secure herself an apartment in
over-crowded Manhattan reflect her strategies for getting herself a
man. For Letty, sexual experience is the mark of equality with men:
she has more lovers than we care to count. And yet she is as
desperate to be married as Teresa, in *For Love Alone*. Even Letty's
broadminded father, Solander Fox, never questions his daughter's
obsession with making herself 'marriageable'.

For Love Alone leaves readers with the impression that Teresa will
go beyond her preoccupation with men and achieve self-
fulfilment.[64] *Letty Fox* does not inspire the same optimism. Not for
one minute do we share Letty's romantic notion that she has found
the 'right man' and will become the 'perfect wife'.[65] When she tells
her young man, Bill van Week, 'We're made for each other', and he
answers, 'I know. This is it',[66] we are not sure whether they are
consciously sending up Grade B movies or not. But Stead certainly
is. She herself would point out later that for all her libertinage,
Letty Fox is no 'heroine of feminist freedom'.

Everyone in the USA understood perfectly that she showed
the error of feminine riot! What end was there for her but
deterioration, a miserable middle age, desperate abandon, or
a total acquiescence with conformity?[67]

Stead offers no solution. Marriage validates women; it also destroys
them. Significantly, Persia and Solander, the only positive picture
of a couple in the novel, are not married. But Persia is also shown to
be vulnerable, for Solander's lawful wife has a hold on him that has
nothing to do with love. Stead's conclusion is clear enough: 'It is a
real inferno we are born into.'[68]

After *The Man Who Loved Children*, Stead had resolved that her
next novel would be less painful to write. But she was becoming
aware that anger fuelled her creative fires. As she was writing *Letty*

Fox, she told Bill Blake: 'I feel splendid, nastier and more Stead-ish each day.'[69]

Progress on the novel was slow during the summer of 1941. Stead had not yet found a way to shape her mass of raw material, and was feeling tense. To escape the New York humidity and write without distractions, she removed herself in early August to a quiet guest house in New Canaan, Connecticut. (Blake, working once again for Alf Hurst, was obliged to stay in New York.) From this 'Department of Old Crocks', as she uncharitably referred to her fellow guests, Christina wrote affectionate, contrite, girlish letters to 'Munx', as she called Bill.

> I miss you very much, but I know it is good for me to miss you and get some work done. I am working, haven't any of that confusion or indecision I have in town.
>
> . . . I appreciate very well what you are to me; I hope when I get this manuscript finished I will be not so jumpy, a better girl to you; you know I am stuck on you but I certainly am a horror. I'll finish as quickly as I can; the place is a bore of course, and it's a good thing.
>
> Try and come the following weekend will you Chick?
>
> Love to Alfish who is so very Alfish; I really love the guy.[70]

Four days later she wrote:

> You ought to be strong and you ought to have all the time you need to write a great book, for you have all that Balzac had, except about 100 pounds (less) avoirdupois.
>
> Dear Munx, I don't deserve such a good guy as you, but I am always hoping that a miracle will happen and I will deserve you.[71]

She is not sure how long she can put up with the place. The food is inadequate. She misses steak. She misses wine. None of the old ladies around her drink, and she abhors 'lone drinking'.[72] But she is making good progress. At last she is satisfied with the character of Letty. The ending of her novel had been giving her trouble, but now she can see a way out.

> I have seen daylight about the end of the book; it was all due to my foolish insistence on having a morally satisfying solution —but I do not need a solution; a woman of twenty-three does not have any solution but marriage—she has got a start in life, and that after all is my subject, a start in life, isn't it?

The published novel ends with Letty making the same point. The general framework of *Letty Fox* seems to have been in place by the end of the summer of 1941, though the novel was not published for another five years.

'I have several tremendous weaknesses,' Stead told Blake, referring to her writing, 'one of which is this feeling that I am solving a moral problem every time I start a book.' She evidently felt pressured to give her fiction an explicit moral dimension, but it was not her bent. What interested her was to convey characters: their voices, preoccupations, jokes. This led to what she considered her other great weakness: her tendency to put everything she knew about the real person into her fictional character, even where it was inappropriate in terms of the narrative.[73]

As someone who aimed to transcribe life into fiction, Stead could hardly have set herself a more difficult challenge with *Letty Fox*. The 23-year-old in whose voice the novel is narrated was to be Ruth Blake—an ambitious task for a 39-year-old Australian. In addition to the problem of language and idiom, there was the psychological challenge, for it required at least a superficial identification with Ruth Blake. Would she be able to portray Mathilde Fox—that is, Mollie Blech, whom she had never actually met— through her daughter's familiar gaze? And would she be able to view characters like Mathilde and Grandma Fox (Rosa Blech) from Letty's less critical viewpoint? Could she portray herself—Persia— from Letty's rivalrous standpoint?

Solander Fox, Letty's father, is 'a gay, ribald, talented man', but underneath even his daughter sees that he is 'not very sure of himself'.[74] She also sees that caught between the emotions and claims of his two women—his wife Mathilde and his mistress Persia—he pacifies each by lying to them.

Persia, we learn from Letty, is clever, reads a lot and speaks several languages. Her love for Solander is not based on self-interest, and she placidly puts up with humiliating treatment from his mother. She and Solander lead a nomadic life, always surrounded by hearty male friends—company Persia enjoys, for she has 'a fondness for men'.[75]

Persia—like Teresa, in *For Love Alone*—is Stead's idealised fictional self. But the level-headed Persia, who holds herself aloof from gossip and family crises, could not have written *Letty Fox*.

★   ★   ★

It seems that Stead carried out her threat to break contract with Simon & Schuster after their indifferent treatment of *The Man Who Loved Children*, for she submitted *Letty Fox* in the autumn of 1941 to Angus Cameron, a distinguished publisher and political radical who worked at Little, Brown & Company. But the pressure to make money prompted her to submit her manuscript too early, and to her chagrin, Cameron requested major revision. By November 1941, the manuscript was 'in the deuce of a shape, torn to atoms for a re-do'.[76]

Dismayed by the delay, Stead urgently tried to think of ways of making money out of her writing. In October 1941, she asked Angus Cameron to act as referee for an application for a Guggenheim Fellowship. He willingly agreed. But she soon found herself writing to him again.

> 212 E. 16th St, New York.
> 8th October, 1941.

Dear Angus,

I feel as if I'm pestering you, but shortness of time makes me do it. Please forgive me.

I am told that I ought to have a wellknown American writer to act as reference [sic] as well. I do not know what American writers have read any of my books. Do you know of one who likes one of my books well enough to act as a reference in the same capacity as you will? If there is such an author among us, can he be reached this week? He does not have to write a letter. He only has to say yes, he is willing to read the papers the Foundation will submit to him in good time . . .

If you know one and could possibly make the request for me, I cannot say how obliged I should be. It would save me a horrible embarrassment: for it is very hard to approach in this way a person one does not know at all. I am now suffering, of course, from my barbarian habits of going nowhere and meeting no one. However, I am hoping for that one chance in three, just the same.

Kind regards,

Yours sincerely,

Christina.[77]

Coming from the author of *House of All Nations* and *The Man Who Loved Children*, the tone of the letter is surprisingly helpless. When it came to self-promotion, Christina Stead was dismally bad at presenting herself in the best light. In the end, Angus Cameron managed to organise an impressive list of referees, including the poet Stephen Vincent Benét, critic Clifton Fadiman, and Louis Kronenberger, the drama critic for *Time*. Five other publishers and critics agreed to write brief references.[78]

Stead's proposal was to collect legends and contemporary lore from diverse regions in the United States, and to base a cycle of stories upon them in the style of *The Salzburg Tales*.

In places settled by Poles, Germans, Dutch, and Swedes are to be found tale-tellers, often old women, who are fountainheads of household, farm and forest tales, partly imported and adapted to this country and partly new. Certain districts are of the deepest interest as having affected American history, manners or religion.[79] She aimed to use newspaper and oral sources as well as the talents of natural tale-tellers, and pointed out that the Brothers Grimm, Hans Christian Andersen and E. T. A. Hoffmann had all collected folk-lore in this way. For a while now she had been planning to bring together the strange and marvellous dreams of their friend Philip Van Doren Stern, production manager at Simon & Schuster and a historical novelist, whom she called the 'talking ghost'.[80]

For once Stead made every effort with the presentation of her application. Usually she would insist that it was content, not form that was important, and submitted work typed single-spaced, with numerous errors and crossings out. The Guggenheim application, however, was double-spaced and without a single mistake.

She was not awarded a fellowship. In many ways, the application was ahead of its time: a selection committee nowadays would appreciate Stead's interest in local history and ethnic subcultures. When, in early April 1942, she saw she was not among the list of successful applicants announced in the newspaper, she shrugged: 'Well, there we are. I am not a winner and that's sure.'[81] She thought it might be because she was not an American citizen. She even wondered whether the judges were put off by the photo she sent, in which her newly permed hair made her look like a woolly dog.[82] What disgusted her was that most fellowships had gone to academics and critics rather than creative writers. To her poet friend Ettore Rella, whose application had also failed, she wrote bitterly: 'Careful, or even superficial inspection of the Guggenheim lists reveals that it is necessary to be at least a sub-professor at Harvard to get one.'[83]

However, there was money in scriptwriting, and in November 1941, Stead sent Columbia Pictures Corporation the outline of a melodramatic romance: *Was it Heaven or Was it Hell?* Constructed with suitably high and low points to appeal to movie-goers, it was, in rough form, the outline of her next novel, *For Love Alone*. When Columbia Pictures indicated they were not interested in the idea, she began to shape the material into a novel, putting *Letty Fox* aside for the time being.

★   ★   ★

For Love Alone involved turning again to the past. *The Man Who Loved Children* had ended with the 14-year-old Louisa running away from home to go 'for a walk round the world'. *For Love Alone* opens with Teresa at 19. She is recognisably an older version of Louisa, with the same manipulative, self-obsessed father. The setting for the first half of *For Love Alone* is Watson's Bay, Sydney: there would be no compromises with publishers about location this time. The second half is set in London, where Teresa follows Jonathan Crow.

It was fourteen years since Stead had left Australia, and nine years since she had completed *Seven Poor Men of Sydney*. She rejoiced in the chance to write again about Sydney, this time with the perspective of her mature years. Sydney had become if anything more beautiful and exotic in her memory, and Australian society more claustrophobic, vulgar and provincial.

Fourteen years had passed since she had seen Keith Duncan, the man she had followed to England. She had heard nothing during this time, apart from a 1934 newspaper cutting from her aunt with the information that Dr Duncan was the new Director of Tutorial Classes at the University of Sydney and that he was (still) engaged in research on immigration and population. Could she recreate his voice after all these years: the emphatic opinions, the seductive shifts of register, the anger, the self-pity? Years later, Stead indicated that she became 'bogged down' in letters when writing *For Love Alone*.[84] Though there is no trace of them today, it is almost certain that she kept all Keith Duncan's letters and perused them as closely as she had her father's writings when she created *his* portrait. Letters were an invaluable reminder of the way people spoke. It is possible that Jonathan Crow's letters to Teresa in the novel contain extracts from Keith Duncan's actual letters—perhaps only vaguely altered.

Never one to back away from bold truths, Stead wanted to portray the repressive sexual attitudes in Australia in the 1920s. Just how courageous she was to broach the subject of female desire is clear from Diana Trilling's review in 1944:

Teresa is not quite nineteen when we first make her acquaintance but Miss Stead shows her to be quite frenzied with sexual desire—and this seems to me to be a healthy defiance of the present-day convention which permits sexuality to married women (or children) but not to very young women ...

And Miss Stead's heroine not only defies the conventions by being fully developed sexually at so tender an age; she is also improperly outspoken in her fear of spinsterhood. I know no novel, including the novels of Jane Austen, which reveals as frankly as *For Love Alone* the frantic need young women have for a husband and the brutal hypocrisy with which society surrounds their efforts to find one.[85]

★   ★   ★

Harry Bloom, the radical pharmacist, had left Brighton Beach in 1940 and bought a dilapidated drugstore on Upper Broadway at Washington Heights. Despite the depressed economy, he was turning it into a prosperous business. The family—he and his wife Anne and two children Janet and Michael—lived above the shop.

Harry Bloom and Christina had pursued their flirtatious relationship, first struck up in 1935. Christina found Harry disconcertingly moody—'one minute on the boil, then flat'[86]—but she admired his strength and extraordinary energy. He was funny and engaging, a brilliant raconteur, passionate about politics, and an affectionate, loyal friend. He told her he loved her.

Stead's deepest longing was to be romantically courted by men. She had no illusions about this: she once told a friend that her father had been goodlooking and that his success with women made him 'a pain in the neck to his wife; he couldn't stop bragging'. She added: 'I talk too much about my men friends, I know; but that is for the contrary reason—I am so staggered and delighted that they even look at me!'[87]

She was flirtatious: her men friends agree about this. And she thrived on dramas—real or imagined. When Blake was in Canada one time, she wrote to him that Henryk Grossmann was acting as her 'Escort', and that Harry Bloom was jealous.

Dear Chick,
    ... My Escort turns up next. I wonder at my temerity
(in private) in going out cheerfully with the world's leading
Marxist, etc. but my Australian brass comes to my aid.
    ... Harry asked (on the phone) if I was lonesome, I said no,
I had an Escort. Who? said Harry. I said who. "Oh, Henry! He's
harmless," says Harry ... I am not being as foolish as I sound.[88]

Bill possibly encouraged Christina's flirtation with Harry Bloom—though if it ever became something more, he was not told about it. Over the years, in letters to Harry, he would call him Christina's 'boyfriend'. Bill himself found Harry extraordinarily lovable.

Anne Bloom was wary of her husband's womanising; Christina was neither the first nor the last of his infatuations.[89] Christina disliked Anne, though they were friendly enough on the surface. To Harry (who rather fostered this image of himself) Christina made it clear that she was sorry he should have a possessive wife who did not understand him. The picture of Harry Girton's jealous wife in *For Love Alone* (based loosely on Ralph Fox's wife) may well have been partly inspired by Stead's sense of rivalry with Anne Bloom.

Harry Bloom's son Michael does not know whether his father and Christina had an affair; he does know that his father was 'not as monogamous as he was meant to be'. He remembers that Christina quite often visited Washington Heights by herself. On one occasion in the early Forties, when he was in his mid teens, Mike was hanging around when she and his father were talking, and his father eventually told him to go and buy some stamps. Mike flung at him: 'I know! You just want to get rid of me so you can have an affair with Chris!'[90]

Letters from Harry Bloom to Christina after Bill's death are sufficiently intimate to suggest that their relationship was at one time physical. From remarks Christina made in letters to Bill in both 1942 and 1946—remarks that almost certainly understated the case—it is clear that she was obsessed with Bloom.

Young Michael Bloom's hunch was probably right: it is likely that Stead and Bloom had some sort of an affair in the early Forties. During 1942, Stead was writing *For Love Alone*, which ends with Teresa having an affair with *Harry* Girton. Exulting in her sexual freedom, Teresa makes a vow to herself: 'She had learnt from Harry and made up her mind, if the chance came, to learn from others. "I only know one commandment, *Thou shalt love*."' Stead firmly believed that writers write best about what they know about, that writers need to experience the world, see things, do things. To write about Teresa's affair with Girton, she needed to know what it was like to have an extramarital affair.

Stead (like Teresa) made love and passion into a commandment, yet she would always suffer immense anguish over men. When she discussed the subject with her friend Edith Anderson in 1944, she told Edith that she believed monogamy to be an 'absolute necessity' for writers, since love affairs caused 'tremendous upheavals'.[91]

However, Stead needed upheavals. Love was essential to her well-being. She needed to be in love, and she needed to feel loved. Without it, she suspected, her creative juices would cease to flow.

* * *

'An acute stage of New-York fatigue' had settled on them. Blake was doing too much, for too little remuneration. Stead was working hard and sleeping little. Her current novel, not yet called *For Love Alone*, was 'spun out of anguished reminiscence'.[92] In a note to Ettore Rella, Stead apologised for their lack of sociability:

Bill has not written (with all his political work) for many a long day, but he is raring to go and as for me—New York is death to me, the "El" wins every time and I have made up my

mind to get out if it's the last act ... We are both so tired that
we consider the movies a fatiguing evening and I haven't had a
person in for a "cup of tea" for 500 evenings.[93]

In addition to his political activities and work with Alf Hurst that
took him frequently to Canada, Blake wrote articles and reviews
for the *New Masses* and still managed to average a book a year. In
January 1941, he taught a course in Historical Fiction at the New
York Writers' School; early in 1942 he gave lectures on economic
history at the newly formed School for Democracy—both 'poor
man's schools' established by the Party.[94] Stead tried vainly to
protect him from endless requests to speak at rallies—by answering
the telephone in a hostile voice or not answering at all.[95]

The League of American Writers had no real function now it no
longer opposed the war, but Blake and Stead remained members
until it folded in the winter of 1942–3. Throughout 1942, Stead was
even a board member of the New York branch, though without
enthusiasm. In the winter of 1941–2, Stead and Blake were both
featured in the League's Friday Night Reading Program, along with
William Carlos Williams and Richard Wright, whose 1940 novel
Native Son had made him the leading black writer in the States.
Blake read from his recently published American Civil War novel,
The Copperheads,[96] which was receiving high praise in leftwing
circles. Stead read from her untitled work in progress.

She had become thoroughly impatient with the 'pious slogans'
and 'dreary political saysos' found in the *New Masses*. The
'politically-minded poets and writers,' she remarked to Ettore
Rella, a non-Party friend, 'are invariably those with least talent'.
She was angry that the editorial clique often turned down Blake's
reviews in favour of 'some threadbare drivel' considered more
politically correct.[97]

She nevertheless wrote occasional reviews for the *New Masses*
herself.[98] Her review of French communist Louis Aragon's novel
The Century was Young in January 1942 created a minor stir among
New Masses readers. Stead claimed that the central character, Pierre
Mercadier, dies without finding a solution to his dilemma: as a
bourgeois intellectual, he has no role in the modern era.[99] Hannah
Josephson, the novel's translator, replied that Stead had misunderstood the author's intention, and that in his dying gasp, Mercadier
discovers the importance of political commitment.[100] Stead stuck to
her guns:

We hunger for the happy ending and the consoling "Credo" of
the dying, but we would laugh at the device in a religious novel
and we cannot take that comfort to ourselves in a political novel

... I fancy socialist writers are of sterner stuff than those who
only let their characters steeplechase through trouble in order to
come out first in the happy ending of moral uplift.[101]

★   ★   ★

The winter of 1941–2 had been mild and the Canadian fur trade
slow.[102] Stead told Thistle Harris that Bill and Alf had been
working with 'an endearing idiot' with no moral compunctions,
who had committed 'catastrophic errors'.

It turns out that *though* he does not know whether the U.S.A. is a
monarchy or a republic (and I'm not fooling) he *does* know how
to sell furs to himself under another name, how to bucket furs,
how to create companies of his own, and other mysteries.[103]

It was depressingly reminiscent of the Travelers' Bank.

Hurst was convinced that the fur trade would pick up the
following winter, especially if the Russian markets, closed because
of the war, were to open again. But Blake was tired of Alf's
exploitative behaviour, his war profiteering and his manic pursuit
of women. (Stead was making notes for a future novel about Alf
Hurst: she would call it *A Little Tea, A Little Chat*, his euphemism
for sexual conquests.) Blake had had little alternative but to go back
into business with Alf: they needed the money. Writing, they now
realised, was 'another word for slow-starvation'.[104]

At least Mollie Blech was no longer dependent on Bill. She had
not worked all these years, though she was a university graduate,
with training both as a teacher and a secretary, but when the United
States joined the war, she took a course and became a factory
inspector. Ruth Blake was now 21, and with her grandmother's
legacy, she was also independent.[105]

Bill Blake had been trying for months to sell the motion picture
rights to *The Copperheads*. When he still had heard nothing by the
end of April 1942, he angrily terminated his contract with his
literary agents, McIntosh & Otis,[106] and decided he and Stead
should go to Hollywood themselves. Stead was pessimistic. To her
the short-term Hollywood scriptwriting contracts with their ruth-
less lay-offs sounded 'worse than typhoid'.[107] Blake told her: 'Every
situation is a challenge except the boredom of living with Don Juan
in a cubicle in a betting office in Wall Street.'[108]

★   ★   ★

Bill Blake left for Santa Fe, en route to Hollywood, in early May,
1942. Stead was to join him within a few weeks, as soon as he had
found work. In the meantime, she was to finish her novel, have

some work done on her teeth, and make arrangements about the apartment.

For ten days before Bill left, Christina lay on her back, while Bill did all the domestic chores. At almost 40, she was pregnant again. And this time, she was trying hard not to miscarry in the first weeks, as she had apparently done several times before.

★　★　★

Bill and Christina wrote to each other regularly. A few of these letters have survived. Tender, sometimes passionate, they reveal a strong mutual dependence.

Their financial plight was worrying, but Blake was still determined to make money from writing. He had had enough of the likes of Alf Hurst. Despite their trials, he and Stead remained optimistic; almost childishly so. But neither was afraid of hard work.

> Hotel De Vargas,
> Santa Fe,
> New Mexico.
> Thursday, May 7, 1942.

Chris darling,

　　I wired you as soon as I got here as I have been fearfully worried about your condition and had Poesque dreams about you on my two days train ride.

After his 'crazed employments' in New York, Blake was recuperating in Santa Fe for a few days. It reminded him of Ronda. At an altitude of 7000 feet, he felt strangely euphoric. The weather was cold, but his health was improving, and the countryside was 'enchanting'. Rents and housemaids were cheap. 'If Hollywood does not work out, I think four months here would make you years younger,' he told Stead, finishing, 'I have so much to write about how much I love you, how much more I understand every day what your life is to me . . . Ever so much love, Billo.'

★　★　★

Stead wrote the same day from New York, probably sending a telegram as well.

Dearest Munx,

　　Our varmint: the creature departed next day and was about one month, that's all. It seemed a pity, why did it have to? . . . it would have been so much hope and joy for us. However I am counting that this summer we surely will go at it wholesale and take into account that I don't seem to have any staying powers in that direction. Oh, my back—after lying around for

10 days! ... It touched me so much that you worked so hard
for me all that time and really seemed to want it: it is the first
time we looked at it this way. Anyhow, no more of this.[109]
She had apparently been happy to be pregnant. Bill, it seems, was
also pleased. Time was limited: Stead would be 40 in July, and
perhaps this was why she wanted to try again that summer. Nearly
all her women friends had children. She had told Florence James she
envied her her two young daughters.[110] When Elisabeth Granich
(Gold) had had a second son in January 1940, Stead had sent love
and 'Mazeltov', adding, 'It seems nature made you to be the mother
of sons: a gift I should like to have'.[111] And now her friend Ruth
McKenney was pregnant. (In December, she would have a daughter, whom she called Eileen, after her sister.) And yet musing about
her father, Stead told Thistle Harris she had decided she was
'temperamentally ... much like the old guy' and concluded:
'I suppose I do not really miss not having children very much.
I should be like him!'[112]

Even at her early stage of pregnancy, Stead had excitedly broken
the news to Alf Hurst, Asa Zatz, Harry and Anne Bloom. When,
shortly after Bill's departure, Alf Hurst rang up, all 'brotherly and
anxious' to enquire how she was, she felt such a fool, she told Bill,
that she could not bring herself to tell him the sad news. 'He still
thinks you a father. It's too stupid.'[113]

Two days later, on Sunday morning, she wrote to Bill that Alf
was coming to tea that afternoon, and she would tell him then. To
make him feel guilty, she would say that the miscarriage was due to
all the work she had been doing.[114] (She could be as manipulative as
Hurst himself, when she put her mind to it.)

'I am glad you love me, my darling; I love you, and you know
it.'[115]

*　　*　　*

Bill had been delighted by Santa Fe. 'For the first time I wanted to
stay somewhere forever.' However, he soon discovered that his
exhilaration was partly due to the altitude. Overstimulated, he
could not sleep at night. After a few days, he left for Albuquerque,
2000 feet lower. Christina's first letter was forwarded to him there,
and having heard the news of the miscarriage by telegram or phone,
he was greatly relieved to hear she was all right. 'I had conjured up
all sorts of dreads as to bleeding, fever.'

From Albuquerque he took a Pullman coach through the Arizona
desert to California, 'a sort of Riviera and Australia'.[116] In Beverly Hills,
he was entertained by New York friends, Hy and Reah Kraft. Earlier

that year, Blake had passionately defended Hy Kraft's Yiddish comedy *Café Crown* after it had been scathingly attacked by Alvah Bessie, drama critic for the *New Masses*.[117] Hy Kraft was also trying to break into screenwriting.

Blake signed up with Nat Goldstone, a literary agent sympathetic to progressives.[118] 'Half the world's writers, including the most brilliant exiles, are here,' he told Stead. Aldous Huxley was in Hollywood. Bertolt Brecht, Lion Feuchtwanger, Thomas Mann, Leonhard Frank, Oskar Homolka—all refugees from Nazi Germany—were in Hollywood. Everyone was hoping for lucrative employment.

The Screen Writers Guild was 'a real militant Union', Blake told Stead. He joked: 'The Dies Committee found that the Screen Writers Guild is run by "reds" and they are right, by enemies of "red ink".'[119] The Dies Committee, named after its chairman, Martin Dies, was officially known as the House Un-American Activities Committee. Formed in 1938, it had already conducted hearings in Hollywood to test the 'loyalty' of film personalities. Now Dies was threatening to hunt out all communists in the film colony.[120]

★   ★   ★

Alf Hurst visited Christina on Sunday afternoon, as arranged. Kissing her twice on each cheek, he gave her perfume, announcing it was Mother's Day. She could not bring herself to tell him she was not in the family way after all. 'What a lunatic I felt.' She would definitely tell him next time he phoned.

> I sleep relatively well, though dream much, weird long dreams: miss you very much. I love you so much. It is wonderful, after so long ... I am so anxious for you to get into the literary game on one side or another: for Alfish, dear old boy, is quite a wash-out for us.[121]

She had told Asa Zatz about her miscarriage, and he was 'as sorry as if it had been his own'. Eventually she told Alf Hurst.

> Alf, a wonderful friend, said, next time I was to remember I am an incubator and if he had known he would have arranged for a maid and a lot more kindly hokum: and we really must have it for between the two of us we would produce a Shakespeare.[122]

She was working extremely hard, hoping to finish her book within a few weeks. Pascal Covici at the prestigious publishing house Viking, had expressed a strong interest in it. Covici was known for his communist sympathies, and Viking was already publishing another Australian writer, 30-year-old Patrick White. *The Living and the Dead*, his second publication under their imprint, had appeared the previous year.

*   *   *

Communist Jerome Chodorov, who had written the popular stage version of Ruth McKenney's *My Sister Eileen*, held a welcoming party for Bill Blake on Sunday 17 May in his grand Hollywood house. Some of the guests—screenwriters Albert Maltz, Lester Cole and Herbert Biberman—would become famous in the late Forties as members of the 'Hollywood Ten'—ten prominent communists tried and imprisoned by the House Un-American Activities Committee.

Blake chatted with Lester Cole about a movie version of *The Man Who Loved Children*. 'He wants Charles Laughton for Sam Pollit and Bette Davis for psychotic Henny.' There was interest too in his own books. 'Herbert Biberman wants to shape *The World is Mine*: he has read it six times.' To Blake's surprise, people seemed most interested in his idea of a movie about the life of George Graham Rice, a glorious swindler, who had written a book called *My Adventures with Your Money*.[123] Things were looking promising.

*   *   *

'How about the title *It Was For Love Alone*?' Stead was not good at titles, and always sought advice. She had come up with *Spring Tide*, but Stanley Burnshaw, when she told him, had scoffed at that. The present suggestion, proposed by Pascal Covici at Viking, came from a calypso song about Edward VIII's abdication: ''Twas for love, love alone, King Edward left his throne.'[124]

Pascal Covici was impressed with the first half of her manuscript, set in Australia. Provided the rest of the book lived up to the first chapters, he had told her, she could consider it provisionally accepted for autumn publication.

*   *   *

Blake was working furiously on a script about Rice, the crooked financier. He was turning down social invitations and not even reading the newspapers. He told Christina: 'I have to look at your picture to know why I am on the job and then I do much better. Write, pliz, for I am turribly lonesome, love Billo.'[125]

It was risky to be working so hard on an uncommissioned script. Sometimes he fell into a panic. Yet it did not seem impossible to live off writing: others could. If between them he and Christina could sell one manuscript a year—the film rights to one of their novels—they would make US$5000 gross ($4000 nett after agency and taxes) and could live quite comfortably in the west,[126] where fear that the Japanese might bomb the Pacific coast had caused rents to plummet. For the rest of that summer, he proposed New Mexico.

Let us make a break for the mountains. I am the more persuaded not to do anything else the more I see that since Ruth is grown up our economic wants can be modest and all boiled down to freeing you from the chores of housework. That we can accomplish this summer for four months at Santa Fé or Albuquerque.[127]

★   ★   ★

In New York, Stead was working hard and living on her nerves. She was talking metaphedrin for bad sinusitis, her constant New York ailment. Her best working time was the evening, when the El was quieter, and she often wrote till 1.30 am. To go to sleep she took half a bromide, but soon woke and lay listening to sirens from boats or factories, wondering whether they were air-raid signals. At night too she was reliving her past: the moist heat of summers at Watson's Bay, the water lapping on the harbour, and the frightful scenes at home; the smell of chalk and schoolchildren and her frantic fears; Keith Duncan's discussion group, their letters, her arrival in London, and the dark days that followed. She thought again how much she owed to Bill. In her novel, she had James Quick (suitably named) virtually restoring Teresa to life.

The publishers at Viking liked the sexually-charged imagery in the first half of *For Love Alone*. 'Old Covici gloated on phone— fairly dripping lechery about some scene where poor Tess is bathing.'[128] From his reading of the first few chapters, Covici intimated that it might make a 'best-seller'.

Stead feared the novel might be 'mawkish'—yet another novel about a female half-deranged by unrequited love—but she was too anxious about money to spend more time on it. She had thrown out 'cartloads of manuscript . . . all messy dreary talk',[129] but the novel was now going to have to stand as it was. 'Nothing on earth would induce me to revise it.' She told Blake in Hollywood: 'I am not sure, but *think* my book will make a movie.'[130]

★   ★   ★

What grand news to hear that Covici is convinced that you have written great literature and that all is well in his bean: not that his opinion moves me but Viking battling for a literary production is different from Simon & Schuster.[131]

The 'Grand Moguls' had organised a private dinner to raise money for anti-fascist refugee writers and asked Blake to speak as guest of honour. Flattered, he had talked for twenty minutes, but hoped such commitments would not snowball: 'I came here to avoid speeches.' Charlie Chaplin had addressed a fundraising meeting for Russian relief and proclaimed himself a communist.

Working like mad on the Rice script: the agent tells me I have a great line, is he lying?

I am glad I am busy—if I were not my absence from you could no longer be supported. Not habit, either, just mad love.[132]

*   *   *

Stead went to the pictures with Anne Bloom and was taken aback, coming home, by the beauty of the city in the wartime dim-out. 'Looked like the primeval Manhatto swamp.'[133]

She was not sure whether to sublet the apartment or to give it up. The apartment was 'terribly pretty' with its dappled sunlight and views of trees and birds. She was sorry to be leaving it, despite the El. However, she reasoned, New York *was* expensive—they were paying $75 a month in rent—and a period in the 'Hollywood-Hades' would broaden her experience as a writer. She was feeling too narrow.

I find my stock of characters is too small ... After this book is finished I must go out and actually fill notebooks with characters. I am short of them. Warning sign: I have written my last two books about my childhood and youth. Bad.[134]

To Bill she was encouraging. Imitating her father's Artemus Ward language, she admonished him: '*Do not* bust in two tears—you will make out there, I am sure of it!' Be sure to eat liver, steak and salad, she reminded him. And he was not to forget his vitamin pills. 'Christ, Baby, do *I* miss *you*! Love, mush-mush for ever, Chris.'[135]

Bill assured her:

Your boy bathes every day, does Toofies three times, cuts nails, does not bite fingers, sends laundry regularly, has cheveux shampoinged every week, is shaven and shorn steadily, even bootshined: all to no avail: watches his suits for spots: Mama's boy 100% until Krisht comes here, when owing to the corset of her management I will become Public Slob No. 1.[136]

*   *   *

Stead had now plunged into the second part of her novel, set in London. She was trying to work up a feeling of complete empathy with Jonathan Crow, so she could 'gaze' upon him. 'I am just at the point of "giving", I think, & you only give when the sympathy is complete. It is wonderful when it "gives" suddenly: such a relief.'[137]

Sympathy was not quite the right word for her complete immersion in Jonathan Crow. 'His seduction has as much to do with love of women as picking the wings off flies has to do with love of entomology.' She was still angry with this man who had rejected her. However, she told herself it would be 'ludicrous' to punish him in order to satisfy herself: 'A novelist is not one of the Eumenides.'[138]

Stead's immersion in her characters, when it worked, generated in her an excitement verging on sexual. The same emotion engulfs Teresa when she sits next to Jonathan Crow at the opera.

> She sat down beside him and looked at him cautiously through
> the dark. Her pulses leaped, how strange he was; complex,
> perverse, ignorant of himself! She drew in her breath sharply.
> He fascinated her.[139]

Stead would often liken the creative act to a love affair. Writing about someone aroused similar sensations in her to those of early infatuation: the fascination, the stalking and waiting, the mulling over and musing. At 74, she would tell an interviewer:

> I only write about certain people who strike me in a very
> peculiar way. It is like a love affair, exactly. I know almost at
> once: love at first sight . . . It's nothing to do with observation,
> it's totally unlike it. It's a reception of some kind of electrical
> impulse from the other person.[140]

She wrote to Blake that thinking about Jonathan Crow was leading her to consider other 'seducers' she had known: Peter Neidecker, Alf Hurst, Mike Gold—though they did not actually constitute a single type. 'The seducer, of any kind, is not well understood by the rest of mankind: there are several of him, to begin with.'

She was taking aspects of Jonathan Crow from Mike Gold. ('There is a superficial resemblance, although M is gifted, mature, and J.C. not.') She had already sketched Mike Gold, as Jean Frère, in *House of All Nations*. Her idea now was to 'clear the ground for a proper fullgrown portrait of Mike in another book . . . You know how I do this, always sketch in a chief character several times before he really appears.'[141]

It worried Stead that her characters were always morally flawed. But she rationalised, 'A truly great character must have meannesses . . . Look at the private, stupid side of Lincoln!'

★   ★   ★

June 5, 1942

Chris my own,

The slowness of tempo here is Mexican . . . it has taken de Mille's expert, Lou Harris, 3 weeks to go half way through TWIM! [*The World is Mine*] If I were to go by pure concrete results, I would be discouraged.

> If w comes to w [worse comes to worst], I can get what
> Albert Maltz does . . . a job that can average me over $100 a
> week, allowing for a vacation of nearly 4 or 5 months a year.
>
> As to divorce: New Mexico is as good as Nevada: . . . 3
> months residence, & the decree looks better.[142]

Blake, an incorrigible optimist, was still anticipating imminent
divorce after fourteen years. And whenever he was beginning to
despair about making it in Hollywood, he would meet up with a
successful 'mogul' and become hopeful again. To Christina, he
constantly cited the success stories. 'Kingpin Ed Chodorov' was
paid $2000 a week for scriptwriting. 'The most touted & best paid
writer in Hollywood, the super-odious Ben Hecht'[143] earned $5000
a week—'stopping for 6 months to write awful stories'.

At a communist social function, Blake told the writer W. L.
Rivers the story of *For Love Alone*. Rivers was enthusiastic, suggesting Hepburn for the part of Tess Hawkins. ('She is feminist.')
And when Blake told him about *Letty Fox* ('the struggles of girls
to get married and get men'), Rivers thought 'it would sweep the
movies'. Blake, who reported these conversations with childlike
credulity, was beginning to think that Stead, with her interest in
women, might have a better chance of making it in Hollywood
then he had. 'I see that I will soon do the housework while you
smoke cigars on the piazza—may it only come.'[144]

In Hollywood he was at last learning something, he told Stead.
He was beginning to realise what his uncritical fraternal affection
for people like Peter Neidecker, Alf Hurst and Mike Gold had cost
him: a great deal of hack work trying to please and impress them.
'I have pushed off at least 10 incipient male crushes, & all to the
good. One lesson learned at last. I will wind up as cool as an Ingres
uncle.'

He added: 'But not for oo. The hour approacheth & the bride
cometh soon I hope, if I am not to enter Bedlam.'[145]

★　★　★

Leo Horney, their dentist from Paris days, had proposed to take out
Stead's protruding front teeth. She happily agreed. An inveterate
woman-chaser, Horney joked that she should get herself out to
Hollywood fast before some woman got hold of Bill. She teased
Bill: 'Has Greta or Marlene got her hooks into you?'[146]

The next day, she received a letter in which Bill wrote nostalgically of their earliest rendez-vous in Lyons Corner House, the day
in snow-covered Cambridge when they first kissed, the week at the
Aigle Noir 'and all the little incidents of courting and honeymoon'.

This, he wrote, was 'soon to come to a higher level'. Surprised by this, Stead wrote back:

I hope you do not think I will think *more* of you if I am married to you legally. That is quite impossible: such ideas do not exist for people like me. Marriage for us has very little meaning, except that if we pass out, we will be buried as "Munx & Mrs. Munx" and that is worth something.

You and Molly in same plot, Jewish writing imposed by Grossman family: "W. Blake, & so-&-so loved wife of above." 'Tis all that haunts my dreams. Because *I* am loved wife of Above.

Of course, Munx, it is useless to say h.m. I want you & need you too. I can see how we get a kind of mental freshness out of each other—at least I do. Your letters keep me going.[147]

*　*　*

Blake's mood was oscillating violently. On 9 June, he wrote with his usual conviction that everything would turn out for the best: 'I still think that Hollywood is the writer's lifesaver.' Three days later, desolate, he surrendered all decisions to Stead:

At the moment I have no clear indication that I will make a cent here. Selling here is not so easy.—*Copperheads*, God no, it would offend the south (they are all convinced that *Gone with the Wind* is the greatest novel ever written & that picture the greatest accomplishment of mankind, incl. Homer). *TWIM*, who cares about Spain now? *The Painter & the Lady*—too psychological . . .

But the query is this: do you want to come here & brave it out? There is a high possibility, of course, of our making a living within a reasonable time, certainly our chances are no worse than in N.Y. So decide, anything you do pleases me, for, candidly, life is not worth living except for you: I am a man in love, I have that as my great joy in life, all other things are subordinate, & whatever else this absence has shown me, it has revealed the root of my adult existence.[148]

*　*　*

June 15, 1942

My dear Munk,

I got your Friday letter in which you say how hard it is to get in—and I know this of course, have seen from your letters what the set-up is. The best thing we can do is go to Santa Fé, get some proper rest, fresh air and working-strength and work at some MSS; and try again. It is much cheaper than living here—we cannot afford this $75 pied-à-terre, with N.Y. scale of expenses. My teeth are nearly finished and Leo will wait for his money, as you know. I have bought two summer suits which will do for anything . . . will last for years, and in Autumn and Winter, under a furcoat.

. . . I am working like a dog on the MS; extraordinary how long it takes to finish. But I suppose they will accept it, with alterations, and if they do I will ask them to advance me a bit of the advance.

. . . Santa Fé is the best thing. You absolutely must have a rest. I cannot travel this week—wd. not be finished in the beginning; the end is my lunar rendez-vous, unsuitable for travelling—but as it is shorter now I wd. be ready to travel on Monday next. Of course, the MS. must be in first.

. . . Cheer up, sweetheart. All is not lost. A few months in a Paradise where you can't spend dough, some peace and quiet and good hard work, work—we will feel wonderful. I feel myself full of books. I know this is but the writer's illusion and that each of these books takes inexpressible months to finish—but we will try, Love, Your Christina. Musk![149]

Stead had her own frustrations. She had handed Pascal Covici a large chunk of manuscript and he had insisted that the novel was now long enough, though she planned at least ten more chapters. And he had taken one look at her untidy single-spaced manuscript and said it would have to be re-typed by his office staff at her expense. This was an unexpected financial blow.[150]

She could not decide whether to sublet the apartment (which would mean placing their furniture and pictures at risk, and putting up regulation air-raid blinds) or to pack the furniture up and place it in storage at $8 a month. She was embarrassed to be letting down Asa Zatz, a dear friend. They had not signed a formal lease, but there was a tacit understanding that they would rent for a second complete year—until October. She had put a sublet notice in the *Villager*, but enquirers lost interest when they heard there was no elevator.

The previous day, she had had sharp pains, an old problem which she took to be the aftermath of her appendix. She had spent the day in bed reading Balzac's *The Middle Classes*, and was reminded, once again, how good Balzac was. 'Every word he writes seems to be spoken in my ear . . . I know him and I understand him, as a man . . . and that is because he is so like you,' she told Blake.[151]

★   ★   ★

In Hollywood, Blake was selling his soul:

I have handed the script to an old pimp at the game, who
came up today and worked out a plot with me, so banal and
so vulgar that it left me shuddering and yet I know that it is
the only chance for money.[152]

Two days later, he went with friends to visit Lion Feuchtwanger,
the German refugee and author of *Jew Süss*, 'the guy we all chipped
in pennies to aid'.

He has a palace and grounds at Pacific Palisades reminiscent
of the Rothschilds and a private library that for the first time
made me green with envy.[153]

Blake felt the irony keenly.

★   ★   ★

Stead was tense, suffering from severe sinus headaches and the high
blood pressure she believed she had inherited from her father. She
had hoped to finish her novel before leaving New York. Now,
even though she had decided to shorten it, she realised with dismay
that she would be finishing the last section in Santa Fe.

She had bought a book on fortune-telling by cards. After telling
Asa's fortune and her own, she believed she had a talent for it.[154] Asa's
short visits were ideal, but other friends, with their invitations to go
out, were a distraction she did not welcome. She was tired living
intensely in her fictional world. 'They don't seem to realise that a
strong-looking, casual person like me can be so worn out that a
social outing is the last straw. I cannot frankly see anyone.'[155] With all
the writing and marathon typing, the housework and visits to the
dentist, packing and cleaning out closets, she acknowledged that a
'varmint' would have been 'utterly impossible'.

But there was one person she *did* want to see: Harry Bloom. His
visits were rare these days. According to his wife Anne, he was
'working like a dog', and the long days on his feet left him tired and
short-tempered.

Anne is really suspicious (like any good wife!) & although he
wants to come downtown & see me, he cannot do it openly
... You know it is not real love on his part for me, but only
the desire to get away from the pharmacy and to expand a bit
in different terms. This I know quite well & of course have
never made the faintest disloyal move—but such are wives
and so one can do nothing, though I know Harry is *suffering*
because he could not see either of us before we left—perhaps
for such a long time. He is the most affectionate guy.[156]

When Stead collected their bank statement, she discovered that the account was down to $747.70. Deeply worried, she told Blake that the only certainty was $675 in July, as her advance from Viking.[157]

* * *

Peter Neidecker ('Old Mercury') had phoned to see how she was. Asa, whom she saw for a few minutes each day, had registered for the army. Meanwhile, he had gone 'back to his old habits, sleeping till 11 or 12—in this awful heat too, in that filthy, smelly room with the windows closed'. Stead suggested he should go to Hunter for the summer, but he said he could not bear it now that only Max and Aida were there.

Two days before leaving for Santa Fe, at the end of June, she sat in a café with their Polish economist friend Henryk Grossmann, one of the 'revolutionary' friends she was planning to write about.[158] 'Count Chatterbox', she called him.

His anxiety to see me was out of utter loneliness . . . He talked for hours: would be talking still, if I had not invented a telephone call and fictitious date . . . Can't make out why he didn't marry a brilliant woman. He is not averse to marriage, women, sex: quite the opposite I should say. Perhaps an unhappy marriage in the background. He needs a wife like nothing else . . . I love him for the way he talks about his work: in his atrocious English makes it all (Descartes, etc) as clear as possible to my feeble brain. A real teacher.

. . . Will tell you about Grossmann later on. Poor lost man. He cannot get over his insignificance here when he was such a figure, a celebrated scholar, in Europe. . . . What he misses most of all are his workshop of brilliant young men and the *café*.

. . . Asked old Grossmann yesterday for some views on the revolutionary . . . He does not think psychologically and what he said was utterly useless . . . So all I can get out of him is *himself* as a revolutionary . . . He's crazy as a bedbug is your Grossmann, wild, excitable . . . but sane, cheerful, brave . . . a splendid fellow, though quite a trial as a conversationalist. He does not give a tuppenny damn for me and my affairs: nothing in the world counts but his work, "Grossmann's Works" . . .

Until Wednesday, my dear boy . . . I have realised this month which has been so hard, what you mean to me. I would work without you, but not for long. I would go to pieces . . . What an extraordinary chance that I met you—I have met a few other men, of course, but only men who would have left me with a torn-up mind. I can't get over how cruel human beings, not are, but *must be*, to each other—for ever and ever, I suppose. It is a real inferno we are born into. [159]

She finished cleaning the apartment. She packed up their books and papers. Asa Zatz lent her a small trunk for their typewriters and promised to accompany her to the station to help with the luggage. And—wonderful moment—dear Harry Bloom came 'sneaking in' to say goodbye.

10

The Besieged Fortress

JULY 1942–DECEMBER 1946

THE REST OF the summer of 1942 was spent in Santa Fe. Stead was enraptured by the fine mountain air and blue skies, the views of the sierras and 'sun-bitten plains'.[1] She tended to feel light-headed from the altitude, but her sinusitis and headaches disappeared completely, and she plunged back into *For Love Alone* without delay. A fortnight later, in mid July, she sent off the last third to Viking— a little too hastily, no doubt.

Her buoyant mood was thoroughly deflated in August. Viking publishers Pascal Covici and Marshall Best thought the final scenes 'quite impossible and unconvincing', and James Quick, the man who saves Teresa, 'a cardboard American'. Readers would understand that Australia was 'fifteen years behind the times', but the dialogue between Teresa and Quick could not possibly have occurred in London at that time. Stead was deeply stung. 'I have not told them the character is Bill, and the scenes ones in which I myself played a part,' she told Burnshaw. 'This is too juicy for them—and what difference would it make?'[2]

Covici infuriated Stead by holding up Viking's latest success, Steinbeck's war novel *The Moon is Down*, as a model of simple, understated writing. 'That brainless pamphlet of monosyllables!' she groaned to Burnshaw, bitterly recalling that six years ago

Simon & Schuster were urging her to write like *Gone with the Wind*. 'This is the sort of nonsense I have to stand every time a book is a best-seller. May the word perish.'[3]

Her agent, Mavis McIntosh, also let her down. 'Instead of trying to put my point of view, she writes me letters telling me how right the publishers are and advising me how to write.' Grim and disillusioned, Stead remained resolute. 'I am fighting the Steinbeck-slick to the bitter end.'

She and Blake had become acrimonious about the 'weary hacks of the publishing trade', whose standard message was 'cut'. With their best-seller mentality, publishers were robbing literature of its most important characteristics: 'freedom, breadth and eloquence'.[4] Blake satirised American publishing in the novel he began that summer, *We are the Makers of Dreams*. And Stead's *Miss Herbert*, written in the late Fifties, would be a savage indictment of the publishing business.

With no income and no savings left as a buffer, they were now in dire financial straits. They wondered whether to return to New York, since their Hollywood agent, Nat Goldstone, had not come up with any work. Stead asked Burnshaw, who as Editor-in-Chief at the Dryden Press had useful contacts, to let her know if he heard of an office job for her in New York. ('Not licking stamps.'[5]) At the end of the summer, they decided to head west.

★   ★   ★

Hollywood, 1942. The big lure for writers was money. Rumours of astronomical salaries circulated freely, and indeed, some screen-writers were paid $1200 or more per week. Income tax was low, and the dollar worth fifteen to seventeen times its 1992 value. But in reality, this salary talk amounted to Hollywood stardust. Writers were employed on week-to-week contracts, there was no security of income, and the majority pocketed pay closer to the median weekly wage of $125. (The Screen Writers Guild, not nearly as powerful as Blake had first thought, had only just won the battle for a minimum wage.[6])

It sounded glamorous to be a Hollywood screenwriter: in fact, it was a hack job, which merely entailed adapting and transforming material handed over by the story department. Producers wanted nothing but dramatic and entertaining scripts, and they wanted them fast. Not unlike alienated production workers, 'scripters' had to clock in, work Saturday mornings, and look busy. There was no room for originality, and they had no influence on the final prod-uct. It was no wonder that Hollywood writers looked forward to the non-salaried part of the year, when they could make for the mountains or return to New York and do *real* writing.

The writers, more than 10 per cent of whom were communists, formed the most radical group in the Hollywood film colony.[7] This was the group Blake and Stead mixed with when they went out socially, though these occasions were rare. It was difficult for them to get around without a car: distances were vast and residential areas remote. And they felt like outcasts in Hollywood, where even in communist circles the social hierarchy was rigidly based on salaries. Stead recalled:

> Even at gatherings of mostly communist writers, a fellow would be classified as a "$1000-a-week man," and therefore important, while another would be dismissed verbally as a "$150-a-week man" and therefore of no particular significance. The hierarchy of the writers was absolute, everybody knew if a scriptwriter was paid $1000 a week or $100.

She added: 'I was a $175-a-week woman, and I counted for nothing.'[8] When Adrian Scott (later notorious as one of the communist 'Hollywood Ten' on public trial) invited them to his Christmas party, they were surprised and touched.[9]

In late November or early December 1942, Stead landed a week-to-week assignment at Metro-Goldwyn-Mayer. In separate interviews later in life, she recalled her earnings as $175 a week and $750 a week.[10] It was most likely the former. For Stead, a weekly salary of $175 would have seemed very good: in four weeks she earned $700—roughly the same as the advance she had anticipated from Viking. Forty per cent of screenwriters were paid less than $250 a week, and only seven per cent were paid over $750 a week.[11] William Faulkner, already famous, commanded a weekly salary of $300 at Warner Brothers.[12] Alvah Bessie, the *New Masses* drama critic whom Stead and Blake thought leadenly doctrinaire, was lured to Hollywood by what he considered the princely sum of $150 a week.[13] Blake told Burnshaw: 'If she holds out a month, we shall clear all debts and have the return fare. If she holds out longer we might actually get ahead of the economic parade, for the first time in years. That remains for her producer to decide.'[14]

At the 'Lion's Roar', Stead's brain was 'racing with torpedo boats'.[15] She was part of a team working on the film *They Were Expendable*.[16] Directed by John Ford and released in 1945, it was to become a Second World War classic, starring Robert Montgomery and John Wayne.[17] Hollywood was now turning out war films, many watched by the 12 million American servicemen stationed around the world.[18] Even the radical Screen Writers Guild (to which Stead belonged[19]) exhorted its members to produce 'fighting words' to spur on the struggle against fascism.[20]

Next, Stead was put to work with a group of eight or so other writers on *Madame Curie*. Her boss, Sidney Franklin, had directed several successful films— *The Barretts of Wimpole Street, The Good Earth* and *Goodbye, Mr Chips*—and was now working for the first time as a producer. The film had a long history. Back in 1938, Aldous Huxley had been put to work on the script. He was paid $15000 for eight weeks' work, and Franklin had scarcely glanced at the script. Later F. Scott Fitzgerald had worked on a new script at $1000 a week; later still the Polish émigré actress and writer Salka Viertel wrote another.[21] Originally, there had been talk of Greta Garbo for the title role; in the end, it went to the redhaired Irish actress, Greer Garson, famed for her role in *Mrs Miniver*, a moving propaganda film which Churchill said was worth one hundred warships.

Stead would later recall her experience on *Madame Curie* with amusement:

> They had an idea I was English and had a scientific
> background. The moguls had also brought out a crowd of
> eminent European scientists, refugees from Hitler, to work on
> the film as scientific advisors. Except they weren't allowed to
> scientifically advise. They did as they were told right up to one
> scene at the end of the movie when Pierre Curie walks into his
> laboratory and all the other scientists line up neatly and clap
> him. The eminent scientific advisors protested that real
> scientists would never do that, that they'd keep on working.
> The moguls told them to mind their own business.[22]

Scriptwriting, Stead discovered, was 'a dreary sort of office job'. The absurdity of the work conditions irritated her: for hours on end the writers and advisors sat around feeling useless. It is not clear whether her contract expired or whether she gave up, but Stead's employment lasted eight weeks.

Blake did not land a Hollywood contract; nor did anything come of his George Graham Rice script. He did give some lectures on the novel at the Hollywood School for Writers.[23] And he took advantage of his free time to finish *We are the Makers of Dreams*. As soon as he had sent it off to the Dial Press, he began a series of essays on imperialism, a subject on which he was exchanging a voluminous correspondence with Henryk Grossmann in New York.[24]

Viking eventually rejected *For Love Alone* outright. The Dial Press also sent back Blake's novel. He would have to wait seventeen years to see it published.

Stead and Blake stayed in Hollywood for three or four months altogether. It was more than enough. For Stead, the only virtue of the place—apart from the clear air and mild weather which reminded her of Sydney—was that it made her appreciate New York.

It also gave her an impression of Hollywood communism, enabling her to set part of her future novel, *I'm Dying Laughing*, in the film colony. Her own impression of the wrangling, doctrinaire communist set with their vast mansions and Japanese butlers would be filled out the following year by Ruth McKenney, who spent twelve months there with her husband Richard Bransten and wrote to Stead regularly.

★   ★   ★

The communist scriptwriters liked to talk as if their films were a powerful weapon in the campaign to influence public opinion, but this was utterly illusory. John Howard Lawson, leader of the Communist Party in Hollywood, had exulted when he was asked to write *Blockade*, a film about the Spanish Civil War.[25] But the producer stripped his script so successfully of political content that audiences were not even sure on which side the hero was fighting.[26]

Influential or not, communists were irrevocably cast as 'baddies' by the House Un-American Activities Committee (HUAC). Though the Russians were America's wartime allies, Martin Dies, head of the HUAC, was convinced that communists posed a much greater threat to the nation's internal security than the Nazis or Japanese. His explanation for communist influence in Hollywood was that the producers were mostly Jews.[27]

When McKenney and Bransten were in Hollywood, from the summer of 1944 to May 1945, they made a considerable fortune as freelance scriptwriters and 'chummed around with the $2,500-a-week radical crowd'. In *Love Story*, her highly sentimental portrait of their marriage, McKenney writes that she and Bransten collaborated on a movie script which sold for $25 000. This success was followed by others. They bought a house two doors down from Joan Crawford in the fashionable suburb of Brentwood and employed servants. McKenney and Bransten now had the care of Eileen's son Patrick, Bransten's son Tom, the issue of his previous marriage, and their own daughter Eileen. The children attended expensive private schools.[28] *I'm Dying Laughing* depicts it all.

Yet their year in Hollywood was a 'low point' in the Bransten marriage. They were living so high that they were soon in debt. They fought incessantly. Ruth (like Emily Wilkes in *I'm Dying Laughing*) ate 'like a cormorant, an elephant, a pelican'.[29] Richard developed severe ulcers. To readers of *Love Story* Ruth McKenney confessed that she and her husband were doomed to a tempestuous marital life. 'We are too passionate, and too blundering, to inhabit any safe and comfortable plateaus.'

There were also fights with the Party, and their comrades denounced them as 'renegades' or 'semi-Trotskyites'. Like Bill Blake, they disagreed with 'Browderism', which to them had come to mean capitulation to American capitalism. Ever since America and Russia had become war allies, Party General Secretary Earl Browder, following orders from the Comintern, had pursued a policy which aimed to reconcile the CPUSA with mainstream American politics.[30] The Party persuaded the trade unions not to strike and asked the negroes not to pursue their struggle for rights. Browder's book *Victory and After*, published in 1942, called for a truce between capitalists and workers.

In 1950, long after they had been expelled from the Party as 'renegades', Ruth McKenney would write about 'the little band of serious Hollywood thinkers' who gave them such a hard time. One memorable evening among the radicals, embellished by Stead in *I'm Dying Laughing*, was first described by McKenney in *Love Story*:

Stacy ... was a big, leading writer and made $2,500 a week when he worked, which was fairly steady; his wife wore sables ... He always had a tendency to be domineering and loud-mouthed, back in the old days of the League of American Writers. But in New York people used to sit on Stacy practically every time he opened his mouth. "Oh, what bilge," was the general cry when Stacy made deep, philosophical comments. The first time we went to a Hollywood party, we were flabbergasted to discover that now everybody formed a respectful, alert circle and listened to Stacy sound off, gruffly, on purple thoughts like "The Motion Picture Is the Art Form of the People," or "The Novel is Esoteric and Dead."
... We were invited to a soirée at the great man's home— quite an honor, we gathered, although I cannot say we felt it keenly. The refreshments were a little buffet of champagne, lobster, and the like—not bad. But before we had half a chance to stuff ourselves on the goodies, Stacy called the party to order, whipped out a little leather-covered notebook and a Waterman pen, and drew up an agenda. This is an absolute fact. It was not a meeting, either, just a cheerful little gathering of higher-paid Hollywood gadabouts, the $2,000 a week set, in fact. Stacy Summed Up. Afterwards, as the jolly fête was breaking up, he took me aside and urged me to be psychoanalyzed before it was too late.[31]

A comparison of *Love Story* and *I'm Dying Laughing* shows the extraordinary resemblance between the voices of Ruth McKenney and Emily Wilkes. Stanley Burnshaw, who knew Ruth McKenney well, was 'astounded' when first reading *I'm Dying Laughing* in the mid Sixties, by the way Stead had captured her voice.

'Stacy Cresswell' in McKenney's story — Jay Moffat Byrd in Stead's — was almost certainly John Howard Lawson, the unofficial leader of Hollywood's communists from 1937 until 1950, when he would be sent to jail as one of the Hollywood Ten. A doctrinaire and bullying character, Lawson would take it upon himself to explain sudden switches in the Party line, to settle internal conflicts[32] and summon wayward members for ideological 'discussions' at which he would 'straighten them out'.[33] One such scene is graphically depicted in *I'm Dying Laughing*.

In February 1943, while Stead and Blake were still in Hollywood, Ruth McKenney's revolutionary novel *Jake Home* was published. Stead sincerely admired it. Israel Amter, reviewing it for the *Daily Worker*, deemed it an 'untimely' moment for a portrait of a flawed communist — especially as its working-class hero, Jake Home, was by no means 'typical'. Stead, even less interested than McKenney in exemplary communist heroes, was dumbfounded by Amter's rigid righteousness and censoriousness, and courageously fired off an angry missive to the *Daily Worker*.[34] A novel is not a pamphlet, she expostulated, and it cannot be 'timely', for the simple reason that it takes at least one year to write a book and a second year to see it in print. It is 'the business of a novel ... to be untimely or timeless'. The idea of a 'typical' character was equally meaningless: 'No book, picture or other work of art can possibly show all types.'

> I will say that *Jake Home* will probably outlast us; it has some
> of the spirit of Jack London's best proletarian novels, and I'm
> certain its author will write yet greater proletarian novels.
> She is probably the best writer of and for the left; and to
> discourage, insult, and attack such a fine writer is about
> the greatest disservice anyone could do to the left.

It was a passionate expression of solidarity with what Stead considered intelligent, rather than uncritical, leftism. At the time, she regarded McKenney as 'a great friend'.[35]

By the time she came to write *I'm Dying Laughing*, ten years later, Stead had changed her mind. By then, it seemed to Stead that McKenney had no political integrity whatsoever — perhaps no integrity of any sort.[36]

* * *

When Stead and Blake returned to New York, in February or March 1943, the Desert War in North Africa was raging and there was active engagement in the Pacific, but the tide of war seemed to be turning: the Germans had just surrendered in Stalingrad, the greatest battle in the war so far. American males under 37 were being called to the armed services. Asa Zatz was about to depart for the Middle East; Ettore Rella had left to serve in the Pacific.[37] Lina Lewin, their Russian friend, was so relieved by the outcome of the Battle of Stalingrad that she offered to teach Stead Russian as a thanksgiving. Stead accepted enthusiastically.

Their top floor apartment in Asa Zatz's house had been sublet to the Austrian playwright Ferdinand Bruckner and his wife, escapees from Nazism.[38] Zatz did not want to throw them out, and through a friend he found Blake and Stead an apartment nearby, at No. 21 E. 14th Street. It was spacious and modern and not so close to the El—though it turned out to be noisy just the same. On the street side, fire engines would tear up and down; on the courtyard side was the roaring ventilator of an all-night bakery.[39] Stead never slept the night through. But they were to stay there almost four years, and later in life she would pride herself on being 'a tried and true 14th Streeter'.[40] She liked the old houses on 14th Street, the cosmopolitan flavour, and the location at the edge of Greenwich Village.

★   ★   ★

Bill Blake had hoped that the shortage of personnel in civil employment might open up an opportunity for him in publishing.[41]. But no. He would find he had to resort to a number of short-term jobs—all unsatisfactory. He worked for Alf Hurst in his grain and fur business. Under the pseudonyms George B. Collingwood and George S. Kent, he wrote about finance and stock investment for *The Magazine of Wall Street*.[42] Then, in the spring of 1944, Stanley Burnshaw as Editor-in-Chief of Dryden Press, came up with an idea to take advantage of Blake's prodigious research skills: a mini-encyclopaedia along the lines of Bernard Shaw's *The Intelligent Woman's Guide to Socialism and Capitalism*, or G. D. H. Cole's *The Intelligent Man's Guide Through World Chaos*. *An Intelligent American's Guide to the Peace* would contain a potted history, geography and economic analysis of every major country in the world. The rationale was that better international understanding would lead to better international relations in peace time.

For the next few months, Blake worked at the Dryden Press offices on Fourth Avenue, 'hammering out' 5000 to 7000 words a day.[43]

Bill Blake's name carried no weight outside communist circles. The book needed someone to give it public authority: Sumner Welles, former Undersecretary of State, whose book *A Time for Decision* made him a leading expert on international politics, was the perfect candidate.

Burnshaw edited Blake's draft, then sent it to Sumner Welles, who made numerous changes.[44] The book came out in January 1945, with Sumner Welles' name on the cover. It sold extremely well—55000 copies—and was widely praised for its vast and useful coverage, clear style and intelligent organisation. All praise and royalties went to Sumner Welles. Blake received no royalties: Burnshaw had paid him a fixed sum.

'Who Done It?' was the headline of a review by George E. Sokolsky, a notorious rightwing journalist, in the Hearst newspaper, the New York *Sun.*

> I recently received from the Dryden Press a copy of *An Intelligent American's Guide to the Peace*, a massive volume of what appears to be objective information. On the blurb the name of Sumner Welles appears in letters one and a quarter inches high. Above that name appears, in letters one-eighth of an inch high, the legend, "Under the General Editorship of." In a "Publisher's Note" I came across the fact that "the research and preparation of the material were entrusted to Mr. William J. Blake." As the research and preparation of the material are the business of an author, it would seem that William J. Blake must be the author.

On close reading, Sokolsky found that the information was not 'objective' at all. The account of the depression in the United States was 'one-sided', and the section on Soviet Russia improbably rosy. Its bias notwithstanding, the journalist declared it an 'extremely valuable reference book':

> So as long as there is nothing better available—and there is nothing better available—this is the book for an intelligent American. And if the publisher was afraid that I would shout "Marxist!" if he admitted that Blake wrote the book, he might get over that inhibition and give the devil his due.[45]

Coming from someone known to attack anything even mildly liberal, Sokolsky's final endorsement of the book undoubtedly helped to increase sales.

*   *   *

Stead spent July 1944 at the Kotlarskys' rambling country house at Hunter in the Catskills, far removed from the terrible events of the world. The old house was surrounded by fields, fruit trees, rust-coloured barns; over the tool shed, and crawling towards the house, a sprawling wild hops vine strangled every plant in sight. Impressed by its indestructibility, Stead would use it, in *The People with the Dogs*, as a metaphor for the suffocating nature of family bonds.

It was an enchanting place. Every few days the air would become hot and steamy, the light would turn a supernatural pink, and an afternoon thunderstorm would break from the west. ('The thunder bowled and hopped in the Catskills, and the rainfalls, like ghosts, real ghosts, on stilts stalked over the hill.'[46]) In the evenings Stead sat on the terrace with Aida and Max, looking across the valley to the mountains, watching the furtive shadows and darting fireflies. Nights on the mountainside were soft and cold, and for once, she slept soundly. To her, those weeks in the mountains were a 'midsummer night's dream'.[47]

Blake, working on the 'Sumner Welles book', had had to remain in the heat-struck city. He caught the bus up for the weekend before Stead's birthday, and stepped off looking pale and enervated. Stead kept trying to persuade him to come again later in July, but he was under too much pressure. 'I have already completed the physiography, resources, ethnology, economics of 46 countries but I have 22 to go and then I must write the political structure and history of 68 and all by August 15th,' he wrote to her from the city,[48] adding that on unbearably hot days, he wrote about Greenland, Iceland, Norway or Antarctica.[49]

Aida was the most hospitable of friends. Stead was left to write in peace, in a room with a view of the mountains. She liked to hear Max Kotlarsky practising his piano in another part of the house. In the late afternoon, the women would walk together, or swim in the small dam ten minutes from the house, returning with glowing skin.

The month at Hunter allowed Stead to observe the 'dog family'[50] at close quarters. She met Aida's sisters and brothers, who lived in cottages dotted around the property, and Stanley Hooper,[51] a dandyish neighbour, in the distant past Aida's suitor, who had created a 'dream garden' of fountains and sweet-smelling blooms.[52] Stead wrote to Blake: 'The immense universal kindness and friendship of the great clan I live in, for goodheartedness I have yet to meet their equals.'[53] She was intrigued that the family had retained something of their Russian ancestors' culture, even their storytelling.

The utopian ideal of a community outside capitalist society interested her. Her notes for *The People with the Dogs* refer to William Morris' vision of an artist community and Fourier's socialist phalanx. She could see real advantages in communal living and work-sharing—particularly for women. However, she was not uncritical of this nineteenth-century enclave, as she saw it, in the twentieth-century world. There was 'an awful boredom in this social pointlessness'.[54]

Back in New York in early August, she wrote to thank Aida for her 'boundless generosity'.

> I deeply, profoundly, sincerely appreciate it and you and the
> great Dolinsky scheme (I can't say Family, for it is something
> beyond a family, it's a scheme of things) which so lavishly
> accepted me and treated me with such indescribable kindness
> ... It was wonderful to me in many ways, seeing the Catskills,
> living on the Farm, getting to know you personally as you
> really are, not as you just seem to be in 12th Street, and getting
> to know the rest of those great Characters I have heard about
> for years but who never have had flesh and form till now.[55]

Aida Kotlarsky had no idea that Stead had been taking notes about those 'great Characters' while she was at Hunter, though Stead *had* told her she was planning to write about her friend Harry Bloom and his Washington Heights pharmacy. Harry had given her a printed silk smock as a late birthday present: 'I am going up this week to start my notes about the drugstore,' she told Aida. In *The People with the Dogs*, Al Burrows, 'big as a prairie breeze', is a pharmacist with a 'great joyous melodious laugh'[56] and a talent for Rabelaisian stories. The imagery associated with him evokes the natural world: vast, untamed and benign.

> His big white shirt, open at the neck, seemed to boil round
> him, like a sail full of wind: his soft muscular chest, without
> a hair, flowed in the opening, polished and broad as an ocean:
> his big face, with little eyes and little mouth, with its
> spectacles and big nose, expressed goodness.[57]

Young Edward Massine and his aunt Oneida Solway are more rounded characters in the novel, which is set in the post-war period, partly in New York City and partly in the Catskills. The return of the soldiers has created a shortage of houses and jobs; there is an atmosphere of disillusionment on the Left. But the 'people with the dogs' are sheltered from these economic and social pressures. Nothing stops Edward from chattering idly until the early hours and sleeping in until midday.

The People with the Dogs is full of humour, but not Stead's usual sharp satire. For once, the central character, Edward Massine, recognises himself more or less for what he is. And though there is plenty of talk in this novel, it is *conversation*—not manic wind-bagging, as in several other Stead novels.

The characters are not idealised. Oneida's love for her dogs is shown to be a substitute for adult love, a spiritual or professional life. Edward is affable and talented, but without purpose. After having tried in vain to throttle the massive hops vine at the country house, he sits back exhausted and angry, musing that it is a symbol of his life: 'the sloth that stretches back into my childhood'.[58] He is unable to commit himself to Margot, the woman he has loved for twelve years. Walt, a happily married man (based on Bill Blake) consoles him, but with an edge of irony:

> "You only understand the communal life, that's why you
> don't want to marry, isn't it? You don't see the reason for
> crawling into a corner with one woman and having one child.
> You need abundant multiple life around you like Whitehouse,
> like the Massines; the perfect still life, eh? Ha-ha. Fruitfulness
> with grapes and rabbits dropping over the edges of an oak
> table on a woven cloth—and many dogs and dishes and many
> children and many days? Isn't that you fundamentally?"[59]

Edward Massine believes he cannot live for himself: he needs to live for others,[60] and, in the end, he decides he wants commitment to one woman. This desire is seen, within the narrative, as a sign of his new maturity.

When Edward announces his impending marriage, his Aunt Oneida is distraught.

> "Children are Frankenstein's monsters! They grow up and leave
> you: but dogs never leave you . . . Edward, oh, Edward! Are you
> going to leave me?"

> "Jesus!" said Edward getting up and strolling to the window.[61]

Interestingly, in this book it is a man, not a woman, who feels unable to live for himself, and who finally discovers a point to his life in marriage. During his last hours as a bachelor, Edward feels 'very happy that this arid stretch of his life was over, and excited, curious to know what the next would be like'.[62] The journey imagery is similar to the ending of *Letty Fox*, though in Edward's case the reader feels optimistic. His marriage takes place on St Valentine's Day. Outside, there is 'the earliest, faintest intimation of spring'. In the final scene, the Massine tribe is gathered together: they are standing around, 'not especially arranged', on the stairs, round the long table, waiting patiently for the toasts. It is the 'perfect still life' Walt once described. But Edward has broken out of the closed circle. If the book has a message, it is that even benevolent, extended families such as this need to be left behind.

★　★　★

Stead had been revising *For Love Alone* in Hollywood, and continued to do so for several more months in New York. She then paid Ruth Blake to type it professionally. Her new agent, Helen Strauss, worked for the prestigious William Morris Agency,[63] and she impressed Stead and Blake as a superb businesswoman, for she quickly sold *For Love Alone* and arranged a three-book contract with Harcourt, Brace. It was Stead's third American publisher in eight years.

For Love Alone appeared on 6 October 1944, a cheap wartime edition. Its title, 'suggestive of the drugstore rental shelf', did not do it a service.[64] The jacket illustration, a drawing of a bare-breasted girl leaning out of her window on a starry night,[65] reinforced the impression that this was a popular romance.[66] As critic Jose Yglesias, one of Stead's admirers, saw it, the book was 'inevitably bound ... for the 49c remainder counter at the Concord bookstores'. He wrote later that the small côterie of Stead admirers were beginning to feel 'like disappointed lovers'. 'We shook our heads about Christina Stead's shortsightedness in allowing her publishers to misrepresent her work.'[67]

Some twenty years later, Patrick White was to read *For Love Alone* for the first time. He thought the first half of the novel even more powerful than *The Man Who Loved Children*. 'It is a *remarkable* book,' he told a friend. 'I feel elated to think it is there.'[68]

But few were so enthusiastic in 1944. Although some praised the 'subtle, lilting prose' and the 'pitiless clarity of vision',[69] Americans did not understand the intense Australian heroine whose passionate Odyssey was a search for Cytherean love. The *New Yorker* rather perversely complained that it had 'none of the wit that glittered through *The Beauties and Furies*'.[70] Yet in the *Nation*, Diana Trilling praised the 'flashes of real wit'.[71] Ruth Page, the *New York Times* reviewer, was more perceptive than most:

> It would be easy to be flippant about this book and miss its
> gravity, or be gross and miss its pathos. Christina Stead does
> not have the stature of D. H. Lawrence, but she has many of his
> qualities, and her new novel suggests his early and best fiction.[72]

The novel's sensuality and poetic intensity would frequently remind readers of D. H. Lawrence: the subject matter and exalted tone were particularly reminiscent of *Women in Love*. Stead greatly admired Lawrence, though she denied any conscious imitation on her part.

For Love Alone tended to be better understood by women critics than men; they could also appreciate the courageousness of its portrayal of female desire. There were, of course, exceptions, and one critic dismissed it as 'five hundred morbid pages of lust and abnormality'.[73]

When Peter Davies published the novel a year later, the reception in England was similarly mixed. Male reviewers often failed to see the point of the book. The anonymous reviewer in the *Times Literary Supplement* (it was R. D. Charques) was damningly negative as usual: he found Teresa 'a most tedious young woman' and the novel 'for long stretches . . . without any significant imaginative purpose'.[74] The *Listener* described Stead as having 'more evident genius than any other living woman novelist', but asserted it was 'an uncriticized and provincial genius'.[75]

The most enthusiastic review for once came from Australia. For the first time since *Seven Poor Men of Sydney*, Stead had set her novel partly in Australia. The *Bulletin* only reviewed 'Australian' books and had not reviewed Stead's other novels. This time though, the anonymous reviewer was Douglas Stewart, the *Bulletin* literary editor and himself a distinguished writer. He was extraordinarily impressed. The style of *For Love Alone* was 'unmistakably excellent', he wrote. The delineation of character equalled Dostoevski, and the novel had 'tremendous vitality'.

> There is a profoundly original talent speaking in *For Love Alone*, something wild and fierce and fearless that tempts one to use the word "genius." . . . It is a work of the highest quality.[76]

More typically, the Sydney *Daily Telegraph* claimed that the book 'just fails', adding, 'yet it is the profoundest book this most gifted and intellectually rich of Australia's contemporary novelists has produced'.[77] The *Sydney Morning Herald*, in one small paragraph, called the 500-page novel 'an admirable little book'. The reviewer, L. V. Kepert, a low-brow Sydney journalist, asserted: 'All her books have been written since she went abroad to live in 1926, which is a pity, because we should be proud to call her an Australian novelist.'[78] It was not enough that Australians wrote about Australia: they also had to stay at home to do it.

*   *   *

Stead had taught a Workshop in the Novel from September 1943 until January 1944, one evening a week, as part of the New York University extramural program. She prepared the workshop with her usual thoroughness, typing pages and pages of notes which fortunately have been preserved, and calling on her thorough knowledge of nineteenth- and twentieth-century European literature as examples of narrative techniques. She was to repeat the course in 1944 and 1946 because she needed the income, but complained it was time-consuming. It always took her a whole day to prepare the two-hour lesson.

'People do not like originality,' Stead warned her students. Nevertheless, she insisted, writers must have the courage to respect those 'ideas that rush up and force themselves into the story'.

Outside critics will tell you to take out these sudden apparitions from below which satisfy you so much, because they "don't contribute to the plot" . . . these critics being quite unaware what original impulse made you start the novel and what critical streak in your temperament is now coming to light. Do not listen to them, whether they are publishers, agents or friends.[79]

By the time Stead wrote *For Love Alone*, her sixth work of fiction, she was quite definite about what she was aiming for in her writing: '*intelligent ferocity*'. Her most striking statement of this *credo* was in a letter to Thistle Harris at that time:

The sensuality, delicacy of literature does not exist for me; only the passion, energy and struggle, the night of which no one speaks, the creative act: some people like to see the creative act banished from the book—it should be put behind one and a neatly-groomed little boy in sailor-collar introduced . . . But for me it is not right: I like each book to have not only the little boy, not very neat, but also the preceding creative act . . . Most of my friends deplore this: they are always telling me what I should leave out in order to have "success." But I know that nothing has more success in the end than an intelligent ferocity.[80]

Her aim was to disturb, even madden the reader, and she believed that a polished style reduced the force of the impact. She did not want to produce carefully wrought, well-balanced 'literature', with a neat plot and a tidy ending. She refused to tie together the loose ends of narrative. Characters are introduced in her fiction, never to reappear—just as this happens in life. Her endings are open; very often they circle back to the point of departure. The moral message is ambiguous, as it is in life. And her dialogue has the fractured syntax, repetition, colloquialisms, facetiousness and bullying of actual speech. As Angela Carter writes, it is 'that chaotic sense of flux that makes reading Stead somehow unlike reading fiction, that makes reading her seem like plunging into the mess of life itself'.[81] This quality of unpolished *rawness* is something Stead's readers either find immensely seductive or immensely irritating.

In so far as Stead believed that a polished style would come between the world and her reader, hers is a naturalist view of art. However, the desire to leave the traces of the 'preceding creative act'—to evoke the author sitting at the typewriter so to speak—is an *anti-realist* impulse, which celebrates art as process. This duality—realism versus anti-realism, life versus art—is ever-present in Stead's universe.

On the one hand, she would talk of 'Jonathan Crow' in interviews as if Crow were the name of the real man. On the other hand, the name Crow, like the name Quick, has a self-conscious fictionality: it is a metaphor as much as a name. There are also other devices in her fiction more typical of modernist than realist writing. The hundreds of allusions to other books in Stead's work suggest that the world is as much about fiction as fiction is about the world. Then there are the thinly concealed self-reflexive passages embedded in her fiction, in which a character who is a writer (most of Stead's major characters are writers) is about to embark on a novel or play that reflects or subverts the very novel Stead has written. In *House of All Nations*, Adam Constant declares he is going to write about the men in the bank and show the 'cynicism and egotism' of their existence. In *The Man Who Loved Children*, 13-year-old Louisa writes a violent little melodrama about a young girl who hates her father.

A typical instance of the intertextual strands in Stead's fiction is when Jonathan Crow, upon hearing Teresa describe her projected novel, asks her if she has read *Sister Carrie* by Theodore Dreiser. '"You must," said he. "There's a woman there who lives with a man for years without being married." '[82] In *I'm Dying Laughing*, when Emily tells her husband Stephen she plans to write a 'cruel book' about political opportunists in the revolutionary movement, he says he has been haunted since boyhood by Edward Everett Hale's *The Man Without A Country*. Stead does not explain the significance of the nineteenth-century novel, but for those who know, Hale's hero's fate reflects that of Stephen: an American who loves his country, he is condemned for conspiracy, and dies in exile, a broken man. Stories within stories, embedded narratives: Stead delighted in building Chinese boxes with narrative.

Stead greatly admired the nineteenth-century realists Balzac, Flaubert, Zola, Tolstoy, Gorki. For her, realism (or naturalism) was about objectivity. Like Flaubert, Stead aimed to rid her fiction of overt authorial judgement. Flaubert once said:

> Human beings must be treated like mastodons and crocodiles; why get excited about the horn of the former or the jaw of the latter? Display them, stuff them, bottle them, that's all—but appraise or evaluate them: no![83]

This suited Stead: she believed herself to have 'a terribly strong moral streak',[84] but in order to immerse herself in her characters, she needed to engineer herself into a state of sympathetic identification. In not making her own moral viewpoint clear, the risk she ran was of being misunderstood, and she often was. In her frustration, she would wish she were writing for socialist countries, where she would be obliged to make her message clear. 'I am tired of muffling my thoughts so that only the initiated understand exactly what I am driving at,' she told a friend.[85] Flaubert had the same problem with his irony.

Stead, unlike Bill Blake, was never translated in the Eastern Bloc, and it was probably because her novels lack an obvious message. Susan Sheridan points out that Stead's 'lack of moral colouring' and 'dizzying lack of narrative direction' often 'unsettles and disorients readers'.[86] This sense of moral vertigo arises partly because Stead herself was often undecided about her characters. From her early childhood, love had been associated with resentment, even hate, and this is a terribly confusing foundation from which to establish emotional commitments. Her major love as a child—her father—was someone she also bitterly resented. Moreover, there was a disconcerting gap between the ideals he professed and his actual actions, and though he was puffed up with grandiloquent talk, his grasp on the real world was decidedly slippery. The other love of Stead's life was Bill Blake, a man full of passionately held socialist ideals, who constantly found himself pandering to self-serving capitalists. Alphendéry, in *House of All Nations*, is not a happy man, nor is he an admirable man, but we sense that the narrator loves him.

In a sense, writing lifted Stead out of her moral dilemmas. In her writing, she suspended judgement: her aim was to understand. Writing the 'truth', which she believed to be neither black nor white, made her feel a more moral person. In *I'm Dying Laughing*, Emily Wilkes speaks in this instance for Stead:

> I think a writer *has* a tremendous responsibility to tell the truth
> and tell it with all the skill and ability and experience—he has
> —to rise above himself ... That's a funny thing, but every
> night I wake up and I think, I want to be better than I am by
> nature. To be a writer in an age when the truth will set us free
> —means to be a writer of the truth; or to be an utter, utter,
> decadent damned soul.[87]

Stead lived for her writing. In describing Edward Massine, one of her writer-characters, she is no doubt describing herself:

> He had an effective method for getting to sleep. It was to
> piece together names, faces, backgrounds, times of day,
> temperatures and seasons, tones of voice, things that had been
> said to him that had caused him emotion. He tried to form an
> idea of any given person's character, temperament.[88]

Another self-portrait is that of the Musical Critic in *The Salzburg Tales*, who tells the assembled group that he looks at life 'as a spectator who looks at a vast stage-setting'.

> If you have five minutes to observe a man, from a secret cranny, you will find out a great deal about him. Does he shake his head, loosen his collar, noiselessly gargle his throat and brush back his hair with his hand, does he take out his handkerchief and refold it, button and unbutton his coat? What is the colour of his eyes, hair, skin: what is the quality of the cloth in his coat, and of what cut is the garment? Is he fat or thin? What are his half-dozen tics? . . . Does he look into jewellers' windows, or bars, or banks? Has he a stick or a bag: what paper does he carry? . . . What is his gait, what his tread? There are a thousand things to observe which will give away the party he votes for and the amount of his bank-balance. And for this reason, I am an inveterate and shameless eavesdropper, I listen at the doors of rooms, I pussy-foot along the corridors, I read private letters and stare at people in their emotion. My own life is too calm for my energy, I suppose that is the reason.[89]

*   *   *

How did Stead go about her writing? As she explained to her students, the germ of a story would 'exhibit' itself to her one day. The idea would nag at her. She would mull it over, usually for several years, read books on the subject, collect newspaper clippings, keep a notebook, talk to the people on whom she thought she would base her characters, make more notes. Generally, she tried to keep all this file-keeping and auxiliary writing to the afternoons and evenings: the mornings were reserved for serious writing.

The subjects she treated would always involve conflict: between a parent and a child, between a man and a woman, or a conflict of values within an individual. She never underestimated the passions these conflicts engendered. 'We have a society that believes in reason or that would like to, and for one reason or another we are obliged to ignore or suppress various human passions, but the novelist must know what they are.'[90]

When she was ready to start on a new book, she would spend several months preparing to write. During this time, she would clarify her aim, her message. She told her students, who were all struggling with a manuscript of their own:

> The *proposition* is something that the author believes—it is one of the vital fluids of the novel. It carries it along: it is your message. Once your message is clear, your novel goes more

easily. If your novel has stuck at a certain place, it is perhaps because you have mis-stated your message. If it is dry, it is because (perhaps) you have not fully interpreted your message or your message is not one you really believe in.[91]

She would choose characters—people she knew or amalgamations of people she knew—and make notes about their physical characteristics and their ages at various stages of the narrative. In the case of Letty Fox, mainly modelled on Ruth Blake, she 'studied' Ruth, asked her questions, examined the letters she had written to her father over the years, discussed her with Bill. In order to find out in what ways Ruth was representative or special, she talked to other young women of Ruth's age, such as Nadine Lewin. Eventually, she would amalgamate and concentrate the various experiences of these young women.[92] It was important that no-one knew at the time that she was writing about them.

For any particular subject, she would read books that might help her focus on the peculiarities of the social milieu she was delineating. In the early Forties, when she was working on *For Love Alone* and *Letty Fox*, she read books by women and books about women: the Journal of Marie Bashkirtseff, *Madame Bovary*, *Mrs Dalloway*, *Anna Karenina*. She read, or re-read, depictions of love affairs and marriages: Ovid's *The Art of Love*, Pierre Louÿs' *Aphrodite*, Defoe's *Moll Flanders*, Chekhov's 'The Lady with the Little Dog', Rebecca West's *The Judge*, Ibsen's *The Doll's House*, Strindberg's collection of stories, *Getting Married*. And she read theoretical works about the social conditions of women: Bebel's *Woman and Socialism*, John Stuart Mill's *The Subjection of Women*.[93] Whenever she was not writing, Stead read vast quantities—mostly fiction, poetry and drama, but also biographies and socio-political books about her times.

She would think of incidents and dramatic scenes ('not plots or story-lines'), and plan her framework, perhaps making chapter headings. She knew she would probably discard the framework later, but it was essential to have something to guide her into the labyrinth of the novel.

To inspire her, she would go back again to the great dramatists: Shakespeare, Ibsen, Chekhov. Reading them always taught her more about dialogue. Above all, she listened. She listened to her character model speak: she listened to friends talking, she listened to people talking in the street, in the trolley car. She made notes as soon as she could after hearing a conversation she wanted to remember. Though she had acquired an excellent verbal memory, she knew that speech was not something one remembered like faces, attitudes and characters.

Eventually, the 'depth charge' would occur which made her impatient, almost feverishly so, to start writing. She described it as an intense emotion, like a shock or the stab of love that grips the belly. When it worked best, she would write in a state of white heat, fast, obsessively and all day long—almost as if in a kind of trance. She explained the 'depth charge' as something which 'blows the whole thing skyhigh, so that it comes down again in a new, and in the creative form'. This 'moment of discovery' was a 'moment of truly physical pain'; in that moment, she would see 'the pain of human relations'. The excitement, the awareness of human vulnerability were like a love affair. Some twenty-five years later, she would describe it in these terms.

> I'm a psychological writer, and my drama is the drama of the person. The start of a story is like a love affair, exactly. It's like a stone hitting you. You can't argue with it. I wait and wait for the drama to develop. I watch the characters and the situation move and don't interfere. I'm patient. I'm lying low.[94]

She gave her first draft all her care, energy and concentration, but she allowed herself to write haphazardly, not necessarily in sequence. (She had a plan to guide her back.) If she was blocked, held up in mid action, she would say to herself, 'Leave them alone for a few minutes and see what they will do'. This meant throwing herself on her bed and staring at the ceiling, while thinking about her characters. Certain valued techniques for thinking herself inside her characters she owed to Konstantin Stanislavski, the director of the Moscow Art theatre, whose experimental method of direction (aimed at achieving psychological realism) was influential in the States.[95] In order to get his actors to identify wholeheartedly with their stage character, Stanislavski had them imagine situations outside the script. Along these lines, Stead told her students: 'Arrange the characters together and make them say "I will." What are they willing at the moment?' She herself found this useful for constructing the dramatic scenes in *For Love Alone*—for example, a crucial scene between Teresa and Jonathan Crow in London:

> An inexperienced young girl is in the room of the young man she is in love with: he has made advances to her and she expects him to say he loves her. If he says he loves her, she will spend the night with him, without any qualms. She does not know that the young man has had many affairs with girls, is quite callous and has made it a rule never to say he loves the

girl. He considers it both more honest and more manly. A long discussion ensues and nothing comes of it because they misunderstand each other. This simple scene can become very moving if the writer keeps remembering what she wants and what he wants: it seems to be the same thing, but it isn't.[96]

After Stead had completed her first draft, she would re-arrange the sequence. Chapter One might become Chapter Four or the ending. Usually she wrote (or re-wrote) the beginning last of all. At this stage a new art came into play: 'the art of throwing away'. She was cautious here: 'By throwing away I do not mean what is called "paring to the bone."'

Stead disliked revision. By then her passion was spent. For the most part, it seems, she preferred to re-write than revise. This meant rolling a fresh page into the typewriter and writing the page again, working alongside the old draft but altering as she went. Among Stead's papers are pages and pages of slightly different drafts, all typed single-spaced on flimsy paper (light for suitcases) and with numerous crossings out. It is usually quite impossible to tell which draft is which.

Not only did this method of revision involve constant typing: it also explains the appearance of spontaneity and the genuine carelessness in Stead's writing. Ironically, this effect of spontaneity, which made it seem as if Stead wrote almost effortlessly, was achieved by monumental hard work.

*   *   *

Stead had been frustrated by the reaction of American critics to *For Love Alone* and sincerely hoped that her current character—she had gone back to her manuscript *Letty Fox*—was a young woman Americans could understand. Letty was a tough-minded New Yorker, intelligent and cynical, who claimed to be a typical New York college girl. However, she is sexually promiscuous, and the picture of American society in the novel is hardly flattering.[97] Once again, Stead had written frankly and daringly about subjects that were still taboo: female sexual aggression and male impotence. The novel, Stead was well aware, was likely to provoke outrage.

In *For Love Alone*, Teresa Hawkins is a heroic figure, with ideals, passion, moral integrity. With *Letty Fox*, Stead was entering a new phase: from now on, she would portray anti-heroines, anti-heroes—with varying degrees of sympathy. The portrait of Letty, while deeply ironic, is not unsympathetic. The sexual, social and political binds in which Letty is caught up are real.

To clarify her ideas for the novel, Stead made pages of notes about the condition of women in contemporary American society.

The question she asked herself: 'What is the solution for the restless, able, lively girl like Letty?' was one she could not answer. Marriage was not a solution for the modern bourgeois woman. Women had no security as mothers in a world in which divorce was always a possibility. If they worked or had a lover, it gave the father an excuse to apply to the court for custody of the children. Some married women prevented themselves from having children to please a husband who still harboured 'bachelor feelings', but this too, Stead noted, was 'a degradation, a crushing, an abuse of them'. (And they could be 'injured for childbearing by abortions'.) She considered the poor girl who wanted to go to night lectures and better herself: 'Who will look after her, as a man is often looked after?' Lowly duties were expected from women: 'Poor slum mothers hope to let rooms to girls, because girls will clean the rooms.' And yet women were physically weaker.[98] These surviving notes show Stead's anger about the situation of women and her genuine compassion. In the novel itself, which is highly satirical, Stead's sympathy is less apparent.

Letty Fox was Stead's first truly American novel; *The Man Who Loved Children*, transferred from Australia, did not arise out of her American experience. This time, she could not risk being told that her characters were 'cardboard Americans'; her challenge was to capture American voices, American behaviour and preoccupations. In preparation for writing, she immersed herself in the world of New York women—their magazines, their talk.

Men's talk interested her too. At the beginning of *Letty Fox*, Stead acknowledges that certain jokes and stories in the novel were taken from conversations heard in midtown Manhattan. She relished the storytelling culture in New York, which she called 'Bagdad on the Hudson'.[99] One evening, a friend had dropped in at the flat and recounted a series of horse stories currently circulating in New York. Stead typed them out the following morning from memory, and several appear in the novel.[100]

In later years, Stead would give quite a false impression of the writing of *Letty Fox*.

> After I'd written *For Love Alone*, which is gloomy and serious, I thought, I must write about another kind of girl. And I also thought, instead of being bogged down in all this stuff, letters and that kind of thing, I must write straight off. I did write straight off, without any pause whatsoever. That's why it's so bad in places.[101]

Far from being written without a pause, the novel was written in two bursts—over a period of five years. And Stead *did* make use of letters in *Letty Fox*, as she always did in her character novels. She was—like James Joyce, T. S. Eliot, like many artists—an indefatigable scavenger.

Ruth Blake, who was now 23, lived in the Village and would often call in at their 14th Street apartment, and talk freely about her rather complicated love life, her reading, the political meetings she had attended. She was a lively, curious, humorous young woman, and her father always invited her to their parties. Occasionally, when Bill was away on a business trip, Christina and Ruth would go out together for a meal or drinks.[102] Since gaining a Bachelor of Arts degree at NYU, Ruth had been working at various jobs. Stanley Burnshaw had employed her for a time at the Dryden Press, but he began to worry that she would 'corrupt' the other office girls with her stories of her sexual adventures.[103] Now she was working for the Free Belgian and the Free French Movements in Exile, using her fluent French.[104]

Stead had access to the letters Ruth had written to Bill over the years—an invaluable reminder of Ruth's evolving preoccupations.[105] Stead had also seen quite a bit of Nadine Lewin, Lina Lewin's daughter, in recent years. After a visit from Nadine one evening, Stead wrote to Blake: 'Nadine told me quite a few interesting men-women stories: [she] has a regular eye for the strange and complex.'[106] Nadine, who studied French and art at Hunter College, was quite different from Ruth Blake. Sheltered and idealistic, she was eager to become an artist. She and a friend of hers would together be the models for Jacky, Letty's younger sister.

Nadine's best friend at Hunter College unwittingly made an important contribution to the novel. She was a passionate young Italian woman, who aspired to be a writer and had an extravagant crush on their French lecturer, an older Frenchman. She would write Nadine long letters in French, detailing the torments of her passion. When Nadine told Christina this story, Christina asked if she might borrow the letters. Nadine agreed.[107]

Among Stead's few surviving *Letty Fox* notes are two pages in French.[108] At the top of the first page is typed: '*Lettre de jeune fille amoureuse de son professeur de français.*' Stead comments (in French) that the girl is 21 and talented. The rest of the page is the letter itself, written in a rapturous, exalted style. In it, a young woman writes that her passion, which she fears is not reciprocated, keeps her awake at night. She has become the slave of *War and Peace*, and particularly likes Natasha[109] (who writes confidential letters to her friend Sonia about *her* infatuation). She is also reading Keats' letters and biographies of Keats.

The same details appear in *Letty Fox*, in a letter from Jacky to her sister Letty.[110] In the novel, the letter is in English, though we are told that Jacky wrote it to Letty in French. Stead has reproduced the original letter at times word for word, at times slightly modified.

In the novel, the two sisters are polar opposites. They also represent the two sides of Christina Stead. Jacky, who cultivates Romantic agony (she even has tuberculosis, that Romantic disease), is 'wild about' Spinoza, Melanchthon, Shelley, Dostoevski, Napoleon, Goethe, Baudelaire. She is compared to Marguerite in *Faust*, whose 'grande passion' is for an older man. Letty, on the other hand, admires Marx and Hegel, distributes the *Daily Worker*, and aspires to write for the *New Masses*. She enjoys Odets' *Waiting for Lefty*, admires Dreiser, and reads Milton's *Lycidas* alongside Barbusse's *Stalin*.

When the jacket designer asked Stead for suggestions for the cover of *Letty Fox*, she, thinking of the two sisters, lent him drawings of Marie Bashkirtseff and Madame de Staël.[111] The parallels are not drawn in the novel itself, but when Stead created Jacky, she clearly had in mind Marie Bashkirtseff, the nineteenth-century Russian painter and diarist who died in her mid-twenties of tuberculosis. The narcissistic, exalted style of Jacky's letters closely resembles Bashkirtseff's journal.

The writer Germaine de Staël grew up in the turbulent years before the French Revolution, in a Paris intoxicated by radical social change. The daughter of Jacques Necker, Louis XVI's Minister of Finances, and a liberal mother, Germaine married at 19 Eric Staël von Holstein. It was not a match of love, but for her it was a point of departure. She was 23 when the Revolution broke out, and already writing fiction.

★   ★   ★

Edith Anderson was an aspiring writer in her late twenties when she and Stead became friends in 1944. The friendship began when Anderson wrote to Stead, whom she had heard read at the League, asking for advice on a writing project. Stead wrote back an encouraging three-page letter,[112] and invited her to the apartment. Edith wrote her impressions in her diary:

> I met Christina Stead last night. She made me feel like a bumptious adolescent, crude, undeveloped and prudish. She is a strange-looking creature. She has a good nose—small light blue eyes with a reptilian glitter, and a mouth which invites peculiar speculation . . . The conventional clothes in which all women disguise themselves succeed also in disguising her to the outsider who doesn't really look . . . But if you care to

look closely you may even be terrified. I don't think there is
any thought that Christina is afraid to think. She thinks, she
draws conclusions constantly. She is not unkind but she is
truthful and this may hurt sharply. [113]

Edith's admiration brought out the best in Stead: Edith believed her
to be a great writer and a great woman—intelligent, mysterious,
experienced. It made a welcome change; few of Stead's American
friends had read her books. With Edith, a fellow writer, Stead could
discuss her intense psychic life: the dreams she had had at the time
of Ralph Fox's death, her intuitions, her telepathic insights. Ruth
McKenney liked to talk; Edith Anderson was happy to listen.

Edith had worked for a time as an editor at the *Daily Worker*; now
she was working on the railways, making her contribution to the
war effort. She had just married for a second time. Her husband,
Max Schroeder, was a communist activist who had fled Germany in
1933 and been in gaol in Paris and a concentration camp in Morocco
before he made it to New York in 1941. Anderson had been
intrigued by the tattered-looking foreigner who moved into her
block of flats. Over time, Max and Edith would become firm
friends of Bill and Christina's.

Edith found Christina extraordinarily generous and kind. Once
she caught a severe dose of 'flu and happened to mention to
Christina, during a phone call, that her flat was very dirty.

What did she do but come over and clean the kitchen herself!
I was in an agony of contrition and shame that this great
woman was on her knees in my filthy kitchen. But there
was no stopping her. [114]

★   ★   ★

On 12 April 1945, shortly after being elected for a fourth term,
Franklin D. Roosevelt died at the age of 63, with Allied victory
only weeks away. Within a fortnight, Hitler committed suicide in
his Berlin bunker and Mussolini was shot by Italian partisans. In
May the Germans surrendered unconditionally. In July, a conference of the victorious powers at Potsdam had Churchill bitterly
complaining that Stalin had erected an 'iron curtain' across Europe.
On 6 August, the world's first atomic bomb destroyed Hiroshima,
followed three days later by another dropped on Nagasaki. When
Japan surrendered on 14 August, carnival broke out in allied cities.
'My guy's come back', crooned a popular American hit song.

But the 'Cold War' was under way. President Harry S. Truman
showed none of Roosevelt's reluctance to prosecute communists.
'Red-baiting' and 'witch hunting' would dominate American politi-

1. (*top*) The Stead family (*c.* 1883). Back row (left to right): Christina, Sydney, Samuel, Jessie. Front row: Samuel (senior), Florence, David, Christina (senior). 2. (*left*) Ellen Butters, Christina Stead's mother, at first communion (*c.* 1890).
3. (*right above*) David George Stead, around the time of his marriage to Ellen Butters (1901).

4. (*top*) Left to right: Doris Weeta, Frederick Huxley, Katharine Ada, David Darwin and Christina Ellen (*c.* 1914). 5. (*above*) A recent photo of Lydham Hill, Bexley, the Stead family's elegant home, originally surrounded by 3½ acres of land. The house was owned by Ada's father, Frederick Gibbins, until 1917. 6. (*right*) Ada Gibbins' family home, Dappeto, where David and Ada married on New Year's Day, 1907.

7. (*below left*) The view over Boongarre of Sydney Harbour in the 1980s. 8. (*right*) The 1991 sale of 14 Pacific Street (Boongarre), Watsons Bay, Sydney, once Christina Stead's home. 9. (*below*) Left to right: Fred, Peg, Weeta, David and Kate.

10. (*top*) Sydney Girls High School (1919). Back row (left to right): Viola Bonnette, Margaret Faram, Florence Quodling, Ruth Hunt. Front row: Christina Stead, Freda Cavell, Tempe Datson. 11. (*left*) David Stead in Malaya (1922). 12. (*above*) Christina Stead in London, her hair newly bobbed (1928).

13. (*below left*) Florence James, aged 21 (1923). 14. (*right*) Walter George Keith Duncan (late 1920s). 15. (*below*) Walter George Keith Duncan (left) in the research common room at the London School of Economics (June 1930).

16. (*far left*) William Blake (Blech) (*c.* 1928).
17. (*left*) Christina Stead in the Paris years (1929-35).
18. (*below*) Letter from Christina Stead to Gwen Walker-Smith (April 1931).

"Café de Flore"

172, B^d St-Germain
PARIS
◙
Tél.: LITTRÉ 55-26
◙

RECEIVED
11 MAY 1931

Dear Gwen

Thank you very much for your letter telling me about Bundanoon; + for the 3 photographs, which are a surprise a great pleasure + Who is this young creature? Don't you ever cease deceiving people — Bill is sure you are about it to look at you + He will not believe you are the person I used to live with, I am very glad you had your holiday at Bundanoon + are so much better + you look in very good shape, — really almost d'but-on

TRAVELERS BANK

18, Rue de la Paix

Adr Telegraphique
TRAVELBANK - PARIS

TÉLÉPHONE

CENTRAL 71·38   GUT. 84·41
LOUVRE 33·43   —   84·42
—   61·55   —   84·43
INTER 70·9

COMPTE CHÈQUES POSTAUX 032·47 B.

R C SEINE 208 433 B

PARIS Twentysixth July, 1932.

Dearest Gwen,

I was very happy to get a letter from you and thank
you for the birthday wishes and the handkerchief. It shows that
good injustice reigns in your bosom, for if you had any sense of
give and take you would not write to me at all after my lapses.
I am sorry you are so tired when you get home from work. Do you get proper holidays
in this work? Do you meet interesting people you can gg out with, at the office?
I should imagine you would: all the newspaper people I have ever met are amusing and
kindly, genteel but saucy. The only other Australian I know in Paris is a young fellow
from Adelaide, who writes articles for an economic journal and haunts Bill at the Bank
from time to time for information. He is slender quickfooted genial chap, full of
backchat, but modest withal: I hold him up to Bill as a pattern of Australians. He
told Bill he was looking for financing for a company to make local beer out of kangaroo
hops: I suppose that is an old one, but it is new in Paris! I told him I preferred
thescheme for making ducks' eggs for wombats, but Bill says that is the worst crack ever
made, and whacked me forthwith.

I have had letters from most people this week,
and a sample of hymeneal printing fromPercia. The family is growing fearfully: I shall
soon have to have my Christmas cards printed by the gross (it is almost time to think
about that, of course!), and I shall have the same difficulty as has the Royal Secretary
i.e. to choose a subject which will be suitable for all eyes and plain enough for all to
seize: if I do not succeed better than he does Heaven help the family - their mail will
be filled with Academy tulips which have stood the test of time, and foxhunting squires
taking the waterjump, and I am certain the latter would be no atmosphere for Elizabeth
Ada at that.   It is most oppressive to be an aunt. I have been called aunt before
this of course, by adventitious nepotisms on my mothers side, but to be a full aunt,
what a disaster: I shall have to study education and lay a little aside for the child's
bottom drawer and inveigle young men into my clutches with tarts and raspberry syrup.
I confess that I hate to be an aunt, although I would not object to putting my sisters
in that embarrassing position,(for it is a heart of stone which does not fob off on others
the incommodities of life), in fact I refuse to be one, and I shall manage that by calling
this child my aunt· Henceforth I shall callit Aunt Elizabeth· I shall no doubt in the
course of many years be so furnished with aunts by this system that I shall not have to
worry about my own bottom drawer at all. Aunt is a detestable word: I don't know why we
can't have the pleasant word the French and Germans have, viz. Tante or Tanta, or Nana, or
Nounou, or Mimi, or Mémé, or any of the other gentler epithets in use among the European
savages.   What a badtempered letter: it is because my coiffeur cut my hair with a razor
by way of being chic, and now it is all ends and xhinkixxxxhknxmgh I feel an oddity and I
have to go and see Bill's mother, who is a charming little person, but has a small head
full of private comment, so that I dress up for her while appearing nonchalant.
It is Bill's birthday on Thursday (day after tomorrow) and I have bought him the usual list
of things bought by a doting wife for an indigent husband, but also a gramophone record
of James Joyce the English littérateur, reading from his own works, a rare thing costing
200 francs: you pay that and youare not allowed to hear the record before buying, on the
pretence that it wears the record (and I suppose once you have had the experience you are

19. Letter from Christina Stead to Gwen Walker-Smith (26 July 1932).

WANTED BANKER IN A YACHT

Police Hunt for Two Men

From Our Own Correspondent

PARIS, Sunday.

POLICE are searching — in Paris and London, on the Riviera, and even on the high seas—for Mr. B. Coles Neidecker, founder of the Travellers' Bank of Paris, and Mr. Aubrey Neidecker, his brother and partner, warrants for whose arrests have been issued.

The doors of the Paris office of the bank in the Rue de la Paix were closed last Thursday and an announcement was made that

MR. B. COLES NEIDECKER.

they would reopen on Friday. They are still closed.

Riviera branches have also been closed, though others in London, Brussels, and Amsterdam were operating until the week-end.

The police have now placed their seals on the Paris office of the bank, and are searching the homes of the Neidecker brothers in the fashionable Avenue Foch and the Rue des Sablons.

The last heard of Mr. B. Coles Neidecker, a former member of the American Air Force in France, who founded his bank in 1923, was that he was at Marseilles, where his luxurious yacht, Etoile Filante (Shooting Star), was moored in the Old Port.

Before Mr. Neidecker could be reached, however, the Etoile Filante had put to sea, with its owner and his wife and family on board, heading for an unknown destination.

The Travellers' Bank of Paris dealt chiefly in exchange operations with New York and London.

It was apparently prospering until a Paris customer went to London to verify certain matters of accountancy, later lodging a charge of fraud against the head of the bank.

Mr. Neidecker assured the examining magistrate in charge of the case that all his accounts were in order and that securities deposited by his customers were in New York. He was allowed his freedom without being asked to produce bail.

The liabilities of the bank are said to amount to about £1,300,000. Its nominal capital when founded was 2,500,000 francs, or £20,000 at par.

It will be recalled that Mr. Bertrand Neidecker had to throw his two children into the sea, and then, with his wife, leap after them when an explosion occurred aboard his yacht Argus in Cannes Harbour last September. They were rescued by other craft.

20. (*left*) *Daily Mail* clipping on the collapse of the Travelers' Bank, Paris (July 1935). 21. (*below*) Mike Gold, 'The Yankee "tribune of the people"' (*c.* 1938). 22. (*bottom*) 'Yiddish'. Stead's notes on Rosa Blech's conversations with her son 'Vill' (Bill). (September–October 1937).

Ist er aus Okraina?

The young couple were out late last night and when Mrs. Segal comes in to breakfast, she scowls and looks into her cup, refusing to say good-morning. When a second cup of coffee is poured, however, and she hears the two idiots mention the word "Chicago," she is glad to speak..

"Chicago! Oy, vaist Du, Vill, das ist cold wie Rossia, das ist wie Moscow..

.........Tomorrow will be warmer but cloudy.... ·Der Goldenweiser is doch

from Okraina, Will?...Hör, Vill, Der Goldenweiser, er ist nit fom Okraina?..

Wie viel gibt's, Vill, provinces in Okraina?..Oy, die Kazaken Oncle

Jule was bei dem for years. Oh, he liked it so much. Oy, Vill, kommt in Neesh (Nice) a junges Mädchen. A zieh nit a English oder a French. Sie zelt

sie ist aus Okraina, oh, a zay beauty, a zay shainhait. Sagt sie,

of course her eltern sind nit hier, sie ist at French school, die eltern sind

dort. Never mind, she was beautiful. What, describe her! Was für narrish-

keit. Ich hab gesagt a beauty. Bhain, das ist eine andere sache, nu, na!

She was a beauty. Um, mwsk! (a kiss). Vell, she had majestic shoulders and her

- and her - arms and body - and alles. She was a beauty and she married a

soldier. Wer künnte es glauben?? "Oh, Mrs Siegel," her mother told me,

23. (*right*) Christina Stead, Brussels (*c.* 1937). Stanley Burnshaw said of this photo: 'It must have been taken by someone who specialised in making women look appealing.'
24. (*below left*) Left to right: Mike Gold, Harry Bloom and Bill Blake – ardent communists (*c.* 1938). 25. (*below right*) Ralph Fox – a life-long passion of Christina Stead. Fox believed in heroes: 'The heroic must come back to the novel.'

26. (*left*) Edith Schroeder
(Anderson) in her railway
uniform, New York (*c.* 1940).
27. (*right*) Ruth McKenney:
Emily Wilkes in *I'm Dying
Laughing*. 28. (*below*) Ruth
Blake c. 1940.

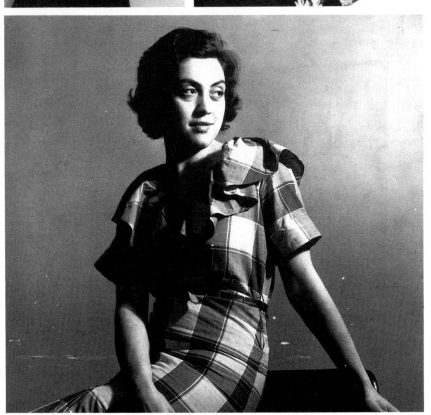

The People with the Dogs.   *Jacob and [illegible] Massine*
OLD DAD   *OLD MUM*

TABLEAU of NAMES.   Cats or Dogs. Scotty.

EDWARD MASSINE.   3½ yrs.   MUSTY, a Scotty.
   (Dr. Edward, father)   dead   WEST FOURTH, a black and white cat.
   (Mildred, Mother   )
   (Uncle Syce Fleming, once guardian.
   (~~Robert~~ *PAUL* Massine,   dead brother. "swine fever."

AMY SOLWAY née Massine & LOU SOLWAY.45/47. yrs.   MADAME X; French bull. Very old.
MME. BUTTERFLY TOY BOSTON   ~~PINCHBECK, Pellotel FUSTIAN Bostons~~
                                     ~~CAMEIS~~, cat just died.
Amy's sisters and brothers as follows:-   *TOBACCO*   *TIGER*
NORAH
MARY COOPER née Massine, eldest   75 yrs.   *DINGY — A SKYE*
BIG JENNY BARNES née Massine   68 yrs.   No animals.
DAN BARNES.   45 yrs.   DARLY, a toy Boston. Old.
THAÏS BURNS née Brns, dtr. of above. 33)yrs.   OLD HANK, red mixed shepherd type
CARMEN BURNS dtr. of Thaïs.   IO)yrs.   SMOKY aged blue Persian.
WHITMORE BURNS husband of Thaïs.   35)yrs.   PIP, a Spitz. Old.   (pups
                                               TEX, Thaïs's Great Dane female with
FLORA BARSTOW, née Massine,   65 yrs.   PIZZY, Carmen's gutter-saved cat.
"Fat" JACK MASSINE   70 yrs.   THE ABBOT, young Manchester;
Whit~~xxxx~~px Aunt" POPPY.   60 yrs.   ~~Xxxxxxxxx~~ ANGUS, Airedale. Old.
LITTLE JENNY MASSINE, née Thomas, 61 yrs.   ~~Xxxxxxxxx~~ BOB an American retriever,
Relict of Edmond Massine, yd.h. sbn JT yrs.   a fighter. Middle aged.
MRS. ~~Thomas~~, mother ~~xx Jenny~~ abxxi ,72 yr. ~~Eksenel~~ No animals.
  (for suppression always called "Mother.)   *"SAMSON SPANIEL*
TWO MASSINES, ~~daughtxxxxxxdx~~ dtr.-in-law
  and son of above Jenny Massine   BOY a wirehaired fox. Young.
OLIVE; "Ollie" ~~Jops~~ *Benson*   55 yrs.   No animals.
~~Jgsxt~~ (only mentioned) husband of above.
~~Rat Cheese~~ MASSINE & CLARE"Beauty" 50/45 yrs. No animals.
LEANDER
Massine Dependents:-   *"OPSE" AND "PALAYGA" COOPER*
MOSTBROOK   *LAUREL " ROSE COOPER*
MRS. ~~Benson~~, "Frankie" has run   *DES. OF MARY,*
  their large paying farm for yrs. 58 yrs. A house-dog.
~~Xxxxxxx~~ her son, a weakling HANNO 35 yrs.
IRENE NORTH, married twice. old friend. 40 yrs.
  appears ten yrs. younger.
VICTOR ALEXANDER (shepney)   52 yrs.   No animals.
MRS. ANNICHINI "Annitchka"   58 yrs.   Takes over Pip and Smoky.
Ben and Aline VAN KILL   40/28 yrs.   ~~farmxxxxxxxxxxxx~~ farm
  Farmer on home-farm.   BONES, Large red crossbreed.
~~Adams~~, squatting neighbor in cabin   CHARLIE, the tied-up ~~foxterrier~~. *SPITZ*
ADAMS
Edward's Friends:-   . . . .

MARGOT ROSSI   45 yrs.
Innocent Faith, White servant of above. 50 yrs.
Painter CHARLIE THE CROAT.   60 yrs.
Agent MISS ~~DENHAM~~ *WALDMEYER* 45 yrs.
The Butcher ~~xxxxxx~~ *CHUBB*   45 yrs.
Friend AL BURROWS, druggist   45 yrs.   MILL, gutter-cat. blue and white.
Friend WALT, his cousin (Ed's)   30 yrs.
Friend MELVILLE,   45 yrs.
~~WILL & MARK MOOKE~~ *WYLIE* 68/61 yrs?   LADY a whippet.
In their lodging-house:
CHASS (Charles McIntyre)   20 yrs.   *DAN BARNES'*
ELLA girl friend of Mark   48 yrs.   *Feathers/ & cat*
Others.
MR. PARKE a painter/[illegible]   *BART AIRMAN*

10. **Subject upon which you propose to write—**

(Define fully the specific programme of work proposed to be carried out. If you contemplate undertaking original research, your scheme of work should be outlined.)

NEW AUSTRALIA. A sort of New World Symphony. (MIGRANTS could be title, but no title at this stage is of value.) A novel situated in various parts of Europe and Australia,illustrating the New Australians, for example, French or Swiss engineers, with colonial experience, or longing to depart from old ways, Dutch people from Holland which is over-populated, Belgian unemployed (perhaps), Italian workers, as a mine-worker from Belluno (Alps) who feels he must go to another country, Argentine, USA or Australia and decides upon Australia, (this has a recall to the famous Italian poular novel Cuore and is part of Italian experience), English workers, as say, an engineer or other worker from, say, Newcastle-upon-Tyne, or xxxxxxxxxxpx Hull, German artisans or printers, etc......The present writer has had some experience of use, having lived some years among such migrants and their descendants in New York City and elsewhere in the USA: and knows Western Europe quite well, having lived for longer or shorter periods in France , Italy,Spain, Belgium, Holland, Germany, England, Ireland,(USA) and round the Mediterranean, but chiefly in USA, France,England: not only knows something of the views, letters home, language and job difficulties of migrant workers but knows many of such persons or has casually known them: is a sort of polyglot without any special language proficiency, and out of sympathy has studied one or two minor languages,without being any sort of talent in this way: the writer feels she has a genuine feeling however for this xxxxxx people (the migrants, that is) on account of long xxx experience, a lifetime, or half that, of experience. If this project is of interest, the writer would be very glad to submit a detailed idea. Nothing would be done or described without personal knowledge.

11. Give the names and occupations of your three referees ..

Dr. Gilbert E. Phillips, xxxxxxxxxxx
xxxxxxxxxxxxxxxxxxxx
Eamonn V. MacAlpine, xxxxxxxxxxxxx
xxxxxxxxxxxxxxxxxxx
Sydney Daily Telegraph.
Maria Beuzeville Byles, Barrister,
Sydney.

Principal,Sydney Teachers'College and
Senior Lecturer in Education,
University of Sydney (1950)
Editor-in-Chief,Consolidated Press,
Sydney

Paris

Date..4th September 1952   Signature....Christina Ellen Blake

30. (*top*) Christina Stead's application for a Commonwealth Literary Fund Fellowship (September 1952). She sabotaged her chances of success with this badly presented application. 31. (*above*) Christina Stead and Bill Blake in the grounds of Foxwarren Park (1959). Beyond is Wisley Common. 32. (*right*) Bill Blake, aged 65, standing on the terrace of Foxwarren Hall at Foxwarren Park (1959).

33. (*right*) Dr Philip Harvey, relaxing in his gardening clothes (*c.* 1970). 34. (*far right*) Christina Stead in London (early 1950s). Her cousin Gwen was shocked by her appearance. 35. (*below*) Christina Stead's FBI file, opened in February 1947.

FEDERAL BUREAU OF INVESTIGATION

Form No. 1
THIS CASE ORIGINATED AT NEW YORK
NY FILE NO. 100-82232

REPORT MADE AT	DATE WHEN MADE	PERIOD FOR WHICH MADE	REPORT MADE BY
NEW YORK	2/18/47	1/28,29,30,31; 2/3,4,10,13,17/47	

TITLE

CHRISTINA ELLEN STEAD, was. Mrs. William J. Blake, Mrs. William J. Blech

CHARACTER OF CASE

SECURITY MATTER - C

SYNOPSIS OF FACTS: Subject, CHRISTINA STEAD, was born in Sydney, New South Wales, Austria, on July 17, 1902, of Australian born parents. She travelled to London in 1928, Paris in 1929, US in 1935, returned to Europe and returned to US on August 2, 1937. Retained British citizenship. Occupation writer. Marital status, single. Sailed for Antwerp, Belgium, on 12/28/46 for ten months stay in Europe. NY residence 21 East 14th Street. Signer of open letter to All Active Supporters for Democracy and Peace in 1939. Committee member of American Peace Mobilization at Chicago, Illinois, in 1940. Appeared on mailing list of Greater NY Emergency Conference on Inalienable Rights in 1940. Signed Call for the 4th Congress of American Writers. Author of "Letty Fox," depicting life of young Communist League member in 1946.

- C -

DETAILS: This investigation is predicated upon a book review appearing in the October 6, 1946, edition of the New York Times. This was a review of the book "Lettie Fox" written by CHRISTINA STEAD and indicated the author had an extensive knowledge of Communist matters.

ALL INFORMATION CONTAINED HEREIN IS UNCLASSIFIED DATE

Background:

Reference was made to Who's Who in America for the following information concerning the subject.

She was born in Sydney, New South Wales, Australia, on July 17, 1902. Her father's name was DAVID GEORGE STEAD, and

APPROVED AND FORWARDED:

DO NOT WRITE IN THESE SPACES

COPIES DESTROYED 8-17-53 R25

100-236179-6

RECORDED

COPIES OF THIS REPORT
5 - Bureau
3 - New York

EX-33

F B I
34 FEB 21 1947

50 MAR 7 1947

36. (*right*) Harry Bloom (left) and Bill Blake at Karl Marx's tomb in Highgate Cemetery, London (May 1965). 37. (*below left*) En route to New York and Puerto Rico on the SS *United States* (February 1966). Christina Stead was at the height of her fame. 38. (*below right*) Christina Stead's favourite picture of the older Bill Blake (*c.* mid 1960s).

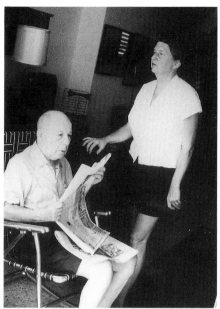

39. (*above left*) At Harry
and Anne Bloom's, Puerto
Rico (March–April 1966).
40. (*above right*) Puerto
Rico (1966): Bill Blake was
often ill; Christina Stead,
bored, drank a great deal
of Scotch. 41. (*right*)
Christina Stead in her
'barn' at Hurstville
(1976).

42. (*above left*) Nugget
Coombs – 'darling Cole'
– and Christina Stead in
Canberra (1982).
43. (*above*) Christina
Stead, posing for her
young American friend,
Jonathan LaPook,
in Sydney (1982).
44. (*below*) Christina Stead
at Heather Stewart's
house, Sydney
(January 1983).

cal life for over a decade and the Left would be relegated to the margins.

Inside that besieged fortress, the Communist Party, members were engaged in their own vilifications and expulsions. A controversy that blew up early in 1946 was to be one of the last 'Old Left' literary wrangles. In the *New Masses*,[115] Albert Maltz argued that the conventional communist view of art as a propaganda weapon had proved a straitjacket to writers. The outrage from communists around the country was such that after two months he officially recanted.[116]

On the whole, Party members dreaded expulsion. In *I'm Dying Laughing*, Emily Wilkes and Stephen Howard's disagreements with local communist doctrine land them in severe trouble with the Party, but Howard abjectly tells his wife: 'If I lost the Party I'd have nothing. I wouldn't know where to go, where to look. I can't live without the Party. I've built my life, my philosophy, my affections, too, on it.'[117]

At the end of the war, 'rightwing revisionism' came to be associated with General Secretary Earl Browder, leader of the Party in America. The abrupt reversal of Comintern policy began with an open letter from French communist leader Jacques Duclos, published in May 1945 in communist newspapers around the world.[118] Duclos' letter, which vehemently attacked Browder, was the signal that Moscow wanted to remove Earl Browder from the American leadership. It was already clear that the Kremlin's main enemy in the coming years would be the United States: Browder's vision of post-war harmony between America and Russia now looked ridiculous. In July 1945, he was ousted from the leadership. Seven months later, he was expelled from the Party as a 'social imperialist'.[119] At branch meetings all over the country, comrades stood up to 'confess' that they had allowed themselves to be misled by Browder.

Bill Blake and his 'old-liner' friends who had been against Browder's 'United Front' policy throughout the war years, formed a discussion group in 1944, composed of like-minded anti-Browderites whose aim was to 'preserve imperilled theory in time of crisis'.[120] They met at Stead and Blake's 14th Street apartment. (Edith Anderson went along once with her husband and found the room full of 'brilliant people'.[121]) At the same time, Blake kept up a demanding schedule of money-raising talks for the Party;[122] he and Stead were both members of the Joint Anti-Fascist Refugee Committee. And in June 1945 they helped arrange a seventieth birthday celebration for Thomas Mann, the main spokesman for the anti-fascist émigré writers.

Blake's 'leftwing sectarianism' was not well regarded by the Party, even when Browder was no longer in favour. Like-minded thinkers Ruth McKenney and Richard Bransten (alias 'Bruce Minton') were expelled from the Party in September 1946. They were deemed guilty of advocating the petty-bourgeois notion of 'freedom of criticism' in order 'to facilitate their propagation of views hostile to the party'.[123] Horrified, Stead wrote to Aida Kotlarsky at Hunter:

> Nine days' wonder here—my friends Ruth and Richard (McKenney and Bransten) were chucked out of the Party. Of course I knew it, but it just hit the press, and the criminals (the State Committee) have been very busy getting their story all over the fences and billposts ... A lot of gangsters have stolen the all-powerful name of the Communist Party: but they are close to a shut-down, I believe, and then something decent and honest will take their place.[124]

Six days later, convinced that their own phone was tapped by the FBI, Stead preferred to write to Edith Anderson:

> The statements even in the D.W. [*Daily Worker*] were the opposite of the truth. At a time like this a wretched clique can think of nothing better to do than make a stink and throw out good Bolsheviks; and lie!!—you should see what lies! ... My chief interest is to tell people that Ruth and "Bruce" are innocent, absolutely innocent.[125]

It is this atmosphere of fierce recrimination that Stead portrays in *I'm Dying Laughing*, portraying the 'besieged fortress' from within.

★　　★　　★

Stead had to put aside *The People with the Dogs* to go back and revise *Letty Fox*, which she handed to Harcourt, Brace in August 1945.[126] After that, she briefly thought of returning to her collection of short tales, tentatively entitled *The Exploits and the Heroic, Gay, Improper, Amorous Adventures and the Lies of Jan Callowjan*.[127] Jan Callowjan (inspired by Till Eulenspiegel, the legendary prankster and man of the people in German literature[128]) was based loosely on Henryk Grossmann.

Bill Blake went to Stanley Burnshaw with a suggestion for a possible money-spinner: an anthology of contemporary fiction about love, with an introduction by Louis Untermeyer, the New York poet and critic. Burnshaw, dubious at first, agreed, and Stead and Blake worked on it together. They selected a dozen short stories and forty-eight excerpts from novels,[129] (including the shotgun wedding scene in *For Love Alone*) and called the collection *Modern*

Women in Love. Stead was more interested in passion than love. 'A strong passion moves in chaos and associates with death ... Venus should be black: that is the colour of love, the rite of the night.'[130]

Louis Untermeyer wrote an enticing introduction: 'The pages run from the purest virtue to the most debased *voyeurism*, from natural fulfilment to almost insane frustration.'[131] Three years later, Stead was to describe the book as 'an excellent ... anthology which bears my name too, but only because they had to have a woman on the title-page ... It was a charming bit of Bill's work.'[132] They found it satisfying to publish in joint names, and the volume did make them some money.

★　★　★

In the summer of 1946, Stead and Blake spent a week in the Catskills with Asa Zatz and the Kotlarskys, and then stayed some time with the Branstens in Westport, Connecticut. Stead took advantage of these visits to make notes for *The People with the Dogs* and her novel about revolutionaries (later called *I'm Dying Laughing*). Blake returned to New York alone in early August, to take up a new job. He was not enthusiastic, but Stead told Aida Kotlarsky: 'I am only wanting him to keep at it long enough to put awful Alf in his place. Awful Alf is batting about as large as life in Canada, at present.'[133]

Bill Blake, famous among New York communists for his fund-raising prowess, had landed a job with the American Birobidjan Committee. His task was to promote and raise money for a Jewish settlement in Birobidjan, a province in Siberia set aside by the Soviet government for Jews already living in Russia. After the holocaust, the American Jewish community was overwhelmingly in favour of establishing some sort of Jewish homeland.

Blake, like most of his Jewish communist friends, had never liked the idea of a Jewish homeland. Ruth Blake recalls that when she once wrote a short story about the Jews needing a home, her father had said to her: 'Beware of false sentimentality.'[134] But during and after the war, Jewish national aspirations were encouraged by the Party. Indeed, the American Birobidjan Committee was openly a communist front.[135]

Birobidjan was a swampy, mosquito-ridden terrain, with winter temperatures of minus fourteen degrees; however, Blake saw it as a wholly generous gesture on Stalin's part. Writing for the Jewish paper *Nailebn* in September 1946, he tried to convince American Jews of its importance.

An almost unpeopled wilderness has been transformed into a
pioneering area, already significant, with cities and settlements
having a rich cultural life and a wide diffusion of modern
amenities . . . For Birobidjan to attain the status of an
Autonomous Jewish Republic, whose prestige would heighten
the world position of Jews, a population of some 500,000 would
seem to be required . . .

   As the Soviet Union (despite its cruel burden of rebuilding the
wasted homes and farms of tens of millions) makes liberal grants, it
follows that ordinary generosity by the fraternal Jewish population
of other countries could make it easy to attain this goal within a
decade. Birobidjan, then, in the heart of the most rapidly
growing industrial area of the world, would be resplendent, and
its early pioneering days remembered with that same romantic
fervor with which Americans recall the Pony Express, the
Covered Wagon, the Stage-Coach and the Cowboy.[136]

In early September, Blake travelled around Michigan and Ohio,
raising money for the scheme. The Zionists he encountered were
not as conservative as he had feared, he wrote home.

   I have not met with a single malicious or clever attack on the
   Soviet Union, as one so often hears from the "wise guys" in
   large cities . . . Wherever I go I find these ex-immigrants,
   former idealists in the ghettos of Europe . . . who remain the
   same unassuming people who believe the system all wrong.[137]

Birobidjan would prove a hopeless venture. After the establishment
of the State of Israel in 1948, Stalin no longer attempted to conceal
his anti-semitism. The Comintern, ruling that Jewish nationalism
was anti-progressive and anti-Soviet,[138] suppressed Jewish institutions in Birobidjan. Those who had settled there, and those who
had sent money, were betrayed once again.

*   *   *

Stead left the Branstens' suburban home in mid August. She found
the heat in New York unbearable. The cafeteria below their apartment had upgraded its airconditioning system and now sounded
like a fleet of low-flying bombers. In desperation she wrote to Aida,
still at Hunter:

   It gets me down: I don't work. I sit there and every fifteen
   minutes or so, heave myself out of my chair and write about
   four bad lines just to fool my typewriter. I have been thinking
   —who has a spare room in N.Y.?[139]

She asked if she might leave her typewriter at the Kotlarskys'
apartment and work there for six weeks, until their return to New

York City. 'I would (if you permitted) arrive there about nine or ten, say, have a sandwich and milk lunch there and come home about four, doing my shopping on the way, or even at five, if busy ... I hardly ever work at night anyhow.' Aida no doubt agreed to this.

In the evenings, too tired to work, Stead would play solitaire or double patience or embroider—the very things her stepmother had always done. She also enjoyed crosswords and puzzles. That summer she was enthusiastic about that bleak and despairing novel, *The Heart is a Lonely Hunter*, written in 1940 by the 22-year-old Southern writer, Carson McCullers. And she reviewed three minor Australian novels for the *New York Times Book Review*.[140]

She was learning Yiddish from Ber Green, one of the editors of the Yiddish-language communist daily, *Morgen Freiheit*.[141] In return, she was helping him translate his Yiddish poems into English. She enjoyed her sessions with this 'highly scholarly and cultivated' man.[142]

When Bill was away on fundraising tours, she would occasionally go for evening drinks with Ber Green or Henryk Grossmann. When he was not in 'one of his black or silly moods', Grossmann was 'a marvellous companion'. As unhappy as ever in his New York exile, he was living for the day when he could return to Europe. Stead wrote to Blake wistfully: 'Why doesn't *Letty Fox* sell like mad and then we could all (three) be over there?'[143]

The imminent publication of *Letty Fox* was making her anxious. Would it be considered scandalous? Stead told Blake she thought she might run away to the Branstens in Connecticut when it came out. After their expulsion from the Party, she was nervous about the communist reaction to her novel, which scarcely presented a flattering picture of communists. From Letty Fox, a Young Communist Leaguer, comes the quip: 'Radicalism is the opium of the middle class.'[144] Stead was worried about libel: what would Nadine Lewin and her Italian friend say about the letter she had reproduced almost verbatim in the book?[145] She must also have been uneasy about Ruth and Mollie's reaction to a novel in which, to all who knew them, they were recognisable as Letty and Mathilde Fox. Fortunately Mollie and Ruth were busy preparing to leave for France. When Ruth did eventually read it, she was very upset, not only because of its indiscretions, but also because Letty appeared to be based entirely on her, whereas she could see that Letty was in fact a composite portrait.[146]

Letty Fox was published in New York in early October 1946. Harcourt, Brace once again presented the novel like a cheap romance, with a soft cameo drawing of two pretty girls on the jacket. On the flap were the words of critic Harrison Smith: 'To read it is like listening through a keyhole to a conversation in a harem. There are no reticences. Miss Stead proves once more that she is one of the greatest novelists of our day.'

The novel caused quite a stir. Some critics were shocked; others were outraged. Letty's claim to be a typical New York college girl angered the locals: Mary McGrory in the *New York Times* accused Stead of 'serious misrepresentation': 'All is distorted, turgid and overblown in her world, with sex rampant and passion unbridled.'[147]

The *New Yorker*'s anonymous reviewer described Stead as 'an Australian and something of a newcomer to America' and bemoaned her 'rather shaky grip on the local idiom and mores'.[148]

The communists were incensed. Stead's former associates at the *New Masses* had this to say:

Letty is only a play-radical, like some of her lovers and friends. That such people sometimes attach themselves to the revolutionary movement is undeniable. As a rule they soon find their way out again, usually through the back door of ultra-leftism which permits them to feel both safe and "militant." At any rate they make not only the most unnatural of revolutionaries but the least interesting and important. To present them as Miss Stead does, without the contrast of one genuine Communist, distorts the picture beyond even the broadest limits of caricature.[149]

Stead was grateful to Harrison Smith, who, reviewing the novel in the *Saturday Review of Literature*, found it 'something of a miracle that anyone who was not born in this country should be able to capture so accurately the American scene and the nuances of American speech'. He agreed that there were 'tens of thousands' of Letty Foxes in New York, and added that if Christina Stead was not accepted by 'comfortable people', it was 'because she has touched too closely and too sharply the nerve centres where our conscience lies'.[150]

In an interview for the Sydney *Daily Telegraph*, which she only saw when her father cut it out and sent it to her, Stead was defensive and angry about the accusations of vulgarity.

"It is a serious, realistic novel, not obscenity. It is meant as a satire on American divorce and sexual customs.

"I was so afraid of what the critics might say that I was actually contemplating leaving town before the book came out. Some American critics don't take kindly to satire on American social habits."

Miss Stead said that she had presented Letty Fox as a Communist "because at the time I wrote about—through the

twenties to the present time—there were so many of that type
of girl in the Communist movement."

Miss Stead added: "Really I am a Puritan. I am not opposed
to free love—and I don't mean wantonness—but I believe
there should be some discipline in behaviour."

She said she had intended to write a third book to become
a trilogy, "but I am sick of women. I am not going to write
about them any more."[151]

Letty Fox, her best-selling book to date, sold well over 12 000 copies
in the States alone.[152] Stead had a least achieved a *succès de scandale*.

★　　★　　★

Stead now put aside her short stories, as well as *The People with the
Dogs*, and began something which she intended to be a short novel,
The Blondine. Later called *A Little Tea, A Little Chat*, it became a
400-page novel, and is a scathing portrait of Alf Hurst. Heartily
tired of his endless empty promises, Stead told Aida Kotlarsky: 'We
have not the slightest faith in him, but we play along with him,
why not?'[153] For years Blake had been struggling with this complicated love-hate relationship, but he could not risk cutting contact
with Hurst altogether.

★　　★　　★

Despite the frightening stories of shortages in Europe, Blake was
impatient to leave the States. There seemed no choice but to go
back into business, at least temporarily, but he believed he had
sufficient contacts in Antwerp to make a decent living 'out of
commerce and not out of favours'.[154] He was sure he would not
have to rely on Alf Hurst.

As a notorious New York communist, Blake was fortunate to
obtain a visa for travel. His application deliberately made the trip
appear a temporary one on behalf of Hurst's Montreal Grain
Union.[155] This was possibly a reason for travelling ahead of Stead,
on his own.

He left for Belgium from Montreal in November 1946, crossing
the Atlantic on a Victory Ship, as the make-shift converted troop
ships were euphemistically known. From Antwerp he wrote to
Stead on 26 November:

> The voyage was a beast. Five days of raging tempests and
> mountainous seas . . . The narrow seas are sickening: dozens of
> masts sticking out of the water . . . dead freighters and troop
> ships. The Nazis blew up the damned world. We had to have

special pilots to sweep and indicate floating mines in the North
Sea and the Scheldt . . .

By this afternoon I am the happiest bugger in many lands.
I wandered among the baroque stones and simply adored the
city . . .

Come over. We have a wonderful home, a beautiful office in
which you can do your best work, a heavenly city, a true, if
miserably poor, civilization. Oh, how rich America is!

His 'New York cobwebs' had completely blown away, he told her.
'I am full of ambition and a new youth.'[156] He added: 'As to Alf,
just keep him amused and fairly sweet for the present . . . In any
event, in Europe, we will have practically nothing to do with
him.'[157] Blake was researching his book on imperialism in Brussels,
only forty minutes from Antwerp by train. 'The documentation in
Brussels is beyond comparison: for my work it is ten times that of
New York, and in saying this I am not exaggerating.'[158]

Stead had a name for Blake's hyperbolic enthusiasms: 'Blakery'.
The home to which he referred was one room above Alf Hurst's
office. And Antwerp, transformed by the war, was hardly 'heavenly'. Before the war, there had been 60000 Jews; now there were
3000, Blake told Stead.[159]

Blake had hoped that his friend Edgar Lallemand, previously the
manager of Alf Hurst's grain firm and now Minister for Food
Supplies in the socialist government, would prove a useful contact,
but Lallemand was up to his neck in a ministerial crisis and under
daily attack in the conservative press. To his chagrin, Blake found
himself waiting for Alf Hurst to return from the States. Moreover,
in the Brussels financial world, he kept running into former clients
of the Travelers' Bank, and he still had not received a formal
clearance from the French courts.[160]

*   *   *

Stead was tying up ends in New York, her home for the last nine
years. She had intended to sail before Christmas, but in mid-
December Ruth McKenney developed septicaemia as a result of an
abortion and was rushed to the Beth Israel Hospital in New York.
For a time it looked as if she might not survive. Richard Bransten,
hovering anxiously at his wife's bedside, rang Christina twice a day
with progress reports. When Ruth eventually regained consciousness, Richard persuaded Christina to postpone her trip and spend
Christmas with them at the hospital.

Stead deferred her sailing date until 28 December. Over the next
fortnight, she spent hours at Ruth's bedside, deeply moved. Mc-

Kenney told her that it had been Richard's desperation that had pulled her through.[161]

Stead was waking at 2 am and unable to go back to sleep till dawn. There was the business of packing up. (She sold some of their furniture and gave other pieces away.) She had to say goodbye to dozens of friends. ('We know too many people.'[162]) She worried about organising income tax payments before she left. They had money for once: Harcourt, Brace had forwarded her $2700 as an advance for her forthcoming novel *A Little Tea, A Little Chat*, and another $2500 in royalties for *Letty Fox*. (University lecturers averaged $3000 a year at that time.)

She was avoiding Henryk Grossmann; evenings with him were exhausting.[163] She was even avoiding Ber Green, though she felt guilty about hurting him, for he had proved one of her most helpful friends.[164] She was tossing all night and taking belladonna for nervous exhaustion. There was only one man she wanted to see, and that was Harry Bloom. He seemed to be avoiding her.

On Saturday, 14 December, the Blooms had a farewell party for Christina. Three days later, she wrote to Bill:

Mr Bloom, Harry, was an amusing spectacle on Saturday night. He did not smile once, looked grave and even stolid, and did not look at me straight once: reason—he told me EVERYONE thinks he is in love with me and he cannot control his expression, so he did not look at all. It is amusing after all for a man of his age![165]

Five days after the party, Christina was in a terrible state, and admitted as much to Bill:

Mr Harry, such a good friend, cannot find time to see me, what a shodheaded scrambled egg he is. He did not even take me to the movies and at the same time, love-love, flon-flon. How annoying he is.[166]

The following day:

I sent Bloom H. a sizzling letter about his goings-on and did not answer the phone, am angry with him. Harry has NOT come to help me.[167]

On a Monday evening, five days before Christina was due to sail, Harry Bloom finally turned up, looking like Abe Lincoln, 'a dark, tall man made taller by a dark, tall hat'.[168] He brought steel-strapping and a sealing-machine, and sealed her trunks. Peace was made.

Poor old Harry—said he rang me 10x on Friday and 6x each other day but I was out. I WAS out—so all my tantrums were for nothing and he said the nasty letter I wrote him should result in my arriving in Antwerp black and blue only he always knew I was crazy.[169]

On Saturday, the day of her departure, Harry Bloom turned up at the apartment one last time.

Asa Zatz took Christina to Hoboken, New Jersey. They crossed the Hudson on the Christopher Street Ferry—a service that was to close for ever in a few days' time. In Hoboken, rusting ships lay idle in the pale sunlight alongside notices in Polish and German left over from the war.[170]

In *The People with the Dogs* it is Vera Sarine, a concert artist, who is leaving for Europe just after the war, seen off by a small group of close friends.

> It was a bitter morning, with a fresh breeze sharpening the waves in the river. The ferry slid along by the moored ships and presently they saw the Victory ship she was to sail on, the Blue Peter flying, faint smoke from the smokestacks. It was a sad gripping sight: for though each had made a promise to see Vera in Europe, part in joke, part in seriousness, and though Vera had promised to return to them next summer ... with the way things were shaping up, as they put it, both in Europe and at home, all felt they might never meet again. Madame Sarine was at home in Europe; and their home was here.[171]

Stead was to travel on a cargo ship, the *Oglethorpe Victory*, with just two other passengers. They were to be at sea on New Year's Day. Just like Vera Sarine's Victory Ship, the boat's departure was delayed. Stead and Zatz went back to New York and spent the day in lower Manhattan, which felt like home to Stead by now. Together they walked the frozen, slippery streets. Asa took her for a last lunch at Luchow's, an old German restaurant she and Blake had always loved.[172] Later that afternoon, at dusk, Asa watched as the ship pulled out into the river, 'black and smoking slightly against the wonderful brocade, the skyscrapers of the city'.[173]

11

From One Perch to Another

Christina Stead, a British subject with permanent residence
in the United States, was an outbound passenger on the SS
Oglethorpe Victory of the Black Diamond Line from New
York on December 28, 1946, bound for Antwerp, Belgium.
    ... A pretext interview with the doorman at 21 East 14th
Street, New York City, reflects the information that
CHRISTINA STEAD resided at that address until the latter
part of December, 1946. She then sold some of her furniture
and left for France, and it was the doorman's understanding
that she would be gone about ten months. He said further,
that she had retained the lease on her apartment ...[1]

For Bill Blake, departing from the States had been a great joy.
Returning to the Old World at last, he had thought himself 'the
happiest bugger in many lands'.[2] Stead was more circumspect,
painfully conscious that she was once again leaving part of her life
behind: a pleasant flat in New York, a literary culture, Harry
Bloom, friends. Nevertheless, she must have felt a sense of excitement as the boat tossed on the rough seas. She as much as Blake
regarded Europe as her spiritual home. It was New Year and a new
beginning. After nine years in the States, she was returning to the
Europe she loved. The war was over.

But the Cold War had only just begun; and for Stead, Blake and their communist friends, the term would be terrifyingly apt. The warmth of anti-fascist solidarity was a thing of the past. Publishers were cold about their books; and poverty was chilling.

In America, J. Edgar Hoover's Federal Bureau of Investigation created an atmosphere of subtle terror, menacing everybody even remotely suspected of leftwing views. Leftists departed from the States in droves. Mike Gold, Richard Wright and their families headed for France. The Branstens and their three children sailed for Belgium in the spring of 1947. Henryk Grossmann left for Soviet-occupied Germany.

Stead was in Belgium by the time the FBI started to assemble a file on her in February 1947, after they read in the *New York Times* that the principal character in her novel *Letty Fox* was a young Communist Leaguer.[3] Stead's case did not interest them for long: investigation of her activities ceased in 1948. But the file on Blake, opened in October 1943, when he was on the 'key figure' list in the New York area, was almost 200 pages by the time it was finally closed in 1962.[4]

Replying to Mike Gold's news that her friend Ber Green, editor of *Morgen Freiheit*, was being hounded by the FBI, Stead remarked that Americans arriving in Europe 'draw a big breath, like former escapees from tsarist Russia'.[5] She believed they were fortunate to escape Hoover's frenzies. But she would soon have her illusions shattered: Europe did not provide the refuge American leftists hoped for. The FBI's activities were transatlantic. It was not only in the States that the US State Department withheld or revoked the passports of Americans suspected of Left leanings; Americans in Europe lived with the same threat. Stripped of their papers, they were ineligible for work and unable to travel elsewhere to look for work. Even with their papers, work was hard to come by for people in their position.

Blake had hoped to leave America's orbit behind, but by 1947, the United States had assumed Britain's pre-war position of global eminence. The 'Truman Doctrine' made the United States the guarantor of the 'Free World'. America would support 'free peoples' against any 'aggression' which threatened their 'freedom'[6]—an ambiguously formulated policy used to justify the ousting of communists from governments in Greece, France, Italy and Belgium. In Greece, the US supported an undemocratic, reactionary regime. Meanwhile, the Marshall Plan installed a progamme of massive economic assistance in Europe—a scheme vigorously de-nounced by the Comintern. Stead was convinced that the 'frenzied

American imperialists' were deliberately creating a food crisis in Europe to starve the Europeans into submission.[7]

* * *

Christina Stead changed after they left the States. That year, 1947, she lost something of her fire, her joy in life. From now on, her letters have a different tone: angry, bored, resentful. The expression is careless, as if written with an invisible shrug. Her typing is worse than ever. Rarely now do we glimpse the lively correspondent who once took such care over the impression she was giving. Occasional gusts of the old warmth blow through these pages, but often her letters to friends and family alike are disconcerting in their coldness.

Stead's fiction also underwent a metamorphosis. Apart from *The People with the Dogs*, a mellow novel conceived in a time of happiness, Stead's post-war fiction is fierce and bitter, devoid of the softer shadings which give relief to her earlier works. The satirical humour has a sharper bite to it. Stead's style, Angela Carter observes, has become 'craggy, unaccommodating, a simple, functional, often unbeautiful means to an end'.[8] This does not detract from its power: Carter considers that *A Little Tea, A Little Chat* and *Cotters' England* equal, and in some ways surpass, *The Man Who Loved Children*. She adds that *Cotters' England* and *Miss Herbert* 'contain extremely important analyses of post-war Britain, address the subject of sexual politics at a profound level, and have been largely ignored in comparison with far lesser novels such as Doris Lessing's *The Golden Notebook*'.

Stead left the States at end of 1946 as a mature writer with an international reputation. At 44, she had seven books to her name, and—except in Australia, where they were rarely celebrated—they had been praised by major reviewers in major journals. During their years in the States, Blake had also established his literary career with a much-praised first book, rapidly followed by others. By 1947, at the age of 52, he had written three historical novels, an important textbook on Marxist economics, and most of an encyclopaedia. However, his last publication in his own name had been *The Copperheads*, the American Civil War novel, in 1941. And now he and Stead were about to have the humiliating experience of one rejection after another—as if they were unknown novices.

There was a book crisis; it was said that with the advent of television, people were reading less. There was a paper shortage. British publishers lacked capital. American publishers, investigated by the FBI, had become conservative. Blake's name was tainted by communism. Neither his nor Stead's work was commercially promising. Stead's fiction, angrier, more relentless than ever, did not appeal to 1950s war-scarred sensibilities, which celebrated femininity, family and hearth. From now on, her fiction offered neither moral integrity nor hope. Instead, it confronted readers with poverty, corruption and self-deception—things they preferred to forget.

That year, 1947, Stead became subject to a low-grade depression that would prove chronic. She would continually complain that she could not settle to her writing. She blamed her listlessness on the poor nutrition in post-war Europe. She blamed their wandering life, which she detested. Always on the move, they were eternally packing up papers and typewriters. They could accumulate nothing. They had no time to make real friends. Stead used her high blood pressure—which she also blamed for her violent blushing and furious angers—as an excuse to stay inside and conserve her energy, and she became house-bound, isolated and bored.

But the listlessness had a deeper-seated cause. Though she did not want to admit it to herself, she was profoundly disillusioned. Her thirst to write something so good that there would be 'no denying it on anyone's part',[9] had remained unassuaged for two decades. Reviewers had not appreciated her: some had been extraordinarily harsh—worse, patronising. It hurt. Stead had begun to refer to her writing quite disparagingly, as she had done early in her career. Self-deprecation came naturally to her.

Nevertheless, the late Forties and Fifties would be productive years for Stead. Despite the lack of recognition and their nomadic life, she could still enter into a state of excited immersion in her fictional world. She told a friend: 'I only think on . . . the typewriter: and while I foot it restlessly round I am longing to sit down on that little chair . . . the keyboard tugs deliciously at me and when I put my fingers on the keys I am childishly happy.'[10]

Why then did they spend the next seven years moving from hotel to hotel, if Stead felt she could not write properly in such circumstances? England seemed the logical place to settle; they had friends there and good libraries, and Stead would always feel the need after a time to be enveloped by the English language. But they had never really liked England: neither the English themselves nor the climate. After the war, food rationing there was severe: one egg a week, one ounce of bacon, two ounces of butter, three ounces of potatoes per person. Stead, a committed carnivore who scorned vegetables, was tempted to write a 'heart-rending and very fervent' ode to meat.[11] They were not good at making do with dried eggs and milk and off-ration meat—kidney, liver, heart and tripe.

Though petrol and clothes rationing did not affect them, gas and coal rationing did. After a brief stay in London, they would tell themselves that such conditions made sustained work impossible and they would flee. Yet on the Continent they were always searching for cheaper and less dreary accommodation, milder winters, better food, good libraries for research. One after another, each place became an alibi, an excuse for their dissatisfaction. It was Blake who was a wanderer by temperament, not Stead, and it was a point of tension between them.

Stead no longer cared about new places: she wanted a congenial environment to write in, sufficient money to be able to write in peace, and some friends around her. But she had none of these. Blake went for long exploratory walks, sat in cafés, worked in libraries and went to the shops. Stead spent the days beside suitcases and behind her typewriter, 'wedged between the hotel bed and the hotel window', in a succession of tiny rooms all over Europe.[12] She scarcely ventured out, except for evening drinks.

They were both sociable people in their different ways, and they were forced to depend on one another for company to an extent that was good for neither. Without the opportunity to make close friends whom she could love and hate as she needed to do, Stead's life lacked passion. For her this was a deathknell.

★   ★   ★

When Stead first joined Blake in Belgium, they lived in Antwerp. But they soon moved to Brussels, where they installed themselves in the dilapidated Hôtel George Scheers, near the station. They lived in one room, but they were grateful that it was heated.

Blake had not intended to work for Alf Hurst again—Hurst's willingness to engage in war-profiteering had finally disgusted him—but he found himself once again playing Alf's factotum, his 'do-all and net-nothing'.[13] Stead, who had learned hard drinking from the New Yorkers, now resorted to it in earnest to calm her anxiety and keep the incipient dread at bay. Every morning she drank a glass of port and a Luxembourg beer in the hotel restaurant before she went upstairs at 9.30, when their room was done, to work on her novel.[14] When Blake and Hurst arrived after work, they would go to a wine café: Stead would have several drinks, Blake would mostly drink coffee, and Alf Hurst would excitedly arrange 'a little tea, a little chat' with some woman. Robbie Grant, in the novel Stead was writing, does the same: 'Ever since his early manhood, since his marriage, he had bought women; most had been bargains and most had made delivery at once. He never paid in advance: "I got no time for futures in women."'[15] Though Stead was making the most of her dismal circumstances by writing about this Don Juan (once again), she was monumentally bored.

She typed all day long. Her only other pastime was to teach herself Flemish from a conversation book. As she banged away on her large manual typewriter, even the hotel cleaning-woman was heard to mutter: '*Est-ce une vie, ça—toute la journée à taper?*'[16] Blake was out all day, doing business with Hurst or examining documents at the Belgian Ministry for the Congo for his book on modern economic imperialism. Some months later, Stead told a friend that she had worked so hard in Belgium she almost had the DT's from writing, and that by the time they arrived in London, in May 1947, she was 'nearly at nervous breakdown stage'.[17]

A Little Tea, A Little Chat was Stead's angriest book to date. Robert Grant (Robbie), a middle-aged businessman who has made his fortune through cotton trading, pursues money and women with equal opportunism. He is arguably the most loathsome character in Stead's formidable collection of dangerous charmers: he certainly has none of the redeeming charm of other characters based on Alf Hurst. Not a single ray of moral virtue penetrates this seamy narrative, set in New York in the early Forties. Stead would tell Nettie Palmer defensively: 'I recognise it's not very "nice". It's merely true. Too bad. (New York City in wartime—everyone was *not* rolling bandages.)'[18]

Grant has a wife and family in Boston, whom he uses as an excuse never to commit himself to his other women. But the 'blondine', a 32-year-old European as cynical and shady as he, temporarily holds him in her thrall. He has met his match.

Politically, he considers himself on the Left. He tells a friend: 'I'm not a Red, mind you, but a bit of a Marxist ... Made money for me, being a Marxist: I know what's coming.'[19] He likes to think he altruistically helps out his brilliant, down-at-heel friends, the 'Flacks'. David Flack, a financial journalist and Marxist, has been 'his best friend for long years'. Flack often works for him (in an exploited capacity), giving him 'intelligent information on financial markets'.[20] Flack's daughter Edda (who has elements of both Christina Stead and Ruth Blake) is a sharp-tongued 17-year-old. She dislikes Grant, and once drew a caricature of him, which he thought 'uncalled for, and unwomanly'.[21] (This may be an allusion to Hurst's reaction to *House of All Nations*.) Edda wants to be a journalist, and Grant tells her: 'A writer? I can give you material! ... I can give you stuff—a best-seller. Just come here every day, any time you like, I'll give you my life.'[22] Alf Hurst used to say the same to Stead, and Stead did write it all down—though not quite as Hurst would have wanted. And it was no best-seller.

David Flack is the usual good-humoured, yielding Bill Blake character, too weak to take an ethical stand. Like all the Bill Blake characters, Flack's laughter covers up moral confusion. In the novel, Pearl Harbor is attacked on 7 December 1941:

> The city was released. The war-tension of months, the uncertainty, were at an end . . . Everyone was downtown. In that morning, Flack and Grant sold all Grant's Government bonds at superb prices, many others being ashamed to sell at that moment, and they bought steel shares which had fallen since people were nervous, not knowing which way things would turn . . . In the next few days they all considered what primary produce would be needed in war, as well as cotton, he went with Flack in a car to look at disused piers and sheds in the Hudson, he wrote letters to all his correspondents in Europe and elsewhere, and considered forming a shipping company in Valparaiso to send contraband of war to Japan. Flack was found sufficiently pusillanimous to shake his head at this idea, while laughing. Grant shouted, "My dear boy, when the golden harvest has begun, take a scythe in your hand."[23]

A wealthy financier asks Flack why he allows himself to be exploited by Robbie Grant. The exchange again reflects Blake's relationship with Alf Hurst:

> "What do you want to lick his behind for? It still sounds cheap, keeping you for a yes-man . . . I offered you a participation. You could have done better with me."
>
> "He keeps me to be his no-man, don't you understand? You know damn well I'm a leftist and I have to speak my mind. Now with your crowd of bums, I have to drink whisky every evening at five and say nothing. I can't do it, Hugo. I prefer that guy with all his faults and his strange, sweet song. I tell him he's going nuts when he begins to think he's Mussolini . . ."
>
> "I still don't see what's in it for you—you got to pay your rent."
>
> "He's asking Edda and me along with him to Rome and to Lake Como after the war."[24]

★　★　★

Later, Stead would say that she and Blake were asked to leave Belgium for political reasons—'rather mysterious'.[25] Or she would say that Belgium, in its war-torn state, did not welcome foreigners.[26] Most businesses, including Alf Hurst's Grain Union, had been taken over by the Germans during the Occupation, and the government was now offering compensation. But Hurst, fearing communist rule and government control, eventually decided to give up business in Antwerp. Clearly there was no opening for Blake in Antwerp business circles, and he and Stead left for England in May 1947.

They found London battered and impoverished. Many of the quarters they had known and loved before the war—like the Jewish East End—were now desolate blitzed areas, with weeds growing on the bombsites. The railway porters looked so thin and weary that Stead felt ashamed to hand them her bags. Rents were high because of the housing shortage. After the resplendence of New York, London was a real shock.

Not everyone had suffered from the war. The 'income tax invaders', sustained by black market transactions, inhabited 'miles of nickleplated apartment houses, vulgar imitations of middle-class New York'.[27] But the working class struck Stead as phlegmatic, more interested in playing the horses, the dogs and football than in Home Secretary Herbert Morrison's announcement that England faced imminent starvation. Since the women all seemed to have heavy bellies as well as babies in prams, Stead surmised that the workers were feeling falsely confident since Labour's overwhelming election triumph.

Blake managed to organise a three-month sublet arrangement on a top-storey flat of a crumbling old house in Primrose Hill. It was close to Regent's Park and two minutes from the zoo, which Stead visited frequently in an attempt to find some inner peace. The shops were further away and Blake, the family shopper, sometimes had to take the bus several times a day to pick up their ration of eggs or meat which had not been available earlier. Feeding themselves was a time-consuming occupation.

Food parcels arrived from Kate and Gwen in Australia. From New York Stead's Spanish friend Pilar Libenson sent three pounds of coffee, though the parcel went astray, and Stead guessed that a customs officer had been lucky. She and Blake sent chocolate, English paperbacks and a subscription to the English *Daily Worker* to Mike Gold in France.

Alone in the flat, Stead was writing *A Little Tea, A Little Chat*; Blake worked in the British Library. He showed his imperialism manuscript to Harold Laski, now Chairman of the British Labour Party, who said he found it impressive.[28]

It did not feel the same to be in London without Ralph Fox, but there were other old friends to see. Stead visited her cousins Jessie and Winnie Martin, now in their late sixties, still living in the same house at Streatham Common. Their mother, Christina's Great Aunt Emma, had died. Living in Primrose Hill were Anne and Patrick Dooley, 'old and true friends',[29] as 'avid, lively, hungry for life' as ten years before.[30] Pat wrote for *Irish Freedom*; Anne, the thin, highly-strung Tynesider whose accent fascinated Stead, had just lost her job on the *Evening Standard*; paper shortage forced newspapers to run on a tight budget. There was also Claud Cockburn and his wife Patricia. Cockburn's influential newsletter *The Week* had recently folded, and he was writing for the *Daily Worker* again.

Peter Davies, his wife Margaret and their three sons were living nearby in St John's Wood.[31] Stead was shocked to find Davies pale and sick, suffering badly from the emphysema that had plagued him since he fought in the Somme trenches. It seemed an opportune moment for Stead and Peter Davies to go their separate ways, which they did amicably and to the relief of both. Stead was convinced another publisher would promote her books more effectively.

The Blakes struck up an acquaintance with their next-door neighbours, Mark and Miriam Risner, who would in time become good friends. A designer and tailor by profession, in his spare time Mark Risner worked with Unity Theatre, the workers' theatre established back in the Popular Front days. Stead became a supporting member. She was impressed with Roger Woddis' satirical play *Dragnet*, which ridiculed the 'Land of Freedom'.[32]

★   ★   ★

'Australia has always taken a strong stand against lewd and salacious literature,'[33] the Sydney *Sun* had boasted in late 1946, in an article headed 'Sydney Girl's Book Called "Quagmire"'. The short article ensured that the censors would eagerly watch for the arrival on their shores of *Letty Fox*. And indeed, in June 1947, the Australian Literature Censorship Board banned the novel. The two-page censor's report stated: 'The general tone of the book is indecent and vulgar and grossly over-emphasises matters of sex ... For adolescents it would be definitely harmful.' Letty is 'over-sexed'. As for a series of lewd jokes which Stead claimed in the frontispiece were actual Manhattan jokes: 'That is no reason for recording them.'[35]

Americans had not understood *For Love Alone*; Australians did not understand *Letty Fox*. 'If this is a true picture of the society in that country,' remarked the novelist Kenneth Seaforth Mackenzie in the *Sydney Morning Herald* a few months before the censorship ruling, 'then we are better off in Australia.'[36] Mackenzie added, with the arrogance so often found in Stead's Australian reviews:

Christina Stead is not a very good writer. She has told the tale ... with about twice as many words as any competent romantic novelist would use; she has, as usual, indulged in vast orgies of written conversation (about money or sex or their material fruits), and the whole is set down in the same reckless babbling style of writing that spoiled her recent *For Love Alone* and other works.

Stead was scathing about the banning, which she must have half expected. 'Ever since I was 17 and began taking an interest in art, they seem to have been banning things in Australia ... Personally, I am unalterably opposed to censorship of any form in art. How can some clerk or government official have authority to ban something he probably knows nothing about?'[37]

*   *   *

Edith Anderson had become Stead's keenest correspondent and closest confidante, though they had been only casual friends in New York. Anderson was about to leave for Paris, from where she would try to arrange permission to join her husband, Max Schroeder, in Soviet-occupied East Berlin. Schroeder was flourishing in socialist Germany. A cultivated, knowledgeable man, he had become literary editor at the Soviet-oriented Aufbau Press, and was busy publishing the best of the German exile literature: Heinrich Mann, Bertolt Brecht, Anna Seghers, Johannes Becher, Arnold Zweig.

With characteristic generosity Stead, who had recently received a cheque for the French and Italian translations of *For Love Alone*,[38] sent Anderson $100 to help with her fare. She passed on Ruth Blake's address in Paris, and added that if Anderson should chance to meet Mollie Blech, who was living near Ruth on the Boulevard Raspail, she should not mention their names. 'She hates us both.'[39]

Mollie Blech remained a thorn in Stead's side. She had returned to the Paris she loved, and was working for the Joint Anti-Fascist Refugee Committee—a relief organisation for Jewish refugees. When Stead heard that Mike Gold and Elisabeth had befriended her, she felt personally betrayed. 'I hear they are pals of Mollie now and all sit together in the Dôme: this "Sun Also Rises" set up bores me to rags.'[40]

Their sublet was due to run out at the end of August, and Blake went round to some twenty-five hotels looking for a cheap place to live. Meanwhile they were staying temporarily in the Dooleys' small attic flat in Chalcot Square, while the Dooleys were away in the country feeding friends' chickens. Stead was desperate to settle somewhere and do some serious writing. 'We have just hopped from one perch to another since we left the U.S.A.'[41]

In September, they decided to head to southern Europe to avoid the English winter and the food rationing. Stead first went to Paris: she needed more dental work done—this time by their friend Fred Loeffler—and she wanted to see Edith Anderson. Blake had research to do in Basle, where they arranged to meet after a week or so.

It was ten years since either of them had seen Paris, and without telling Christina, Bill had written to Fred Loeffler and given him her arrival time. To Christina's surprised delight, Loeffler was at the station to meet her in his new Ford.

She wrote to Bill on 29 September, from the Hôtel Alexandra:

The last few days (week) of running about after all the formalities made you look tired. I was quite absorbed by that thought and no other and that you wept, at the station, you know, and so the trip seemed short, for I was only thinking of you.

Entering France, one sees Boulogne . . . a terrible sight of rubble; and the factories in all that part blown up, skeletons. All this first part of the trip I felt a sort of fixed horror . . . I thought of you, too, all the time and felt a real—heart-pain you could call it—to think you were not seeing it. So I saw it with your eyes.

She continued:

Last night after we had dinner Edith and I walked all through shining, sweet and lively Paris, all the parts we knew all those years and I felt so very gay and intelligent, simply tiptop . . .
I told Edith I didn't dare really think where I was and about it all for I should burst into tears that you were not there.[42]

Edith Anderson was living in a cheap attic room at the Hôtel Alexandra and also working for the 'Joint', as a clerk. It seemed that she had adapted to Parisian life in an admirably short time. 'She is not the ordinary American exile,' Stead told Mike Gold afterwards, possibly a little pointedly.[43]

*   *   *

Blake and Stead were put off Basle by reports of the harsh winter there, and decided to spend winter in Montreux instead. By early October, they had found cheap and pleasant accommodation at a small hotel called the Hôtel de Londres, with a balcony looking over the lake. 'La haute montagne right in our eye, and we can enjoy it without having to put on hobnail boots and get heart-failure.'[44] Stead was inspired by the thought that Byron and Shelley had lived in the region for a time.

The food, French-style fare, made them instantly feel stronger and fitter. By the end of the year, Stead had *A Little Tea, A Little Chat* ready for Harcourt, Brace, and Blake sent his imperialism book to Reynal & Hitchcock, where his friend Leo Huberman worked as an editor.[45]

At weekends they went for walks, taking a tram to the Château de Chillon, Villeneuve, Clarens, and walking at the other end before stopping to sample the local wine. They took a steamer to St Gingolph and Evian-les-Bains.[46] It was a beautiful part of the world. But Stead felt restless. She told herself that it was almost as if the place harboured a sinister spirit.

> The climate does not suit me at all: it is dull, sedative, yet
> unnaturally stimulating in an underhand way ... This town
> creaks into bed at 9.30 ... Even after theatre they scoot home
> as if the Devil was after them ... I am having a dreadful séjour
> but can't put my finger on it. We are happy, we are working
> hard, everything is organising itself, as to work. Well, maybe
> when winter comes it will be better.[47]

In their isolation, they avidly devoured newspapers and letters from friends. Political news from the States was intensely depressing. A witch hunt had begun in Hollywood. Notable conservatives Walt Disney and Ronald Reagan, President of the Screen Actors Guild, had testified about the communist threat in the studios. Thomas Mann protested that the congressional hearings resembled the first measures undertaken by the Third Reich. Several of Blake and Stead's Hollywood acquaintances—Alvah Bessie, Herbert Biberman, John Howard Lawson, Albert Maltz and Dalton Trumbo—were on trial as 'subversives', and threatened with gaol for 'contempt of Congress'—that is, refusing to answer questions and name names. The Hollywood moguls had met at the Waldorf-Astoria hotel in New York to discuss the issue. When the doors were opened at the end of the meeting, they issued the statement that Hollywood believed passionately in free speech and civil liberties, but would 'not knowingly employ a Communist or a member of any party or group which advocates the overthrow of the government of the United States'. The 'Hollywood Ten' were fired from their jobs. The notorious Hollywood blacklist was in place.[48]

One weekend at the end of October, McKenney and Bransten flew from Brussels to see their adopted son Patrick (Eileen's child), now 10, at an exclusive boarding school in nearby St Prex. To Stead they seemed to have changed. Their rhetoric was as leftwing as ever, but Ruth and Richard had become obsessed with luxury and commercial success. McKenney and Bransten, in Belgium, had supply parcels sent regularly from the States. They were 'living like princes' in a sumptuous house with servants,[49] and had no compunction about buying blackmarket goods. Bransten was teaching courses in American history to the 'wide-eyed Brussels liberal bourgeoisie' and McKenney was selling stories to popular magazines back home.[50] The day after they left, Stead wrote to Mike Gold:

> The Branstens, for the moment, are flat out for money success
> ... Do not think me cynical. I regard Ruth as the greatest
> American of all in many respects (Richard really does not count,
> he is not in the same scale), outrageously venal, ferociously for
> her ideas, gangster à outrance when she must ... and capable of
> volte-faces—in a word, we don't know yet.[51]

Stead had gone back to her short story collection, *Jan Callowjan*. Jan Callowjan (sometimes spelled Kalojan) was modelled on Henryk Grossmann, about whom she had been intending to write for a long time. In the end, only one story, 'The Azhdanov Tailors', has a hero called Jan Kalojan, son of a half-Jewish family, who learns Yiddish to organise the Jewish tailors in Cracow.[52] Other stories were based on incidents in Belgium, Switzerland, the States. To Edith she explained that her puppet Nello had become her subconscious and was helping her to write.

They had left their other puppets behind in London in various trunks and depositories, but Stead could not bring herself to part from Nello, the 'wonderful little wooden man' in the yellow pantaloon. Patrick Bransten stayed overnight on his way to Brussels for Christmas, and was captivated by Nello. Stead was charmed by the boy: he is 'a darling', she told Edith Anderson: 'sex-appeal, and really a dear, quite smart, though how smart one does not know'.[53] In her amusing and ironic story 'Trains', probably written at this time, Joe, a 10-year-old American boy who attends an élite school in Switzerland, is coming to stay for the night with the narrator and her husband. His humorous, overbearing mother writes with detailed instructions. The narrator—Stead in her most benevolent aunt mood—writes:

> I conceal my extreme animation from my husband; for
> husbands may not like wives to become excited about other
> people's children; and then there is the expense, which wives
> do not think of. When I see a strange child, I become lavish.
> I become a heady greedy giddy six-year-old, the sort I never
> was. I have fantasies about buying icecream, orangeade,
> comics, magic tricks, cake and circuses.[54]

When a Christmas card arrived from her 'little brother', Gilbert—the first sign of life from him for fifteen years—Christina wrote back, imploring him for details about the family. He and David

Darwin had both divorced, but Christina had been told almost
nothing. She only ever received polite little letters—'all except the
Old Man who of course is a wretched hothead, but at least writes
about something real'. And even her father tended to write these
days about 'the Art of being Grandpa'—'I keep getting records of
the tots, including foreign tots who apparently have taken over the
backyard at Boongarre.'[55] Around the same time, Christina wrote
to Gwen reproachfully: 'I have been away for twenty one years and
during that twenty one years have hardly learned one solid fact
about the family.'[56]

Summing up the past two decades for Gilbert, Christina still
portrayed Bill's role in her life in almost fairytale terms:

I look my age pretty much and can't say that the past twenty
years of happiness have in any way effaced the peculiar looks
given to me by previous conditions. My career almost ended at
25, on account of the four years I had saving up to go to England;
but I was very lucky, met Bill the week I went to England. I have
never quite got over this piece of luck; it doesn't seem possible.[57]

One cold day in late January, they returned from their apéritif
outing to find a letter from England, which produced a 'very
wonderful amusing evening' of reminiscences. Stead replied the
following day.

Dear old Firenze, Well, by jove, you could have laid us out
with a feather yesterday evening when we returned from
cocktailing and discovered your letter. We didn't know it
was your letter but as Bill tore the letter out of my hands
(he ALWAYS reads my letters first) your photo fell out and
I positively shouted, "It's Florence."

Florence was back in London with her girls, divorced from Pym
Heyting. During the war years in Australia, she and her friend
Dymphna Cusack had written a children's story, *Four Winds and a
Family*. Now Florence was trying to find a London publisher for
their thick novel *Come in Spinner*, set in wartime Sydney. Stead's
comment on all this literary activity was written as a postscript:

The most important I left out. I am awfully excited about it
and simply must get a copy of *Four Winds and a Family*. . . .
And as for *Come In Spinner*, I know it is asking much, but
could I get a copy in galleys? . . . I am very much interested
and fascinated in this; and I have not forgotten one day of your
literary life in London. You worked so much and with such
endurance, and hope too, now fully justified. You are really
a woman I like, you kept it up in spite of family and all.[58]

*　*　*

Reynal & Hitchcock rejected Blake's book on imperialism. Blake was dismayed: the book was the product of ten years' research and writing, and he believed it by far his most significant work to date. He was obliged to send it to Helen Strauss, their New York agent, to have it do the rounds. Meanwhile, he went to Italy in March to do some preliminary research for an historical novel on the *Risorgimento*, Garibaldi's movement for Italian unification. His letters to Stead, still in Montreux, were full of enthusiasm for Italian life. Hers reveal her concern for him, and express the self-reproach that seemed to surface whenever she thought about their relationship:

> Well, sweetie, it seems you are really having a good time for once, and I rejoice. You deserve it, you are a poor old mite and you don't have much of a good time; especially with the Australian Nasty you are tied up with. I hope you are eating something nice old boy, none of your Italian versions of hamburger and corfee.[59]

For her own work, Stead was keen to spend time in England. She had been wanting for years to write a novel about the English working classes, and the desire was becoming more urgent. She planned to visit the coal-mining area in the north of England with Anne Dooley, 'a splendid girl and pal who knows the working class inside out'. Anne's family, 'pure grind-and-drudge working class',[60] lived in Newcastle-upon-Tyne, the coal town.

The obstacle to the trip was money, and prospects were not promising. *A Little Tea, A Little Chat*, which was due to appear in the States in September, was proving too strong a brew for English publishers, who were not interested in a grim novel about wartime New York. Stead must have been regretting her decision to leave Peter Davies.

For the first time since 1925, Stead tried the Australian publishers, Angus & Robertson. All she had ever received from Australian sales of her books was the ludicrously small 'colonial fee' offered by British publishers for distribution of the book in Australia. But she had what she considered an 'impudent' reply from A & R editor Colin Roderick,[61] and she was still indignant when she wrote to Nettie Palmer:

> A & R were offered my first book ... by my father ... about 1924 or 1925 ... and this firm has not yet made up its mind to take anything of mine: and who else is there? I consider it disgraceful, and the disgrace is not mine.[62]

Since she could not afford the English trip, Stead joined Blake in Bologna. They were enchanted with the mediaeval university town, where the politics were as red as the local brick. It was early April 1948: the spring was delightful. In Italy, with luxury leather and silk goods in the shops and the pastries in the cafés, it was almost as if there had never been a war. Living costs were about a third lower than in Switzerland, an important consideration. Nevertheless, Stead observed, though the rich were able to 'stuff themselves to death' in Italy, there was genuine poverty: the workers seemed to live on pasta and 'green stuff'.[63]

For the first month, she worked 'like old Nick' to learn some Italian. After that, she took it more calmly.[64] Immersing herself in Italian literature in translation, she was impressed by Natalia Ginzburg, whose portraits of women and families she thought among the most poignant and penetrating she had ever read.[65] She and Blake were elated by the colourful May Day procession, which reminded them of New York.[66]

She had returned to the manuscript begun in New York, *The People with the Dogs*, inspired by Asa Zatz and the Kotlarskys. It bored her a little; she felt she had been 'dabbing' at it for years.[67] But the more likely reason for her lack of enthusiasm was that this mild and affectionate novel did not tap into the stronger emotions—ambivalence and anger—which best galvanised her creative energies. Having finished *A Little Tea, A Little Chat*, she had thought 'I can't go on criticising', but the truth was that she needed to be worked up in order to write. She told Florence James she was longing 'to get down to a big dramatic subject'. She did not yet know what.[68]

At the beginning of the summer of 1948 they left for Basle, where Blake wanted to examine documents at the Bank for International Settlements. He was making minor revisions to his imperialism book, which he believed already required updating. Simon & Schuster had rejected it as too 'deep' for their readers. George Joel at the small Dial Press praised it and talked of publishing it, but decided the financial risk was too great. Angus Cameron at Little, Brown, had said he would perhaps be willing to publish if Blake made some revisions. But he too rejected it in the end, and so did Stanley Burnshaw at the Dryden Press, now limiting itself to college textbooks. The book that Blake considered his most significant work was doomed never to find a publisher.

Meanwhile he was writing another historical novel, *The Angel*, a fictional biography of Tsar Alexander I of Russia, Napoleon's great antagonist. He sent the completed manuscript to Helen Strauss in September 1948, and this time, the manuscript was accepted in both the States and England.[69]

Their four-month stay in the Hotel Krafft-am-Rhein in Basle was not a particularly productive time for Stead, who was 'paddling along' with *The People with the Dogs*.[70] She blamed the 'boorishness' of the Swiss-Germans, the endless rain which swelled the Rhine, and the lack of meat. Their diet was mostly potatoes with veal fry or pot-roast once a week. She told Edith Anderson: 'Bill says that beef is out of date, and in generations to come the world will get down to beansprouts and rice, but I was born in the dark ages.' Only later in the letter did she realise that her complaints were 'rather indelicate', since Edith was far worse off in Berlin.[71]

She again attacked the local language with demonic energy, setting herself the task of learning 200 to 300 German words a day, 'hail or shine'. She was reading the contemporary Marxist critic Georg Lukács in German, and though she found the language 'a trial', she was pleased with the progress she was making.[72]

A Little Tea, A Little Chat was published in New York in August 1948, the third book in Stead's three-book contract with Harcourt, Brace. The chorus from reviewers was more or less unanimous: 'There are some individuals in whose company one can remain only to a point. Miss Stead takes the reader far beyond that point.'[73]

Americans did not want to hear about war profiteering just then. Reviewers righteously agreed that the novel portrayed 'the most loathsome and amoral characters' that could possibly be 'dredged up from the cocktail bars and brokerage houses of New York'. *Time* commented: 'Christina Stead's prose is as hard and cold as a cake of ice. She specializes, with the murderous calm of a hangman slightly bored with his job, in dissecting egotists.'[74] Stead wondered what the reviewers would say about the affable characters in *The People with the Dogs*. They were sure to find something wrong.

In June, Florence James had written with the news that *Come In Spinner*, the novel co-written with Dymphna Cusack, had won the A£1000 Sydney *Daily Telegraph* literary prize. The Editor-in-Chief of the conservative *Daily Telegraph* was Stead and Blake's old friend E. W. MacAlpine, now living in Sydney. Having awarded the prize, he had suddenly become concerned about Australia's obscenity and libel laws, and asked the authors to make certain deletions. They had refused.

Stead, referring to MacAlpine as 'our onetime friend', agreed that the charges were ridiculous. 'We are from a stupidly backward small, small country in these matters.'[75] She herself was always worried about libel, and after her Australian experience with *Letty Fox*, Stead certainly had every reason to feel strongly about the obscenity charge. Bill Blake too was later criticised for his 'scrotal approach' to Alexander I, when *The Angel* appeared in the States in 1950.[76]

Stead sent warm congratulations on the prize, but she did not write to Florence James again that year. It was Blake who wrote to Florence in October and December, explaining that Christina was busy putting the finishing touches to *The People with the Dogs*.[77] He added that his own book on imperialism had been turned down by several American publishers.

> At the moment in the States the censorship is so violent . . . that it is hard to place not merely a "red" or a "pink" book but any book critical of any value established in God's own country . . . The amount of liberty in our much touted Western democracies is such that we are seriously wondering whether it is possible for two people like ourselves, both working, and without family obligations, to make a mean living given these circumstances. I would hate to give up writing for a living . . . Chris has finished (or nearly done so) her first quiet novellete [sic] in a long time: it is a change from her incisive pictures of hideous New York society and may be more welcomed. Her last novel was reviewed by the American press with *fear* although it describes the life of one millionaire whoremaster. None dared to say it was not true: they suggested rather that such truth was too pervasive to be "artistic."[78]

Blake's *Copperheads* had finally been published in England, seven years after its American publication, and was well received by the British Left. But the income was small, and by now Stead and Blake were completely disillusioned with the publishing industry. As Stead explained to her cousin Gwen, English publishers waited to see if the book was a success in the States before committing themselves, and then at much lower author's rates.[79] And the income from the 'colonial edition' was a scandal. Authors' royalties were halved for Australian sales, though the sales were just as lucrative for the publisher.[80] Australian sales of *The Copperheads* had brought the British publisher Cassell almost £400, and Bill Blake a mere £3.[81] Moreover, Stead complained, the publishing industry practised tacit censorship. The English were such 'daffodils' that they could not stomach *A Little Tea, A Little Chat*, and they would be sure to dislike the trenchant novel she planned to write about working–class England.

She and Blake left Basle for Lausanne, and at first were pleased to be back in French-speaking territory, with French cuisine. Soon, however, Stead was bemoaning the dullness of the place. She longed for some interesting social connections to relieve the daily monotony of writing books and letters, cooking meals, and feeding the sparrows on their window–sill. There were moments when she actually wished she had some house-keeping to do. In these dreary times, Bill was the emotional mainstay. When Stanley Burnshaw, who composed his poetry and criticism in the evening after work, wrote from New York complaining of the unremitting struggle, Bill responded with the same stoic optimism with which he consoled Christina: 'Stanley, despite your boredom at times, weariness with sordid struggle, and so on, it is true that you are one of a happy breed, those who can write their vision, so that their lives have value, heard or unheard.'[82]

They left Lausanne and its 'milky spring' at the end of April 1949, having decided to give London another chance.[83] Blake went first to Milan to research his *Risorgimento* novel, spending his days in the library of the ruined Palazzo di Brera and his evenings looking up Communist Party documents in the Casa della Cultura.[84] He returned via Basle, where he checked more documents for his imperialism book. Stead went straight to London, taking cubes of sugar wrapped in paper as presents from Switzerland.

When Florence James was in hospital for several days, Christina looked after her daughters, Julie and Frances, now young adolescents. Julie, aged 12, found her uncomfortable and aloof.[85] Florence herself found Christina much changed: colder, more brittle. For her part, Christina felt closer to Florence again now she was divorced. She told her brother Gilbert that Florence had 'tended to the suburban model matron for a while', but had remained 'one of the best of women' and 'a left type'.[86]

When Blake arrived in London in mid May, he found them a ground floor flat in a large Victorian house at No. 6 Downside Crescent, Belsize Park. For once there was space for their trunks. From Belsize Park Station, it was a fifteen-minute tube trip into the centre of the city, and from their flat it was a short walk to Anne and Pat Dooley in Chalk Farm. The Branstens had left Brussels and were living in Chelsea, 'Hollywood style'. Richard Bransten had a modest job as an editor with a small English publishing firm, but they rented a large, handsome house, all white and gold inside and furnished with heirlooms; they paid exorbitant gas bills, imported extravagant food from the States, Denmark and Belgium, and mixed with the publishing crowd. Stead went there as rarely as possible; McKenney irritated her these days. Blake, with his 'heart of gold', visited more often.[87] From now on he often visited friends by himself.

Stead complained that London was 'oafish, suety' and 'dull', but she had no desire to leave it—at least not before the winter. She felt an urgent need to 'get some hold on life', and told Edith Anderson:

This life abroad unclasps all my contacts with life. I get friends
and they are cast adrift, not by my will, but by this travelling
mania. I hate it. Bill is sweet about it and knows this is my
need: it isn't his, you see.[88]

England was in a mess. In September 1949 the pound sterling
would be devalued by an incredible thirty per cent. Meat, vegetables and fruit were still in short supply, and Stead had to rely on
tripe and 'grandfatherly Australian wild rabbit' for her stockpot.

American publishers, one after the other, were turning down *The
People with the Dogs*. It was set in New York, it was Stead's most
positive, benevolent book: why did they not want this one? Stead
felt the despair rising. Her progress was slow; she was sick of
'writing such weak tea, such dillywallying trifles'[89] and 'fed up with
waiting for books to sell'. She told Florence James bitterly: 'I have
been a writer, quite unsuccessfully for twenty years.'[90] Yet she
dreaded the idea of taking a dull office job, and wanted to make a
start on her English working-class novel.

She accompanied Anne Dooley on a brief visit to Newcastle-
upon-Tyne, staying with her family, the Kellys. Stead was intrigued by this eccentric working-class northern family who were
always at each other's throats: alcoholic 'Pop Kelly' with his 'face of
fire', timid and prematurely aged 'Ma Kelly' who had just had a
stroke, and their plump, dark daughter Zena, in her mid thirties.
There was also Uncle Tom, 'a wee bowed man' of 78, and Peter the
black, hairy dog, 'foolish and noisome', who belonged to Zena.
From Newcastle in June, Stead wrote to her sister Kate: 'It is a
decaying family you might say. The two lively ones, Anne and
Peter, left home, went to London fifteen years ago ... Both are
now and have been for many years C.P. members.'[91]

Anne Dooley, in her early forties, was tall, thin and garrulous.
Her black hair was gathered into a top-knot, and with her buck
teeth and long legs, she reminded Stead of a marsh bird.[92] She
showed Stead the working-class suburbs of Newcastle, the little
university town of Durham, the seaside at Tynemouth. After a few
days among the Tynesiders, straining to catch every detail of the
dialect, Stead was talking like a girl from Jarrow herself. In her
letter to her sister, she repeatedly called Kate 'old girl', 'dear girl'
and 'poor old girl'.

Stead took every opportunity to see the English working class.
She accompanied Anne Dooley's brother Peter to Norfolk, where
he was to be interviewed for an engineering job. He liked to talk to
Christina about his family and his future, and she found his boyish
face and open, caressing manner immensely appealing.[93] She went

with Anne to the London docks, where Anne was reporting on the
Canadian seamen's strike for the *Daily Worker* under her maiden
name Anne Kelly. To see more of the countryside, Stead joined
McKenney and Bransten on a weekend car trip to King's Lynn and
Norfolk. They were writing an American guide-book on South-
East England, undeterred (Stead observed) by their almost complete ignorance of the country. For the most part, McKenney
would write all day in their luxurious Chelsea house; she disdained
public transport and ordered deliveries of food and library books
over the phone. 'She got $5000 berries, five thousand, count them,
for this bit of embroidery,' Stead told Edith Anderson with envy
and disbelief, 'so this will keep the Branstens going for the next
week.'[94]

McKenney did most of the writing—in the jaunty, personal style
her readers loved. Moreover, she projected herself as a loud and
pampered American who found England's smallness cute and its
lack of good food and heating deplorable. It was as if she had never
been a communist. Her former Hollywood comrades were in gaol,
and she presented herself in her Introduction as a proud American
citizen:

> *Here's England* is no mealy-mouthed, judicious guide-book; my
> husband and I are not in the least neutral. We love England;
> but love has not totally dewed over our approach. Richard and
> I are American tourists: we belong to the great Solidarity of
> the Green Passport, long may it wave.[95]

These days, Stead considered McKenney a traitor—politically and
morally. As well as planning her novel about working-class England, Stead was now making detailed notes on 'Emily Wilkes' for
the novel she was to call *I'm Dying Laughing*.

★   ★   ★

Blake and Stead did not have the money to take advantage of
London's cultural life. They had been to the theatre only once since
they had been in England.

> I find our lives dull, selfish and inactive; we really do not do
> enough and have shifted so much that we are quite out of
> touch: then, as usual there are the plans for being *somewhere
> else* say next spring at the latest—ouch, what a stupid pair.[96]

But Stead had at least decided she need go no further than the Kelly
family for her picture of English working-class life. The Kellys
were not exactly *typical* of the English working class: on the
contrary, they were 'far from repressed, not at all reticent, very
unreasonable, very fantastic, emotionally turbulent and amazingly

immoral in an old-fashioned sixteenth century style'.[97] They strangely aroused her emotions—perhaps because they reminded her of aspects of her own family.

No doubt Stead told Anne that she wanted to write about the English working class generally, rather than about the Kelly family specifically. Anne arranged for her to make another visit to Newcastle-upon-Tyne—for several weeks if necessary—to research her novel. Stead decided to go as soon as possible, not wanting to spend winter in that damp region, which had the highest rate of tuberculosis in the country. She left in late October, and stayed a fortnight. At first she enjoyed the family's abrupt manner and appreciated their 'decent simple manners' and cheerful generosity.[98] But the house was cold, food was rationed, and she soon found the constant family dramas degrading. The dog tore up a pair of her silk stockings. Zena, she told Bill angrily, was a pyromaniac, selfish, and verging on insane. Brother Peter, who visited at weekends from Norfolk, was 'very sweet indeed, but too weak', and this made her 'really angry'.[99] Anyone in their right mind would have fled from that family and that area, yet the parents and Zena considered Peter and Anne 'selfish' for escaping Yorkshire. 'This is insanity! Stupidity! I do despise families.'[100]

Bill, who visited briefly, was worried about her. Back in London, he urged her:

> Leave as soon as you think you have had whatever minimum experience you need. Your situation there is so miserable that unless you see a genuine fictional source in staying, come as soon as you can ...
>
> Get out of that icebox ... Lastly, your old monk is ready to take care of you in every way you think you need him. I am your lover. That is my job in life.[101]

Though Blake may not have realised it at the time, Stead *needed* to immerse herself in the family dramas and work herself up into a rage. It was the way she wrote best.

In London, Blake had given up the large Belsize Park flat and was staying with the Branstens. He was finding 'Emily', as he and Stead now called Ruth McKenney, hard to bear. McKenney was eating ferocious quantities and, too fat to be comfortable in ordinary clothes, sat around all day in her dressing gown. Richard was ravaged and miserable. Blake, after working on his *Risorgimento* novel at the British Library during the day, spent the evenings correcting proofs for the McKenney-Bransten guide book, *Here's England.*[102]

He eventually found Ruth and Richard all too much and escaped to the Dooleys' flat. This was scarcely an improvement. Patrick

Dooley had just left for Bucharest, where he was going to work for a time for the Comintern. Anne could not decide, from day to day, whether to join him. Blake commented that everyone but Anne herself could see that her marriage was in tatters. Stead returned from the North; Anne continued to dither. Eventually she left, going via Sofia, Bulgaria, from where she was to report to the *Daily Worker* on the trials currently being conducted there.[103] There had been a wave of purges, trials and executions since 1948; Blake, Stead and their friends continued to view the thousands of political victims as ignominious turncoats.

The 'mad excitement and upset over getting Anne off to Sofia' exhausted Stead and 'quite broke Bill down'. Anne Dooley, Stead decided, was a 'human maelstrom'.[104] While the Dooleys were in Bucharest—seven months in all—Blake and Stead occupied their attic flat.

At her typewriter in the Dooleys' flat, Christina Stead's head was full of the Kelly family. She told Gwen Walker-Smith: 'I am (more or less) engaged in shaping them up for writing—of course at the other end they will come out quite different, but it doesn't matter.'[105] It was rare for her to admit that the creative act inevitably transformed life.

She complained that the effort of capturing 'life's grey warp' and the miles of moors and hills and 'bleak blasted ridges' was turning her into 'a drivelling halfwit'. She had set herself an awesome challenge: to capture the atmosphere of the Newcastle region, its physical qualities, and, above all, the speech and preoccupations of the Tynesiders. It was her first wholly English novel, and she was plunging into a world as foreign as any she had encountered anywhere. Her interest in languages served her well. Ma and Pop Kelly were old-line Geordies, and Ma Kelly used a 'very complex old style English with pluperfects and conditionals' that Stead had thought occurred only in grammar books, whereas Anne and Peter's speech had been diluted by their time in the South. Stead began by trying to record phonetically exactly what she heard, but soon gave this up as an absurdity. 'Dialect novels are a bore.'[106] She decided to aim for impressionistic veracity.

In 1982, British critic Rodney Pybus would claim that *Cotters' England* is one of Stead's great novels, its intense psychological power, dense texture and originality reminiscent of Dostoevski and Lawrence.

As someone who was born in Newcastle and lived there for a total of more than 20 years I can vouch for the fidelity (more important in this context than literal accuracy) with which the harsh sounds, both guttural and flottal, and sing-song part-

Scandinavian rhythms of Tyneside speech have been given
form and resonance on the tongues of the Cotters ... All this
... enables Christina Stead to tap the energies of areas of
English society still largely neglected in the novel.[107]

Peter Kelly, Anne Dooley's brother, now worked in Norfolk and
often came to spend weekends at the Dooleys' London flat, with
Blake and Stead. He was that powerful mix of political radicalism
and masculine gentleness which always attracted Stead. She told
Edith Anderson:

When I see him on some weekends, I have a delightful feeling
that my own brother is around the house. He behaves like a
brother too: I mean unobtrusive and dependable and understands
everything without being told, but just as if we had grown up
together. Don't think I am saying something else: I am saying
what is.[108]

Peter Kelly had a close relationship with his sister Anne, and Stead
had always tended to idealise the brother–sister relationship. In *For
Love Alone*, Teresa feels great tenderness for 'adorable' brother Leo.
In *Seven Poor Men of Sydney*, Catherine and Michael are half-
siblings who talk of fleeing across the world and living together as
lovers. Philip and Nell Christy in *The People with the Dogs* are New
York anarchists in their late fifties, and when Philip is killed by a
trolley car attempting to save his dog, his sister Nell wants to be
buried with him. In *Cotters' England*, Nellie Cotter and her brother
Tom are so close that neither can have successful relationships with
others.

While writing her novels, Stead inhabited a world somewhere
between reality and fiction. Now she was imagining Peter Kelly as
her brother. In order to write about Nellie Cotter, she was project-
ing herself onto her, at times, even talking like 'Nellie Cotter'. For
Stead the process of creating fiction from life involved intricate
psychological blurrings and layerings.

*   *   *

Christmas that year was an Australian affair. Blake and Stead had a
small Christmas Eve party in the Dooleys' flat, with Florence James
and her two girls and Florence's co-writer Dymphna Cusack and
her partner Norman Freehill. Florence Walker-Smith had sent a
rich Christmas cake from Sydney. Nello the puppet distributed
presents.[109] The guests were in a buoyant mood: *Come in Spinner*
had just been accepted by Heinemann, after a series of rejections.
Other English publishers had not been interested in a book set in
Australia, about a 'group of women with barnyard morals'.[110]

Stead was not impressed by *Come in Spinner*, written for a popular readership. She did not like Dymphna Cusack: neither her socialist moral righteousness nor her commercial success. She would later tell a friend that Cusack's fiction was ridden with 'valueless clichés'.[111] While she tried to be pleased about Florence James' success, she found it 'a boiling shame' that Blake should have such difficulty selling his 'serious book on imperialism and his good book on Alexander I'.[112]

McKenney and Bransten had invited them for Christmas Day in Chelsea. But Stead 'broke down' after their own party and refused to go. She told Aida Kotlarsky:

How mean of me. I spent Christmas Day in bed or armchair
—and why, goodness knows, there weren't any cocktails to
account for it. But I actually had a good time. Bill went, said
they had the biggest Christmas tree he has ever seen outside
Radio City and Washington Square, also imported delicacies
and lord knows what, lots of fun, great excitement. She raised
a toast to herself: "To Mummy who has sold two books!"
What do you think of that?[113]

★   ★   ★

Eighteen months earlier, Stead, writing to Florence James, had called Ruth McKenney her 'dearest American friend, female' and Anne Dooley her 'best English friend female'.[114] Now she was making detailed notes on their characters for novels in which she intended to portray them with all their flaws and contradictions. A few years later, she would be making notes on Florence James.

Stead's attitude towards the friends she wrote about was profoundly ambivalent: one minute admiring and the next vehemently antagonistic. Her oscillation from one pole to the other is reminiscent of the fervent adolescent who was driven to write out of both love and a desire for revenge. One day in January 1950, feeling bored with the 'doormat islanders' who surrounded her (she meant the English), Stead headed to Chelsea 'to see Mme. Gargantua perform'. She told Edith Anderson:

She longs to be anti-Soviet and to decry the Cominform—it
makes her sheer raving mad to think of the money you can
make by being anti-Soviet and she is prevented by shame ...
I laugh at her—I like her, Edith. She is big, noisy, ravenous
and alive ... I have a lot of fun when I visit Ruth.[115]

A year later, Stead and Blake went to see *Jericho*, a film about the Resistance, and Stead—who by then had begun to write *I'm Dying Laughing* in earnest—'wept like a fool'.

I'd never known until then how far this "traitor" theme I am treating had got under my skin ... I felt how dreadful dreadful dreadful it is for R McK (the only friend I have in that category) to betray. I never thought her anything but Gargantua, a crazy out-of-size drawing ... (Of course I'm writing about the whole thing, so I'm not normal about it.)[116]

What exactly had Ruth McKenney allegedly betrayed? McKenney was disillusioned with Soviet communism and the dogmatism of Party politics. In Europe, she and Bransten tried in vain to organise an anti-Stalin opposition, which Blake and Stead certainly would have opposed.[117] It horrified Stead that McKenney admired George Orwell, whose post-war novels *Animal Farm* and *1984* made him a treacherous renegade in the eyes of the Stalinists. And she was shocked to hear that Ruth's 'mamma-in-law'—Richard Bransten's wealthy mother—had demanded a list of their friends, wanting to check that no 'reds' were among them before she agreed to lend the couple money. Bransten had possibly obliged her with the list.[118] In 1952, Stead would comment to Edith Anderson that the Branstens had managed to renew their passports, unlike many of their communist friends: 'I think I would be afraid to know what declarations were made by ONE of them, to get the passports. I have an idea.'[119]

In *I'm Dying Laughing* Stead has the fictional Stephen summoned to the American Embassy in Paris, in April 1950, to name names. He does so and goes home 'pleased because there is no more ambiguity'. Stephen and Emily are described with bitter irony as 'the renegade husband and wife, the perfect American couple, loyal to each other and to the country'.[120]

Seventeen years later, when Stead was revising *I'm Dying Laughing*, she equivocated as strongly as ever, commenting to Stanley Burnshaw, who had been a close friend of Richard Bransten:

I'm re-reading material from the past—and it's borne in on me how much more brilliant Emily was than I make her ... She was very incisive, hardminded, and with—until the end— a high sense of integrity and what people should be doing as opposed to what they do do. Part of her decline came from that terrific struggle.[121]

*   *   *

Stead was excited about *I'm Dying Laughing*. For the first time since *The Man Who Loved Children*, she allowed herself to hope it would be a great novel—though she no longer hoped for commercial success. The subject embodied the kind of conflict she thrived on in her writing: Emily Wilkes, strong and freckled, who likes to say she comes from 'Hix-in-the-Stix' (she is from a small town in Arkansas), marries Stephen Howard, tall, effete, peevish and rich. Both are 'pickled in contradictions'.[122] Their marriage degenerates. Their socialism degenerates. Their preoccupation with money and success as well as freedom and individualism is portrayed as quintessentially American: Emily herself calls it the 'American dilemma'.

Embedded in the novel is a short self-reflexive passage in which Emily Wilkes talks of writing a novel about revolutionaries:

"I'd like to write a book about the revolutionary movement, the way I see it and what's wrong with it . . . Are there too many labour opportunists, too many finks and goons? . . .

"You could do it," said Stephen without force . . . "You could have me for one of the characters; a clay figure covered with the fine patina of soft living . . . a radical dandy, dispensing the amenities of another caste, paying his way into the labour movement."

. . . "This would be a cruel book. I wouldn't spend much time on theoretical errors or an analysis of our peculiar applications of theory; but I'd try to put a finger on essential human weaknesses; the ignorance and self-indulgence that has led us into Bohemia . . . I ought to say how everything becomes its opposite not only outside the besieged fortress but in: how we misinterpret the mission of America, the position in the unions, ourselves; and what our lives are, that are going so far astray."[123]

It is Emily Wilkes who declares she is going to write this novel; yet in *I'm Dying Laughing*, she is the very person who best exemplifies the self-indulgence and hypocrisy of the revolutionary movement. Stead told Edith Anderson:

It's a fascinating subject. Here is a gargantua who marries $1.000.000—and decides to go in for Despair, and it *is* a tragedy, it's not just talk . . . What dimensions! I hope I'm able to do it, that's all.[124]

She told Edith about the 'queer problems' she faced in building up the character of Emily Wilkes: problems that stemmed from the contradictions in Ruth McKenney's own personality. 'They're all real, not invented by me in a nightmare moment.' McKenney believed hummingbirds came from the union of moths and birds, and she would talk of spraying American forests with DDT to kill off the bees, birds and butterflies. She disliked Nature, which she could not control. Although a communist, she loved splendour and high living; there was nothing she liked better than to stuff herself with food in the finest restaurants in Europe. Stead was intrigued by McKenney's 'tumbrils obsession', which seemed to reflect her guilt about her high living.

In *Tour d'Argent* restaurant she hears "tumbrils"—in an
expensive Swiss hotel where some rucksack gentry are at the
gate she hears "tumbrils"—in Versailles, surrounded by several
millionaires of the family, she sees Louis XIV (meaning Louis
XVI) on a balcony surrounded by grovelling simian courtiers
... looking down at the "restless mob"—and she "hears
tumbrils" again ... I didn't invent it: in fact, I wouldn't dare
... I attribute it to the torturing conscience of the traitor plus
the terror of this epoch for a bourgeois.[125]

In the novel, Stead gives Emily Wilkes the same obsessions. The
tumbrils image works beautifully as a metaphor: in post-war Europe,
the Branstens' pampered existence did bring to mind Louis XVI and
Marie Antoinette ensconced at Versailles, indifferent to the plight
of the starving peasants.

As preparation for writing, Stead read all Ruth McKenney's
letters to her, which dated from the late Thirties. When McKenney
was in Connecticut, then Hollywood, she had written to Stead in
New York; after the war, they kept in touch.[126] Stead eventually
destroyed these letters. We will never know to what extent McKenney's own words were incorporated into Stead's fiction. McKenney,
like David Stead, revealed herself so brilliantly in her own writing
that it would have been hard for Stead to resist letting her speak for
herself.

★   ★   ★

In February 1950, Bill Blake made a trip to the German Democratic
Republic, formally established by Stalin in October the previous
year. Henryk Grossmann, now living in Leipzig, had nominated
Blake for a lectureship in American literature to be established at
the university there. Although East Germany was depressed and
neglected by comparison with West Germany, and controlled by
Soviet troops and the Secret Police, Blake fervently hoped the
appointment would come off. He told his daughter Ruth that he
was 'mad about living in a country directed towards socialism'.[127]
Leipzig was in ruins, but Blake thought it a lively town, and told
Stead he was sure they would find some intellectual life in Germany
and that it would be good for their writing. She was willing to take
his word for it; she even quite looked forward to it. They had a
number of friends in East Germany—friends who had been in exile
in New York or Hollywood during the war years. Blake would be
in his element as a lecturer, paid to teach and write: he was already
eagerly planning a Marxist-Leninist book on American literature.[128]
The salary, though very modest—1200 Deutschmarks a month,

the equivalent of $70 a week in the States—would solve their financial problems once and for all. But it all depended on the approval of the Soviet Occupation Authorities.

In East Berlin he stayed a few days with Edith Anderson and Max Schroeder, and their young daughter Cornelia. They lived on the outskirts of the city, and Edith was suffering from the isolation of motherhood in the suburbs. She was unhappy, trying unsuccessfully to write fiction. Max Schroeder was about to bring out Blake's novel *The Copperheads* with the Aufbau Press, and Blake spent his evenings editing it in preparation for the German translation, called *Maria Meinhardt*. His friends told him the German publication would surely swing his case.

He gave seminars in Berlin and Leipzig—one in English, on Cotton Mather and Puritan American literature; the other in German, on the Italian *Risorgimento*. He wrote to Stead: 'My German is fluent—few grammatical errors. Within a month's study I should be able to lecture better in Gm than I did in Lausanne in Fr.'[129]

But it was a sad trip for Blake. Henryk Grossmann was dying in hospital. He had returned to Europe in 1947, having been appointed Professor of Marxian Economics at the Planned Economy Institute in Leipzig. But in 1949, he was found to have cancer of the prostate. At the age of 68, when Blake saw him, he was prematurely worn out. The years of neglect in New York had been followed by the shock of Europe after the Holocaust. His family and friends were dead. Blake told Stead, 'When he came back to Europe, he found his ex-wife had been murdered by the Nazis, and son (of 16, of whom we never heard) had been barbarously killed.'[130] While in Leipzig, Blake visited his friend in hospital every day, and came away crying.

By the end of Blake's sojourn in East Germany, the Leipzig lectureship looked doubtful. He did not lose hope for several more months, but his chances were eventually dashed by the Noel Field affair, a scandal created by communist authorities afraid of employing Americans in their midst. Noel Haviland Field, an American who since the war had been helping refugees in the Eastern Bloc (mostly orphaned children of communists and Jews), was denounced as an American agent. In October 1950, the East German authorities sent word to Blake that although he was a comrade they greatly honoured, the widespread poison injected by the US government had forced them to make a general ruling: not to employ Americans.[131] Several years later, Noel Field's reputation within East Germany would be cleared.

*   *   *

At the beginning of June 1950 Christina received a tentative letter from her sister Kate. She was planning a six-month trip to Europe the following year, but knew that her elder sister was always on the move and was not wanting to be an imposition. Christina was offended that her hospitality was in question:

Dearest Kate, Well, thanks for your funny letter. You're very welcome, wherever we may happen to be. I have only had one place in my life where there wasn't a spare bed, it's a cult with me to have a spare bed and an extra plate. So once you get here, we'll take care of you. I only got your letter last night and my first thoughts were, "Oh, gosh, where are my bachelor friends?" For in New York, where we had a regular plunder of friends ... I always had four or five bachelors ... to get into parties, and even kept one or two as pets—but here![132]

Stead was somewhat unbalanced by the news that after twenty-one years a member of her own family was at last crossing the seas. Her letter must have seemed offputting to Kate, who was now 42 and had never been a good-time girl. Nor was Stead's reaction to Kate's 'funny letter' entirely reasonable: despite her protestations of hospitality, she and Blake had not had a spare bed for years on end, and when Kate eventually arrived, she would find herself staying in a hotel. In truth, Stead was not good with guests: she desperately needed her own space. She told Nettie Palmer she had become a hermit. 'Friends cause me to scowl for the most part, "get out of my life while I WRITE." You see how disagreeable I am.'[133]

The demands on one's time were something she discussed with Edith Anderson, who was finding that her baby daughter made progress on her novel almost impossible. Stead agreed that it was not easy for women, particularly mothers.

I guess I wouldn't know how to do it myself. We always talk about having a home when we get to the hotel stage—it's cheaper, it's nicer, it's more fun for me, cooking, than just sitting on a threadbare hotel carpet and tapping away: but the fact is, the minute I'm surrounded by "the home", even with a man who is not overwhelmed with his own preoccupations in the evening and who even—in one way very surely—lives for me more than for himself, even so, once in "the home" I get practically nothing done.[134]

*   *   *

The summer of 1950, spent in London, was a trial. After being scratched by a cat, Stead felt exhausted and suffered heart palpitations. She wondered whether it had anything to do with the tetanus injection; only later did she learn that cat scratches can cause debilitating viral diseases. Blake, who had rheumatism, patiently nursed her for two months. By the end of summer, he wanted to go to Belgium, where the food and climate were better. In London, they were about to face the prospect of flat-hunting again: after seven months, the Dooleys were returning from Eastern Europe. ('They don't get on too well abroad—no languages, for one thing. And NO TEA!'[135]) An acquaintance in Brussels had offered them half her house for a time, free of rent. This was lure enough. But Stead regretted leaving London.

> I like it here, I have had some pleasure, some personal approaches, have begun to feel my way about . . . On the continent, I am in that lonely life which deprives me of that casual contact of friendship which I like and of the intense contact of character-hunting whch is everything to me. Bill does not understand this at all.[136]

Once again, they had to store clothes, books and other belongings. Stead hated always having to leave her reference books and dictionaries behind, but now that they had decided to move, she was anxious to get it over with. The one good thing about going to Brussels was that McKenney and Bransten had lived there for some months, and Stead would be setting part of *I'm Dying Laughing* in that city.

The Angel, Blake's fictionalised biography of Tsar Alexander I, was published by Doubleday, New York, in June 1950, the week the Korean crisis flared up. Blake was sure this was the reason it did not sell well. In England, it was published the same year by Cassell. Angus Cameron at Little, Brown had accepted *The People with the Dogs*: Stead was sent an advance for which she had waited three years, and they could at last buy some warm winter clothes. There were some changes to make to one section ('A Night in Town'), which Stead had feared might have to be cut. 'Bill is manfully holding back his shrieks while I re-hack Section III. (He doesn't believe in rewriting: it's my only religion.)'[137]

Before they left England, they struck up a warm friendship with Jack Lindsay. Stead had first heard of this *Wunderkind* back in her twenties. The eldest son of painter Norman Lindsay, he had been one of the editors of *Vision*, the Dionysian magazine that had so inspired her in her Teachers' College days. He had left Australia two years ahead of her, and in the late Thirties they had met briefly in the offices of the *Left Review*. Over the years he had proved an extraordinarily prolific writer—of fiction, biographies, books on literature and art.

Stead initiated the contact, asking Lindsay to include her name on a list of Australian expatriate writers protesting against Prime Minister Menzies' new Bill to outlaw the Communist Party in Australia. In mid July they met Jack Lindsay in Lyons Corner House, and talked for hours, over prodigious quantities of red wine.

Lindsay was active in the newly formed Writers' World Peace Appeal, which Stead and Blake had also signed. The Peace Movement, officially not associated with any political movement, was in fact Moscow-inspired, and rapidly achieving the status of a global crusade. Lindsay had just returned feeling very positive from a trip to the USSR. (He had no inkling, he said later, of the Stalinist repressions behind the scenes.[138]) Now he and his wife, Ann Davies, an actress from Unity Theatre, were on the point of leaving for a holiday in Czechoslovakia.

'Is he a lovable chap!' exclaimed Stead, who thought him very like Bill Blake in many ways.[139] They met several times in the next weeks. Stead, walking with Ann Davies behind the men, was warmed by the sight of the 'two short energetic polymaths, excited scholars, borne along rapidly by their legs and whirling arms and their hot exegetics'.[140] She and Blake would write several affectionate letters to Lindsay and would see him again on their return to England, but the first flush of friendship was not maintained.

Blake went by himself to the Peace Demonstration in Trafalgar Square on 23 July 1950. That evening he visited Dymphna Cusack and Norman Freehill to say goodbye before he and Christina left for Belgium. Stead was still feeling weak from her virus, and ventured out only rarely. She did go to Chelsea to say goodbye to Ruth McKenney, who, despite the love for England she had professed in her guide book, had finally had enough of its hardships. The family was going back to Connecticut.

> She's too tired to fight all the day. Of course, poor us: only
> central heating, hot and cold, refrigerator, fully furnished with
> carpets, broadloom style, diamond-cut glass, Belgian wine
> glasses, pink-bordered and embroidered linen sheets, servant
> daily etc.—all in—what a pity, we're not in the U.S.[141]

It was, Stead sensed, the end of their friendship.[142] However, Ruth McKenney—with all her brilliance, quirks and hypocrisies—was to loom large in Stead's mental universe for years to come.

*   *   *

They left for Brussels at the beginning of August 1950. Their apartment was in a house belonging to Miss Hitchcock, an English friend of Mitzi Enders, the one woman for whom Hurst had once

seriously thought of divorcing his wife. The affair had eventually
gone the way of his others. One day Mitzi, whom they saw from
time to time, asked to borrow *A Little Tea, A Little Chat*; she had
heard it was based on Alf Hurst. Stead told Edith Anderson: 'She
knows "Grant"—knows more than anyone about certain aspects
and again less than anyone about others. It's quite a story, I can't tell
you in writing.'[143]

What did Mitzi Enders think of the novel? We will never know,
but the effect may well have been powerful. In the novel, her
fictional counterpart, Myra Coppelius, a small, honest and genteel
brunette who is humiliated by her physician husband's numerous
affairs, falls for Robbie Grant, who is full of promises about a
possible future together. When she discovers just how false these
promises are, she throws herself out of a seventh floor hotel
window. One or two years after reading Stead's novel, Enders too
would commit suicide.

Stead had still not completely recovered from her cat-scratch
virus, which had been like a severe bout of influenza. When they
first went to Brussels, she could do little more than move herself
from chair to chair. After a while, she started to work again. At the
end of August, she sent her revised manuscript, *The People with the
Dogs*, to Little, Brown. Angus Cameron, her publisher, had written them a woeful letter about the political situation in America.
(He himself would be grilled by the House Un-American Activities
Committee the following year and forced to resign from his job.)
Stead was horrified by it all—and disgusted that Australia under
Menzies was following the same path. 'I used to be proud of being
an Australian with industrial action and political freedom. Imagine
that they now take passports away and threaten jail for mere
opinion ... What have we come to?'[144]

Having sent off *The Dogs*, Stead went back to reading and taking
notes for *I'm Dying Laughing*. All she wanted was to immerse
herself in it properly, but for this she needed to be settled. It would
require her complete concentration. The other problem was that a
novel about communists (even if the characters were *bad* communists) was not likely to sell in the United States, so that it was a
luxury to spend time on it. She really needed to move on to a 'less
angry' and more marketable subject.[145] American and English sales
of Blake's novel *The Angel* had brought in a small sum, and the
Norwegian translation of his novel *The Painter and the Lady* netted
$500, having been voted a Norwegian Book Club choice. But their
financial situation was grim.

After two months in Belgium, she still felt weak, and Blake

wanted to try the famous healing properties of Swiss air. The trip, via Paris, was tiring. In Paris, Stead, to her chagrin, was constantly taken for a German. Her sedentary life had caused her to put on weight: tall and fair, she did not look like a half-starved *Anglaise*. She solved the dilemma by wearing a pin with an Australian flag.

When Kate heard that Christina had been ill for so long, she offered to give up the money she had saved for her fare to Europe, so that Christina could have a holiday in Australia instead. This generous gesture greatly touched Christina, who was not entirely looking forward to her sister's visit.

★ ★ ★

Blake and Stead stayed in the Hôtel Metropole in Montreux, then moved round the lake to Lausanne, where library resources were better. Both needed a good library; they had no reference books at home. Their living conditions were good: two heated rooms on top of a modern apartment house, with a view of the misty lake and the Alps across the water in France. Stead cooked their meals in the kitchen they shared with the landlady, Mme Pinay. The winter was exceptionally harsh that year, and the landlady kept turning off the hot water. Truman was shamelessly rattling the atomic bomb over Korea, and everyone was worried about a Third World War.

Stead was working on *I'm Dying Laughing*, and managed almost to complete a first draft within the next year. It entailed massive research: reading documents, personal letters and books on contemporary American history, including the recently published and controversial book *The God that Failed*, six accounts by disillusioned former communists including André Gide and their old friend Richard Wright.[146] It did nothing to shake her own faith in communism, but it was useful to know the renegades' viewpoint.

At the same time Stead was taking notes for a short novel based on their experience of the international rightwing expatriates they had met in Swiss hotels. Blake continued to nurse her as if she were 'a sort of hothouse product'. In an attempt to shake her out of the doldrums, he took her to see some plays and films. She told Edith Anderson, 'Dear old Bill is trying to pull me over the rough spots. I expect it's good for me to be treated this way: I expect I'd be climbing the walls in a padded cell if not.' She consoled herself: 'Dostoevsky had a *TERRIBLE* time in Switzerland, and so did Lenin.'[147]

Blake's spirits were untamed and there were times when Stead wondered what strangers must think of them.

You know him, imitating Senator this and Congressman that, imitating an angry husband and a lying tradesman, and all in the

first person . . . Bill was followed around the street the other
night, it was the night when the Truman gang spoke of using
the atombomb first—because he was imitating "an American
talking to his wife"—oh boy. I hustled him round the corner:
look out, you're going to get HIT . . . Ai-ai-ai! But I'm fairly
hardened to living with 64 plays, all written, produced and
acted, and even applauded by Little B.B. I must have NO stage
ability at all, for with this life I ought to have written dozens.[148]

Her novel, still called *The Renegade*, was causing her problems. She
noted in her diary:

In the night I worry: I have exposition laid out and plan for
my book *The Renegade* but where is the plot? Death of the
conscience? Am proceeding nervously and for the count of
pages well, but plot advancing scarcely. This is only a rough
draft, and so much work![149]

In another entry, she noted that she was thinking of writing a story
about her father ('Uncle Morgan'). 'Read some of the material I
have on the old man, cried a bit.' She had still not said all she had to
say about her childhood: the memories still pained her. She probably wrote 'Uncle Morgan at the Nats' around this time—the story
in which Morgan tries to persuade his 3-year-old niece to put her
hand in the fire.

So worried was she about *The Renegade* never selling that she was
working on several things at once. As well as occasional short
stories, she was continuing to make notes and plan her novel on
England's industrial North-East. Her loneliness and intense immersion in her fictional world plunged her into a strange emotional
state. She reproached herself for drinking too much. But she was
waiting for a letter from a man. Her diary gives him the code-name
'Elie' and Bill is called 'Walt'—the name of his fictional counterpart
in *The People with the Dogs*. She noted that she thought of Elie every
day, longing for him—'though without reason'.[150] The object of
her obsession was Peter Kelly, Anne Dooley's brother. On 16
January 1951, she noted in her diary:

In night, sickening feeling of doubt about Elie, why do I send
cards he doesn't answer? Felt his sister controls him, must have
made mischief, yet all may be sick. He's really only a boy
nonentity. Wish I had more friends to forget this maternal
obsession, yet misery of their lives bothers me.[151]

On 3 February, she wrote:

Said to Walt, "It wasn't the cat that hurt me, it was Elie, he
withers and blasts all the women he's close to." Walt said, "Cut
out that Elie stuff and stick to me, I never did you any harm."
I came back and said "I love you," he put his hand on his heart

sincerely and said, "Thank you." I said "Are you surprised?"
"Very surprised," said he, but he kept his hand on his heart.

⋆　　⋆　　⋆

In December 1950, Blake heard within the space of a week that he
had lost two fathers. He had written to his father for the first time in
years to congratulate him on his eightieth birthday. Eventually a
reply came from his wife in Chicago: Gustavus Blech had died over
a year before, in August 1949, and had been buried in Arlington
Cemetery among the national war heroes. Stead mused that physically Gustavus and William were similar, though the father's eyes
were 'uncompromisingly field-Marshal blue' and the son's 'Latin
brown'. Intellectually, they could not have been more different:
General Gustavus Blech had written books about supply-lines and
the organisation of field hospitals; his son, also a writer, was a
Marxist and pacifist.

The real loss was Henryk Grossmann, who had died in November
1950. 'A release,' his doctor wrote. Bill wept. Christina stayed
awake all night, angry with the world.[152] She thought of the tragic
lives currently being led by former communists and resolved: 'All
this must be in *The Renegade*.'[153] And she reproached herself for not
treating Grossmann as well as she might have. 'Thought of the ugly
things I had done to him incidentally, the day he was very wet, I let
him stay in the lobby because the flat was untidy, and so on.
Horrible. I really have no heart.'[154] Death always made her feel
guilty—a legacy perhaps from her childhood.

Blake wanted to put together a volume of Grossmann's writings,
which he proposed to translate from German.[155] He wrote to
Leipzig to ask for information about Grossmann's literary estate. In
time, the reply came from Leipzig. The next day, the Lausanne
security police, in contact with the FBI, arrived and questioned
both Blake and Stead about their 'extremist political frequenta-
tions'. What had Blake earned as editor of the *Magazine of Wall
Street*? What had Stead been taught in her history class at school?
Stead explained that all she did was sit at a typewriter. But she was
so dumbfounded and intimidated by the whole affair that she
answered politely—much to her regret when she thought about it
afterwards. After this episode, they both heartily disliked Lausanne.
Before, it had been a 'dull town'; now they were keen to 'quit the
wretched village'.

In March 1951 they went to Paris, and from there to St Germain-
en-Laye, an old cavalry town, half an hour away by train. Near the
huge château, where Louis XIV lived until he moved to Versailles

in 1682, was a large forest. Blake and Stead found themselves a modest but warm two-room flat, in a villa owned by an old French army officer, who lived there with his daughter, his servant and her little daughter and a boisterous dog called Yac. But they had to produce three months' rent in advance, and it was more than they had intended to pay.

They worked. They took daily walks along muddy tracks in the forest, with Stead pointing out the early spring flowers.[156] From the upstairs window, she liked to hear the forest 'sigh and rustle' at the onset of evening.[157] At first Blake disliked the large exuberant Greenland dog, Yac—he did not think much of animals —but after a while he took to feeding him remnants of their dinner. Stead wrote a story set in that place called 'Yac, Yac'.

Another story, 'The Captain's House', also gives a good impression of the old royal town that spring, the cobbled streets and high-walled houses. The characters Aldo and Laura are English-speaking guests staying in the Captain's villa: after dinner they go to a café and return about eleven. One night Aldo slips on the stairs and hurts himself: the Captain does not want to call a doctor, because if it becomes known that he has tenants, he will have to pay tax.[158]

Blake was delighted to be back in the vicinity of Paris. After spending spring in the countrified outskirts, he and Stead intended to move to Paris permanently. 'It's Bill's favourite spot,' Stead told Aida Kotlarsky. 'He really doesn't feel at home elsewhere. I must admit he's tried a lot of other places.'[159] Ruth Blake, 30 that year, and well established as a simultaneous interpreter, regarded Paris as her home, as did her mother. The surprise, when Bill visited Mollie, was that after all this time—Bill had lived with Christina for twenty-two years now—Mollie finally agreed to a divorce.

But Stead was worried about Blake. For once it was he who was tired and depressed. Every day he went into Paris to organise papers for the divorce, trudging from office to office to obtain the stamped approval of various departments. He was anxious to get the case through before Bastille Day, when the courts would go into recess. Stead noted in her diary:

> It is twenty minutes over cobbles to station, he insists on doing all the shopping before he goes, and he walks back at night and I suspect walks all over Paris to save fares and does not eat much.[160]

One evening in a café he almost wept after a liqueur. Alcohol tended to upset him when he was tired. At night he would groan and snore.

In mid-March, a general transport strike put a halt to his trips to

Paris. Then, at the end of the month, just as the strike was about to
be resolved, Blake was incapacitated by a fall. One night, he was
'on his way to the antique invention they think here is a toilet'—in
stockinged feet so as not to wake the house—when he fell down the
polished wooden stairs.[161] He was in bed for a week and still not
quite fit when he resumed his Paris trips in mid April.[162]

Stead was frustrated by the transport strike for another reason.
They now heard that Janet Bloom, Harry and Anne Bloom's 22-
year-old daughter, had been living in Paris for the past month. For
Stead, she was a precious link with Harry, from whom letters came
all too rarely. Back in the days when the Blooms had lived at
Brighton Beach, Janet had been impressed by Stead and Blake's
enthusiasm for French culture. She had ended up majoring in
French at NYU.

Stead and Blake invited Janet out to St Germain-en-Laye one
Sunday early in April. They were waiting on the platform when the
Paris train came in. Stead scanned each passing face. She was
looking for Harry's features, and she found them.

A remarkable figure, very tall, slender, dark crop, black
sunglasses, flat shoes, graceful large steps . . . Eyes made up.
She looks older than 22, beautiful eyes, colour of her father's,
but bigger, husky pure variable voice like H's.[163]

Young women always interested Stead. She told Edith Anderson:

I have been lonely, my loneliness is maternal. I like all kinds
of stray young sad people . . . Daughter of an old friend of
mine has escaped to Paris for the old America escape—she's
really a nice brave attractive funny naive type . . . One of my
consolations in life is to meet the youngsters of the men who
once loved or might have loved me—this letter is not for
general use, you see—and to feel very happy when I am with
them, because these kids in a way either know or sense that I
liked their papa and vice versa and they're so kind to me—it's
strange, it's the modern world: I think it very nice of them.[164]

Stead often spoke of her 'maternal' love for others—including
grown men like Peter Kelly, or even Bill. She seems to have meant
there was an element of tenderness in her affection, an empathy
with the person's vulnerability. For her part, Janet Bloom was
intimidated by Stead, whose empathy was more a writer's than a
mother's.

Later, Stead would hatch the idea of a collection of novellas about
'stray, young sad' women. It would become *The Puzzleheaded Girl*,
a collection of four novellas, eventually published in 1968. One of
the stories, 'Girl from the Beach', is about 22-year-old Linda Hill,
who is modelled on Janet Bloom in the spring of 1951.

The irresponsible children of Stead and Blake's radical friends were the new 'lost generation'. When Janet lived at the Beach in her early childhood, everyone seemed to be a communist, but by the time she was in her late teens, Cold War fever had hit America. Janet, at 22, was something of a dislocated drifter. She felt she did not belong in America, and yet abroad she was totally the American girl. She was wary of French food; her parents sent her provisions from the States. She had been earning money by playing guitar and singing in bars, and when her repertoire of folk songs ran out, she sang the old union songs her father had taught her in her childhood.

That first day, she told Blake and Stead matter-of-factly that she stole 'creamers' (little silver or metal cream pots) from cafés or hotels. She hid them in the deep pockets of her full pleated tartan skirt, intending to take them back to the States. Stead did not say much at the time, but she woke up in the night and said to Blake: 'My gosh, what a bandit!'[165] Eventually Janet's landlady discovered the hundreds of creamers hidden in her room and told the police. Blake and Stead vouched for her, and Janet was fortunate to escape with a reprimand.

Stead did not realise it at first, but modern girls did not like their father's girlfriends any more than girls in her own generation had done. She was to discover that Janet Bloom resented her complicity with Harry. Before leaving for France, Janet had come across several letters from Christina to her father, in which Christina made a casual reference to his women friends.[166] For Janet, it had been a terrible shock to discover that her father had dallied with someone other than her mother. She 'adored' her father, finding him more interesting than any of her boyfriends.[167]

According to Janet Bloom, the details about Linda Hill in the novella are extraordinarily close to the facts. It was not from her that Stead prised most of the details; it was from Henry Jordan, a middle-aged Czech-American crime reporter whom Janet met through Blake and Stead.[168]

Almost twenty years later, in 1967, Janet's brother Michael Bloom, read about the novella in the *Saturday Review of Literature*, and recognised the characters and the details.[169] He rang his sister and said: 'Feel like a book burning?' Stead's tactic, as always, was openness. When the book appeared in New York, she had her publishers send a copy to the Blooms. Anne Bloom, her son recalls, was 'outraged'.[170] Janet herself was flattered by the attention: Stead's knowledge of her, she admits, was astounding. She showed the story to her psychiatrist, who was equally awed by Stead's perceptiveness.[171]

★   ★   ★

Stead, always interested in the relationship between fathers and daughters, was disconcerted to discover the power her own father could still exert from across the world. It all came back when she saw her sister Kate.

At the end of May 1951, Stead and Blake returned for a few weeks to Brussels—probably for residence reasons. Kate arrived in London and stayed with Florence James and her daughters; then in early June, she took the boat to Antwerp. Christina had sent her three closely-typed pages of instructions about currency, tipping, food on the train, how to reply in French to the customs officers. One paragraph was 'How to recognise us'.

> A smallish roundish whitehaired man with big brown eyes,
> and me, same brown wig, same smallish suspicious greyish
> eyes as before. I'm a bit taller than Bill. Will probably wear a
> brown suit of British cut (feel like saying alas to that) and a
> very colourful large scarf which I may wave, if I think it right.
> Bill has a big big grin, me a strained expression.[172]

Kate was 19 when Christina left Australia, but on the railway platform in Brussels, Christina recognised her sister instantly. Small, thin, wiry and dark-haired, she looked just like her mother. Ada had been 49 when Christina left Australia: Kate was now only seven years younger. Christina told Gwen, who was very close to Kate:

> The old Kate was not there. She is someone different, altogether
> different, with a number of Mother's traits—it's quaint. Kate
> spent a few days with us here and then went off to Switzerland,
> having so much to do and see in so short a time and so short a
> purse. But she is managing very well, quite unusually so, is very
> self-reliant and quick: she seems to have a taste for language: it is
> a pity she had not learned one or two. Certainly she has no foolish
> embarrassment, but is quite lively and comes forward, smiles,
> makes a pleasant impression and is quick to make friends.[173]

Kate spent a few days in Brussels, staying in a hotel nearby. Then she left for Montreux, with two more pages of typed instructions. The three had arranged to meet in Paris in July.

Soon after Kate's departure, Christina had a letter from Gilbert announcing that Ada had died. Christina worried that Kate would want to catch the first boat home. They decided that Bill should go on ahead and break the news to her. When Christina arrived later, she also fussed over Kate. But Kate took the news with fortitude, saying she had almost expected it.[174] Ada was 72 and had always been frail: her children never thought she would reach that age. Moreover, she had been ill and mentally confused for some time.

The Paris holiday was not a success. Bill so wanted Kate to love Paris that he flooded her with explanations and details. The sisters were tense with one another from the outset. They had no interests in common. Kate was unmarried and worked as a machine telegraphist at the Sydney GPO: Christina could regard her 'spinsterdom' only as a 'defeat', and her letter the previous year about not knowing available bachelors suggests that she would not have been entirely tactful on this score.[175] Kate's lack of curiosity about European history appalled her. And she was also appalled (according to the fictional notes) when Kate, sitting in a French restaurant, would say things like: 'I'm waiting to go back to England to have some oats, some porridge. I miss my oats.' She and Blake wanted her to dislike England and love France, just as they did.

Kate was also not without ambivalence towards her sister: she disliked Christina's books ('terribly wordy')[176] and had not been at all happy about some of the family details in *The Man Who Loved Children* and *For Love Alone*—and no wonder. In *The Man Who Loved Children*, dark-eyed Evie, modelled on Kate, is the one child Louisa openly dislikes. Evie is her father's pet, and Louisa cannot stand the feminine wiles and the 'dolly voice' which the little girl cultivates to please him.[177] In *For Love Alone*, Kitty, younger, prettier and more docile than Teresa, is once again the daughter their father prefers.

From thinly fictionalised accounts among Stead's surviving papers it is clear that Kate was impatient with Blake. She disliked his loudness, his verbosity, his mini-lectures. In Stead's notes, Meg hurts her older sister Sally (a writer) by telling Sally that her companion Tony is just like their father.

> He's like Dad because he's always saying a thing's the best in
> the world, the finest in the world, the greatest in the world
> ... I can't stand it when someone is always boasting that
> something is the best in the world. It makes me boil.[178]

Later there is a bitter exchange between the two women:

> "He's just like Father and that's why you yes him. You yes
> each other. You have no independence."
> "Well, I didn't yes Father."
> "Oh, you understood each other."[179]

If this conversation ever took place, Christina would have found the situation very painful. She was fiercely proud of Bill, and she depended on him heavily to act as social mediator between her and the world. It is significant that he was the one to go ahead and tell Kate the news of her mother's death. But Christina herself must have realised that Bill had several of her father's qualities. Both were autodidacts with extraordinary energy and enthusiasm; both shared a love of language, both had fine, melodious voices, both had a tendency to be know-alls, both exaggerated. Bill dominated conversations; his need for attention drove even Christina mad at times. So the spectre of their father came between the two sisters in the form of Bill Blake.

Moreover, in the fictional notes, Meg tells her older sister: 'You went off without thinking of us. I could have done what you did but I was not so selfish. Poor mother slaved for you and you went off like that.'[180]

After Kate left Paris, Stead was still tossing at night in anguish. In her notes, 'Sally' says to 'Tony' in bed: 'I am living through agony: why is it?' A few weeks afterwards, Stead confided to Edith Anderson: 'I was heart-sick, sick, and feverish for ten days. What a haunt! To no one but you and Bill would I dare declare this effect of a sister.'[181]

* * *

Stead and Blake stayed on in Paris for several months, living in a series of hotels. Stead had completed a first rough draft of *I'm Dying Laughing*, but calculated that she needed at least a year to revise it. She felt obliged to put it aside now and write something that might sell. But it was like putting aside a love affair: it meant losing the original rapture. When she did eventually return to the novel, it had gone slightly stale.

They urgently needed a publication. They owed $500 to a Wall Street man who had offered it to them a year before as a small tax avoidance scheme. (Who this was remains a mystery.) At the time they had leapt at the offer; now it seemed that most of the income from *The Dogs* would be swallowed up by the debt.

Stead dreaded taking a job and rationalised that her real earning power lay in writing: the sale of a book could keep them for almost a year. She was working on novellas, hoping to finish a volume more quickly this way. But *The Puzzleheaded Girl* would not be published for another fifteen years.

* * *

From Australia came the news, in June 1951, that communist writer Frank Hardy, author of *Power Without Glory*, a semi-fictional novel about the millionaire Melbourne businessman John Wren, had just been acquitted after a nine-month court case for criminal libel. The case had caused a national sensation. Jack Lindsay and Dymphna Cusack, who supported Hardy's case, sent the book to Stead. She admired it and was delighted that Hardy had defeated the libel laws, 'the gag that has ruined English and Australian literature, the privilege of the propertied and the corrupt'.[182] Since she herself risked libel charges with almost every novel she wrote, Stead was adamant that libel laws were a sham.

★   ★   ★

There was family news from Australia too. On 30 June 1951, the same month that Ada died, David Stead married Thistle Harris at Boongarre. He was 74; Thistle was 49, the same age as Christina.

In her will, Ada Stead had left her children £300 each—her *own* children, that is. There was nothing for Christina. It was a cruel gesture, for Christina had never enjoyed any benefits from her own mother, and it provides a glimpse of the exclusion to which she had been subjected as a child. Kate Stead, who had just returned from her trip abroad and could doubtless have done with the money, immediately offered to share her inheritance with her sister. Stead was 'all for turning it down', but she and Blake needed the money so badly that she was obliged to swallow her pride and accept the offer. Kate sent the money to England. As a British resident, Stead was not allowed to take money out of the country. And so, in December 1951, feeling as emotionally buffeted as ever by her family, Stead once more left with Blake for London.

12

Literary Hacks

DECEMBER 1951–DECEMBER 1959

BACK IN LONDON, they stayed two months with Mark and Miriam Risner, generous communist friends who had a spare room at the top of their house in St John's Wood. 'A dark, dank weary town it is,' Stead told Gwen Walker-Smith.

It's the mystery of all the world how the centre of a great old civilisation can closely resemble the liveliness and gaiety of a pig-village ... Bill and I can't help feeling that they make the people miserable purposely to keep them down. There are clubs for the rich and grand homes, balls, parties: and as for the rest, let them rot. It's such an old world in England, so nineteenth century, so old baronial, so out of date.[1]

Money was so short that they felt they could hardly even afford to see friends. 'Friendship is next to impossible in London—it takes half the night and too much money for anyone to travel to dinner.'[2] McKenney and Bransten had returned to the States. Stead had fallen out with Anne Dooley, who had implied that her writing was 'trivial paperwasting'. Peter Kelly had told Stead things that did not warm her to Anne. Later she would tell Ron Geering (using the fictional name as she always did): 'Nellie [Cotter] seduced her brother and sister to sex, when they were little.'[3] Rightly or wrongly, she had decided that Anne was a lesbian,[4] and she did not conceal her irrational animosity towards homosexuals, particularly women.

In January, they went to dinner at Jack and Ann Lindsay's and met Guy (R. G.) Howarth, a visiting Australian from the Department of English at the University of Sydney. He was the founding editor of *Southerly*, a quarterly literary journal that since the war had focused on Australian literature. Not having access to the magazine, Stead would not have read Howarth's recent (1950) review of Patrick White's novel, *The Aunt's Story*, which concluded:

> Christina Stead having committed formal suicide, Patrick
> White challenges Kenneth Mackenzie as the most expert
> Australian stylist in the novel . . . It is gratifying to know that,
> after his war service and European wanderings, White has now
> returned to settle down in his native country.[5]

That January evening, Howarth, moved by Stead and Blake's obvious financial hardship, encouraged Stead to apply for an Australian Commonwealth Literary Fund Fellowship, worth up to £600. He even checked that she was eligible, residing as she did in England. She was, for she still had an Australian passport. He also asked her for a story, and a few months later published 'The Hotel-Keeper's Story' in *Southerly*.[6] Stead was grateful for speedy payment.

The friendship with Guy Howarth would become strained in 1958 when Howarth, who by then was Professor of English at the University of Cape Town, wrote a chatty article on Stead for *Biblionews*, the magazine of the Book Collectors' Society of Australia. In this he wrote that he had met Stead and Blake in London and discovered they were puppet enthusiasts. He understood that they assembled their cast of puppets 'to act the plot out' before Stead started writing—an approach that might explain the 'relative planlessness and formlessness' of her novels.[7] He added: 'Any such composition of course benefits from the jolly or caustic contributions of the irrepressible Bill.' Stead would write back in high dudgeon:

> The notion that I just sit down and write my novels without
> knowing what I am going to do next, is so untrue, and even
> ridiculous, especially to me, considering how I sweat blood
> over them and write and rewrite and rewrite and that I make
> for each one a thousand plans . . . that I feel quite annoyed.[8]

★   ★   ★

In February 1952, not wanting to impose on the Risners any longer, Blake and Stead moved to a cheap room in nearby Woronzow Road. The house looked pretty enough from the outside—painted white, with a little green balcony, and just around the corner from exclusive St John's Wood villas. Inside, it was 'a disgusting slum', with 'the dirt of generations'. The landlady was a 'frightful old monster' who looked capable of murder. The carpet reeked of her tomcat.[9] The thin blankets were dirty. (Stead and Blake had left their bed linen and typewriters in Paris.) For water, they had to go upstairs to a freezing bathroom, and they were forever putting shillings in the meter for gas and electricity.

An Australian journalist friend, Anne Matheson, who worked for Consolidated Press, arranged for Stead to work in a heated office in Fleet Street during the day.[10] 'By the time I got there,' Stead told Edith Anderson afterwards, 'I felt as if I could not live any more; the old sinking feeling.'[11]

It was while they were living in that dismal 'hole', with Stead fighting off severe depression, that Blake and Stead eventually married. The bitter irony of it all would not have been lost on Stead. She had waited twenty-three years for this divorce—for years she had longed for it—and now, when the final decree came through from Paris, their conjugal life had sunk to its lowest ebb ever. The French divorce proceedings had been slow. The non-conciliation order had gone through in June 1951; the Prefecture de la Seine ruled the divorce on 17 October (naming Mollie Blech as the wronged party), but the certificate was not finally signed and stamped by the French Civil Authorities until 14 February 1952.[12] Soon after receiving it in the mail, Blake and Stead went off to the St Pancras Registry Office. They were married on 23 February 1952. The groom was 57; the bride was 49. The witnesses, G. Banks and A. Oxley, were probably Registry Office employees.[13]

Six years earlier, Stead had portrayed the wedding of Teresa Hawkins and James Quick in *For Love Alone*. It was prescient writing: the fictional marriage is described as one of those 'lonely distant unions known to wanderers'.

> The wedding ceremony means nothing, the man is there
> before and there after, he and she have looked after everything
> themselves. The witnesses are two street cleaners and a
> messenger boy. They take a bus or taxi and eat their wedding
> breakfast alone ... The whole move is made in the heart of a
> great city, where no one knows whether they were united
> yesterday or last year.[14]

What did marriage mean to Stead after all this time? She did not mention the ceremony in her letters; it no longer had any romantic connotations. She had become a married woman too late to enjoy the psychological security marriage would once have brought her. Mollie Blech was no longer a threat. Children were now out of the question. She was beyond caring about the social stigma of separate passports in hotels. There was a time when marriage to Bill Blake would have facilitated her residence status in the States, but she had no interest in an American passport now, and as a communist, Blake himself was in danger of losing his American citizenship. On the other hand, Stead's Australian passport, which gave her automatic British residency, conferred residency rights on her husband.

The marriage in *For Love Alone* is a cheerful, even if anonymous occasion. Was theirs? On that drab February day, as they returned to their dreary lodgings without so much as a marital bed, a cosy lamp or a writing desk to call their own, Mrs Blake, as she liked to call herself, must simply have had a leaden heart.

She was torn apart to see 'poor dear Bill . . . calling round hopelessly to 101 places' looking for work and getting nowhere.[15] As a foreigner, he was not legally entitled to work in England. And when Stead scrutinised the jobs for women her age, she despaired.

England is stuffed with very well-educated women,
Cambridge, Girton, all that, who are struggling for the
meanest jobs: there's a terrible unemployment of that sort.
You can get matron's jobs etc. but very often it's next door
to *au pair* and always live-in. But I'm a married woman.[16]

Because social security premiums were higher for older people, employers preferred applicants below 40. Stead was about to turn 50. And though they dyed Blake's hair to make him look younger, they could not conceal the reality. Their only consolation was the bitter one that their situation was shared by thousands of talented Americans both at home and in Europe—'really brilliant people who were best-sellers who now do not know where they can eat'.[17]

Stead advertised herself in a newspaper as a writer looking for work. Not surprisingly, it produced nothing. Blake believed they should stretch their money for a few more months and try to write something that would sell. Stead retorted, 'That is what has ruined us!'[18]

As Stead told friends, she could have produced much faster if only they could afford a professional typist to do the final draft. She saw the issue as one of speed, but in fact the constant rejections she was now encountering from publishers may have been due in part to the dreadful presentation of her manuscripts. Viking publishers had had to re-type *For Love Alone* before they could read it. Stead was terribly impatient with what she considered a vacuous obsession with presentation. To her, publishers seemed 'like schoolteachers' when they returned her manuscripts with the comment that the typing made a bad impression. She felt like retorting: 'But what about the BOOK, you nitwits!' When she asked for her manuscript back after the publication of *The People with the Dogs*, an editor at Little, Brown had the 'insensate pertness' to write to her: 'Your MS. is in a very dirty condition and I hardly think it is worth keeping.'[19]

Typists were expensive; furthermore, they were 'so spoiled' these days that one or two had even refused to work from Stead's drafts.[20] This problem was a constant lament in letters. She told Edith Anderson: 'I've got such stacks of stuff, but by James, they want everything so beautifully typed these days that I don't really know what we are going to do. Look at the outlay before we can even send things in for their lordly approval!'[21]

She and Blake talked of escaping to the Australian sun, but they did not have the means. The fare was high, and so was the cost of living there. Australian law, unlike British, discriminated against women in that marriage to an Australian woman did not entitle her foreign spouse to Australian nationality or right of residence. As an American, Blake needed £400 and a return ticket in order to stay six months, as well as a clean bill of health—which also had political implications. (Kate Stead's political credentials had been checked by ASIO before she was granted leave of absence to go overseas in 1951.[22]) Stead was not convinced that Blake would like life in Australia. She told Nettie Palmer, 'He even gave up USA for Europe so I don't believe all my charm stories about Manly and Newport etc. would compensate. Besides, how would we make a living? It's impossible. It's a pity though. I'm getting tired of this lifelong wandering.'[23]

She herself had mixed feelings about Australia, which was scarcely surprising, since Australia felt the same about her. She found the country parochial and culturally on the defensive, yet she angrily repudiated any notion of an Australian sense of inferiority. Nettie Palmer had recently sent her two 1950 issues of the cultural and literary magazine *Meanjin*, thinking they might be of interest to her. Stead wrote to thank her, but confessed she was irritated by Arthur Phillips' article 'The Cultural Cringe', which argued that Australian writers and artists suffered from 'the centrifugal pull of the great cultural metropolises'. Stead told Nettie Palmer that in her early years in Australia she had only ever encountered 'an honest ... hatred and contempt for the seat of a vicious Empire'. If the 'cultural cringer' really did exist, was he perhaps 'the Menzies type of Australian?' she asked. But she was missing the point.[24]

In the same letter, she had asked Nettie Palmer if *Meanjin* would be interested in a regular 'Letter from Paris', where they would soon be living again. (Dymphna Cusack's recently published 'Letter from London' had made Stead ashamed of her own inertia.) Nettie Palmer replied that she had no formal connection with *Meanjin*, so Stead should write to the editor, Clem Christesen, but she suspected there might not be space for a regular Paris Letter. Stead (who had just railed against the idea of European cultural metropolises) privately thought this 'silly and even mean'. Furthermore, she was insulted by Nettie Palmer's comment: 'I always meant to write something about you, but never seemed to get round to it, though I do sometimes unexpectedly drop a mention of your books into the middle of one of my lectures.'[25]

Stead told Florence James she thought this 'impudent'.

This was uncalled for; I did not ask her if she wrote about me. I am quite finished with her, taking this with the thing I mention above . . . Of course, I recognise she may be a flutterbrain and be quite confused, but I don't care.

Stead was angry about many things these days, and would probably have been even more upset had she read Nettie Palmer's account of their 1935 Paris meeting in *Fourteen Years*, Palmer's diary, recently published by the Meanjin Press in Melbourne.[26] Palmer made it seem as if the elegant Christina Stead was obsessed with hats and fashion. This was a tragic irony: Australian readers could scarcely have been given a more false impression of her current circumstances. How far away the Parisian Christina Stead seemed now!

★   ★   ★

In early March 1952, the Blakes left for Paris, buoyed by hopes that Stead was to be given work at UNESCO. In three months in London they had had no success with finding work, and had merely spent Kate's precious inheritance. But they had been introduced to an Australian, Mr Bellew, who worked in the cultural section of UNESCO, and he had assured them that 'nothing would be easier' than finding Stead work at UNESCO in Paris. It was arranged that they should come and see him in March, when he would be back from a holiday in Australia.

They crossed the Channel thinking their troubles were over. But Mr Bellew did nothing for Stead: he merely palmed her off on to someone else who also could not help. 'Bill was terribly upset,' Christina told Edith Anderson. 'Me too. We were ruined.'[27] Every expense was now 'lifeblood'.[28] They spent the next few months in Paris moving from one cheap hotel to another—a 'shifty life'[29] brought about by a new rental law which, aiming to protect tenants, decreed that hotel rates should be lowered for clients staying longer than a month. In practice, it meant that hotels accepted clients only on a short-term basis.

Ruth Blake thought she could find them enough translation work to keep them going, but she managed to find only two small jobs for her father. In their anxiety about money, Blake and Stead were overworking: it was not proving productive. Unable to concentrate with Stead banging away on her typewriter in the same room, Blake worked at Ruth's during the daytime.

The Ronkins, interpreter friends of Ruth, sublet their apartment cheaply to the Blakes for the three summer months. It was in an old working-class district on the outskirts of Paris.[30] Stead was overjoyed to have a 'home' again, and admitted to Florence:

> I spent two and a half blessed days doing housework, cooking,
> washing, and all the other things that you itch for when
> cooped up in one small bedroom in a hotel, the rest of the
> time tramping the streets or sitting in cafés, to pass the time
> until lunch or dinner or bed.[31]

Food was plentiful again in France. On fine summer days, they would sometimes walk to the nearby park, taking a picnic with the treats they so missed in England: ham, pâté, black olives, brie.

Blake had two manuscripts doing the rounds of publishers in the States. The problem, as he saw it, was that if a book contained 'even contingent praise of any communist character' or if it did not show 'intense enthusiasm for the American way of life', it was not acceptable to publishers. Several publishing houses had been 'assailed by the McCarthyite barbarians', and most had become conservative and censorious. Yet—he told himself—Arthur Miller and Nelson Algren were still managing to be published: it was not completely impossible for leftwingers.[32] However, neither his imperialism book nor his *Risorgimento* novel would ever find a publisher.

Stead admired Blake's courage. He rarely descended into self-pity, and he never stopped working. He was currently writing a novel about Egmont, the Flemish general, friend of Philip II of Spain. At the same time, he was turning out stories. So was Stead:

> I am always starting a story that is to be done: "today without
> fail"—it invariably takes a week if not longer . . . and then
> [I] start all over again. Bill is very amiable under such trying
> conditions. He meanwhile has taken to writing stories that
> genuinely take only one day and are posted the same day or
> the next. Admirable! We will see how they turn out. Perhaps
> he will work out his own genre.[33]

At the same time she was finishing the short novel she had begun in Lausanne in 1950, *Mrs Trollope and Madame Blaise* (later *The Little*

Hotel). Set in a modest Swiss hotel in the late Forties, the 200-page narrative focuses on an eccentric group of characters who are 'running from doomsday'. As Diana Brydon puts it:

> The English are fleeing from a Labour government at home and the collapse of their Empire abroad; an American from the South wishes to avoid "racial contamination"; and everyone is trying to second-guess the newest symbol of doom, the Russians. Among the servants, hostilities are continually breaking out between the French and the Italians and between the Swiss-French and Swiss-Germans. As Europe enters the Cold War this little hotel represents, as if in microcosm, the ambiance of the times.[34]

There are wonderful miniature portraits in *The Little Hotel*, which in some ways resembles *House of All Nations*. It explores the fear of loneliness and old age, and the effect of money and class on human relationships. The characters are lonely wanderers, a 'sad lot of scarecrows', trapped by their fear of commitment. (The mature Stead was no longer celebrating the unattached, free and easy wanderer.) Mrs Trollope complains to her companion Robert Wilkins, 'At times you seem to me a complete stranger. I am living with a stranger.' He replies: 'We all are.'[35]

Mrs Trollope and Madame Blaise was close to completion in May 1952. 'Perhaps Little Brown won't take it,' Stead told herself anxiously. 'They're so very moral ... And who cares about Switzerland anyway?'[36] It was probably an untidy manuscript that she sent to Helen Strauss, who wrote from New York that she did not much like the novel and doubted whether publishers would be interested.

In July 1952, Clem Christesen wrote to Stead inviting her to write a Paris Letter for *Meanjin*.[37] She had offered it, in need of money, but it was not the sort of article she liked to write. Stead left it until the September deadline fell due before eventually sitting down at her typewriter and producing two and a half untidy pages. She told Christesen that since her letter was late, he should take it as a personal letter to him. Christesen, who had no time to clarify what she meant by this, plucked out a lengthy extract and printed it in his editorial column as a letter he had received from abroad, without attaching her name to it.[38] He wrote and thanked her warmly and suggested she write another—next time an open letter which he could attribute to her. Stead was dismayed at not being paid. She was not to know that *Meanjin*, regarded as a socialist journal, had its government subsidy cut in half that year and that Christesen had already put in £2000 of his own money.

Stead's 'Letter from Paris' was such uninspired polemic that it is surprising Christesen asked for another. She wrote mostly about the Camus-Sartre controversy—the talk of Paris that summer. But the article was muddled, and too prejudiced to be good journalism. It expressed impatience with the 'backyard quarrel' of the two Existentialists—both of whom she regarded as anti-communist.

This was quite misguided. Indeed, the issue of communism was at the heart of the feud. In his latest book, *L'Homme révolté*, Camus had taken a stand against Stalinism and condemned Western intellectuals who remained silent about the Soviet forced labour camps and the show trials in Eastern Europe. Sartre, on the other hand, had moved toward the Communist Party and his journal *Les Temps Modernes* advocated solidarity with Soviet communism. Not surprisingly, the review of Camus' book in the May issue of *Les Temps Modernes* was highly critical.[39] Camus, who despite their political differences had thought Sartre a loyal friend, was terribly offended. The August issue of *Les Temps Modernes* contained an open letter to Sartre from Camus, followed by Sartre's reply. The exchange was cruel and bitter.

Stead explained none of this. She merely scoffed that Existentialism was a 'middleclass movement', representing 'normal postwar pessimism'. She had nothing good to say about Jean-Paul Sartre:

Sartre is a smart pedlar with a few varied goods in his pack, he is not selling any of them particularly, till he sees which line takes, and so he offers tears for the poor, home-truths, the wickedness of French colonial policy, Soviet oppression of the Turkmens, and so on, a remarkable stream of bright rubbish.[40]

Camus, she grumbled, was leaning towards mysticism.

Arthur Levy, an Australian working in UNESCO in Paris, told Clem Christesen that Stead's piece was 'hopelessly inaccurate', whereupon Christesen asked Florence James: 'By the way, could you tell me what are Christina Stead's politics?'[41] The following year, 1953, Dymphna Cusack would write a 'Paris Journal' for *Meanjin*[42] in which she expressed admiration for Sartre, then active in the Peace Movement.

Stead had not yet registered the strength of anti-communism in the post-war world. She did not seem to realise that a pro-communist 'Letter from Paris' would reflect badly both on herself and on *Meanjin*. Her naivety in this respect is surprising, for along with Jack Lindsay, Florence James and Dymphna Cusack, she had become a member of the newly formed Australia & New Zealand Civil Liberties Society in England, in which anti-communism was frequently discussed. The Society made formal protests about such matters as censorship, the position of Aborigines and Maoris and the confiscation of alleged communists' passports. Meetings were usually held in the congenial atmosphere of the Bull and Mouth, in Bloomsbury.[43] Stead was for a time one of four Vice-Presidents. Dymphna Cusack was President.[44]

In September 1952, just three days before she sent her Paris letter to Clem Christesen at *Meanjin*, Stead sent off her application to Australia for a Commonwealth Literary Fund Fellowship. She could not have applied at a worse time. In February that year, Robert Menzies had instructed the Australian Security Intelligence Organisation (ASIO) to investigate the political colouring of all writers applying for grants. ASIO had opened files on numerous writers—Katharine Susannah Prichard, Vance Palmer, Judah Waten, Eric Dark, Frank Dalby Davison, Jean Devanny, Stephen Murray-Smith (editor of *Overland*), Nina Christesen (Clem Christesen's Russian wife) and Christina Stead.

Stead heard in November that her application had not been recommended. Guy Howarth, who was on the selection committee headed by Vance Palmer, told her that her long-term residency abroad had been an issue after all. Stead told Florence James: 'It went to Menzies for decision, he's Chairman, he said if I had been *travelling* [it] would have been OK: otherwise I was the designee.'[45]

Did she believe this implausible explanation? Menzies and his parliamentary committee did influence the final decision, and her politics may well have had something to do with it. The selection for Literary Fellowships caused a major scandal in the press that year. Vance Palmer was branded a Red, accused of favouring communist writers, although the only actual Party member to be awarded a grant was Judah Waten. One MP protested that the liberal progressive Kylie Tennant, another grant recipient, would be spending hers on communist activities. Palmer resigned his Chairmanship, ill and disillusioned.[46] At the London Annual General Meeting of the Australia & New Zealand Civil Liberties Society in November, Dal Stivens suggested they investigate political discrimination in the awarding of Commonwealth Literary Fellowships, as well as the general smear campaign in Australia against leftwing writers.[47]

Neither her communist politics nor her residency abroad would have helped Stead's case. But the more likely reason for being knocked back—which Guy Howarth perhaps felt he could not have told her—was that her application simply had not impressed the committee. She had sabotaged her chances of success with an extraordinarily badly presented application, obviously written in haste. Her project outline, typed onto the official Commonwealth

Literary Fund form, was inchoate notes, marred by clumsy expression and crossings-out. Although the subject she proposed was extremely interesting—a novel about immigrants to Australia, set in Europe and Australia—she portrayed herself as a kind of dilettante.

> The present writer has had some experience of use, having lived some years among such migrants and their descendants in New York City and elsewhere in the USA: and knows Western Europe quite well, having lived for longer or shorter periods in France, Italy, Spain, Belgium, Holland, Germany, England, Ireland, (USA) and round the Mediterranean, but chiefly in USA, France, England: not only knows something of the views, letters home, language and job difficulties of migrant workers but knows many of such persons or has casually known them: is a sort of polyglot without any special language proficiency, and out of sympathy has studied one or two minor languages, without being any sort of talent in this way: the writer feels she has a genuine feeling however for this people (the migrants, that is) on account of long experience.[48]

Although Stead did not know this, her referees further weakened her case. She had nominated her old Psychology supervisor, Dr Gilbert Phillips, now Principal of the Sydney Teachers' College, but he was ill and told the committee he would forward his reference later. Another referee was Stead's old university friend Marie Byles, a well-known Sydney barrister, who told the Committee that she was aware of Stead's international reputation, but she herself was no novel reader and had scarcely read Stead's work. Only their 'onetime friend' E. W. MacAlpine, now Editor-in-Chief of the conservative Sydney *Daily Telegraph*, produced a reference that was at all persuasive.[49] Faced with this embarrassing situation, Thistle Harris, whom Stead had asked to collate the application, hastily asked Sydney author Eleanor Dark for an additional reference. Dark wrote a brief but generous reference; however, it would not have helped that her husband Eric was listed by ASIO as a leftwing subversive.

★   ★   ★

When the Paris sublet ran out in September, Stead and Blake moved to Brussels. These days, in order to stay longer than six months in France, they needed residence cards. For this they had to prove financial resources, which they could not do.

In Brussels, they had hoped to stay a second time in Miss Hitchcock's house, but in winter, with the high price of coal, she had to charge more than they could afford. They found accommodation at the Hôtel Junon. On the front door was a lead-light picture of Juno, 'powerful and half naked'. The ground floor was a tavern with drawn curtains. They did not at first realise that it was a 'half and half place'. But the amorous goings-on did not affect them. The hotel was quiet and warm, and the furnishings—dark blue velvet curtains and peacock blue wallpaper—were sumptuous. There was stout clean linen every two days, and it was cheap. Stead made friends with the room-maid, Louise, a young Jewish woman from whom she heard the 'inside stories'.[50]

Stead's English agent, David Higham, wrote to say he could not sell *The People with the Dogs* in England. Stead was disgusted: 'What a jellyfish he is.' She felt like reminding him that she had published nine books in the States and seven in England, and that the two not published in England were the two he 'shepherded to a miss'. Nor had he been able to find a publisher for *Come in Spinner*, which had since sold upwards of 48 000 copies. But what was the use of saying so? One London publisher had commented on *Dogs*:

I do not understand who the various persons are, or why they are rushing about up and down town singularly dressed, and talking about subjects which have not been explained to us and to the meaning of which we have no clue at all.[51]

British publishers were put off because *The People with the Dogs* had sold badly in America—fewer than 3000 copies—even though it paid affectionate tribute to New York City. The *New Republic* called it a 'thin-blooded thing'.[52] The *New York Times* reviewer declared himself 'more than somewhat disappointed'.[53] Only Rose Feld, in the *New York Herald Tribune*, closed the book with a sense of regret that it was over.[54]

Brussels was a lively city; Stead liked it, but the autumn days seemed grey that year. There was no word yet from New York about *Mrs Trollope*, and she and Blake were paupers, living on cheques still coming in from their 'Wall Street man'. This time the money was a gift, she told Edith Anderson.

We're getting a little help, not repayable, from someone who must be nameless, who admired Bill's work in the old days: it's incredible, and a sort of miracle, and miracles don't really happen. So we never have more than a month ahead of us. The money doesn't quite cover, but we can do much better here than in England, for the time being.[55]

Ruth Blake believes the cheques were for $150 a month.[56]

In Belgium, the 'two months rule' applied: after this time they either had to leave or acquire official residency papers. In November, an old friend of Blake's, Arnold Spur, visited from Holland. Shocked to find them living above a brothel, he pressed them to move to The Hague, and found them first-rate accommodation in the Pension van Son, an inexpensive hotel opposite the Peace Palace,[57] where they had a fine sitting room with a large balcony facing the Palace, and a bedroom in the attic. Hot baths were readily available. The meals were heavy but nourishing Dutch-style food. And there was no housework to do. Stead and Blake gratefully moved there in late November 1952.

Stead's agent, Helen Strauss, had predicted correctly: Little, Brown did not like *Mrs Trollope and Madame Blaise*. Since *The People with the Dogs* had not sold well, they now wanted to cancel their three-book contract with Stead. It was one blow after another. With no money either for typing or the luxury of spending time on manuscripts that would not sell, Stead had begun several projects that she had put aside. Several short stories were lying around 'half-dead', and she was still lugging about a complete first draft of *I'm Dying Laughing*, which needed 'such heavy work' that she could not face it just then. She was waiting until she had money and strength. These days, she would often begin letters then put them aside, sometimes to be finished weeks or months later, sometimes to be abandoned altogether.[58]

Now she decided to have a run at *Cotters' England*. She had been reading and drafting bits for months: it was ripe for writing. There was no desk in their sitting room: Stead was obliged to type on her lap supported by cushions and books. Nevertheless, the first few months in Holland were a period of intense productivity reminiscent of the summer in Ronda, Spain, seventeen years before, when she worked on *House of All Nations*. The conditions in The Hague were excellent. ('It's charming, gay and so much cheaper for poor writers to eat in!'[59]) Blond lads wolf-whistled along the street. Young and old cyclists passed the window: 'They twine their arms round each others' necks or waists, and still pedal along on an even keel and with a perfect rhythm.'[60]

Stead seldom breathed fresh air, except to feed the sparrows on their balcony or visit the American Library. Blake, happy to have a new city to explore, went for long walks by himself. They knew no-one except Arnold Spur, who had once been a successful Berlin wheat merchant. As a Jew, he had fled in the mid Thirties to Paris, then to Belgium, where their mutual friend Mitzi Enders had hidden him throughout the German occupation.[61] Stead rarely joined the men for evening drinks; Arnold liked to 'talk wheat' in fast Berliner German and she became 'hard of hearing' after half an hour of this.[62] For company she had only Nello, whose wise sayings were cited in letters to friends, and Corrie the hard-working young maid, with whom she spoke German.[63]

By mid January 1953 Stead had written over 100 pages of *Cotters'*
England, and was greatly encouraged when Blake pronounced it her
best novel to date. 'It's a pretty little Strindberg type of comedy,
filled with tears of blood,' she told Florence James sardonically, 'but
Bill likes it, I think he really does, it's not just the kindness of a
husband.'[64]

She was excited by *Cotters' England*. This time her egocentric
monster was a woman, Nellie Cotter. One of Stead's manipulative
charmers, she—like Sam Pollit, Robbie Grant and Emily Wilkes—
is dangerous enough to precipitate suicide by someone close to her.
Nellie's brother Tom was another of Stead's seducers: 'a queer
character who entangles all the women by suggesting that he can't
make good as a lover: they're fascinated'. She was worried that
American publishers would not be interested in a novel set in
working-class England. 'As for the wretched British publishers,
they don't publish anything now unless it's published first in U.S.
and then they don't.' She thought she would try Australia, which
had just set up a Left Book Club.[65]

Cotters' England caused Stead 'weeks of moral struggle'. She
asked herself: 'Is it fair to show the good so bad? Is it not
sentimentality to show the bad so good?'[66] It is a question others
have asked in relation to Stead: was it fair to take a real-life
individual who is both 'good' and 'bad' and create a fictional fiend?
Was it moral to use details from life to enhance the reality-effect,
and at the same time to transform and distort reality? Stead often
complained that the libel laws made writing burdensome, but she
never wanted to change the minor details that made real people
recognisable.

The German classics that lined their mantelpiece, and the long
dresses and picture hats of Dutch society women reminded Bill
Blake of the backwater German culture of his childhood, and he
was inspired to write a sentimental novel set in turn-of-the-century
New York. Stead explained later:

> When Bill was a child in New York, his gossipy elders
> laughed spitefully at the love between an elderly German
> doctor and a middle aged Viennese lady, living in Brooklyn.
> They courted, married and his aunts coarsely scoffed, "And
> now she will be a legitimate widow!" Bill never forgot this
> cruelty . . . Years later he wrote the story of these lovers.[67]

His novel *Evergreen* would be rejected in America and England.
Jonathan Cape found the story 'charming', but like the other
publishers, Cape regretted that no-one was interested in old people.
That it was a serious study of old age and class was only recognised
by the East Germans: Aufbau would publish the novel as *Späte*

Liebe.[68] The translation added to Blake's store of Ostmarks, but (except for occasional cheques that came through in pounds sterling) this money could be spent only in East Germany. In a mood of desperation, he dashed off a sequel to his 1938 best-seller, *The World is Mine,* but it aroused no interest from publishers.[69] Stead hoped that Dutch publishers might be interested in her Australian books: there were many Dutch migrants in Australia, and Frank Hardy and Frank Dalby Davison had been translated into Dutch. But she had no luck.

In January 1953, hurricane winds and high tides created havoc in Europe. In Holland, dykes burst, causing over 1000 deaths. Bill Blake answered Florence James' concerned letter:

> The crisis is, of course, the one talk of the country. I am afraid it is being used to cover up secret military deals with the U.S. ... Every time I see the newspapers obsessed by one subject I ask what is missing from their columns.[70]

He trusted only the communist press.

On 6 March 1953 the flags in The Hague were at half-mast. The editorial in the British *Daily Worker* proclaimed: 'Long live the immortal memory of the greatest working-class leader, genius and creative thinker that the world has ever known!'[71] Shortly afterwards, Stead wrote to her brother Gilbert and his new wife Sylvia:

> As to the death of Stalin, that was a very great event, so strange and so close to millions! Lenin established the Revolution but the socialist state has lived and firmly been founded with Stalin ... It will take a *long time* for Stalin to leave the world; he is so firmly fixed in it ... Most of the people here were so happy and relieved when J.V.S. died: they thought their happy days were back again or would be soon. It's a strange and pathetic sight to see them wasted in years and living in a fairy tale.[72]

Liberal newspapers noted that Stalin might well have been responsible for more deaths than any man in history, with the possible exceptions of Genghis Khan and Hitler. The months before Stalin's death had seen the trial of fourteen leading Czechoslovak communists, branded as Trotskyists, Titoists and Zionist-American spies, and a new series of purges in Moscow had eliminated more 'enemies of the people'. In January 1953, nine prominent Kremlin doctors, seven of them Jews, had allegedly confessed to murder and conspiracy. However, the 'doctors' plot' caused a scandal even in the Soviet Union, where anti-semitism was rife, and four months later, the world was informed that the doctors were innocent after all.

Nevertheless, Blake's faith in Stalinism never wavered, and if Stead had private doubts, she would never say so publicly. But she became very worked up about the terror in the anti-communist West. She was haunted by the trial in New York of Julius and Ethel Rosenberg, faithful communists of Jewish immigrant backgrounds, accused of transmitting atomic secrets to the Soviet Union. 'I dream about the Rosenbergs every night,' Stead told Edith Anderson in February, 'that I am visiting them in jail.'[73] Early in June, she wrote to Jack Lindsay and Dymphna Cusack asking them to join her in sending a last-minute Save the Rosenbergs telegram to the American Ambassador in London: 'Because of new evidence justifying strong doubts of Rosenbergs' guilt, we beg you to request clemency and re-trial for Ethel and Julius Rosenberg.'[74] She wrote to Florence James: 'Do you know that the execution date now fixed June 18 is their fourteenth wedding anniversary: a shocking piece of cynicism.'[75]

On 19 June 1953 the Rosenbergs were executed in the electric chair at Sing Sing prison. Stead was horrified. 'This *will out*,' she told Ettore and Jessie Rella. 'It was the knockout blow of America's prestige: but they don't care, do they?' She added that most of their other American friends no longer even mentioned politics in their letters. 'They are afraid if they say "it's damn hot weather," they will be taken (by the censors) for Reds.'[76]

By the end of the summer, Stead had finished *Cotters' England* and felt stale. 'What's wrong,' she admitted, 'is total ennui.'[77] She wondered whether she had exhausted herself by writing so fast at the beginning of their stay in The Hague. Florence James had found her an inexpensive typist in England, and for once Stead sent off a neat manuscript to Helen Strauss. But it was greeted with silence. The novel did the rounds of publishers unsuccessfully, and eventually was added to the pile of abandoned manuscripts in trunks. Stead would not touch *Cotters' England* again for twelve years—not till 1965.

In The Hague they enjoyed a level of luxury they knew they would never find in England. But they now found the town dull, and told themselves they were tired of the 'soggy sort of over-steamed potato-bolstered cooking'.[78] Most of all, they were sick of being so cut off from friends. And there was an immediate reason for going back to England: Ruth Blake's wedding at Aldershot, Hampshire.

Ruth married Laurence Hall, an Englishman working in Civil Aviation, on 23 September 1953. Bill and Christina hurried over to England for a wedding to which Christina was not invited. Even though she was now Bill's legal wife, it remained the rule, twenty-five years after Mollie and Bill's separation, that Christina's name was never mentioned in front of Mollie, an agreement Laurence Hall admits he found tedious.[79]

It must have hurt Christina that she was not invited to the wedding. Earlier that year, Ruth had travelled to Australia as interpreter at an International Civil Aviation Organisation Conference in Melbourne. Afterwards she had gone to Sydney and met the Stead family. She went to Boongarre; Christina's father had shown her his snake collection and terrified her by placing a snake on her shoulder; she had been entertained by Thistle, Kate and Gwen. 'Everyone liked everyone,' Christina told Florence James, 'quite a surprise.'[80]

*   *   *

In London, the Blakes were again living in a one-room flat. This time it was a large attic room in a condemned house at No. 103 Broadhurst Gardens, in West Hampstead, a narrow, tree-lined street with the railway line across the road. The house was so dilapidated that friends wondered whether it would hold up, but it was cheap.[81]

Housing was still in short supply in London. Large, once-grand houses were divided up and partitioned off to cram in boarders. These cold, bleak rooming houses recur in Stead's late fiction. In a short semi-fictional piece, '1954: Days of the Roomers', the middle-aged Watsons are 'literary hacks' who type most of the day on a rickety table on the bare floor, ashamed to disturb the people below with the banging. The landlords are saving up to educate their children in private schools.[82] When the Watsons walk around the streets to feel the weak rays of sun on their faces, they are always on the look-out for a better place to live. But everywhere is the same.

These rooms had never had the sun since the roof went on.
The front room underneath, never heated, even in midwinter, sent up the cold. The landlords were saving money ...
    Tens of thousands of people, even families with one or two children, live just so, in one room, in the great city. In all the houses of London, it seemed, behind white facades with pillared porches and lofty railed steps, with high walls and handsome windows that promised significant space, were thin partitions making cubicles for roomers.[83]

Ruth and Laurie Hall lived in a two-storey house—'an almighty castle of boxes upon boxes, landings and stairs'[84]—at Willesden Green, two stations away on the tube. It was in this thin-walled 'draft-catcher'[85] that Blake and Stead spent Christmas 'toting large bronze scuttles up and down steps', while Laurie and Ruth were in Paris. Christina, who had been immobilised for a while with a sprained ankle, told Gwen that they felt like 'crabbed old people' beside the blooming couple. Ruth was looking 'remarkably beautiful' and Laurie, 'tall, very blond with a fascinating stammer and a lively mind', was 'simply madly insanely in love'.[86]

★   ★   ★

By November 1953, Stead had begun to realise the full implications of being stereotyped as a communist in the Cold War world. Several of their American acquaintances had had their passports withdrawn. The 250 or so blacklisted Hollywood writers and actors were having difficulty scrabbling together a meagre income, whether in America or England. There had been breakdowns and suicides.

Stead became very nervous when Dal Stivens, a fellow Australian writer in London and member of the Australia & New Zealand Civil Liberties Society, called on them and in the course of his visit intimated that he knew Blake was a communist. Shortly after this, a journalist from the *Sydney Morning Herald* asked Stead if she and Blake had left America because of political pressures. Stead suddenly started to worry. How had Australians heard that Bill was a communist? Had Florence James (who was in contact with the Australian literary set) said something? She sent her a semi-accusatory letter, saying she was 'rather hesitant about how to put something'.

What's strange is that the Australians . . . think that Bill is a
Communist. How would they get that idea? He's quite unknown
to them. I know Dal Stivens thought there was political business
in my not getting the Fellowship (I don't know this), but that
would be on account perhaps of the Civil Liberties — What else?

I don't know whether you ever have occasion to discuss my
(our) political attitudes with anyone, but if it ever crops up,
I hope you would do your best to remove any such ideas.[87]

Florence James replied patiently but firmly:

Chris dear,
. . . You write as though you were a couple of nonentities whom
no-one would be likely to speculate about, which is very far from
the case. Bill's brilliant talking is enough to set him upon people's
tongues and your own light doesn't hide naturally under a
bushel; it doesn't take much speculation to place either of you on
the extreme left with or without labels . . . Your place in
Australian letters would make Bill interesting to them even if he
weren't already so as a writer. And he's personally known to
quite a few people in Australian journalism.

I'm sorry it's distressing you, but the fact that two cases have
come to your notice needn't mean anything sinister at all.[88]

Stead's reply two days later, still tetchy, shows how defensive and jittery she had become. Florence had said nothing about England being a 'free country' nor had she called Stead 'nervous', but she was accused of both:

Dearest Florence,

. . . Please don't brush away the difficulties of this time for many people by saying I am nervous: or that we live in a free country. As Nello said about another and greater land—"You can say anything you like in this country if you keep your mouth shut." True this is a free country for, say, my aged cousins who regard the royal family as sacred and spend their time at church bazaars.

Why are so many thousands of people in London now busy saying that they had "a Spanish phase"—they were misled by the communists but since Beria, police-chief in Russia, was deposed they have seen how wrong they were etc. . . .? Because we live in a free society? Where your job is *not* dependent on your opinion? How many people who once supported the communists now say "I once had a *Labour Party phase*" etc. . . . (Do you know for example that the American police have hounded Americans in all countries . . . I am unable and unwilling to go into details about hundreds of things I know—and whether they happened to me or to close friends, is of no account.) The very best service anyone can do anyone at this moment is to say nothing.[89]

In the rest of the letter, Stead railed against a second Australian journalist (an 'impudent, brassy dame') who, when Stead had said she could not afford to return to Australia, had suggested the Ten Pounds Immigrant Scheme. Stead felt humiliated.

Two established writers . . . are to go out there in their middle-age as charity cases—my revolt at such shameful treatment is physical. The bourgeois and the philistine has always loved to see the "artist in the garret."[90]

A few days later, Stead apologised to Florence for her 'hotheaded note':

You see I have cooled off. I don't know why I got so choleric—I AM choleric to begin with and then this enforced inaction—and I should be writing, all this messing about is no good. However, I must make a humble apology and beg some more of your infinite goodness and patience. Love, as ever, Christina.[91]

★　　★　　★

'My last manuscripts and Bill's haven't had a nibble, and we are really on the beach,' Stead wrote to Edith Anderson in September 1953.

I hope to get a job at the minimum wage anyway, but not office work I hope and literary devilling is getting to be the lowest paid of all possible jobs . . . I hope I can get a job say in a parrot and monkey shop or something like that. Bill can't get a job here.[92]

Florence James' experience of 'literary devilling' had removed any illusions they might have had about this way of life. She worked at home as a reader for Constable, reading manuscripts seven days a week, often till midnight, and scraped together about £6 a week. (Bus conductors and ticket collectors were paid £8 or £9 a week.)

Whereas Florence James had exceptional physical stamina, Stead and Blake did not. Stead tired easily these days and Blake had started to hold books three or four inches from his eyes. His trouble would later be diagnosed as glaucoma.

Stead had practised her shorthand in preparation for work, but her typing was neither accurate nor fast. An employment agency found her work as a domestic to a 'hoity-toity TV and radio family' but Blake would not hear of it. For a few weeks that winter she worked in the office of a hospital on the other side of Hampstead Heath, catching a bus across Hampstead in the mornings. One memorable day in February, there had been rain, and a sudden freeze had caused an ice-storm: 'Every trunk, branch, twig and fibril was coated in thin glass and shining in the sun —a woodland in glass.'[93]

Max Schroeder, at Aufbau, had managed to send Blake £250 as royalties for *Späte Liebe*: it had been quite a feat to get the money out of East Germany. This unexpected cheque saved them for a time. Stead wrote to the *Times Literary Supplement* asking for review work[94] which required her to swallow her pride, since the *TLS*'s reviews of her own books, except for *The Salzburg Tales*, had been singularly ungenerous.[95] But it seems they did not send her anything.[96] Things had come to such a sorry pass that Stead— once the prestigious author—found herself turning to Peter Davies to ask whether he would recommend her as a publisher's reader. He wrote to A. S. Frere at Heinemann:

I don't suppose for a moment you are in need of a reader, but Christina Stead, whom I used to publish years ago and whom I still regard as a species of genius though impossible to sell, is in the market for any job of that sort which might be going.[97]

Literary hack work seemed the least unpleasant of the available jobs, and at first, Blake and Stead went at it with their usual determination and energy. There were two of them, they reasoned, and they had no dependants. Surely they could make enough to live on?

Blake had acquired a temporary work permit, and soon they had a stream of editing and translating jobs. It was irregular work and badly. paid. They reported on books in German and French for Frederick Muller, Hutchinson and Cassells, and took on some translating—Stead from French, Blake from French and German—and editing work and proofreading. Translations were preferable in that they provided work for several months, but they had to wait until the job was finished for payment. Blake was pleased when Muller commissioned him to write a light, humorous book about Americans for a series on different peoples of the world. But he dismissed *Understanding the Americans*, published later that year, as a 'sorry tidbit'.[98] In 1954, Stead edited a book of short stories set in the South Sea Islands[99] and translated a reportage on the Far East by a Swiss-French journalist.[100] But she told Gwen despairingly: 'It really won't do—they do not pay enough to feed a small louse.'[101]

They had little time and no energy in reserve for any writing of their own. With both of them working flat out, they were managing to scrape together a living equivalent to the wage of one skilled worker: about £10 a week. But the pay was irregular and it was 'hackwork pure and simple'.[102]

Bill and I are hacking it in the most disagreeable way:
publishing, our side of the water, is a mean, contemptible
business and depends a great deal upon sweated labour, that is,
jobbing out editorial and other work. If the actual work is not
contemptible, the conditions are and remind me of the lace-
workers of Calais, who did the finer work, not the machine
work, producing lovely webs in hovels.[103]

Their demeaning situation gave Stead insight into a new and shabby world: Grub street, 'where you grub in the garbage of literature for a living'.[104] It was this world of drafty rooming houses, humiliating job interviews and the wretched struggle for money by sweated and inky labour that Stead would portray in her next novel, *Miss Herbert*.

Food rationing had just ceased in 1954, but the life and spirit seemed to have gone out of England. Nevertheless, as Blake pointed out, the country was at least humane compared to 'the silent land beyond the seas'.[105] Their American friends were saying almost nothing about the activities of that 'unconscionable egocentric' Senator McCarthy,[106] though communists were hunted, oaths of loyalty imposed, university professors ousted, welfare benefits denied to communist veterans and their widows, and passports confiscated. Confronted in court by the House Un-American Activities Committee, members of the Old Left usually dodged the questions—afraid of losing their livelihood.[107] In that atmosphere of terror, everyone distrusted everyone else. The FBI suspected all communists of being Soviet agents; leftists suspected new acquaintances of being FBI informers masquerading as communist sympathisers.

Reflecting the prevailing spy-film atmosphere, Jacques Coe, a Dutch-born Wall Street friend who saw Blake at least once a year on business trips to London, had the 'strong feeling' in the Fifties that Blake was 'an undercover Russian agent'. Coe comments: 'There were times, after his disassociation with Alfred Hurst, when his funds seemed to come out of the woodwork.'[108] It was a schizophrenic life Blake led, befriending communists and right-wing businessmen alike.

In June 1954, Blake's application for a renewal of his American passport provoked renewed FBI investigation. In September, he was obliged to submit a sworn affidavit to the United States Embassy in London about his communist past. In it he declared that he had written articles and reviews for the *New Masses* until 1942, but had never been on the magazine's editorial board. He had been a member of the Communist Party in New York for one year, from March 1938 to April 1939. He concluded:

> I am not now in politics, have no political affiliations, belong
> to no organizations whatever, have not for many years. I am
> not and was not a member of the Communist Party except for
> the period mentioned above.

On 19 October, he was called back for more details. This time, in a second affidavit, he named the branch of which he had been a member: 'To the best of my recollection, it was the James Connolly Branch on Upper Broadway, New York City.' He stated that he had attended only three or four meetings during the whole year, because he had mostly lived outside New York. 'Under the circumstances I had almost no contact with the Branch aforementioned except that I believe its Chairman was William Browder, a brother, I think, of Earl Browder.' He had decided that his best strategy was vagueness.

Two months later, the State Department informed him that it was still not satisfied with his affidavits: its officials wanted 'further details regarding the members of the unit with which he was connected'. On 20 December 1954, Bill Blake submitted a third affidavit. This time, he had had enough of the humiliation.

> With reference to my membership in the Communist Party
> during parts of the years 1938 and 1939, I am astonished that
> you have impeached the completeness of my affidavit upon no
> evidence whatsoever except your own assumptions. I have

sworn to the truth and the whole truth and stand to face the consequences of this veracious statement, and I regard as a personal insult your statement that it is incomplete.

I repeat that I attended only three or four meetings casually, scarcely remembering them. I do not remember what persons were in the unit. It is immaterial to me whether you believe or not, this is the fact.

With respect to my own activities there, all I can say is that I was present and I remember once being asked to deliver a speech, but I could not as I was going to the country. If there were any other information to give in this matter I would furnish it, but there is no more.

His boldness worked. On 11 January 1955, the Department authorised a passport valid for one year. Subsequently it was extended to the full two-year period. And when Blake applied to renew his passport again, two years later, the FBI did not object. By 1957 that particular form of Government harassment was coming to an end.[109]

★　★　★

Mark and Miriam Risner had introduced the Blakes to the Friedmanns, who became the Blakes' closest friends. The Friedmanns were South Africans who had come to England in 1949. Boyce Friedmann (known to his friends as 'Boy'), a biochemist by profession, was very interested in politics and economics. Years before, he had used Blake's book on Marxism when he taught evening classes at the Left Book Club in Johannesburg. Boy Friedmann was another talented raconteur. He was dark and Jewish; his wife Tella, blonde and lively, was of Dutch Huguenot origin. She worked as a dress designer at Marks and Spencers, and she also had a flair for colourful story-telling. Tella was the only one of their friends who actually read Stead's books. For years, she and Christina wrote each other letters across London,[110] though Stead was easily jealous of the elegant Tella.

By December 1954, Stead had still not been paid for the two big jobs she had done for publisher Frederick Muller that year. She had been trying to write a screen script of *The Man Who Loved Children*, but it was a dispiriting task. The producers seemed to want to make it both into a Hollywood version (with the villain defeated) and a British movie version (with the villain triumphant, but the tragedy blunted).[111]

The Branstens also were back in London, and they spent Christmas together. Ruth and Richard were quite neurotic these days, with no friends left. Stead and Blake felt they could not desert them, despite 'their false position'. It would have been 'too upstage'.[112]

★ ★ ★

In 1955, Stead translated from French one humorous book, *The Candid Killer*,[113] one children's book, and a scientific book, *In Balloon and Bathyscaphe*, by deep sea explorer Auguste Piccard.[114] She had a row with Frederick Muller about one of her translations: the publishers wanted the text modified—'falsified' as she saw it. It was a sore subject, for she had just been sent the Italian translation of *Letty Fox*, and was dismayed by the way it had been 'hacked, compressed, vulgarised' without her permission—in order, she supposed, to please Catholic Italian ladies.[115]

Stead was attending German classes, with the idea of translating from German as well. Blake was talking of a holiday in East Germany, which would enable them to spend his pile of Ostmarks and live in luxury for a time. He was translating a German book on Albert Schweitzer—'one of the charlatans of the age'.[116] But he hoped to do research work for the American television producer Hannah Weinstein, who had recently formed a London company, Sapphire Films Ltd, with the intention of employing blacklisted Americans as screenwriters. At the time, the British Board of Trade was pressuring her to employ Britons, and so temporarily there was 'no run for Willy' (as he put it), but his response was characteristically lacking in rancour:

> One can hardly blame the Brits: their intelligentsia do not share
> even in the wretched income of the workers: unemployment
> among actors is fully a half and among scenarists, television
> writers, etc, despite Commercial TV, really serious.[117]

Weinstein suggested that Stead should try a treatment of a television script based on Edgar Wallace's cycle of stories *The Four Just Men*. Stead read Wallace and sent an outline to Weinstein in November 1955,[118] but she did not like it. The American Ian McLellan Hunter ended up writing the series, starring Jack Hawkins.

Professionally, the bright spots of the year were two articles by American critics. Well-known poet and critic Randall Jarrell briefly mentioned *The Man Who Loved Children*, 'a wonderful novel', in the *New York Times* in July 1955:

> I've been getting people to read it for ten years, with the most
> dazzling results; so many have bought it for themselves that
> Simon & Schuster wrote one a letter saying: "Would you be

kind enough to tell us how you happened to order this particular book? In recent years there has been a small but steady demand for it."[119]

Then in a three-page article in the August issue of *New Republic*, Elizabeth Hardwick, wife of the poet Robert Lowell, reminded readers of the existence of a remarkable author who had been unfairly neglected.[120]

> The dust seems to have settled rather quickly upon the works of Christina Stead. Her name means nothing to most people ... At the present time none of Christina Stead's work is in print ... The dust, grimly, meanly collecting, has fallen upon a work of sheer astonishment and success.

Coming when it did, when Christina Stead had almost been forgotten, Hardwick's appraisal of the 'truly radical power and authenticity' of Stead's fiction was like rain in a desert. Stead and Blake were touched by the article, and Blake proudly sent it to friends.

★   ★   ★

They moved twice in 1955, once to a squalid basement flat at No. 10 Primrose Gardens in Hampstead, where they put up with all sorts of discomfort simply because the landlady was in the Peace Movement. They washed with a bowl on a chair in the freezing cellar-kitchen, and by the beginning of winter Stead was putting on a dressing gown, sweater and topcoat to make a cup of coffee. Every morning, they would wake up with back or neck ache from draughts.

In December, a friend of a friend offered them a groundfloor flat in an old whitewashed cottage at low rent. Tella Friedmann, who was there with Christina waiting for their boxes to arrive, thought it a nice place. But there was a problem. In the sitting room was a small fireplace, in which a sheet of newspaper had collected some drops of soot. Tella, who until then had not been aware of the extent of Stead's superstitiousness and occultist learnings, recalls:

> Chris was restless, pacing up and down. She said: "This will never do. We can't stay here." I asked her why, and she said: "Can't you see the soot? Don't you know what that means? This woman is in her menopause and she has got it in for me."[121]

Stead refused to stay there. The next move was to a Dickensian rooming house in Adelaide Road, Hampstead. This time the house was inhabited by night workers, and the Blakes felt mortified to be typing during the day when through the thin walls their neighbours were trying to sleep. The common bathroom and toilet were next to their room, and the noise of people coming and going kept Stead awake most of the night. Only after they had left did she admit how bad it was:

> It was one merry-go-round: very bad for writing: and the exhaustion of trying to turn one room from bedroom to bathroom to livingroom to receptionroom to diningroom and back to bedroom—I think I made 100,000 little turns like a mad white mouse, every day.[122]

In July 1955, Gwen Walker-Smith made a long-planned trip to the northern hemisphere. Christina, who once had been so keen for her favourite cousin to share the delights of her European life, must have been profoundly embarrassed to be seen in such poverty. And there was no question of Gwen staying with them.

Gwen was shocked by the Blakes' living conditions. She was also taken aback by her cousin's appearance and evident poor health.

> She had changed so much I could scarcely recognise her. Her hair was a different colour. It had been fair, and now it was dyed almost black. And she'd put on such a lot of weight. She was a big woman now, and she'd been so painfully thin when she left Australia.[123]

Photographs from this time confirm that Stead had put on weight. It did not suit her. Her hands and wrists were puffy. The keen, hooded eyes, arched eyebrows and knowing mouth were padded by plump cheeks. Her short hair was tightly permed in an unflattering Fifties style. She looked weary, sad. The American writer Hortense Calisher, who arranged a meeting with Stead around this time, thought she looked like a country matron in town for the day.

> The woman who came toward me might have been one of those, amply bosomed in her tan twin-sweater set, big-boned rather than fat, a good strong face. I could see her in a suburban garden.[124]

★   ★   ★

In December 1955, Richard Bransten gassed himself in his car. Only a few days earlier he had been talking to Bill. A week later, Blake told Max Schroeder:

> Richard Bransten ("Bruce Minton") ... committed suicide last week. Whatever our sharp differences on politics (he never abjured his faith and yet did not maintain it: this twilight caused him intense pain and wrecked his life), I simply had to take care of the children and speak to his widow, despite the fact that I have a real dread of her: she is a demon of verbosity, vanity, and, although she was very much in love with her husband, had that sort of love that can express itself only by mad quarrelling, mad gadfly bites.[125]

A month later, Stead commented to Edith Anderson that Ruth was 'in a very strange state of mind', and it was not caused by Richard's death.[126] Ruth McKenney had began to lose her mind. In the next few years, she would be in and out of mental asylums.

Bransten's suicide did not soften Stead's attitude to Ruth McKenney. In November 1956, McKenney, back in the States, sent her a pre-publication copy of *Mirage*, a book about Napoleon's campaign in Egypt which she and Bransten had written in collaboration. Stead told Edith Anderson furiously that McKenney, 'that greedy pig',[127] had written 'a monstrous prefabricated best-smeller' [sic]:

It's got lush sex scenes and summer-tourist French and all kinds of Hwd [Hollywood] garbage about the French Revolution and absolutely hackneyed types and comic-strip conversations and it was all done purposely, every word done purposely to make a best seller, done by Richard and Ruth consciously, with the intention of *being* garbage but just the right sort to appeal—not too low, mind you.[128]

McKenney's sell-out as a writer irritated Stead even more than her political sell-out. For Stead, writing involved honesty, probing beyond the surface; this was what gave writers their moral integrity. She once told an interviewer: 'I'm not moral when I'm not writing. When I'm writing . . . I'm a thoroughly moral being.'[129]

★　★　★

The idea that writing which merely caters for the market is a form of prostitution, with literary agents and publishers acting as treacherous pimps, is one of the themes of *Miss Herbert*. In 1955, Stead was embarking on this novel, which gave vent to her bitterness and humiliation about their situation as hack writers, the new educated proletariat. As usual, minor characters in the novel are based on herself and Bill Blake, and for the first time in her fiction, the portrait is a bleak one.

The Blackstones, two middle-aged writers, were living in a foul bed-sitting room in a side street of St John's Wood, with a 'bachelor's oven' in the fender. The bed was made with the landlady's coarse, patched and grimy bedclothes, thin, old blankets, yellow and gray. The couple translated from French and German, and read books in foreign languages for publishers.[130] Millia Blackstone works in a hospital in the mornings and writes reviews for the *Times Literary Supplement* in the afternoons. Ben Blackstone is 'a very gentle soul' whom people 'can't help liking'.[131]

The main character, Eleanor Herbert, is inspired partly—but only partly—by Florence James. For the rest the fictional character is an amalgamation of various women, including the landladies Stead had met as a 'roomer'. Eleanor epitomises the Cold War conservatives whom Stead had already portrayed in *The Little Hotel*. Stead would later tell a friend she also had Dymphna Cusack vaguely in mind.[132] (In real life, Cusack was a committed socialist; Florence James, a liberal, mistrusted the Left.)

Eleanor Herbert despises the Blackstones for their poverty. As she tramps from one job interview to another, she tells herself proudly: 'I won't go so low as Millia Blackstone, I'm no defeatist.'[133] The remark reveals Stead's utter sense of humiliation.

A pragmatist, Eleanor Herbert considers the Blackstones partly responsible for their fate; they are Reds, after all. As a publishers' reader, she identifies with the interest of publishers:

"You can hardly blame people, publishers and editors for not paying for unpopular minority opinions—that is," she added hastily, "for opinions they are in violent contradiction with; it wouldn't be human, and after all, they must think of reader opinion ... Freedom of opinion is one thing, but to impose the beliefs of a sect and a fanatic sect on the general public would be a little too quixotic! ... I don't think outsiders give publishers enough credit for being warmly and simply human —that is, when the cash is the same."[134]

Eleanor Herbert is shamefully exploited: her long hours of work for a pittance constitute sweated labour, no less. Even so, she has a slight edge over the writers on whose material she is dependent. In one job interview, she tells the publisher savagely:

I love to rip into manuscripts, tear them to pieces, rip out the flummery, show them the top-heavy stuff that simply has got to be jettisoned ... and tell them that writing is guts, nothing but guts.

The chief editor looks pleased at this, and she continues 'more sweetly':

I never lose sight of the publisher's point of view. I consider a writer, once he has written something and offered it for publication, has formed a kind of unwritten pact with the publisher to conform to the rules.[135]

Charming, persuasive Eleanor manages to land herself a commission. The publisher, Mr Ambrose, tells her:

"I have a book here which was a success in the United States and which we've bought. It's for a certain public, a religious public. It needs rewriting. We have permission to rewrite. Will you rewrite it for four guineas and do it in eight or ten days?"

"Give it to me," said Eleanor. "I'll be glad to do it."

"If you can do it in a week or under ... it would be convenient. You'll see what's needed: there are passages that won't appeal to English taste; they can be taken out. The principal thing is to cut it from a hundred and twenty thousand words to seventy thousand."

... With pleasure Eleanor took it all in and could hardly wait to get the book into her hands. "This is right up my street," she told Mr. Ambrose.[136]

Miss Herbert, like *Letty Fox*, depicts cut-throat competition, though in this novel it is for employment, not for men. Jaunty Eleanor Herbert prides herself on being hardworking, businesslike, and understanding the 'elementary economics' of supply and demand.[137]

As a Marxist, Stead was attuned to the issues of production, exploitation and power involved in the publishing industry. Indeed, it is surprising that so few novels treat this crucial aspect of the production of literature. *Miss Herbert*, with its sombre vision of commercialised culture, stands with Balzac's *Illusions Perdues* and Gissing's *New Grub Street*. It was time for a twentieth-century novel on the subject.

But Stead's novel is more than a satire on publishing: its other interest is the complex character of Miss Herbert, who in some ways also represents struggling, rightwing post-war Britain.

Exceptionally beautiful, Eleanor Herbert (reminiscent even in name of narcissistic Elvira Western in *The Beauties and Furies*), sees her life in terms of the clichés of women's magazines and acts out two contradictory roles: the old-fashioned 'lavender and musk' romantic virgin, and the 'modern woman' who has 'the right to have fun'. Miss Herbert (like Letty Fox, like Nellie Cotter) typifies the self-deception—'bad faith'—which Simone de Beauvoir so brilliantly analysed in *The Second Sex*. Stead had read Beauvoir's book, in the mid Fifties, with admiration.[138]

Eleanor Herbert's marriage to a Swiss reactionary is miserable, but Eleanor tells herself she is 'radiantly happy'. She works hard at making a success of their boarding house, even deciding, for the sake of respectability, that she will exclude dark-skinned foreign students. (Her prejudices against blacks, Jews and displaced persons represent post-war England generally.) However, she cannot avoid being exploited herself. Legally, her earnings belong to her husband. When they eventually divorce, he becomes an 'alimony-skipper', and with two children to support, Eleanor joins the ranks of penurious hack writers living in mean, drafty rooming-houses.

Miss Herbert (The Suburban Housewife) is another of Stead's ironical titles: why is *Miss* Herbert a *wife*? Eleanor is not sure whether she wants to be married or not. She believes she does, but lets several opportunities pass her by. One of Stead's cold Venuses, she is afraid of passion, afraid of losing her rigid control on life.

As usual, Stead immersed herself in Eleanor Herbert, to the point where she was writing partly about herself. She told Edith Anderson:

> Yesterday I was involved in a scene with my heroine "Miss Herbert" which although it has no relation to anything personal—I don't even like her, although I've got to know her —upset me. Poor girl! After all, she has just lost her husband and although she lost him in a hefty mood, by no means a hysterical person, still I really think I *felt* the loss—for her! It upset me. Besides I've been fighting this off for some time— I identify myself with the character, unwillingly, and it does me no good whatever for characters to lose husbands.[139]

The fictional Miss Herbert has a number of real-life models, as Stead herself admitted,[140] but again there were enough similarities between fiction and life to make Stead worry about libel, and it seems she did not want the book to be read by Florence James, who had once protested about the way Stead interwove real life with fictional fabrication to create hurtful caricatures. When the book was accepted for publication in the States in 1976, Stead asked for it not to appear in England or Australia. It did, nevertheless, and Florence James was duly hurt.

★   ★   ★

David Darwin Stead was coming to London on business in the spring of 1956. He was almost bald these days, he warned his sister. For his part, he had been forewarned by Gwen that Christina and Bill were living in grim conditions. Still, he was shocked by what he saw. Their poverty was so palpable that when Bill and Christina once gave him sardines on toast, he suspected they were depriving themselves of their own lunch.[141]

He talked to them about the prospect of going out to Australia, suggesting they could live with Gilbert and his wife for a time, and that the family as a whole would keep them until they were established. 'How's that,' wrote Christina, deeply moved. 'And I have been squalling and yelping because they didn't seem to know I was a writer.'[142] In early October, she wrote to Gilbert and put it to him straight:

> I am putting it simply because I feel embarrassed about it and I should like you to say yes or no ... We wouldn't want to put off going to Australia too long, if we were really going.
> Australia attracts us, not only because it's my country and I

feel (even now) I understand Australians, what they are up to, mentally and temperamentally, but because of the climate.

Against this we must put a. the question of getting a living, b. where to live, c. the fact that Bill is an outlander. However, he isn't at home anywhere, so why not Australia where the climate would be good for him.[143]

Gilbert replied that he and Sylvia would be moving the following year to a house in Mortdale, in Sydney's western suburbs. He offered to build an extension for them, saying he would be happy with a nominal rent to cover costs.

The letter brought Blake and Stead back down to earth. Mortdale was a long way from the city centre. And they did not want Gilbert to make alterations that would tie them down. Then, in December, they heard that Bill would qualify for an old-age pension if he remained a British resident and paid social security contributions for three more years. It seemed 'a poor thing to stick for',[144] but they had become more practical these days. They would think again about Australia in three years' time.

In the immediate future, their break from poverty and England would take the form of a three-month holiday in East Germany, to spend Blake's accumulated Ostmarks. It was planned for autumn of the following year, and Blake talked of little else. Stead was reading Goethe's *The Sorrows of Young Werther*, and was pleased to be able to appreciate its beauty in the original. In September 1956, they saw the Berliner Ensemble performance of *Mother Courage*, in German, with Helene Weigel as Courage. The Friedmanns had booked front row seats weeks ahead. Shortly before the British tour, Bertolt Brecht had died, but Weigel, his widow, performed nonetheless. She was given a roaring ovation. Stead was disappointed to understand as little as she did, but the performance turned her into an admirer of Brecht.[145] Next she read *Galileo* in German.

In mid September, they spent two weeks on a farm in Devon, their first real holiday for a long time—and 'all for the cheapest rates in England'.[146] The farmers were a delightful youngish couple, who took boarders in the summer months.[147] The wife was a regular Mrs Beeton cook, and the Blakes enjoyed elderberry wine, homemade bread, giblet pie and clotted cream. Stead read, made notes for *Miss Herbert*, and dug in the garden. She and Blake went for walks in and around Dartmouth and the beautiful Dart Valley. Back in London, feeling stronger after the holiday, Blake told a friend he had been truly exhausted by the unremitting hard work: 'I just about had to go to Devonshire before I fell into the arms of Jesus but right now it looks as though the Nazarene's kisses are a long way off.'[148]

⋆   ⋆   ⋆

The year 1956 was a watershed for communism. In February, Khrushchev, successor to Stalin, revealed to the Twentieth Congress that the rumours of frame-ups, torture and murder in Stalinist Russia were substantially true, and that no less than seventy per cent of the members of the Central Committee elected in 1934 had been eliminated on anti-revolutionary charges. Stalin, it transpired, was a brutal despot and criminal murderer.

The speech caused havoc. There was a mass exodus from the Communist Party throughout the Western world. Those who left declared themselves disgusted at having been unwitting apologists for tyranny. Those who stayed saw Khrushchev's speech as grounds for optimism that Soviet Russia was undergoing genuine liberalisation. But then came 4 November 1956, when Soviet tanks rolled into Budapest, crushing the Hungarian workers' movement for democracy. Soon hundreds of Hungarians were facing death penalties for distributing leaflets or carrying arms. When the major European communist parties defended the Soviet invasion, there was a second mass exodus from their ranks.

Ten days after the invasion, Stead wrote to Edith Anderson, who, living behind the Iron Curtain, had reason to be anxious.

> Don't let politics faze you, is Bill's opinion: he doesn't think the present crisis will be "historically significant" however much of a "hurly-burly" . . . it looks now . . . Many intellectuals who regard party activities as "part of my picaresque life," are jumping off the train at this station. It's quite a clean-out of the soft element . . . Bill and I were discussing the curious traits of intellectuals, the liberal bourgeoisie—why are they so immoral? For they are. To jump off every time you're threatened is immoral. Of course it's hard for an unromantic like myself to realise that these people are sincere when they think feudalism changes to capitalism by soft methods: but they are.[149]

It was, Stead admitted, Bill's opinion, and in politics she would only ever echo him. To regard those who jumped off the locomotive of history as immoral was understandable in previous years (though a bit preposterous coming from someone who had never clambered on to the train), but after 1956, it was difficult to defend this position. Yet from now on, Blake and Stead were more impatient than ever with those who criticised the USSR. When, two months after Hungary, Charles Humboldt, editor of *Masses & Mainstream*, the successor to the *New Masses*, asked Stead about the European attitude to Jean-Paul Sartre, who had vehemently denounced the Soviet invasion of Hungary,[150] she replied disdainfully:

'An indifferent writer, a bogus philosopher, that's J.P.S. but high-rating publicity talent. He's been debunked continuously and often in France.'[151]

*　　*　　*

At the end of 1956, Hannah Weinstein, the American television director, gave Blake a job researching the fifteenth-century Siege of Florence for a television script, *The Sword of Freedom*. It was the sort of project he enjoyed, but it was still piecemeal work and under-paid, and it ran out after six months.

They moved again—a few blocks away, to No. 14 Glenmore Road. They considered themselves fortunate because the rent was below the market rate. Stead liked the 'funny little Hanseatic doll's street', and here they had a separate kitchen where Stead worked, near the oven for warmth, her large typewriter on the kitchen table. She hoped to be able to get some real work done at last.[152] She was still writing *Miss Herbert*.

Boy and Tella Friedmann wanted to buy a small weekend house in the country, and they discussed the possibility of buying a house as a foursome. The Blakes could live there permanently, and the Friedmanns at weekends. The prospect of getting out of London appealed to Stead, and the communal aspect appealed to Blake. The problem was that the house would have to be on the main transport line for Blake, not too far from London's libraries, and yet it would have to be cheap. In the spring and summer of 1957 they piled into the Friedmanns' car at weekends and motored all over the country-side looking at houses in various stages of dilapidation. Stead told Edith Anderson:

> We saw some old bush shanties, with kerosene lamp (one) and tarpaper toilets and marsh-grass a yard high and one string of wire in the fence last weekend—you'd think such places were only in the upcountry of South Africa or the Never-Never of dear old N.S.W.[153]

One of the bonds Stead enjoyed with the Friedmanns was that they too came from a southern continent with vast spaces and blue skies. None of them felt at home in England.

*　　*　　*

On 2 August 1957, Christina's father died at Watson's Bay. He was 80, outlived by his brother Sam and his sisters Jessica and Florence. His last years had been difficult: he was hard up and had suffered from arthritis and poor eyesight. For the last two years, he had been seriously ill following a prostate operation. Thinking back over her father's life, Christina told a friend, sadly:

He had become really old and needed so much care and was so
unlike himself that we all knew he could not live long. He was
eighty. After a lifetime in the Civil Service, he was thrown out
... a few months before due for his pension, convenient for
them as it would have been a reasonable one, for he had a high
position, good pay. It quite broke him.[154]

She had empathised with her father's plight in the last years. Bill's
life, and her own, in some ways resembled her father's. Most
importantly, her father's death freed Christina from her anger
towards him—something that writing *The Man Who Loved Children* had not achieved. From now on, she would talk of him quite
affectionately to friends. In the short pieces she was still to write
about her childhood, the portrait of her father is gentle and loving.

★   ★   ★

They had planned their trip to East Germany for months. Blake
was longing to travel again. It was Stead's first visit to a socialist
country. They both badly wanted a holiday: Blake's eyes were
weak and Stead had 'sprung high blood pressure', and was feeling
tense and lethargic. Menopause was causing her problems: 'Like
you,' she told Edith Anderson, 'I detest the superstitious attitude
towards middle life. Of course, there are *some* physical changes, but
surely the body in health can take care of them; it's nothing sickly.
But is the body of the housebound woman in health?'[155]

Blake had accumulated nearly 30 000 Ostmarks in East Germany.
Späte Liebe had done quite well, and *Maria Meinhardt*, the 1952
translation of *The Copperheads*,[156] had been reprinted five times and
sold 10 000 copies—partly because it explored the role of German
immigrants in the American Civil War. (There would be a sixth
edition of 10 000 copies in 1962.) Blake planned to spend two-thirds
of his Ostmarks and leave the rest intact; from time to time Aufbau
managed to send him a cheque in sterling, and it often proved a
'life-saver'.[157] They were hoping, while in socialist Germany, to place
several of Stead's books for translation. As she explained to Edith
Anderson, it would mean 'small regular money from HONEST
people'.[158]

They arrived at Friedrichstrasse, the border station, on 30 August
1957, and stayed a few days with Max Schroeder and Edith Anderson,
who were living in a large apartment ten minutes from the centre. The
atmosphere in the house was heavy. Max, always a gaunt figure, was
fatally ill with lung cancer. He was to live only five more months.

Edith Anderson recalls that she and Christina got on well,
though they never had an intimate conversation, despite the years
of letters. When it came to tête-à-tête conversations, Stead was

reserved.[159] Her last truly intimate friendship had been with Florence James, back in the Thirties; now Stead was transforming her old friend into 'Miss Herbert'.

It was the second time Blake had come to East Germany to find a friend dying, and it cast a pall on the holiday. Nevertheless, they had a wonderful break. For once they had plenty of money. They had friends, who made them welcome. They found the countryside beautiful and the socialism admirable.

They went to Schierke in the Harz Mountains, where they stayed in the elegant Heinrich Heine Hotel, and told each other wryly that the bathroom alone was the size of their Glenmore Road flat. Stead found the regional German 'delightful'. She loved the ubiquitous chime of cowbells. And she was fascinated by the ancient pagan traditions and legends of the Harz region—the origin of the famous Walpurgis Night legend. Edith and Max Schroeder joined them there. Max was in pain and his voice was almost inaudible, but he had retained his sharpness and his wit, and his 'pithy remarks' delighted the Blakes, who admired his fortitude.[160]

In Leipzig, they had a suite in the Hotel Internationale, sat a great deal in cafés, went to the zoo and spent time with Hermann and Hannah Budzislawski, whom they had known in New York during the war, when Hermann was amanuensis to the journalist Dorothy Thompson.[161] He taught sociology at Leipzig University.

They made the most of the opportunity to buy things: Stead bought herself a winter coat, a blue German suit, Czech shoes, blouses, a nightdress, stockings, underwear. They bought four puppets. They even bought a typewriter.

Through Hannah Budzislawski they made arrangements to have a thorough medical examination by a senior doctor, Professor Tietze. They had great faith in socialist medicine, particularly in Germany. Stead was told she suffered from hypertension, with dangerously high blood pressure. The doctor, who presumed they were wealthy, prescribed a 'cure' in Bad Tölz, West Germany. Stead told Edith Anderson: 'I hope the *Oberarzt* Tietze can suggest some simple line for me to follow until I graduate as a West German millionaire.'[162] He did, and Stead was horrified:

No meat, fish, eggs, no protein of any kind, and I have always lived on protein! No tea, coffee—it goes on and on. But he says four strict months and then Bad Tölz (I don't know how we'll do it) and one year altogether plus taking RAUWULEIN and other things and I will be able to work properly for a long time. And that is consideration number one.[163]

He recommended an eye-wash for Blake's bloodshot eyes and told him he might have a tendency to cataracts. (This would prove correct.) And he told Blake to give up coffee. This was a rude shock—Blake was as dependent on coffee as Stead was on alcohol—but he cut back his intake radically and eventually gave it up altogether, drinking strong black tea in its place. Tietze also told him he had poor circulation and needed regular massages—an equally unaffordable cure. The Blakes would return to England very impressed with the holistic approach of socialist medicine.

Before they left Leipzig, they visited Henryk Grossmann's grave, now seven years old. Blake was 'exhausted and upset' all over again. [164]

In Dresden they stayed at the Hotel Excelsior and were entertained by Eva Schumann, who had translated Blake's *Späte Liebe*. She was hospitable, energetic and, Stead complained, a 'great organiser'. Stead let Blake go alone on Eva's excursions, while she read German socialist novels in the hotel, using her lack of energy as an excuse.

Early in November they went to Weimar, at the edge of the Thuringian Forest, and stayed a week in the luxurious Hotel Elefant, with a balcony overlooking the city square. They went for daily walks in the pine forests, devoured the art museums and historic buildings, visited Goethe's house, and saw Schiller's *Räuber* at the Weimar Theatre. On a bitter foggy day they went on a tour to the remains of the concentration camp at Buchenwald. Over the large entrance gates was the sign '*Arbeit macht frei*'. Inside, they saw 'all the horrors ever mentioned'. Blake was too upset to complete the tour. Stead stayed on. She 'wanted to know the reality of it'. [165]

Apart from all else we have heard, it was so meanly vilely
SMALL. The gallows, about the size of a double children's
swing, but not a big one, stood in a tiny backyard like a slum
backyard—and that was the impression, vile slum imaginations,
small low brains, hideously abnormal executioners. [166]

Finally they returned to Berlin for two more weeks, staying this time in a hotel in the centre. But they had no luck placing Stead's books for translation. Eva Schumann did not like them. About *Seven Poor Men of Sydney* she remarked: 'It sounds as if Bill wrote it.' Stead pretended to take this as a compliment, but she was hurt by the insinuation. [167]

At the end of the trip, Stead told Edith Anderson:

I feel Bill and I *owe* it to the Republic to write something
about our visit: we have had such a good time; and (I know
this will seem perhaps infantile to you) we have been so happy
to be in a socialist state. [168]

It was to be their last happy holiday abroad together.

★　　★　　★

Tella Friedmann organised a welcome home party in London in early December. She remembers thinking that Christina and Bill looked wonderfully well and refreshed.[169] The returning travellers were proud of having kept to Dr Tietze's rigorous diet for two months, though Christina complained that it took her far longer to prepare a 'carrot toothsome' than to fry a juicy steak.[170]

But they returned to a cramped room and the London winter. Stead found it depressing to take up *Miss Herbert* again: the novel had definitely reached 'the Albatross stage'.[171] Jonathan Cape had seen part of the manuscript and expressed cautious interest; Stead hoped he would become her next English publisher.

Christmas that year was spent with the Friedmanns in Hampstead, and soon afterwards, they resumed country-house hunting. But by February 1958, the Friedmanns were beginning to realise the idea would never work. Friends declared they must be 'daft': 'Chris would be hell to live with.'[172] And it did not seem likely that the Blakes would be able to borrow enough money for a mortgage, though the money question was never properly discussed. The dilemma was solved when Hannah Weinstein, the American television producer, offered the Blakes free accommodation at Foxwarren Park, her country estate at Cobham, Surrey.

The Blakes left the city in March 1958 without regret. Foxwarren marked the end of their days as London roomers.

*　　*　　*

Foxwarren Park was one of England's large estates. The Victorian Tudor-style manor in which Hannah Weinstein lived with her companion, John Fisher, and her three adolescent daughters from a previous marriage, boasted fifteen bedrooms and numerous ornate reception rooms. The Blakes moved into the adjoining cottage, once the stables, and were merely obliged to pay the cost of fixing up the cottage. For them it was wonderful to have more than one room again, even if it meant buying furniture and doing housework again.

The grounds, tended by a team of gardeners, were magnificent. The hyacinths, daffodils, azaleas and rhododendrons were just coming into bloom, and beyond the gardens stretched the woodland and heath of Wisley Common, once the haunt of highwaymen. This was the view from their windows. Stead, who thought herself in paradise, was not surprised when a young man called at their door and asked: 'Is this Shangri-la?' It transpired that a cottage down the road had that name.

Stead made a point of learning the names of the flowers, ferns and fungi. Outside their kitchen window was a large holly bush where she spread crumbs for finches, robins, blackbirds and sparrows. Occasionally she would see cock pheasants. And she was very excited when one evening she heard a nightingale for the first time.

It was a lively place. Gardeners cut hedges, pathmakers tarred paths, horse-sellers brought horses. When the Blakes took a walk they were likely to meet Robin Hood, Little John, or the Sheriff of Nottingham in full dress. For the last four years, Hannah Weinstein had been producing the highly successful series *Adventures of Robin Hood* for American television, and the estate was full of film sets, including a two-dimensional baronial castle. Richard Greene, the boyishly handsome British actor who played Robin Hood, would be seen in the distance riding his horse up to the gallows to rescue a condemned man, or scaling a high wall and shooting an arrow at the same time.

The historical research Blake was doing for Weinstein required him to make regular trips to the British Library, and in this respect, their rural retreat was far from ideal. Foxwarren was twenty miles from London on the road to Portsmouth, and poorly served by transport. The bus trip to London took fifty minutes and cost almost six shillings return. Even the local Cobham shops were a bus trip away, which meant planning the shopping carefully. Nevertheless, Blake, in particular, enjoyed the communal life at Foxwarren. Apart from the staff who lived on the property, there were constant American visitors: Weinstein commissioned scripts from a number of talented writers on Hollywood's blacklist and would always be inviting the Blakes for 'high tea' or drinks to meet people in the film industry. Some were communist screenwriters the Blakes had met in Hollywood: Jerome Chodorov, Albert Maltz, Adrian Scott. The last two had since served a year in prison as members of the Hollywood Ten.

The Blakes' old Hollywood friends Hy Kraft (the Yiddish playwright) and his wife Reah were staying at Foxwarren when the Blakes first arrived, but they scarcely saw each other. After they had left, Stead noted in the diary she kept at this time: 'The Krafts were in residence, but never visited us during the whole time, a hanger-on must kick another, poorer hanger-on, in the teeth.'[173] She still felt keenly humiliated by their poverty and dependence.

*   *   *

Early in May, a few weeks after they had moved to Foxwarren, Stead was distracted from the daily grind on *Miss Herbert*. Harry and Anne Bloom were in London for a few days.

It had been eleven years since Stead had said goodbye to Harry

Bloom in New York; she had left the States still in love with him. In Europe, restless and unhappy, she had at first been hurt that he had not written. Eventually she and Bill had heard from him, and he proved as lively in letters as in the flesh. In the mid Fifties, the Blooms had moved to Puerto Rico, where Harry Bloom had opened an electrical goods business—mostly selling lights. He was doing very well these days. He had taken up sculpture as a hobby, and sent them a photo of himself at his art class, his long hands dripping with clay. Stead thought them beautiful hands.[174]

She and Bill were at Waterloo Station to meet Harry and Anne, their arms full of spring flowers from Foxwarren. Stead described the scene in her diary. Harry Bloom leapt out of the first carriage and hugged them 'in his graceful style'. He had the same animated face; he even wore the same hat. Anne looked older and had adopted a 'mid-western' style of dress. Bill had booked the Blooms in at the Cumberland and had arranged for him and Christina to sleep at the Risners that night. But Harry would not hear of it, and insisted on getting them a room at the hotel. They had dinner in a French restaurant and went for a walk. The city was 'splendid and bright'. Stead hardly slept. (In her diary she attributed it to the overheated room.) The following morning, she accompanied Anne Bloom to the American Embassy to make visa arrangements; Harry and Bill walked the streets of London together. That afternoon, Ruth Blake joined them all for drinks at the hotel. To Stead's acute embarrassment, Harry Bloom was paying for everything.

Over the next few days, Bill caught the train into London to spend as much time as possible with Harry; Christina stayed at home, broodily writing in her diary: 'Two's company, four's none.' On Sunday, the Blooms came to Foxwarren for a picnic with the Friedmanns and the Risners. 'Harry with cold. No chance to talk,' Stead noted cursorily. The next day Bill went to London to see the Blooms off to Paris; Christina did not go. 'Letter from him [Harry]. Regret I felt too,' writes Stead briefly. But if Harry regretted they had not had time to talk, he was being careful about Anne.

The following Saturday morning, Christina and Bill were out walking in the Foxwarren grounds when they were handed a telegram by the stable master. Harry Bloom was inviting them to Paris. France was in crisis: they must be there.

The issue of Algerian independence from France had come to a head. De Gaulle had just been recalled from his retreat at Colombey-les-Deux-Eglises to take power. Harry knew how Bill would enjoy witnessing the making of history.

Bill and Christina were touched, but Bill left for Paris on his own the following morning. Christina told herself she did not want 'one of those sleazy foursomes'.[175]

Blake left on Sunday, 1 June 1958, the day de Gaulle was voted into office. The Left held a massive demonstration opposing him. Policemen were everywhere. De Gaulle's investiture as Premier took place the following evening: the National Assembly gave him full powers for six months. France's Fourth Republic was dead.

The three stayed at the Lutétia, where Bill and Christina had honeymooned some thirty years before. While in Paris, Bill did some research at the Bibliothèque Nationale. For him, the 'bourgeois cowardice' of the French over Algeria called to mind Germany in 1933.[176] He did not mention the political situation in his brief letter to Christina, merely telling her that the cost of living in France was hugely high and to expect him back on Sunday evening, the day after the Blooms were to sail home. He signed off: 'xxxx to my own dearest girl from her petit Willy.' It is the last surviving letter between them.

After Blake's return, Stead noted in her diary: 'We were talking much of Harry, how unusual for a man to keep on developing; Bill said he . . . really got to know him for the first time, he is a big man in all ways, he fell in love with him.'[177]

She had just begun to recover from Harry's visit and the subsequent nights of restless insomnia when a spring storm flooded the cottage. It created mayhem and her work was held up again. Stead eventually sent *Miss Herbert* to Jonathan Cape in July 1958.

After their 1958 reunion, Harry Bloom would correspond regularly with the Blakes. Some of their letters to him have survived—written sometimes by Blake, sometimes by Stead, with the other invariably adding a note at the end.[178] They are the most consistently affectionate letters Christina and Bill ever wrote to anyone.

*   *   *

It is amusing to think that *Robin Hood*, a series that everyone thought so very British—about that gentlemanly British outlaw who robbed from the rich and gave to the poor—was written mostly in New York by two blacklisted American communists. They wrote under the pseudonym 'Oliver Skene', though they even had to change this name from time to time, to be safe. Ring Lardner Jnr, the main scriptwriter, had been among the Hollywood Ten. His passport had been confiscated for almost a decade, but in 1958 the State Department was loosening up, and Lardner's papers were validated. One day he turned up at Foxwarren with his co-writer, Ian McLellan Hunter. Less notorious than Lardner, Hunter had been issued with a passport in 1955. Since then he had commuted between London and New York, acting as the liaison.

Stead was impressed by Ring Lardner Jnr, whom she described in her diary as dark and tall, with a lank, Indian-looking face. At the age of 31 he had earned $2000 a week; now, at 44, he was struggling to support his wife and five children. (He would later script *The Cincinnati Kid* and *M.A.S.H.*) Stead had already encountered Lardner in the mid Forties, when he had written a screenplay for *The Man Who Loved Children*; but with the advent of the blacklist, nothing had come of it. Stead had not been entirely sorry about that, as she disliked the liberties Lardner had taken with her text.[179]

A casual visitor to Foxwarren in 1959 was Paul Robeson. After nine years, the State Department had finally given back his passport; now he was in England to play *Othello* at Stratford-on-Avon. His life had been savagely affected by the blacklist: listed writers could take on pseudonyms and still attempt to scrape together a living from writing, but singers and actors were not able to conceal their identity.

*   *   *

The Blakes had a three-year rental lease from Hannah Weinstein, but her company, Sapphire Films Ltd (which owned Foxwarren Park) looked as if it were heading for bankruptcy, and they feared they might have to leave the cottage at any time. They did not want to accumulate furniture they could not use in the future, and so the stone cottage remained rather bare. In winter, it was cold and damp. But it was a pretty cottage and in magnificent surroundings, and for the first time in eleven years they had a spacious dignified home. They ended up staying 'three blissful years'.[180]

They would seem blissful in retrospect, but in fact, all the old problems remained. Stead, who had been dabbling with *Miss Herbert* for five years now, had hoped that the country air would cure her writing lethargy. It did not. After finishing *Miss Herbert*, she intended to complete her collection of short stories. But instead, she became 'entangled' in a novel based on Hannah Weinstein and John Fisher that eventually led nowhere.[181]

Later, Stead would resort to the old excuse: 'I had no place to write.' But the conditions for writing were fine. Moreover, in the past Stead had written some of her best work on kitchen tables, squashed in bedrooms, even writing on her lap. In their cottage, she and Blake shared a magnificent hand-carved oak partners' desk, which he had bought at an auction for twelve pounds. It was not the physical conditions, it was the motivation that was lacking. It had been lacking ever since they came back to England in 1952, and

Stead tended to blame England. She had not enjoyed writing *Miss Herbert* (though the novel does not seem to suffer from this). In her frustration, she became thoroughly worked up about the Hollywood-style goings-on in the manor house. She maintained her rage for three years, but for once it did not result in a book. It ate her up, but unproductively. After she left Foxwarren, she told Edith Anderson:

> Our life was spent, frittered away, on a lot of trivialities not originated by us ... It was a great episode. Now that we have moved we have almost forgotten the people we were so involved with: it is washed away; though I know they are going on in their terrible fever-fit just the same. But I don't want to know any more about it.[182]

From the beginning of March 1958 to January 1959, Stead kept a handwritten diary, a 'secret notebook'.[183] She destroyed it the following year, but not before she typed out a second version of it. (No doubt she omitted the more intimate entries, just as she had in the revised version of her Belgian diary.) The typed diary has survived, and although the badly typed single-spaced text is difficult to decipher, the 'Foxwarren Hall' diary, as she called it, gives a sense of their daily life there, and Stead's obsessive involvement in the characters around her. Hannah Weinstein and John Fisher had something of the crazy qualities of the McKenney-Bransten ménage. Hannah was charming and hardworking, tiny and full of energy, but she had an 'unquestioning egotism'[184] and a weakness for luxury. John Fisher was empty, authoritarian, fraudulent and an incurable spender. He was to bring about their financial ruin.

Hannah Weinstein married John Fisher soon after the Blakes moved to Foxwarren. The Blakes attended the wedding: a Jewish ceremony, with readings in Hebrew. Hannah's father, 'Papa Dorner', and her three daughters were present. No expense was spared on the wedding attire, and the banquet afterwards was sumptuous.

Stead soon decided that John Fisher was a sadist and an extortionist. Even when she and Blake had been living in their cottage for seven months, Fisher kept fetching away the carpenters who were working on the fittings to have them work on the manor instead:

> They are still confectioning our stable home. Every time John (the boss) sees them he yanks them out for some job which he avers will take ten minutes to two hours but which really takes four days to two weeks. Just a spoiled selfish brute we have to endure with a grin. He's got the idea I like him, am charmed by him, although a general sourpuss, cantankerous uneasy snarling suspicious drunken zany ... he's hard to handle and a beast to anyone employed by them, a bully and coward, no brains at all

... It's like being in a little court, smaller than Weimar; all the appanages, fights for power in the kitchen-secretariat, toadies.[185] She noted details in her diary. John Fisher squandered money on himself, yet was astoundingly mean with others: 'Bill says he'll soon begin to look into how many nails the workmen use.' He was imperious and dominating. 'He said to servants immediately after marriage, if you call her Mrs. Weinstein, I'll dock you two weeks' salary.' Stead wondered why Hannah was so blind to his flaws: 'She's going down with him, down, down to the devil.'[186] She mused: 'He may be very sexy, can be with some insane criminal types. (Also *undersex* has great value in attracting women.) *I* feel no sex in him.'[187] For Stead, the sexual drive was a crucial aspect of personality.

Stead's opinion of John Fisher is supported by Ring Lardner Jnr: 'Fisher was obviously a phony, full of bluff. Anyone could see it except Hannah, who was completely taken in.' He adds: 'Fisher was an even bigger spender than she was. He ran the business into the ground. Everyone was completely confused as to what was spent on the film business and what on the estate.'[188]

In the notes for her Foxwarren novel—alternately called *Fan Pearl* or *The Golem*—Stead speculated that company money was diverted for household expenses. *Robin Hood* had made huge profits, but Weinstein's other swashbuckling productions—*The Buccaneers*, *The Adventures of Sir Lancelot*, *The Sword of Freedom* and *The Four Just Men*—were running at a loss.[189] Soon after the marriage, everyone associated with Sapphire Films was expecting black disaster.

Hannah Weinstein saw herself as a communist; was she being philanthropic or exploitative in the Foxwarren days? According to Ring Lardner Jnr, she was both. Howard Koch, another blacklisted writer in London at the time, observes that if Weinstein provided employment for blacklisted writers, 'the benefits were mutual'.[190] She was taking a risk. As an independent producer she had no formal connection with Hollywood, but would have found herself in severe trouble had it become generally known that she employed blacklisted writers. She was paying highly-talented writers Screen Writers Guild wages; it was a mere fraction of their former earnings, but then again, she was not Hollywood, and no-one else would employ them.

Bill Blake certainly considered himself exploited, despite the free accommodation. He did considerable research for Sapphire Films: Weinstein's movies all had historical settings, and his knowledge and research were invaluable.[191] Stead's notes for her novel *Fan Pearl* show that she certainly did not see Weinstein as entirely altruistic. 'Fan Pearl', in these notes, is Hannah Weinstein; the cruelly named 'Catchbone' is an unidentified blacklisted writer:

> Because of her past which, because of her connections with the great radicals, people thought of as a radical past and because she was a clever convincing talker, talents like Catchbone and many others, with better names, saw their future and fortune in her. She enjoyed creating her own society, was charming, gave parties and was believed to have helped many people: at least she helped them in little ways, or at least in her company they met "useful" people. The poor, degraded, frightened could for the first few months find a sort of welcome with Fan: at that time she was feeling her way, she had an idea; she would build a new theatre empire out of the free-floating and high-paid talents of the radical world. The persecutors had done her a favour: they had thrown these brilliant talents on the labour market and denied them all employment: they had once worked for fantastically high wages, now they must work for nothing and find doors shut, or must work under assumed names ... These highstarred gentry found in her a foster-mother; they were anxious to work for reduced wages.[192]

★   ★   ★

Miriam and Mark Risner sometimes visited Foxwarren with their two children, who liked riding the horses. Mark Risner, a tailor, would give the Blakes clothes his clients had ordered but never claimed. In this way, Stead acquired a smart winter coat and Blake some new suits, but they never quite fitted him, despite the alterations.

It was through the Risners that Bill and Christina met the Harveys. Leah Harvey was Miriam Risner's cousin; Philip, her husband, was Senior Resident at St Stephen's Hospital. Politically active, extroverted and goodlooking, Philip Harvey rapidly became Stead's favourite man in the circle. She disliked Leah Harvey.

The Risners, the Harveys and Boy Friedmann were all Jewish— and all communists, though none were still active Party members. They were delighted when the Russian rocket 'Lunik' flew past the moon in January 1959, putting Russia ahead in the space race and thereby (in Stead's words) demonstrating what a 'workers' state and workers' science' could achieve. There was heated discussion in the group about Boris Pasternak winning the 1958 Nobel Prize in literature for *Dr Zhivago*—a novel hostile to Soviet communism.[193] Stead followed the newspaper controversy with interest, and read a wealth of material on the book. At first she could not help being impressed by the power of Pasternak's writing. He was 'a real poet', she told Neil Stewart, an Australian communist they had befriended in London. She added dutifully: 'Many good poets are very very weak in the head.'[194] By the time she finished the novel— and reviewed it for *Friendship*, the Australia-Soviet Friendship Society journal that Neil Stewart edited—she had decided that it was 'true old-fashioned, dyed in the wool anti-socialist propaganda'.[195]

Despite her nervousness a few years before about Australians labelling her a communist, in the late Fifties Stead reviewed a number of Soviet novels for *Friendship*, and with no remuneration.[196] Blake also occasionally reviewed for the magazine but under a pseudonym[197]—perhaps because he did not want to ruin his chances of entering Australia.

Politics was the passionate topic of conversation among the men. And in 1961 Blake could still say:

Not all the mistakes of Socialism, not its crassness, vulgarization, bureaucracy, tyranny, errors in humanity as in theory, can ever cause me to lose the Celestial Vision and I am not by nature Apocalyptic, Utopian or Messianic. I see the millennium as Marx saw it, as struggle, ever widening and ever deepening.[198]

Apart from Miriam Risner, the women were less devoted to political talk, though they were more vocal about current affairs than Christina. According to Tella Friedmann, when Christina made a comment, it was invariably about personalities. It was people who captured her imagination.

The Blakes saw the Friedmanns most often. Boy and Tella had eventually found a pretty country house at Braughing, thirty miles from London, and Bill and Christina would sometimes go to their Hampstead flat on a Friday evening and drive out to the house with them for the weekend. 'They were easy guests,' Boy Friedmann recalls, 'though they never partook in the renovating and gardening. Bill was happiest sitting and talking. Chris would read or play patience.' Sometimes the Friedmanns would arrange a lunch party on Sunday. 'Bill loved these occasions,' Tella says. 'By 11 am he would be pacing up and down saying, "When are they coming?"'[199]

It was Bill this group of friends loved. They found Christina rather odd, self-contained and awkward. Whenever the Blakes entertained at Foxwarren, Christina spent most of the time in the kitchen preparing food. Bill used to boast that she was a marvellous cook, but guests never sat down to full meals; Christina would make an array of little courses—things like pickled oysters and curried eggs. Tella Friedmann imagines that she was happier fussing in the background than sitting down and talking. Stead admitted as much to Edith Anderson:

I have been with too many great talkers in my life and it gives me the heeby-jeebies. I must get up and leave the scene of inaction occasionally; and I never had any sitzfleisch ... I need much quiet, a lot of quiet and after a certain time with people I get "removed"—I do not hear them.[200]

Quite often Bill would turn up to lunches or dinners by himself, saying 'Chris sends her apologies: she's crashed', or 'Chris is totally exhausted'. There was never any forewarning and Bill never said more.

They were all aware that Stead prided herself on her psychic powers. At Foxwarren too, it became known that Mrs Blake could tell fortunes. In her diary, Stead mentions reading Hannah Weinstein's hand and, on another occasion, telling her fortune with cards. Talk of communication with the dead or with alien worlds fascinated Stead as much as it appalled Blake. Stead told friends: 'He would not like, really, anything to crop up that is not accounted for by Hegel and Marx.'[201]

* * *

From East Germany Aufbau had managed to send Blake £617— more royalties for *Späte Liebe*. Victor Gollancz in London and Simon & Schuster in New York were now expressing interest in *We are the Makers of Dreams*, the novel Blake had written in Hollywood in 1942. Blake was dismayed by the exploitative deal offered him by Gollancz, the notoriously tight Left Book Club publisher of old days. 'That Christian Yid offered me the sum of 100 pounds on *publication* and, in the meantime, insisted on cutting over a third of its length as otherwise he couldn't sell it at 18 shillings,' Blake told a Jewish friend in New York.[202] Simon & Schuster paid better, but they also wanted changes, *different* changes. It all took 'oceans of time'.[203] This was Blake's first publication in nine years, and it was to be his last.

Jonathan Cape turned down *Miss Herbert*. Stead, bitterly disappointed, wondered if it was because of its grim portrayal of the British publishing industry. Blake joked that it was 'like sending ethical tracts to whorehouse proprietors'. [204] In the States, her agent Helen Strauss liked the novel, but for more than eighteen months— from October 1958 to April 1960—the manuscript went from publisher to publisher without success. Stead had come to detest the book, a symbol of her failure. She told Edith Anderson: 'I can hardly face Bill, when I think of him struggling away at research at his age and with his poor eyes.'[205]

Bill tried to console her. He was convinced that the resistance to *Miss Herbert* was because it was saying something important—both about publishing and about women. He told Stanley Burnshaw that Stead revealed female experience in a way no woman writer had dared to do before her.

Women have had little personal expression in letters to date: and even those most gifted, Sand, Eliot, Gaskell, Austen, Colette, have not revealed too much of the feminine world. Colette could have, sometimes did, but drew back. The dread and stormy revelation of men has only rarely been equalled. This is not due to lack of capacity but even hussies like Sand, even cats like Colette, have allowed a man like Racine to portray a Phèdre with an intensity and sureness that none of them *dare* to equal. It is Christina's gift and misfortune alike that in her books she bares the feminine needs and nature.[206]

Stead's daring was that she 'went for the jugular'—as Blake put it.[207] This was true, and the anger in her recent novels—*A Little Tea, I'm Dying Laughing, Cotters' England, Miss Herbert*—was more disconcerting than her earlier anger, less driven, less obsessive. When *Miss Herbert* was eventually published, in 1976, reviewers would praise its many qualities, but they would always mention the anger: 'The fury in her books is rarely the anger that feminists promote as a step toward liberation,' writes Stephen Koch. 'It is the rage that drives people to death, the rage of the headache that won't go away, the check that is never large enough, the coat that never fits properly.'[208] Thomas Shapcott implies that Stead repudiates Miss Herbert because she repudiates herself:

One of her outstanding qualities is her ability to translate herself deeply into her characters. I feel that she dislikes and repudiates Eleanor Herbert; in some ways, almost enviously (the classroom beauty brought down, good and proper).

'And yet,' he adds, 'there is also such a full understanding of the woman's plight in her self-defeat.'[209]

Despite his faith in it, Bill Blake would not live to see the publication of *Miss Herbert*, sixteen years later. And neither he nor Stead would see *I'm Dying Laughing* in print—a book which Blake had vigorously championed.

Stead's anger made her unpalatable to publishers. Blake's eyesight was getting worse, and he worried about Christina, who had lost her optimism, her spark. He refused to see it as depression; to him, ever the stoic, this would signify defeat. When Stanley Burnshaw enquired after Stead's health in 1959, Blake attributed her problems entirely to physical causes.

Two years ago we found that she suffered from essential hypertension, it was really quite serious, and she has been taking proper medicines which have, at least, reduced the crisis factors. She fluctuates a good deal. Some weeks she is in poor condition, sometimes in a really bad state, then there are long and good rallies . . . But what remains is a lack of strength: not due to nourishment which is superb, but making it difficult for her to complete big jobs of work. She has done so much and the actual novels themselves (there are three and some *nouvelles*) do not get to completion because she lacks the physical resources. However more than a year in the wonderful Surrey countryside has done much and I am an optimist.[210]

He clearly found it hard to contend with his companion's bitterness and disillusionment. When *We are the Makers of Dreams* came out in England, he had asked Gollancz to send advance copies to certain friends. Stead told Edith Anderson:

Bill's book came out Monday. He sent copies to best friends. No acknowledgments. He got hot in the collar. I said, "Pooh, that's human nature. Writers pull it out of the air; why thank them!" Bill said, "You're beaten, that's all." I said, "I know Marxists ought to believe in changing the world but I know a few corners it will be hard to dust out and this is one of them! I'm just a realist."[211]

Their disappointments and struggle were taking their toll.

13

'Bill, My True Companion'

JUNE 1960–FEBRUARY 1968

BY MID 1960, Hannah Weinstein and John Fisher were on the verge of bankruptcy, and the Blakes were expecting to have to leave their Foxwarren cottage at any time. In August, the tranquillity of the estate was disturbed by a deluge of photographers, reporters and 'transatlantic snoopers':[1] Elizabeth Taylor was in England to play in the Twentieth Century Fox blockbuster *Cleopatra*, and she and her husband Eddie Fisher were going to rent 'the dump' (as Blake called the manor) while Weinstein and Fisher were in the States for six months. The rent was to be a phenomenal £225 ($660) a week. But the actress changed her mind—she claimed the security was not tight enough—and Foxwarren was left empty when Weinstein and her husband left in November. 'We are so rural,' Blake told friends, 'that we will soon hear only the Pipes of Pan.'[2]

Culturally, the Western world seemed to reflect their dreary personal circumstances. Marxists were now 'a despised minority'. Only the anti-nuclear campaign in Britain attracted any sort of mass following. Blake bemoaned the absence of politics in contemporary British writing: where were the larger social questions? Where was the passion? The French literary scene was more lively, especially in the theatre—but French universities were bitten by an arid new 'fad', structuralism. 'The intellectuals having decided that all values are "unprovable" are pretty much out of it,' Blake told Burnshaw.[3]

The previous year, when Blake turned 65, he had managed to obtain some financial relief. Though he was not technically eligible for it, with the help of Harry Bloom (who had probably put him on his payroll at some point), he received an old-age pension from the United States.[4] (From July 1964, when she turned 62, Christina, as his wife, would also receive an American pension—about A$90 a month.) In addition, Blake had been making small payments to a British social security fund since 1953, and he now received a monthly pay-out. Though a bare minimum, these pensions at least provided a regular income.

Blake's eyes had become a serious problem: he had developed chronic glaucoma and a cataract. His sight had degenerated rapidly. It was too blurred for proofreading, and his typing was full of errors. But his London eye specialist did not want to operate just yet. Stead bought a tape recorder and tried to persuade him to work by dictation; but Blake, concerned about the effect this would have on his style, refused to use it. Still an omnivorous reader, he held the pages a few inches from his nose, sometimes using a magnifying glass.

Though he rarely complained, he, too, was depressed these days. His spirits would not have been lifted by his wife's growing obsession with their medical friend, Philip Harvey—which he could hardly have failed to know about. The Harveys were the focal point of their group of friends. Energetic, sociable people, they had a large, pleasant house and garden in Roehampton, and an Austrian housekeeper who would do the catering for lunch and dinner parties. At 44, Philip Harvey was in his prime. He worked five and a half days a week as a senior consultant physician at St Stephen's Hospital, Fulham, seeing patients and lecturing to medical students. In the evenings he regularly studied for three to five hours, to keep abreast of medical developments. A committed communist, he was active in organising medical aid to Castro's Cuba, and had even learnt Spanish to lecture to Cuban medical students.

Christina Stead, her English friends observed, was capable of substituting fantasy for reality with quite extraordinary blindness. Philip Harvey had known his wife Leah since their schooldays. The friends in the circle, who were all aware of Stead's passion, wholeheartedly agree today that the Harveys' was a happy marriage and that Philip did not have a roving eye. Leah Harvey was a calm, confident and compassionate woman, with a busy life of her own and many friends.[5] Over the years, Stead would come to detest her with an ardour almost equal to her infatuation for Philip. Leah Harvey, she would tell friends, was a lesbian.[6] This fictional embellishment enabled her to construct the myth of a long-suffering Philip, whom only she, Christina, knew how to love. A few years later, she would tell Norman Rosten, an American poet with whom she had struck up a friendship by correspondence:

> When you love several people truly, there is always one who is La Traviata (and a man can be too) ... I think these are the people we love most. They need us, our love, and we cannot do the slightest thing for them: that is very troubling.[7]

★　★　★

Some time during 1960, the Blakes had a visit from Edith Anderson, whom they had last seen in 1957, in East Germany. After the death of her husband, Max, early in 1958, Edith had wanted to return to the States, and she and their 12-year-old daughter Cornelia had just been to New York for three months to assess their situation. Edith would have liked to stay, but Cornelia did not want to leave her friends in East Germany. Conscious that Cornelia had already suffered the trauma of her father's death, Edith had decided not to uproot her. They returned to Berlin via London, and stayed overnight at Foxwarren.

To Edith it seemed a happy reunion, though Stead made one comment which (she recalls) 'went through me like a knife'.[8] When they were preparing for bed, Christina admired Edith's white satin peignoir. Edith told her that it was synthetic and cheap: she had bought it in the States for six dollars. Christina said, 'I wish I had six dollars.' Only then did it dawn on Edith just how poor the Blakes were. The cottage was pleasant, but it *was* rather bare. In bed she remembered the $100 that Christina had once sent her for her trip to Europe after the war. Determined to pay it back, Edith wrote to her brother, who lived in England, to ask for the money. (She had no Western currency of her own.) Her brother obliged. 'But then Chris carried on about accepting it.'[9]

Later that same year, Edith experienced a rather unpleasant, though seemingly trivial, incident. In December, Philip Harvey made a trip to East Berlin with a medical colleague. At the Blakes' instigation, he contacted Edith, and spent an evening at her flat. On his return, he reported that she was lonely and still grieving for her husband. Did the comment suggest a familiarity which piqued Christina, who was aware that Edith was attractive to men? Or was she annoyed by Edith writing that she had found Harvey bourgeois and cold? When Philip, Leah and their two sons came to Foxwarren on Christmas Eve in 1960, Christina told Philip that Edith had described him as 'an English middleclass bourgeois doctor'. Then, in her next letter to Edith, she told her she had passed on this comment, adding (in a voice strikingly reminiscent of her manipulative character Nellie Cotter): 'This was just to cut you out, pet: knowing your penetrating charm.'[10] Anderson was 'puzzled and discomfited' by Stead's behaviour—though she chose not to make anything of the incident.[11]

★   ★   ★

In the winter of 1960–1, the South of England was swept by violent gales and storms. The Blakes' Foxwarren cottage had cold cement floors and plenty of spaces for draughts, and they could afford to heat only two rooms. Then Weinstein and Fisher returned from the States early, in January 1961, declared bankrupt. Two months later, Stead wrote to her brother David:

> Our unfortunate friend John Fisher fled to Scotland where
> he tried to commit suicide, nearly succeeded, has been
> incapacitated ever since: our unfortunate friend Hannah Fisher's
> companies are in receivership ... Hannah's thud was received
> by us with complete indifference: gone are the hectic years
> when every move they made signalled a crash.[12]

While the receiver showed potential buyers around Foxwarren, the Blakes looked for another place to live. Ruth Hall drove her father around in her Ford jalopy, looking at flats in the Aldershot area where she lived. Bill was keen to live close to Ruth and his two young grandsons, Louis-Antoine and Nicholas.

It was Ruth who secured them a flat in Hawley, near Camberley, five miles from where she lived.[13] The flat occupied the entire upper floor of an old villa, and it was pleasantly light and airy. Though the views did not compare with Foxwarren's glories, they overlooked trees, a green common and a farm courtyard. Stead thought it a great improvement on their 'Foxwarren stables'.[14] Since they were thirty-three miles out of London, the rent was low.

They had dreaded a return to inner-city rooming houses. But this was a different hell: this was the dreary outskirts. Stead had no need to complain of the noise here. Nor, indeed, would she complain that 'nothing normal' ever happened in this environment. However she would soon be complaining about the deadly dullness of 'Hawley, Queen of the Yawnies'.[15] Hawley was poorly served by public transport, and with the last bus at 8.30 pm, an evening in London would mean staying overnight with friends. For groceries they depended on deliveries from Camberley. The one shop within walking distance was a nightmare for Blake to reach, with his poor eyesight. 'No footpaths on the road, you hug the hedge as the traffic whizzes past,' Stead lamented.

At first, nevertheless, she was enthusiastic about the move. 'I had no place to write at Foxwarren. Here I have. I hope I'll work. Also I'm so calm. It's lovely,' she told Edith Anderson.[16] Blake was less sanguine about the 'bucolic idiocy' into which they had plunged.

> We read no newspapers, have no radio or television, live in a
> hermit's world ... Our neighbours are all of the "intellectual"
> middle class, doctors who never attend the sick but work at
> "research", etc, the dread "nice" people of Bertrand Russell's
> celebrated essay. Our other neighbour Miss Carter tried to get
> us to attend the services of that dear old Church of England
> but gave up: she is not clear as to how Satan's emissaries got
> into this parish ... but like all the British, Thank God, she is
> polite and respects one's attitude, at least formally.[17]

The Blakes spent four years in Hawley—four years of isolation from the literary world, from London and from friends. Outings to the theatre or cinema were too expensive and complicated. And Stead complained that having friends to stay at Hawley for the weekend involved so much cooking, cleaning and serving meals that the pleasure evaporated. 'Ruth lives a few miles away and she and the grandchildren toddle over often: that is our company,' Blake told the Burnshaws.

> The butcher's boy wears the traditional straw hat and advises us
> on our gardens, the grocer's boy approves of us, says our orders
> are "jolly good", the milk boy likes us, the "dustmen" (Garbage
> collectors to you Yankees) speak happily to us already
> anticipating their "Christmas box." ... Not since Virgil has
> a more imbecile life been led in the countryside but we are,
> Thank God, remote from the lunacies of American city life with
> its emphases on psychic "problems." Nary a problem seems to
> bother the various human fauna about here.[18]

In their isolated and penurious circumstances, social contact interested Stead less and less. According to Ruth Hall, their only regular visitor, Stead sometimes didn't leave the house for up to two weeks. At home, hidden away from the world, she wore tracksuits and old sweaters, and when she was not at the typewriter, she cooked, did housework, and played interminable games of patience. On Sunday afternoons, Bill went to see Ruth and the grandchildren; Christina usually stayed at home.[19]

By May, Stead's spirits were sinking.

> We're a bit cut off here, I worry more for B than for me, since

>he lives by contact and talk and visits and libraries: but even
>patient C—I'm so patient I'm a threadbare doorman—gets a bit
>low at times. No car, no TV, no radio, not even a newspaper!
>I have been driven back to the classics—Darwin! so perhaps it is
>a good thing. But sometimes I get a bit sorry for myself.[20]

After a few months, friends gave them a television set. The Blakes
were delighted with this breeze from the outside world.

In February 1961, Stanley and Leda Burnshaw passed through
London. Burnshaw, who had not seen the Blakes since they left
New York in 1946, was appalled by their poverty. He promised
himself that he would do his best to persuade his publishing firm—
he had sold the Dryden Press to Holt, Rinehart & Winston—to re-
issue some of Stead's work. In February 1962, when Burnshaw was
again in London, they agreed they should begin with *The Man Who
Loved Children*; Blake told Burnshaw that Blanche Knopf, of A. A.
Knopf, had considered re-issuing *The Man Who Loved Children* in
her 'Vintage Books' reprint series in 1956 and had come up with the
idea of a preface by Randall Jarrell.[21] Back in the States, Burnshaw
spoke to his old friend Robert Frost, to enlist his help in persuading
Holt's Senior Vice-President:

>Did you ever hear of Christina Stead's *The Man Who Loved
>Children*? If not, you will ... It's a *rare* novel—published in
>1940, quickly hailed, then quickly ignored because of the War,
>and except for a writers' underground—Robert Lowell and
>especially Randall Jarrell—wholly forgotten. She and her
>husband barely manage to survive. We can rescue the book
>and resuscitate a truly remarkable writer. But we'll have to
>move carefully, slowly.[22]

It would prove a slow process. At first the prospect seemed bleak:
Holt was not keen to risk the venture. The company's financial
situation was not strong. Robert Frost, who had a major influence
on editorial matters, died in 1963. But Burnshaw persevered.

Negotiations were long and tiresome. Burnshaw wrote to the
Blakes asking for details of Stead's contracts with previous publishers, print runs and sales figures. Blake, who acted in all business
matters as Stead's literary manager, did his best. But the saga had its
ups and downs. The Blakes relied too heavily on Burnshaw, their
sole friend in the New York publishing world: they were always
asking advice, information and favours. On one occasion Burnshaw received a letter from Blake, asking him to please contact so-
and-so and do such-and-such. The letter was typed by Stead
(Burnshaw knew her typewriter, which had smaller print), but
there was no word of greeting from her.[23] Burnshaw was a crusty

character, as blunt as Stead was tactless, and he told them what he thought of being treated as a secretary. Stead hurriedly apologised. 'Do not be angry please. I should have written to you myself; at that moment I was doing some insignificant thing—we were in London—and I asked Bill to write.'[24] Blake added a note, hand-written in large capital letters. 'The Blake ménage does ask you to do a great deal and imposes too much but it is because you are our best friend in New York and friendship, as Humpty-Dumpty said, pays extra.'

Soon after this incident, Burnshaw invited them to join him and his wife Leda on a short trip in France and Italy, all expenses paid. Stead did not like the idea of being beholden. ('I WON'T go around as a poor relation picking out the cheapest dish—or the one next to the cheapest to make it nice,' she told Edith.[25]) It fell to Blake, who would dearly have loved to go, to write back with an excuse. Burnshaw made it clear that he was piqued. Stead finally felt compelled to explain her point of view:

I am sorry about the trip "planned six months ago"—as you
say; but allow me to add one word of my own. (Bill would kill
me!) I did not want to go on that trip; and I told Bill to tell you
so. Not because of you or Leda, of course; but because I find it
very forbidding the notion of two married couples going about
together on the Continent or elsewhere . . . The idea of two
wives, two husbands; the husbands walking ahead talking over
important stuff . . . and the wives behind, no, no: even when the
other wife is a dear charming woman like Leda.[26]

The Burnshaws were hurt, but they were becoming used to Stead's eccentricities.

The silence of Hawley was deadly. In their isolation, Stead and Blake relied on the hearsay of passing American friends. Their hopes were raised when Blake's friend Leo Huberman told them Lillian Hellman was trying to organise some funds for Stead. But nothing happened. On another occasion, Leo Huberman met Elizabeth Hardwick at a party. Afterwards he told the Blakes that Hardwick was thinking of putting together an anthology of Stead's writing. Blake wrote and thanked Hardwick, but there was no reply. Feeling frustrated and helpless, Blake told Burnshaw: 'I didn't tell Chris I was writing as Chris dreads publicity although, God knows, she could use some.'[27]

Though Blake was 69 and half blind, he still saw himself as the indefatigable researcher he had always been. To Burnshaw he proposed various projects that he thought might make money. All involved vast research. One suggestion (a decade in advance of the times) was a Women's Encyclopaedia. Another, which interested him less but which he thought would appeal as a gift item, was a Jewish guide to Europe. A third proposal was a biography of Engels. He discussed this last plan with Burnshaw in July 1963, in his shaky block print:

My view of Engels differs from the canon. He was Marx's alter ego but Marx was a genius beyond compare and Engels does not rank with him. But he is a fascinating *man*, a great and original theorist, a seeker after omniscience, the variety of his interests and speculations was astonishing; I am prepared to write that life; it will be widely discussed. My eyes are good enough for this—I will just be somewhat slower than my old lightning speed self.
I could not do the "Welles" book in six months, as I did, but I could do its up-to-date version, say, in a *year*.[28]

He was being optimistic, as always. The fact was, he was now typing by touch, so that even his typed letters were difficult to decipher. Every four hours, he put drops in his eyes for his glaucoma. If he was in London for the day, he would call in at his friend Paul Koston's bookshop, on Newman Street, to administer the drops. But his visits to London were rare. The English winter of 1962–3 was the most severe in over eighty years: birds froze in the trees. Even when spring came Blake scarcely ventured into the city, except for visits to the Royal Eye Hospital. Stead worried about him.

And Blake worried about her. She sat at the typewriter and typed furiously, just as she always had, but she never finished anything. A number of full-length manuscripts in first draft form were packed away in trunks; she had lost interest in them. Most days, she admitted to Edith Anderson, she felt 'lazy, soggy, even weak'.[29] Though she herself never admitted as much, there is little doubt that she was chronically depressed.

Blake was a staunch old-fashioned stoic. He would often make some disdainful comment about the American preoccupation with self and with popular psychology. A very private man, he rarely talked about himself or others. He considered it 'gossip' to air people's private lives. He did not even like to mention to friends if he or Stead were ill. In this too, he influenced Stead. If they commented at all on one another's health, it was done almost stealthily, as if they were breaking a pact by disclosing their private suffering. Blake told Burnshaw:

Chris has been quite poorly lately—her hypertension has resulted in dizziness and even staggering so I am taking her to London soon for a checkup. Do not refer to this in answering.[30]

In later years, when Blake was seriously ill, Stead would write to her editor at Secker & Warburg:

Bill has been quite sick. (In hospital, which means trouble for him and many visits to town for me, but I am not complaining.) . . . Do not write about this.[31]

This fierce sense of privacy was linked to their wretched situation, which they saw as fallen. They did not want others to see them in this state. For Blake it was less a question of pride than a refusal of self-pity. But Stead was deeply humiliated by their poverty. As a romantic and ambitious adolescent, she had envisaged a very different future for herself.

Left to herself, Stead tended to give psychological explanations for things. As a younger woman, when she had fallen ill on her visits to London for the Travelers' Bank, she believed that London's soot and greyness had affected her, when in fact she had appendicitis. Blake was the opposite. He did not like to probe the psychological sphere. Thus he preferred to believe that Stead's depression and lethargy had a purely *physical* origin. Whether or not she privately thought otherwise, Stead outwardly adopted Blake's view. Apart from anything else, it provided an excuse to visit her favourite doctor.

Dr Philip Harvey suggested Stead should come in for observation at St Stephen's Hospital. For her it was a welcome rest, and pleasant to have her indolence regarded as a physical illness. She told Edith Anderson: 'Dr. Harvey inspires a childlike trust in me.'[32]

Harvey and his medical team found no physical cause for Stead's listlessness. They observed a mild post-menopausal hormone imbalance. Harvey also noticed signs of her once having had tuberculosis, which had obviously cured itself. He privately believed that Stead's main problem was alcohol, and he tried to suggest that she abstain. This was not a suggestion she appreciated.

Neither Stead nor Blake ever seemed to consider her dependence on alcohol a problem. It is possible that Blake was privately concerned, and that it was not the sort of thing he would mention to others. More likely, he closed his eyes to it. Perhaps he did not even realise the extent of her private drinking, which began in the mornings.

Stead's drinking was never an embarrassment. On social occasions friends noticed that she drank 'like a fish', but no-one ever saw her unsteady on her feet.[33] Leah Harvey and Pera Koston both recall that Stead would always turn up to parties with a carton of cream, which she would drink before she started imbibing in earnest. They presumed she thought it would cushion her stomach.[34] (She also believed that cream gave her skin a flattering glow, but they did not know this.) Philip Harvey comments that Christina's facial colour was always ruddy; when she had drunk too much, her skin would become mottled and her nose would shine.

After her stay in hospital, Stead joked that Harvey had given her pills to make her 'tick faster'. A few weeks later, she told Harvey she was suffering from terrible insomnia. Worse still, she said to him pointedly, was the randiness—with no-one to fix it on.[35]

* * *

As always, she and Blake were 'feeling dank about Britain'.[36] 'If only the country were vital enough to be *hated*, that would be something,' Blake would grumble.[37] They became quite excited when they received an unexpected letter from Peter Neidecker, hinting that they should join him in foreign purlieus. Neidecker had retired to Nice after two serious motor accidents severely curtailed his financial and sporting adventures.[38]

But the free health services kept them in England. Moreover, despite Stead's complaints about dreary England, it was really only Blake, the more dedicated Gallophile, who wanted to 'fly the coop' and move permanently to France.[39] Stead was still haunted by the memory of 'those frightful years going from hotel to hotel'.[40] And she was too tired and lethargic to contemplate moving. When the Bakwins (the wealthy American friends who owned a gallery in New York) invited them for a trip to Europe in the summer of 1963 (all expenses paid), she again refused. Harry Bakwin persevered, saying he wanted Bill to bid for him at art auctions in Paris, and eventually Blake took the train to Paris. He came back sparkling. Paris made him so happy. He and Harry had had wonderful gourmet meals; he had seen old friends. He had had several Montparnasse lunches with Ben Shahn, the socialist-realist painter, an old friend from the Thirties. And he would have seen Mollie. Whenever she came to England to stay with Ruth, he always visited her.

He did some research at the Bibliothèque Nationale, and after he returned to England, he started work on a novel, Balzacian in scope, about the scurrilous activities of the bankers during the French Revolution.

* * *

Stead shared her inner world with nobody. She prided herself on being 'more silent than the grave (for posthumously how many silly secrets come out!)'. But there was something in her life she finally had to tell a friend. She chose Edith Anderson:

I *had* to mention that thing to someone ... I'm not going
soft in the head either. It's just that—you'll have to take my
word for it as I can't go into it—this is real. And I sound like
Letty Fox, don't I? "This is it." I assure you I'm blushing from
embarrassment and probably shame.[41]

Letty Fox was 23: Stead was 62. Stead was in love with Philip
Harvey, as she continued to be for the next ten years. Edith
Anderson would not be the only one to know. Stead's infatuation
became an open secret.

Any social occasion without Philip Harvey seemed dull. One
week before Bill's seventieth birthday party, organised for his
actual birthday, 28 July 1964, Stead told Edith Anderson: 'Many
people, too many, are coming; I hope I get through it, but no one I
love among the guests, too bad. I won't have time to love anyway.'[42]

In December that year, she told Edith, 'I know you are shocked
at my loving anyone besides Bill—but you don't know anything
about me really, do you? It is no underestimation of Bill. Nothing
to do with it.'[43]

That year, Paul Koston became a confidant. The Blakes had met
Paul and Pera Koston through the Harveys. Paul Koston, originally
a New Yorker of Latvian Jewish parentage, and his second wife,
Pera, had come to England from South Africa in the mid Fifties.
Koston managed Hatchard's bookshop in Piccadilly before he set
up his own business, a bookshop dealing mostly with international
mail-orders, on Newman Street, off Oxford Street. He was one of
those inestimable booksellers who read voraciously and know their
books. It was he who introduced Stead to William Empson's book
of literary criticism, *Seven Types of Ambiguity*, which she thought
quite marvellous.[44]

Koston, himself a frustrated writer, was fascinated by writers and
the 'spring of creativity'. He admired Stead and Blake, and he (like
Tella Friedmann) was one of the few friends who had actually read
their fiction. His other passions were food and gambling. A generous fellow, who prided himself on his gallantry, he liked nothing
better than to invite Christina and Bill, together or singly, to lunch
in a restaurant near his bookshop.[45] He could also be irascible and
difficult—though this was a side of him the Blakes rarely saw. On
social occasions, when he had drunk too much, Paul, a Trotskyist,
would berate Blake and Harvey for being 'Stalinists' who were
preventing the Workers' Revolution.[46]

Christina flirted with Paul Koston, though not seriously; she
thought him physically unprepossessing. The perception was mutual:

Koston found her *interesting*. He comments: 'There's nothing like plainness to sharpen a woman's wits.'[47]

In November 1964, Stead and Koston enjoyed a well-lubricated lunch of oysters and steak, and Stead found herself confessing her passion for Philip Harvey. With Koston, she could say what she liked. Indeed, he rather encouraged a comradely lewdness. In the note she wrote afterwards to thank him for the meal, she told him she intended to buy Harvey a present of a little Chinese box. 'Being the straightforward wholesome type he is, he won't start to wonder why I am always giving him lovely little boxes.'[48]

* * *

Throughout 1963 and 1964, Stead was working on four novellas. Three of them were about young American women and their inconsistent attitude to sex. Stead was interested in a phenomenon she called the 'Diana complex'. In several young women she had observed a kind of chastity complex, a 'tug-of-war between wanting and not daring'.[49] The novellas would eventually be published under the title *The Puzzleheaded Girl*.[50]

The fourth novella was the ghost story Stead had begun at the Putnams' house at Lambertville in 1938, 'The Right-Angled Creek'. It sits incongruously in the collection, but Stead rationalised that it was a good thing to 'break up the tightness of a single idea controlling the book'.[51]

As she reflected on the young women she had known, Stead re-read the letters she had received over the years from Edith Anderson. She had kept them all in a file, chronologically arranged. Struck by their frankness and lively tone, she wrote and told Edith she would like to write about her, asking permission to use her letters. She posed the delicate question clumsily:

> I have a question to ask, and want to formulate it, put it the right way. No, with this introdn I will put it badly; will you mind if I use your letters as a source? I wish they could be printed as they are: they are unusual (with your frankness and gift of forcible and personal expression) and they give an excellent purely personal idea of Berlin in the early days. But that cannot be, I expect: my idea is not to use them for that, in any case. I hope you will say yes. (Not to print them, I don't mean that, good gracious.)[52]

Though it was not quite clear what Stead *did* mean, Edith was flattered, and consented.[53] That was August 1963. A year later, when the signs all pointed to a cooling in Stead's affections, Edith changed her mind and asked to have the letters back, saying she might use them in a novel herself. Stead returned them in November

1964. 'I have no other correspondent now,' she told Edith (meaning no other close woman friend). About the letters, she commented: 'When I read through them with an eye to story-writing, I saw that I could not use them—they are too much yours; it would be quite wrong.'[54] In fact, she kept a thick bundle—almost a hundred.[55]

At Christmas in 1964, Anderson made an impetuous visit to England. Her meeting with the Blakes was not a success. Afterwards, Stead felt contrite for appearing so ungrateful for Anderson's little gifts.

I am sure we let you go without saying thankyou properly.
I don't know why we were so *rough*. And I am sure you were not happy about the visit. But what can one do, short visits at such long intervals? Unhappy things.[56]

For six months they did not write to one another. In mid July 1965, it was Bill who wrote to Edith. In September 1965 Stead wrote one last amicable letter. Then, in November, Stead wrote a tirade about the evils of bohemia. She added:

I was not going to write to you. I was very angry with you for coming into my affairs; and for taking advantage of a confidence, you should not have done it. But you would do it again! You can't help it . . . You are so girlish. You'll never grow up.[57]

Anderson, flabbergasted, asked what she was supposed to have done. A week later, on 8 December 1965, came the 'terrible letter' (Anderson's words) in which Stead 'lowered the portcullis with a crash'.[58]

You have asked me what it is that you have done that has made me angry. I am sure you know. I won't elaborate. We have jogged along a considerable time with a very vast disagreement between us over things that cannot be reconciled.[59]

Edith Anderson claims she does not know to this day what she was supposed to have done. She was devastated.

Though Anderson did not know it, she was not the only woman friend of Stead's to receive this treatment. She had lasted longer than any of Stead's other female correspondents. Florence James, Anne Dooley and Ruth McKenney, once intimate friends, had all been written off—literally. All three were now hanging in Stead's fictional gallery of monstrous characters.

Stead's difficult relationship with women reflected her uneasy relationship with herself. Elvira Western, Letty Fox, Nellie Cotter, Eleanor Herbert and Emily Wilkes all contain aspects of herself. Deep down, she raged at one person: herself. She upbraided Edith Anderson for betraying a confidence, but this was something she herself had done five years earlier, when she told Philip Harvey what Edith had said about him. She accused Edith of being 'girlish', yet she admitted she herself had begun to sound like 23-year-old Letty Fox. Her tirade against Edith was in the very voice that Stead, eternally plagued by self-recriminations, used in relation to herself.

Among Stead's papers are notes for a story based on Edith Anderson. They include passages that have been copied from Anderson's letters to Stead, though Max Schroeder has become Ernst, and Edith is Agnes. Here Agnes alludes to the unconventional behaviour and allegedly unbridled sexuality of bohemian circles:

I share your feelings about Bohemia, but I also think it's the only place in society that has accepted certain people, and that it isn't so simple to state that Bohemia has ruined people ... Maybe it's American Bohemia and English Bohemia that are so especially revolting. Ernst is a product of Berlin's Bohemia of the twenties, and I've met a couple of the leading spirits of that Bohemia ... I found them charming and admirable and fine. ... They would horrify the Communists even more than the respectable bourgeois; you know how easily horrified most Communists are. And yet there is nothing horrible about these people, on the contrary—I hope that everybody will be like them in the Utopian future when human beings will be permitted to be beautiful without having to be ashamed of it.

Later in the letter, Agnes writes that she is working on a novel that is 'an investigation into the social meaning of Lesbianism'. She explains: 'I think Lesbianism is a disease that springs from the inequality between the sexes,' adding: 'I don't think Lesbians are any more vicious in their behaviour than anybody else who has been warped by injustice. The usual argument is that Lesbians corrupt "normal" girls. That's silly.'[60]

Lesbianism and bohemia, which Edith Anderson spoke of too approvingly for Stead's liking, appear to have been the focus of Stead's hostility.[61] She would later refer to Edith Anderson and Max Schroeder as 'dreadful bohemians—the real Berlin Bohemia'.[62] To friends she would say that she once knew a woman living in Berlin who was a 'horrid horrid lesbian'.[63] (It was a bizarre conclusion to draw, considering Edith's obvious liking for men.)

In the winter of 1964–5, Stead put aside her novellas about young women and sex, and returned to an old manuscript, *Cotters' England*, in order to develop the picture of Nellie Cotter as a bohemian and a lesbian. About the novel she told Burnshaw: 'Much of what it attacks is purely British; though I am quite sure it has its sisters and brothers in New York, Paris, Berlin.'[64] The reference to Berlin suggests that Stead had Edith Anderson in mind as much as Anne Dooley. Nellie Cotter, Stead wrote to Burnshaw, is 'married to a husband she admires'. She added: 'This is very typical of aggressive lesbians. They use the husband in many ways ... This kind of "male" Lesbian does not hate men, she uses them, when she is tired of the perverted practice.'[65]

Stead's imaginative world was once again impinging on her perception of reality. Eventually, her fictional characters became more 'real' to her than the flesh-and-blood individuals on whom they were based.

She told Paul Koston she was 'worrying about the morality' of *Cotters' England*.[66] She had first raised the issue when she drafted the novel in the Fifties, but it was never quite clear what she meant. Was it the way she manipulated reality that worried her? Did it trouble her that Nellie Cotter *appeared* (to all who knew her) to be based on Anne Dooley, whereas she was in fact a mixture of different women, and heavily laced by Stead's imagination? For once, Stead admitted that the 'truth' in *Cotters' England* was 'a poetic interpretation of life, not unreal, quite true, but as poets see truth'.[67] Indeed, the characters were suffused with folklore, even 'Freudian folklore',[68] and thus were often far removed from the real-life models on whom they were based. To portray Nellie's brother Tom, Stead studied Freud on impotence. Though she claimed to have little time for Freud, she certainly embraced his central thesis: that sexual behaviour is a major determinant of personality.

Revising *Cotters' England* meant plunging herself back into the character of Nellie, and the experience was again proving 'nerve-wracking'.[69] In February 1965, she confessed to Burnshaw that she was 'suffocating in a wood of hate and other bad feelings'.[70] Nellie Cotter was a person she 'detested'.[71] Seven months later, she commented that the novel was meant to be 'an attack on mental moral and physical squalor enjoyed in Bohemia, an attack on bohemia which I detest'.[72] In 1967, she would tell Ron Geering, in response to a letter he wrote her about *Cotters' England*, 'I detest lesbians'.[73] In her fiction lesbians are always portrayed as aggressive and predatory.

It seems as if a deep, repressive pathology was at work here. Why was Stead—who had always vigorously championed sexual freedom—so hostile to lesbianism and bohemia?

Why did she react so violently to something that surely did not threaten her? Or did it? She had left Australia precisely to avoid the suburban life she now found herself living. She had fallen in love with an erudite cosmopolitan, who now seemed weak and dull.

Did she rail against unconventional lives because she was appalled at how boring her own had become?

Stead saw herself as ugly, something of a monster. Unable to come to terms with the monster within herself, she made her characters monsters. In their manic talk and manipulative behaviour there is both her father and her own fragmented identity. Her characters reflect the irresolvable tensions within Stead between the self and other.[74]

She had long ago internalised her father's misogyny. In 1973, at the age of 71, she would tell a woman interviewer that she disliked women because of their smell. Her biologist father looms large:

> There is something (it's purely physical, I think a sense of smell is very strong in our make-up, especially some of us), there's something about women's skirts, I mean there's too much smell of material, I don't know what it is, something like that—I don't like it. Whereas, well this is a purely sexual thing, you see, I'm sure that the men we like ... I'm sure there's something—we're animals after all—that attracts us ... Now I'm sure that the reason I don't like women is that I don't get this particular stimulation, you see.[75]

In her adolescence, Stead had written love poems to women, though later she would shrug this off as immaturity. Most of her novels are about women. She spent years of her life musing about women: their bodies, minds, needs, desires. How could she maintain so emphatically that she did not like them?

Naturally, Stead's protestations about disliking women made her friends wonder. Ruth Hall comments that her father would sometimes tell friends, in front of Christina, that Christina seemed to attract women: 'There would be great gusts of laughter from him and Christina.' Their wealthy friend Ruth Bakwin (probably the model for the lesbian, Lucy Headlong, in *Letty Fox*) gave Stead one of her mink coats in the early Thirties, and was thought to be keen on Stead.[76] Stanley Burnshaw recalls that his late wife Leda was convinced that Christina had lesbian proclivities. She and Christina were sitting on a sofa and playing with a puppet in the Burnshaws' New York apartment one night in the Forties, and Christina— Leda was sure she was not imagining it—began to flirt with her in an intense, rather uncomfortable way.[77]

Pera Koston remembers a bizarre incident at one of the Blakes' parties in Surbiton in the mid Sixties. Christina was in the kitchen and Pera went to ask if she could help. Christina ignored the question, walked over and shut the kitchen door, leaned against the sink and said to her: 'You know, you have a beautiful body.' Pera (who intensely disliked Christina) made for the door, embarrassed.[78]

Stead described Pera Koston to her cousin Gwen as 'a magnificent woman' with a 'physique of the sort loved by Henry Moore'.[79] Certainly, Stead was extremely conscious of beauty in women; she profoundly envied it. But it is interesting that she appraised beautiful women with the sexualised gaze normally associated with males. A scene in *The Beauties and Furies* is particularly striking in this respect. Elvira, alone in her Paris hotel room, is contemplating her body as another might look at her. She does not know it, but her lover Oliver has come in, and is gazing at her from the doorway. It is one of the most overtly erotic passages in Stead's fiction:

> She got up, walked languidly to the dressing-table, undressed
> and made poses before the long mirror. Then she walked slowly,
> with a childish swagger, to the bathroom, turned on the water,
> and lay naked on the bed till the bath filled. She spent a long time
> in the bath, massaging herself, washing herself over and over
> with love for her soft skin, watching herself floating in the green
> water, like a strange sensuous water-animal, and got out to get
> her hand-glass so that she could see how she looked to strange
> eyes . . . She got out of the bath with reluctance, letting the water
> run slowly off her limbs, held up her arms in the warm air to see
> how slowly they dried, put her hands beneath her breasts and so
> carried them, glad to feel their weight, into the bedroom. She
> folded her hands round her waist, passed them round her thighs
> and looked at the profile of her belly. She glanced sideways at her
> olive shoulder and kissed it. She kissed her arms, tried to reach
> her breasts with her mouth, but could not. Then she threw
> herself across her bed, and with her arms raised above her head,
> imagined an old ivory female idol . . . she imagined children
> clustering over her like grapes, curtaining her.[80]

Along with the often expressed hostility towards lesbians and, increasingly, towards women in general, went Stead's often expressed liking for men. It is scarcely surprising, since she openly flirted with their husbands, that Leah Harvey and Pera Koston never much liked Christina Stead. 'If she hadn't hung out for the admiration of men, she would have been more relaxed,' says Pera, who sensed that Stead was 'very knotted inside'. She adds:

> Christina would adopt a coy manner with men. It was a
> coyness that seemed to go along with her liking for frills and
> lace and crêpe de chine blouses with bows. She lived in a kind
> of time warp as far as women were concerned.[81]

There was a desperation in Stead's behaviour—a terrible insecurity about her own appearance which left her with a lifelong need to convince herself she was attractive to men. Her preference for men was so often and so emphatically stated that plainly it had more to do with her self-image than with men. It was more about power (or, rather, powerlessness) than sex—though she always expressed it in blatantly sexual terms. Significantly, the men she loved—with the exception of Harry Bloom—were all passions of the head.

★ ★ ★

These days, Stead was humbly grateful for any attention she received in the literary world. In 1962, the Sydney journal *Southerly* had printed a *Christina Stead Special Issue*, containing a short story of hers,[82] a chapter from the forthcoming novel *I'm Dying Laughing*,[83] and an article about her by R. G. Geering.[84] In his sympathetic appraisal of Stead's work, Geering concluded by asking (as Hardwick had done before him) how it was that a writer of such quality could have been so unjustly neglected. Why were her books out of print? Why had Stead never been published in her own country? Why had there never been a thorough analysis of her work?

A surprise that had arrived in the mail early in 1963 was a stage version of *The Man Who Loved Children* written by Eldon Branda, from the University of Texas. Stead approached the manuscript with trepidation. She had disliked the liberties taken by Ring Lardner Jnr in his screenplay. (In true Hollywood style, he had insisted on giving Sam Pollit his come-uppance at the end.) But she thought Branda's play 'charming, sensitive and absolutely authentic'. She read it straight through, and 'not without tears'.[85] But nothing would come of the play that had taken Branda four years.

By the end of 1963, Stanley Burnshaw had finally persuaded Holt, Rinehart & Winston to re-issue *The Man Who Loved Children*. It was to be in hard cover instead of the paperback Burnshaw had envisaged, and he was embarrassed that Stead's advance was a token $250, but he was determined to make this as successful an exhumation of a buried author as possible. He had arranged for the distinguished poet and literary critic Randall Jarrell to write an introduction.[86] The re-issue was due to appear early in 1965.

In England, no publisher was prepared to re-issue the book. Peter Davies, Stead's sole champion in the British publishing world, had committed suicide four years before. His brother Nicholas Davies would have liked to publish the novel again, but Peter Davies Ltd had been amalgamated with Heinemann for several years, and his Heinemann colleagues did not think it worthwhile.

Secker & Warburg considered it. Writer and critic James Burns Singer was given it to read, and he wrote to Fred Warburg, 'she could easily have the kind of success which Lawrence has had . . .

I think her a much better and more central writer than Lawrence'.[87] But Fred Warburg agreed to the British re-issue only after the book did so well in the States.

Publishers on both sides of the Atlantic believed that a serious attempt to launch Stead again would require a new book as well. Fortunately, Stead had two manuscripts almost ready for publication, *Cotters' England* and *The Puzzleheaded Girl*. In each case, Secker & Warburg in London would lag a year behind Holt, Rinehart & Winston in the US.

Before 1965 none of Christina Stead's books had been published in Australia. By then, the English editions were out of print and almost impossible to obtain. *A Little Tea, A Little Chat* and *The People with the Dogs* had been published in America alone, and virtually no-one in Australia had ever read them. Eventually, Ron Geering persuaded Beatrice Davis, at Angus & Robertson, to re-issue the two 'Australian' novels, *Seven Poor Men of Sydney* and *For Love Alone*. These were to appear in 1965 and 1966 respectively. In 1966, Geoffrey Dutton, at Melbourne's paperback publishers, Sun Books, would bring out *The Salzburg Tales*. All these publications involved a long correspondence between the Blakes, the publishers and Stead's two new agents—Cyrilly Abels in New York, and Laurence Pollinger in London.

★   ★   ★

'It is a small edition,' Blake told a friend at the end of 1964, referring to the forthcoming re-issue of *The Man Who Loved Children*, 'but one hopes a harbinger of better things'.[88] After fourteen long years of publishing drought, Stead too was optimistic:

I should like to clear the decks a bit in 1965, because I have
a feeling, though nothing to back it up, that I will get into a
more creative frame of mind.[89]

The galleys of Randall Jarrell's Introduction, entitled 'An Unread Book' (it would also appear in the *Atlantic Monthly*), arrived at the end of 1964, a few weeks before the book was due out. Several days passed before Stead sat down to read it. She dreaded the feeling of 'quiet nausea' which nearly always overcame her when she read criticism of her books. But she was overwhelmed by Jarrell's 'wonderful sympathy' and 'profound understanding'. So moved was Stead that she could hardly read it to Bill. When she read him Jarrell's description of Henny, she broke down and sobbed. At other points they laughed together.

With Jarrell, Stead had found her 'perfect reader'. She told people that when she read his Introduction the same delightfully warm feeling would creep over her that she had when she felt loved.[90] When she read it a third time, slowly this time, to savour it, she wept and wept, 'a regular fountain'.[91] She found it difficult to write to Jarrell about it. Four months later she managed to thank him:

I wrote to Stanley that I felt as if I had received the one letter of a lifetime; there was a letter one was going to get and I had got it . . . It is quite the loveliest thing that ever happened to me in "my literary life." That is only an expression. I do not have a literary life different from any other life. I have not really become very integrated and am still easily gulled, have to clamp down on the fever fits, etc. I feel as if I did not learn very much. Does one?[92]

In February, several copies of the book arrived in a large airmail parcel from the States. It was a handsome edition. The jacket was illustrated by Milton Glaser, the most fashionable book designer around, and on the back were tributes from Hortense Calisher, Robert Lowell, Elizabeth Hardwick, Jean Stafford and Peter Taylor. Stead told Burnshaw gratefully: 'It is a miracle to have a book reprinted after 25 years.'[93]

Randall Jarrell made Stead able to read again a book she had not opened for twenty-five years. For the first time she could see it 'not as a miserable story, but as it looked to a sympathetic outsider'. Several months later, she wrote to him a second time:

Thank you for recreating that book for me and making me able to read it with some creative feeling. The worst thing about books for the author is that once done, he can't bear to look at them again, not only for their errors, the incredible oversights and indiscipline; but also that they are no longer creative, they are now dead.[94]

Jarrell had written:

Where *The Man Who Loved Children* is concerned, I can't help myself; it seems to me as plainly good as *War and Peace* and *Crime and Punishment* and *Remembrance of Things Past* are plainly great.

There was only one statement in Jarrell's Introduction with which Stead disagreed. He considered *The Man Who Loved Children* to be her last great book, and he attributed this to the lack of critical response.

When the world rejects, and then forgets, a writer's most profound and imaginative book, he may unconsciously work in a more limited way in the books that follow it; this has happened, I believe, to Christina Stead. The world's incomprehension has robbed it, for twenty-five years, of *The Man Who Loved Children*; has robbed it, forever, of what could have come after *The Man Who Loved Children*.

Stead protested, but only halfheartedly.

I do not think the absence of appreciation of *TMWLC* stopped me writing. I have grit. But you may be right after all.

Perhaps you are. You are on the outside and see.[95]

Jarrell could not have known that Stead had hurried *For Love Alone* because she was in a panic about money. Nor could he have known that for years she had put off revising *I'm Dying Laughing* because she and Blake were in desperate need of money and she knew it would not sell well. She *had* written other significant books. But she liked to write in the sweep of a powerful emotional current; it was not emotion recollected in tranquillity. And this gave her writing a raw, unpolished quality.

She had continued to write vigorously for some fifteen years after *The Man Who Loved Children*—until the mid Fifties. Then, it is true, she had lost her impetus. Perhaps Jarrell was right that Stead would have written better had she had the praise due to her. She always reacted to praise like a schoolgirl, with the determination to do better still. Her emotional response to Jarrell's Introduction shows how parched she was for empathetic appreciation.

* * *

In April 1965, while the New York literati were all discussing the Stead novel Randall Jarrell had championed, Jarrell was in hospital, having slashed his wrists. It was there that he received Stead's first letter, thanking him profusely.

Six months later, on a mid October night, Jarrell was struck by a car in North Carolina and killed. It was the tragic end, at 51, of a 'noble, difficult and beautiful soul', as Robert Lowell described his friend.[96]

Jarrell's death made Stead feel sad and guilty. She believed they could have been friends, at least by correspondence, and she felt sorry that she had never been able to do anything for him.[97] In September 1966, Stead wrote to Jarrell's widow, Mary von Schrader Jarrell:

About that Introduction, allow me to say one word. It is so extraordinarily friendly and close to me that if I ever need encouragement I just look at a little part of it and I feel ready to work again.[98]

* * *

'How does it feel to be famous?' Stanley Burnshaw asked Stead, in March 1965.[99] Harry Bloom wrote: 'You must be walking on air. Floating. Do you talk to people?'[100]

This time round, American reviewers raved about the novel. The *Saturday Review* called it a 'long-neglected masterpiece'.[101] The *New*

York Review of Books termed it 'a marvelous neglected novel'.[102] The *Nation* pronounced it 'a funny, painful, absorbing master-piece'.[103] (The reviewer, Jose Yglesias, conjectured that Stead had been neglected because she was a Marxist. This amused her, though she liked the review.[104]) In a single week in April, the book sold almost 1200 copies.[105] There were several reprintings. In Australia, Patrick White read Christina Stead for the first time, and commented:

> In *The Man Who Loved Children* Christina Stead has written a book as chock-a-block and as recognisable as private memory. The humiliating part of the whole business is that most of us overlooked her genius till Randall Jarrell fought the battle for it.[106]

★   ★   ★

'I am NOT walking on air,' Stead told Harry Bloom indignantly. 'You say that to me?—and you know me?' She added:

> I do not give a 2d. darn about what hired hacks say about me. My business is a certain kind of work; and I am *very glad* to be doing it. And I am very glad to have someone to love; indeed for me (I am quite crazy), that comes first. By someone I mean "some ones".[107]

Despite Stead's show of indifference, it is significant that it was the burst of recognition and the pressing requests of publishers for more work, rather than Philip Harvey's pep pills, which revived her spirits and made her eager to write again. She still lacked physical energy, and would complain that she was easily exhausted (especially if she had to entertain people or go into the city on some errand), but she had a new lease on life. For the first time, she felt the impulse to polish all her unfinished manuscripts. 'Now I am being pursued by myself,' she told Burnshaw.[108]

★   ★   ★

Early in 1965, *The Puzzleheaded Girl* was at Holt's. Burnshaw thought it a 'stunning collection'.[109] At Secker & Warburg in London, Oliver Stallybrass pointed out to his colleagues that Stead was an intransigent writer:

> It is important if we are going to take on this very strange author, that we all realise just how strange, and commercially difficult, she is likely, on the strength of this collection, to be. Christina Stead is a writer who makes absolutely no concessions to the reader.

He concluded his report:

> A vision of hell, in fact, but what a vision! For all its faults, this is the sort of writing one broods on, returns to, and finds hidden depths in. For there is subtlety as well as demonic

strength, though Christina Stead is the last person to draw attention to her own cleverness. As an explorer of certain dark areas of the soul she is comparable only to Dostoyevsky.[110]

For a brief period, until he left Secker & Warburg early in 1966, Oliver Stallybrass was Stead's editor. They became friends. Early in their professional acquaintance, Stead concluded a letter to him: 'I'll say it plainly: I think your name is the most beautiful in all England. I think about it.'[111] Philip and Leah Harvey recall that they were taken aback the first time they saw Stead with Oliver and his Norwegian wife, Gunnwor. The Stallybrasses were *her* friends, not Blake's. Instead of being in the background, as she was in *their* group of friends, she was talking and joking with an animation the Harveys had never seen before.[112]

It was Oliver Stallybrass who had to argue with Holt, Rinehart & Winston about the title *Cotters' England*. Stead liked it, and Fred Warburg thought it 'a good strong oak-like title'.[113] But the Americans objected that it sounded like a novel about the seventeenth-century wool industry in England. Exasperated, Stallybrass wrote back:

> I immediately recall such titles as Kafka's *America*, Dos Passos's *U.S.A.*, Dreiser's *An American Tragedy*, Graham Greene's *The Quiet American* and Linklater's *Don Juan in America*, all of which have triumphantly survived these titles on this side of the Atlantic. Are Americans really so anglophobe?[114]

The Americans stood their ground, coming up with titles including *Things That Will Never Come To Light Now*. Stallybrass thought this 'a heavy handicap for any book to bear',[115] and suggested alternatives. The Americans then suggested *Dance in a Hall of Mirrors*. Fred Warburg insisted this was 'meaningless'.[116] In the end, the novel carried a different title each side of the Atlantic, and Stead never liked the American one, *Dark Places of the Heart*.

The title was not the only problem Burnshaw had with *Cotters' England*. He wanted Stead to condense Nellie Cotter's talk. Nellie was worse than Sam Pollit, he told her. Stead compromised on some of his minor criticisms, but on this last point she dug her heels in:

> About Nellie's talking. Stanley you may not like it . . . but I am going to leave it almost entire. Cyrilly [Abels] told me she read *every word* of it twice and enjoyed it. Mr. Woodburn [Harcourt, Brace] could not stand "Auntie Bea" in *For Love Alone* and wanted me to cut it out: others could not get enough of it: "I wish you had put in more Auntie Bea." So I must choose for myself, mustn't I?[117]

For the first time Stead gave her novel a dedication: 'To my friends Anne and Harry Bloom.' She really meant Harry Bloom, of course. She was delighted when she heard he responded 'with wild joy'.[118]

★   ★   ★

Meanwhile, Blake was having no success whatsoever with publishers. He was delighted that Stead had at last been recognised as one of the twentieth century's major writers, but he himself had been doggedly working for years entirely in vain. His last publication, *We are the Makers of Dreams* (written in 1942), had been in 1959. He would never have another publication.

Yet he never stopped working. In 1965, he took time off his French Revolution novel to produce another college students' guide to Marxism, which his friends Leo Huberman and Paul Sweezy, editors of Monthly Review Press, had asked him to write. He worked hard on the project, which strained his eyesight, and when he finished, he thought it 'a damned good book'. However, after some prevarication, Monthly Review Press rejected it as 'too deep' for American students.[119] Stead told Aida Kotlarsky that Bill was 'dreadfully upset'.[120] It was worse than the usual rejection because Monthly Review Press was a last bastion of Blake's kind of accessible, non-academic Marxism.[121]

By 1965, at the age of 71, his health was flagging. He had always prided himself on being able to walk for miles and work late into the night without noticing it. Now he was distressed by his declining energy. With the aid of a strong light and magnifying glass, he still spent most of the day reading and writing, but he had become more dependent, and Stead was not patient. Now that she was motivated to work on her old manuscripts, she resented demands on her time. In April Blake had influenza and became so despondent that Stead felt quite 'harassed', as she told Burnshaw afterwards.[122]

> I had rather a bad time with Bill—had a touch of 'flu and it
> looked to me like a touch of something like hypochondria
> which as you know is a disease: I don't want him to get it.[123]

She could not bear it when Blake was not cheerful: he had always been the one to rally her when she was depressed. She was terrified of losing him. When Max Kotlarsky died, she told Aida, 'I am afraid to think what it is to lose a life companion'.[124] Christina's insistence that Bill's problems were psychosomatic made her a harsh and patronising nurse, and her unsympathetic attitude shocked her friends on occasion. Tella and Boy Friedmann recall a dinner just before they left England to live in Italy, in 1967. Blake, by this time, was seriously ill with stomach cancer, though no-one knew it. In the middle of the meal, he abruptly got up and went out. Stead made no move to follow him. The Friedmanns wanted to go after him, but Stead held them back, explaining that he felt nauseated and that it was psychological: he was jealous of her literary success and not finding it easy to adjust. 'This was the only time she appeared to us unfeeling about Bill,' says Tella Friedmann, but they saw the Blakes seldom these days. [125]

Ruth Hall, who does not conceal her hostility towards Christina Stead, believes success *did* turn Stead's head. In 1965 she became the 'great writer', and felt that from now on, nothing should stand in the way of her writing.

Philip Harvey recalls Blake and Stead quarrelling late one evening, when he was taking them home after dinner at his house. Christina flung at Bill that he had hindered her as a writer; Bill sat on the edge of his seat, his hands gripping the leather tightly, and said nothing. Harvey also recalls another occasion when Bill kept saying to Christina, apparently trying to justify himself: 'It was all for you, Chris, you know. I did it all for you.' [126] There seems little doubt that Stead had begun to blame Bill for their problems. Their wandering life in Europe now seemed a terrible waste. Perhaps, in bitter moments, she also blamed him for the grim poverty of their last twenty years.

In early May 1965, Harry and Anne Bloom visited London again from Puerto Rico. A photograph from this visit, presumably taken by Stead, shows Bloom and Blake standing under the imposing head of Karl Marx at his tomb in Highgate Cemetery. Blake, grey and fragile, looks stiff and sad; Harry Bloom is tall, loose-bodied and strong-looking.

Christina Stead had allowed herself to become painfully distracted by her completely unrealistic infatuation for Philip Harvey. Because she no longer had a confidante, her fantasies tumbled around crazily in her own head. She did not dare to tell Philip Harvey her feelings about him. And she could not talk to Bill about it. They no longer shared their intimate thoughts. So it was a relief to be able to tell Harry Bloom. At the same time, it enabled her to show Harry that he was not the only love in her life. When it came to promoting jealousy, Stead was an able strategist.

Later, she would describe that period to Leda and Stanley Burnshaw:

> I had AN AWFUL time. Comes along my big brudder Harry
> Bloom (who fights people for me) and I felt better ... Alas,
> his years and terribly hard work are telling and he has *angina*

pectoris. It is strange to see a big tall strong man, a fighter—
he was a terror with his fists, a union organiser in NY and I
can't say blacker than that!—and also an artist, a humane,
reasonable and intensely keen man—to see such a man getting
older, beginning to crumple. It makes me feel so bad ...[127]

Three weeks later, a second letter to the Burnshaws reveals the
same proclivity for mythologising.

I had a big skyride with my mad passion, Mr. X. [Philip
Harvey], all in the air, too—I was so entangled I sent for (well,
all but) my old friend and cobber (Australian for the closest and
best friend) Harry Bloom. He came from P.R. I am still
humble, I can tell you, at this devotion: I really am. I am
thinking over human life and love. I couldn't tell him all; it hurt
him too much; but the fact that he was there, enabled me to see
things in a normal way. It was very necessary, I assure you.[128]

★   ★   ★

The Halls had recently moved to the South London suburb of
Surbiton. They now had a third son, Simon, who was the image of
Bill: small and rotund, with dark, animated eyes. Bill missed the
contact with Ruth and his grandsons, and he and Christina decided
to move to Surbiton themselves. Ruth found them a flat at No. 12A
Elmers Court, Avenue Elmers, and Laurie Hall covered over the
grime on the kitchen walls with a fresh coat of paint.

They moved at the beginning of June 1965. The flat was in a
dilapidated tenement building, a fifteen-minute walk from the Halls
and just sixteen minutes from Waterloo by express train. It was
smaller, much less pleasant and more expensive than the Hawley
flat and up three flights of stairs, but after seven years in the remote
countryside and London's suburban outskirts, they were relieved to
be closer to libraries and friends.

June was taken up with settling in. Perhaps it was this drudgery,
so soon after the excitement of Harry Bloom's lightning visit, that
prompted Stead to remark to an Australian journalist that when she
was writing she sometimes wished she were not married. ('Only then,
mind you.')[129] These days she was impatient with her married life.

Throughout July, Blake was obliged to do everything in the
house. Stead had slipped, breaking a bone in her foot. Told not to
put any weight on it for a fortnight, she walked with crutches, and
after this had her foot in a reinforced cast for several more weeks. It
did not improve the state of her nerves. She admitted to Burnshaw
that she was 'mad as a hornet all day long with being thwarted' and
kept blowing up 'like a volcano'.[130]

Bill wanted them to take a holiday. They had some money now—though they cautiously regarded the recent windfall as no more than a lucky break. The hardcover re-issue of *The Man Who Loved Children* sold 20 000 copies, and an editor who was then at Holt estimates that Stead would have made about $25–30 000 from it—enough to live modestly on for two years.[131] Holt also paid her $19 000 as an advance for *Cotters' England* and *The Puzzleheaded Girl*, which seemed to Stead a phenomenal sum. (In England, Secker & Warburg's advance for the same two books was £1000.) Cyrilly Abels, Stead's New York agent, sold 'The Puzzleheaded Girl', the title story in the collection, to the *Kenyon Review*[132] and 'The Dianas' to the *Saturday Evening Post*.[133] This last seemed a coup, for the magazine paid extremely well, but they chopped the story around without Stead's consent—to her fury. 'The arrogance of money,' she fumed.[134]

When Harry Bloom received a copy of the *Kenyon Review*, he wrote affectionately to Bill:

Good title. As soon as I finish this I'll dive into it to see what the Witch has brewd up now. I'm sure it must be a whopper. Tell me Bill . . . is there any real tranquility around that domicile? I mean isnt there always something stiring in that noodle of hers like a cauldron of all kinds of herbs, bones, captured gestures, words that flew out of open mouths . . . But take special care as you probably know when that left eyebrow goes up at a 90 degree angle . . . then its really time to put on the lead shielded armour.' [sic][135]

Stead finally agreed to a fortnight's holiday in Yorkshire in September. Blake looked forward to exploring old villages, Norman castles and ruined abbeys. They booked an inexpensive bed-and-breakfast (abstemiousness had become a habit) and travelled north by train. On 27 September, Stead sent Paul Koston a postcard of Richmond Castle. Three days later they were back in London. The cold damp climate of Yorkshire had given Blake such painful lumbago and fibrositis that he was almost crippled, and they had had to come home. Stead had not wanted to be there in the first place.

Stead was stifling in what she described to Burnshaw as the 'ever-tightening airless circle of our lives'.[136] She was trying to persuade Blake to make the trip to Puerto Rico. Harry Bloom wanted them to go for a visit, and it was warm there. For once, it was Bill who was hesitating: Puerto Rico was a long and expensive trip, and he was feeling ill. He suggested the South of France instead, but Stead baulked at this. She confessed to Burnshaw: 'I could not tell him that the idea of a S. of France holiday à deux, more little cafés, little hotels, cosy walks, talks would SUFFOCATE me.'[137]

She was making it more and more plain to a number of their friends—and doubtless to Bill as well—that his company no longer excited her. To Harry Bloom she lamented:

I am so horribly lonely! My books are coming out all over
the place in reprint and new; and it doesn't mean anything to
me. I mean it. I need "a drinking companion" as you said.
I thought that very cute: since neither of us drinks more
than 2 at a sitting.[138]

In the autumn of 1965 she was still 'ironing out little wrinkles' in *Cotters' England*. It embarrassed her that Nellie Cotter was yet another 'monster'. From now on, she would rather 'praise famous men', she told friends.[139] But the 'greathearted' never made her creative juices flow. Indeed, when Bill went to Paris for a week in November, invited by Alfred Hurst to hear his son George conduct a concert at the Salle Pleyel, Stead was inspired to write one more time about her favourite target.[140] Alf, now in his late seventies, was living in Paris and feeling sorry for himself. Stead told Harry Bloom:

Guess poor old Casanova is no longer up to it. . . . I said to Bill,
Alf ought to come to London to live, gloomy as it is. Paris is
the capital of SEX and it must be pretty depressing for him.[141]

Her story *The Palace with Several Sides*[142] is about a wealthy old man whose speech is recognisably the same as Henri Léon's and Robbie Grant's, but he is mentally distracted and physically weak. His womanising and power-mongering are things of the past.

By October 1965 they had decided to go to Puerto Rico early the following year and see the Blooms. Stanley Burnshaw suggested they go via New York, making it partly a business trip for tax purposes, as well as to meet Holt publishers and Stead's agent, Cyrilly Abels. This seemed a good idea, though Stead felt shy at the thought of the publicity. The English re-issue of *The Man Who Loved Children* was to appear while they were away.

★　　★　　★

They sailed on 27 February 1966, travelling tourist class on the SS *United States*. It was a rough crossing, and they had scarcely recovered when they were plunged into the whirl of New York literary society. 'The first time I ever rated a literary New York life,' Stead told Paul and Pera Koston, evidently rather pleased by it all.[143] They were in New York for twelve days, staying with their friends the Steinbergs, and had 'a very very pleasant time . . . with a very full calendar'.[144] Stead was blooming, rejuvenated by her success.

Holt, Rinehart & Winston threw a party for their brilliant and neglected new protégée. Stead bought a 'beautiful cream ribbon dress and fluffy little jacket' for the occasion. 'I am told I made a very good impression,' she told her brother David's former wife, Percia Stead.[145] Jose Yglesias, a tall and 'most serious man', bent down briefly and asked her: 'Was I right in what I said?' (that she had been neglected because of her Marxian views). She replied: 'Yes, you were right,' and laughed.[146]

Ettore and Jessie Rella organised a cocktail party for Stead in their split-level 14th Street apartment. Ettore, still a devoted puppeteer, manipulated his three-headed puppet, the Three Fates, for Stead, who was so gripped by the performance that she felt 'quite scared'. Robert Lowell was there. On the dust jacket he had praised *The Man Who Loved Children* as 'a classic, a big black diamond of a book',[147] but he had a 'dull effect' on Stead, who conjectured that he was temperamentally unsuited to his position of 'grand man of letters'.[148] The poet and playwright Norman Rosten, a young man when the Blakes first met him in New York political circles in the early Forties, enjoyed a playful conversation with Stead. It was the beginning of a warm, flirtatious friendship.[149] Stead also liked his wife, Hedda.

Another party was at the home of Philip Van Doren Stern, the man whose fantastic dreams had so beguiled Stead in her New York days. Hortense Calisher, who had met Stead briefly in London in the Fifties, would later recall that wintery Sunday afternoon in March 1966. As an outsider to the group, Calisher's observations are all the more interesting:

> It was a "brownstone" party, recognizably of an era ... Stead, handsome in a long dress and taller than I remembered, was the happy center of her old crowd. The crowd itself, older now, and roughly treated by history, might look frowsty to younger eyes, and unduly acerb—a bohemia that knew itself for a backwater now. Maybe all bohemias ended like this— slapping each other's backs and spirits on a jaunty Sunday afternoon? Or was this crowd, in its mix of inherited money, applied radicalism, and determinedly international know-how, slightly adolescent even in age?
>
> I could picture a younger Stead in their midst, gawky with talent, their red-cheeked colonial. Her face, bent now towards theirs in nostalgic pleasure, seemed the most vigorous, and planed by broader sympathies; she was deservedly their star.[150]

The Blakes left for Puerto Rico on 16 March 1966. This was the first time these seasoned travellers had ever flown in an aeroplane. Blake, who suffered from vertigo, had always been convinced that flying would terrify him, but he was persuaded to try it by the Steinbergs, who accompanied them on the flight, to spend a few days with the Blooms. It was 'fair sailing' all the way, and Stead was absolutely thrilled by the views. Even Blake was 'converted' to flying[151]—though this was to be his only flight.

The Blooms lived on the top floor of a modern penthouse flat in Hato Rey, a suburb of San Juan. The weather was hot, humid and sleepy. It rained and rained. Puerto Rico was having a building boom, and the bulldozers started up at 6 am, even on weekends. Stead slept badly. Blake had no energy, and occasionally 'sprang a bit of appendicitis'.[152] Harry Bloom was preoccupied with his electrical business. In the evenings, his angina left him tired.

Stead, bored, drank a great deal of scotch.[153] In the first few days she occupied spare moments by checking the galleys of *Dark Places of the Heart*, due out in September. When she finished this task, she wrote to Burnshaw (in Florida for the winter): 'Am already showing signs of violence, so must do *something*.'[154] According to Michael Bloom, who heard about the visit later from his parents: 'There was a bit of a set-to in Puerto Rico. Chris told mother she was not the woman she used to be—meaning she'd become conservative.'[155]

The Blooms must have hoped that their guests would be more independent and energetic than they turned out to be. Bill had never been so lacklustre. Public transport was difficult. And the price of everything horrified the Blakes. They tended to rely on Harry and Anne taking them around in their car. Then they were charmed by the pastel-coloured Spanish-style bungalows with their ornate grilles, the banana and coffee plantations, and the bright blue ocean.

What did Stead hope for from the holiday? When she wrote to Judah Waten, the Russian-Australian Jewish writer whom they had met briefly in London the previous year, she did not conceal her disappointment. Waten was writing an article for the Melbourne *Age* on Australian writers living in London and had written to Stead asking for a photograph.[156] Her flurried reply, written amid the suitcases shortly before they left, is one of the few letters she wrote from Puerto Rico.

> We were nearly seven weeks here, a very long time and nothing worked out as I imagined it. This is, for one thing, a car town, like Los Angeles, vast empty sandy lots between supermarkets, and foot pilgrims unknown. WE have no car, and our friends, though most kind, have a car that is needed for business . . .
> We have been cut off from everything and have not seen the island . . . We're in the rainy season. Much rain.[157]

The days before their departure brought the sort of drama Stead seemed to have been wanting. She and Harry Bloom spent some passionate time alone together. They may have made love. By the time she stepped aboard the *Flandres*, a French liner destined for Le Havre, Christina was in quite a state. Eighteen months later, she gave an oblique account of her departure to the Burnshaws:

> My *Orlando Furioso* in P.R. who has been so close to me for over 30 years, suddenly got into a passion and said he would kill me if I left him and he would do such and such and I would never get on the boat. Ungrateful for this, I made up my mind to get on the boat, even with four broken limbs (which he promised—you think it's a joke? No.). But he did manage to stab me to the heart the morning I left and I did not get over it for many months.[158]

She added, in the margin: 'Don't refer to this when writing back. Of course, Bill, my true companion, knows something, but I managed to make it fairly light-hearted.'

It was early May 1966 when they reached Paris. They spent three weeks there, cold and bored, so that Stead could see their dentist, Fred Loeffler. They had to be patient as dental sessions were interrupted by holidays and a general strike.

After the large glass windows and oceanic views at San Juan, they had been dreading the 'dark, pinched little flat' in Surbiton.[159] But it was a 'splendid summer afternoon' when they arrived in London. The trees were flowering, and Ruth Hall had filled their refrigerator with supplies. They were strangely relieved to be home.[160]

*　　*　　*

Blake was not at all well, and Stead was miserably unhappy. Her only chance, she thought, was to try to write herself out of her gloom, and she returned to the big project that had been hanging over her for sixteen years, *I'm Dying Laughing*, based on the turbulent lives of Ruth McKenney and Richard Bransten. A year later, she told the Burnshaws that the circumstances had been 'something like those that made me write *TMWLC* in a very bleak period . . . I hauled myself out of that Slough of Despond with my hand round my own neck'. Her fame did not help: she felt there was nothing in her life. Harry Bloom was the other side of the Atlantic with his wife Anne. Philip Harvey, in London, was equally inaccessible. For months she mooned about Harry Bloom. Eventually, after 'a lot of stiffneckedness and courage and whatnot', she told herself: 'I am never going to get over this!' and she began to improve. She told the Burnshaws: 'I'm much better now, though I won't get over it! I guess there's no age at which all passion is spent, after all.'[161] She was 65.

Without sexual passion, Stead had no passion for life or writing. Nevertheless, she was eager to deliver *I'm Dying Laughing*, and she put in one final intense burst. 'This is a book full of anguish,' she told Percia Stead. 'It takes a lot of work. I know exactly what to say; in this case, it is cutting down the excitement and drama and conflict.'[162] In the evenings she read it to Bill, who thought it magnificent.

By the beginning of November 1966, Stead had the revised manuscript ready to send to Stanley Burnshaw. Ruth McKenney was still alive, and Stead may have been worried about libel. She wanted Burnshaw to read it before she officially submitted it to Holt. 'You are the only person I know who knows part of the story,' she told him.[163]

> I should be very glad to have your views if you will be so good
> as to spend time on it. It is in two sections—a rather long book;
> but I don't doubt I will cut some. I just wanted to go ahead to
> get the fling. At any rate, say what you like and I *do* mean it this
> time. I am very serious about getting this book right.[164]

She knew that a book about communists during the McCarthy period would not be seen as 'timely', but she told Burnshaw: 'No matter—it is there. And I felt I had to write "the truth"—and this is it, expressed in my own way.'

Burnshaw was awe-struck by the way Stead had captured Ruth McKenney and Richard Bransten; the characters' voices were 'uncannily real'.[165] But he thought she should change some of the details for fear of prosecution for libel. Did Stephen Howard have to commit suicide just like Bransten? Could she not invent an illness for him? Burnshaw, though he was very impressed with the novel, again recommended considerable pruning. He also wanted Stead to build in more information about the political atmosphere of the late Forties.

> The whole Hollywood situation sounds incredible today, and so
> does all the kowtowing to the party hacks through the forties
> and fifties. The CP and the radical movement are absolutely nil
> here; you wouldn't believe it. And your novel will come upon a
> reading public that regards the American experience with the
> CP and the radical left as nonsensical, idiotic, meaningless.[166]

Stead's agents and publishers all agreed that the novel had great power, but everyone wanted changes. Cyrilly Abels, her New York agent, considered that certain details needed elaboration: Emily Wilkes and Stephen Howard's disagreements with the Communist Party were not clear, and she wanted to know more about Emily's past, in order to understand what made Emily the person she became.[167] At Secker & Warburg in London, Maurice Temple

Smith pressed Stead to make substantial cuts and re-think the first half of the novel.[168] Stead agreed to revise, but the barrage of advice quite paralysed her.

Nevertheless, it was understood that the novel was almost ready for publication. By mid 1967 Stead's American and English publishers were discussing the possibility of a co-production. Yet the novel was not published for almost twenty years—not until after Christina Stead's death.

I'm Dying Laughing clearly presented libel problems and Holt could not have published it as it was. Emily Wilkes was instantly recognisable to those who knew McKenney. But Stead could have changed personal details easily enough (though she would have hated the idea). It was the request for more political detail that bogged her down: building in explanations went against her grain. The 'fling' of writing the first draft was behind her, and she was not at all convinced by the revisions requested. Over the next few months she wrote three totally different bridging chapters ('to bring back the past to those who have forgotten') and did not like any of them. *I'm Dying Laughing* would become her worst albatross ever.

* * *

Dark Places of the Heart was published in New York in September 1966. The reviews tended to be halfhearted, and sales would not have been lifted by Joseph Mathewson's damning review in the *New York Times Book Review*: 'The reader is Nellie's victim ... a blurry-eyed victim, with hands too weak to support ... so leaden a volume.'[169]

But Stead had conquered the literary establishment, and an Australian academic, Ron Geering, was writing the first analytical study of her work. On study-leave in London in 1966, he made several visits to Surbiton to talk with her. He was depressed by the dismal flat, and though he found Blake charming and animated, he was frustrated that Blake dominated the conversation, making it difficult for him to ask Stead questions about her work.

In later years, Geering and Stead would become firm friends. Eventually, he was to be her literary executor.

* * *

Mike Gold's death in May 1967 brought back nostalgic memories of the passionate political camaraderie during the New York years. When Stead read the news in the communist *Morning Star*, she was surprised by the force of the blow. She wrote to Elisabeth, his widow, and the letter was published in the American *Daily Worker*, alongside a tribute from another oldtimer, John Howard Lawson.

My dear Elisabeth,

. . . It is dreadful to think that you will feel this total loss for so many years. The only consolation possible is that you know Mike was so loved, so justly famous, was truly a great man and this great man, so loved, so well known, was your husband and life companion.

. . . I am sure we can all still and will always, too, hear his warm genial voice, hesitating, drawling, goodnaturedly laughing, explaining, excusing, telling his knowledge of humanity, as he remarked on actions of friends and enemies. I learned a lot from him in this way, though never able to be as goodhearted and accept all he accepted from people; but then he loved them more.

He did not excuse treason but he knew its origins; he knew when to be angry in the right way—and what a man he was! Such a natural, straightforward, keenwitted man; and over everything, when he was feeling well and at his best, he shed this glow. He had genius. There was no one like him in the movement.[170]

It was through Mike Gold that Stead had first met Harry Bloom, one of the men who still 'hexed' her thirty years later.[171] The other was Philip Harvey. In the spring of 1967, Harvey went to North Vietnam as a medical witness with the International Association of Democratic Lawyers and was shocked by what he saw. On his return, he appeared on television and in the newspapers decrying America's use of chemical and bacteriological warfare. In his spare time, he turned his energies to raising money for medical supplies for the North Vietnamese, which involved lectures all over the country. In Stead's eyes, Philip Harvey was more of a hero than ever.

* * *

Bill Blake had done vast quantities of work on his French Revolution novel, but his eyesight made progress depressingly slow. And now he was having trouble swallowing food. Thinking that a change might help to restore his spirits, he tried to persuade Christina to take a holiday with him. She told him she could not face the packing. She suggested that he go and stay with Alf Hurst in Paris, but he refused to go without her. Eventually, in September 1967, she agreed to go away for a week to the Midlands. They caught trains and buses to Leamington Spa, Warwick, Coventry and Stratford-upon-Avon and visited old castles and cathedrals.

Back in London, Bill's discomfort in swallowing became acute, and he began to panic. Christina did her best to make special mashed dishes or broth, and he would eat a few spoonfuls, and say, 'It's very nice, but that's all I can take now'. Stead, describing herself to friends as 'half-wild with the work and anxiety',[172] persisted in believing that the problem was psychological. She observed with impatience that Bill was behaving exactly like his mother in the years before she died, when Rosa had been falsely convinced she had tuberculosis. Friends were told that his illness was 'a rejection of age',[173] and 'a form of depression'.[174] She told Paul Koston:

> I think part of it is that, with his very bad eyesight and the difficulty in getting things written, he feels ill at ease; and this translates itself, with him, into this slight (it's really very slight) eating difficulty. . . . I think that when we get his novel typed and sent off, he will feel a lot better in spirits.[175]

Because she regarded Blake's problem as 'a refusal to eat' and a form of 'hypochondria', Stead acted like a harried mother with a recalcitrant child of 73. A constant refrain in her letters was her lack of time: Bill's perversity made it impossible for her to get on with her writing. 'It has been very difficult even for me, trying a hundred preparations, most of which are refused.'[176] She told Aida Kotlarsky: 'Bill knows he is taking all my time and energy, he regrets it, constantly mentions it—but his own need is greater than his conscience; so it is with sick people.' She added: 'Bill wants to believe there is something serious that is taking his appetite . . . No one wants to think he is a hypochondriac.'[177]

* * *

Life is certainly a lottery. The $10 000 Britannica Australia Award for Literature was Australia's most generous literary prize.[178] Sponsored by the Encyclopaedia Britannica company since 1964, the award was presented annually for the most outstanding contribution to Australian literature. Winners had been Judith Wright in 1964, R. D. FitzGerald and A. D. Hope in 1965, and Hal Porter and Randolph Stow in 1966 (after Patrick White had turned it down[179]). The Britannica constitution stated:

> The Award in each nominated field is intended to be for a contribution of outstanding merit in the field in question involving an original contribution or development and having a direct connection with or benefit for Australia or some aspect of Australian life. The Award shall be open to any Australian National, irrespective of his place of residence during the year of the Award or during the period in which the contribution for which the Award is recommended was made.[180]

A six-person Literary Committee[181] chaired by Clement Semmler, Deputy General Manager of the Australian Broadcasting Commission and a well-known literary critic, had met in May 1967 and Stead's name had been mentioned in relation to *Cotters' England*, published that year. In September, the committee's unanimous vote was for Christina Stead, 'the outstanding Australian novelist of this day'.[182]

Following the decision of the Literary Committee, the General Council for the Britannica Australia Awards met on 27 October. Its Chairman, Sir Leonard Huxley, was a physicist, newly retired as Vice-Chancellor of the Australian National University. The Deputy Chairman was Sir Macfarlane Burnet, the prominent immunologist. With the agreement of the four other members present, they overturned the Literary Committee's decision to award the prize to Christina Stead. The relevant minutes read:

> Sir Leonard . . . said that this was the first time a nomination had been made which was not within the requirements laid down in the Awards Constitution. The Chairman of the Literary Committee, Mr C. Semmler, had proposed for the literature award a person who had not lived in Australia for forty years and whose Australian citizenship was in doubt. On available information it was also doubtful whether the proposed candidate's contribution to literature was of sufficient and specific relation to Australia to satisfy the importance attached to this qualification in the Awards Constitution.[183]

The meeting agreed that the Literature Award for that year should be withheld.

Clement Semmler was abroad in October. When he heard about the decision on his return, he was shocked, but did not formally protest, and his letter to the General Manager of Encyclopaedia Britannica was weakly acquiescent:

> While I would argue against the decision (since Christina Stead is accepted internationally as an Australian author and is still regarded as such by the Australian literary community—and this latter proposition was that which particularly prompted our recommendation), I nevertheless, now that the decision has been made, unequivocally accept it as a decision of Council of which I am a member.[184]

Two Melbourne members of the Literary Committee, Professor Sam Goldberg and the poet Vincent Buckley, did make a public protest.

> We feel sure that this decision was not made by the management of Encyclopaedia Britannica itself, who have shown the keenest interest in encouraging literature as well as the other fields covered by the awards. It seems to have been made by men whose competence in literature is very doubtful

indeed and who do not seem to know the normally accepted conventions affecting a writer's relationship to his homeland.[185] Barbara Jefferis, from the Australian Society of Authors, told the *Australian* with mild irony: 'It seems sad that Christina Stead should be rejected in Australia as a non-Australian when the rest of the world regards her as one of the shining lights of our literature.'[186]

The most outspoken critic of the decision was Patrick White. He had suffered as much as Stead from his compatriots' obsession with 'Australianness', and now he wrote an enraged, mocking letter to the *Sydney Morning Herald*:

Sir,

If the Higher Junta of Australian Intellect considers a novelist of genius like Christina Stead ineligible for its much-juggled American award, it helps explain to me why, for some time past, I have felt a foreigner in this pathetically chauvinistic parish.

And what about Sidney Nolan? Ineligible too, because he doesn't squat around the pump along with the other blokes?

Patrick White.

Centennial Park.[187]

(Sidney Nolan, the eminent Australian painter, was frequently abused for spending most of his time in London and New York.[188])

Early in December, Kate Stead heard that the Literary Committee had recommended Christina Stead. She immediately wrote to her sister congratulating her. The letter, which arrived on 12 December, was the first Christina Stead heard of the whole affair. She imagined that Kate was referring to the small bursary of £1200 she had just received from the Arts Council of Great Britain.

'How very astonishing that you should know about that grant on Friday last!' Stead wrote back, perplexed. The Arts Council grant was hardly the stuff of international news. She herself had not seen anything about it in the British press.[189]

The mystery was unravelled later that same day, when two Australian journalists rang Stead in Surbiton. The next day, she told Harry Bloom about the Britannica prize, adding that the reason for the change of mind was probably some 'inner shenanigans' of which she was 'happily unaware'.

$10,000 Ausn. is not a small sum—hard luck! But I really don't give a hoot. (Hoot, hoot.) I am not working well, because we don't hear from you and I don't know how you are.[190]

Stead would always be impatient with the notion of 'cultural cringe', but this was an unmistakable instance. Strident nationalism and a reactive defensiveness towards Australia were obverse manifestations of the same phenomenon. There was a long tradition of resentment in Australia about its 'overseas talent drain'.[191] As much as possible, expatriates were punished for living abroad. This made it extraordinarily difficult for Australian expatriate artists to find funding, since America and Britain (which tended to patronise colonials) looked after their own citizens first—though that year the British Arts Council put Australia to shame by awarding a grant to Stead (the equivalent of a good year's salary) as well as to Jean Rhys, born in Dominica.[192]

Had Stead received the Australian prize, it would have been the first time she had in any way been honoured by her own country in thirty-three years as a published writer. Not until 1965 had Angus & Robertson decided to publish two of her books. Even then, the company was only interested in the novels set in Australia.

The new nationalists of the Sixties were no more interested in Christina Stead than the Thirties' nationalists had been. In 1966, Clement Semmler and Derek Whitelock had edited a 200-page book called *Literary Australia*. In the Introduction, Semmler remarked: 'Perhaps in retrospect the 1960s will be remembered as a period of full tide in Australian literature.' The book is full of literary names: Lawson, McCrae, Paterson, Slessor, Henry Handel Richardson, Nettie and Vance Palmer, Patrick White, Judith Wright, Kenneth McKenzie, Douglas Stewart. Christina Stead is not even mentioned in passing. It was as if she had never existed.

Stead would later express impatience with the notion of 'Australianness'. 'Would you call Byron an expatriate writer because he wrote in Italy?' she asked. 'He's English. I am Australian.'[193] She was right. D. H. Lawrence is not left out of the English literary canon because he set novels in Australia and Mexico. Joyce was still Irish, even if he lived in France and Italy.

There was not even consistency in the judges' decisions. The previous year, Randolph Stow had won the Britannica Australia Award, yet he also lived abroad. Presumably, he had redeemed himself by returning to Australia for brief intervals, but Stead could never afford the trip.[194] The following year, 1968, the Britannica Award would go to Douglas Stewart, a New Zealand-born poet. Patrick White would rage that he was 'staggered by the logic of the minds which have made these latest decisions'.[195]

Stead dismissed the whole affair with a shrug. She had other, more serious, concerns on her mind. In retrospect, these concerns make the Council's decision seem even more tragic.

* * *

At the beginning of November 1967, Philip Harvey had Blake in hospital for three days for a series of tests. His stomach cancer was diagnosed. Blake was not told, but Harvey is convinced that he made it clear to Stead at this point that Bill might not have long to live.[196]

In mid November, in a letter typed by Christina, Bill described the tests to Harry Bloom. It was, he said, a 'science fiction run of x-rays'.

I was tilted, spun about, forced to lie recumbent, suddenly jerked up, and felt like a 21st century robot. These technicians found out that my neck-bones, owing to age, impinge on the oesophagus (or gullet), thus making swallowing difficult. There is nothing any doctor can do about this; and so I have to adapt myself and I am doing so. It takes some of the fun out of living; but once you live with it, you forget about it.[197]

A few days after Christmas, in 1967, Philip Harvey rang and asked to speak to Bill. The patient was in bed and told Christina he felt too weak to go to the phone. Harvey was surprised. 'If he's too weak to come to the phone, he ought to be in hospital.' He called for Bill the following morning, 30 December, and took him to St Stephen's Hospital in Chelsea.[198]

Left by herself, Stead collapsed with the 'flu.[199] She was exhausted. 'I have not the strength for this enormous effort of care,' she told Aida Kotlarsky.[200] For four days she was confined to bed, and for another week she scarcely went out. She wrote tender letters to her 'darling boy', in which she told him how much she loved him[201]—something she could only ever do in writing. Bill rang her when he could, and told her he loved her.

On 8 January, Stead wrote to 'darling Aida' that Bill was:
... suffering from a form of depression that shows itself as a rejection of food ... It comes, we all think, from the failure of his eyesight—you know what reading, analysing, always was to him ...

Bill is in hospital with a friendly doctor, a clinician, trying to cope with this. It is much more difficult to cope with than say migraine (which is difficult enough) or stomach disorder, anything "real", as we say. Because it stems from sorrow, sadness. He always wanted to be so active, and he is cut off.[202]

Now that her health was restored, she visited the hospital every day, but begrudged the time and energy these visits took. When Bill underwent an operation, a few weeks later, Christina shocked Ruth Hall terribly by telling her that if Bill survived, she would put him in a home: she could not possibly continue to nurse him. Ruth would never forgive Stead for her attitude in the last weeks of her father's life.[203]

Blake was in St Stephen's Hospital for three weeks. Paul Koston called in every day. Alf Hurst wrote and rang from Paris. Blake, a much-loved man, had no shortage of visitors. His Texan friend, Bill Ash, thought he looked 'terribly wasted' but was impressed that he had not lost his spirit. Blake joked about the humiliation of taking weak tea by the spoonful. They discussed 'the financial crisis of British imperialism and the opportunity this presented for a genuine Marxist-Leninist party to provide revolutionary leadership for the British working class'. Blake also spoke of death, Ash recalls, but 'lightheartedly, as a matter of no concern to a convinced materialist'.[204]

On 19 January 1968, Blake was moved to the care of a specialist surgeon at Westminster Hospital. Stead appeared to believe—as Blake himself did—that he had a severe ulcer. She told her sister Kate that he looked thin and old, but was 'quite cheerful, considering', and that she was hoping surgery would restore him to a normal living.[205] She wrote to Aida that Bill had a stomach ulcer:

It never crossed my mind that Bill, always the good eater,
always the eupeptic, might have a thing like that. He foresaw
it—no one believed him. It seems we do know our own
bodies. (And our nearest and dearest misunderstand us!)[206]

It is possible that Stead could not bear to 'know' what she really knew. She had to steel herself, not allow herself to think about the future, so that she could face Bill in hospital without breaking down. Before Bill was moved to Westminster, Philip Harvey had told her that tests revealed cancer of the upper stomach and lower oesophagus, and that he did not have long to live. Bill himself knew he might die. In the last weeks, he told both Ruth and Christina that he wanted his ashes scattered to the wind—no funeral.

When Christina brought him a book by Che Guevara sent by his friend Leo Huberman and held it close to his eyes for him to see, Bill told her he did not want to look at it just then. 'I've been thinking only about myself,' he told her. 'I haven't thought about anything outside.'[207] This was quite unlike him.

It was Philip Harvey who persuaded Professor Ellis to perform surgery. Ellis was not keen: Blake was very weak and wasted. But Harvey knew it was his only chance. Ellis operated on 26 January, removing part of Blake's stomach. Afterwards, Christina hung over his bed, watching Bill 'reaching out feebly for life, almost like a sea-animal attached to a rock'.[208] It seemed that he would not survive. Christina and Ruth expected to be called at any time during the night.

Five days later, there were flickers of his old spirit, and Stead began to hope again. Bill, once so proud of his powerful voice, asked her in a frail whisper: 'Do you think my voice is getting stronger?'[209]

When Philip Harvey called in that day, fussed over him and gave him a kiss, Bill gave him 'a bit of a grin'—his feverish eyes seemed to be twinkling—and he whispered: 'Hey Philip, we're going to beat this, 'aint we?'[210]

On 1 February 1968, Bill asked for the newspaper. The Vietnam War was at its height and the Viet Cong had just attacked Saigon in the Tet Offensive. That morning, Stead wrote to Burnshaw:

> I do hope that in about three weeks he will be home. I have been told that it will not be for long; but he does not know that and hopes to recover; and as I said, is in good spirits now.[211]

That evening she spoke to Bill for the last time—a visit she would later describe to Burnshaw:

> He was lying down on a couch in the corridor-end they used as a sitting-room (nicely furnished). I hung over him, holding his hand and saying those things I knew to be untrue but that would help, for instance that he would soon come home to me. He looked at me with such a "trusting believing" sweet expression and smile—it was about to be our anniversary and that made it easier for him to believe.[212]

It would be the thirty-ninth anniversary of their life together that year. Bill was 73.

Christina left the hospital when Ruth arrived. Ruth and her father talked briefly about the war in Vietnam. An interpreter friend had just given Ruth a Spanish bible, which she showed Bill. They smiled about Saint John being 'San Juan'. She tucked him in and put drops in his eyes. He told her she did it better than the nurses. He never woke up.

The hospital rang Christina at 5 in the morning, on 2 February 1968. Bill, who had developed a major pulmonary embolism as a result of surgery, was close to the end. Ruth and Laurie rushed over to collect Christina. While Laurie was parking the car below, the two women watched Bill take his last breath.[213] They just had time to kiss him. He was unconscious, but Stead thought it was 'as if he had waited' for them.[214]

14

Hundred Thousand Regrets

FEBRUARY 1968–AUGUST 1974

'BILL'S DEATH WAS just like a heart attack,' Stead would tell friends ten years later. 'Part of me died.'[1] Over the years, she had often dreamt about a little boat that would determinedly travel on, whatever the elements. When Bill became seriously ill, the little boat sailed into her dreams and sank. 'I see now the little boat was Bill,' she wrote to Stanley Burnshaw.

> Did I tell you that after travelling a long way suddenly the little
> boat sank on Thames-side? I called it and called it—all the fleets
> came, liners, warships, but it did not come, Did I tell you that?[2]

Bill was cremated at Golders' Green on the afternoon of 5 February. According to his wishes, there was no funeral service—no-one was present. Christina was glad to be spared 'that quite harrowing theatrical ceremony'.[3] The Harveys thought a funeral might have helped her come to terms with the death. 'People seem to need funerals.'[4]

On the day Bill died, Stead went to stay with the Harveys for a few days, and for the next few weeks she would go there for weekends. Leah Harvey remembers a sad, lonely figure staring out of the windows for hours on end.

In her bewilderment, Stead wrote twice to Aida Kotlarsky announcing Bill's death—on 3 February and again on 5 February.

'I am tempted to say to myself, "He is only away for a long time",'
she told Aida, 'but that is a wrong attitude. I must not do that.'[5] She
kept saying to herself: 'I must get organised and then decide what to
do.'[6] She thought she might not stay in that 'cold country' which
neither she nor Bill had ever liked. But where would she go?[7] She
knew only that she must not think about Bill for the moment. It
hurt too much. She told Stanley Burnshaw:

> He telephoned me every day from the hospital while he could
> and kept saying "I love you so much"; and I ask myself and I
> did ask then, who else ever was so good to me? Or ever will
> be? I didn't deserve it. But then I know that none of us
> deserves the gifts of that sort that are carelessly and without
> any reason thrown at our feet. No more. I am trying to avoid
> this kind of thinking.[8]

When Burnshaw gently admonished her not to block her feelings,
she replied firmly:

> My dear Stanley, the time will come when I can think about
> it: but I know only too well, by instinct, that NOW it would
> be useless, incapacitate me and do no one any good. What
> good are the traditional things "I did not do enough"—
> "if I had known"—you cry and you get no farther.[9]

Kind letters arrived from the family in Australia. Thistle Harris told
her family would like to have her home again. Tella and Boy
Friedmann invited her to stay a while in Tuscany. When Stanley
Burnshaw, in London for a brief visit, suggested she make a trip to
the States to see old friends again, Stead knew that was what she
wanted to do. She could not face the Friedmanns, who would
remind her of Bill and, being a couple, of all she had lost. She was
afraid she would do nothing but weep. More than anything, she
wanted to see Harry Bloom. She thought vaguely that she might
move to the States, but she needed to see Harry first.

By early March she was making travel plans. At least it gave her
something else to think about.

*   *   *

A week after Bill's death, Stead and Ruth Hall quarrelled bitterly.
The issue was Blake's novel about financiers in the French Revolution. Both women were pained, as Blake himself had been, that he
had not been able to bring to fruition the solid work of several
years. In his last weeks, lying in his hospital bed, Bill had wondered
whether Ruth might finish the novel, and he asked her to write a
summary of the events he had described to her over the years. He
seemed pleased with the four pages of notes she produced.[10]

When her father died, Ruth asked Christina for the manuscript. The task was virtually impossible. Blake's typing was full of mistakes, with his sight so poor, and there were hundreds of pages of notes in his almost illegible handwriting. The book was Bill's vision alone; and then there was the problem of continuity of style. Moreover, Ruth, as a part-time interpreter and mother of three, had very little time.

Stead handed her the manuscript on a five-year loan, and as soon as she had done so, worried that she might never see it again. For Bill's sake, she even entertained the idea of trying to finish the novel herself. Ruth resented what she considered Christina's patronising attitude towards her; Christina thought Ruth grasping. Eventually Stanley Burnshaw stepped into the breach. He wrote to Ruth that publishers in the States were interested in the manuscript: would she please lend Christina the manuscript to bring with her to the States? (In the States, Burnshaw would make a copy of it. The era of xeroxes had dawned at last.)

A year later, Christina angered Ruth by writing to ask for a progress report. Ruth complained that Stead was harassing her, and asked for their 'vague' arrangement to be clarified.

Dear Ruth,

Thank you for your letter.

There is nothing vague about Bill's French Revolution MS. and you. I am Bill's executor and gave you this MS. on loan, at your request, a week after Bill's death, to see what you could do with it. At the end of one year (in February this year), I asked you what progress you had made. I have not harassed you in any way. (If you think authors do not get constant queries about the progress of their work, you do not know their life; there is nothing at all humiliating about it.)

At the end of the second year, February 1970, I will find out what progress you have made and if it is not satisfactory, we will have to think what to do.

If within that time, you have finished a MS. acceptable to a publisher and which is in agreement with Bill's ideas (which are known to me), and you have been offered a suitable contract (and you would be wise to employ a good agent), then, if I am satisfied, I will consent to your having complete rights.

You do not know the literary world and do not understand that this is a generous offer. I told you, I think, that I had two offers from two friends of Bill, both established authors, just after his death, offering to work on this same MS. These authors would have naturally made an arrangement with me, financial and otherwise, and giving Bill all credit for the remarkable and dense groundwork done by Bill. All this is not required of you; but you must show that you can do suitable work on the MS.

That is how it stands at present.

Kind regards and I trust you all are well,

Sincerely,

Christina Blake[11]

Relations between the women would remain strained—though both made token efforts at friendship.

* * *

Blake would have been profoundly moved by the effusive two-page obituary devoted to him in the *Monthly Review* of June 1968, written by his Texan friend William (Bill) Ash, a novelist and journalist. In it, Ash paid tribute to Blake's 'lovable and selfless personality', and wrote of 'the delightful privilege of hearing that brilliant conversationalist free-wheeling informatively and wittily over the enormous range of his interests'.

Unlike certain other experts in Marxian economics his interest was never merely academic. He was always a revolutionary. He understood Marxism as the science of changing society radically in order to end the inhumanity of every form of exploitation . . . "Weightier than Mount Tai" is his death, but in cherishing his memory and recalling his contribution his friends at least share the burden—and it is the lighter because there are so many of them.[12]

Reading this, Stead remarked that 'Bill would have cried with delight . . . Tough in his intellectual exercises, he had a soft heart and most wanted to be loved by his friends. As he was.'[13]

Before he died, Blake, who may have foreseen the rivalry between his wife and daughter, asked Bill Ash to be an unofficial literary executor.[14] Over the next few years, Ash, who sincerely loved Blake and greatly admired his work, tried unsuccessfully to interest a number of publishers in Blake's unpublished manuscripts. Finally, Blake's book on imperialism, his novel about Garibaldi's 'Mille', and his unfinished French Revolution novel were all to be relegated to packing boxes to gather dust.[15]

* * *

Soon after Bill's death, Stead received a letter from Florence James. Back in Australia, Florence had heard nothing of Blake's sudden illness and death, but she *had* heard about the Britannica Award fiasco, and told Stead she was pleased that 'Patrick White's scathing comments' had 'put the record straight'.[16] She was now a doting grandmother, she reported.

Margaret Stead, David's daughter, had recently visited the Blakes in London. Stead now wrote to her niece in Sydney, asking *her* to reply to Florence's letter. 'I do not feel I can prick this great healthy jolly bubble of her joy in life by saying Bill is dead,' she told Margaret. 'So would you write for me—or ask someone?'[17]

Florence James had been with Christina when Bill began to court her thirty-nine years earlier. With Florence, Christina had excitedly shared her 'dearest secrets' about her cultured, cosmopolitan boss. Now Christina could not bring herself to write Florence a short note.

As usual, anger served to deflect Stead's anguish about herself. Haunted by her uncharitable behaviour towards Blake in his last few years, she was suffering agonies of self-reproach. 'I have very little to console myself with,' she told Ettore Rella six months after Bill's death. 'We always look back and think, "I should have noticed this and that, I who knew him so well"; and you think, "And so how well did I know him?" '[18] Three years after Bill's death, she wrote to the Burnshaws of the '100,000 regrets' of her 'recent life':

> In fact, everything is a regret, until I say to myself, "But surely I must have done something kind for Bill?" and I try to think of something—but then at once clouds of vicious little black birds with beaks and wings assail me, quite visible to me though not to others—remorse, regret.[19]

In order to bear the pain and remorse, Stead tried not to think about Bill. She believed she was being stoic. In June 1969, she told an interviewer: 'I refused to crack up when Bill died, that would have been mere self-indulgence ... It wouldn't have helped me, and certainly wouldn't have helped him.'[20]

Throughout her life, Stead had only ever been able to express powerful or convoluted emotions through the medium of fiction. Now her tragedy was that not only had she lost Blake, her muse had deserted her too. She had written very little in the last ten years, and she would write almost nothing after Blake's death. She *wanted* to write: indeed, when she was not writing, she did not feel 'moral'. She would not feel quite moral for the last fourteen years of her life. Not a day would pass without her talking about writing and worrying about not writing. But her motivation, drive, willpower were gone. Like many writers abandoned by their muse, she relied heavily on drink to assuage her frustration. But it brought only temporary relief.

Though she tried not to complain, her thoughts from now on

were to be one long lament. She missed Bill, she was lonely, she was frightened to live alone, she was repelled by women living on their own, she wanted to be loved, she wanted a man, she was not working, she felt lazy, she hoped to start writing again soon.

She was 65 when Bill died. Alone, Stead was beset by the same panic she had felt as a young woman; the prejudices of her childhood had not weakened over time. Women on their own were pathetic creatures, devoid of dignity.

While other widows could take comfort from women friends, Stead all too frequently reiterated her negative views about her own sex. To journalists and friends, she would make swaggering comments such as: 'I adore men. While there is a man left on earth, I'll never be a feminist.'[21] Where her friends were couples—the Rellas, the Burnshaws—it was the men she loved, as their wives well knew. She told Ettore Rella she would hate to go on a holiday with a woman. 'Must be something wrong, a hormone deficiency ... I love men.'[22]

She was vehemently opposed to the burgeoning Women's Liberation Movement. In this, however, she was not atypical of many intellectual women of her generation. Mary McCarthy, though ten years younger than Stead, was equally uncomfortable with what she saw as the shrillness of feminists, though she (like Stead) powerfully portrayed in her fiction the secondary condition of women. As a socialist, Stead had to admit that women lacked certain rights, and she was particularly sympathetic to the lonely plight of suburban mothers.[23] But she insisted that the women's movement was 'purely middle class' and a 'waste of time'. Men and women complemented each other, and that was that.

> The worst thing about some of the so-called women's liberationists is their hatred of men, but men and women are made to love each other. It's only by loving each other that they can achieve anything. This separation of women from men is the most disgraceful thing and disorderly thing in the movement, and that's why I'm against it.[25]

Several women friends eventually grew tired of Stead's misogynist ways. After Bill's death, Pera Koston, fed up with seeing Christina openly flirt with her husband, while she herself was ignored, refused to have her in their house again. Anne Bloom put up with Christina's rudeness during the Puerto Rico visit in 1966. But when Stead's novella 'Girl from the Beach' appeared in 1967 (in which Anne Bloom's fictional counterpart is a mindless housewife), Anne wanted nothing more to do with her. No doubt she sensed the affection between Christina and her husband, and probably guessed that Christina would willingly have taken her husband.

★　　★　　★

On 5 February 1968, Stead wrote to Anne and Harry Bloom, who had already heard the sad news from Ruth Hall. Harry Bloom rang Christina from Puerto Rico. A week later, Stead wrote him a letter, evidently passionate, and sent it to his post office box. He replied on 14 February:

> Dear Darling,
>
> I've reread your letter many many times. For now better left unsaid all the things I would want to say. Of course you are constantly in my thoughts.
>
> I know you pretty well. I'm afraid you will do something impulsively now. Please wait a little while. Things have changed for you. Let raw edges heal a bit.
>
> In one of your letters you said that you may come to the States in the spring. Will you be coming? If you do I want to be there when you come. I want to see you so much and its much too long since I've last been with your great tenderness and that great volcano inside of you.[26]

Over the next few years, Stead's days would revolve around the postman's early morning visit and the hope of a letter from Puerto Rico. The 'clandestine correspondence' with her 'lover-brother'[27] made her feel alive. Not that it was so very clandestine. She told Burnshaw:

> He goes to the P.O., memorises my letters and then tears them up leaving them in the trash-basket there. It is all very funny, I laugh at us, he is very funny, and yet such romances are quite romantic, too, if you're thinking of lifetimes.[28]

Bloom's letters brought Stead back from the dead. And she took them much more seriously than she let on to Burnshaw. The trip to the States was principally to see 'dear Harry'. She allowed herself to hope that he would come up with some proposal that would make sense of her life. She hesitated to travel just then: the arrangements tired her. In the past Blake had always dealt with these. There were all sorts of formalities: she needed permission from the Bank of England to take money out of the country, and the American Embassy wanted evidence that she had sufficient capital to cover her stay. It seemed foolish to spend so much just then. But she had to see Harry.

At the end of April, a cryptic letter arrived from Puerto Rico:
Darling Christina,

We will be coming to N.Y. about May 15th.

... I reread your letters about 4 or 5 times. Sort of devour
them and commit them to memory and then destroy them.
All at the Box.

... The doctor gentle soul told me a tale; "beware of the
Wild Cats but a pussy is allright." So bring me kitten like the
one that we had in P.R. or when you were on 14th St. Crazy?

Love, Harry. XX[29]

Aida Kotlarsky had invited Christina to spend the summer in the
Catskills. It had been a firm invitation for two years now, and Bill
had talked of their going there that summer. Kind Aida wrote to
say she had borrowed two typewriters, one electric and one manual,
in preparation for Christina's visit. She even pressed her to move
permanently to the States: she could live half the year at Hunter
free, Aida suggested, and the rest of the year she could live in a
studio in downtown Manhattan. Stead was moved, but reasoned
that the offer was made because Aida was lonely. 'Youngest of a big
family, mostly gone, even her dogs and cats are gone—and a
widow some years since.'[30]

Before she left for the States, Stead wrote a will in which she
made Stanley Burnshaw her literary executor. It was not entirely
sensible, she realised. He was only three years younger than she
was, and she warned him that her family had a proclivity for living
well into their nineties.[31] But she felt she owed him a great deal. She
bequeathed him her published and unpublished works as 'an absolute gift', though she expressed the hope that if the money ever
justified it, Burnshaw would 'set up a fund for money to be given
to writers who need it, whether young or old'.[32]

She put Bill's clothes in mothballs, thinking she would give them
away when she came back. The sad task made her reflect all over
again that she had not given the 'dear boy' enough affection; she
had been 'too unbending'. She felt terribly tired: tired of sadness,
tired of being stoic. 'To be honest with you,' she told Burnshaw in
mid May, 'if the Little Bill came through the door, put out his hand
and said "Come with me", I would gladly go with him to the land
of shades.'

I know I'll keep going, but really my life was for that, wasn't
it? To live with Bill. I didn't know that was it, but it was. I'm
glad to say I told him so just before the end and he liked it.

Must stop: of course, I'm crying my eyes out.[33]

Her days, only rarely lightened by a letter from Puerto Rico, were
lonely, sad, and full of self-reproach.

Paul Koston was a comfort, giving her avuncular advice and inviting her to lunch in the city at least once a week. She looked forward to his company and the good wine which temporarily restored her spirits. And Philip Harvey did his best to help where he could. When he went on holiday in April, she suffered from nervous stomach pains—an old complaint that seemed to occur when she felt she was entirely on her own. She told Burnshaw:

I rang Philip (doctor friend) the other day. He said, "Come over for supper and stay the night" (which I often do) but later I rang again saying I was too tired; and he said, "Are you in a state? Because if so, I'll come over and hold your hand," (meaning have a talk). I said, "I am not in a state and am never in a state." But he said, "You are always in a state, and so you don't know when you're in a state." A highly medical conversation. But oddly enough, I think he is right.[34]

★　　★　　★

She crossed the Atlantic by ship early in June 1968. Harry Bloom did not meet her. Stead stayed alone in the Burnshaws' 11th floor apartment, at No. 32 Washington Square West. Stanley and Leda were at their summer house on Martha's Vineyard, where Christina was to visit them later.

Bloom was stuck in Puerto Rico with bad angina. He wrote to her: 'I think of you in the daytime and dream of you at night.'[35]

New York was steamy, and Washington Square was noisy, full of brightly dressed hippies playing guitars until the early hours of the morning. The newspapers were full of Vietnam and anti-war demonstrations. Earlier that year, there had been riots at Columbia University. In April, Martin Luther King had been assassinated in Memphis. In June, Senator Robert Kennedy had been fatally shot in Los Angeles, after winning the Presidential Democratic primary election in California. It was a different country from the one Stead had known in the Thirties and Forties.

Her letters did not mention political events. She was absorbed by her own problems that year. The days yawned ahead. Stead had brought *I'm Dying Laughing* with her, but she was in no mood for work. Instead, she read her way through Burnshaw's library and saw friends: Ettore and Jessie Rella, Isidor and Polly Steinberg, her agent Cyrilly Abels,[36] her Holt editor Charlotte Mayerson, her writer friend Norman Rosten. But she was terribly restless.

She took the bus to Hunter on 2 July, and told Aida everything. Aida pressed her to invite Harry to Hunter. Stead wrote to his post-office box on 15 July, and Aida, an enthusiastic matchmaker, hatched all sorts of plans for when Harry would come. But there was silence from Puerto Rico. At the beginning of August, Stead wrote a curt four-line letter to his house. (She probably arranged to have it posted in England. Anne Bloom must not know she was in the States.)

At Hunter Stead had a large studio room with a balcony. Red squirrels clambered around on the roof, and tame chipmunks sat on her shoulders. Aida was generous and affectionate ('an unadorned good heart'[37]), and Stead loved to hear her beautiful piano playing. The women went for walks together. Yet Christina was far from calm. She attacked the garden vigorously. And she spent hours each day cooking—so obsessively that she apologised afterwards to Aida, explaining that her 'cooking mania' was probably due to having spent so many hours preparing food for Bill at the end of his life. 'I expect it set up an obsession in me, I am sure it did ... It must have annoyed you. Blessings on you for all your human understanding.'[38]

The days were hot and steamy, punctuated by dramatic Catskill downpours, but the nights were cool, and she slept almost 'too much'.[39] In the evenings, they would sit in white rocking chairs on the verandah, looking out at the wooded mountains. They would sip 'sours', and discuss life, love and men.

One evening they rang Asa Zatz, who now lived in Mexico City with his Guatemalan opera singer wife and their two sons. Asa had a doctorate, and was an interpreter and translator from Spanish. There had been an earthquake in Mexico, but Asa reassured them: 'It just rocked me to sleep.'[40]

Stead felt cooped up in Hunter. By mid August, when she took the rickety plane to Martha's Vineyard to stay with the Burnshaws, she was extremely tense. Later she would tell the Burnshaws that staying with them on that beautiful New England island had enabled her to calm down and remember 'Aida's many good points'.[41] But with them, too, she could be irritable and contrary. It became a joke with Stanley and Leda to count the number of times she said, 'My dear, you're wrong'.[42]

Life on the Vineyard was sociable. Fashionable New York left-wing society formed a colony there in the summer months. Lillian Hellman owned a house on a bluff overlooking the water; Cyrilly Abels and Jerome Weinstein rented a cottage, and Leo Huberman, Bill's friend from the Monthly Review Press, came to dinner one evening. At a big party Burnshaw held for her, Stead was delighted to meet people who had actually read her books. It was a blow to the Left when Soviet tanks moved into the Czech capital in late August, crushing the 'Prague spring'. But Stead made no mention of it in her letters.

Back in New York, Stead still waited for Harry Bloom. It turned out that he had not picked up her 15 July letter from his post office box until 5 August—by which time it was too late for him to go to Hunter. He had been seriously ill, in hospital. His angina, which he referred to, mock-lovingly, as his 'Angelina' or 'Angina Doll', had occasioned several stays over the years in intensive care wards.[43] Now he told Christina that he planned to come to New York early in September, alone or with Anne. ('I'm not pressing her to come,' he added.)[44]

Stead tossed and turned at night, and changed rooms several times in her attempt to escape the noise of the street and the neighbours' air-conditioners. During the day, the heat confined her to the Burnshaws' apartment. She told Jonah Raskin, who interviewed her over gin and tonics the day before she left, that she had read more than a hundred books in the three months she had been in the States. Malcolm Lowry was a 'genius', she ventured. (She had bought *Lunar Caustic* as a present for three different friends.)[45] She admired Joseph Heller's *Catch 22* and Gunter Grass' *The Tin Drum*. And she was impressed with Thomas Berger's *Little Big Man* and Wallace Stegner's *Wolf Willow*—recent American novels that reappraised the myths of the old frontier.[46] She had been reading works by American blacks. James Baldwin played up to whites, she thought, but Eldridge Cleaver's *Soul on Ice* 'gives an outsider a lot of inside'.[47]

She spent two pleasant evenings at the Rellas' W. 14th Street apartment. They sat outside in the small terrace garden on the roof of a Spanish bar, the Oviedo, and chatted over 'Manhattans'. Stead was not impressed when Cyrilly Abels and her lawyer husband Jerome Weinstein took her to a wineless restaurant in the Village, and she made up for it by doing some 'serious drinking' in a bar in the Village with Charlotte Mayerson, her editor at Holt. Mayerson, a much younger woman, thought Stead 'rather forbidding looking, but striking'. She dressed in a 'conventional, dowdy, British way', but carried herself well. To Mayerson's surprise, they talked like old college chums—about men and sex. Stead told her she was worried that her life from then on would be spent among women. When Mayerson outlined her own relationship troubles, Stead joked that Mayerson's problem was that she liked tall men. She should try little men, she told her. The implication, Mayerson recalls, was that little men like Bill were lusty. Stead gave her the impression that 'she got around quite a bit'.[48]

Stead's return to England was scheduled for 12 September; it was early September and Harry Bloom still had not appeared. It was hurtful, terribly disappointing. Stead may have been reminded of another fateful trip across the world, forty years before. To Philip Harvey she wrote bitterly that her 'mythical friend Harry' had not appeared. Their romance was 'just a fable and a myth together'.[49]

And then the phantom turned up. He had been in New York for some days, but had been ill. His wife was with him—they were staying at their son Mike's—and it was difficult for Harry to phone. It was a tender meeting. Afterwards, Bloom wrote to her: 'It was so short ... I was so overwhelmed. All the things I wanted to ask you ... It was wonderful.'[50] They hoped to meet again, but Harry was too ill. Stead summed up her American sojourn as a 'curious mellow season in hell'.[51]

★   ★   ★

Stead disembarked in Southampton early in the morning on 17 September. Miriam Risner drove down to meet her. There had been floods in the south of England. It was cold and windy and the streets were like rivers.

The trip to the States had made her more realistic about Harry Bloom. He had wanted her to move to New York, but she told him she was put off by the cost of living. She did not tell him that she did not want to be a 'floater', living in a modest one-room apartment, waiting for him to visit. His 'noble affection' and 'romantic visits' would make her ill, she was sure. In a mood of grim realism, she told Aida: 'To tell the truth, whatever he may think, Harry cannot do anything for me that would suit both him and me. (It's a beautiful dream!)' Evidently, it was a dream she had often dreamed.[52]

Her fantasies now settled again on Philip Harvey. 'We're devoted to each other in a nebulous romantic genuine manner and in the manner described by the inimitable D. H. Lawrence, "every friendship is a kind of marriage".'[53]

Soon after her return, Ettore and Jessie Rella visited London, and Stead had them to dinner in Surbiton with Philip and Leah Harvey. Jessie Rella recalls: 'It was clear that something was going on there.'[54] Later, Stead would tell the Rellas: 'That fatal dinner was a sort of turning-point.'[55] She implied that Harvey was jealous of her friendship with Ettore Rella.

Dr. Philip is a demon lover; he could kill anyone but a demon lady like me; "he means no harm." Something about you— well he was horribly rude to me the next day and I thought, "All right, friend, I'll wait till you call"—and he did of course. But somehow your demon ... made him curious; and impressed him. I think myself you are quite impressive. This sounds garbled—but it is the truth without a novel attached. If you think I'm joking—I—no, no, I won't say it.[56]

In her acute loneliness and distress, Stead was building up a picture—in her own mind as well as in her friends'—of a complicated love-life, beset with rivalries and jealousies. Harry Bloom encouraged this propensity:

My darling Chris,

I miss you dreadfully. You're a great woman. Really very strong and some of it seeps into me. You have verve and it sets off vibrations. Of course I'm jealous of the bookman and the postman and the tailor and all the other men that even look at you. I'm pretty tough and I was smacked from the first time I saw you.[57]

When Aida Kotlarsky wrote, making coquettish mention of *her* admirers, Stead replied with enthusiasm:

How are you, my dearest girl, and all your boyfriends! My goodness what a roll call! And to think you have kept them all from your girlhood. "Aida keeps her men." This makes me like you even more than before. I respect such women. No matter if we can't marry them all. It's a pity.[58]

Stead was flattered when Ettore Rella (in his mid-sixties and 'apparently happy with an understanding wife') told her he loved her. She took Rella's effusiveness as a serious declaration, and spent many pleasant hours musing why it was that men liked her. It seemed to her that her male friends—with the exception of Harry Bloom—regarded her as an elder sister or mother figure.[59]

Paul Koston was one of her brother figures. In the brief notes Stead wrote him, usually to thank him for an extravagant and boozy lunch, he had become 'darling Pauli'. At her request, he would often act as host at the lunch parties she felt obliged to organise when Australian and American acquaintances came to London. (She was very embarrassed when he insisted, as he sometimes did, on paying for everyone.) Occasionally she would even shop for clothes with 'Pauli' in attendance, providing 'a man's eye'.[60] According to Koston, Stead once asked him over lunch why he never 'made a pass at her'. She patted her hips and said: 'I'm not fat.' For his part, he insists, he was never interested in her in that way, but he enjoyed her company—'in small doses'.[61]

In February 1969 Stead was bold enough to write a note to Philip Harvey asking if she might join him on an excursion he was about to make to the country, to give a speech on behalf of the Medical Aid to Vietnam Committee. ('If Leah sees no objection.') She explained that it was just to see the sights, adding: 'I may after all quit the country sooner or later.'[62]

Harvey willingly agreed, thinking it would help her to take her mind off her grief. Indeed, it was the beginning of a new interest.[63] Harvey lent her books on Vietnam; Stead kept a file of newspaper cuttings.

Over time, they would make more than twenty trips together. In May, they went to Porthcawl for the day, where Harvey addressed Welsh miners. They made day trips at weekends—to Coventry or Manchester. Usually they went to evening meetings in the London area. Harvey lectured to universities, schools, charities and trade unions, condemning American involvement in the war and collecting money for medicine and medical equipment for North Vietnam. The US Defence Department denied using plastic-coated fragmentation bombs: Harvey caused a stir when he brought one back and showed it to the British Press. Harry Bloom even saw him on the American television news.

For Stead, these trips in the car were precious—when she and Harvey were alone together. She would have her hair set in the morning, and look forward all day to the evening adventure. For his part, he enjoyed her company. 'You could have a really good conversation with Chris, an *excellent* conversation, when she was on the reality plane—provided you were determined not to let things stray out of control.'

He was aware of her interest in him, and probably flattered. But he claims that though she would have loved physical contact, he would have 'run a mile'. One evening, according to Harvey, Stead 'made a pass' at him in the car, stroking his cheek and trying to kiss him. He said, 'Please Chris, don't.' She withdrew and said, 'All right, no sex'. He discussed the incident afterwards with Leah. They thought it best to act as if nothing had happened.[64]

Harvey's brilliance as a speaker must have reminded Stead of her father and Bill. As a young girl, she had often gone with her father when he lectured. She told Aida Kotlarsky that Harvey was no 'dingdong rabble-rouser'.

He is a most serious speaker, with those details only a doctor could give (he was in Hanoi under the bombing, to inspect the devastation and war-wounds) and speaks quietly and dispassionately just because he is fully passionate about this business. It makes a tremendous effect.[65]

In 1970, Michael Wilding, an English lecturer at the University of Sydney, would ask Stead, as an Australian writer, to contribute to an Australian anti-war anthology he was co-editing.[66] It was published the following year. Stead willingly agreed. In her essay, 'What Goal in Mind?', she condemned the American involvement in Vietnam and sang the praises of the paramedical services in 'democratic Vietnam', paying special tribute to the work of the Medical Aid to Vietnam Committee and the 'socialist doctor' Philip Harvey.

At first she thought of calling the piece 'Doctor in Vietnam',[67] and her rough jottings were about Harvey the man:

> The doctor, a burly powerful person in his fifties, amiable and
> at times much like the medical student he must have been,
> gay, rough, argumentative, resolute and with that particular
> subtlety of observation which comes from a passion for the
> truth, appears defenceless against private criticism. He is not.
> Hurt by insensitivity, he instantly recovers himself, believing
> that everyone has some truth, sifting the criticism, looking for
> reality and anxious to make things plain.

Though she was more interested in the man than the cause he espoused, Stead eventually realised this was scarcely appropriate material for the anthology and, after several drafts, she cut out the character sketch of Harvey. Her published article merely quotes Harvey, and presents a passionate indictment of American war crimes.

★   ★   ★

Clem Christesen, editor of *Meanjin*, had nominated Christina Stead for a Creative Arts Fellowship at the Australian National University in Canberra. Stead explained to Laurence Pollinger, her English agent, that the Britannica Award saga had caused 'a lot of sore feelings' in Australia, and that in the end the publicity had done her a service. *Meanjin* and *Southerly* had requested stories from her, and she asked Pollinger not to quibble about the low fees she would be receiving. Australian journals could not compete with American rates.[68]

Early in 1969 Stead heard that the Creative Arts Fellowship at the Australian National University had come off. She was offered a short-term 'B class' fellowship: a category for Australian expatriate artists of international repute. The lump-sum stipend, $5000, was to cover her fare and expenses. The only previous Fellow had been artist Sidney Nolan, in 1965.

The letter from the university stated that there was 'no obligation to give lectures or talks', but it was hoped that fellows 'would meet and talk, at least informally, with members of the academic staff and students'.[69] Stead would be given an office in the English Department.

Inevitably, perhaps, the Australian press inferred that Stead had been offered the fellowship because of the protests over the unfortunate Britannica episode.[70] Whether or not the Britannica episode actually played any role in the committee's decision, the university was embarrassed by the inference.[71]

Stead, more nervous than excited, tried to postpone the trip until 1970, thinking she would try to finish *I'm Dying Laughing* before she left. But a deferral was not possible, since the budget had been planned for the year. After that, it seemed like the hand of fate. She told Harry Bloom: 'I am at a Whistle Stop ... waiting for the first express to take me somewhere, I don't know what will be the destination, but I will take it.'[72] She opted for four months, rather than the full term of six. It was an opportunity to see something of Australia, and to make up her mind whether, eventually, she could live there.

Feeling guilty that she had done nothing for a whole year, she resumed desultory work on *I'm Dying Laughing*, still hoping to have the manuscript ready before she left for Australia, but it had become 'a large albatross' and she 'a reluctant sailor'.[73] The Secker & Warburg files contain numerous letters from Fred Warburg to Christina Stead asking about her progress with the novel. In March 1969 she told him: 'Oldfashioned people would say laziness, Americans would (and do) say "a block"—and the British say it's "the weather"—and it may be a combination of these three.'[74] He then asked her to aim for delivery by 30 June 1969. She replied: 'Dear Fred: You were right, no doubt, to give me a dead-line. Perhaps the old firehorse will now snort and gallop. We'll see.'[75] It did not. By mid July, just before her departure for Australia, she told Burnshaw (who had left Holt two years before to write full-time) that she was abandoning the novel for the time being. Her additions had merely ruined the original dramatic tension, and now the manuscript was only good for the 'garbage can or the deep freeze'.[76] It was to be the deep-freeze for seventeen years. When in was published in 1986, after Stead's literary executor had succeeded in piecing the bits of draft together, the book was praised as a forceful and wonderfully exuberant portrait of the poisonous betrayals of the McCarthy years; but it was generally deemed 'one of those loose and baggy monsters than can try one's patience even as it impresses itself in memory'.[77]

For once, reviews were generally very favourable in Australia, and much less so in the US and Britain. Don Anderson wrote in the Sydney *Times on Sunday*, 'It is, it goes without saying, a great novel, and proves, if proof were necessary, that Christina Stead is Australia's greatest novelist.'[78]

Stead, anxious about the prospect of being a visiting literary expert, spent the next months devouring contemporary fiction. She read Updike's *The Centaur* and Mailer's *An American Dream* and was surprised how good they were. Günter Grass' *Dog Years* she thought 'first rate, wonderfully good'. She was less impressed with *Herzog* than with Saul Bellow's earlier novels. And was no-one except Norman Mailer prepared to criticise America's foray into Vietnam?[79]

★   ★   ★

Stead left for Australia on the evening of 28 July 1969. Philip Harvey drove her to Heathrow. She had left instructions that if anything should happen to her, there was a suitcase in her flat marked Paul Koston, which contained love letters and 'a lot of manuscripts' to be destroyed.[80]

After forty-one years she was going home, alone. Bill Blake had always wanted to see Australia and meet her family and friends. They had talked of retiring to Australia. She felt terribly sad to be making the trip without him.

She had left Australia at the age of 26, a budding writer. Now she was 67, a writer with an international reputation. In Australia, however, most of her books had been out of print until 1965, when there were Australian re-issues of *Seven Poor Men of Sydney*, *For Love Alone* and *The Salzburg Tales*. The revised *The Man Who Loved Children* arrived from England. But several of her books remained virtually unobtainable, even in libraries.

The trip was long and tiring. First, the departure from Heathrow was delayed. Then there was a seventeen-hour delay at Bangkok. The plane was 'close-packed as a crate of eggs'. Sitting next to Stead was a Greek-born mother who talked across the aisle to her friends about 'the good life in Australia'. Mentally picturing the woman delivering this 'rich boast' to the grandparents somewhere outside Athens, Stead looked out of the window, fascinated by the 'distant earth, every spine and wrinkle visible in the dry air'.[81]

They stopped in Darwin at 3 am, and eventually arrived at Sydney airport twenty-four hours late. Stead felt like a rag. To her horror, a sprinkling of reporters and press photographers were at the airport to greet her, as well as a small crowd of family members. Wanting only to run away, Stead was obliged to give a short interview in the airport press room. The journalists pressed her about her feelings towards Australia. 'No, no! I didn't go to England full of resentment that my great talents weren't being recognised in parochial Australia,' Stead told them. And when

asked about her reaction to the withholding of the Britannica
Award, she assured them, 'I didn't mind. After all, it was only fairy
money, wasn't it?'[82]

Stead had arranged to spend the first few days with her maternal
cousin Elsie Ford, rather than with her immediate family. Elsie and
her husband Robert had visited her and Blake in London in 1967,
and the two couples had formed an easy friendship. Elsie Ford
believes Stead wanted a 'breathing space' before more emotional
meetings with the family.

'I had forgotten the Australian splendour, the marvellous light,'
Stead would write later.[83] The Fords lived in Pymble, on Sydney's
North Shore. Where once there had been green hills, there was a
'rash of red roofs'.[84] But trees were everywhere, and glimpses of
blue harbour. The following year, she would write her impressions
in an essay, 'Another View of the Homestead'.

> The most exquisite thing in my recent life was a giant eucalypt
> on the North Shore as we turned downhill, the downward
> leaves so clear, the bark rags, so precise, the patched trunk,
> so bright. "Look at that tree!" It was outlined in light. It was
> scarcely spring, but the lawn outside the house was crowded
> with camellias, magnolias in bloom, even falling; at both dawn
> and dusk the kookaburras thrilling high in the trees, the
> magpies—I had quite forgotten those musicians and their
> audacity . . . Too long in London! Everything was like ringing
> and bright fire and all sharpness.

Culturally, everything had changed. Modern Australia was only
twenty-four hours from Europe. The post-war influx of European
immigrants had created cosmopolitan cities: the choice of food was
as great as in New York. Driving into the city over the Harbour
Bridge (opened in 1932, after she had left), Stead looked at the
skyscrapers and thought to herself: 'Is this Sydney? This is New
York.'[85] Much of the early colonial architecture had been destroyed, and the electric trams were no more. Instead there were
buses, an overhead railway station at Circular Quay and the Sydney
Opera House at Bennelong Point.

Christina called to see Florence Walker-Smith. Her favourite
aunt was very frail now at 90, and was living with Gwen in a flat in
harbour-side Cremorne. Gwen was at work that afternoon, but she
gathered the meeting was slightly strained. Six weeks later, in
September, Christina would be back in Sydney for Florence's
funeral. Gwen would never forget that moment: in the middle of
the service, during a violent thunderstorm with torrents of rain and
flashes of lightning, Christina suddenly appeared, and thrust some
beautiful flowers into her hands.[86]

Christina was awkward with her family, and though she was painfully shy about meeting Australian literati, she was relieved to leave Sydney for Canberra. A. D. Hope and Dorothy Green, well-known writers from the English Department, met her at the airport and drove her to University House, a residential college for academics and postgraduates.

The 'bush capital' had been officially declared the federal capital in 1927, the year before Stead left Australia. The city, which had sprung up behind her back, was a dramatic reminder that she had been out of the country a long time.

Surrounded by hills and mountains, Canberra struck her as very beautiful. The air was crisp, clear and dry—quite different from Sydney's humidity. The nights were cold, and in the mornings the grass was covered in frost. The campus had only native trees, between which flitted multicoloured rosellas. Some mornings there would be a 'dawn chorus of hellish laughter' from the kookaburras.[87]

The flat in University House comprised a living room, bedroom and bathroom: Stead had not expected such comfort. There was a large wooden desk, but she sensed she would not be able to write there. She had told the Creative Arts Fellowship Committee, as well as the press at Canberra Airport, that she was going to work on Bill Blake's French Revolution manuscript during her four-month term.[88] But if she lacked energy for *I'm Dying Laughing*, she certainly lacked energy to work on a novel that was not her own. She read a great deal: she made notes on Patrick White's *The Living and the Dead* and *Voss*, neither of which filled her with enthusiasm.[89] She wrote letters. She was lonely, she told the Harveys.

> It is not hard to think of you, for I really have no links here.
> Sydney is jewelled, a wonderful city, (though smog) and full of
> friends and relations—but I don't at the moment contemplate
> settling there—all alone. This "all alone" business when you
> have had someone to understand, "to forgive" (to forgive the
> ineptitudes, etc.) is a new state, an odd state.[90]

Australians, seemingly obsessed with being 'cut off', talked incessantly about the 'cultural cringe'. It irritated her, yet she told Paul Koston: 'I hear words, names, I haven't heard for 40 years. But no feeling of nostalgia ... One could not live here—some do and like it, but it is "erewhon" and "never-never-land".'[91]

Australians were curious about this famous writer, briefly back from her long exile. All sorts of people wrote her letters: people who wanted to meet her, people she had known in the past. Her telephone rang with requests for talks or interviews. Interviewers were struck by the musical intonation of her voice and her slight American accent. 'It is a mellow contralto, deep for a woman, yet

not too deep,' wrote Stuart Sayers. 'A beautiful instrument, beautifully used.'[92] In the *Australian Women's Weekly*, Anne Matheson
commented on Stead's 'soft, well-modulated voice', and gave a
flattering description of her appearance:

Christina Stead is a handsome woman. Her hair is strong,
short, and only touched with grey. Her eyes are blazing blue,
yet soft. She has an upright figure that looks so well in tailored
clothes that I was not surprised to learn she wore trousersuits
from the moment Paris decreed pants.[93]

Stead would have been delighted by such comments, for the official
photographs taken in Australia caused her great distress. Old age
suited her: her craggy features lent her a noble profile. But she was
as painfully self-conscious as ever about her appearance, and vehemently resented the airport photographs. Cruelly, fate afflicted
her with a skin problem throughout her stay. Near the end of her
trip, she admitted to the Burnshaws:

I have stacks of "official" photographs taken with a wen on the
very end of my nose, nothing could be more noticeable . . .
I suffered tremendously in my shyness having to appear as a special
"Fellow" before all sorts of curious and talented audiences.[94]

Her role as 'Official Personage' made her uneasy. Unused to being
treated as a celebrity, she encountered it at a time when she had
neither Bill nor current writing projects to make her feel good
about herself. She worried that she was not carrying out her
obligations satisfactorily. 'I have a dreadfully immoral feeling that I
am worse than chaff,' she told Harvey.[95] To the Burnshaws she
wrote, 'Since I have not been writing, I am not myself, I am in fact
no one at all and have no reason for having friends fond of me.'[96]
The old feeling of worthlessness had returned with a vengeance.

Stead was not good at public speaking, nor was she skilled at
conversations with strangers. A student interviewer found her most
intimidating:

Conversations with her are apt to lapse into occasional silences.
She is not herself inclined to gloss over these pauses with the
veneer of normal social trivia, and those with her, unable to
fall back on these standbys, sometimes search around in vain
for something which seems worth saying.[97]

Stead made two trips to Melbourne, a city she had visited only
briefly in her student-teacher days. She liked what she saw. She
made several trips to Sydney, where she was invited to talk at a
meeting of the radical writers' group, PEN, and at a meeting of the
Fellowship of Australian Writers. At this meeting, she exchanged
passing greetings with Florence James, but left without saying

goodbye.[98] Nor did she answer a letter from Florence inviting her to stay a few days in the Blue Mountains.[99]

Patrick White invited her to lunch, which passed very amicably. When she told him she was vaguely thinking of returning to Australia to live, White told her she should 'give it plenty of thought before burning her bridges'.[100]

Dymphna Cusack asked Stead to become a patron of the Fellowship of Australian Writers. She accepted. But the strain of being treated as a celebrity was taking its toll. She began to turn down and cancel engagements, yet felt guilty because everyone was so pleasant. In Sydney the family treated her with 'extraordinary courtesy', yet for some reason she avoided Thistle Harris, and never once visited the house at Watson's Bay, which Thistle shared with Christina's brother Kelvin and his family. She was uncomfortable with her two sisters, Kate and Doris (Weeta), and much preferred the company of her brothers, David and Gilbert. In letters to 'dear, dear Philip' she grumbled: 'I don't care to remember how I'm filling in this dreadful time . . . It's long and dreary.'[101]

Nevertheless, there were moments of genuine pleasure. She drove to Melbourne and back with Dorothy Green, poet and critic, who lectured in English at the ANU and was writing a book on Henry Handel Richardson. (Stead grumbled to Burnshaw that 'HHR' might as well be 'Her Highness Royal' in Australia, adding: 'They dislike her best book about her musical time in Leipzig, *Maurice Guest*, 1908. Like most young countries they don't care about foreign countries and romances written for "foreigners".'[102])

Dorothy Green had been married to H. M. Green, the eminent critic of Australian literature. Now a widow, Dorothy was a 'sweet, pure, serious and absolutely darling little creature', who dressed 'charmingly' and drove with 'great competence'.[103] What won Stead over—even more than her generosity and kindness and the detours she took to show Stead the countryside—was that she said there were one or two men whom she loved.

Stead enjoyed lunch with Dr H. C. Coombs, Chancellor of the ANU, whom she had once met in London. She was hugely taken by this 'small sunbaked personage' with his nuggety build, widely known by his West Australian nickname 'Nugget'. One of Australia's most impressive public figures, Coombs, who had a doctorate from the London School of Economics, had played an active role in Australia's post-war financial policies. He was an enthusiastic patron of the arts and Chairman of the Council for Aboriginal Affairs. In 1972, when she met him again in London, Stead would send him a copy of *House of All Nations*, and it was his turn to be impressed.

She rang an 'old boyfriend', Colin Kenneth Lawson, who had managed Henderson's hat factory where she once worked, and brought her roses, calling her his 'Tosca'. Later, he had given up business and become the manager of the Sydney Symphony Orchestra. Stead commented: 'It was as if we had met only yesterday—although he is twice the size.'[104]

A less welcome, totally unexpected confrontation with her past occurred when Stead found herself sitting at the same table as Professor G. W. Keith Duncan at dinner. He was in Canberra for a conference, and was staying at University House. Stead, sitting with the Geerings, left straight after dinner, embarrassed. According to Duncan, when his wife (who knew virtually nothing of the whole story) asked him why he did not speak to his old friend, he retorted: 'I will never talk to that woman!'[105]

A pleasant fortnight was spent with Gilbert Stead and his family in a holiday house in Mollymook, on the coast south of Sydney. With her brother David and his wife Doris, Stead drove west, towards Broken Hill, and was thrilled by the copper-red and sunburnt country. She stayed two days with a cousin, Enid Wall, who lived on a wheat station near Narrabri, in north-western New South Wales.[106] But despite these brief flights into the bush, by mid November Stead was flat and exhausted. 'Everyone very kind here,' she noted, 'and I am beaten into the ground with it.'[107]

In 'Another View of the Homestead', she would write of Australia's 'melancholy' in a tone reminiscent of *Seven Poor Men of Sydney*:

I don't understand the settled sadness of some intellectuals, artists and academics. The heat mystery, black shadows in the tropics, the long bright road ending in a mirage? Deserts? Not belonging to ourselves? Not united with our nearest neighbours?[108]

* * *

Stead left Australia on 3 December 1969, flying to London via Rome. She was going to spend a few days with the Friedmanns, near Florence. But now she was anxious to be home again—Australia definitely was *not* home—and Florence seemed like another hurdle to cross.

Tella and Boy met her at Rome airport, a three-hour drive from where they lived in Greve-in-Chianti, north of Florence. It was the beginning of winter and there was snow on the Apennines. Their renovated Toscana villa, 200 years old, was in the middle of rolling hills of vineyards. Stead privately thought it 'too lovely'—'like a dream'.[109]

In 1967 when the Friedmanns left England, Bill had seen them off with a bouquet of violets in his hands and tears in his eyes. They still found it difficult to accept that he was gone. Stead told them that she did not want to talk about Bill; it would upset her too much.

Stead did not sleep in Italy. She was plagued by an urgent feeling, 'Get on, you must be getting on'. For the first time, Tella Friedmann found Stead's drinking excessive. She would have several hard drinks in the middle of the day—gin, martini or dry vermouth—and again in the evening. At dinner they drank the local chianti.

Stead had always thought Boy Friedmann a 'lovable man', though he was not one of the men with whom she flirted. She had once written affectionate letters to Tella, but now she felt strangely hostile. Perhaps it was jealousy: Tella, after all, had what she most wanted—a loving male companion.

One morning they had a row. According to Tella Friedmann, they were talking in the kitchen while Tella was cooking. 'For something to say', Tella asked Christina: 'How do you create characters? How does one set about making a character in a novel that is not recognisable to others?'

Was Tella being provocative? The ensuing argument was reminiscent of a heated one Stead had once had with Florence James over *Power Without Glory*, when James argued that it was wrong of Frank Hardy to create recognisable characters. It rapidly escalated into a full-scale row. Tella, almost 50, took the opportunity to tell Christina she did not appreciate being referred to as a 'sex kitten'.

The friendship between the two women 'more or less died' after this visit.[110] It was the last time Stead ever saw the Friedmanns.

★　★　★

Stead returned to Surbiton to find a letter from Frederick Warburg, her publisher:

> I cannot help wondering what has happened to that new novel which you were re-working, whether you are still at it, whether you have scrapped it, or what has happened? Somebody said you have made a trip to Australia and this may of course have interfered with working on the novel. In any case I would very much like to know whether it will be ready in the next few months for publication in the autumn of 1970.[111]

Stead's reply was vague:

> I wouldn't say I have scrapped the novel; I just put it away and there it is on the shelf. Now that I have completely recovered from those four months as an official person (you might say) and the travelling, I am quite ready to begin work again; and I can only say, I hope that novel will be the novel.[112]

Warburg did not pester her again.

Christmas that year was spent with Oliver and Gunnwor Stally-brass. Stead went there the following Christmas too, and for Easter and weekends, always taking with her a crate of bottles. She greatly appreciated Gunnwor's warmth, energy and creativity as an interior designer. Oliver reminded her of Jesus Christ and D. H. Lawrence: 'tall, thin face, deep eyes, beard, unruly hair, sandals'. Alongside this passionate aesthete, who lived for art, literature and music, Stead somehow felt 'puritanical' and 'severe'.[114]

*   *   *

When Stead had written from Australia saying she felt inadequate and harassed in her role as an 'Official Personage', Harvey reassured her. It did not matter; she was timid, that was all. Stead found this verdict strangely comforting—perhaps because, in one small domain, it allowed her to accept herself. Before, her timidity had been partly concealed by Blake's sociability. After her return from Australia, she embraced her 'timidity', using it as an excuse. She told Burnshaw in January 1970:

> I had a severe shock from that Australia visit—still get a
> violent headache from "society", "company", can hardly
> endure more than half an hour of the company even of my
> dear Doc. It just shows what a timid person I really am.[115]

In January 1970 she was working on the essay about her return 'home', commissioned by *Hemisphere*, and finding it 'strangely difficult'. How could she explain that she had never had a home other than Bill? And how could she explain 'the useless misery I was in the whole time? I can't explain it to myself'.[116]

Later that year she began work on a short piece about her father, 'A Waker and Dreamer', commissioned by Stephen Murray-Smith, editor of the socialist literary magazine *Overland*. At first she was not enthusiastic—she felt she had said everything in *The Man Who Loved Children*—but she asked Gilbert Stead for some material about their father's family, and in the end she enjoyed imagining her grandfather coming to Australia, and her own father's childhood. Looking back this time, she saw her father as 'an unusually gifted man', with 'great courage'.[117]

That same year, 1970, she wrote the article on Vietnam. It turned out to be an unusually productive year. But she found writing a strain these days.

Over the next years, Stead revised old short stories for various Australian and American magazines.[118] She did not touch *I'm Dying Laughing*, but it remained a burden on her mind. She believed it was preventing her from writing other things.

She toyed with other ideas. She had a thick sheaf of notes on Hannah Weinstein, but she did not want to write any more about 'fools and crooks'. She had 'folios and folios of notes'[119] on Philip Harvey, 'an Honest Man', but she had not got 'a line on the story yet'.[120] And she wanted to write a book about Bill. It would be a 'simple unaffected book' about the 'funny things his mother did' and the many things Bill taught *her*, Christina. Having resolved to write the book, she felt better: 'I had been carrying such a load of guilt,' she told an acquaintance in August 1972.[121] But guilt and affection were not emotions that stoked her creative fires: she never wrote it. Nor did anything come of the other projects. Her anger, one of the important sources of her creative vitality, had subsided into depression.

She read a great deal. Having made her way through the French books in the local Surbiton library, she started on German. William L. Shirer's *The Rise and Fall of the Third Reich* was 'very very readable, a fascinating book'.[122] To Alexander Solzhenitsyn's *The First Circle*, a blistering portrait of Stalin and the Soviet treatment of dissidents, her reaction was much the same as it had been to Pasternak's *Dr Zhivago*. 'Though written with a lot of eagerness, skill, imagination . . . and you are carried along by his energy, you keep saying, "How many? Where? Prove it."' It seemed to her that it was 'very saleable' these days to run down Stalin and the Soviet Union.[123]

★   ★   ★

Stead heard almost monthly from 'dear Harry', though he was often laid low with his angina. He wanted to visit her in London, and even had a good excuse for a trip to Europe, since his son Michael and daughter-in-law Barbara were temporarily playing in the Lucerne orchestra. In 1970, he and Anne planned a visit to Switzerland, but then the young couple flew to Puerto Rico instead.

Harry Bloom was full of plans, but nothing much came of them. Either he was ill, or his wife was. He grumbled to Christina that Anne had taken to her bed, and though no-one could find anything wrong with her, she refused to travel. Disappointing though it was to have her hopes constantly dashed, Bloom's letters went some way towards filling the emotional void in Stead's life. His letters were passionate, warm and tender. He wrote as he talked—in colourful, racy American. He told her about their mutual friends, the political situation. He related amusing anecdotes. He worried about her. He encouraged her. He missed her. He wished he could hold her hand and talk to her. When the press reported heavy snowfalls in England, he worried that her flat would not be warm enough. Was she managing to shop? 'Why couldn't I snuggle in bed with you and let all those cold winds blow as much as they wanted to?'[124]

He even made her feel desirable. 'Nobody I can think of can fill your shoes, your heart, your mind and your beautiful body,' he told her. 'Much love and kisses I send to you my darling.'[125] Five days later, he assured her: 'Think of me as always loving you. I live on it.'[126]

Stead still thought of Harry Bloom as the 'Faithful Henry', the King's loyal servant in the Grimms' tale 'The Frog Prince'. She thought she would like to write about him. 'I have not told him,' she confided to Burnshaw, 'since I don't want to make it difficult for him to write freely.'[127] However, she could not. Although she spent her last years wishing she could write about the men she loved, to please them, she could not.

★   ★   ★

Stead did not complain about ageing; she accepted it with the rationale of a good naturalist: it was natural. 'I do not understand people who think about age,' she told Aida Kotlarsky. 'It's like saying, "I can't stand [it] that the sky is up and the earth is down." '[128] Her existence was a 'thin grey soup', and she longed for a 'richer brew',[129] but her health was good at 68. She was too heavy, and conscious that she ought to lose weight, but she did nothing about it. Her staple diet was steak and alcohol.

But late one Sunday night in October 1970, she suffered a mild heart attack. Philip Harvey was on holiday in Yugoslavia at the time and the local GP told her it was angina of the chest. When Harvey returned, he took her to hospital for observation. Tests revealed she had had a coronary. She spent three weeks in a private room at St Stephen's Hospital, 'treated like a princess'.[130] With 'almost daily views and news of that nutty Doc. I am so fond of', she enjoyed her stay, though she felt 'quite a fake', for she seemed perfectly fine again.[131] Paul Koston brought her a 'ravishing night-gown' and slippers with roses on them. (Stead told this with great delight to all her friends.) And the 'Doc' would come to see her—'all instruments and horse-laughs'.[132] She felt much loved by her men.

However, the reality—and she knew it—was less cheerful. Back in Surbiton, she conjectured that the heart attack might have been caused by the bottling-up of her feelings. She told Burnshaw:

Since everything in this house reminds me of Bill—we bought this, said this, and I am not mentioning all the things that call out regret and sorrow—I have to be firm all the time with

myself. I feel quite cheerful and normal, and even appear
lighthearted or lightminded, I don't doubt; but I should not
be surprised to know that these three years of suppression
(is it only two?) cause the HBP [high blood pressure] and
heart attack, for what else did?[133]

After the attack there was a new dimension to her life: fear. She
became more sedentary than ever, afraid that exertion might cause
another attack.

★　★　★

The highlight of the following year—at least Stead *thought* it would
be—was a two-week trip to Albania, in an organised group with
the Harveys. In May 1971 she received a royalty cheque from the
United States for $1200—*The Man Who Loved Children* was still
enjoying steady sales—and she felt able to treat herself to the trip in
August. She told Burnshaw that she had not been working well and
she suspected 'that part of the brave and good Doc's invitation' was
to give her 'a new start in life'.[134] Excited letters were posted to
Ettore Rella, her 'Albanian friend'. Where was his father born? ('I
should like to see it—then I could tell you; I know how you miss
your ancestors.'[135]) The only book about Albania she could find in
the local library was *Illyria Reborn*, by Dymphna Cusack, who had
visited the country in 1965. Stead told Rella:

She's a facile enthusiastic journalist when doing travelogues;
very easy reading, she tends to greatly praise the country
(leftist countries): is sold there, makes a profit and is able to go
back there again on her earnings! Good idea. (But she would
not dwell on the shadows in the picture.)[136]

Stead herself was not known for dwelling on the shadows when it
came to socialist countries. Once in Albania, she would have
several arguments with Leah Harvey, who was critical of the
Stalinist-style regime, whereas Stead opined that repressive measures were necessary for the country's development. (Afterwards,
she told Australian communist Judah Waten that they had seen 'a
fresh new Socialism struggling hard'.[137]) It was *other* shadows that
would haunt Stead. Though she was never prepared to elaborate,
she made it clear to all her friends that the two-week trip was an
unmitigated disaster.

The party of sixteen left for Albania on 21 August, among them
several archeologists from Cambridge. The group flew to Dubrov-
nik, the seaport in Yugoslavia, and after that, they travelled over
rough, cliff-hanging roads in a bus decked with photographs of
Lenin, Stalin, Marx, Engels and Enver Hoxha, the Albanian head

of government. As musical accompaniment there was the horn, blown as they approached each turn.

The tourist industry was newly emerging. Americans were still not permitted into the country. The visitors were confined to special locations. ('I am not one to complain about that,' Stead told Waten. 'Would we allow ignorant visitors to roam around our factories and workshops, without guides and with cameras?') The hotels were primitive, the food was undistinguished, but the beer and *raki*, a potent kind of slivovitz, aided its digestion.

Physically, the country was extraordinarily beautiful, with steep, rocky mountains and a narrow, ancient coastal plain. Stead was struck by the 'old yellow cities, mud-coloured and as old as Mud', and the 'dark, thronging people' in traditional dress.

But she was bitterly unhappy. Back in England, she told Burnshaw she felt 'sick' when she thought about the trip. 'I will never forget it or get over it.' She added: 'It is perhaps too private, can only be said in *public* (writing).'[138]

What happened in Albania? Remaining remnants of Stead's Albania story, entitled 'On the Beach', suggest that Stead was offended that the Harveys went their own way, leaving her to make friends among the group. She felt lonely and abandoned. Instead of being one of a trio, she felt that she stood out in the group as a pathetic figure, a woman on her own.

Leah Harvey was studying at that time to become a barrister, and was preparing for her final exams. She would sit on the beaches and study. Philip Harvey was preparing for his next term's medical teaching. Another of his favourite pastimes was to swim to the point of exhaustion. These were not sociable pursuits.

Stead's fictional notes are written in the first-person. 'Marigold' and 'Reed', old friends of the narrator, invite her to accompany them on their holiday to Albania. Though Stead changes minor details, it is quite clear whom she is describing:

He is tall, muscular, burly, once an athlete; he has tender dark shortsighted eyes, a pale skin, a big nose and chin and he is quite well known in his profession . . . he's a physicist with a laboratory in his charge. He's about 55.

Marigold is younger, middlesized, dark . . . with the . . . colouring of an antique Graeco-Roman painting on wood . . . She has fine white teeth which she has been told to show and she does so continually, when talking, in a strange wolfish manner . . . and her voice, usually coarse and dull, then takes on a ringing precision, with the tone of the bell in the committee rooms she is fond of.

In the airport, Reed, who calls himself "a chronic swot" sat at a small table studying physics, while Marigold hurried about collecting our allowances of dutyfree liquor and cigarettes, which she intended to carry all through the trip to bring back home.

One evening, at some coastal town—it seems to be the ancient Adriatic town of Durres—the three of them go for a walk. Then comes the first hint of crisis:

> Next morning I was early on the beach waiting for my friends and was presently breath-taken to see them lying ready for the sea under an umbrella. I stared. I was sitting on a tussock, easy to see. Mortified, I returned to the hotel to sit under an oleander.[139]

It is obvious that she resented Leah Harvey throughout the trip, and was furious with Philip Harvey for ignoring her. Writing about it afterwards was Stead's way of coming to terms with anger and pain. (If she could publish it, it would also be a means of revenge.)

Stead, it seems, made up for Philip Harvey's obvious preference for the company of his wife by throwing herself at the other men in the group. Two months later, when she wrote to Burnshaw about the Albanian trip, she could not bring herself to say exactly why the trip was so infernal. Like Burnshaw, we are obliged to read between the lines:

> I was sick in bed for six days after I returned and for four or five weeks after (morally sick only); and I can say now that I am better, but it took the same amount of froth and foam and sweat that a hurdle race takes. There was I in full public, making friends with one chap after another, for company—and all very nice, mind you, all splendid "shipboard" friends, all inveterate travellers who knew their way about and how to behave on a package trip or any other trip in fact—I would go with them to the moon, these unknown blokes I will never see again—but the despair, horror of it! Each single day a new thought struck me and then I realised it was always the same thought: "This is Hell."

As a postscript she added:

> I felt sucked down hopelessly in a suffocating thing, maybe like the caves, those frightening caves in 'Passage to India' (Malabar Hills) [sic]. It was SO dreadful; I tremble now when I write about it. Must not. Must one day write a long-short for myself and so cure myself.[140]

If the trip constituted a terrible crisis for Stead, it was in all likelihood because she, who liked to think of herself as a 'man's woman', who painted herself in this light to all her friends, including the Harveys, felt she had been exposed. It made her feel 'morally sick'. The 'very severe "rejection" anxiety' Stead had once analysed in herself (attributing it to her childhood, when her love and her appearance were constantly rejected), caused her intense distress.[141]

How interesting that at such a time Stead should think of the dark, echoing Marabar caves in *Passage to India*, the climactic scene in which young Adela Quested imagines herself attacked by her Indian friend Dr Aziz. For Adela, the novel implies, the caves were frightful because it was in those pitch black caves (her unconscious?) that her repressed sexual desires took the form of hysterical hallucination. Later, Adela feels terribly guilty as she begins to think she imagined the whole incident. Stead was certainly aware of the ambiguity of the caves scene in E. M. Forster's novel. For her to make the comparison was tantamount to an admission that she could not bring herself to face the indignity of her sexual desire and emotional desperation. Albania had become her Marabar cave.

Unable to write her long-short story, she could not cure herself. She could not rid herself of the feeling that she had degraded herself. She struggled with the story for weeks, but could not finish it. The only other way she knew to relieve the pain and embarrassment of the memory was her standard ploy: to repress it.

The *Sydney Morning Herald* had asked her for a story. As she could not write the Albania story, finally, on the day of the deadline, she switched to a story based on herself and Bill in their old age. A sentimental story about the romantic love between Jenny (a tall fair woman) and Gill (a square-cut, dark man) after forty years of marriage, she called it 'Street Idyll'. It was the kind of thing Stead had never written before, and if she wrote it now it was because she felt the need to purify herself, as it were, to revive the memory of her love for Bill, to lessen the guilt she felt toward him, to eradicate the memory of her recent desperate behaviour, and to bring back some dignity into her life.[142] Having sent it off, Stead felt embarrassed by it, thinking it 'coy and weak'.[143] But the newspaper liked it, and published it in January 1972. It gave Sydney readers a highly romanticised view of Stead's relationship with Bill Blake in their last years together.

Stead avoided the Harveys for several months, 'not having quite digested their behaviour in Albania'.[144] Over time, she came to the more digestible conclusion that her misery in Albania was due to the depressant drugs she had been taking to keep down her blood pressure, and that she had missed Bill, who had always been her travelling companion. However, the trip marked a turning point in her relationship with Philip Harvey. Things would never be quite the same again. By 1973 she scarcely saw the 'splendid fellow' any more; she was no longer invited on his lecturing trips.[145]

*   *   *

For Christmas 1971 Paul Koston gave Stead a year's membership to a dining club, so she could entertain people in the city. Le Petit Club Français, a modest little house in St James' Place, near Piccadilly, had been the headquarters of the Free French during the war and was now 'the haunt of those who are fond of France'.[146] It became Stead's favourite eating place. She took visitors there, like Elizabeth Harrower and Michael Wilding, Sydney writers. And she had a birthday party there on Bastille Day, 1972, inviting the 'Doc' and 'His Dishrag' (she meant Leah),[147] and Ruth and Laurie Hall.[148]

In December 1972, she told Burnshaw, with unusual honesty, that her relationship with Harvey had become very painful for her:

I don't see that fellow any more than necessary, for he tends to ridicule me for my ancientness, lack of beauty and I don't know what else—curious fellow. I know he wanted to love me once, but could not because of my age; now he is sticking pins in me ... But I remember every day how marvellously good he was to me for four years after Bill died, as if he had taken on a charge—and I believe he had.[149]

The disappearance of the Harvey factor in her life had badly affected her morale. She felt old now. 'My affection for the good Doc. filled in the cracks and puttied the falling panes of the old building. Now that does not work.'[150] It was the lack of romance, more than any other factor, which prompted her to think of leaving for Australia after all.

The building metaphor was not a random image: her mind was on old buildings. The old tenement houses in her street were being demolished all around her, to be replaced by modern high-rise flats. The building next door was almost down. Her own, a rambling brick house, was due to be wrecked within a year or so and already had an enormous crack from attic to basement. Stead's downstairs neighbour, Marjorie Way, a retired nurse who would call in each day for a chat over a drink and a few cigarettes, used to lie awake imagining the chimney falling through her flat. The other occupants of their building had gradually found somewhere else to live. Stead and Marjorie Way were 'hanging on', partly because they had not decided what to do next, and partly because they had heard that the landlord was obliged to pay substantial compensation to evicted tenants. Stead was hoping it might be enough to pay her fare to Australia.[151]

Marjorie Way had been lending Stead romantic novels by Lucy Walker, who set her stories in Perth or the outback. Stead was contemptuous of them, but admitted the descriptions of the bush made her nostalgic. She told Judah Waten, in Melbourne, that Marjorie Way was all for taking the next boat to Australia.

I keep telling her it is not all splendid bachelors, owners of stations. But there is some fascinating scenery in L.W.'s books and grand detail ... Then her girls are spunky, full of grit, and grit from dust storms too ... And they get their man (the tanface station owner).[152]

The upstairs neighbours, the Frazers, left the sinking ship in October 1972. Barbara, a secretary, had typed the manuscript of *I'm Dying Laughing*; James was a retired policeman. Stead spent Christmas with them in Leicester that year, anxious to save London friends the embarrassment of asking each other, 'What about Chris?'[153]

'I am basically awfully lonely my dears,' Stead told the Rellas.[154] After the mailman passed, at 7.30 or 8 am, the day stretched wearily ahead. The highlight of her week was Thursday morning, when Hilda Adamson, 'a little tired half-pint Durham girl',[155] arrived to clean the flat for two hours. Stead usually detained her for a sherry afterwards.

She was not particularly well. She had had another scare in the night in the summer of 1971, just nine months after the first. Elizabeth Harrower, who saw Stead several times in 1972, remembers her in pain in the London Underground, having to stop in a tunnel and take a pill for her angina.[156] In August 1973, she suffered a more serious attack. The fear was making her into a 'cautious valetudinarian'.[157] The hill on the way to the shops worried her, so did the steps up to her flat. She even worried about serious mental exertion. Ruth Hall did her shopping once a month with the car— and her 'huskies', as Ruth called her three boys, were there to help if necessary.[158] The Halls, Stead had to admit, were remarkably good to her, inviting her to dinner on Bill's birthday and at other times. But they were not intending to remain in England permanently. Ruth, like her mother (who had died in Paris in February 1971, three years after Bill), was happiest in France, and she and Laurie were buying a house in the south, in the hills near Nice.[159]

Harry Bloom still wrote, though less often. His health was very poor. After a bad attack early in 1972 and another stint in an intensive care ward, he told her: 'I had made up my mind that this is it and I only came out of it because I thought, I mustn't die, Chris needs me.'[160]

Later that year, he planned to visit Switzerland, then come to her in London. Christina wrote to Gwen, enclosing a letter to the Blooms, and asked Gwen to post it from Sydney. This ruse was Harry's idea: if his wife believed Stead was in Australia, he would be let off the leash for a visit to London from Switzerland. He did get to Switzerland, but he did not manage to make it to London after all.

As the buildings around her came down, and a return to Australia became almost a certainty, Stead was going through her papers: 'big dollops of paper, hundreds'. It was probably at this time that she destroyed a vast quantity. At her death, she would leave behind complete files of correspondence from Ettore Rella and Stanley Burnshaw, beginning in the 1930s, and all the letters she had ever received from Philip Harvey, a friend since 1952. There were letters from Bill and from Harry Bloom. But there were none from the people on whom she had modelled her major characters: Keith Duncan, Florence James, Anne Dooley or Ruth McKenney.

During the sorting process, Stead came across *Mrs Trollope and Madame Blaise*, the short novel about British expatriates in Switzerland which she had written in Lausanne in 1949. Little, Brown had rejected it back then. Early in 1967 she had given it to her new agents in New York and London, but again, there had been no interest. Now Stead decided to give it to her friend Oliver Stallybrass as a 'token of esteem'. She sent it to him on 14 February 1972, jokingly telling him it was a Valentine gift.

Stallybrass liked it very much, and though he no longer worked in a publishing house, he told her he would try to have it published. He edited it carefully, suggested minor changes, altered the title to *The Little Hotel* (which Stead never liked), and sent it around to publishers. This time, it was accepted by Angus & Robertson in London and Sydney, and published in 1973. (Holt published it in the States in 1975.) Its reception was remarkably positive in all three countries.

In 1972, Holt sent Stead an advance of $4000 for the re-issue of *House of All Nations*. In early 1973 she decided to abandon *I'm Dying Laughing* for good. Quite firm this time, she told Burnshaw:

My "forthcoming novel" is now in the dustbin or as good as. I ploughed it under—instead of dying laughing it was dying of boredom and overwork and what Bill used to call ree-search. It is not my métier and it got me down, so low I could not even read a book—any book.[161]

Ruth McKenney had died in July 1972, after years of mental instability. When she heard the news, Stead, who had spent twenty years (off and on) musing about McKenney's strengths and weaknesses, wrote to Harry and Anne Bloom:

What a wonderful personality she had; what a marvellous friend she was! I never met anyone like her, gay, clever, astute, and pithy: as well as pithy, she could be a torrent, an

endless talker—a phenomenon. You couldn't always endure it
—but it was unique—(probably led to her mental disorders;
there was no limit) . . . Then how charming, cunning in her
impulsiveness! I have had few women friends: she was the
best, wisest, and as a personality, much the most gifted . . .
Her generous and politically sensitive nature made her a
communist: she WAS a rebel; she was in nature great.[162]

There was no mention of McKenney being a 'traitor'; there was no
sign of any anger at all. Stead's judgements could be as whimsical as
they were intransigent.

In August 1972 she was asked by the New York journal *Nation* to
review Quentin Bell's biography *Virginia Woolf*, just published by
the Hogarth Press. She had never liked Woolf's fiction, nor did she
have much time for literary biography, but she agreed to take on
the review. She thought Bell's biography good, like an interesting
novel—but instead of discussing it on its own terms, she started to
make notes on Virginia Woolf as if she were a character in her own
fiction. And in a sense Stead made her into one.[163] She read all
Woolf's essays and several of her novels; she read Roger Fry's
recently published *Letters*; she even went so far as to steep herself in
the 'unreadable' Jane Austen[164] (that 'tiresome chronicler of the
country marriage-hunt'[165]) to try to understand why Woolf so
admired her. She was following far too many tangents, and felt
inadequate, wishing she had the 'brilliance, thoroughness' and
'good sense' of her scholarly Canberra friend Dorothy Green. She
told herself she was going mad with it all: 'boring myself steadily
to death'.[166]

Virginia Woolf became the new target of her anger. The beautiful
Woolf was a 'beast' when it came to remarks about the appearance
of other women writers. Woolf was a terrible snob. Her feminism
was a 'narrow and savage passion'. *A Room of One's Own* was
'ridiculous even when it appeared in 1929, with its notion that to
equal men in fiction . . . a woman must have not only a room of her
own but £500 yearly. (Ben Jonson was a brick-layer, Keats a clerk.)'
Three Guineas was a 'bitter, and intolerable attack on men'. Virginia
Woolf 'had no notion of history'. Worst of all, *The Years* revealed a
'coarse and unnecessary anti-Semitism' which made Stead 'absolutely
furious'.[167] She also took it as an indication of outrageous anti-
semitism that Woolf told Violet Dickinson she was going to marry
'a penniless Jew'.[168] She ignored the next line in Woolf's letter,
quoted in Bell's biography: 'I'm more happy than anyone ever said
was possible.'

Stead's behaviour was no longer rational: she had become one of
the Furies. She wrote to Burnshaw:

Well, I said to myself, when I saw my furious red face in
the looking glass, "You are right but calm down" and I was
surprised at my intense feeling.[169]

In December 1972 she abandoned the review, asking her agent
Cyrilly Abels to make some excuse to the *Nation*. Not only did she
feel a miserable failure, she simply could not understand why she had
had 'to fight 100 devils', why the whole thing had upset her so.[170]

Yet she did have some idea. In an abandoned draft of a letter to
Emile Capouya, book review editor of *Nation*, she tried to explain
why she felt unable to write the review.

I took it harder than necessary perhaps, because I too married
a Jew (though I would never have thought of saying so),
I married a fine man who in a sense was my creator too: he
did everything for me, as L.W. did for V.W. You see, I could
not bear her mean behaviour.[171]

To her cousin Gwen she wrote:

I was held up three months on a piece about Virginia Woolf,
got snarled up horribly, because of the dreadful subject (as I
saw it eventually). She was mad and tortured her husband in
every way (partly through her own agonies)—he was a Jew as
you know and she was beastly about it . . . and I became very
upset about her horrible behaviour: so it all fell through . . .
Naturally, V.W. who had been mad all her life, and
cottonwooled all her life, was extremely spoiled and thought
she could do and say anything. Well, no more of that.[172]

Clearly, Woolf's aristocratic upbringing, snobbery and alleged
anti-semitism were not the *real* issue. Her sin was that she was
'unbalanced, strange, unreliable, malevolent as the sick are, especially to those closest to them who are caring for them'.[173] In other
words, the *real* issue was that Stead unconsciously identified with
Woolf. Reading about Woolf, a woman writer with whom she had
several things in common, from a deep insecurity to a Jewish
husband, had brought all the remorse she felt about Bill to the
surface again. It caused her agony. Stead was dealing with her self-
hatred in her habitual way: she deflected it into fury against others.
'Virginia Woolf'—a very different figure from Quentin Bell's
Virginia—nearly became one of Stead's fictional creations.

★   ★   ★

When she was not angry, Stead suffered from 'horrible mental and
moral lethargy'. Reading Coleridge's poetry one spring day, she
was comforted to see that he suffered from the same malaise. She
quoted his poem 'Work Without Hope' to Gwen:

> All Nature seems at work. Slugs leave their lair—
> The bees are stirring . . .
> And I, the while, the sole unbusy thing,
> Nor honey make, nor pair, nor build, nor sing.[174]

Whole days went by without her doing anything much. She would feed the birds, snip the flowers at the window box with a pair of scissors, write distracted letters, have drinks with Marjorie Way, her neighbour, and then sit wondering what to do next. Sometimes the radio played one of Bill's favourite pieces of music, and she would sadly mark down on the radio guide 'Bill'.[175]

Stead believed she had suffered 'some sort of a breakdown'.[176] Mentally she was much more fragile than she revealed to others. Though she admitted to terrible loneliness, she rarely revealed the extent of her desperation. To Dorothy Green she wrote that she had become 'indifferent to writing—because there is no love in my life'.[177] She told Joan Lidoff, an American scholar who interviewed her at Surbiton in June 1973, that Bill Blake's death had stopped her writing.

In July 1973 she was interviewed by Ann Whitehead, by telephone from Australia. She told Whitehead she was a 'goodnatured sort of person' who was 'never irritated', and that she believed a reader had the right to make 'whatever judgements he thinks'. Then Whitehead asked her about *For Love Alone*:

Q: In *For Love Alone*, your semi-autobiographical novel— would that be fair, to call it that?

A: Yes, yes.

Q: Teresa leaves Australia because she feels that the insularity and the restrictions of the society are crushing her . . .

A: No! That's not an interpretation that I care for.

Q: But how do you see it? You know . . .

A: Well, it's explained in the novel. I assume you've . . . I know you have read it, of course, because you're talking about it.

Q: Yes.[178]

After such occasions, Stead suffered agonies. She did not sleep for two nights after the interview with Whitehead and on the third night she told herself: 'This has to stop—I must forget it!'[179] Interviews, she told Burnshaw, made her feel 'seasick'.[180] ('I always make a fool of myself, some way or other.'[181]) The fact is, she *did* care what people thought. She cared very much.

Hiram Haydn, editor of the *American Scholar* and a close friend of Stanley Burnshaw, planned a special issue on his poet friend. He asked Burnshaw whom he could suggest to write a portrait of him. Burnshaw suggested Stead: she had read all his work, and Burnshaw considered her an astute critic. Haydn wrote to Stead, asking her 'to try to get a *feeling of the person*, within the scholar and poet'.[182] Stead accepted, feeling she owed this to Burnshaw.

From July 1973 she struggled with the article, supposed to be anything from 2000 to 4000 words. She told Burnshaw she would use his letters to her as a basis for writing about his life and character. In addition, she asked him to provide her with brief autobiographical notes. He sent her a closely-typed twelve-page mini-autobiography.

Stead intended it to take six weeks. It eventually took seven months. She chided herself on being a 'slothful worthless friend'.[183] She apologised for taking so long. She made excuses. She complained: 'My lifelong disease ... re-writing, gets worse as my powers weaken.'[184] The heart attack she suffered that October was caused, she was convinced, by the mental effort of it all. Though she had a deep appreciation of poetry and had always impressed Burnshaw with her sensitive insights, it was the kind of scholarly exercise she was not good at. In March 1974, shortly before she left for Australia, she sent Burnshaw some fifty pages, saying she was unable to cut them herself. Burnshaw was in the awkward position of having to hone a piece about himself. He was pleased, nevertheless, with her warm, beautifully written portrait, which taught him things about his own writing. When he had finished with it, it was a much condensed, fine piece of writing. Stead was embarrassed: 'I do not know why I did not simply copy out the generous notes you sent me and send them back with my name attached!'[185]

Hiram Haydn had just died. His successor as editor, Joseph Epstein, commented that though Stead's article was handsomely written, he wanted a critical piece on Burnshaw's work, and less of a personal portrait. After all that, the article was relegated to Stead's and Burnshaw's respective files.

Ten years later, after Stead's death, the London magazine *Agenda* decided to bring out a *Stanley Burnshaw Special Issue*. The editors were shown the Stead piece and were delighted. It appeared in 1984. Stead never saw in print the sensitive tribute she had written to her long-standing literary friend.[186]

★   ★   ★

By the end of 1973 she was making plans for her return to Australia. Winter was approaching; she hated the cold, and there was a world oil crisis. She did not want to return to Australia at 71:

it was more a question of having nothing to live for in England. Under Gough Whitlam's new Labor Government, the country was flourishing culturally, and Patrick White had just won the Nobel Prize for Literature. But Stead was obsessed with one thing only: finding a companion. For a while she hesitated: should she go to Australia via the States? She was frightened by the stories of hijackings. But she decided she wanted to see Harry Bloom one more time. Since he had not come to her, she would go to him. She knew it would probably be the last time she ever saw him. Her plan was to go to New York for three weeks. To Aida Kotlarsky she wrote wryly that she and Harry Bloom would probably meet in a Greenwich Village café over glasses of tomato juice—since they both had heart trouble and angina.

Uprooting herself from England made her anxious, and she suffered from 'the three a.m. worries'. She went at the task slowly: she had to give away her furniture, sort through remaining papers, pack trunks, farewell friends. 'It is only now that I know all that Bill did for me, for us,' she told Aida Kotlarsky.[187] Paul Koston arranged for her books to be packed up and sent off. And the Halls helped with the heavy work. At first Stead planned to fly in March 1974; then she postponed the trip.

On 2 May 1974, Philip Harvey and Ruth Hall accompanied her to Heathrow. Stead was flustered and nervous. She was leaving for good the country in which she had arrived, full of hope, almost exactly forty-six years ago. There was nothing to stay for; she felt an outsider in these people's lives. But they had known her for years. They had loved Bill. And now she was going to a country where only a handful of people had ever set eyes on the man she had lived with for almost forty years. She was cutting herself off from her past as radically as she had done at the age of 26.

She guessed she would never see Ruth or Philip again. She and Ruth had never loved each other. But they had both loved Bill, and this had created a significant bond. It was touching to watch Ruth walk along beside her. Ruth, short and plump with smiling eyes and animated gestures, looked just like her father. The burly, cheerful man cajoling her and carrying her luggage was another man she had loved—for over a decade now. It had been a painful passion, a 'great waste of time and heart'.[188] But he had been good to her.

Only Bill had ever given her the greatest gift a man could give her: his love. She had scarcely been able to believe in it at first. And England was the country, London was the city, where it had all begun.

* * *

Stead spent a miserable time in the air. Once through the barrier, she lost her boarding card. She eventually found it in her handbag. Over the Atlantic she worried about the whereabouts of her health card. Surely she would be asked to produce it in New York. Eventually she found that it was in 'the right place', and they did not even ask for it.

In New York she stayed with Ettore and Jessie Rella in the downstairs section of their double-storey apartment. Full of plants and flowers, the Rellas' world always seemed magical to her. It was a 'little clearing in the forest . . . a curious heavenly place a bit like the everlasting moment on the Grecian urn'.[189] Hidden away in their cupboards and drawers was a 'secret life': the fine glove puppets they had made together over the years. (Ettore did the 'beautiful faces' and 'fine long elegant hands'; the dressing was done by Jessie, a skilled dressmaker.)[190] Over the furniture stalked their haughty Siamese cats. Stead called them the 'aristo-cats'.

For the first week she 'went into a trance and did nothing'.[191] She wrote to Philip Harvey meaningfully: 'NY is very dear; but pleasant. I am very much at home here, much more than in London and much much happier. Thank goodness.'[192] He answered her from Corsica, where he and his family were on holiday.

> You lived in close association with all that is best in the
> American character for many years . . . Your present environs
> must be striking answering points that have not sparked since
> Bill died. Fancy living with 10 million Bills around you, not but
> that the lovely man was not unique & not really capable of
> being duplicated. But one friend will hint at his level of
> generosity of mind & Spirit, another will smack of his bubbling
> humour, a third will whisper of his scholarship & profundity &
> perhaps most will reflect his optimism & vigorous affirmation
> in their joy of life & for the human scene.[193]

Stead was profoundly moved by his letter. She liked American male voices, and she would often hear traces of Bill's rich accent. She *was* partial to Americans because of Bill, Harvey was right. And for the same reason, she felt particular warmth towards Jewish people. She commented to Stanley Burnshaw, who was writing a trilogy based on three heroic Jewish lives, Moses, Uriel Da Costa and Stanley's own father:[194]

> What is absolutely fascinating is that you are studying the
> means by which the Jews managed to survive; what *does*
> explain their special characteristics? Intensity, energy, talents,
> warmth, self-expression. I don't know what forms any
> national characteristics. Pressure, training; but why anyhow?
> . . . It is the warmth and ardour and ingeniousness and love of

talent in others which makes the Jews so dear to their friends.
(I know about bad Jews and dumb Jews—I am not idealising;
but I am talking of all the others.)[195]

She also liked to speculate that small men were more likely to show
geniality and brilliance.

Harry Bloom had written: 'Darling Xris, Now soon I will see
you in the flesh and hear your lovely voice and touch you!'[196]
He had told her he would be in New York on 10 May, one week
after her arrival. But he had been ill again, and his wife Anne had
had a heart attack. For the moment he was stuck in Miami, and
once again, Stead found herself waiting for Harry Bloom.

By 6 June, around the time Stead had planned to leave for
Australia, there was still no sign of Bloom. She told herself 'it
would be useless to come here and go off without seeing him, after
all this'.[197] She sent telegrams to Australia. When Aida Kotlarsky
went to Hunter for the summer, Stead moved into her twelfth-floor
apartment on E. 18th Street. She had always liked Aida's furnishings: the carved ebony chairs, oriental lamps and rugs, the brocades
from ancient China, the handsome pianos. This time Aida's apartment seemed 'faded, as a pale story'.[198]

She read all the 'readable' books in Aida's apartment, and various
books by American radicals sent her by her publishers. She found
Cedric Belfrage's book *The American Inquisition* highly informative
about the McCarthy era. And she was shocked by *All the President's
Men*. ('It simply leaves one wondering how long this has been
going on and what goes on in the "white" house.'[199])

Eventually, on 12 June, Harry arrived in New York. His wife
had come with him, and they were staying with their son Michael,
so once again, his movements were restricted. He managed a brief
visit. When he stood at the door in the half-light, Stead was
shocked by his appearance: she imagined she had seen the Egyptian
horror 'Thoth' at the door.

Bloom arranged to have lunch with her at Luchows, a favourite
old restaurant of hers, but then he telephoned to say he was ill.
For the first time, Stead, in a letter to Aida Kotlarsky, expressed
irritation. But even now she took out her annoyance entirely on
Anne Bloom, fabricating a picture of a wicked wife that smacked of
fairy tale:

If this goes on, though I am truly anxious for Harry's health and
good spirits, I will have to think of moving on. She (the wife)
does not know I am here—but she is suspicious of any trip
Harry makes . . . She doesn't want him to see anyone, any old
friends; for she has got a mania about his MONEY. She wants

to be a rich widow and does not want him to give presents etc. maybe to old friends (like me, eh?). That is the sordid fact. And that is why she keeps him under lock and key . . . I am not telling this to the Rellas—it is too sordid, and makes this whole thing, which was a blessed thing, a real tender farewell between two old lovebirds, old lovers, something unpleasant. Well, let us hope things will improve in a few days.[200]

Two days later she apologised to Aida for her badtempered letter. She was happy; she was buoyant. She even felt like writing fiction again, and had already written a funny piece based on a story Harry had told her the day before. He had eventually turned up at the apartment and they had 'a fine long time together'. He looked a little better. She was planning a story called 'Lover's Meeting'. She told Aida:

Suddenly you see I have begun to see everything as a story; and that is why we get on. Not only does he love me but he turns me into a Scheherazade; which is what by nature I am.

She would stay in New York as long as Harry was there; when he went south to Miami, she would leave for Australia. In the meantime, she decided she was enjoying New York. 'If it were possible for me to live here, I feel I would be happy here; many very good old friends. But that cannot be.'[201]

Harry's return to Miami was delayed, but not because of Christina, as she would have liked. Soon after his visit, the 'honeytongued' Harry was admitted to the coronary division of St Luke's Hospital. He sent her a letter via a nurse. Once, Ettore Rella telephoned the hospital on Christina's behalf. When he started to improve, Harry rang her. On one occasion he even arranged for her to visit him in hospital. Three weeks passed. Stead was having nightmares. She told the Harveys:

Harry . . . gets his night nurses (noy-ses) to telephone me and tell me how he is; but though I am sure he loves this cloak-and-dagger work, I am quite tired of it; no one's fault.[202]

In Australia the family had planned a birthday party for 17 July. Stead sent another telegram and spent her seventy-second birthday with the Rellas at the Plaza Hotel.

She had booked a flight to Australia on 3 August, but told herself she could always postpone it. Now she was waiting for Harry Bloom to come out of hospital. The nurses told her he should be out in three or four days. She saw friends. The Rellas were 'great comforters'.[203]

But when Bloom came out of hospital in late July, he was 'under observation' by his family, and they had no opportunity to meet.

Stead decided to keep to the 3 August departure date. She had been in New York three months, not three weeks as planned, and had seen Harry Bloom just three times. From Australia she would write to Aida that the trip to New York had been worth it to see Harry, but it was not what either of them had expected.

> It seems certain that I will not see him again; so it was well that I managed to see him those few times. Things end—one knows it; but it is an odd experience to feel.[204]

A few months later, living at her brother's house in Sydney's dusty western suburbs, she called her New York sojourn 'a sort of heaven-haven ... between the limbo of London and this strange little suburban wilderness'.[205]

15

Humping Her Own Bluey

AUGUST 1974—MARCH 1983

CHRISTINA STEAD WAS tired. She was tired, in particular, of loneliness. At the age of 72, after forty-six years in the northern
hemisphere, she had returned to Australia to live in her brother
Gilbert's house in Hurstville, just one suburb down the railway line
from Bexley, where she had spent her first fifteen years. From her
1969 visit she remembered Hurstville as a dreary, hot and dusty
suburb, a long way from the city.[1] She knew there was no deep
affinity between her and her family. But with her heart condition,
she was so frightened of living alone that she had paid approximately
A$7000 for an extension to be built at the back of Gilbert's house.

By 1974 Hurstville was so built up that the glistening blue of
Botany Bay could be glimpsed only from high vantage points, and
then over a myriad of red rooftops. These days Hurstville, thirty
minutes from the centre of Sydney by train, epitomised working-
class Australian suburbia. It had few trees; the corner shops were
going broke. 'New Australians' (as European immigrants were
then called) had settled in the area, their brick-veneer houses
sporting white doric columns and newly concreted backyards. The
sky roared with the sound of jets boring in and out of Sydney's
Kingsford Smith Airport to the north-east—a far cry from the beginning of the century when Christina Stead had lived there.

511

Christina's new quarters comprised a long, narrow room, much like a barn, with a small bedroom off to the side. A large sliding aluminium window at the eastern end looked out onto a small backyard with a lemon tree, banana-palm, pepper tree and ferns. Stead would sit by the window and watch the birds come for the birdseed she put out. At night, she derived some comfort from the patter of birds on the tin roof and the ping of berries as they dropped from an overhanging tree.

The ceiling was unfinished: Stead looked up at silver lining and rough wooden beams. The light was a naked bulb hanging from the rafters, and the furniture was cheap. But she hardly noticed these things any more. For years her surroundings had been austere, often grim. Dorothy Green had been shocked by Stead's dingy flat in Surbiton, especially when she saw pigeons strolling around in the kitchen.

Gilbert took a week off work to help his sister settle in. She paid for, and he installed, an electric stove, television, refrigerator and filing cabinets for her papers. Christina felt immense relief at being looked after by her 'baby brother', strong at 56, though he too had suffered a heart attack. They had a congenial relationship. When Gilbert came home from work, he would join Christina for evening drinks. Betty, his third wife, worked long hours in a catering business, often at night as well. Their two boys bore the traditional family names: David was 12; little Gilbert, a spoilt, cheerful fellow, was 7. For the first two or three weeks, Christina sincerely believed her loneliness was over.

It was wishful thinking. In all Stead's fiction (behind her now), there is no glimpse of cosy family life. 'Family life is poison,' declares Emily Wilkes, a wife and mother, in *I'm Dying Laughing*.[2] Christina had almost nothing in common with her half brothers and sisters. After a month in Australia she wrote to Rella: 'I am very welcome and well-received here, Ettore, but they are not "my own." They are not the brothers and sisters I picked up along the way of my life, whom I miss.'[3] When Stanley Burnshaw asked if she was beginning to feel at home in Australia, she replied emphatically: 'I left my life lying on the shores of other countries and I came to Australia. No question of coming back—you can't come back . . . I am not home.'[4]

Kate lived alone in a flat in harbour-side Cremorne, not far from Gwen Walker-Smith, with whom she was close friends. Weeta had converted to Catholicism when she married a Catholic (to her father's horror) and had four children, now grown up. She lived in Wollongong, on the south coast of New South Wales. Christina was happier with her brothers: they were men, they enjoyed drinking, they appeared more broadminded. Gilbert was a finance officer at the Metal Workers' Union; for relaxation he made endless alterations to the house in Hurstville. David, a metallurgist, lived on the affluent North Shore in a house set in bushland. Christina saw nothing of Kelvin, the middle brother, whose family shared Boongarre, at Watson's Bay, with Thistle Harris. (Thistle lived at the back, quite independently.) David and Gilbert had read Christina's books and were proud of their famous sister; the two sisters could not quite forgive her for what she had written about the family. To Ettore Rella Christina mused about the neuroses of the 'Pollit family', as she called them. Convinced that their peculiar childhood had scarred her and all her siblings, she made notes, 'The Bones the Parents Left'. She believed she herself had been wilful enough to stand up to her father, but some of her siblings were less forceful. ('If it did that to me, what did it do to certain gentler members?') All seemed 'marked with the iron ring'.[5]

Over the years, Stead had occasionally written to Thistle Harris from the northern hemisphere, but now that she was back in Sydney, Stead ostentatiously avoided her—just as she had in 1969. Thistle never knew why. Only once did Christina go back to Boongarre. It was in May 1976, two years after her return. *Miss Herbert* had just appeared in the States and *Time* magazine's article would praise it effusively. Their photographer, David Austen, rang Stead and suggested he come out to Hurstville to photograph her in her home environment. Gilbert Stead was in the throes of renovations and the house was dusty and noisy. For Christina, it was anything but 'home'. Austen then came up with the idea that they should go out to her childhood home at Watson's Bay. Stead concurred, admitting she had not seen 'the old patriarchal hut' for forty-eight years. Watson's Bay had changed dramatically. In Christina's youth there had still been large areas of dirt road and bushland; now the harbour-side settlement was filled with the houses of the well-to-do. She and Austen walked down the drive of Boongarre, and through the garden to the harbour beyond. He photographed her walking on the jetty in front of the house.[6] Thistle came out and spoke to them, but Christina was distant and awkward. The incident left Thistle dumbfounded.[7]

★   ★   ★

In her autobiographical piece 'Another View of the Homestead', which told of her four-month return to Australia in 1969, Stead played down the 'going home' aspect and portrayed herself—in strikingly Nietzschean terms—as a wanderer. She was enthusiastic about being 'a temporary citizen of a flying village with fiery windows, creaking and crashing across the star-splattered dark'.[8] She made clear that 'home', for a traveller like herself, was only ever a temporary arrangement.

> I have had many homes, am easily at home, requiring very little. My first novel (before *Seven Poor Men of Sydney*) was to be called *The Young Man Will Go Far* and then, *The Wraith and the Wanderer* . . . The Wanderer, once he has started out in the company of the Wraith, the tramp and his whisperer, does not look over his shoulder. He does not think of where to live, somewhere, anywhere; anything may happen, awkward and shameful things do happen; he does not believe it when life is good; by thirty all is not done, neither the shames nor the lucky strikes. He takes no notice, it is his equal but different fate, he marries a stranger, loves an outlaw, neighbours with many, speaks with tongues. So that if he should cross the high bridge of air sometime, going homewards, he is also on the outward path.

Whereas Nietzsche's intrepid wanderers strike out alone, Stead's travel with a 'wraith', a companion. Returning to Australia after her protracted exile, Stead compared herself with Ulysses.[9] The difference (though she did not say this) was that unlike the Greek hero, she was not eagerly awaited by a faithful companion. She had left Australia hung with the dreadful spectre of spinsterhood; she had returned as a widow—more respectable but no less bleak. She could not help herself: women without men, whatever their age, seemed pathetic figures to her. (The only glimpse in her fiction of an elderly woman on her own is the tragically lonely and distracted figure of Solander Fox's mother in *Letty Fox*.) Could she write without her 'whisperer'? Soon after her return to Australia in 1974, she told Ettore Rella:

> I have no great instigator—Bill was; and there have been some others (not necessarily lovers!) and I am hoping that certain lovely present day instigators, like yourself will keep me going, sting me (but only with honey, please) to keep me buzzing.[10]

In the next few years, because she was constantly typing letters, people thought she was 'writing'. To the last, she clung to the hope that she would soon start to write again. But, she told herself, in order to write she needed someone to 'sting' her—she needed the love of a man.

*   *   *

Ettore and Jessie Rella, in 'lovely New York', became Stead's confidants; she wrote to them at least fortnightly, sometimes more often. To friends she spoke of Ettore Rella as her 'Albanian boyfriend'. As summer approached, she would type letters during the night, sometimes at 3 am, or 'nightride' through a book.[11] She liked the early mornings, the coolest hour of the day, when she could watch the dawn come up through the window. Writing letters made her feel less alone. Her thoughts were often with Harry Bloom, but he could not keep up with the Rellas' letter-writing pace. Invariably, he was too ill to fetch her letters from his post office box.

It was a twenty-minute walk up a slight incline from Gilbert Stead's house at No. 10 Donald Street to Hurstville's main street and railway station, and Christina no longer walked that far. She found it a strain to take a taxi to the station and the train into the city, and preferred, despite the expense, to take a taxi straight to the city. She made the trip once a week or so—necessary, she was soon telling herself, for her sanity. She would meet David at The Green Jade, his favourite restaurant in Chinatown. They both liked food and enjoyed a good bottle of wine. Or she would meet Gwen or Kate, who would help her shop for an item of clothing or a present, before having lunch in a café.

Gradually Stead made friends. Ron Geering, who had visited her in Surbiton in 1966 when he was researching his book, *Christina Stead*, invited her to lunch at his house in the leafy North Shore suburb of Gordon, and Stead met his wife Dorothy, a lecturer in Early Childhood Training. Geering, a warm, unpretentious man with a keen sense of humour, taught English at the University of New South Wales. He soon found himself playing the avuncular role men so often assumed with Christina. He and Dorothy regularly had her to lunch at Gordon: they would sit on the terrace overlooking their magnificent garden. Sometimes they invited Christina to stay for the weekend. They celebrated her birthday, invited her for Christmas. With 'Ron-Ron', as she called him, Stead could talk about books and nature: she could relax, joke, grumble about her family. She flirted with him, of course—and he indulged this, kissing her hand and fussing over her—but above all, she treasured him as a 'pleasant, kind, brotherly' friend. 'Doro' was a 'sweet person' and a 'great cook',[12] but it was to Ron that Christina wrote letters. One woman friend observed that she could be brusque with Dorothy.[13]

Through the Geerings, Stead was re-acquainted with the novelist Elizabeth Harrower, whom she had met several times in 1972 in London. Stead admired Harrower's fiction and thought her 'a good sweet dear woman'.[14] This was an ominous sign, but they became friends. Harrower was close to Patrick White and his companion, Manoly Lascaris, and occasionally they would meet as a foursome.

*   *   *

In mid October 1974, Harrower rang to invite herself out to Hurstville on a 'mysterious mission'.[15] On arrival, she announced to Stead that she came as Patrick White's emissary: he wanted her to receive the first Patrick White Literary Award.[16] Would she please accept? The $6000 award came from a trust fund that White had set up when he won the Nobel Prize for Literature the previous year. Now that the Britannica Award had ceased, it was the richest annual award open to Australian writers. White stipulated that he particularly wanted to help older writers who had not received the critical acclaim they deserved, and he and his fellow judges, historian Geoffrey Blainey and librarian James Allison, agreed that Christina Stead was 'the most brilliant and deserving of any Australian writer'.[17] Afterwards, Stead told the Rellas wryly that Patrick White and his fellow trustees wanted to hand 'a certain person' ('whom I do not name until it is published') $6000 'as a reward for being an older writer'.[18]

The prize brought a brief burst of publicity, but Stead did not even mention it in a letter to Stanley Burnshaw later the same month. It made her feel more comfortable financially, for she still regarded herself as poor—more from habit, these days, than from necessity.

With her customary helplessness, she had handed her financial management over to her brother David, who says today that she had little idea about the state of her finances though she did complain, probably influenced by him, that the 'income-tax crows' picked her bones.[19] Apart from occasional cheques from royalties or lending rights—these varied from year to year but rarely exceeded $10 000—she lived quite well on three different pensions: an Australian old-age pension ($96 monthly), the British one to which she and Bill had made small payments (about $20 monthly) and an American widow's pension (about $200 monthly in Australian currency). She rarely touched the capital she had amassed in recent years, and at her death she would leave over $70 000. She remained impulsively generous: she was always buying gifts for the family, her friends and their children. When Ettore Rella had a stroke the following year, she sent him and Jessie $2000.

★　★　★

Patrick White had championed Stead since the re-issue of *The Man Who Loved Children* in 1965, when he had first discovered her writing. No other Stead novel had quite the same impact on him, but he thought *For Love Alone* 'a remarkable book',[20] and when he

read *Letty Fox*, he remarked to Geoffrey Dutton: 'It's quite extraordinary to think of that quiet, sedate woman writing anything so
hilarious.'[21] Stead was always nervous about their social encounters.
White had invited her to lunch during her 1969 visit and afterwards
told Geoffrey Dutton that they 'got on very well'. He commented:
'Christina Stead's characters . . . are all people she has known. She
wasn't prepared to believe that mine, the important ones anyway,
are latent bits of myself.'

> To talk to her is more like talking to a man than a woman,
> although there is nothing overtly masculine about her, and I
> shouldn't think anything lesbian. Her marriage seems to have
> been one of the best kind.[22]

In that short encounter, Patrick White had been quite mystified. He
did not know it—perhaps she did not either—but her characters, as
much as White's, contained latent bits of herself.

Stead sensed that White, 'sensitive' and 'somewhat withdraw-
ing', listened and observed with the same sharp-eyed awareness
that she did—and she feared it.[23] When, soon after her arrival in
Sydney, he and Lascaris invited her to lunch at their house in
Centennial Park, Stead kept postponing it, pleading dental troubles.[24] To add to her shyness, her skin problem had returned:
several keratoid spots had appeared on her face, and she turned
down most social engagements that summer.

Embarrassed that she had read so little of White, her patron (as
she saw it), that summer she was 'stuffing' and 'cramming' herself
with his work. It was not the ideal frame of mind in which to read
White, and it left her unenthusiastic. Back in 1969 she had found
Riders in the Chariot 'consoling',[25] but only *The Cockatoos* ever
inspired her. She could not get beyond the first few pages of *The
Vivisector*. Two years later, when White invited her to a small party
in November 1976, Stead hastily read his latest novel, *A Fringe of
Leaves*. She did not like it, though when she talked to White about
it, she concentrated on the section she did like. She did not tell him
that she 'couldn't stomach' Mrs Roxburgh wearing her wedding
ring attached to the fringe of leaves she wore round her lower
middle parts. 'Pat has some odd ideas about women, even though
he has some very good and true women friends,' she told Ron
Geering.[26] She would not have dared to call him Pat to his face,
either.

After reading *A Fringe of Leaves*, she told the Rellas:

> He is a devoted noble soul, etc. but he is trying to spread
> altar-juice all over Australia's dark and bloody history hoping

that up will come lilies (of the soul), whereas it was those very Anglicans he admires so much who created the crime, the penal system, the brutal floggings etc.

'A lot of hard work and honest craftsmanship has gone into this hardwon bilge,' she conceded.[27] Scathing though she was, she had completely misunderstood White's intention. It was exactly the sort of opinion, hotly defended, that used to madden Stead's friends. Another was her assertion that Patrick White was not a homosexual, and that Elizabeth Harrower and Dorothy Green (who knew White far better than she did) had got it wrong. Yet letters to the Rellas as early as 1975 make it quite clear that she knew that Lascaris was not simply a companion. (White's homosexuality was never hidden, though it was not openly proclaimed until he published his autobiography, *Flaws in the Glass*, in 1981.) Stead was sufficiently perverse to make dogmatic statements she herself did not believe.

Patrick White was impeccably polite to her, but privately she thought him 'a courteous and friendly cuss'.[28] Moreover, Stead was convinced that, as a homosexual (which she saw as being 'anti-woman'), White would look upon a plain woman without generosity.[29] She described one of his 'delectable lunches' with more admiration than warmth:

Everything is perfect, he is perfect, the long room where one sits and dines is delightful—all the paintings chosen by one man—and one cannot help feeling the stage-man in him, who gets everything to a pitch of perfection for the performance . . . He must be a *cordon bleu*—his cooking is also perfection.[30]

★   ★   ★

Deprived of a stimulating male companion, Stead was finding life 'very very dull'. She kept saying to herself: 'I must write my way out of this.'[31] She badly *wanted* to write: to an interviewer she explained that writing produced in her the same sort of euphoria as being loved.[32] She did not add that the first depended on the last. The Patrick White prize had jogged her conscience, and she began to talk of polishing and collating some short stories still in camphor balls. Back in the late Fifties she had planned a collection called *The Talking Ghost*; now she returned to the idea and even wrote to Philip Van Doren Stern in New York for permission to use his dreams in the stories. He willingly consented, but nothing came of the project.

It was not easy to start all over again, in a new place, with new friends, at the age of 72. 'Fact is,' she told her friend Dorothy Green in Canberra, 'I have to build up a new world, I suppose . . . What remains is ancient history, barrel-scrapings.'[33] That first summer the roar of the planes overhead drove her mad. To add to her misery, the family had purchased a portable swimming pool and the backyard was full of the 'demoniac shrieking' of young Gilbert and his friends. A sulphur-crested cockatoo hung around the 'hellish pool' and shrieked in imitation.[34] 'I'm of strong nerve, good heart and indifferent spirit,' Stead grumbled to the Rellas, 'but tomorrow, no later, I'm buying some ear stopples.'[35]

She found preparations for Christmas 1974 at Hurstville tiring. In honour of her return, there were to be twenty-six guests, two turkeys, six chickens and one ham. Christina was put in charge of the drinks. She had a brief moment of pleasure when buying plastic beakers in the local hardware store. Hearing them speak Italian, she said something in Italian herself, and was promptly 'smothered' with 'celestial storms' of the language. She had already fished out her Greek dictionaries to exchange words with the Greek owners of the corner shop, but some months later, to her dismay, her friends went bankrupt.

Early in 1975 came the blow she had been expecting for some time: Harry Bloom died. Fearing he would not survive heart surgery, he had written to Christina on 21 January from a cardiac unit in Miami. After that there was silence. She was filled with dread, but dared not write to his wife for news. Eventually Polly Steinberg wrote to say that Harry had died on 6 February. Stead was 'quite stricken'.[36] She told friends it was as if she were widowed a second time. To Aida Kotlarsky, one of the few who knew how much she had loved Harry Bloom, she wrote:

He was always at my side, even when we were thousands of miles apart, always the best of friends to Bill and to me. I want to thank you again, Aida my dear for what you did for us.[37]

She told Stanley Burnshaw:

I would tell him all sorts of things, for he always responded and we spoke the same language. An *amitié amoureuse* which went on for just on 40 years, one way and another. I am only just now getting over my habit (of which I was unconscious) of saying to myself (inside the head), "Harry would laugh at that" and "I'll tell Harry that." He wrote to me every year on the anniversary of Bill's death saying something like "I stayed awake nearly all night, I could not sleep for thinking of Bill and what is lost."[38]

★ ★ ★

The Little Hotel, written in the early Fifties, came out in the States in April 1975—two years after England this time. It received enthusiastic reviews in both countries. Lillian Hellman bought the option for a screenplay.[39] In New York, Holt, Rinehart & Winston had just re-issued *House of All Nations* in paperback, and Angus & Robertson published it in Australia in 1974. On the strength of all this, Cyrilly Abels, Stead's American agent, encouraged her to take *Miss Herbert* out of its box. Gwen Walker-Smith re-typed the manuscript, untouched for over a decade, and it was sent off to the States.

When Cyrilly Abels read it, she was disturbed by Miss Herbert's anti-semitic comments, and made the point to Stead that many readers would see Miss Herbert as something of a heroine—beautiful, hardworking and sexually 'liberated'—and would thus assume that the author condoned her anti-semitism. Stead, who regarded Eleanor Herbert as anything but a heroine, was horrified. Thinking, perhaps, of her own reaction to Woolf's novel *The Years*, she immediately agreed that if there was any chance of misunderstanding, the comments would have to go. She cut nearly all, leaving in just enough to show Miss Herbert as an overall racist.

Holt rejected the novel, convinced it would not sell—perhaps because it was set in England. But Random House liked it and paid Stead an advance of $5000. (Charlotte Mayerson, previously Stead's editor at Holt, now worked at Random House.) Stead dedicated the novel to Cyrilly Abels, not only because of her role in the revision and publication, but because Abels had not long to live. She had been ill, with a persistent cough, when Stead was in New York the previous year. She was to die in November 1975 from lung cancer, a few months before the book came out.

*　　*　　*

'She cannot love,' Stead wrote disdainfully to her editor Charlotte Mayerson, about her character Miss Herbert.[40] Her dislike for this woman (and her main model, Florence James) was mingled with envy: she admitted to Stanley Burnshaw that it 'riled' a plain woman 'to see another woman beautiful and senseless'.[41] The two magnificent beauties in Stead's fiction—Elvira in *The Beauties and Furies* and Eleanor in *Miss Herbert*—are both portrayed as emotionally frigid Venuses. Each of them is exposed, in the end, as a dull woman 'with an ordinary suburban face and ordinary suburban remarks'.[42]

Stead believed that she herself, in contrast to Miss Herbert, was a woman who loved. More accurately, she craved love. If there was no love in her life, she imagined it. 'All love stories are ghost stories,' she rationalised to Stanley Burnshaw.[43]

For the most part, Stead believed her own elaborate fictions. She transformed 'ghost stories' into 'love stories' with an insistence that bordered on the truly delusional. One such story arose from a rare visit from a man. Kel Semmens was a medical doctor in his mid fifties, a tall goodlooking man with kind blue eyes, whom Stead had met briefly on her 1969 visit to Melbourne. At that time, she had warmed to him instantly. In 1975, on a visit to Sydney, Semmens rang David Stead and asked for Christina's address. On the first day of May, he appeared at the door of No. 10 Donald Street. He was shocked by what he saw: the cheap and ugly furniture, the rows of empty bottles. He thought sadly of the Place Vendôme days she had told him about. He proposed a meal out. The weather was mild, but Stead donned the mink coat given to her forty years before by Ruth Bakwin. She knew it suited her.

Over lunch, she did not conceal her utter loneliness. Kel Semmens, who liked to think of himself as a 'Mr Fixit', could see how out of place she was in suburban Hurstville and suggested that one of the university residential colleges in Canberra might provide a more suitable social environment for her. He added that he regularly travelled to Canberra from Melbourne, where he lived with his wife. Back at Donald Street, he felt no inclination to go inside a house that depressed him. While the taxi waited, he saw her to the front door.[44]

Stead's version of the meeting was heightened and embroidered. Two weeks later, she wrote in great excitement to her brother David, promising him a good bottle of wine:

Not only out of gratitude and proper family feeling; but because you put me in touch with you know whom!—he telephoned and it turned out to be the work of young Cupid himself. He wants me to go to Canberra to be near him, remembers me from a slight visit to Melbourne in 1969 and says he loves me. He is such a charming, able, delightful, sweet sort of chap, I said I would . . . I will go if everything works out. Don't say his name, if you remember it, to other friends or family members . . . Don't want any scandal (for him—for me, it's a *credit*!) I was feeling rather poorly in spirit. This is already helping me.[45]

She added that the meeting had made her start work again on 'that old (and fine) novel of mine, which has been in the ash-heap for so long'. (She meant *I'm Dying Laughing*.) By August, she was quite bewildered. She told the Rellas she had had 'the most extraordinary declaration of love—and then the man . . . vanished into the blue beyond. So strange.'[46]

A year later, the story had become more colourful. She told Burnshaw that her 'suitor' ('strikingly handsome') had 'hung around' at the front door for a 'fervent farewell salute'.[47] To Aida Kotlarsky she wrote ambiguously that she had found a 'Lover'.

> I'm not kidding though I would only dare tell people at a great distance who can't laugh at me (or at least I can't *hear* them laughing) and I would be doing wrong if I did not say he is a dear fellow and most unusual and very ingenious (a doctor of medicine and a poet).[48]

The advantage of friends 'at a great distance' was that they could not confirm or refute Stead's stories. Eighteen months after the original meeting, having seen Kel Semmens again in Melbourne, Stead would fill half a letter to Stanley Burnshaw about her 'strange spectral lover'.

> He is an able M.D. with a well-paid official job, he is tall, goodlooking (though nervous face, so that I am reminded of Richard Bransten) bronze-haired (curly and thick), sweet voice, graceful, exceedingly passionate when in presence—and then total absence.

She had decided that Semmens was a mythmaker:

> He loves "the princess in the distance" (me, in this case) and I fully believe if I took up any position where he could see me every day, that he would take off for Finland or Fiji or France or—and then from there, come to see me once a year—but no, I won't do it.[49]

Kel Semmens is warm and effusive. His affectionate manner, combined with the friendly farewell kiss at the front door, prompted Stead to imagine that here was another man who loved her. Semmens sensed that she wanted far more from him than he could give, and for this reason did not write to her afterwards.[50]

*   *   *

Even without a knight to rescue her, Stead had had enough of backyard suburbia.[51] She was greatly relieved when Dorothy Green rang in September 1975, offering her house in Canberra. Green was going to Tasmania to be with her pregnant daughter, who was seriously ill. Kate Stead offered to accompany Christina and stay with her for a fortnight. Later, David would come down for a few days. Gilbert drove the two sisters to Canberra.

Christina, in her shyness, liked to be accompanied; she had turned down an invitation to the Adelaide Festival of Arts because Gwen was unable to go with her. For the first two days in Canberra, she felt she had to adjust to the higher altitude and was pleased to have Kate there to look after her. But her sister soon got on her nerves. 'We have NOTHING in common,' she wrote to Stanley

Burnshaw, adding ungratefully: 'This company is not for me. Is any company for me but a good man? No.'[52] Early in November, Elizabeth Harrower came from Sydney to spend a few days with her. Christina, always up with the sun, would be playing at least her third game of patience by the time Harrower rose around 7 am.[53]

'Politicians battle and do murder to each other,' Stead told the Rellas in October 1975.[54] It was a time of great political tension in Australia: the Senate was blocking supply, making the Government's position untenable. But no-one was prepared for the events of 11 November 1975, when the Governor-General, Sir John Kerr, sacked Labor Prime Minister Gough Whitlam and dissolved Parliament, and within the hour, Liberal leader Malcolm Fraser announced that he had been commissioned as Caretaker Prime Minister. Stead was as disgusted as her friends that a representative of the Crown had the power to dismiss an elected Head of Government. Elizabeth Harrower, like many intellectuals a fervent admirer of Whitlam, was devastated. They had just come back from a picnic with Dorothy Green's friends Patricia Walker and Clare Golson when a friend telephoned with the news. The following day, Pat Walker drove them to the vast lunchtime rally outside Parliament House, Whitlam climbed onto a table-top truck and gave the victory salute; the crowd gave a deafening cheer and shouted 'We want Gough'. A week later, Stead wrote to Dorothy Green in Tasmania:

> Had a delightful time with that lovely (innocent too) girl
> Elizabeth Harrower. She had the great good luck of
> supernatural foresight to be here exactly in time to see her god
> (Gough W) in the flesh and manfully speaking from a lorry-end
> after his ignominious and ignoble dismissal, laughing (he) and
> all-embracing. She has gone home filled with the Message![55]

Few believed that the coup would come off. However, on 13 December 1975, Malcolm Fraser triumphantly won the general election. Long gone were the heady Whitlam days of the early Seventies; the Liberal–National Country Party Coalition was again in power.

Stead spent Christmas with the Walkers and the Golsons in Canberra. Dorothy Green came home at the end of December. She had been through the most painful time of her life: she had thought she would lose her daughter, and the baby was born handicapped. Stead stayed on another week. She was 'sympathetic and tactful', but Green wanted to be by herself, and Stead's restlessness and dogmatism irritated her.[56]

★　　★　　★

Harry Bloom had died; Cyrilly Abels was dying. Aida Kotlarsky had serious osteoarthritis. In July 1975, Ettore Rella had a stroke. Stead told Ruth Hall: 'He used to fly up and down the stairs and round the town and come back with extraordinary amusing Commedia dell'Arte stories, about nothing, about incidents—it was his Italian theatre—and now he can't.'[57] It would be months before he could even manoeuvre himself downstairs. Faced with these sobering reminders of human mortality, Stead arranged for her papers to go to the National Library of Australia, in Canberra, after her death.

* * *

After 'the calm and cool of beautiful Canberra' and the company of new artistic and intellectual friends, Stead could not settle in suburban Hurstville. Feeling guilty about not working, she defensively told Random House editor Charlotte Mayerson:

> My brother's house, in which I have a flat of my own, is so near a big international airport that I may as well live in an airport. The extreme noise, squealing, screaming (of planes) "a sound of iron in the air" (as poet Rella says) is hellish and breaks down my fresh fine mood (which I awake with) every morning and all day. Do not blame me. I am NOT lazy and [am] as anxious to work as anyone.[58]

Worse, there was domestic tension between Gilbert and Betty. Christina now referred to Hurstville as 'Curstville'.

Letters to friends—trifling and digressive—reflected the emptiness of her life. She would tell little anecdotes, sometimes scarcely coherently, then say: 'How did I get on to this trash?'[59] or 'I don't know what I am raving about'.[60] From March 1976 onwards, the Rellas and Burnshaws were treated to letter after letter about her new idols, H. C. Coombs and Premier Don Dunstan. Both, she told them, were small in stature but with enormous presence.

Herbert Cole ('Nugget') Coombs wrote to Stead in March 1976, inviting her to lunch with him and his daughter-in-law Margaret.[61] Stead had first met Coombs, then Chancellor of the ANU, in London in 1968. She saw him in Canberra in 1969, then again in London in 1972. From their first meeting, Stead had been charmed by the wiry, boyish-looking man with the sharp blue eyes, gravelly voice and mischievous smile. Despite his prominent status in Australian political and cultural life, he was devoid of airs and graces. In June 1976, Stead wrote to him from Newcastle, telling him that he ('King Cole') and 'dashing Don' (Dunstan) were her heroes.[62] By June 1977 she was addressing letters to 'Darling Cole'. Coombs' replies were friendly but reserved.

That Stead admired Nugget Coombs is not surprising. He was her type of man: intelligent, fiery, energetic. He was no leftwing radical, but he was committed to good causes, a man of quite astounding diversity and energy.[63] He had made his mark in Australia during the Forties as Director-General of Post-War Reconstruction, doing much to establish the welfare state. When the Reserve Bank was established in 1959, he became its Governor. From the Fifties through to the Seventies he played a major role in persuading the government to support the Arts. An omnivorous reader, he admired Stead's work. As an economist, he was hugely impressed with *House of All Nations*, and he liked *Miss Herbert*, which he read twice when it came out in 1976.[64]

Coombs had been concerned about aborigines since his schoolteaching days in Western Australia in the 1920s, and more than anyone else in Australia, he was responsible for establishing Aboriginal Land Rights. For months each year he would go 'on walkabout', as Stead called it: travelling with aborigines in tribal areas in the outback. He became 'recharged' in the bush which, he told friends, generated a powerful spiritual energy.[65] In May 1976, at 70, Coombs retired as Chancellor of the ANU and took up a Visiting Fellowship in the University's Centre for Resource and Environmental Studies, having become an outspoken conservationist. In 1977, he would be elected president of the Australian Conservation Foundation[66]—a society that owed a great deal to Stead's father, David G. Stead.

Coombs was a busy man. When he was not away in the desert, he was writing books, giving speeches, chairing committees. Stead saw him only occasionally, either in Sydney or Canberra, but she thought about him a great deal.

To friends, Stead also made much of her admiration for another highly talented man, 50-year-old Don Dunstan, Labor Premier of South Australia. This time, her crush was more playful than genuine. She had been told he preferred men. To Stead, he was 'the most colourful and unusual personage' in Australian politics. She admired his 'immense voice of bronze'.[67] (She called him Demosthenes, after the Greek orator.) Dunstan was hardly a typical Australian politician. He was interested in the classics and gave public poetry readings. Under his influence, Adelaide ('the Athens of the South') had entered a new era of cultural libertarianism.[68]

Stead heard Don Dunstan speak on the steps of Parliament House after Whitlam's dismissal, and was deeply moved. They had dinner together in August 1976. The Premier found her charming, a delightful conversationalist. He recalls discussing Greek and Latin poetry and the influence of Cicero's speech "Pro Caelio" on Shakespeare.[69] He encouraged her to write some short stories for the South Australian Film Corporation he had founded, with the idea that they could be used for scripts. For a while, Stead thought she was at last inspired to write again. She typed out a cover page for a book of short stories, 'The First Hundred Tales', and dedicated the manuscript to Dr H. C. Coombs.[70] But she needed more than distant muses.

★   ★   ★

In April 1976 Stead was invited to the English Department of Melbourne's Monash University for a week. The trip was a strain. Recently, she had had all her teeth removed and new dentures fitted. From now on, her gums were often ulcerated, and she could eat only soft things—painstakingly slowly. Her staple food had always been steak; now it became steak tartare. When she had her own cooking facilities, she would buy fillet steak, singe it rapidly in a frypan, then cut it up with nail scissors. She was embarrassed to eat in public, and when asked out to dinner, would think to herself: 'Oy, another hungry night.'[71] At Mannix College, where she stayed that week, she sat in a corner and ate with her back to the throng. If somebody joined her her food lay untouched and she 'starved'.

For Easter she went to Clem and Nina Christesen at their beautiful old house in Eltham,[72] then a rural suburb on the outskirts of Melbourne. They celebrated with Russian Easter bread, painted eggs, sweet delicacies and 'endless drinks'. Nina, born in St Petersburg, had come to Australia with her family at the age of 13 and later introduced Russian Studies to Australian universities. Small and roundfaced, goodhearted and hospitable, Nina reminded Stead of Aida Kotlarsky. Nina and Clem were gracious and thoughtful hosts, and Stead loved the cosy house, with its redwood panelling, embroidered cushions, books and nicknacks.

At the beginning of June 1976, Stead went for a nine-week term to the University of Newcastle. She was their second Writer-in-Residence; Xavier Herbert had been there the previous year. She stayed in a hotel near the campus, and this time, because it was only a few minutes' walk from shops, she managed to eat properly. Evening meals in her room were steak tartare with a raw egg on top, and several drinks. This time the problem was the twenty-minute walk (through pleasant bushland) to her office in a building without lifts. She walked slowly these days. She had become quite weak.

At weekends Stead was entertained by colleagues and shown the surrounding Hunter Valley and coastal region—an area she had often visited in her childhood. In company, her spirits would lift and she would sparkle and joke, but her letters were as desolate as ever. While Stead was in Newcastle, *Miss Herbert* appeared in the States. The *New York Times Book Review* hailed her as 'one of the most distinguished novelists writing in English'.[73] A more general article on Stead in *Time* (with David Austen's photograph of Stead at Watson's Bay) alluded to Stead's 'extraordinary craftsmanship' and 'the touch of the sadist' in her characterisation of Miss Herbert.[74]

Stead had decreed that the novel should not be published in England and, therefore, not distributed in Australia (where people might recognise Miss Herbert), but it turned out that American Random House copies were freely available in Australian bookshops. She told interviewers she had been carrying the manuscript around in a trunk for thirty years.[75] It made everyone wonder what else was at the bottom of her suitcases. Several articles referred to her 'new novel', *I'm Dying Laughing*. She told herself she really should return to it.

★   ★   ★

In Hurstville again, she was interviewed by Marion McDonald for the *National Times*. The article was headed: 'Christina Stead: the exile returns, unhappily'. Stead admitted to McDonald that she had written only one short article in the two years since her return.

"I lost everyone, that's why," she said (with such an unguarded grief that it seemed indecent to be a stranger with a tape-recorder and a list of questions). "I lost my husband and our best friend and all my contacts and I have nobody to talk to— of my sort, you know. To be in sympathetic touch with.

"... You must have somebody to love, of your own. You can't sit out in a sucker suburb like this and be happy about it."

The article continued:

Moved by pity and Manhattans and rain, and the bottle of Ribena on the sideboard for the infant relatives who run through her flat all weekend, and the lowering vista of marigolds, carports, stunted shrubs and hard little houses, I said that it must be a comfort to have her family. This had the virtue of restoring her to full acerbity:

"Family means nothing to me. Don't get me wrong, they're very good to me. But what Goethe meant by elective affinities —the relatives you pick up in the course of life—are my real family."[76]

The one article Stead had written was on Australian literature, commissioned by the same newspaper, the *National Times*. In it, she spoke warmly of various younger writers. That way, she admitted to friends, she could avoid commenting at length on her 'benefactor Patrick White', about whose literature 'I am not as wild as I should wish to be'.[77] The article was uninspired.[78]

★   ★   ★

The interview with Marion McDonald contained such a *cri de coeur* that Stead received letters from complete strangers offering advice or friendship. An unusually entertaining letter of consolation came from John Dillaway in Hawks Nest, on the mid-North Coast of New South Wales. Dillaway was Stead's own age; he also suffered from hypertension and a bad heart, he too read and wrote in the 'wee small hours' of the morning, and enjoyed puns, witticisms and foreign languages. He sent her a photograph of himself, bent over a stick, with thick white hair. Stead told a friend he seemed to have many of the 'traits of all the charming small men that have grown along my path of life, coaxing, imperious, self-knowing, loving'.[79] He called her 'Veet', the sound the sparrows made, she told him, when they asked her for food. At one point he sent her a poem and signed it Sacha; thereafter Stead called him by that name. His French was not perfect, but it was passionate: one letter was signed 'ton slave à toi, Sacha'.

Before long they were writing to each other every second day, a correspondence which helped to fill the vacuum in both their lives. Dillaway remarked to Stead: 'There seems to be a strong mutual attraction.'[80] She started to bloom, to be playful again. She told the Rellas in January 1977:

> What keeps us both up at 3 a.m. and points towards dawn, is the muggy, fuggy, torrid, horrid weather (and he is closer to the equator than me). He is trying to write stories at 4 a.m. and he sends me simple maths queries just to show I don't know everything—so I haste to my very latest edition of Webster's unadulterated unabridged and I can surprise him . . . I have now moved on to cryptograms at which I am fairly fair.[81]

He invited her to visit him and 'read poetry' to him, warning her that his was a humble house.[82] In January, she had Gilbert drive her there. They stayed one night in a motel on the coast, and visited Dillaway the following morning, finding an old man, ill and living in squalor, unable to look after himself properly. But the visit did not entirely disappoint Stead, who told Dorothy Green:

> He lives in a poor shack on one-quarter acre of ground, only partly cleared, and was waiting at the top of his three or four wooden steps, with the elegance of a man waiting to receive

you in his fine old home—and no pretence, a real grandness,
generosity and emotion.[83]

The correspondence with Dillaway continued apace.

*   *   *

The domestic tension at Hurstville was extremely distressing, and in
March 1977, when Stead left for ten weeks as Writer-in-Residence
at Monash University in Melbourne, she resolved never to return
to Hurstville. It meant leaving her manuscripts, most of her books
and some clothes behind; a couple of years later, Ron Geering
would take four filing cabinets full of papers to his house. At 75,
without Bill, and in fragile health, Stead was a wanderer again. From
March 1977 until her death in March 1983—six years in all—she
would be 'map-hopping', restlessly moving from place to place.[84]
The constant moving was exhausting, mentally and physically. She
briefly considered renting a flat in the city, but she was anxious
about living alone and worried about the cost. Gilbert was not in a
position to pay back the $7000 she had invested in his house. She
decided to take a trip to New York in October, at the end of the
northern summer, but this left several months to fill between
Monash and New York. From now on, she was forever worrying
about where she would be staying in a few weeks' time.

*   *   *

Monash would become her favourite Australian university. The
campus was lively and friendly. She lived in Mannix College,
across the road from the university. Every morning she walked to
the Menzies Building, ten minutes away, and took the rattling
escalators to her office on the seventh floor. Her window overlooked many kilometres of flatlands, with the Dandenong ranges in
the distance. Monash's heyday as a radical university was over, but
Stead liked to see the communist booths in Orientation Week. Less
pleasing were the 'outrageous raging ridiculous feminist rampages',
in which female students carried notices declaring: 'All men are
complicit in rape.'[85] She was horrified.

She enjoyed meeting new people. Her door was always open,
and when students called to see her, she was welcoming and
helpful. Afterwards, in a letter to Michael Costigan, the Director of
the Australia Council which had arranged the Writer-in-Residence
program, she claimed the main purpose of a resident writer was to
undo the negative effects of literary studies at tertiary level:

I may have helped one or two confused and hesitant young
writers by talking over their hesitations—but I don't know. My

feeling still is that the gifted student does not need help—except in only one particular: He needs to have it confirmed that literature is by writers and not by critics, that critics should be thrown out the window ... In any case, the gifted student will soon come to the conclusion that criticism has nothing to do with creative writing, but he may waste some time before that.[86]

Stead (like Patrick White) was openly scathing about academics, whom she tended to regard as uninspired dullards. But she warmed to several of her colleagues in the English Department who were affable and hospitable. There were dinners, parties and weekends away. Mary Lord, a lecturer, proved a particularly kind and caring friend.

While in Melbourne Stead renewed contact with Judah and Hyrell Waten, who had visited her and Blake in Surbiton in 1966. A warm and loving couple, they became affectionate friends. Judah, in his mid sixties, was the type of man Stead most missed in her life: a man in many ways like Bill, though the physical impression of bulk could not have been more different. A Russian-Jewish Australian, Judah loved conversation. Like Bill, he was self-educated and astonishingly erudite. He too was a passionate communist. And his main interest was one that Stead shared: Jewish migrant life in Australia.[87] Waten also provided a precious link with Stead's past. Not only had he met Bill and liked him; when he was in London in the early Thirties, he had met Ralph Fox.

For the second year in a row, Stead spent a 'marvellous Russian Easter' with the Christesens at Eltham. At the end of April Stead was invited for a weekend to the bush home of painter Clifton Pugh and his wife Judith. But she was finding the constant sociability a strain, and was ready to be leaving Monash and its 'high old doings'.[88]

Her correspondence with John Dillaway, which Stead acknowledged was 'honey to the heart for us both', had continued for seven months. In May 1977, Dillaway died, and it was one more death that upset Stead grievously. She did not think she could settle down until she had seen Hawks Nest again, and she wanted to write a story about Dillaway. As soon as her ten weeks as Writer-in-Residence at Monash were up, she returned to Sydney, and David drove her up the coast. He left her in a pleasant motel near the beach, with ample supplies of food and drink, she intended to stay for two weeks. She even thought of settling in that beautiful place. Twice she walked past the shack her 'dear Sacha' had lived in; she spoke to a couple of people about him, and was warmed by their affection. The woman in the grocery store, Mrs Elaine Hughes, remembered her from her previous visit and came to dinner at Stead's motel. Dillaway, she told Christina, had improved in spirits recently: 'You made him happy in the last six months of his life.'[89] But to hear how Dillaway died was a 'terrible blow' to Stead. He had had a stroke and several days passed before he was found. Nobody knew how long he had lain there, still alive. The thought haunted Stead: it also reinforced all her fears about living alone. The following day a fierce wind began to blow. She imagined she heard Sacha telling her to 'get out'. She did.

John Dillaway had left a bequest to the Hawks Nest library. Back in Sydney, as a tribute to a man she had loved, Stead supplemented his bequest with her recently purchased set of Encyclopaedia Britannica and over sixty other books in her personal collection.

Stead then spent an 'uneasy month' at her sister Weeta's in Wollongong,[90] before she returned to Melbourne for five weeks with her 'excellent friends' at 'lovely Eltham'.[91]

★   ★   ★

'Christina was the most uncomfortable guest we have ever had,' says Clem Christesen candidly. He and Nina were used to house guests, and they were genuinely fond of Christina, but there were moments of exasperation. On the second day, she asked to borrow Clem's typewriter: to his annoyance she kept it for her own use for five weeks. After breakfast, she would type letters. Between ten and eleven she had her first gin and vermouth. Initially, Clem gave in to her entreaties to join her, but soon admitted defeat. In the afternoons she would usually squat in an armchair in the lounge, her legs drawn up to her chest, and watch television at high volume. Clem would occasionally try to persuade her to talk about her past, her travels. Once he suggested taping a discussion and she allowed him to set up the tape-recorder and record the identification of tape message, but the interview went no further. She would answer his questions with three words. To his frustration, if she ever talked about her past, it was over the television, in her low, husky voice.

Clem and Nina agree they never had a 'profound talk' with Christina. She was 'earthy' rather than analytical or introspective, happiest when exchanging stories about people and their lives. She got on well with Nina's mother Tatiana (Tanya) Semeonovna Maximov, who lived in a little white cottage up the drive. At 88 she was frail but still full of vitality. She and Nina's father had loved each other from childhood, and Stead was charmed by this romantic story.

Stead would ask Nina questions about *her* past: Nina had worked at two jobs during the Depression, supporting her mother who had tuberculosis, before she established the Department of Russian at the University of Melbourne. Nina was both merry and earnest, and her earnestness, Stead told the Rellas, had the virtue of not making her feel guilty. Clem was 'excitable, friendly, hot-tempered but engagingly humane and kind'.[92]

Stead enjoyed speaking French and learning Russian phrases. Nina was impressed with her smattering of Russian. Stead spent quite a bit of time in the kitchen and would show Nina how to make little things. Her omelettes were the best Clem had ever eaten.

Nina believes that she and Christina got on well because Christina did not see her as a competitor for male attention. When they entertained, Nina would deliberately sit her beside some charming man. 'I would tell him beforehand: "For goodness sake, kiss her hand. She likes it."'

The Christesens witnessed a couple of 'uncomfortable' dinners, when Christina seemed to want to dispute every remark anyone made. 'She would point-blank contradict you,' Clem recalls. '"No, no, you're wrong," she would say, and then she would contradict herself after fifteen minutes, no less dogmatically.'[93]

Stead turned 75 while in Melbourne, and Stephen Murray-Smith, editor of *Overland*, hosted a party on her birthday.[94] Stead particularly liked Nita Murray-Smith, her hostess.

> She is Russian Jewish, very good cook, had some most tasty
> salads, stuffed potted meats etc.—every kind of party dish,
> lots of drinks. "It's going to be a booze-up," she said, greeting
> me in my battered mink coat (which however always pleases
> Pipple) [people]—but it wasn't a booze-up, just lots of liquor,
> wine—and a beeeautiful huge Sachertorte made as my
> birthday cake by friend Judyth Pugh.[95]

Twenty or so people came—some close friends, some strangers.[96] (Coombs was invited, but he had caught 'flu in Central Australia. He was 'probably wearing a fringe of leaves' with his tribe, Stead joked.[97]) Stead cut the cake and went home laden with gifts. The occasion had been 'very pleasant' and 'very soothing'. She felt she had made some real friends in Australia at last.

She was leaving for the US on 8 October 1977, arriving a month before Ettore Rella's seventieth birthday. To Dorothy Green she explained she had to see Rella: 'We have an old fond friendship with love mixed in it.'[98]

A brief return to 'Curstville' was necessary to pack for the trip. It had been a most distressing year, she reflected: domestic squabbles (a divorce was looming), John Dillaway's death, the constant moving around. Back in her old quarters, she was wide awake at 2 am with 'the horrors and anxiety'.[99] The American trip worried her: arrangements were still up in the air. Neither the Rellas nor Aida Kotlarsky had extended an invitation to stay, and only three weeks before she left, Stead was obliged to write to the Rellas asking tentatively if she might stay with them, 'for a short while at least'.[100] Kindhearted Jessie Rella, fully occupied with looking after Ettore, had been ill herself, with suspected breast cancer, and surely did not relish the idea of a tense Christina under their roof, but she wrote a welcoming letter back. Stead was grateful. 'On this ticket I have, I can stay away a year—so no hurry.'[101]

Two weeks before her departure Stead flew to Melbourne for one night to attend the National Conference for a Democratic Constitution. In the wake of Whitlam's dismissal, leftwing intellectuals were to debate the issues of political rights and democracy and how these could best be incorporated into a new Australian constitution. Stead was on the list of sponsors, with, among others, H. C. Coombs, historian Manning Clark, writer Frank Hardy, Patrick White (who had been a vocal Whitlam supporter) and Bob Hawke, then President of the Australian Council of Trade Unions. It was not the conference that interested Stead so much as H. C. Coombs, who was chairing the opening session. She wanted to write a story about him and she needed 'to penetrate his system'.[102] She told Coombs: 'I want to know you, I don't feel I do know you; I feel you are unique.'[103]

★   ★   ★

The trip to the States, Stead's last trip abroad, was a catastrophe. She had overestimated her strength. Too embarrassed to eat on the plane in company, she arrived weak and wobbly. Her chronic anxiety did not go away at the Rellas: despite her overwhelming jet fatigue, she lay awake in a state of nervous agitation. She had been shocked to find Ettore so helpless, much more so than she had imagined from his letters, and only now was she conscious of the extra burden she placed on Jessie. Perhaps, too, it pained her to see the contrast between Jessie's devoted nursing of her husband and her own behaviour when Bill was ill. After a fortnight at the Rellas during which she scarcely went out, unable to walk more than two blocks, she moved for a few days to Polly and Isidor Steinberg's small studio apartment. From there she wrote her first letter in three weeks, to her brother David:

> Since Jessie has everything to do for Ettore who has NOT
> recovered (though mentally all there) and though I was in the
> downstairs flat, not in their way, I thought it wiser to go

elsewhere for a while. Ettore tries to get downstairs, almost every day ... but only with real difficulty, wheelchair to top of stairs, handing himself down on handrail installed for him and then that "spider" sort of walking-stick to the downstairs flat and if possible (more great difficulty), out on to their terrace, which they have made into an Italian garden.[104]

The Steinbergs threw a party for her, and one of the guests was Mary Kathleen Benét ('Markie'), grand-daughter of writer Stephen Vincent Benét and daughter of an old acquaintance of the Blakes, Mary Benét. Markie Benét cautiously did not say anything that evening, but Stead had been told that she wanted to write her biography, and had decided not to co-operate. On a later occasion, however, after drinks with Markie and her English husband, Julian Hale, she agreed after all, and signed a note giving permission for Benét to interview friends and see letters. By the following year her benevolence had evaporated: no name would raise her hackles so dramatically as that of Markie Benét.

The next month saw her 'to-ing and fro-ing between kind friends'.[105] Aida could not accommodate her in her small studio apartment. Stead had dreamt of basking in the love of New York friends, and instead she felt an imposition, 'an all-out nuisance'.[106] On 26 November, she was back at the Rellas when she woke up at 4.30 am, feeling she was about to suffocate. She struggled and panicked and eventually summoned Jessie on the intercom system to the upstairs apartment. Two days later, it was from bed in St Vincent's Hospital that she wrote again to David Stead:

> I began to sniff the pearly gates it seemed to me and a very bad smell I thought it—so unwilling, at last, I buzzed poor dear friend Jessie (at about 4 a.m.)—the good girl came downstairs, went up, rang the police & ambulance (it's the system) dressed, went with me to hospital, waited & returned that same day—& next day.[107]

It was a frightening experience to be put on a stretcher and rushed to hospital with the siren screeching. Perfectly alert, Stead knew she was being given oxygen and morphine. It was congestive heart failure, brought on by water in the lungs. At the hospital she underwent a series of electrocardiac tests. She had no medical insurance and Joan Daves, the agent who had taken over at Cyrilly Abels' death, was obliged to advance her hospital fees—almost $3000—before Stead could be discharged. Stead wired David, in Sydney, to send the money urgently from her Australian account.

The New York episode left her more afraid of being alone, and with a new fear of drowning in her own fluids, for the doctors told her that Jessie Rella's quick action had saved her. When, after four days, she was discharged, she was told not to get over-excited or strained and to limit her fluid intake. Since fluids included soups and stews, among the few things her dentures allowed her to eat, she felt uncertain about any food. What *could* she eat? Joan Daves' mother was away in the country and so Stead was taken to her apartment on E. 55th Street, where she lay around miserably until 9 December, when she had her next appointment with the doctor. She was anxious to get back to Australia, but where would she live back there? It worried her terribly. She was upset by a letter from Betty Stead, which apparently made it plain she was no longer welcome at Hurstville.[108] When Ron Geering wrote to New York inviting her for Christmas, Stead accepted with relief. She had asked Dorothy Green to enquire about residential colleges in Canberra. She had friends there, and her 'preux chevalier',[109] Nugget Coombs, was there, when he was not in the outback. She thought that having her own room in a communal college might be the solution to her problem. 'I do think, that in view of my having become a water-drunk and having to be careful about that, I had better be in a place where people can look out for me and say, "What happened to our beautiful neighbour today?"' Joking aside, she hated the idea of being discovered 'out cold on the coir matting'.[110]

Writing a letter exhausted Stead for the rest of the day. She was far too weak to attend a dinner party at Lillian Hellman's, and was glad of the excuse. What with her timidity and her embarrassment about eating in front of others, the dinner had given her 'the horrors'.[111] Though they never met, Hellman was a loyal admirer. That December, she was asked by the *New York Times Book Review* which writers she most admired:

> Of the older generation I have long believed that Christina Stead is first rate. I share with Randall Jarrell—it is interesting that so many of her admirers were poets, Lowell and Roethke were among them—his great admiration for *The Man Who Loved Children*. If ever the Nobel Prize Committee could get off the highwire of trying to balance world literary opinion with the diplomatic consideration of which-country-should-it-be-this-year, they will give her what she deserves.[112]

When Saul Bellow was awarded his Nobel Prize for Literature in November 1977, he had said he would like to see Christina Stead receive the laurels.

The heart attack in New York left Stead considerably weakened. When she returned to Australia in mid December 1977 and stayed at her brother David's, she felt so unsteady she would not walk without someone at her side. The heart attack haunted her. 'I'm not a mollycoddle and I'll get over it. But it's extraordinary how it stays with me.'[113]

Dorothy Green had enquired about Stead living in Bruce Hall, a residential college at the ANU in Canberra. An undergraduate college, it accepted a small number of senior academics and was considerably cheaper than University House, which catered exclusively for postgraduates and academics. Bruce Hall also had a reputation for the best food among the undergraduate colleges.

In early February 1978, Ron Geering drove Stead to Canberra, along with her huge electric typewriter, some books and a large suitcase. She was installed in Room 40, slightly bigger than the standard tiny undergraduate cell, with her own telephone, and a balcony overlooking Mount Ainslie. The bathroom was shared with the inhabitant of Room 41—at that time a male professor in economic history.

Stead was pleased with the arrangement. In her red brick college under Black Mountain, she was 'not degraded by domestic conflict' and was close to intellectual life.[114] The warden, Bill Packard, an energetic, kind man, had hoped she would occasionally eat at the High Table and contribute to the intellectual tone of the college, but she always ate in her room. In 1969, when she had lived briefly on campus, she had walked into town to the shops; now she had to order a taxi, and even this 'short sally' left her 'knocked out'.[115] An obstacle she had not anticipated was that University House, where Nugget Coombs lived, was across the campus, too far for her to walk. Being near Coombs had been an important reason for coming to Canberra. She saw him one morning in the distance, jogging in a tracksuit. At 70 he still jogged or swam every day.

At the end of March, 'Eponym', as she called him—referring, presumably to his nickname 'Nugget'—was officially invited, as patron of the college mountaineering club, to dinner at Bruce Hall. He rang Stead the day before and said he would call in for a drink. She rushed out in a taxi and bought expensive French champagne and two champagne glasses. Then Coombs rang back and invited her to join the dinner party. They did not drink the champagne. She sat among the 'comely' climbers at the High Table, feeling terribly self-conscious about the keratoses on the end of her nose, but happy to be among the men. The food was good and the wine plentiful. 'Eponym', though he seemed tired, was 'burning hot with energy and zeal'.[116] Usually, he was 'merry, larky, amiable'; this was the first time she had witnessed his serious self—and she felt this 'slight out-of-tuneness' allowed her to 'see into the slightly stirring volcano'.[117] Just back from three weeks in northern Australia, he talked mostly about the aboriginal question. Stead told Geering the following day:

> I sat all meal-time beside him and achieved a new and
> momentous feeling about le phénomène . . . There's an effluence
> from him . . . which shows an immense strength and personality
> —a deep power which no doubt helps him to his victories.[118]

Shortly afterwards, Stead spent four days in hospital having her 'sunburnt nose' repaired.[119] For some years now, she had had trouble with cancerous spots on her face. The spots were removed and skin was grafted from the delicate, white skin behind her ear. It created a white patch on her otherwise rather red nose, which she, disgusted, compared to a strip of bacon.[120] Afterwards she hid herself from view at Dorothy Green's. Green comments: 'She set a lot of store by her appearance. She could look enormously impressive even in her old age, but her father had hammered it into her that she was ugly. So Chris told me.'

Dorothy Green invited Stead to stay on a number of occasions. Christina 'got on her conscience'.

> I'd have her here to stay, thinking it would be peaceful, and
> thinking that, like most writers, she'd most like tranquillity
> and peace to read and write. At the time I was enormously
> busy, lecturing, and writing. I'd be in my study and waves
> and waves would come at me. When I went out of the study
> she would trap me, want to talk. She was desperately lonely.

Stead said she wanted to meet people, and so Green had two or three dinner parties, inviting people she thought would interest her. But Green found these occasions most awkward. Stead would either sit on the edge of her chair and say almost nothing,[121] or else she would be in one of her contradictory moods. 'She had strong views, strong prejudices, some of which she maintained in the teeth of all evidence.'[122]

Dorothy Green's friends the Walkers, an English couple with two young daughters, lived in Aranda, near the university. Donald Walker was Professor of Bio-geography; Pat Walker, a wood sculptor, worked as a co-ordinator at a women's refuge. Stead appreciated their generous, communal style.[123] Pat would take Christina into town and help her shop, or bring her back to their house in Aranda, which looked out onto dense bushland. Sometimes she stayed for the weekend. Stead enjoyed going there; at one point, she suggested to them that she come for a week every month. But when Coombs once rang, out of the blue, to invite her to dinner, she was terribly glad she was at home, and not out 'in the wilds of Aranda' 'childsitting' and 'stove-poking'.[124]

She often felt dizzy and uncertain on her feet. It worried her, and she decided to write to her favourite doctor, back in London, for advice.

> One day (night) quite recently I was dining with the Warden
> (of this Hall) and wife in their lodge. I did not drink more
> than I can usually accommodate, but when I got up to go I
> was tottering, and the Warden had to help me all the way back
> to the corridor where I live (though he left me there, did not
> take me to my far-distanced door). This was embarrassing,
> I know, but why did it happen? For not only that, but every
> day I feel very unsure of my balance.

She explained to Philip Harvey that she was taking diuretics to prevent another attack of dropsy and that she had hypoglycaemia. Might these cause her to lose equilibrium? All she seemed capable of doing was to write two or three letters a day. 'I don't want to trouble you, but you know me and maybe you would know what it is.'[125]

Four years had passed since Philip Harvey had seen Stead, and many more since he had thoroughly examined her at St Stephen's. He could hardly be expected to diagnose pulmonary oedema. But he knew her well, and believed he knew what her problem was:

> Try hard to limit the intake of alcohol and, if possible, give
> it up entirely. We know now that the bodily resources which
> treat with alcohol are finite and are lost slowly so that what
> was once an easily processed intake, becomes a level which is
> toxic to heart, nerves and kidneys and precipitates disease,
> which at our age is compounded with that arising from other
> changes. Try it, you may find, to your joy, that you may
> regain much physical prowess that you had thought to be lost.
> Certainly imbalance and totteriness should improve.[126]

Stead must have been irritated by his letter, for she did not reply. Only when Harvey wrote again, two months later, was she stirred to write a friendly letter. She made no reference to alcohol.

★   ★   ★

The new feminist Virago Press in London had re-issued *For Love Alone* and *Letty Fox* in 1978. *For Love Alone* appeared with a preface by Markie Benét, which Stead thought 'mere shameless puff ... outrageously journalistic stuff'.[127] Although she had given Benét formal permission to proceed with her biography, when Charlotte Mayerson at Random House sent her Benét's written proposal, Stead changed her mind. And when she heard that Benét was

contacting her friends, she sent telegrams requesting them not to
see her. To Ruth Hall, now living in the south of France, she wrote:

Markie has no idea of decorum . . . and is behaving in a most
indiscreet and intrusive way in which you and Bill are involved.
1. In her proposal she identified you as Letty. I was very much
shocked and wrote to her at once that she MUST NOT, ever,
identify you or anyone else. If she does, I shall make it clear to
everyone that her story is false. I have already written to her,
to my agent and to Charlotte Mayerson . . .
2. She had the impudence to advertise in the *New York Times*
asking for anecdotes, reminiscences, etc. of Bill. She is not
supposed to be writing about Bill or you—only me. At any
rate, it's done; so I asked her to have the courtesy to let me
comment upon any Bill material.
. . . She plays upon the fact that we were friends with her father
and mother. I am so disgusted and annoyed I cannot tell you.[128]

Stead was dismayed to learn that the Steinbergs and Oliver Stallybrass
had shown Benét letters. She told Burnshaw:

In the meantime she has written me one of her pussycat purring
letters, saying she wants to please me in all and I can read the
whole MS. every word—that's great, isn't it? But I must, after
having seen her methods. She wants to come out here and indeed
Joan Daves says she must—but I say she must not; and I shall not
receive her, nor introduce her nor aid in any way. I am fed up.[129]

Two years later, she heard that Markie Benét was 'still on the
warpath'. 'Blow this spoiled stemmed up fantastic Markie,' she
exclaimed, 'who like many a third-rate journalist cannot tell fact
from fiction or romantic dream.'[130] Markie Benét persevered against
all the odds, but the project was to come to an abrupt end with her
premature death, soon after Stead's.

*   *   *

Christina Stead stayed eight months at Bruce Hall, but soon
realised that an undergraduate college was really not suitable for
her. 'I felt and looked an anachronism beside that moiling, toiling,
ambitious young lot.'[131] She was sorry to leave Canberra and
friends, but she had seen very little of Nugget Coombs; and Mary
Lord, from Monash, had invited her to live with her in Melbourne.
Mary, 50 that year, divorced with four grown-up children, was
about to have her rather large house at No. 28 Wilmot Street, East
Malvern, to herself, and she told Stead she would welcome the
presence of an interesting woman friend. Christina was 'a sunrise to
sunset person'; she herself was 'a sunset to sunrise person', so they

ought to be able to keep each other company without getting in one another's way.

Stead stayed twenty months with Mary Lord. It was one of the paradoxes in her life that she vastly preferred the company of men and fervently hoped that the end of her isolation would come from them, yet the closest she came to escaping isolation in her last years was with women friends, especially with Mary.

> She is a warmhearted lively soul, loves Mozart (like me, but she is a natural musician) and a practised Mamma; hence, does not worry very much about housepride and is a great hand at looking after people, while not knowing the word coddle. She is a good companion.[132]

Mary Lord was busy with teaching, administrative matters and a book on Australian writer Hal Porter that she was editing, but Lord was a sociable woman, who disliked the idea of living on her own as much as Stead did. In other ways too, she and Stead were alike. Lord was large-boned and practical, with a reputation for being forthright, tactless and difficult. Both women enjoyed stimulating company; neither suffered fools gladly. Both could be scathing about academics. They both liked to laugh. Moreover, Mary was tolerant and patient with Christina. Looking back, she describes herself as 'Christina's nurse, mother and servant'. According to her friends, Mary did things for Christina in such an unobtrusive, natural manner that neither she nor Christina was fully aware of the extent of Christina's dependence. Mary's friends and children called in frequently; it was a lively household, and Stead welcomed the change from life in an institution.

For the first time in years, she wrote and completed a story—the last complete piece she would ever write. 'The Old School' was based on her experiences at Bexley primary school, below Lydham Hill.[133] This poignant story, which describes the way under-privileged children were cruelly scapegoated by the others, reveals an older, mellow Stead reflecting on her past.

Since her bedroom was too small for a desk, Stead's typewriter was kept on a table at one end of the living room, in front of a picture window looking onto the garden. It was a choice location but in time the arrangement became an excuse for not writing: when visitors or children came, there was no peace or privacy.

Stead suffered from chronic inertia. Even opening the back door for visitors or emptying the hearth tired her. She made it her task to bring in logs from outside; then she would build an enormous fire, making the lounge (already heated) unbearably hot. There was no way Mary could restrain her.

Preparing the hearth in winter and hosing the garden in summer were Stead's only physical activities. Though she felt listless, she told friends: 'I still hope to beat that Uncle who disappointed us by dying at the age of 99½!'[134]

Some weeks passed before Mary Lord became conscious of Stead's eating problems. 'Chris was vain,' she explains, and 'very proper, modest, in a Victorian kind of way.' Christina liked to eat by herself, and because she ate inordinately slowly, eating took up several hours each day. Breakfast—bread soaked in milk with sugar, or packaged desserts with cream—was eaten in her dressing gown, sitting at her desk watching the birds attack the birdseed she had spread in the garden. Before lunch and dinner she would have what she called her 'poison': equal quantities of gin and cinzano rosso, with double the amount of water, and ice. At dinner, which she usually ate sitting in an armchair, she would drink red wine or rosé. If there were guests, or if Mary had cooked something Christina particularly liked, she would join the table, but it meant that she hardly ate anything: she ate so slowly. Mary persuaded her to see a dentist only with great difficulty; Christina hated the idea of a male dentist seeing her without her teeth. The new set of lower dentures he provided made no difference to her ulcerated gums.

The Geerings had invited Stead for Christmas 1978, but at the end of November she had yet another scare with her heart, exactly a year after the New York episode. She stayed in Melbourne. The house was full of grown children and their partners. Mary Lord was ill in bed. Stead had been buying presents for all and sundry— including each of the family doctor's seven children—and was exhausted. On Boxing Day, she found herself gasping for breath, and was taken to Moorabbin Hospital with pulmonary oedema. When she came out twelve days later, she was given an oxygen tank to keep in her room for emergencies.

Mary Lord had taken on a great deal: Stead no longer walked more than a few metres. She relied on Mary to drive her to the shops, to the post office, to friends. A doctor, a large, big-hearted man, called at the house every second Wednesday morning. Dr Donald Macdonald, a family friend, was even known to bring his boys round to attack Mary's garden, and he was always ready to attend in emergencies, at any time of night. Stead found him a reassuring, calming presence. From Canberra, later, she paid him her highest compliment: 'One feels that there cannot be a better doctor or a better brother-friend than you are.'[135] He thought Christina charming and old worldly. She seemed to him to be making a valiant go of things, though she was obviously lonely.

If she was drinking more than was good for her, he was indulgent: alcohol seemed preferable to Serepax.

With Christina in the house, Mary found it difficult to work. She had her own study and a door that closed, but it was hard to get to it, and after Mary had been at university all day, Christina was naturally eager for company in the evenings. If Mary headed for her study, Christina would ask: 'Will you be finished soon?' Christina had adjusted her sunrise to sunset patterns to resemble Mary's: she now got up later, had a nap in the afternoons and went to bed later.

One night Mary, still up working at 3 am, came out of her study to find Christina walking around looking upset. She told Mary her 'Artie' (heart) was playing up. Mary rang Dr Macdonald there and then. On another occasion, Stead thought she was suffocating. She panicked, gasped and drew deep breaths from her oxygen tank. Dr Macdonald, when he arrived, told her she had been hyperventilating, and advised her, if it should happen again, to sit and listen to Mozart and take shallow breaths. It was a very frightening condition.

★　★　★

In July 1979, her birthday month, Stead spent four weeks in Sydney. Afterwards she admitted to the Rellas: 'I stayed away for this time thinking it might give Mary dear a rest from my company—always wise, even though she is faultlessly kind.'[136] She stayed a week with the Geerings, and during this time she asked Ron Geering to be her literary executor. Fifteen years younger than Stanley Burnshaw, whom she had appointed ten years before, Geering also lived in Sydney, where her papers were. He had done a great deal to promote interest in her work in Australia and struck her as the ideal person for the job.

Stead had become totally dependent on her, but Mary Lord claims she did not want her to leave. There were moments of irritation, certainly. Stead was now afraid to be alone at night. When Mary went out Stead would ask when she would be back and not sleep until Mary came home. It was awkward too when Katharine, Mary's 20-year-old daughter, later diagnosed as schizophrenic, came home to live. According to Mary, Christina did not complain when Katharine was spectacularly rude to her—and not even when she played her guitar all night long. But Stead was a light sleeper at the best of times, and could not have put up with much of this kind of behaviour.

On Sundays the women would go to friends' for lunch or entertain at home. They often went to Box Hill to visit the Watens, Stead's closest friends in Melbourne. 'Judah would tell Russian-

Jewish jokes; Christina would chortle.'[137] They would visit the Christesens at Eltham, the Pughs, and Monash friends. Stead would arrived armed with exquisitely wrapped presents: scents, liqueurs, flowers. Before social occasions, she would apply perfume to the back of her hand, telling Mary: 'You never know when a fella will kiss your hand!' (The way she held out her hand was a sign for men to do so.)

Occasionally, Stead would back out of something at the last minute, invariably because she was feeling fluttery in the heart. Whenever they had guests to the house, she would ask Mary in advance to 'rescue' her (let her disappear to her room) after a certain time.

Stead seldom reminisced, but Lord remembers one occasion when she talked about Bill and suddenly burst into tears. 'Something swept over her. She told me she hadn't been good enough to Bill. "Poor darling Bill. I was not kind to him."' It was the only time Mary Lord ever saw Stead weep.

More often, she talked about Ralph Fox. He was the other half of herself, her twin, and she never quite believed he was dead, even though she knew he was. She told Mary Lord, Ron Geering, and the Watens: 'I firmly believe that he will turn up at the door, the day before I take off for some other planet.'[138]

★   ★   ★

In December 1978 a letter came from the Official Secretary to the Governor-General offering to make Christina Stead a member in the General Division of the Order of Australia.[139] The honours were to be announced in the press on Australia Day, 26 January 1979. Stead declined. She had never been impressed by the monarchy, and the memory of 11 November 1975 still stung leftwing Australians like Patrick White, who had also withdrawn from the Order of Australia in 1976.

In 1981, Virago re-issued *A Little Tea, A Little Chat* and *The People with the Dogs*, making these American publications available to readers in England and Australia for the first time. The following year, the same firm re-issued *The Beauties and Furies*, long out of print, and *Miss Herbert*. Whatever Stead's qualms about a publishing house focusing exclusively on women's writing, Virago did a great deal to restore her stature. For the first time ever, most of her work was available in paperback.

Stead was a name not only in English-speaking countries. In 1978, *The Man Who Loved Children* became one of the first Australian novels to be translated into Italian. The response was enthusiastic.[140] *Miss Herbert* was being translated into Spanish. Stead was amused: 'They probably think it is a real picture of an English-woman. Well, never mind.'[141]

Another film treatment of *The Man Who Loved Children* was being considered in the States. In Australia, producer Margaret Fink was working on *For Love Alone*, negotiating with Fay Weldon to write the film script.[142]

★   ★   ★

H. C. Coombs wrote to Stead to say he would be visiting Melbourne in September 1979, on his way to Yugoslavia. Stead and Mary Lord invited him to dinner. Stead still talked a great deal about Coombs. She carried a picture of him in her wallet, and told him as much.[143] Every so often, she would say to Mary, in that clairvoyant way of hers, that she sensed 'Cole' was back from a trip to the Centre: the air felt warmer.[144]

Over dinner, Coombs asked about her work, and Stead admitted she was not writing. Coombs, concerned about her, may have intimated that University House in Canberra might suit her better. He could not have known—on social occasions no-one ever knew—the extent of Stead's physical frailty. After his visit, she developed the fantasy that Coombs wanted her in Canberra. Mary Lord comments: 'She was fantasising what she would like things to be. I found it terribly sad and terribly moving.'[145]

With the air of helpless passivity she tended to cultivate where men were concerned, Stead told the Rellas that Coombs was now taking her in hand.

He wants me to go to Canberra, University House, where he thinks (I know) I will have more creative quiet than here. He didn't say all that; but I know what the Nugget is thinking ... Mary is a dear, very kind, and but for the In-and-Outs and the considerable traffic at Grand Central East Malvern, I would not think of moving.[146]

A month later she told them:

He's a very decent bloke, companionable—but (inside) oh, dear, fierce as Stromboli, which I call him to myself ... At any rate, this dangerous man thinks I would be better off for my writing by being in Canberra—don't ask me why. It isn't his affection (which possibly exists) (but his is a spotless career—so no blurred marks, eh?). No, I think, he thinks I'm not working because of this in-and-out family atmosphere. Don't know, loves. He wants everyone to succeed—like himself ... Alas, my dears, I cannot tell him how really weak I am ... Though nearly 75, the dear boy ... does not seem to know anything

about human frailty. (I mean, here, age!) Well, never mind—
I was born under a wandering star, that is more than clear.[147]
Mary Lord mentioned to Michael Costigan, Director of the Australia Council for the Arts, that Stead wanted to go to Canberra, but was anxious about money. The Australia Council had replaced the old Commonwealth Literary Fund, with a greatly increased budget since Whitlam's days. At a Council meeting in October, it was agreed that Stead should be offered an 'Emeritus Fellowship'— a recently coined term for a literary pension. The Chair of the Literature Board, Dr Robert Brissenden, announced this to Stead over the phone, but when he told her that the award was means-tested, and that she was required to provide information about her financial position, she expressed misgivings and told him she did not wish to appear to be begging. In a subsequent letter, Brissenden explained that the award was 'a means of recognising senior writers who have made outstanding and lifelong contributions to literature'.

It is designed to ensure that these writers are able to enjoy some measure of comfort and security. It is our hope also that a lack of financial worries may give them the freedom to continue writing, should they wish to do so ... The Board is aware that, in spite of advances made in the social security area, writers are still unfairly disadvantaged to the extent that they rarely have the benefits of superannuation, and they have often been poorly rewarded in financial terms for their life's work ... I must assure you that we do not in any way see potential recipients as "beggars".[148]

The full award was $7500, but each case was assessed individually. In December 1979, Stead wrote to Brissenden giving her earning for the previous year as $19 000. In March 1980, she corrected this figure: her tax return (which she enclosed) revealed that her income for that year had been $8354. Her Fellowship was raised accordingly, from $1500 per annum to $4200. Stead did not at first realise that, provided her income did not radically change, the Fellowship, paid in monthly instalments and slightly increased each year, was for the rest of her life.[149]

She was convinced that Coombs had arranged the Fellowship. Mary Lord said to her, mildly: 'I don't think he did. It's a Literature Board thing.' But Stead replied: 'Oh, yes he did, dear.'[150] Having persuaded herself that Coombs wanted her in Canberra, she was looking forward to his 'dear company',[151] but she was terribly anxious about the coming move. During the last few months at Mary Lord's she felt 'rattled', slept badly, and was 'under the queerest gloomspell'. Her courage was failing her along with her strength: 'What I don't like about my present life is I think all the time "Will I make it?"'[152] Leaving Mary, being on her own again, was frightening. 'I am so lonely you wouldn't believe!' she wailed to the Rellas, stricken with self-pity.[153] She continued to hate herself for not writing: writing had always been her weapon against despair.

In March 1980 she attended the Adelaide Festival of Arts. Though she did not give a talk, the Festival Committee paid her fare and accommodation, and she enjoyed meeting Australian and overseas writers. But the constant sociability tired her, and with people milling round her, she could not eat properly.

She met Don Dunstan again: 'a remarkable brilliant lovable man, who has had some bad luck'.[154] He had retired as Premier amid health problems and scandal. His wife, Adele Koh, had died of cancer. He was now editor of the glossy Sydney magazine *Pol*, which he planned to make into a magazine of opinion and literary merit, while retaining its excellent visual presentation.[155] He asked her for a story, and she promised one, but the promise worried her for months, and nothing came of it.[156]

In February 1980, Rodney Wetherell interviewed Stead on ABC radio—one of the most nerve-wracking interviews in his life. Stead showed just how contrary and dogmatic she could be.[157] Various exchanges:

Q: There must have been a great restlessness in you . . .
   right from early days.
A: No, not at all.
Q: You were very determined to leave Australia, for example.
A: No, not at all.

Q: Do you have a professional sort of writer's interest in
   psychology?
A: No, I was never a professional writer, and I am not now.
   This is quite true. It's a thing I do, but I'm not a
   professional.

About *House of All Nations*:

Q: It's a very glittering world you portray in that book,
   very sophisticated, and corrupt, I suppose.
A: Well, corrupt is the way you may see it. If you have
   very strange ideals about any kind or part of the world,
   you don't know it. You've got to be in it to know it.

Q: Would you say there was a definite political intention
   behind that book?
A: None whatever.

The Australia Council for the Arts wanted to include Stead in their series of video interviews with Australian writers, and Stead, as a recipient of one of their Emeritus Fellowships, felt she could not refuse, though she hated the idea. Researcher Gai Steele came to see her at Mary Lord's to discuss how they would proceed. She wanted Stead to talk in the film about her attitude to the women's movement and Marxism; Stead refused point blank. It took her three days to recover her nerves after this preparatory interview, and she worried that she would not be able to cope with two days of filming. Mary Lord promised to take the film crew away for lunch so that she could rest between shoots.

The video was filmed on 10 April and 11 April 1980, partly in Mary Lord's garden, partly in the house. Elizabeth Riddell, who had interviewed Stead before, in Surbiton, asked the questions. Stead gave one word answers: twice Riddell gave up in despair. It was the cameraman, Haydn Kernan (a 'nice-looking young fella'[158]) who eventually got Stead to thaw.

The forty-minute video, carefully edited, shows none of this. As posterity's only glimpse of Christina Stead talking, moving and laughing, it is a precious documentary. In still photographs, Stead tends to look austere; it is in movement that she charms. The video captures her whimsical humour and the mischievous glint in her keen blue eyes. Her most striking feature is her voice: soft, sing-songish, the voice of a skilled storyteller. She is shy, nervous, dressed in an elegant trouser suit. Talking about Bill and Paris and the writing of her early books, she almost becomes young again. She is close to tears when she tells how she lost consciousness at the very moment when a friend of hers was killed in Spain. Then she makes a joke, covering up her emotion. The image she projects is that of an easy-going wanderer.

> I never think about my life. The idea of death was never present to me, because of the fossils in the rocks. We are probably taught a fear of death ... I don't expect anything, because I don't care. I take everything as it comes.[159]

*   *   *

By mid April 1980 Stead was back in Canberra, installed in University House. The fellowship covered most of the cost, but she was nevertheless worried about the expense and had decided to take a small flat without a kitchen. It was an impractical decision: she knew she would not go to the dining room for meals. But the most important thing for her was that she lived close to H. C. Coombs. And as it happened, their flats were on the same stairwell in the north wing: hers on the second floor, his on the first. Opposite her, on the same landing were former Prime Minister Gough Whitlam, now a University Fellow, and his wife Margaret. They exchanged friendly words when they met. Stead liked to think of herself surrounded by illustrious presences.

Her balcony looked onto the Fellows' Garden below. From the window she could see over the treetops to the Telecom tower on the top of Black Mountain. Lit up at night, this 'Arabian Nights tower' was strangely comforting. It reminded Stead of Watson's Bay Lighthouse, which she had seen from her window at Boongarre. She never pulled her curtains.

Stead hardly even glimpsed Coombs in the first month. When Mary Lord drove up from Melbourne, bringing the rest of Stead's belongings, Stead wrote a note inviting him to join them for a meal at her favourite fish restaurant, the Seven Seas. If he could not make the dinner, then 'a short drink, before you go for your evening meal? Nothing to say. Just like to look at you'.[160]

The Master of University House, Professor Ralph Elliott, was a specialist in mediaeval English literature. He was delighted to welcome Christina Stead to the college and expressed the hope that she would mix with the other residents, who always made up an interesting group. But though her loneliness was palpable, she never went to meals. Elliott thought her 'rather a sad, pathetic figure'.[161]

Friends rallied round. The poet Rosemary Dobson became one of her 'collectors'—picking her up from the hairdresser, doctor or dentist. Then they would go to lunch. Dobson was embarrassed that Christina never ate anything, but she found her humorous, meandering conversation 'wonderful'.[162] Dobson's husband, Alec Bolton, a printer and engraver, called in to see Stead when he could.

Clare Golson, an ex-nurse, partly assumed Mary Lord's role of nurse and mother.[163] Clare worked at the University crèche and would call in on Stead on her way home. She took her cooked food, and lent her a crockpot, encouraging her to make nourishing soups and stews. It was obvious that Stead was not eating properly.

Clare's husband, Jack Golson, Professor of Archaeology, whom Stead described as a 'big boned delightful "beau-laid",'[164] dropped in after work, sometimes with his colleague Douglas Yen. 'The boys drink deep,' Stead told Burnshaw, 'and I am not opposed to the stuff as you know.'[165] The evening drinks were the highlight of her day. It pleased her to think she was once again among scientists, 'the most humane of people'.[166]

Dr Coombs was rarely around. Stead told Philip Harvey, a little pointedly: 'I don't see him often—he's far too busy saving the

Aborigines where the foreign industrialists are trying to grab their land for mining . . . But he lights up the landscape for me—you know me.'[167] She admitted to Geering: 'I'm so lonely that when I know *for sure* that Dr. H.C.C. is not in (I can look through the brick screen down on his place) . . . I telephone him. No answer. But I know that.'[168] Coombs did call in for a sociable drink every so often. Once or twice he asked her to dinner in his flat—he was a good cook—but he found it disconcerting that she ate almost nothing. He enjoyed their conversations, but found her difficult. 'There were times when she was quite intolerant,' he recalls. Once he invited her for a drink without explaining that he had invited another woman writer whom he thought she would like to meet. 'It was an absolute disaster. Christina was obviously annoyed that another woman was there. She was pretty rude.'[169]

Stead soon realised that she had deluded herself about Coombs' desire for her presence in Canberra. After a few months there, she was wishing herself back with Mary Lord again. Mary Lord had resigned from Monash University and was moving to Sydney at the end of the year to work as a freelance writer.

Stead fell in love with men who seemed to have infinite reserves of energy, but she herself had none any more. It worried her that she had promised a story to Don Dunstan, and she told the Rellas helplessly: 'Am quite rusty, right out of gas—have been trying to write a story—don't know which one—wish I did know—for months; don't know what is wrong.'[170]

In desperation she dug *I'm Dying Laughing* out of its box to see whether she could send him a chapter of that instead. She had not looked at it for years, and reading it depressed her. For the first time she saw that it did need substantial revision. She had written it fast—up to 20 000 words a day, she told Burnshaw. 'The spirit of the heroine had indeed got into me.'[171]

Now her 'terrible lassitude' never left her. Mornings were the worst time. The diuretics she took to control the excess fluid in her system—combined with her diet of meat and alcohol, without fruit or vegetables—brought on an attack of gout. Her foot was inflamed and painful. Then the antidote pills caused digestive problems: pills were a risky business. The only reliable relief was her 'therapeutics'. She told the Rellas: 'At least the docs. all say—no exception, that alcohol is good for you.'[172]

Ron Geering believes Stead's semi-starvation reflected a deep self-punitive drive. He would tell Philip Harvey, after her death:

She ate too little and drank too much . . . She gave many reasons for her anorexia (trouble with dentures . . .) and no doubt her

physical disabilities played some part, but there was some obscure
psychological factor at work too ... Again and again it seemed as
if her denials and troubles were a form of protest against her
personal loneliness (about which she rarely complained).[173]

In her twenties, feeling alone, worthless and unlovable, Stead had
half starved herself. Was the same impulse driving her now? Her
letters ache with self-reproach. She told friends loneliness made her
lazy. Perhaps she also believed the reverse. From University House
she wrote to the Rellas:

I'm lonely and I'm wasting my time—and get up in the morning
seeing all the usual things ahead and think "another wasted day—
I'm a shame and a disgrace"—for I have a sort of bursary to this
cursory nursery, as it were—and I'm doing nothing in return.

Later in the letter, she upbraided herself for complaining:

This is a beautiful place, a very attractive bed-sitter (though very
expensive) and appears to have all the conveniences. But "a widow
has no home"—and I am glad to catch on to the floating skirts of
friendship such as come my way ... What am I complaining
about? Loneliness, I guess ... Forgive me, dear ones both. I hope
I shall feel better after having nagged you like this. The weather is
beautiful, everyone is nice to me—what *am* I going on about?[174]

As a hobby, she briefly took up Russian again, taking private lessons
on Tuesday mornings from Mark Higgie, a postgraduate in the
Russian Department, whom Nina Christesen recommended. She
told Higgie she wanted to read Russian poetry in the original—she
seemed particularly interested in Mandel'shtam at the time—but
the lessons, in her flat, rarely lasted longer than ten minutes before
Stead suggested that Higgie fix drinks. They would chat. Sometimes she asked him to put on a record, usually Mozart.[175]

One morning early in February, Stead was walking to the
postbox, waving cheerfully to a room-maid, when she tripped on
the broken cement path. She heard a cracking noise as she fell. The
maid and a young man helped her to her feet. To her surprise, no
bones were broken and she was able to continue on her way. She
noticed nothing for a few days except that she tended to forget the
names of her visitors, but after a week she developed a bad
backsprain. For weeks it hurt her to sit at the typewriter to write
letters, and a year later, she still complained of back ache. It was a
stumble toward death.

Soon after this incident, Anne Chisholm interviewed Stead for
the *National Times*. Chisholm, a shrewd observer, draws a vivid
picture of Stead: 'a woman of generosity and warmth ... beneath a
prickly carapace'.

Christina Stead appears genuinely indifferent to the attitude of the public. She in any case prefers private to public life, being very fond of a drink and a good meal with friends, and enjoys talking about anything from the quality of East German caviar to Chinese art . . .

She is a handsome, strong-faced woman with a small, hooked nose, a high colour, thick grey curls and the profile of a Roman emperor, or an eagle. She has a low, sometimes hoarse voice, and it is not always easy to hear what she says.

She lives in a small corner room at University House . . . [Its] brown woodwork is brightened by colourful bits and pieces—a spray of lemons, a wicker duck, a stuffed wombat-like creature—a few books, several pot plants, some postcards.

Crimson rosellas live in the trees outside her window, and she feeds them devotedly from a large bag of sunflower seeds.

. . . Sometimes . . . in what followed I felt that her dislike of the enterprise, combined with her wish not to send me away disappointed, made her answers erratic, or she was perhaps demonstrating her instinctive disbelief in the value of discussion by facetious, or random, answers.

As I was explaining that I wished to talk primarily about matters of technique such as whether she typed or wrote longhand, or how much revision or rewriting she did, she broke in briskly: "OK, that's simple. Yes, I type, no I don't revise."

. . . Despite her annoyance, I had to get the point clear. Did she never, ever, go over what she had written, and correct, revise or cut? "Never, Done. Bores me stiff," she said shortly, then laughed. "I *mean* that."

And did she keep carbons or take copies of the work? "No sir, no madam, never."

. . . My next question was clumsily put, and led to trouble. "When you started to write for publication . . ." I began. Stead bristled. Her eyes flashed. "I never wrote for publication, kid, *never*."

She had already told me that she loathes the sight of any of her books in print, that she believes, with Ambrose Bierce the American essayist, that "achievement is the end of endeavour, and the beginning of disgust."[176]

★   ★   ★

To Coombs, Stead had promised she would write a book of short stories dedicated to him. (Writing now represented a gesture of love.) Then, since people kept suggesting she write her autobiography, she considered writing more about her childhood. But she told Burnshaw:

I *won't* write that autobiog. I am sure. I get too angry with
the old man (Papa) when I think of the dumb things he did,
including nearly killing me by taking me a 15-mile walk when
I was about 13, not understanding anything (in his puritan-
atheist modesty—atheists can be the very worst puritans)
about . . . a young girl putting on flesh—you can't believe
it, can you? But I get mad at him and so I'd better not.[177]

Stead could still be quite overwhelmed by old griefs and grievances;
but she no longer had the energy to induce in herself the heightened
feelings of anger she needed for writing.

Stead was probably as happy in University House as she would
be anywhere, under the circumstances. In the first half of 1982, her
heart played up on two more occasions, and she spent some days in
Canberra Hospital. The second time, in May, the doctors agreed
that the problem was partly alcohol. University House had a bottle
shop on the premises, and the cleaners complained about the
number of empty bottles in Stead's flat. Stead was pressured to
return to her family in Sydney.[178] H. C. Coombs, who had thrilled
Christina by visiting her in hospital, was 'terribly angry' about the
decision. He could not see that she was doing anyone any harm.[179]

*   *   *

After Stead's departure from Canberra, her life darkened. Back
with her family, she was 'shovelled about', as she put it, from one
relative to another.[180] She felt she was a burden on them all. First
she stayed with David and Doris, then she was passed for two
months to her sister Weeta, recently widowed, who lived in a small
brick house in Wollongong, an hour from Sydney. Though Weeta
was kind and her grown-up children called in often, Stead felt 'all
but a prisoner'. She missed friends with whom she could have 'a
little booze, a little chat'.[181] She depended on it, yet she resented her
family's 'helpmongering'. When she had the strength, she typed
desolate letters to friends in Canberra, pleading with them to get
her back there. In more realistic moments, she told herself she was
about to turn 80. 'I can't keep on humping the bluey, carrying my
tent along the track can I?'[182]

No-one in the family wanted to have Christina permanently; she
was not an easy companion. She could be quite demanding and
imperious, and would ring Ron Geering or her siblings with
constant requests to take her here or there. One Sunday morning,
early, Ron had been urgently summoned to her sister Kate's:
Christina, in a kind of delirium, kept saying that Ralph Fox had
come for her.

At one point, Christina asked Thistle Harris if she could live at Boongarre. Her brother Kel was ill at the time, and Thistle (whom Stead had ignored all these years) had no illusions about Christina; she said no, and felt bad about it for years. Stead also asked Elizabeth Harrower if she could live with her. Harrower liked to live alone, and felt she needed her house to herself in order to write. She also felt terrible about saying no.

* * *

From the Rellas came the news that Aida Kotlarsky had collapsed and died during a walk. Stead was becoming used to friends disappearing for good, but she was sad to lose this 'best of friends'.[183] It impressed her that Aida had adoring young men in her life, around her piano, to the end. Aida's loving companion in her eighties was Don Shaw, a talented concert pianist in his late twenties.[184]

* * *

When the writer Barry Hill came to interview her in Wollongong, in honour of her eightieth birthday, it brightened up Stead's day. She found him charming, and their impressions were mutual:

We sat in the sunroom. Her sister's African violets were in bloom. Christina Stead found a shawl, because the radiator had to give up its plug to the tape recorder. She is an exquisitely frail woman these days, and not at all like those plump, sporty shots of her with her husband, taken on cosmopolitan jaunts. Her fingers in the morning light were translucent and coral pink, like the bow of her blouse.

But when she spoke, the frailty disappeared. Her features sharpened, and the New York timbres of her voice deepened. When she got up to pour vermouth, her step, in the fawn slacks and black kid pumps, had a snap to it; one could imagine her clicking her heels as she left the room—cocktails, olé![185]

* * *

The interview was published on her birthday. The literary establishment also made a fuss of her. She had declined a big birthday party in Melbourne proposed by Stephen Murray-Smith. Nor would she go to a celebration in Sydney planned by the political writers' group, PEN. But she did go to Canberra, where the Golsons had a party for her. Mary Lord and Elizabeth Harrower drove down from Sydney. Coombs was there, of course, and gave a speech. Dorothy Green and the Walkers and Douglas Yen were there. It was a joyous occasion, and Stead was happy to be among friends—until she had to retire, ill.

The next day she was back in hospital. The heart specialist at the Royal Canberra Hospital told Dorothy Green (who also felt bad about not taking Stead to live with her) that the patient needed professional attention close at hand.[186] Stead returned to Sydney.

*   *   *

Patrick White saw Christina Stead as Australia's literary giant. He and Manoly Lascaris befriended her, inviting her usually with Elizabeth Harrower to their house. Lascaris used to give Stead friendly advice about denture problems. When she left for Melbourne, the two men sent her an electric blanket: a thoughtful gift, it was perhaps also a pointed joke about the winters there. They were concerned about her, and Stead was touched.

Over time, White lost patience with Stead. He was unimpressed by her restless moving about and her almost boastful drinking; above all, he was impatient with the way she depended on others and yet blamed them for her inability to write. Elizabeth Harrower comments that White 'liked people to be in control of their own lives, to "front up" to adversity and soldier on'. His 'slow turning-away' from Stead was 'part of a general attitude: he admired extravagantly and was extravagantly disappointed'.[187]

It came, one day, to 'words'.[188] Stead was staying with David and Doris Stead in Lindfield, and had been invited to lunch at Centennial Park with Elizabeth Harrower. Stead arrived in a taxi, with a bag of empty bottles which she asked White to put in his rubbish bin. Later, over lunch, she boasted, 'I've always humped my own bluey'. White snorted, 'Like hell you have.'[189] He made some sharp comments about her living arrangements and her dependence on others. According to Harrower, 'Christina defended herself in a dignified and calm manner.' The storm passed, and they adjourned to the sitting room for coffee. Afterwards, sharing a taxi with the loyal Harrower, Stead tactfully attributed the outburst to White's bad health.[190]

It was to be the last encounter between White and Stead. After her death, Patrick White would send David Stead his condolences, with the comment: 'I'm sorry I did not know her earlier on when she was at the height of her powers.'[191]

*   *   *

As well as the losses, there were new friendships in the last months of Stead's life. One was Jonathan LaPook. A 29-year-old gastroenterologist from Columbia University, he came bearing gifts to Stead from his close friend Lillian Hellman. One was *Pentimento*, a volume of Hellman's memoirs, with the inscription: 'To Christina Stead. Perhaps her greatest and oldest admirer, Lillian Hellman.'[192] The other was a cheque for $10000.[193]

Stead was 'very uneasy' about accepting the cheque, says LaPook. She protested that she did not need it; she even offered to give it to him. 'In the end, she accepted it only with the logic that it would become part of her estate which she could then give to somebody else.'[194]

LaPook was working at the Royal North Shore Hospital in Sydney for three months, and he and Stead saw quite a bit of each other during that time.[195] Stead was proud of her new friend, nearly two metres tall, and 'very humane'. She told Burnshaw that when he heard about her difficulties in finding a home, this 'attractive' and 'delightful' man had offered to share his flat in New York with her. 'Remember he is twenty-nine, I am eighty.'[196]

★   ★   ★

Then there were honours. In September 1982 Stead was awarded a NSW Premier's Award for her services to literature.[197] Feeling fragile, she asked Elizabeth Harrower to attend the ceremony on her behalf.

A more prestigious honour was being made an Honorary Member of the American Academy and Institute of Arts and Letters. Honorary Foreign Membership of the Academy, intended to strengthen cultural ties with other countries, was limited to seventy-five. The other new member that year was Chinua Achebe from Nigeria. Famous Academy members, past and present, included Isak Dinesen, T. S. Eliot, Doris Lessing, Bertrand Russell, Alexander Solzhenitsyn and Rebecca West.

The Academy award presentation was at the American Consulate in Sydney on 24 November 1982. Heather Stewart, the Cultural Affairs Adviser, collected Stead from David Stead's house in Lindfield, and drove her to the Consulate. In the car, Stead told her that she hated living with relatives and was looking for somewhere to live. Heather, who had a large house in inner-city Glebe, said 'I have a room—you might like it.'[198] In conversation, Stead appeared quite vigorous. Stewart had no idea what she was offering to take on.

After the ceremony, there was lunch at the Washington Club, attended by Consul General Horowitz and his wife, Justice Harold Glass and his wife, and Heather Stewart.[199] Amid these Jewish New

Yorkers, with 'pics of George on wall and menus' and a 'huge bust of Old Abe' in the foyer, Stead sparkled.[200] Afterwards, Heather Stewart said to her, 'We must have lunch again'. Stead answered, 'What about tomorrow?' She came in to the city the very next day by taxi, wanting to talk seriously about the house proposition.

They walked one block from the Consulate to a restaurant, and Stewart noticed that Stead was gasping for breath. Stewart then broke the news that she did not live alone at Glebe. 'What's his name?' 'Archibald.' 'Congratulations!' Stead exclaimed. 'You won the Archibald Prize!'

To Stead's dismay, she was not able to move in until after Christmas: there was work to do on her room, which had damp patches and needed painting. 'At New Year, then?' Stead asked. Heather Stewart agreed.[201] A month later, Stead told Rosemary Dobson: 'If all goes well, I shall have a home there. How I hope for it! I can't tell you how bad this has been.'[202]

It was a strange existence for a woman of 80. Stead had met Heather Stewart twice before she moved into her house. Only after her new acquaintance moved in, did Stewart realise that she was considerably more helpless than she had seemed.

The house, at No. 17 Wigram Road, Glebe, was a beautiful three-storey terrace, but it was the hottest time of the year, inner-city Sydney was plagued, as usual, with summer cockroaches, and Heather's partner Archibald Zammit-Ross was hammering loudly on the roof. Stead left again, saying she would stay at Kate's until the repair work was finished. While at Kate's in Cremorne, she had another heart attack and was back in hospital. It did not stop her from moving to Glebe in the middle of January.

The arrangement was utterly impractical. Heather Stewart worked full-time at the Consulate and, a violinist in her spare time, re-hearsed with the Macquarie University Orchestra two evenings a week. Stead's room downstairs was next to a toilet and basin, but the bath was upstairs, and she had to be helped up the stairs and helped into the bath. She would not let Heather Stewart do this, so David, Gilbert or Kate had to come to help her. Stewart, who had fondly imagined Stead could walk to the shops, had to do the shopping on Saturday mornings. Stead hardly ate anything, she recalls, except steak tartare. She drank—sometimes fortified milk, mostly alcohol. She was lonely, there all day on her own, and was pleased to have company in the evenings. She warmed to Zammit-Ross, a goodlooking sculptor whom she called Archimedes.

*   *   *

Susan Molloy arrived in Glebe in January 1983 to interview Christina Stead for the *Sydney Morning Herald*. She rang the bell. Slow footsteps came down the hall, and an old woman opened the door with 'fine chalk hands'.

> The face is creased with life, a humping of the shoulders sometimes makes it hard for her to straighten, the ankles are puffed with age, but the hands are soft and white, young and unlined.[203]

An Artists for Peace Exhibition had just opened in the city, the proceeds to go to the Association for International Co-operation and Disarmament. H. C. Coombs was one of the patrons, as was Stead. She told Molloy: 'I do not feel strongly . . . I just feel it is a good idea. Nugget Coombs . . . is a very close friend of mine and anything he says is good.'[204]

She had been writing to Coombs about her will. She wanted to leave her money to a good cause: what did he suggest? His passion was aboriginal rights: should she leave her money to an aboriginal organisation? 'Anything you say,' she told him, in May 1982.[205] Coombs found it difficult to counsel her: aboriginal organisations tended to be shortlived.[206] He advised the Australian Conservation Foundation, and suggested that she specify the money should be used (in consultation with aborigines) for national parks in aboriginal land.[207]

In the end, Stead kept to the will she had made on 2 August 1979, which she had also discussed with Coombs. In it she left $3000 to each of her five siblings, as well as her cousins Gwendolin Walker-Smith and Elsie Ford. She gave another $3000 to David for being her executor, and she 'forgave and released' Gilbert from a total debt of $7800 for the annexe at No.10 Donald St, Hurstville. Her books and paintings were to go to David Stead and Ron Geering, Bill Blake's manuscripts to Ruth Hall, and all English royalties from Stead's own books were to go to Ruth. Any income derived from the recently published *A Christina Stead Reader* was to go to Charlotte Mayerson, Stead's editorial friend at Random House who had seen it through to press.[208] The residual estate and royalties or film rights other than in England were to go to the Australian Conservation Foundation—an ongoing bequest.[209]

She loved nature, but conservation had never been one of Christina Stead's passions. Her first will, made in England in 1969, had decreed that her money should be given to writers in need and this would seem to reflect her own interests more accurately. However, in her will as in life generally, she was her father's daughter. Politically and intellectually, she always allowed herself to be guided by the man she loved.

*   *   *

When Mary Lord called to see Christina in Glebe in late January 1983, she was shocked at how much her condition had deteriorated, and immediately rang her doctor friend, Helena Berenson, and asked her to look at her. Berenson took Stead to see Dr John James, a specialist in cardiology and respiratory medicine, who admitted her to Balmain Hospital for several days of tests. She had a history of ischaemic heart disease, myocardial infarction, cardiac failure and longstanding hypertension. Now, at 80 and an alcoholic, she had gouty arthritis and severe swelling round the ankle joints, due to an accumulation of uric acid. She was short of breath and unsteady.

Helena Berenson, in her early thirties, had a talent for bringing home stray people and caring for them. Stead could not have fallen into better hands. Berenson, who regarded her as 'a very great lady', collected her things from Heather Stewart's and took her to the rambling Victorian home on Johnson Street, Annandale, where she lived with her husband, Geoff Davis, also a doctor. Like something out of a fairytale, The Abbey, as it was called, was a High Gothic castle, with a Gothic spire, Gothic church windows and gargoyles guarding the tower. Stead had always had a taste for the Gothic: now she was entering the castle of her imagination.

Her tiny groundfloor room, the size of a monk's cell, was formerly the butler's pantry. Next to it was the dining room—or, rather, the banquet room. On the heavy wooden table, Stead had her typewriter. On one wall was a Gothic fireplace; on the other a large traceried bay window, through which filtered light fell on the patterned floor. Propped against the wall was a series of grotesque Charles Blackman paintings, belonging to a friend. A door opened to the outside verandah, where Stead would sit and watch the birds. Sydney was particularly humid that summer. It rained and rained.

Geoff Davis was gradually restoring the house, and the place was chaotic. Planks of wood and lumps of marble and building materials were piled all over the garden. In the house, books and paintings were stacked beside antiques from the Davis family estate. Cats and dogs chased each other through the house; Geoff Davis' young children from a previous marriage regularly came to stay. It was not unlike the atmosphere in *The People with the Dogs*.

Helena Berenson was home during the day; she ran an after-hours practice, in Leichhardt, from 6 pm till midnight. Geoff Davis worked during the day and was at home in the evening. Consequently, Stead was never without a doctor in the house.

In this Gothic mansion, her past unreeled before her. Her childhood had been spent at Lydham Hill, with visits to Dappeto—both grand old Sydney houses. She was ending her days at The Abbey, featured in the book *Fine Houses of Sydney*.[210] Lydham Hill had been owned by Frederick John Gibbins, Ada Stead's father; his wife's family, the Picketts, were related by marriage to the Davis family, from the Gosford area. Though neither Stead nor Davis made the connection, this was Geoff Davis' family. Things have a strange way of coming full circle.

Helena Berenson supplied the European element in Stead's life. Most of Stead's northern hemisphere friends had been Jewish: Berenson's family was Polish Jewish. As a child Helena had spoken Yiddish before she learnt English, and Stead liked to get her to speak a few phrases of Yiddish. And then, like Aida Kotlarsky, Berenson was a gifted pianist—in her teens, she had regularly beaten Roger Woodward in competitions at the NSW Conservatorium of Music—but finally she had chosen medicine as her career.

Berenson became Stead's nurse, doctor and friend. When Stead got up in the morning, Berenson would wash her—either helping her upstairs to the bathroom or bringing a bowl downstairs. (Very modest, Stead had never allowed anyone such intimacy before.) Berenson supervised her pill-taking—there was a row of pill bottles by now—then helped her into the lounge. While Stead sat on the sofa with her feet up, Berenson played to her—mostly Mozart, by request. When she stopped playing, after an hour or so, Christina, whose thoughts had been wandering with the music, would talk in her low voice. She mentioned a great romance across a crowded room, a romance with a man who was killed in the Spanish Civil War. Berenson never knew whether it was fiction or fact, but she was just as enthralled as Geoff Davis' children were when Stead told them a story. It all sounded very beautiful and mystical. Though she longed to, Berenson never broke the spell by asking questions.

In the afternoons Stead would nap; in the evenings she would type in the dining room. The household went to bed at odd hours and Stead, probably woken by the strange noises, would be wandering around in the early hours of the morning, drinking, or making steak tartare in the kitchen. She had a supply of 1½-litre bottles of cinzano rosso, and got through one and a half of these a day. Berenson and Davis did not interfere.

One night in mid March, they were woken by the sounds of clattering and banging downstairs. Geoff Davis hurried down to find Stead stumbling around the dining room in her nightdress. She looked extraordinarily excited. Her face was shining, she was quite unco-ordinated, but she was not drunk. (They never saw her drunk.) To Davis' amusement, she had put her foot right through one of the Charles Blackman paintings. 'He's here! He's come for me!' she kept saying. She hardly registered Davis' presence, and struggled when he tried to take her back to her room. 'You don't understand! He's come for me!'

Davis had seen delirious patients before, but never like this. It could have been a combination of fever, dehydration and alcohol consumption, he says, but there was something else. 'It was,' says Davis, 'very, very impressive.'[211]

*   *   *

They took her to Balmain Hospital the following day. Stead's condition rapidly worsened. From the ulcerated gouti tophi on her feet and ankles she developed septicaemia, and though she was given massive doses of intravenous antibiotics, nothing worked. She refused to eat, and she complained of chest pains and shortness of breath. She had difficulty remembering recent events, and she showed signs of dementia. The nursing staff thought her a cantankerous old woman and doubtless treated her thus. Helena Berenson was sad to observe their hostility.[212]

Stead was able to register that the University of New South Wales was offering her a doctorate. 'They're making me one of you,' she joked to Ron Geering, meaning the dreaded category of academic drones. She told him she was anxious to leave the hospital as she had an idea for a story she wanted to write.

When Mary Lord visited Christina for what turned out to be the last time, she seemed at first to be asleep. Mary sat quietly by the bedside. After a while, Christina opened her eyes. 'It's lovely to open my eyes and see your face, you dear thing,' she told her. Then she said: 'He came for me.' Mary knew whom she meant.

*   *   *

Easter was early in 1983. On Maundy Thursday, 31 March, Ron Geering went to see Stead in the early afternoon. He had retired, but he still gave occasional lectures at the University of New South Wales, and he had just been lecturing on *The Man Who Loved Children*. He found Stead in a terrible state, distressed and in pain, finding it hard to breathe. Drawn and haggard, her face looked like a skull. She was in a panic, convinced the nurses were not giving her the heart tablets she needed. She put her thin hands on Geering's and looked at him wildly: 'Unless I get the tablets this will do for me.' He rushed out to fetch the nursing sister and doctor: they brought in an oxygen cylinder. Christina Stead lost consciousness. Ron Geering stayed for an hour or so, listening to the sound of her wheezing breathing. Then Kate Stead arrived and he left.

That same afternoon, Helena Berenson was at the Easter Show with Geoff's children. She watched them go down the big dipper, and suddenly went quite cold. She immediately rang Balmain Hospital. Christina Stead had just died.[213]

*　　*　　*

Heather Stewart had bought Christina an Easter egg, which she intended taking to the hospital that evening. When she got home from work, there was a message from David Stead on her answering machine. She has never rubbed it off.

Stead died at 80, the same age as her father. There was no announcement in the press until after the burial, and because of the Easter holiday, the obsequies had to wait until 6 April. The body was cremated at the Northern Suburbs Crematorium: there was no ceremony, there were no speeches. Just seven people witnessed the coffin sliding into the flame: David and Doris Stead, Gilbert Stead, Ron and Dorothy Geering, Mary Lord and Elizabeth Harrower. The man she loved was not there. Stead's sisters were not there: David Stead had told them that Christina did not want them to attend. They were extraordinarily hurt, and out of loyalty, Gwen Walker-Smith, Christina's 'sister-cousin', also stayed at home. The women, who had done so much for Christina, were dismayed by this last gesture from the grave.

After the ceremony, there were drinks at David and Doris' home in Lindfield. Christina's name was barely mentioned. Her friends were mortified by the utter bleakness of the occasion.

Forty years earlier Christina had written to Bill, 'Marriage for us has very little meaning, except that if we pass out, we will be buried as "Munx & Mrs. Munx" and that is worth something'.[214] It was not to be.

On another occasion Christina had told her brother David she would like her ashes to be scattered in Botany Bay. But her final will left no instructions, and after a year, when the family had not come to collect them, the ashes were tossed by an official onto the grounds of the crematorium.

Epilogue

CHRISTINA STEAD NEVER thought death the end of everything. As the daughter of a naturalist, she always knew she would go the way of 'the coral-insects, . . . the ancient leaves and saurians that had left only a small imprint in the kerosene shale'.[1]

Like dreams, Stead's books do not have definite endings; they leave us with a sense of recurrent patterns, endless cycles, 'terrestrial eternity'. Christina Stead thought of herself as a Scheherazade, conscious of 'the powerful story rooted in all things', and forever spinning tales. Scheherazade, the legendary queen in the *Arabian Nights*, told stories to retain the interest of the man who held her life in his hands. By telling stories, she held life in *her* hands.

Christina Stead's natural habitat was the 'ocean of story'. As she once said, 'It is the million drops of water that are the looking-glasses of all our lives'.

Notes

Abbreviations

Note: Source details are given in the Bibliography.

Anderson	Edith Anderson
Beauties	*The Beauties and Furies*
Blech/Blake	Bill Blech/Blake
Burnshaw	Stanley Burnshaw
Coombs	H. C. (Nugget) Coombs
Cotters'	*Cotters' England*
Dogs	*The People with the Dogs*
Geering	Ron Geering
Herbert	*Miss Herbert*
Hotel	*The Little Hotel*
House	*House of All Nations*
FJ	Florence James
Laughing	*I'm Dying Laughing*
Letty	*Letty Fox: Her Luck*
Love	*For Love Alone*
McKenney	Ruth McKenney
The Man	*The Man Who Loved Children*
NLA	National Library of Australia
NSW	New South Wales
Ocean	*Ocean of Story*
Rella	Ettore Rella
CS	Christina Stead
DDS	David Darwin Stead
DGS	David George Stead
Salzburg	*The Salzburg Tales*
Puzzleheaded	*The Puzzleheaded Girl*
Poor Men	*Seven Poor Men of Sydney*
SL	*Selected Letters*
Tea	*A Little Tea, A Little Chat*
FW-S	Florence Walker-Smith
GW-S	Gwen Walker-Smith

Prologue

1. Stead's notes on Quentin Bell's biography of Virginia Woolf, NLA, Box 7, folder 53.
2. Vladimir Nabokov, 'Good Readers and Good Writers', *Lectures on Literature*, ed. Fredson Bowers, Harcourt Brace Jovanovich, New York, 1980.
3. *Beauties*, p. 159.

1: Ocean of Story

1. CS, 'Lydham Hill'. (Unpublished notes.) NLA, MS 4967, Box 6, folder 38.
2. The details are reconstructed from Stead's unpublished piece, 'Lydham Hill'. The little girl is called Laurel, and her mother says 'Yes, go, Lossie.'
3. CS interview with Giulia Giuffré in Giulia Giuffré, *A Writing Life*, Allen & Unwin, Sydney, 1990, p.81.
4. 'Lydham Hill'. Stead admired Flaubert. The ending of *The Man*, when Henny, bewildered and badly in debt, takes the cyanide her stepdaughter offers her, has echoes of *Madame Bovary*.
5. CS to Anderson, 22 iii 1963. (Anderson private papers, Berlin.)
6. Preface to *Ocean*, first published in 'International Symposium on the Short Story', *Kenyon Review*, vol. 30, no. 4, 1968.
7. 'A Waker and Dreamer', *Ocean*, pp.481–93; Preface to *Ocean*.
8. *Immigrants, Sydney, 1860–1879*, NSW Archives. Also: *Plymouth Paper*, 12 April 1862, courtesy DDS. The *Hotspur* left Plymouth on 31 March 1862, and arrived in Sydney 19 July 1862 (ninety-eight days later). Samuel Stead was born on 6 May 1846 in Ramsgate, Kent, and died in Sydney on 18 August 1921.
9. Christina McLaren was born on 30 December 1848 in Alloa, Scotland, and died 25 August 1893 in Sydney. (GW-S papers.) In Australia, Christina McLaren's widowed mother had married Mr Broadfoot and the daughter's name was changed to Broadfoot, but McLaren remained her registered name.
10. Sydney John (1868–1952), Samuel Leonard (1871–1970), Christina Maude (1873–1949), Jessie Broadfoot (1875–1964), David George (1877–1957), Florence Emma May (1879–1969). (*Index to Births 1870–1879*, NSW Archives, and information from GW-S.)
11. 'A Waker and Dreamer', *Ocean*, pp.484–5.
12. The first Odd Fellows Lodge was formed in Sydney in 1836. See Geoffrey Blainey, *Odd Fellows*, Allen & Unwin, Sydney, 1991, ch. 1.
13. The Plymouth Brethren, founded in Plymouth, Devon, in 1831, were also known as Darbyites, after their founder, John Nelson Darby (1800–1882).
14. 'A Waker and Dreamer', *Ocean*, p.483.
15. Unpublished draft, NLA, Box 6, folder 38.
16. She died on 25 August 1893. Later, Samuel Stead married again. The only son of that marriage, Harry, died at Poisières aged 21.
17. 'A Waker and Dreamer', *Ocean*, p.485.
18. Gilbert Stead's rough notes for the entry on David George Stead in the *Australian Dictionary of Biography*, are in the Rare Books section of the Mitchell Library, Sydney. David George Stead papers, MS 5413, I. (Several details were omitted in the published version.)
19. Elsie Ford (née Butters) to me, 18 viii 1991.
20. Elsie Ford to me, 23 iv 1988. (Elsie's father, Duncan Cameron Butters, was Ellen's brother.)
21. This is according to Stead's semi-fictional notes, 'Lydham Hill', and it seems, from all accounts, that this was so.
22. 'Lydham Hill'.
23. See 'Nature Notes' (by 'Physalia'), *St George Call*, vol. 1, no. 7, 20 February 1904, p.5.
24. The marriage was announced retrospectively in the *Sydney Morning Herald*, 2 May 1859.
25. The children were Archibald Cameron, Duncan Cameron, Mary Evalina, John, Zoe, Florence, Thomas, William, Ellen and Henry. (Elsie Ford papers.)
26. Brian Hodge, *Valleys of Gold*, Cambaroora Star Publications, Penshurst, 1976, p.61.
27. Elsie Ford to me, 23 iv 1988.
28. Ellen's brother William Butters was Vice Regal poet to the NSW Governor during WWI. Several of his 'Australian poems' (full of glorious, royalist, pro-British sentiment) are published in a slim volume entitled *For God and King*, Thompson Printery, Sydney, 1913.

29. Ellen Stead's death certificate is in Gilbert Stead's family archives.
30. Elsie Ford to me, 23 iv 1988.
31. Sigmund Freud, 'Dostoevsky and Parricide', (1927), *Art and Literature*, The Pelican Freud Library, vol. 14, Harmondsworth, 1985, p.441.
32. Unpublished notes. NLA, Box 6, folder 38.
33. There are Michael and Catherine in *Poor Men*, Tom and Nellie Cotter in *Cotters'*, and Philip and Nell in *Dogs*. David Stead's third wife, Thistle Harris, was the same age as his daughter Christina, which gives the incest idea a new slant.
34. Hugh Walker-Smith went to practise in Cessnock. Eight years later, in 1912, just when he and Florence were talking of living together as a family, he caught pleurisy and died, aged 35. In Cessnock, there is a public memorial to him and his work.
35. CS, 'A Waker and Dreamer', *Ocean*, pp.487–8.
36. Ibid.
37. CS, Preface to *Ocean*, p.4.
38. CS, 'A Waker and Dreamer', *Ocean*, p.493.
39. Preface to *Ocean*.
40. Ibid.
41. In *Poor Men*, Michael Bagenault hears 'long conversations carried on between his teeth and his tongue, between the towel and the washstand, the mosquito and the ceiling he was hitting' ... 'Interminable, stupid conversations.' (pp.14–15)
42. Preface to *Ocean*, p.6.
43. Ibid.
44. Unpublished notes, NLA Box 6, folder 38.
45. 'Lydham Hill', NLA, Box 5, folder 37. (Stead mentions the incident again in a letter to GW-S, 12 ix 1972.)
46. NLA, Box 3, folder 19.
47. In *Love*, Andrew Hawkins (based on David Stead) declares: 'An ugly face is usually the dried crust of a turbid, ugly soul.' (p.9)
48. *The Man*, p.383.
49. From the beginning of 1904 he wrote a series of weekly nature notes in *St George Call*, under the pseudonym 'Physalia'.
50. It was published in 1908. Five thousand copies were published, more than 3000 distributed in the UK and US. (D. G. Stead to Under Secretary, 22 x 1918, NSW Archives, 5/5363.8.)
51. Gilbert Stead's notes for the entry on his father in the *Australian Dictionary of Biography*.
52. Conversation with DDS, 20 September 1991. See Charles Swancott's four-volume *The Brisbane Water Story*, Brisbane Water Historical Society, 1953–1955.
53. 'Dappeto', NLA, Box 6, folder 38.
54. 'Early Days', NLA, Box 6, folder 38.
55. Her younger brother Percy died in early childhood in 1885, just before the family moved to Dappeto.
56. 'Dappeto', *St George and Sutherland Shire Leader*, 29 October 1985. (Also: Gilbert Stead's archives.)
57. John Gibbins married Ann Meredith in Sydney in March 1840. (Record of Births, Deaths and Marriages, NSW Archives.)
58. 'Still Life', NLA, Box 5, folder 37.
59. DDS still has a book his mother won as a prize at Hurtlands. *The Complete Poetical Works of Henry Wadsworth Longfellow*, 1893. It is inscribed to Ada Gibbins by J. T. Hooper, Hurtlands, Christmas, 1896.
60. GW-S says her 'voice was thin, somewhat colourless'. (GW-S to me, 13 xi 1991.)
61. This is Christina Stead's surmisal in her fictional notes, 'Two Steps In, Two Steps Out', NLA, Box 6, folder 38.
62. 'Two Steps In, Two Steps Out'.
63. CS interview, recorded Melbourne, 23 March 1976. Australian Writers series, Program 2, Copyright No. 76/AW/2.
64. The announcement of the marriage was in the *Sydney Mail*, 6 February 1907.
65. 'Dappeto', NLA, Box 6, folder 38.
66. 'Old Bexley', NLA, Box 6, folder 38.
67. The house at 18 Lydham Avenue, Rockdale, later renamed Lydham Hall, was one of the few original stone houses in the area to survive. It was bought by the Rockdale Municipal Council in October 1970, and is now open for public inspection at week-

ends. The brochure advertises it as the 'childhood home of the authoress Christina Stead'. There have been major alterations to the house, and the furniture, on loan from the National Trust, dates from the time the house was built, 1855. The land around has been sold off. Christina Stead visited in 1979 and found it greatly changed.

68. CS to Nadine Lewin, undated, 1938. Published in *Meridian*, vol. 8, no. 2, October 1989. (*SL*)
69. 'The White City', NLA, Box 5, folder 37.
70. 'A Waker and Dreamer', *Ocean*, p.492.
71. CS to FJ, 2 xii 1933. (FJ papers)
72. CS interview with John B. Beston, September 1975, *World Literature Written in English*, vol. 15, no. 1, April 1976, p.93.
73. *The Man*, p.155.
74. GW-S to me, 13 xi 1991.
75. *The Man*, p.156.
76. NLA, Box 5, folder 37.
77. This is actually Louisa's memory of Henny, but it is likely to have been Christina's own memory. She was 5 when David Darwin was born.
78. CS to Geering, 29 viii 1982. (*SL*)
79. 'On growing old', NLA, Box 15, folder 113.
80. GW-S believes Stead's story 'The Old School' exaggerates the poverty.
81. 'The Old School', *Ocean*, p.16.
82. These trials are recalled in the story 'The Milk Run'. Matthew, who goes to fetch milk at Dappeto, is based partly on Stead and partly on her brother David, who later took over the errand. (*Ocean*, pp.27–39.)
83. CS to Nadine Lewin, undated, 1938.
84. DGS to his children, Singapore, 27 v 1922. (Gilbert Stead archives.)
85. DDS grimaces when asked about his father's wordplay.
86. Conversation with DDS, Sydney, 20 September 1991.
87. CS to Burnshaw, 5 iii 1981. (*SL*)
88. 'The Triskelion', in *Salzburg*, is set in this area. Stead wrote the story in Paris in 1933.
89. 'Still Life'.
90. 'Early Days'.
91. In her novel *Dogs*, CS probably had this painting in mind when life at the country estate is described as 'the perfect still life ... Fruitfulness with grapes and rabbits dropping over the edges of an oak table on a woven cloth.' (*Dogs*, p.95.)
92. DGS to CS, Malaya, 15 xi 1922.
93. *The Man*, p.421. It is actually Miss Aiden who thinks this, but plainly CS did too.
94. 'A Waker and Dreamer', *Ocean*, p.486.
95. CS to Nadine Lewin, undated, 1938.
96. Conversation with DDS, 9 January 1987.
97. Ibid.
98. Ibid.
99. 'A Waker and Dreamer', *Ocean*, p.484.
100. CS to Thistle Harris, 7 vii 1939. (*SL*)
101. Unpublished draft of 'A Waker and Dreamer', NLA, Box 10, folder 75.
102. 'We men are all weak as water before the primitive devices of Eve,' Sam Pollit complains. (*The Man*, p.160.)
103. Thistle Harris interviewed by Chris Williams for an ABC Radio documentary on David George Stead in the *Sunday Feature* series, broadcast on 1 and 8 June 1986. The text appears in *Meridian*, vol. 8, no. 2, October 1989, as 'David Stead: The Man Who Loved Nature'.
104. Michael Bagenault, in *Poor Men*, has a naturalist father whose character resembles Sam Pollit's. 'His father, whom he despised, with his orchids and surveying, still had entire dominion over him. If he spoke an idea out aloud and his father guffawed, he felt nauseous.' (p.10)
105. Conversation with DDS, 20 September 1991.
106. *The Man*, p.487.
107. Ibid., p.52.
108. Ibid., p.356.
109. CS to the Rellas, 3 iii 1980.
110. Conversation with GW-S, Sydney, 16 January 1987. Gwen was too young to remember the incident, but her mother told her about it.

111. *The Man*, p.480.
112. Ibid., p.164.
113. Ibid., p.92.
114. CS to Burnshaw, 15 i 1981.
115. *NSW Parliamentary Papers*; Royal Commission on Food Supplies and Prices, Interim Report on Supply and Distribution of Fish (1912), p.xxvi. Cited in H. V. Evatt, *Australian Labour Leader*, A & R, Sydney, 1954, p.505.
116. He established government-owned brick works, metal quarries and bakeries.
117. 'Report on the Fisheries of NSW for the year 1914', *NSW Parliamentary Papers 1915–1916*, vol. 1.
118. DGS to his children, Paris, 20 xi 1914. (Gilbert Stead archives.)
119. Ibid., Stavanger, 24 xii 1914. (Gilbert Stead archives.)
120. Conversation with DDS, 9 January 1987.
121. This was published in 1920 by the American Unitarian Association of Boston.
122. Unpublished notes for 'A Waker and Dreamer', NLA, Box 10, folder 75.
123. For more on Starr Jordan see Donald K. Pickens, *Eugenics and the Progressives*, Vanderbilt University Press, Nashville, Tennessee, 1968. DDS has his father's autograph book. Louie quotes from it in *The Man*, p.502.
124. DGS to Mrs DGS, Boston, 24 ii 1915. (DDS papers.)
125. The play's Oedipal undertone is reinforced by the use and reversals of classical mythology. Antaeus (as it is usually spelt) was a belligerent giant, ultimately strangled by Heracles, who, in a fit of madness, also killed his own children by Megara, his wife, one of the Furies.
126. *The Man*, pp.408–9.
127. Ibid., pp.170–1.
128. Ibid., p.372.
129. CS to Thistle Harris, 7 vii 1939. (*SL*)
130. 'Report on the Fisheries of NSW for the year 1915', *NSW Parliamentary Papers 1916*, vol. 2.
131. 'A Waker and Dreamer', *Ocean*, p.490.
132. DGS made this point in a leaflet dated 6 September 1916, 'A few facts about the NSW State Trawling Industry'. (Gilbert Stead archives.)
133. Holman's unpublished reminiscences, quoted in H. V. Evatt, *Australian Labour Leader*, p.506.
134. Unpublished draft of 'A Waker and Dreamer', NLA, Box 10, folder 75.
135. 'A Waker and Dreamer', *Ocean*, p.490.
136. CS, 'A Writer's Friends', *Ocean*, p.495.
137. She claimed that the headmaster at Bexley School, horrified to hear this statement coming from so young a girl, wrote 'Church of England' in his records. CS to Kathleen Grieves, 15 vi 1976, NLA, Box 7, folder 50.
138. Stead's unpublished novel, *The Wraith and the Wanderer*, written in the early 1930s, contains this poem, called 'Green Apricots', probably reconstructed from memory, and perhaps improved slightly. (NLA, Box 6, folder 40.)
139. CS, 'A Writer's Friends', *Ocean*, p.495.
140. Ibid.
141. Angela Carter, Introduction to the Virago edition of *The Puzzleheaded Girl* (1968), London, 1984.
142. *The Man*, p.70.
143. These details are reconstructed from *The Man*, unpublished notes ('Two Steps In, Two Steps Out') and conversations with GW-S and DDS.
144. Conversation with GW-S, 24 September 1991.
145. Ibid.
146. CS interview with Rodney Wetherell, broadcast 24 February 1980. Published in *Australian Literary Studies*, vol. 9, no. 4, October 1980, pp.431–8.
147. *The Man*, p.45.
148. CS interview with Joan Lidoff, Surbiton, England, June, 1973. In Joan Lidoff, *Christina Stead*, Ungar, New York, 1982, pp.182–3.
149. CS to Nadine Lewin, undated, 1938.
150. *The Bulletin*, 17 March 1888. Quoted by Manning Clark in *A History of Australia 1851–1888*, vol. IV, Melbourne University Press, Melbourne, 1978, p.387.
151. At 15, Jessie was sent to teach in a country town in western NSW. It was a stark, lonely life for young female teachers. (Conversation with DDS, 20 September 1991.)

152. CS interview with Ann Whitehead (1973), *Australian Literary Studies*, vol. 6, no. 3, May 1974, p.243.
153. CS interview with Rodney Wetherell, (1980), *Australian Literary Studies*, vol. 9, no. 4, October 1980, p.438.
154. Mary McCarthy, 'Framing Father', review of *The Man, New Republic*, vol. 104, no. 2, 13 January 1941, p.61.
155. Clifton Fadiman, review of *The Man, New Yorker*, 19 October 1940, p.84.
156. Charles Poore, review of *The Man, New York Times*, 18 October 1940, p.19.
157. Randall Jarrell, Introduction to *The Man*, Holt, Rinehart & Winston, New York, 1965.
158. CS to Thistle Harris, 7 vii 1939.
159. CS interview with Rodney Wetherell (1980), p.441.
160. Ibid., p.444.
161. Conversation with GW-S, 24 September 1991.
162. *Beauties*, p.255; *Love*, p.490.
163. 'Christina Stead', Australia Council Video Series on Australian Writers, 1980. Producer: Haydn Kernan.
164. CS interview with Rodney Wetherell (1980).
165. The term is used by B. K. de Garis in *A New History of Australia*, ed. Frank Crowley, Heinemann, Melbourne, 1974, p.258.
166. CS interview with Joan Lidoff (1973), p.203.
167. CS to Dorothy Green, 8 viii 1977.
168. 'A Waker and Dreamer', *Ocean*, p.485.
169. CS interview with Joan Lidoff, p.185. The collection of stories is called *Getting Married*, tr. Mary Sandbach, Quartet Books, London, 1977. In *Poor Men*, Joseph reads *The Spook Sonata* and is reminded of his parents. Stead probably confused this play with *The Father* or *The Dance of Death*—both about married misery. The Captain in *The Father* is more likely to have reminded her of her own father.
170. *The Man* p.389. Given Stead's love of Shelley, it is likely that this has autobiographical authenticity. On the function of *The Cenci* within *The Man*, see Jonathan Arac, 'The Struggle for the Cultural Heritage: Christina Stead refunctions Charles Dickens and Mark Twain', in *The New Historicism*, ed. H. Aram Veeser, Routledge, New York and London, 1989, pp.116–31.
171. CS interview with Rodney Wetherell (1980), p.445.
172. CS interview with Joan Lidoff (1973), p.187.
173. Dappeto was bought by the Salvation Army and used as a children's home until 1968. Now called Macquarie Lodge, it is a home for senior citizens.
174. David Stead later asserted that he had never wanted Christina to become a journalist, for he recognised an 'original thinker' in her. On 8 January 1950, he wrote to GW-S and Jean Saxelby: 'From 1902 onwards I became very familiar with journalism and journalists, and had particularly noted the effects of frustration upon many women who had started out bright eyed in the profession, expecting that it would be a means or a vehicle for expressing *themselves*; soon—very soon—to discover that their writings must be shaped to the will and demands of others ... I had already seen many of Christina's schoolgirl efforts and recognised an original writer, and one who would demand an expression of her own feelings and thoughts as I would myself.' (Walter Stone Collection; Jean Stone (née Saxelby) papers.)
175. H. V. Evatt, *Australian Labour Leader*, p.389. See also pp.505–6.
176. The Steads' house, Boongarre, was sold in March 1991 (after Thistle Harris' death) for A$2.7 million.
177. Conversation with Kelvin Stead, Boongarre, 15 January 1987.
178. Conversation with DDS, 20 September 1991.
179. 'Overland', NLA, Box 15, folder 113.
180. *Poor Men*, p.17. Stead was probably thinking of Nietzsche, whose refrain this is: 'One has still to be as close to the flowers, the grass and the butterflies as is a child.—He who wants to partake of *all* good things must know how to be small at times.' *Human, All Too Human*, tr. R. J. Hollingdale, CUP, Cambridge, 1986, p.323.
181. *The Man*, pp.334–5.

2: Embarkation for Cythera

1. 'Overland', NLA, Box 15, folder 113. King Boongarre is described in P. Cunningham, *Two Years in New South Wales*, London, 1828, vol. 1, pp.41–3.
2. *Poor Men*, p.1.
3. CS interview with Rodney Wetherell (1980), published in *Australian Literary Studies*, vol. 9, no. 4, October 1980, p.437.
4. *Love*, p.189.
5. Graeme Kinross Smith, 'Christina Stead—A Profile', *Westerly*, no. 1, 1976, pp.67–75.
6. Ibid.
7. Conversation with DDS, Sydney, 9 January 1987.
8. Fish oil was used for medicinal purposes and paint. David Stead, *Fishes of Australia*, William Brooks & Co, Sydney, 1906, pp.250–3.
9. Conversation with DDS, 27 September 1991.
10. Peggy Stead, 'The Hill', *High School Chronicle*, October 1918, p.7. (Sydney Girls' High School papers.)
11. CS describes it in *Poor Men*, p.69.
12. CS interview with Rodney Wetherell.
13. *Poor Men*, p.250.
14. Though these are Teresa's imaginings (*Love*, p.61), given that it was wartime, they are likely to have been Christina's own.
15. CS to Thistle Harris, 7 vii 1939. (*SL*)
16. Conversation with DDS, 9 January 1987.
17. CS interview with Thomas Keneally, 'Conversation Piece', *Vogue Australia*, vol. 21, no. 4, 1977, pp.91–3.
18. GW-S and Jean Saxelby wrote a piece on CS in *Biblionews*, vol. 2, no. 14, December 1949.
19. Weeta Stead to Dorothy Green, 9 v 1983.
20. I owe several of the details about the school to Lilith Norman's book *The Brown and Yellow*, Oxford University Press, Melbourne, 1983.
21. 'Why I am an Expatriate', NLA, Box 15, folder 113.
22. In 1915 eighteen girls won University Exhibitions.
23. Lilith Norman, *The Brown and Yellow*, p.241.
24. Kathleen Grieves (née Nyman) to CS, 3 vi 1976. (NLA, Box 7, folder 51.)
25. *Poor Men*, p.170.
26. CS interview with Ann Whitehead (1973), *Australian Literary Studies*, vol. 6, no. 3, May 1974, p.240.
27. *Poor Men*, p.54.
28. Ibid.
29. Ibid., p.132.
30. CS to Geering, 20 vi 1964. (*SL*)
31. S. J. Kunitz & H. Haycroft, *Twentieth Century Authors*, H. W. Wilson, New York, 1942, p.1330.
32. CS interview with Rodney Wetherell (1980).
33. 'Overland', NLA, Box 15, folder 13. (See also: CS interview with Joan Lidoff, Surbiton, England, June 1973. In Joan Lidoff, *Christina Stead*, Ungar, New York, 1982, p.201.)
34. CS interview with Rodney Wetherell (1980), p.433. Stead alludes to the general practice of ticket-collecting in *Poor Men*, p.42.
35. Conversation with Phyllis Barnett (née McEwan), Sydney, 21 January 1987.
36. CS to Philip Harvey, 12 ix 1979.
37. Conversation with DDS, 9 January 1987.
38. *Poor Men*, p.2.
39. CS, 'A Writer's Friends', *Ocean*, p.496.
40. Ibid.
41. The fictional Clare Meredith, modelled closely on the real-life Clare Tarrant, is the only character in Stead's fiction to bear her real name: Stead could not think of any other which suited her as well. (CS to Pauline Nestor, 8 vi 1975; Nestor papers, Melbourne.)

42. CS to Pauline Nestor, 8 vi 1975.
43. Conversation with Tempe Mann (née Datson), Sydney, 25 January 1987.
44. Conversation with Phyllis Barnett (née McEwan), Sydney, 21 January 1987.
45. Mary Gilmore to Hugh McCrae, 22 ix 1936. Cited in *Letters of Mary Gilmore*, selected and edited by W. H. Wilde and T. Inglis Moore, MUP, Melbourne, 1980, p.125.
46. Stead translated this freely as 'Go forward wherever your fortune points, with ever greater courage'. (CS to Nadine Lewin, undated, probably 1935.) (*SL*) In *Poor Men*, a priest writes this in Joseph's school prize book.
47. CS to Burnshaws, 20 ii 1975.
48. CS interview with Ann Whitehead (1973), p.234.
49. *Love*, p.14.
50. Ibid., p.74.
51. CS interview with Robert Drewe (1982), *Scripsi*, vol. 4, no. 1, July 1986, p.22.
52. *Poor Men*, p.243.
53. Conversation with Thistle Harris, 15 January 1987. (Also: ABC Interview with Thistle Harris, 25 October 1983. ABC Talks and Documentaries.)
54. 'A Waker and Dreamer', *Ocean*, p.492.
55. CS, draft notes for 'A Waker and Dreamer'. NLA, Box 10, folder 75.
56. Ibid.
57. 'Fourth Sectional Report of the Royal Commission (Mr G. Mason Allard) to inquire into the Public Service of NSW upon the State Trawling Industry', *NSW Parliamentary Papers 1920*, vol. 1, p.48.
58. The State Trawling Industry ceased operations in February 1923. The undertaking had not proved profitable.
59. DGS wrote the articles well in advance, for they continued to appear at weekly intervals for the thirteen months he was away in Malaya. The articles—from 25 September 1921 to 8 April 1923—are among the David G. Stead papers, Rare Books Collection, Mitchell Library, MS 5413.
60. Dymphna Cusack. *A Window in the Dark*, ed. Debra Adelaide, National Library of Australia, Canberra, 1991, pp.36, 44.
61. She meant Professors Arnold Wood and James Bruce.
62. The lecturer was Dr Perceval Cole.
63. Having attended a high school where the teachers took pleasure in challenging young minds, Smith found the 'switch from education as inquiry to education as method' dull and demoralising. Bernard Smith, *The Boy Adeodatus*, Penguin, Melbourne, 1984, p.176.
64. The ideas expressed in his book were nevertheless quite conventional. A. Mackie (ed.), *The Groundwork of Teaching*, Teachers' College Press and A & R, Sydney, 1924.
65. 1921 NSW Government Annals, section on 'Teaching'.
66. She underwent a course of voice training with Mr Laurence Campbell in 1922. (CS, 'Report on Vocal Defect and Course of Training', 21 February 1923, NSW Archives, Darlinghurst Public School files, 1917–1926, S/15655, B.)
67. *The Kookaburra*, vol. XIII, November, 1921. (Editors: Christina E. Stead and John H. Deane, BA.) (Sydney Teachers' College.)
68. *The Kookaburra*, vol. XIV, December 1922.
69. On his return he produced a report: *General Report upon the Fisheries of British Malaya with Recommendations for Future Development*, issued by authority of the Colonial Secretary, Straits Settlements, and of the Chief Secretary, Federated Malay States, 1923. (Gilbert Stead archives.)
70. DGS to Tan Kah Kee, 6 xi 1922. David G. Stead papers, Mitchell Library, MS 5413 1.
71. His health was never very good: he had suffered from appendix trouble since his youth, and from 'hot pressure', as his daughter put it, at sea-level. (CS to Thistle Harris, 7 vii 1939.) (*SL*)
72. DGS to CS. (Handwritten at top: 'First six lines for Woit and the rest for Pedler.') Singapore, 5 vii 1922. [Woit is Weeta.] Christina Stead included this letter almost verbatim in *The Man*. There are minor changes—mostly improvements to his style. In order to make Sam Pollit convincing as a contemporary American she made small alterations. For example, she altered the last sentence to 'Let's strip Jack naked!'— which DGS, who clung ferociously to his puritanical Victorian upbringing, would never have said.
73. 'A Waker and Dreamer', p.491.
74. DGS to Weeta and Christina, 5 vii 1922.

75. DGS to CS, Singapore, 12 ix 1922. (Gilbert Stead archives.)
76. DGS to CS, Pagi Pagi, 15 xi 1922. (Gilbert Stead archives.)
77. 'A Waker and Dreamer', *Ocean*, p.491.
78. DGS to CS, Pagi Pagi, 15 xi 1922. (Gilbert Stead archives.)
79. *The Man*, p.85.
80. CS to Margaret Mackie, 24 iii 1980 (courtesy Margaret Mackie). (*SL*)
81. One of Stead's reports, dated 6 December 1922, is in Rare Books, Fisher Library, University of Sydney. The test was conducted on Trevor Martin, at Bondi Superior Public School for boys. Trevor, aged 9, was found by CS to have a mental age of 16 years and ten months and an IQ of 182.
82. *Poor Men*, p.90.
83. Dymphna Cusack comments: 'Freudianism, which we approached through the lectures of that very good teacher, Professor Tasman Lovell, was to shake many of us to our foundations.' (Dymphna Cusack, *A Window in the Dark*, p.42.)
84. Conversation with FJ, Sydney, 11 July 1987.
85. These observations are based partly on photographs of Duncan at the time and partly on FJ's description. (Conversation with FJ, 3 July 1989.)
86. *Union Recorder*, 14 September 1922. (Fisher Library, University of Sydney.)
87. 'Sea People', Preface to *Love*.
88. *Love*, p.196.
89. Ibid., p.117.
90. Ibid., p.63.
91. Ibid., p.67.
92. Unpublished notes for *Love*, Box 1, folder 2.
93. *Love*, p.76.
94. Unpublished notes, Box 1, folder 2.
95. *Love*, pp.18–19.
96. David Walker, *Dream and Disillusion*, ANU Press, Canberra, 1976, p.214.
97. CS to NSW Education Department, Superior Public School, Darlinghurst, 21 February 1923. NSW Archives, Darlinghurst School files, 1917–1926, S/15655, B.
98. The leave was from 26 February to 6 March 1923. Darlinghurst School files, ibid.
99. See *Sydney Morning Herald*, 20 October 1924, 1 November 1924, 6 January 1925.
100. CS interview with Joan Lidoff (1973), p.188.
101. *Love*, p.81.
102. CS interview with Ann Whitehead (1973), p.235.
103. *Love*, p.112.
104. Ibid., pp.81–2.
105. 'Question of the acceptance of the resignation of Miss C. E. Stead, Ex-Student', NSW Archives, William Street Public School files, 1919–1928, S/18122.1 B.
106. *Love*, p.137.
107. Ibid.
108. Conversation with DDS, 9 January 1987.
109. This was Dr John A. O'Keefe, 189 Macquarie St, who opined that Miss Stead would be unfit to resume her ordinary duties for at least a month. Medical report, 24 June 1925. (NSW Archives, William Street Public School files. S/18122.1 B.)
110. William Street Public School files, ibid.
111. Dr O'Keefe's report, 15 July 1925. William Street Public School files, ibid.
112. *Love*, p.136.
113. Department of Education, Application for Sick Leave for Three Days or more, 13 July 1925. (NSW Archives, William Street Public School files, S/181122.1 B.)
114. Ada Stead to Department of Education, Boongarre, 7 October 1925. William Street Public School files, ibid.
115. Medical report from Dr O'Keefe, 5 October 1925. William Street Public School files, ibid.
116. S. H. Smith, Director of Education, 14 October 1925. William Street Public School files, ibid.
117. Conversation with Thistle Harris, Watson's Bay, 15 January 1987. According to Harris, she met Ada Stead only once, and it was nothing like the meeting described in 'About the House', in *Ocean* (probably written in the early 1930s, after Thistle Harris moved in with David Stead). Interestingly, the narrator of this story understands both women: there is no judgement.

118. Among CS's unpublished fictional notes is an account of the courtship that concurs with the broad outlines of Thistle Harris' account much later. It proves that David Stead talked to her about it. Garric Fairchild, a scientist, tells his three eldest children that he went camping with his sweet Alison and that he was in love. 'It was a thing, like other things in their parents' lives, that they accepted calmly.' (NLA, Box 1, folder 3.)

119. *WEA of NSW. 12th Annual Report, 1925.* (WEA (Workers Education Association) Library, Bathurst Street, Sydney.)

120. Conversation with FJ, 11 July 1987.

121. H. D. Black, 'An Australian Institution or "If I could a tale unfold"', *Economic Review* (Sydney University Economics Society), vol. 15, 1969, pp.6–7.

122. 'Mr. Duncan ... dwelt for a moment on his beloved Russia ... Fortunately time prevented an exposition of his usual panacea.' *Union Recorder*, 10 July 1924.

123. *Union Recorder*, 26 July 1923, p.6.

124. Ibid., 29 April 1926, p.52.

125. *The Australian Highway*, the monthly journal of the WEA of Australia, 1 July 1926, pp.83–4. (And *Union Recorder*, 1 April 1926.)

126. *Union Recorder*, 19 July, 1923. In the States, in the 1940s, Stead would defend the notorious White Australia Policy for the same reason.

127. H.D. Black, *Economic Review*, vol. 15, 1969, p.7.

128. FJ to me, 2 iv 1992.

129. *Love*, p.179.

130. Interview with Joan Lidoff (1973), p.213.

131. Axel Clark, *Christopher Brennan*, MUP, Melbourne, 1980, p.235. In *Poor Men*, Stead makes an obvious allusion to Brennan. 'Pumblecherri' is 'the one genius the University has: always liquored up, of course.' He had given a lecture on Beauty in Art, in which he celebrated 'the state of chaos, art unborn', rather than 'scholastic art, rigid art'. (p.163)

132. George Robertson to DGS, 21 vii 1925. (A. W. Barker, *Dear Robertson*. A & R, Sydney, 1982, pp.137–8.)

133. DGS to George Robertson, 1 x 1925. A. W. Barker, *Dear Robertson*, p.138.

134. CS to Nettie Palmer, St Germain-en-Laye, 9 v 1951. (NLA, Palmer papers.) (*SL*)

135. Dymphna Cusack, *A Window in the Dark*, p.52.

136. Marie Byles, born in England in 1900, wrote about her climbs in Norway, the United States, Burma and China.

137. *Union Recorder*, 13 May 1926.

138. John Beaglehole to his family, 30 viii 1926. (Tim Beaglehole's unpublished article about his father: '"Home"? J. C. Beaglehole in London, 1926–1929'.) Article courtesy of Hugh Stretton.

139. John Beaglehole to his family, 18 ix 1926. 'J. C. Beaglehole in London', ibid.

140. CS interview with Joan Lidoff (1973), p.190.

141. It is possible that Stead included passages from Duncan's actual letters (vaguely altered and embellished) in the novel. There is evidence that she made use of real letters in her fiction on more than one occasion.

142. Conversation with GW-S, Sydney, 12 December 1986.

143. GW-S and Jean Saxelby, *Biblionews*, vol. 2, no. 14, December 1949.

144. Nettie Palmer, *Illustrated Tasmanian Mail*, 30 July 1930, p.4. Quoted in Vivian Smith, *Vance and Nettie Palmer*, Twayne Publishers, Boston, Massachusetts, 1975.

145. See C. Hartley Grattan, *Australian Literature*, Seattle, University of Washington Chapbooks, 1929. Foreword by Nettie Palmer.

146. *Love*, p.285. Her cousin Gwen somehow sensed Christina's great destiny: she was different from other young women, artistic and brilliant.

147. I owe the name to Chris Williams' research: *Christina Stead: A Life of Letters*, McPhee Gribble, Melbourne, 1989, p.50.

148. CS to Philip Harvey, 16 x 1969. (*SL*)

149. *Love*, pp.284–5.

150. *Letty*, p.427.

151. CS interview with Joan Lidoff (1973), p.191. Many of these details emerged from interviews with DDS, Gilbert Stead and GW-S.

152. *Love*, p.278.

153. Ibid., p.277.

154. It is one of the stories she re-wrote partly from memory and included in *Salzburg*.

155. P. R. Stephenson, *The History and Description of Sydney Harbour*, Rigby, Adelaide, 1966, pp.56–7.
156. 'Day of Wrath', *Salzburg*, p.466.
157. Conversation with GW-S, 12 December 1986. Gwen stresses that Stead built up the wedding scene. There was certainly no rugby scrum scene when it came to the tossing of the bouquet. Nor does she remember Ettie crying—though she admits it was an unhappy occasion.
158. In 1922, CS wrote contemptuously to her father (in Malaya) that her maternal cousin Edna (from Narara) was marrying the neighbour's son. Her father replied: 'Don't be too hard on the people who marry their next doors.' (DGS to CS, undated, 1922.)
159. NLA, Box 4, folder 24.
160. These are books mentioned in *Poor Men* and *Love*. Considering Duncan and Stead's interest in psychology and philosophy, it is likely that this was her own reading matter —as well as a great deal of fiction, drama and poetry.
161. CS to GW-S, 25 i 1931. (*SL*)
162. CS interview with Joan Lidoff (1973), p.202.
163. *Poor Men*, p.207.
164. Friedrich Nietzsche, *Thus Spake Zarathustra*, Penguin, Harmondsworth, 1969, p.46. Stead quotes this in *The Man*.
165. Friedrich Nietzsche, *Human, All Too Human*. (Aphorism 422) tr. R. J. Hollingdale, CUP, Cambridge, 1986.
166. Ibid.
167. Diana Brydon, *Christina Stead*, Macmillan, London, 1987, p.2.
168. Jean Williamson, 'Christina Stead Tells of Her Latest Book!', *Australian Women's Weekly*, 9 March 1935, p.6.
169. CS interview with Ann Whitehead (1973), p.233. There were only four issues, and it quickly became a collector's item.
170. In *Love*, the *Quarterly* is an obvious allusion to *Vision*: a magazine 'written and illustrated by the young artistic set in Sydney . . . in which, with imitations of Marlowe and Shakespeare, Donne, and free verse, it was chiefly a question of free love and naked women; on each page were drawings of voluptuous, fat-faced, naked women, running away from a crowd of satyrs, carried off by centaurs or tempted by evil-eyed fauns.' *Love*, p.209.
171. See Jack Lindsay, *Life Rarely Tells* (1958, 1960, 1962), Penguin, Harmondsworth, 1982.
172. Dorothy Green, 'Chaos, or a Dancing Star? Christina Stead's *Seven Poor Men of Sydney*', *Meanjin*, 113, vol. 27, no. 2, 1968, p.159.
173. Diana Brydon makes this point in *Christina Stead*, p.15.
174. *Poor Men, Love, Beauties, The Man*.
175. *Love*, pp.192–3.
176. *Poor Men*, p.165. In contrast to this joyful trope are recurrent negative images in Stead's fiction—impenetrable forests, vines with strangling grip, snakes—all of which symbolise the obstacles impeding the 'free spirit'.
177. NLA, Box 4, folder 24.
178. Ibid.
179. GW-S to me, 13 xi 1991.
180. 'Why I am an Expatriate', NLA, Box 15, folder 113.
181. NLA, Box 4, folder 24.

3: Port of Registry: London

1. 'A Night in the Indian Ocean', *Ocean*, pp.53–66. The manuscript is typed on the back of 'American & Foreign Discount Corporation' paper, Stead's Paris office between 1929 and 1932.
2. 'Why I am an Expatriate', NLA, Box 15, folder 113.
3. CS to Rellas, 10 x 1979.
4. *Love*, p.189.
5. C. J. Koch, *Crossing The Gap*, Hogarth Press, London, 1987.
6. Charles Loch Mowat, *Britain Between the Wars, 1918–1940*, Methuen, London, 1955.
7. Henry Handel Richardson, *Myself When Young*, London, Heinemann, 1948, p.87.
8. Katharine Susannah Prichard, *Child of the Hurricane*, A & R, Sydney, 1963.
9. Jack Lindsay, *Life Rarely Tells*, (1958), Penguin, Ringwood (Victoria), 1982, p.504.

10. CS to GW-S, 11 vii 1928. (*SL*)
11. CS to Nellie Molyneux, 1 iii 1929. (*SL*)
12. 'J. C. Beaglehole in London, 1926–1929'. (Tim Beaglehole papers, Wellington, New Zealand.)
13. Ibid. John Beaglehole to his family, 2 xi 1926. (Tim Beaglehole papers.)
14. Duncan had begun his doctoral research under the supervision of Professor Leonard T. Hobhouse, the pioneer sociologist, whose 1911 book *Liberalism* stamped him as a progressive liberal philosopher in the mould of Locke, Bentham and John Stuart Mill. Before Hobhouse died, in 1929, Laski took over. (Appointment docket of Dr G. K. Duncan (73/1950), Registry, University of Adelaide.)
15. John Beaglehole, undated letter home (1926). (Tim Beaglehole papers.)
16. Tim Beaglehole makes this point in his unpublished article, 'J. C. Beaglehole in London, 1926–1929'. (Tim Beaglehole papers.)
17. CS to GW-S, 12 vi 1928.
18. Stead describes it thus in *Love*, p.305.
19. Anne Matheson, 'Christina Stead coming home', *Australian Women's Weekly*, 23 July 1969, p.7.
20. CS to GW-S, 30 ix 1929. (*SL*)
21. CS interview with Joan Lidoff (1973), in Lidoff, *Christina Stead*, Ungar, New York, 1982, p.193. The opening of the novella 'The Puzzleheaded Girl' is based on this scene, transferred to New York. Augustus Debrett, 'a stubby dark man with large hazel eyes, ... round head ... pale face' interviews a diffident, plain young woman carrying a book (on French symbolism!). Debrett is a 'married bachelor' who feels that 'he was not loved and never had been'.
22. CS makes this comment in the video *Christina Stead*, the Australia Council Archival Film Series, produced by Haydn Kernan, 1980.
23. CS to FW-S, 17 vi 1928.(*SL*)
24. Ibid.
25. CS to GW-S, 11 vii 1928. (*SL*)
26. Ibid., 12 vi 1928.
27. Ibid., 30 ix 1929.
28. Conversation with Jack Bermond (Alfred Hurst's son-in-law), London, 17 October 1988.
29. *House*, p.7. According to Jack Bermond, the description of Henri Léon is an accurate, if slightly amplified, description of Hurst.
30. 'Why I am an Expatriate', NLA, Box 15, folder 113.
31. Unpublished notes for 'A Waker and Dreamer', NLA, Box 10, folder 75.
32. 'Why I am an Expatriate', NLA, Box 15, folder 113.
33. CS to GW-S, 15 x 1928. (*SL*)
34. Ibid., 1 i 1929.
35. Patrick J. Kearney, *A History of Erotic Literature*, Macmillan, London, 1982, p.174. The illustrator was Serge Czerefkov.
36. CS to GW-S, 1 i 1929.
37. *Poor Men*, p.45.
38. *Beauties*, p.74. When Elvira sees Francesca in Paris, she muses: 'It doesn't pay to see old friends in another setting: they lose all their charm. In England she was delightful, an elegant bas-relief of her countrywomen: here she's just a dumb little office-girl.'
39. FJ says the portrait of Jonathan Crow in *Love* made her sorry for Duncan. 'Everyone at uni. knew it was him.' She added: 'Chris had a cruel streak, a lack of compassion.' (Conversation with FJ, Sydney, 11 July 1987.)
40. *Love*, p.445.
41. Nora Ephron, 'Revision and Life', *Nora Ephron Collected*, Avon Books, New York, 1991, pp.213–16.
42. Stead's only confidante in the first few months was Francette Hubert—and my attempts to track down the French woman (by writing to every Hubert in the Asnières-sur-Seine region) were in vain.
43. *Love*, p.360.
44. Ibid., p.395.
45. Ibid., p.402.
46. Ibid., p.333.
47. Ibid., p.23.

48. Ibid., p.333.
49. Ibid., p.320.
50. CS to FW-S, 17 vi 1928. (*SL*)
51. CS to GW-S, 11 vii 1928. (*SL*)
52. Ibid., 19 vii 1928.
53. Sigmund Freud & Joseph Breuer, *Studies on Hysteria*, Pelican, 1974, p.295. (Stead read about hysterical phenomena when she studied psychology at Sydney University.)
54. 'Why I am an Expatriate', NLA, Box 15, folder 113.
55. CS interview with Rodney Wetherell (1980), *Australian Literary Studies*, vol. 9, no. 4, October 1980.
56. Stead reveals this in 'A Writer's Friends', *Ocean*, p.497. As Dorothy Green argues, in 'Chaos, or a Dancing Star? Christina Stead's *Seven Poor Men of Sydney*', (*Meanjin*, 113, vol. 27, no. 2, 1968, pp.150–61), the number seven is obviously not chosen arbitrarily. 'One remembers among other myths, how Dionysus was torn into seven pieces before his re-integration. The figure of Dionysus, the god of disorder, chaos, the irrational, is omnipresent in the book.' Equally, Stead might have been alluding (tongue in cheek) to the Seven Wise Men of Greece. Perhaps she was thinking of her own family: she was the eldest of seven children.
57. Conversation with FJ, 11 July 1987.
58. CS interview with Rodney Wetherell (1980), p.447.
59. *Love*, p.348.
60. Ibid., p.343.
61. Ibid., p.346.
62. Ibid., pp.419–21.
63. Portrayed as shadows of each other, they recall their tragic precursors, Catherine and Heathcliff.
64. *Poor Men*, p.201.
65. Ibid., p.233.
66. Ibid., p.136.
67. Ibid., p.52.
68. Ibid., p.249.
69. CS interview with Rodney Wetherell (1980).
70. In *Beauties*, Oliver says this about meeting Elvira, explaining that it was an image from Theodor Storm's novella *Immensee*, read during his schooldays.
71. CS to GW-S, 12 ix 1928. (*SL*)
72. Ibid., 15 x 1928. (*SL*)
73. *Love*, p.390.
74. CS, *Christina Stead* (video), Australia Council Archival Film Series (1980).
75. Blech mentions these Corner House meetings in an undated letter to CS, May or June 1942. (NLA, Box 16, folders 119–20.)
76. See Geering, *Christina Stead*, Twayne World Author series, Twayne, New York; A & R, Sydney, 1979, p.14.
77. *Love*, p.430.
78. Ibid., p.429.
79. Ibid., p.432.
80. CS was haunted by a scene in one of the dreams of her American friend, Philip Van Doren Stern. On a note dated 27 June (1940?) she wrote down: 'Phil is walking down the street, in the dark: lamps are on . . . on the other side of the street a man walking: he seems to recognise him. When the man approaches the lamp he turns his face and looks at the dreamer: Phil feels he ought to know the face, but cannot place it.'
   Later, she notes: 'a deformed man, hunchback, a grotesquely strangely familiar face'. (NLA, Box 15, folder 112.)
81. Conversation with Professor W. G. K. Duncan, Adelaide, 27 February 1987.
82. Hugh Stretton to me, 26 vi 1990.
83. FJ to her mother, 8 xi 1928. (FJ papers.)
84. Conversation with FJ, Sydney, 11 July 1987.
85. FJ to her mother, 19 xii 1928.
86. Ibid., 12 xii 1928.
87. Ibid., 19 xii 1928.
88. Ibid.
89. CS to FJ, 31 xii 1935.

90. I owe some of these details to FJ. (FJ to me, 15 v 1992.)
91. It was not so kind. H. E. Bates' brief appraisal of his relationship with Margaret Dunbar-Smith in the second volume of his autobiography, *The Blossoming World* (London, Michael Joseph, 1971) is patronising and disparaging.
92. CS to GW-S, 1 i 1929.
93. Conversation with FJ, Sydney, 11 July 1987.
94. CS to FW-S, 9 i 1929.
95. Ibid.
96. Conversation with FJ, Sydney, 11 July 1987.
97. Unpublished paper, NLA, Box 10, folder 73.
98. FJ to her mother, 19 xii 1928.
99. CS to GW-S, 25 v 1930: 'Few Jews like their race being mentioned, Wilhelm [William] being quite exceptional in his enthusiasm for his race.' (*SL*)
100. FJ to her mother, 23 i 1929.
101. Blech refers to the incident and to the snows near Canterbury and Peterhouse in an undated letter to CS, May or June 1942. NLA, Box 16, folder 119.
102. *Love*, pp.453–4.
103. Ibid.
104. CS to Dorothy Green, 3 x 1976. (NLA, Green papers.) The general parallels between the two couples are striking. Blech and Stead would live together out of wedlock for twenty-three years.
105. FBI file on William James Blake: File no. 100–236179. The file was opened on 1 October 1943.
106. I owe most of the following details about William Blech's family to conversations with Mrs Ruth Hall (née Blech) at Chateauneuf-de-Grasse, France, in October 1987 and September 1988.
107. CS wrote a short story based on Rosa Blech's life called 'Life is Difficult'. Included in the posthumous collection *Ocean*, it was probably written in the late 1960s or early 1970s. Stead calls the character Emma—perhaps because of the parallels with that other dreamer, Emma Bovary.
108. Henry Roth, *Call It Sleep* (1934), Avon Books, New York, 1964, p.143.
109. Moses Rischin, *The Promised City*, Harvard University Press, Cambridge, Massachusetts, 1962.
110. William Blake, *The World is Mine*, Cassell, London, 1939, pp.48–9.
111. CS tells this story in a letter to E. F. Patterson, 16 v 1975. The Goldsmith poem is 'The Deserted Village'.
112. Mike Gold, *Jews Without Money*, Horace Liveright, New York, 1930.
113. CS to E. F. Patterson, 16 v 1975. (*SL*)
114. William Blake, 'Ticker Tape and Old Lace', *New Masses*, 18 February, 1941, p.27.
115. Gustavus Blech published three medical textbooks.
116. The marriage date is recorded on their divorce certificate: 28 February, 1952. (Ruth Hall papers.)
117. Conversation with Ruth Hall, 5 October 1987.

4: *La Parisienne*

1. FJ to her mother, 14 ii 1929. (FJ papers)
2. CS to GW-S, 22 v 1929.
3. CS to Burnshaw, 30 iv 1974. (*SL*)
4. CS to Rellas, 16 xii 1979.
5. FJ to her family, 14 ii 1929.
6. Dora Russell, *The Tamarisk Tree*, Virago, London, 1975, p.69.
7. Rebecca West to Dora Marsden, late 1913, in Victoria Glendinning, *Rebecca West*, Weidenfeld & Nicolson, London, 1987, p.51.
8. CS to GW-S, 22 xii 1929.
9. *Beauties*, p.91.
10. These phrases come from *Beauties*. William Blake would refer nostalgically to their 'first week at the Aigle Noir and at Moret . . . and all the little incidents of courting and honeymoon' in a letter to CS, undated (May or June 1942). (NLA, Box 16, folder 119.)
11. *Beauties*, p.99.

12. *Love*, p.73.
13. Ibid., p.457.
14. CS to Kate Stead, 14 ii 1951.
15. *Love*, p.457.
16. *Beauties*, p.22.
17. Ibid., p.18.
18. CS to Anderson, 2 ix 1958. (Anderson papers, Berlin.)
19. CS to Nellie Molyneux, 2 iv 1929. (*SL*)
20. Ibid., 1 iii 1929. (*SL*)
21. Ibid., 2 iv 1929. (*SL*)
22. *Laughing*, p.38.
23. CS interview with Rodney Wetherell (1980). Published in *Australian Literary Studies*, vol. 9, no. 4, October 1980, p.440.
24. Interview with CS, ABC program, 'Australian Writers', recorded in Melbourne, 16 March 1976. Copyright No. 76/AW/2.
25. *House*, p.87.
26. From 'In Paris, Our Bistrot', an unpublished piece written probably in 1930 or 1931. NLA, Box 11, folder 79.
27. Putnam is probably the model for the translator in *Salzburg*, and for Laban Davies, the alcoholic translator in the novella 'The Right-Angled Creek', in *Puzzleheaded*.
28. Samuel Putnam, *Paris was our Mistress*, Viking, New York, 1947.
29. Stead's diary, 18 April 1931. (NLA, Box 15, folder 112.)
30. Stanley J. Kunitz & Howard Haycraft, *Twentieth Century Authors*, H. W. Wilson, New York, 1942, p.1329.
31. Notes, 'Stephen Daedalus resolved', NLA, Box 7, folder 49.
32. These details are from 'A Writer's Friends', (*Ocean*, p.499), and 'Lost American', (*Ocean*, p.137).
33. 'Lost American' gives a fictionalised portrait of Townsend's oddities and his strange marriage. Townsend was also the model for Tom Withers in *Poor Men*, and Andrew Fulton in *Beauties*.
    In her non-fictional piece, 'A Writer's Friends', Stead paid tribute to Townsend's friendship, leaving out most of the negative details.
34. Frederick Sard was the model for the 'Centenarist' in *Salzburg* and Marpurgo in *Beauties* —a cabbalistic character with *Arabian Nights* colouring. Letters from Sard published in *Transition* (16 July 1929, pp.120–1, and vols 19/20, 1930, pp.391–2) show the dogmatic and eclectic style of his diatribes, captured by Stead in *Beauties*.
35. CS interview with Joan Lidoff (1973), in Joan Lidoff, *Christina Stead*, Ungar, New York, 1982, pp.216–17. One of Sard's sons, Robert, a brilliant mathematician, lived in the same apartment house as the Blechs in the rue Jean Bart. He was probably the inspiration for the 'mathematician' in *Salzburg*.
36. 'Lost American', p.137.
37. CS to GW-S, 25 v 1930. (*SL*)
38. The piece, entitled 'Paint and Bread', is among Stead's papers. NLA, Box 11, folder 79. CS also wrote bits of her dialogue with the painter in a letter to GW-S, 22 xii 1929.
39. Polianski is recognisable as the 'anarchist poet' in 'In Doulcemer', (*Salzburg*, pp.148–9) and as the starving artist, Cancre, in *House*, scene 79.
40. CS to FW-S, 5 vi 1929. (*SL*) There is a minor character modelled on Haroun in *House*.
41. 'In Paris, Our Bistrot', NLA, Box 11, folder 79.
42. CS to GW-S, 3 vii 1929. (*SL*)
43. Elisabeth Granich, Michael Gold's French wife, claims that Stead's spoken French was excellent. From the late Thirties through to the Sixties, Stead wrote occasional letters to her in French—some of which have survived. (Elisabeth Granich-Humeston papers, San Francisco. Telephone conversation with Elisabeth Granich-Humeston, July 1988.)
44. *Transition*, 14, Autumn 1928, p.97.
45. CS to GW-S, 18 ix 1929. (*SL*)
46. Noel Riley Fitch, *Sylvia Beach and the Lost Generation*, New York, W. W. Norton & Co., 1983, p.72. Stead would have heard these stories. Years later, in *Cotters'*, she had lesbians dancing in the moonlight, though she made them grotesque figures.
47. Conversation with Ruth Hall, Châteauneuf-de-Grasse, 5 October 1987.

48. CS to GW-S, 25 v 1930. (*SL*) In *Beauties*, Elvira goes to the *Folies Bergère* and comments that the 'stageful of beautiful naked young girls, dark, with nipples like raspberries . . . satisfied you like a good French dinner'. (p.109)

49. CS to GW-S, 18 ix 1929. (*SL*)

50. Conversation with Ruth Hall, 5 October 1987.

51. CS to GW-S, 5 vi 1929. (*SL*)

52. Ibid., 26 vii 1932. (*SL*)

53. Conversation with Ruth Hall, 5 October 1987.

54. CS to GW-S, 3 vii 1929. (*SL*)

55. Conversations with Nadine Lewin, New York, 12 October 1987 and 6 July 1988.

56. CS to GW-S, 30 ix 1929. (*SL*)

57. Ibid., 18 ix 1929. (*SL*)

58. Dymphna Cusack would write: 'The only two people I have known in my long life who have an encyclopaedic knowledge and a comprehensive culture, were William Blake, Christina Stead's husband, and the remarkable man who has been my tax agent and friend for over forty years, "Sammy". Interestingly enough, they are both Jewish, unorthodox in their views, the one German in origin, the other Russian.' *A Window in the Dark*, NLA, Canberra, 1991, p.55.

59. Stead's diary, 26 March 1931. (NLA, Box 15, folder 112.)

60. Michel Alphendéry and James Quick share these mannerisms. Quick 'had acquired a few habits during his bachelor life, small and insignificant, like the twiddling of his fingers and a quiet talking to himself of which he now had to break himself'. *Love*, p.459.

61. CS to GW-S, 11 i 1932.(*SL*)

62. Ibid., 22 vii 1929.

63. *Salzburg*, p.41.

64. CS to GW-S, 18 ix 1929. (*SL*)

65. Blech to CS, undated. (September 1929.) (NLA, Box 16, folder 119.)

66. CS to GW-S, 18 ix 1929. (*SL*)

67. Letty Fox says this about her father, Solander (based on Blech): 'My father's genius as a conversationalist is such that no one can remember later whether or not he, too, was witness of all the events and conversations Solander describes.' (*Letty*, p.15.)

68. FJ to her family, 25 ix 1929.

69. Ibid.

70. CS to GW-S, 18 ix 1929. (*SL*)

71. Frederick Sard, 'Let us have order in vertigo', *Transition*, 19/20, 1930, pp.391–2.

72. CS to GW-S, 30 ix 1929. (*SL*)

73. CS interview with Joan Lidoff (1973), p.204.

74. CS to GW-S, 30 ix 1929. (*SL*)

75. Ibid., 26 vii 1932. (*SL*) In later life Stead would denigrate Joyce.

76. Sard in *Transition*, 16 July 1929.

77. Clifton Fadiman, reviewing *Beauties*, would compare Annibale Marpurgo with Stephen Daedalus, adding: 'Marpurgo supplies the keenest and most fantastically witty conversation since *Ulysses*, and the great Somnabulists' Club episode, in which he discourses on "The immateriality of the Earth and the Reality of the Beyond," will take its place just below the *Walpurgisnacht* scene of Joyce's masterpiece.' Randall Jarrell was to observe several 'Joyce-ish sentences' in *The Man*. (Introduction to *The Man*, Holt, Rinehart & Winston, New York, 1965.)

78. The term is Patrick White's. See 'The Prodigal Son' (1958), in *Patrick White Speaks*, Primavera Press, Sydney, 1989, p.16.

79. These and other details are in a letter from FJ to her mother, Paris, 28 xi 1929.

80. FJ to her mother, 5 xii 1929.

81. FJ to me, 15 v 1992.

82. In Bill Blake's novel *We are the Makers of Dreams*, written in 1942 and published in 1959, this is what Peggy Hume (modelled loosely on Christina Stead) says of Jim, her husband: 'I tremble at Jim's humanity. One of these days it is going to blow up our marriage, which, silly as it sounds, is the most beautiful union I know. He will think that deep as his love for me is, he has purchased it too dearly, for it has been paid for with cruelty. And so he will be cruel to me. That woman who dulled his wife, waits, waits.' (Simon & Schuster, New York, p.147)

83. 'A Writer's Friends', *Ocean*, p.500. (Sadly, Christina would not recall Florence's sacrifices with equal gratitude.)
84. Conversation with FJ, Sydney, 3 July 1989.
85. NLA, Box 16, folder 119.
86. I have added punctuation to make Stead's rough diary notes more comprehensible. They are also replete with typing errors which I have corrected.
87. *Poor Men*, p.152.
88. 'La Toussaint', *Ocean*, p.70.
89. *Beauties*, p.238.
90. CS to GW-S, 25 v 1930. (*SL*)
91. Jean Williamson, 'Christina Stead Tells of Her Latest Book!', *Australian Women's Weekly*, 9 March 1935.
92. Susan Sheridan, 'The Woman Who Loved Men: Christina Stead as Satirist in *Tea* and *Dogs*'. (Paper delivered at the Modern Language Association, San Francisco, 1991. In press, forthcoming edition of *World Literature in English*.)
93. CS to GW-S, 30 ix 1929. (*SL*)
94. CS interview with Ann Whitehead (1973), *Australian Literary Studies*, vol. 6, no. 3, May 1974, p.236. See also the interviews with Joan Lidoff (1973) and Rodney Wetherell (1980).
95. CS to GW-S, 25 v 1930. (*SL*)
96. FJ to her mother, 26 vi 1930.
97. CS to GW-S, 23 ix 1930. (*SL*)
98. FJ comments: 'I have no detailed memory of the early draft. My general impression is that it was not altered substantially, but was put on "hold" while she wrote *Salzburg*. (FJ to me, 15 v 1992.)
99. FJ to me, 15 v 1992.
100. Dorothy Green, obituary for Christina Stead, *Sydney Morning Herald*, 8 April 1983, p.6.
101. Jean Williamson, 'Christina Stead Tells of Her Latest Book!'.
102. CS to GW-S, 5 viii 1930. (*SL*)
103. Blech to CS, 6 viii 1930.
104. 'At last a card announcing your address!' writes Blech, 21 vii 1930. NLA, Box 16, folder 119. Nine brief letters from Blech survive, but none of Stead's letters to him.
105. CS to GW-S, 5 viii 1930. (*SL*)
106. Blech to CS, Paris, 31 vii 1930.
107. Blech to CS, undated. (It was August 1930.) James Quick says this in *Love*.
108. Blech to CS, 4 viii 1930.
109. Ibid., 14 viii 1930.
110. Ibid.
111. Ibid., 19 viii 1930.
112. Ibid., 14 viii 1930.
113. Ibid., undated. (August 1930.)
114. CS to GW-S, 23 ix 1930. (*SL*)
115. Ibid., 24 xi 1930. (*SL*)
116. Ibid., 25 i 1931. (*SL*)
117. Ibid., 25 v 1930. (*SL*)
118. Ibid., 25 i 1931. (*SL*)
119. Jean Williamson, 'Christina Stead Tells of Her Latest Book!'.
120. NLA, Box 6, folder 38.
121. 'Overcote', *Salzburg*, p.482.
122. CS to FW-S, 26 vii 1932.
123. CS to GW-S, 22 vii 1929.
124. Ibid., 30 ix 1929. (*SL*)
125. NLA, Box 6, folder 40.
126. CS to GW-S, 20 vi 1931.
127. CS to FW-S, 7 iv 1931. (*SL*)
128. Andrew Birkin, *J. M. Barrie and the Lost Boys*, Constable, London, 1979, and Denis Mackail, *The Story of J.M.B.*, Peter Davies, London, 1941.
129. CS to FW-S, 7 iv 1931. (*SL*)
130. Ibid., 25 ii 1934.
131. CS to GW-S, 6 iv 1931.

132. CS to FW-S, 7 iv 1931. (*SL*)
133. FJ to her mother, 4 iii 1931.
134. Nietzsche wrote about the 'Wanderer and his Shadow' in *Thus Spake Zarathustra* and *Human, All Too Human.*
135. 'Lovelace': Stead probably had Samuel Richardson's treacherous rake in mind—see *Clarissa.* (This insight courtesy of my editor.)
136. CS to GW-S, 25 i 1931. (*SL*)
137. FJ to her mother, 4 iii 1931.
138. CS diary, entry is 18 April 1931. NLA, Box 16, folder 119.

5: In the Phantom Buggy

1. CS interview with Ann Whitehead (1973), *Australian Literary Studies*, vol. 6, no. 3, May 1974, p.238.
2. *House*, p.195.
3. Ibid., p.130.
4. Peter Neidecker is the model for the 'banker' in *Salzburg*, Antoine Fuseaux in *Beauties* and Jules Bertillon in *House*.
5. Stead liked this image of recklessness. Emily Wilkes in *Laughing* also says she wants to go out 'looping the loop'.
6. Blake to CS, 1 vi 1942. NLA, Box 16, folder 120.
7. FJ, 'Australian Writer Wins Success Abroad', newspaper or magazine article, source unknown. NLA, Palmer papers MS 1174 series 28 item 566.
8. Adam Constant is an imaginative blending of Stead herself (the second time she invests aspects of her experience in a male character), Stanley Burnshaw, and the man she had come to regard as her spiritual soulmate, Ralph Fox, who in real life had nothing to do with the bank.
9. *House*, p.511.
10. Ibid., p.521.
11. Ibid., p.80.
12. 'House of All Nations' is mentioned twice in the novel (pp.29, 388), and we are given to understand that the allusion is to a brothel. It was the popular name for Le Chabanais, which Brassai describes in *The Secret Paris of the 30s* (tr. Richard Miller, Thames & Hudson, London, 1976): 'This, the most famous of Parisian brothels ... soon became the center of elegant life, a national institution, a kind of League of Nations. It was a place which the great names of society, high finance, diplomacy, and even crowned heads made sure to include in the official program of their visits, and where they met. The obese and jovial Edward VII, to console himself during his endless years as Prince of Wales ... had a "Hindu Room" set up in the Chabanais in homage to his mother [Victoria], the Empress of India.' Nathanael West mentions 'House of All Nations' in *A Cool Million* (1934).
13. CS to Nellie Molyneux, 1 iii 1929. (*SL*)
14. FJ to her father, 10 xii 1931.
15. CS to FJ, 17 x 1935.
16. See, for example, the review of A. H. Hurst, *Bread of Britain*, Oxford, 1930, in *Times Literary Supplement*, 13 February 1930, p.123.
17. FJ papers.
18. CS to GW-S, 11 i 1932. (*SL*)
19. CS to FJ, 23 viii 1933. The Centenarist tells several Jewish tales. There is also 'The Amenities', told by the Solicitor, and 'The Prodigy' (set in Russia during the time of the pogroms and the great migration to America), told by the Musician.
20. *Salzburg*, pp.37–8.
21. In 1941, in a Guggenheim application, Stead claimed that only 'Morpeth Tower' survived from the original volume. In 1971, she told Hal Porter that 'Morpeth Tower' and 'On the Road' were both written in Australia. (CS to Hal Porter, 27 x 1971. Mitchell Library.) The other Australian stories are 'The Triskelion', 'Day of Wrath' and 'Silk-shirt'.
22. Stead had moved out of a hotel, too sick to take all her luggage with her. When she returned to reclaim the pieces, the hotel keeper demanded a sum of money she could not possibly afford. She wondered afterwards if he had already sold the things. (CS interview with Ann Whitehead, *Australian Literary Studies*, p.235.)

23. This is how Stead describes Ernest Jourdain's story-telling in the story 'The Mirror', in *Salzburg*. (Jourdain is loosely based on Blech.)
24. Geering makes this point in *Christina Stead*, A & R, Sydney, 1979, p.45. See also Ian Reid, Introduction to *The Salzburg Tales*, A & R, Sydney, 1974.
25. CS to FJ, 19 xi 1935.
26. Ibid., 13 v 1933.
27. Ibid., 25 iv 1933.
28. Stefan Zweig, *The World of Yesterday*, Cassell, London, 1943, p.275.
29. CS to FJ, 8 xii 1933.
30. Gide's 'conversion' was to come to an abrupt end in 1936, after his visit to Soviet Russia.
31. CS to FJ, 8 xii 1933.
32. Ibid., 20 xii 1933.
33. See Robert Shaplen, *Kreuger. Genius and Swindler*, Garland Publishing Inc., New York & London, 1986, p.165.
34. Jacques Coe, a financier friend of Blech's, mentions Blech's Kreuger windfall in his book *Fame, Fraud and Fortune, 74 Years in Wall Street*, Exposition Press, Smithtown, NY, 1983.
35. William Blake, *We are the Makers of Dreams*, Victor Gollancz, London, 1959, p.14.
36. *House*, p.619.
37. The London branch, Neidecker & Co., was on Old Broad Street in the City, directed by Sir Duncan Orr Lewis. Much of the information in this section comes from French and English newspaper articles from July 1935, when the bank crashed.
38. CS to FJ, 29 viii 1933.
39. Letter from Travelers' Bank to Mrs Florence Heyting, March 1933. FJ papers.
40. CS to FJ, 10 iii 1933.
41. Terms used by Alphendéry in *House*.
42. CS to FJ, 12 xi 1933.
43. *Poor Men*, p.179.
44. *House*, pp.244–5.
45. Ibid., p.588.
46. Ibid., p.354.
47. Ibid., p.64.
48. CS to FJ, 13 v 1933.
49. CS to FW-S, 26 vii 1932.
50. CS to FJ, 24 xi 1933.
51. Ibid., 25 ii 1934.
52. Ibid., 5 x 1933.
53. Ibid.
54. Ibid., 6 iii 1934. She thought of calling the novel *Confession of Women*. The project, which never came off, strongly resembles *The Testament of Women* which Teresa writes in *Love*.
55. CS to FJ, 7 iii 1933.
56. Ibid., 10 iii 1933.
57. Ruth remembers long walks over the West Sussex downs with Bertrand Russell, and Dora Russell's natural history lessons in which she had the children put their hands on her pregnant belly and feel the baby move. The children could choose not to go to lessons; in summer they played in the nude.
58. Ruth never liked German. Her parents used to talk German when they argued in front of her, and it did not endear the language to her.
59. Conversation with Ruth Hall, 5 October 1987.
60. Ibid.
61. CS to FJ, 25 ii 1934.
62. Ibid., 28 xi 1933.
63. Ibid., 16 i 1934.
64. In *Salzburg*, 'The Little Old Lady', 'Poor Anna', and 'The Wunder Gottes' are all loosely based on Rosa Blech.
65. CS to FJ, 2 xii 1933.
66. Ibid., 16 v 1934.
67. Ibid., 12 xi 1933.
68. Ibid., 10 iv 1934.

69. Ibid., 25 iv 1933.
70. Ibid., 26 ix 1933.
71. Ibid., 8 xii 1933.
72. CS to Anderson, 5 i 1965.
73. CS to FJ, 10 iii 1933.
74. *Times*, 30 January 1934, p.9. (Unsigned.)
75. *Times Literary Supplement*, 15 February 1934, p.106.
76. Rebecca West's comment is quoted in the back of Peter Davies' edition of *Seven Poor Men of Sydney*, but it seems to have been a widely publicised reader's opinion rather than a formal review.
77. See Ian Reid, Introduction to *Salzburg*, A & R reprint, A & R, Sydney, 1974.
78. CS to FJ, 17 iv 1934.
79. Fadiman qualified his praise later: 'I imagine that every writer who has a dozen unsaleable short stories in the bottom drawer has played with the notion of stringing together a modern Decameron. The form has always seemed to me dull, and so has Boccaccio, the most overpraised writer of an overpraised literary epoch. When I say that Miss Christina Stead's *Salzburg Tales* are far better than the *Decameron*, I intend nothing but disrespect to Boccaccio, prince of bores.' *Reading I've Liked*, Hamish Hamilton, London, 1946.
80. Clifton Fadiman, *New Yorker*, 29 September 1934.
81. Stead wrote this as an inscription in the copy she sent GW-S.
82. H. E. Bates writes of Margaret's 'torture and torment' in *The Blossoming World*, Michael Joseph, London, 1971, p.70.
83. CS to FJ, 6 iii 1934 (and 10 vi 1934).
84. CS to GW-S, 16 iv 1934. (*SL*)
85. CS to FJ, 2 ii 1934.
86. Ibid., 16 v 1934.
87. Samuel Putnam, *Paris Was Our Mistress*, Viking Press, NY, 1947, pp.250-1.
88. CS to FJ, 2 xii 1933.
89. Ibid., 17 iv 1934.
90. Ibid., 1 vi 1934.
91. Ibid., 10 vi 1934.
92. Ibid., 6 iii 1934.
93. Ibid., 10 vi 1934.
94. Ibid., 20 xii 1934.
95. Ibid., 16 vii 1935.
96. *Beauties*, p.135.
97. CS to Burnshaw, 31 vii 1973.
98. CS to FJ, 6 vi 1934.
99. CHG, *Saturday Review of Literature*, 23 March 1935.
100. Edwin Muir, *Listener*, 5 December 1934.
101. William Plomer, *Spectator*, 21 December 1934.
102. Montague Grover, *Bulletin*, 28 November 1934.
103. J. S. Southron, *New York Times*, 10 March 1935, p.6.
104. CS to FJ, 22 xi 1934.
105. *The Fairies Return* or New Tales for Old By Several Heads, Ed. Peter Davies, London, 1934.
106. 'Lemonias', *Salzburg*, p.231.
107. CS to FJ, 20 xii 1934 and CS to Anderson, 20 vii 1950.
108. CS to FJ, 22 xi 1934.
109. Ibid., 22 xi and 20 xii 1934.
110. Ibid., 26 xii 1934.
111. Ibid., 22 xi 1934.
112. 'In this way, I had the rare pleasure of seeing a museum of the most exquisite lace in the world, both handmade and machine-made.' CS to Nadine Lewin. Undated. (Probably 1938.) (*SL*)
113. CS to FJ, 22 xi 1934.
114. *Beauties*, p.134.
115. Ibid., p.93.
116. Ibid., p.29.
117. Ibid., p.175.

118. In *Love*, Marian, James Quick's abandoned wife, complains of living 'a vegetable life'.
119. *Le Temps* (Paris), 21 July 1935, p.5.
120. Blech to CS, no date. (Early May 1935) (NLA, Box 16, folder 119)
121. Conversation with Jacques Coe, New York, 19 July 1988.
122. Blech to CS, no date. (Early May 1935.)
123. CS to Blech, 9 v 1935.
124. Ibid., 16 v 1935.
125. Ibid., 17 v 1935.
126. Founded by Montagu Slater, Amabel Williams-Ellis and Tom Wintringham, *Left Review* would fold in May 1938.
127. *Love*, p.465.
128. Ibid.
129. In a letter to Blech (28 iii 1935) Stead says she is off to hear Dooley speak at a rally.
130. See *I, Claud . . .*, Penguin, Harmondsworth, 1956, p.150.
131. CS to Blech, 9 v 1935.
132. Nettie Palmer papers. Unpublished notebooks. NLA, MS 1174; and *Fourteen Years* (1948), ed. Vivian Smith, University of Queensland Press, St Lucia, 1988, p.156.
133. *Love*, p.465.
134. Ibid., p.466. Ralph Fox asserted that T. E. Lawrence was the only hero the English ruling classes had produced in modern times. ('Lawrence the 20th Century Hero', *Left Review*, 1 July 1935.)
135. *Love*, pp.466–7.
136. Ibid., p.458. These features are shared by Teresa Hawkins' father (based on David Stead), who is described in the first chapter of the novel as tall, broadchested, with 'brilliant oval blue eyes'. Both men too, have exceptionally rich, seductive voices.
137. *Love*, p.467.
138. Ibid., p.468.
139. Mulk Raj Anand, Preface to *The Novel and the People* (1937), Cobbett Publishing Co., London, 1944, p.10.
140. Ralph Fox, *Storming Heaven*, Constable, London, 1928.
141. The British Communist Party was founded in 1920. In 1921, the Australian P. R. Stephensen was briefly a member of the Oxford branch, along with British historian A. J. P. Taylor. Craig Munro points out that 'to be a communist at Oxford was unusual as well as risky'. Members risked 'physical intimidation and assault'. (Craig Munro, *Wild Man of Letters*, MUP, Melbourne, 1984, p.37.)
142. John Lehmann, 'Ralph Fox, the writer', *Ralph Fox. A Writer in Arms*, Lawrence & Wishart, London, 1937, p.107.
143. Mulk Raj Anand, Preface to *The Novel and the People*.
144. Jean Lacouture, *André Malraux*, tr. Alan Sheridan, André Deutsch, London, 1975, p.187.
145. Huxley to Victoria Ocampo, June 1935, *Letters of Aldous Huxley*, ed. Grover Smith, Chatto & Windus, London, 1969.
146. See Hugh Thomas, *John Strachey*, Eyre Methuen, London, 1973.
147. It was Vance Palmer who had been asked to represent Australia at the congress, but since he was immersed in a writing project, Nettie went instead.
148. Nettie Palmer, 'A Reader's Notebook' in *All About Books*, vol. 7, no. 2, 11 February 1935, p.22.
149. Nettie Palmer papers, NLA MS 1174/16/1935–39. This and several other passages about Stead were not included in the published version of her diary, *Fourteen Years*.
150. Palmer papers. NLA, MS 1174, 17/11.
151. 'I'd arranged to go to a hotel with three blokes who belonged to the English delegation.' *Christina Stead*, Australia Council Archival Film Series (1980). Nettie Palmer to her mother, 29 vi 1935. NLA, Palmer papers, MS 1174/1/4657–4702.
152. Unpublished journal. Palmer papers, MS 1174, 16/1935–39.
153. Unless otherwise indicated, the quotations in this section come from Christina Stead's article, 'The Writers take sides', *Left Review*, vol. 1, no. 2, July 1935, pp.435–62.
154. Nettie Palmer, 'A New International', Palmer papers, NLA, MS 1174/25/72. (It is not clear where the article was published, if at all.)
155. *Argus*, 27 June 1935, p.11.
156. Hobart *Mercury*, 27 June 1935, p.6.
157. CS to FJ, 31 xii 1935.

158. CS to Dorothy Green, 17 iii 1971. Green papers, NLA, MS 54678, Box 6.
159. Nettie Palmer, *Fourteen Years*, pp.155–6. *Fourteen Years* was published in 1948 by the Meanjin Press in a limited edition of 500 and not reprinted until 1988, but given that she appeared in it, someone would probably have sent Stead a copy.
160. The date at the top of the passage about Stead, Friday 21 June (the date they arrived in Paris), indicates that accuracy was not Palmer's main concern.
161. CS to Kate Stead, 17 ii 1950.
162. Patrick White, *Flaws in the Glass*, Jonathan Cape, London, 1981, p.38.
163. Christina Stead did not seem to make the same striking impression on Mike Gold. About that same evening he wrote in the *New Masses*: 'We toasted [Andersen Nexo] in champagne and told him (Ralph Fox, James Hanley and Pearl Binder of England, two Australian authors and myself were there) what his books had meant to us in the English-speaking lands.' (*New Masses*, 13 August 1935, pp.18–21. Quoted in *Mike Gold: A Literary Anthology*, ed. Michael Folsom, International Publishers, New York, 1972, p.236.)
164. Ralph Fox, 'Great Paris Congress of Writers', *Daily Worker* (London), 29 June 1935.
165. Nettie Palmer papers. Unpublished diaries. NLA, MS 1174, 16/1935–39.
166. CS to Hal Porter, 12 vii 1982. (Geering papers. Unsent letter.)
167. Conversation with Ruth Hall, Châteauneuf-sur-Grasse, 25 September 1988. In a letter to Ruth Blake dated 15 xi 1950, Bill wrote that his situation in the bank ended 3 May 1935. There was a sentence by default on 11 May 1939. He added: 'For some reason no one knows, this sentence was not communicated to the Parquet of Paris until June 1944, just prior to the Liberation.' (Ruth Hall papers.)
168. *Daily Mail*, 22 July 1935, p.14.
169. *Le Matin*, 24 July 1935, p.3.
170. Ibid., 23 July 1935, p.3.
171. The London bankers were Vickers and Goldschmidt, friends of Blech. (CS to FJ, 19 xi 1935, and conversation with Ruth Hall, 5 October 1987.)
172. Scene 102 in *House* is an imaginative reconstruction of this scene. Bertillon is discovered not in New York but Estonia. Stead was obviously sent the newspaper cuttings.
173. *Le Matin*, 25 July 1935.
174. Unpublished notes, 'America', NLA, Box 11, folder 79.

6: Manhattan Peaks

1. 'America', NLA, Box 11, folder 79. (Printed for the first time in *Australian Book Review*, June 1992.)
2. Ibid.
3. CS to Burnshaw, 23 vii 1973. (*SL*) She mentions the episode in the article, 'America'. The hotel was Filene's.
4. CS to FJ, 4 ix 1935.
5. 'America'.
6. Ibid.
7. CS to FJ, 19 xi 1935.
8. Ibid., 29 ix 1935.
9. Ibid., 17 x 1935.
10. Ibid.
11. 'America'.
12. *Letty*, p.151.
13. CS to FJ, 19 xi 1935.
14. *Laughing*, pp.16–17.
15. CS to FJ, 29 ix 1935.
16. Ibid.
17. Samuel Putnam, *Paris was Our Mistress*, Viking, New York, 1947.
18. CS to FJ, 29 ix 1935.
19. 'General principles of marionetting', NLA, Box 6, folder 45.
20. CS interview with Joan Lidoff (1973). In Joan Lidoff, *Christina Stead*, Ungar, New York, 1982, pp.218–19.
21. 'Nello the famous clown', NLA, Box 6, folder 44.
22. CS to FJ, 19 xi 1935.

23. Ibid., 31 xii 1935.
24. Ibid., 20 iv 1936.
25. Ibid., 4 ix 1935.
26. Ibid., 19 xi 1935.
27. 'Workers and Writers', NLA, Box 15, folder 113.
28. CS to FJ, 19 xi 1935.
29. Georges Polti, *The 36 Classic Dramatic Situations*, Mercure de France, Paris, 1924. Stead made copious notes from the book. NLA, Box 7, folder 47.
30. She originally intended to call the three short novels *Student Lovers*, *The Student of Naples*, and *The Travelling Scholar*.
31. CS to FJ, 17 x 1935.
32. Ibid., 29 ix 1935.
33. Ibid., 31 xii 1935.
34. Ibid., 19 xi 1935.
35. Ibid., 17 x 1935.
36. In *Laughing*; Emily and Stephen (who are otherwise not modelled on the Golds) meet on the ship going to France. Stephen is heading for the 1935 Paris Writers' Congress.
37. CS to Gilbert Stead, 30 viii 1938.
38. Blake mentions Michael Gold by name in *The World is Mine* (1938). 'He writes of Jews without money, and he writes as simply as a bard, a people's poet, with none of our high European style, yet with none of the American rough or cynical reactions.' (p.532)
39. Joseph Freeman, *An American Testament*, Victor Gollancz, London, 1938, p.225. See also Max Eastman, 'Journey through an Epoch', Unpublished manuscript, quoted by Daniel Aaron, *Writers on the Left*, Oxford University Press, Oxford, 1961.
40. Stanley Burnshaw to me, 18 ix 1992.
41. *House*, p.67.
42. Phone conversation with Elisabeth Granich-Humeston, San Francisco, 18 July 1988.
43. CS to GW-S, 21 ii 1972.
44. Bloom's son, Michael, comments that his parents' was 'hardly a monogamous marriage, though it was supposed to be'. Conversation with Mike Bloom, New York, 5 August 1988.
45. In the novella 'Girl from the Beach', the beach is Brighton Beach and the girl is modelled on Bloom's daughter Janet. 'The Doc' is loved by everyone, even the 'bad boys, the handbag snatchers and razor-boys'. (*Puzzleheaded*, p.221) His amorous activities are slightly curtailed by a jealous wife.
46. Max Eastman, *Love and Revolution*, Random House, New York, 1964, p.420.
47. Stead's article on Burnshaw was eventually published after her death, in *Agenda* (London) vol. 21, no. 4–vol. 22, no. 1, Winter-Spring 1983–4, Special Issue on Stanley Burnshaw, pp.125–40.
48. Stanley Burnshaw, *Robert Frost Himself*, George Braziller, New York, 1986. (In this, Burnshaw also writes about himself.)
49. *Proletarian Literature in the United States*, eds Granville Hicks, Michael Gold, Isidor Schneider, Joseph North, Paul Peters, Alan Colmer, International Publishers, New York, 1935. Mike and Elisabeth Gold sent the book to Christina and Bill in 1936: To 'two of the tops', wrote Gold.
50. Mike Gold, *New Masses*, vol. 6 (September, 1930), pp.4–5. Blake and Stead never had a good word to say for Proust either.
51. Michael Gold, 'Go Left, Young Writers!', *New Masses*, January 1929, quoted in *Mike Gold: A Literary Anthology*, ed. Michael Folsom, International Publishers, New York, 1972, pp.188–9.
52. McKenney, from a working-class family in Indiana, had married Richard Bransten, the son of a wealthy family. Her hero, Jake Home, is born in a Pennsylvanian mining town and marries a rich woman, whose world he tries to live in, but fails.
53. Granville Hicks in *New Masses*, 2 May 1939.
54. CS to Burnshaw, 2 x 1936. (*SL*)
55. She was referring to Sinclair Lewis' novel *Babbitt*, about George Babbitt, a middle-class stereotype: a prosperous real-estate broker and good republican.
56. 'Workers and Writers', NLA, Box 15, folder 113. Since her Brooklyn address is on a separate piece of paper which seems to belong to the piece, Stead may have written the talk early in 1936, while still in New York. But she was definitely writing for an English audience.

57. CS to FJ, 19 xi 1935.
58. Ron Geering, 'Christina Stead's description of her books' (taken from a curriculum vitae she wrote in 3 August 1961), *Southerly*, no. 4, 1990, p.423.
59. See Geering, 'The Bank Novel. House of All Nations', *Southerly*, no. 4, 1990.
60. CS diary, 12 November 1935. NLA, Box 15, folder 112.
61. CS to FJ, 31 xii 1935.
62. Ibid.
63. Ibid.
64. Ibid., 8 i 1936; 13 viii 1936.
65. Ibid., 31 xii 1935.
66. CS to Nettie Palmer, 8 i 1936. (*SL*)
67. Conversation with Burnshaw, New York, 29 June 1988.
68. CS, 'Workshop in the Novel'. NLA, Box 11, folder 84.
69. CS to FJ, 31 xii 1935.
70. Ibid., 20 iv 1936.
71. Christina Stead, 'The Impartial Young Man', *New Masses*, 17 March 1936.
72. CS to FJ, 20 iv 1936.
73. When she left for Europe later that year, Stead wrote to him. Unfortunately, these letters have been lost.
74. Extract from Clifton Fadiman's letter to me, 15 vii 1988.
75. Unpublished handwritten notes of Max Lincoln Schuster, Schuster Collection, Rare Book and Manuscript Library, Butler Library, Columbia University.
76. CS to FJ, 20 iv 1936.
77. Harold Strauss, review of *Beauties* in the *New York Times Book Review*, 3 May 1936, p.7.
78. J. G. Conant, review of *Beauties*, *New Masses*, 4 August 1936, pp.25–6.
79. Clifton Fadiman, review of *Beauties*, *New Yorker*, 25 April 1936, pp.84–6.

7: 'A Harmless Affair'

1. CS alludes to the banana seller in her diary, Algeciras, 4 June 1936. NLA, Box 15, folder 112. See 'Extracts from a Spanish Diary', *Southerly*, no. 4, 1990, pp.399–400.
2. CS to FJ, 15 vi 1936.
3. Ibid.
4. Hugh Thomas, *The Spanish Civil War*, Eyre & Spottiswoode, London, 1961.
5. CS diary, Ronda, 4 June 1936.
6. Ibid. (Ironically, Malraux was in Spain himself in August 1936, fighting with the Republican air force. It would be the subject of his novel *L'Espoir*.)
7. CS interview with Rodney Wetherell (1980), *Australian Literary Studies*, vol. 9, no. 4, October 1980.
8. *House*, pp.182–3.
9. CS to FJ, 20 iv 1936.
10. *House*, pp.370–1.
11. Ibid., p.785.
12. CS to FJ, 18 vii 1936.
13. Ibid., 13 viii 1936.
14. CS to Burnshaw, 2 x 1936. (*SL*)
15. CS, 'Journal of *The Blackmailer*', in Geering, 'The Bank Novel: *House of All Nations*', *Southerly*, no. 4, 1990.
16. CS, 'Uses of the Many-Charactered Novel', Paper delivered at the Third American Writers' Congress, 4 June 1939. Rare Books and Manuscripts, Bancroft Library, University of California.
17. CS, 'Uses of the Many-Charactered Novel'.
18. See Samuel Hynes, *The Auden Generation*, Faber & Faber, London, 1976.
19. Harold Strauss, 'A Novel of Frenzied Finance', *New York Times Book Review*, 12 June 1938.
20. CS to FJ, 20 vi 1936.
21. CS interview with Thomas Keneally, *Vogue Australia*, May 1977, pp.91–3.
22. 'Terror in La Ciudad Imbecila', NLA, Box 15, folder 113.
23. CS to FJ, 30 vii 1936.

24. Stead's Spanish diary, 30 July 1936. NLA, Box 15, folder 112.
25. CS to FJ, 30 vii 1936.
26. Spanish diary.
27. CS to FJ, 13 viii 1936.
28. See Nettie Palmer, 'The Spanish Struggle' in the booklet by Maurice Blackburn, Nettie Palmer, Helen Baillie and Len Fox entitled *Spain. The Spanish People Present their Case* (1936). See also Vivian Smith, *Vance and Nettie Palmer*, Twayne Publishers, Boston, 1975, p.29ff.
29. Stead's original diary, August 1936. NLA, Box 15, folder 112.
30. CS to FJ, 13 viii 1936.
31. Ibid., 27 viii 1936.
32. Interview with Jacques Coe, New York, 19 July 1988.
33. CS to FJ, 13 viii 1936.
34. Ibid.
35. According to his son-in-law, Jack Bermond, Hurst was not at all pleased with *Tea*. (Conversation with Jack Bermond, London, 17 October 1988.)
36. *House*, p.725.
37. These books are in the private collection of Jack Bermond. In *Modern Women in Love* (1945) Bill called Alfred 'our beloved friend'. The dedications stop around this date.
38. CS to FJ, 13 viii 1936.
39. This passage is in the revised diary—the only intimate comment she makes here about Bill's defects.
40. CS to FJ, 13 viii 1936.
41. Ibid., 27 viii 1936.
42. Antwerp diary, 11 August 1936. NLA, Box 15, folder 112.
43. Dorothy Van Doren, *Nation*, 10 June 1936.
44. My translation.
45. Original Antwerp diary, NLA, Box 15, folder 112.
46. Ibid., 25 August 1936.
47. In Stead's scarcely fictionalised story 'Private Matters' (*Ocean*), Jack Brame (like Alf Hurst) has a nephew living in the village of Gheel, who has been taken to the lunatic asylum. In the story, Lallemand is called Bosch.
48. *Love*, pp.459–60.
49. I am grateful to Shane Youl and Paul and Susan Nulsen.
50. CS to FJ, 6 ix 1936.
51. CS to Burnshaw, 2 x 1936. (The date at the top of the letter is misleading; it was begun in Antwerp, and posted from London later.)
52. His report would be published posthumously as *Portugal Now*, Lawrence & Wishart, London, 1937.
53. Ralph Winston Fox, *Genghis Khan*, Harcourt, London, 1936.
54. Ralph Fox, *The Novel and the People*, Lawrence & Wishart, London, 1937. (It was published only days after his death.)
55. *Left Review*, February 1936. Quoted in Valentine Cunningham, *British Writers of the Thirties*, OUP, Oxford, 1989, p.214.
56. Stead's original diary, NLA, Box 15, folder 112.
57. CS to Burnshaw, 2 x 1936. (*SL*)
58. *Letty*, p.355. At the end of *Letty*, Luke Adams has lost his shine. In a passage reminiscent of Jonathan Crow at the end of *Love*, Letty meets Luke Adams 'shambling down Eighth Street' looking like 'a bit of ambulating pemmican, or a lost red herring'. (p.490)
59. 'A Harmless Affair', *Ocean*, p.184.
60. Ibid., p.192.
61. Ibid., p.194.
62. Conversation with Ruth Hall, Châteauneuf-de-Grasse, 5 October 1987.
63. CS to Blake, 24 vi 1942. Jack Goodman was a senior editor at Simon & Schuster, a leftist, who was destined to appear before the House Un-American Activities Committee in the early Fifties. (See Arthur Miller, *Timebends*, Methuen, London, 1987, pp.310–11.) Clifton Fadiman comments: 'Jack Goodman was head of advertising during my tenure as editor at Simon & Schuster. A most attractive, indeed a brilliant young man, he may well have been fancied by Christina, as he was by many other ladies.' (Clifton Fadiman to me, 22 i 1991.)

64. CS to Geering, 14 xii 1980. (*SL*)
65. *Love*, p.488.
66. Ralph Fox's will can be seen in the Wills Register, at Somerset House, London. His address was the same as his wife's—No. 17 Lucas House, Albion Road, SW 8.
67. See Samuel Hynes, *The Auden Generation*.
68. Ralph Fox to Madge Palmer, Albacete, 10 xii 1936. (Original held at the Marx Memorial Library, London. See also Valentine Cunningham (ed.), *Spanish Front*, OUP, Oxford, 1986, pp.277–8.
69. Judith Cook, *Apprentices of Freedom*, Quartet Books, London, 1979.
70. Ibid.
71. Valentine Cunningham, *British Writers of the Thirties*, p.421.
72. Caroline Ruth Fox, 'Ralph Fox: International Brigadier. October 1936–January 1937. A Study of his fight for freedom in the Spanish Civil War', BA Hons Thesis, The College of St Paul and St Mary, Cheltenham. Kept at Marx House, London, Box 50/FX/1.
73. Draft of a letter in memoriam for Ralph Fox, NLA, Box 7, folder 52.
74. In John Lehmann, T. A. Jackson & C. Day Lewis (eds), *Ralph Fox: A Writer in Arms*, International Publishers, London, 1937.
75. Virginia Woolf, 'Remembering Julian', 30 July 1937. In Valentine Cunningham (ed.), *Spanish Front*, p.234.
76. In Valentine Cunningham (ed.), *Spanish Front*, p.228.
77. Lydia feels this about Paul Charteris in 'A Harmless Affair'.
78. Edith Anderson, 'Cold War Marriage', Part I. (Unpublished Memoir.) (Courtesy Anderson, Berlin.)
79. 'Judith's Sorrows for Adam Constant', NLA, Box 1, folder 4.
80. *Christina Stead*, Australia Council Archival Film Series, 1980.
81. Untitled poem, NLA, Box 1, folder 4.
82. NLA, Box 1, folder 4
83. CS to Burnshaw, 9 vii 1960. (*SL*).
84. CS to Gilbert Stead, 25 i 1937.
85. There are several responses among her papers. NLA, Box 7, folder 52.
86. Jack Lindsay to Chris Williams, October 1987. See Chris Williams, *Christina Stead*, McPhee Gribble, Melbourne, 1989, p.115.
87. NLA, Box 7, folder 52. The questionnaire is dated 11 January 1937, and undersigned by M. R. Anand, James Hanley, Geronwy Rees, Montagu Slater, C. Stead, A. Williams-Ellis.
88. Malraux was interviewed by Aragon in *L'Humanité* in September 1934. For Gide's statement, see J. E. Flower, *Literature and the Left in France*, Macmillan, London, 1983, p.105. When the Popular Front years were long since over, and no-one talked of the political responsibility of writers any more, Stead would say emphatically: 'I write to please myself, to exprsss my own ideas, and not those of a magazine, or a social or political group.' (Interview with Jonah Raskin (1968), *London Magazine*, February 1970, p.72.)
89. Conversation with Hugh and Pat Stretton, Adelaide, 1 March 1992.
90. Among Stead's papers (NLA, Box 3, folder 35) is a page of notes, in diary form, dated 12 November 1937. When she was back in New York, in 1937, she saw a lot of the Golds, and would also ask Elisabeth about her husband.
91. CS to Burnshaw, 2 x 1936.
92. CS to 'Ted', Gilbert Stead, 25 i 1937.
93. See Dudley Collard, *Soviet Justice and the Trial of Radek and Others*, Gollancz, London, 1937. He expresses deep sympathy with the Soviet Government's position.
94. See Stephen Spender, *World Within World*, (1951), Faber & Faber, London, 1977, p.211. See also Samuel Hynes, *The Auden Generation*, p.262ff.
95. In April 1938 some 150 American intellectuals issued a statement linking support for the Moscow verdicts with the cause of progressive democracy in the United States. Among the signatories were several friends of Blake and Stead, including Samuel Putnam. See David Caute, *The Fellow-Travellers*, Revised and updated edition, Yale University Press, New Haven and London, 1988, p.131.
96. See Max Eastman, *Love and Revolution*, Random House, New York, 1964, p.626. See also Daniel Aaron, *Writers on the Left*, OUP, Oxford, 1961, p.320.

97. Blake to Mike Gold, 13 vii 1938. (Elisabeth Granich-Humeston papers.)
98. Blake to 'Cosette, Mike and Nikolai' (Elisabeth and Mike Gold and their son Nicholas), Montpellier, 11 vi 1937. (Mike Folsom papers.)
99. CS to Burnshaw, 2 x 1936. (*SL*)

8: The Battleground of Life

1. CS to FJ, 13 xii 1937.
2. CS to Gilbert Stead, 7 xi 1937. (Instead of a date, Stead writes: '20th Anniversary of the Russian Revolution'.) (*SL*)
3. Conversation with Ruth Hall, 25 September 1988.
4. CS to FJ, 13 xii 1937.
5. CS to Kate Stead, Lambertville, summer, 1938. Undated. (The beginning of the letter has been censored by Kate Stead.) (*SL*)
6. 'Shiksa' is a derogatory Yiddish term for a non-Jewish woman.
7. CS to Harvey, November 1969—exact date unclear. (*SL*) For the same conversation, see *Letty*, p.203.
8. Lili Spontini, in *Letty*, is modelled on Jenka.
9. NLA, Box 5, folder 30.
10. See *Letty*, pp.201–3, 226–7. However, a similar passage of Yiddish-German-English mixture (written by Letty) occurs in *Letty*, p.359.
11. *Letty*, p.82.
12. Ibid., p.196.
13. Ibid., p.200.
14. Jacques Coe mentions the incident in his book *Fame, Fraud and Fortune*, Exposition Press, Smithtown, NY, 1983.
15. CS to FJ, 13 xii 1937.
16. Stead's diary, 3 January 1938. NLA, Box 15, folder 112.
17. See *Letty*, Chapter 24.
18. CS to Burnshaws, 17 xii 1937.
19. CS to FJ, 13 xii 1937.
20. Ibid.
21. The inscription was dated 2 May 1938. In March 1943, DGS donated the book to the Mitchell Library in Sydney.
22. CS to FJ, 13 xii 1937.
23. Ibid.
24. Ibid.
25. Blake to Burnshaw, undated. At the top of the letter, in Bill's ungrammatical German, is written: 'Weissnichtswo, Gott weiss wen'. (Lambertville, June or July 1938.)
26. CS to Burnshaw, 7 vi 1938. (*SL*)
27. CS to Burnshaws, 13 vii 1938.
28. CS to Kate Stead, Lambertville, July or August 1938. Undated. (Beginning censored.) (*SL*)
29. CS to Burnshaw, Lambertville, 7 vi 1938. (*SL*)
30. CS review of Vladimir Pozner, *Bloody Baron*, tr. Warre Bradley Wells, Random House, New York, 1938, in *New Masses*, 29 September 1938.
31. The novella was not published until 1967, in the collection *The Puzzleheaded Girl* (Holt, Rinehart & Winston, New York, 1967).
32. Pocahontas is the name of an American Indian princess, born in Virginia. According to legend, she saved the life of Captain John Smith, about to be clubbed to death by her father's warriors. Stead refers to the story in her novella.
33. Conversation with Ruth Hall, 25 September 1988. Samuel Putnam (1892–1950), radical and writer, was best known for his translations from French, Spanish, Italian and Portuguese.
34. NLA, Box 1, folder 6.
35. 'The Right-Angled Creek', in *Puzzleheaded*, Virago, London, 1984, p.149.
36. CS to Burnshaws, 13 vii 1938.
37. CS to Maurice Temple-Smith, Secker & Warburg, 19 viii 1967. (Courtesy Michael Bott, Archives & Manuscripts, University of Reading.)

38. Elliot Paul, 'Parisian Panorama', review of *House*, *Saturday Review of Literature*, 11 June 1938, p.5.
39. Alfred Kazin, *Books*, 12 June 1938, p.1.
40. Harold Strauss, 'A Novel of Frenzied Finance', review of *House*, *New York Times Book Review*, 12 June 1938.
41. Clifton Fadiman, *New Yorker*, 11 June 1938.
42. Edwin Berry Burgum, *New Masses*, 21 June 1938.
43. Henry Hart, *Direction*, vol. 1, no. 7, July–August 1938, p.28.
44. CS to FJ, 12 xii 1938.
45. Ibid.
46. Peter Davies to CS, 7 ix 1938. NLA, Box 7, folder 51.
47. I am indebted to Margaret Harris for pointing this out in her article '"To Hell with Conservatories": Christina Stead and the Fiction of William J. Blake', *Meridian*, vol. 8, no. 2, October 1989.
48. When Blake wrote the novel in 1942, Stead had just suffered a miscarriage. It was probably on his mind at the time.
49. *Publishers' Weekly*, August 1938, p.498.
50. See Jacques Coe, *Fame, Fraud and Fortune.*
51. Mike Gold, *Daily Worker*, 4 June 1938.
52. Private comment. Simon & Schuster papers.
53. Stephen Vincent Benét, review of *The World is Mine*, in *Saturday Review of Literature*, 6 August 1938.
54. Harold Strauss, review of *The World is Mine*, *New York Times*, 7 August 1938.
55. In press interviews, Stead must have been calling herself the wife of Bill Blake. See the *Wilson Library Bulletin*, vol. 13, no. 4, December 1938, p.234.
56. Edd Johnson, 'His First Novel May Bring Him Fourth Fortune', *New York World-Telegram*, 31 August 1938.
57. Conversation with Gilbert Stead, Sydney, 8 February 1990.
58. Fred Stead had worked in a motorcycle factory, and when he was stood down during the Depression, he organised political resistance at the factory. He did not play the guitar. (Conversation with Gilbert Stead, 2 February 1990.)
59. In September 1937 Bill signed a letter to the *New Masses* about stock exchange activities 'Stephen Blake', and he used the same pseudonym for an article entitled 'Wall Street Strategy and Congress' in *New Masses*, 30 November 1937. The Notes on Contributors cause confusion: 'Ben Blake is an economist with international banking experience'.
60. CS to Gilbert Stead, 30 viii 1938.
61. CS to Blake, 15 vi 1942. NLA, Box 16, folders 119–20.
62. *House*, p.167.
63. William Blake, *The World is Mine*, Cassell, London, 1939, pp.433–4.
64. Stead, amused by this, told Gilbert Stead: 'We are giving a Christmas Party ... on Christmas Day, exclusively attended by Jewish friends—stay—there is a dim possibility of a gentile arriving, a young modeller-and-painter working at the American Museum of Natural History.' (21 xii 1937)
65. Conversation with Burnshaw, New York, 29 June 1988.
66. Stead's diary, 4 January 1938. NLA, Box 15, folder 112.
67. When Blake applied to renew his American passport in 1954, he was obliged to make several sworn affidavits at the American Embassy in London, outlining his earlier communist activities. His statement is contained in his FBI file, dated 24 January 1957.
68. Burnshaw, although not a Party member, was a good friend of William Browder, chairman of the Upper Broadway branch and brother of Earl Browder. Burnshaw helped to extricate Blake from the Party diplomatically. (Conversation with Burnshaw, New York, 5 June 1988.)
69. When Blake joined the Party, Stead noted in her diary: 'Myself: at a loss. Can't join branch for status reasons: where to go to get social background. No-one cares! Will have to "join something" v. soon.' 4 January 1938. NLA, Box 15, folder 112.
70. CS to Burnshaw, 29 ix 1938.
71. CS , review of *L'Espoir*, in *New Masses*, 15 November 1938.
72. CS, review of *Meek Heritage* by F. E. Sillanpaa (tr. from the Finnish by Alexander Matson, Alfred A. Knopf), in *New Masses*, 11 October 1938.
73. The extracts, entitled 'The Prometheans of the Novel' and 'Socialist Realism', were printed in *New Masses* in May 1937.

74. Ralph Fox, *The Novel and The People*, Lawrence & Wishart, London, 1937, pp.109, 134.
75. Ibid., pp.109–10.
76. Ibid., p.112.
77. Ibid., p.24.
78. CS to FJ, 12 xii 1938.
79. Barnard Eldershaw comments that Stead's first three books 'bring a new note into Australian fiction', but claims there is a 'failure to create living people', and that Stead's books 'are like Ankor, the city overwhelmed in the jungle'. M. Barnard Eldershaw, *Essays in Australian Fiction*, MUP, Melbourne, 1938, pp.158–81.
80. P. R. Stephensen, 'Export of Genius', *The Foundations of Culture in Australia*, W. J. Miles, Sydney, 1936, p.122.
81. H. M. Green, 'Australian Literature, 1938', *Southerly* 1939.
82. NLA, Palmer papers, MS 1174.
83. CS diary, 10 February 1936. NLA, Box 15, folder 112.
84. CS to Thistle Harris, 7 vii 1939. (*SL*)
85. Fay Zwicky, *The Lyre in the Pawnshop*, University of Western Australia Press, Perth, 1986, p.149.
86. Mitchell Library, Rare Book Collection.
87. Virginia Woolf wrote in her diary, 28 November 1928: 'I used to think of [my father] and mother daily; but writing the *Lighthouse* laid them in my mind. [. . .] I was obsessed by them both, unhealthily; and writing of them was a necessary act.' (*A Writer's Diary*, ed. Leonard Woolf, Hogarth Press, London, 1954, p.138.)
88. CS to Thistle Harris, 7 vii 1939. (*SL*)
89. Mariann Heimans, 'Christina Stead . . . Writer Courageous', *Sun* (Melbourne), 11 April 1977.
90. CS to Blake, 14 vi 1942. NLA, Box 16, folders 119–20.
91. Interview with Christina Stead, Melbourne, 23 March 1976. ABC series, 'Australian Writers'. (Christina Stead. Programme 2.) Copyright no. 76/AW/2.
92. CS to FJ, 15 vi 1940. FJ papers.
93. CS to Thistle Harris, 7 vii 1939. (*SL*)
94. Ibid.
95. These phrases are from *The Man*.
96. CS interview with Rodney Wetherell (1980), *Australian Literary Studies*, vol. 9, no. 4, October 1980, p.437.
97. Conversation with Thistle Harris, Sydney, 15 January 1987.
98. NLA, Box 1, folder 3.
99. CS to Richard Kopley, 9 x 1972. (*SL*)
100. CS interview with Ann Whitehead (1973), *Australian Literary Studies*, vol. 6, no. 3, May 1974, p.242.
101. Stead once commented: 'I was very lucky in that whenever my books came out I was always in another country, so I'm never concerned.' (Wetherell interview, p.437.)
102. CS to Thistle Harris, 7 vii 1939. (*SL*)
103. Jose Yglesias, 'Marx as Muse', *Nation*, vol. CC, 1965, pp.368–70.
104. *The Man*, p.327.
105. In his review of *The Man* in the *New Yorker*, 19 October 1940, Fadiman wrote: 'Miss Stead, an Australian, has lived among us only four years. Her powers of assimilation are like an ostrich's, but are not equal as yet to the task of completely digesting an American background. Despite the spate of carefully studied detail, her Washington and her Annapolis have little reality, and her Pollits are not Americans, though they are so labelled. The key throughout is just detectably false.'
106. Mary McCarthy, 'Framing Father', *New Republic*, 13 January 1941, p.61. It was Blake who spoke of 'Teddy' Roosevelt. (See his review of Matthew Josephson's *The President Makers* in *New Masses*, 29 October 1940, p.26.)
107. CS to Eldon Branda, 2 iii 1965. (*SL*)
108. CS to Thistle Harris, 7 vii 1939. (*SL*)
109. Randall Jarrell, Preface to re-issue of *The Man*, Holt, Rinehart & Winston, New York, 1965.
110. This letter arrived after the novel was published. However, DGS must have sent other letters earlier. He probably did not realise that CS had finished her novel. Obviously he had not yet read it.

111. The letters from Malaya, mostly typewritten, were kept in Gilbert Stead's private archives until his death in October 1991.
112. The letter from Sam Pollit to 'Looloo-Dirl' (*The Man*, pp.258–9) is copied from a longer letter that DGS wrote to CS ('Pedler Dirl') from Singapore on 9 ix 1922. (Gilbert Stead archives.)
113. Modernist and post-modernist writers celebrate 'intertextuality'; however, their systematic borrowings are from published works, usually well-known, whereas appropriating unacknowledged, unpublished letters, as Stead does, involves an element of usurpation.
     There was considerable controversy about the verbatim use Robert Lowell made of the letters of Elizabeth Hardwick (his ex-wife) in certain poems in *The Dolphin* in 1973. The parallel is not exact, for the American public (for whom Hardwick was a well-known figure) were aware of the appropriation, though no-one knew the proportion of fact and fiction. (See Ian Hamilton, *Robert Lowell*, Faber & Faber, London, 1983, pp.418–36.)
114. Clifton Fadiman, *New Yorker*, 19 October 1940, p.84. (There is no record of Stead's reaction to Fadiman's review.) The critics did not agree on this. Charles Poore declared Sam Pollit's letters 'spectacularly dull'. (*New York Times*, 18 October 1940.)
115. CS interview with Joan Lidoff (1973). *Christina Stead*, Ungar, New York, 1982, p.202.
116. CS to FJ, 15 vi 1940.
117. CS to Thistle Harris, 7 vii 1939. (*SL*)
118. *Letty*, p.229.
119. Conversation with Ruth Hall, 25 September 1988.
120. Ibid., 5 October 1987.
121. *Letty*, p.231. The same detail recurs in the short story 'Life is Difficult': hence the title. *Ocean*, pp.151–69.
122. Conversation with Ruth Hall, 5 October 1987.
123. See *Letty*, p.227. Grandma Fox tells Mathilde, 'I want to give all my dear ones something . . . and I don't want her [Persia] to get it.'
124. CS to FJ, 15 vi 1940.
125. Ibid.
126. The Bulgarian communist Dimitrov was arrested in Nazi Germany on the charge of complicity in the burning of the Reichstag. Acquitted, he was now living in the Soviet Union—a member of the Supreme Soviet, and on the executive committee of the Communist International.
     Stead's paper is among the papers of the League of American Writers, in the Bancroft Library, University of California. The first draft is also there—rough typed notes, with many crossings-out.
127. The letter was published in *Nation* on 26 August 1939. See Daniel Aaron, *Writers on the Left* (1961), OUP, Oxford, 1977, p.363.
     That Christina Stead signed the letter is noted in her FBI file. (File No. 100–82232. Report made in New York, 18 February 1947.)
128. Total US membership of the League after the Nazi-Soviet Pact was approximately 750.
129. *New Masses*, 19 September 1939, p.2.

9: Dearest Munx

1. CS to FJ, 15 vi 1940.
2. Ibid.
3. Ibid.
4. *Dogs*, p.19.
5. CS to Blake, 7 v 1942. NLA, Box 16, folder 119.
6. Ibid., 23 v 1941.
7. *Dogs*, p.3.
8. Conversation with Asa Zatz, New York, 14 October 1987.
9. Aida Kotlarsky died on 2 January 1982. Asa Zatz wrote her obituary in the *New York Times*: 'She lived a long life but never aged. A beautiful, caring adult who remained always a wide-eyed elfin child, she found joy always in her music, her mountains and in those she loved. She brought fantasy, delight, humor, warmth to many lives. All who knew her will miss this irreplaceable spirit.'

10. CS chose the name Oneida as an echo of the nineteenth-century radical community by that name.
11. CS to Thistle Harris, 6 iv 1942. (*SL*)
12. Stead was writing to Isidor Schneider to thank him for his review in the *New Masses*. (CS to Isidor Schneider, 7 xi 1940. Schneider Collection, Rare Books and Manuscript Library, Butler Library, Columbia University, New York.)
13. Clifton Fadiman, review of *The Man*, *New Yorker*, 19 October 1940.
14. Louis B. Salomon, 'Scalpel, Please', *Nation* (NY), 26 October 1940, p.399.
15. Charles Poore, *New York Times*, 18 October 1940, p.19.
16. Isidor Schneider (1896–1977) was a leading leftwing novelist, poet and critic in New York in the Twenties, Thirties and Forties. CS and Blake would include an extract from his novel *The Marriage of Venus* (1928) in their anthology *Modern Women in Love* (1945).
17. Isidor Schneider, review of *The Man*, *New Masses*, 12 November 1940, pp.19–20.
18. Pearl K. Bell, 'A neglected master', *New Leader*, 11 December 1972, p.7.
19. Mary McCarthy, 'Framing Father', *New Republic*, vol. 104, no. 2, 13 January 1941, p.61.
20. Clifton Fadiman, review of *The Man*, *New Yorker*, 19 October 1940, pp.84, 86.
21. CS promised to send GW-S a copy (CS to FJ, 15 vi 1940), but she did not.
22. Conversation with Thistle Harris, Sydney, 15 January 1987.
23. The letter has not survived. I am surmising the content from CS's letter to Blake, undated. (Monday, 1942—probably 6 April, since Blake was in Canada in early April.) Stead writes: 'But she still loves the guy.' NLA, Box 16, folder 19.
24. CS to Thistle Harris, 6 iv 1942. (*SL*)
25. Conversation with Thistle Harris, 15 January 1987.
26. Conversations with Gilbert Stead, 1990.
27. Conversation with DDS, 9 January 1987.
28. *Sydney Morning Herald*, 20 September 1941, p.10.
29. Louis B. Salomon had written in the *Nation*: 'While I have every reason to hope that Sam Pollit is an exaggerated figure, he is drawn convincingly enough to make a lot of men want to crawl away into a corner and die. But of course the Sam Pollits never know when a barb is aimed at them.' (*Nation*, 26 October 1940, p.399.)
30. Christopher Ricks, 'Domestic Manners', review of *The Man*, *New York Review of Books*, 17 June 1965, p.14.
31. Cecil Hemley, 'Unhappy with the young at heart', *Saturday Review of Books*, 10 April 1965, p.44.
32. Robert Lowell, quoted by R. J. Scholfield in his review of *The Man*, *Bulletin*, 22 May 1965, p.29.
33. Pearl K. Bell, 'A neglected master', *New Leader*, 11 December 1972.
34. Conversation with Asa Zatz, New York, 14 October 1987.
35. Ibid. Gibbon's book is mentioned in *Dogs*, p.206.
36. Cordon Press, New York, 1939.
37. Simon & Schuster, New York, 1939. 'To the memory of my dear friend Ralph Fox, killed in action at Cordoba. *The dead shall live, the living die.*'
38. Blake to Burnshaw, Lambertville (exact date unknown), 1938.
39. Conversation with Asa Zatz, 14 October 1987.
40. Ibid.
41. Carl A. Bristel to Blake, 4 iv 1941, NLA, Box 7, folders 50–1.
42. Stead to Rella, 30 vi 1953. (*SL*)
43. Pilar Libenson comments that Harry Bloom was the kind of man everyone loved— kind, gentle, with a wonderful laugh. (Telephone conversation with Pilar Libenson, Pittsburgh, 2 August 1988.)
44. Conversation with Asa Zatz, 14 October 1987.
45. Rella is the model for Roselli in *Dogs*.
46. CS to Burnshaw, 10 iii 1965. (*SL*)
47. See Martin Jay, *The Dialectical Imagination*, Heinemann, London, 1973.
48. CS to Burnshaw, 19 ii 1965. (*SL*)
49. CS to Blake, 14 vi 1942.
50. Telephone conversation with Pilar Libenson, 2 August 1988.

51. Ruth McKenney, *Love Story*, Harcourt, Brace & Co., NY, 1950, p.49.
52. Ibid., p.50.
53. Burnshaw to me, 31 vii 1992.
54. In *Laughing*, Emily Wilkes says this (p.52).
55. *Current Biography*, H. W. Wilson, New York, 1942, p.549.
56. 'Three Decades. Life and Times of the *Masses*, the *Liberator* and *New Masses*. Samuel Sillen discusses the fight for the American Dream from 1911 to 1941', *New Masses*, 18 February 1941, pp.8–10.
57. The list of signatories was published in *Clipper* (Hollywood), May 1941.
58. 'A Communication to all writers from the League of American Writers', *Clipper* (Hollywood), August 1941, editorial.
59. CS's membership, in 1941, is noted in her FBI file. (NY 100–82232)
60. *Bulletin of the League of American Writers*, 3 January 1942. Cited in Larry Ceplair & Steven Englund, *The Inquisition in Hollywood*, Anchor Press, New York, 1980, p.174.
61. There is a note among Stead's papers about Teresa and Letitia. (NLA, Box 2, folder 7.) See, further, Anita Segerberg, 'A Fiction of Sisters: CS's *Letty Fox*', *Australian Literary Studies*, vol. 14, no. 1, and R. Geering, '*Letty Fox* (and *For Love Alone*)', *Southerly*, no. 1, 1991.
62. Angela Carter, 'Unhappy Families: Angela Carter on the scope of Christina Stead's achievement', *London Review of Books*, 16 September–6 October 1982.
63. *Love*, p.454.
64. Sex, in *For Love Alone*, is 'romanticised as the key to the heroine's self-awareness'. (See Susan Sheridan's Introduction to the A & R Imprint Classics edition of *Letty*, Sydney, 1991.)
65. *Letty*, p.14.
66. Ibid., p.513.
67. CS to Walter Stone of the Book Collectors' Society of Australia, 24 iii 1958. (Walter Stone papers.)
68. CS to Blake, 28 vi 1942.
69. Ibid., 25 v 1941.
70. Ibid., 2 viii 1941. NLA, Box 16, folders 119–20.
71. Ibid., 6 viii 1941. The self-humbling tone reappears in a letter written to Blake in Canada some months later. (Bernard Myers was to introduce Bill before he gave a speech; Christina had been asked for some details about Blake.) 'Much love, my dear Munx: I think of you, think what a fine man you are. Writing out the list of your perfections for Dr. B. Myers, I was overcome. Oh, gosh, I'll have to pack a valise and sneak off: I am not good enough for this citizen, I felt.' (4 iv 1942.)
72. CS to Blake, 6 viii 1941.
73. Ibid.
74. *Letty*, p.286.
75. Ibid., p.297.
76. CS to Burnshaw, 18 xi 1941.
77. John Simon Guggenheim Memorial Foundation, New York. Courtesy of Margaret Harris.
78. These were M. Lincoln Schuster and Philip Van Doren Stern from Simon & Schuster; Edwin B. Burgum, Quincy Howe and Willard Waller. Their letters, and Stead's application, are in the archives of the John Simon Guggenheim Memorial Foundation, New York. (Courtesy of Margaret Harris.)
79. John Simon Guggenheim Memorial Foundation, New York.
80. CS to Burnshaw, 19 xii 1966. As late as 1976 Stead was still intending to use Stern's dreams in a book of short stories to be called *The Talking Ghost*. CS to Dorothy Green, 23 xii 1976. (*SL*)
81. Undated letter from CS to Blake. (Monday, 1942.)
82. CS to Thistle Harris, 6 vi 1942. (*SL*)
83. CS to Rella, 16 iv 1942. (*SL*)
84. CS interview with Joan Lidoff (1973), *Christina Stead*, Ungar, New York, 1982, p.195.
85. Diana Trilling, 'Women in Love', review of *Love*, *Nation*, 28 October 1944, p.535.
86. CS to Blake, undated. (June 1942.)
87. CS to Elizabeth Harrower, 21 vi 1976. (*SL*)
88. CS to Blake, 11 iv 1944.

89. Conversation with Michael Bloom and Janet Ladenheim (née Bloom), New Jersey, 17 August 1988.

90. Conversation with Michael Bloom, New York, 5 August 1988.

91. Stead's words are cited in Anderson's diary, 15 April 1945. (Anderson papers.)

92. Blake to CS, undated (June 1942).

93. CS to Rella, 16 iv 1942. (*SL*)

94. CS to Thistle Harris, 6 iv 1942. (*SL*)

95. CS to Rella, 16 iv 1942. (*SL*)

96. Dial Press, 1941. Northern 'Peace Democrats', who advocated compromise with the Confederate States to end the war, were popularly known as 'copperheads'.

97. CS to Rella, 16 iv 1942. (*SL*)

98. She praised Kylie Tennant's novel *The Battlers* for its 'simple style of reportage' and authentic use of the Australian vernacular. (*New Masses*, 30 September 1941.)

99. *New Masses*, 20 January 1942, pp.23–5.

100. 'Pro and Con on Aragon', Hannah Josephson's response to Christina Stead's review, *New Masses*, 17 February 1942, p.23.

101. 'Pro and Con on Aragon'—Hannah Josephson and Christina Stead in *New Masses*, 17 February 1942, pp.23–4.

102. CS to Burnshaw, 8 i 1942.

103. CS to Thistle Harris, 6 iv 1942. (*SL*)

104. Ibid.

105. Conversation with Ruth Hall, Châteauneuf-de-Grasse, 5 October 1987.

106. Annie Laurie Williams of McIntosh & Otis wrote back (4 v 1942) telling him she had submitted the manuscript to nine different movie companies. She enclosed extracts from the letters from Twentieth-Century Fox, Columbia Pictures and Warner Brothers. They all made kind and flattering comments, but none wanted to buy the film rights. (The letter is in Ruth Hall's papers.)

107. CS to Thistle Harris, 6 iv 1942. (*SL*)

108. Blake to CS, Beverly Hills, 14 v 1942.

109. CS to Blake, 7 v 1942. NLA, Box 16, folders 119–20.

110. CS to FJ, 12 xii 1938.

111. CS to Elisabeth Gold, 21 i 1940. (Elisabeth Granich-Humeston papers.)

112. CS to Thistle Harris, 6 iv 1942. (*SL*)

113. CS to Blake, 8 v 1942.

114. It worked: he gave her a camel hair coat two weeks later. CS to Blake, 2 vi 1942.

115. CS to Blake, 10 v 1942.

116. Blake to CS, no date (May 1942).

117. 'Blake dissenting', *New Masses*, 17 February 1942.

118. Nat Goldstone was head of the Goldstone Agency. One of his colleagues there, George Willner, would be blacklisted by the House Un-American Activities Committee. (See Victor S. Navasky, *Naming Names*, Viking, NY, 1980.)

119. Blake to CS, Beverly House, Beverly Hills, 14 v 1942.

120. See Ian Hamilton, *Writers in Hollywood 1915–1951*, Heinemann, London, 1990, p.234.

121. CS to Blake, 11 v 1942.

122. Ibid., 12 v 1942.

123. Blake to CS, 18 v 1942. Blake had already mentioned George Graham Rice in *The World is Mine*, p.294. In *Laughing*, Axel Oates is writing a script on George Graham Rice. (p.60)

124. Years afterwards, Stead claimed she was not responsible for the title. 'I'm always embarrassed about that title.' (CS interview with Joan Lidoff (1973), p.195) But she kept it, though the publishers were ultimately not Viking but Harcourt, Brace.

125. Blake to CS, 21 v 1942.

126. Ibid., 5 vi 1942.

127. Ibid., (Beverly Hills), 20 v 1942.

128. CS to Blake, 1 vi 1942.

129. Ibid. Thursday, May 1942. Undated.

130. Ibid., 1 vi 1942.

131. Blake to CS, 1 vi 1942.

132. Ibid., 23 v 1942.

133. CS to Blake, 5 vi 1942.

134. Ibid., Sunday, May 1942. Undated.
135. Ibid., 5 vi 1942.
136. Blake to CS, Wednesday. Undated.
137. CS to Blake, 2 vi 1942.
138. Ibid., 22 vi 1942.
139. *Love*, p.329.
140. Marion McDonald, 'Christina Stead: the exile returns, unhappily', *National Times*, 22–7 November 1976.
141. In fact, she did not return to Mike Gold, but concentrated on other revolutionaries— McKenney and Bransten—instead.
142. Blake to CS, 5 vi 1942.
143. Stead would use these very words in *Laughing*, p.60.
144. Blake to CS. Undated.
145. Ibid., 1 vi 1942.
146. CS to Blake, 10 vi 1942.
147. Ibid.
148. Blake to CS, 12 vi 1942.
149. CS to Blake, 15 vi 1942.
150. Ibid., 24 vi 1942.
151. Ibid., 16 vi 1942.
152. Blake to CS, 20 vi 1942.
153. Ibid., 23 vi 1942.
154. Among Stead's papers are several pages of notes on patiences, for fortune-telling. (NLA, Box 4, folder 28.)
155. CS to Blake, 24 vi 1942.
156. Ibid., 21 vi 1942.
157. Ibid., Thursday evening. (Undated, but it is clearly 25 vi 1942—Stead's second letter to Blake that day.)
158. In the end, CS wrote a brief portrait of Grossmann in her story 'The Azhadanov Tailors', in *Ocean*. He is also the model for Simon Gondych in *Letty*.
159. CS to Blake, 28 vi 1942.

10: The Besieged Fortress

1. Letty Fox uses this term to describe Santa Fe. (*Letty*, p.182)
2. CS to Burnshaw, 31 viii 1942. (*SL*)
3. Ibid.
4. CS, 'Workshop in the novel', NLA, Box 11, folder 84.
5. CS to Burnshaw, 31 viii 1942.
6. Nancy Lynn Schwartz, *The Hollywood Writers' Wars*, Alfred A. Knopf, New York, 1982, p.173.
7. Larry Ceplair & Steven Englund, *The Inquisition in Hollywood*, Doubleday Anchor, Garden City, NY, 1980, p.332.
8. Peter Smark interview with CS in London, *Australian*, 13 June 1969, p.9.
9. CS, *Foxwarren Hall*. Memoirs. 1958. NLA, Box 3, folder 21.
10. CS had told Peter Smark, in June 1969, that she earned $175 a week. She told Anne Matheson, in July 1969, that she was 'doing time' in Hollywood on $750 a week.
11. Leo C. Rosten, *Hollywood*, Harcourt, Brace, New York, 1941, p.324.
12. This was in the mid 1940s. See Tom Dardis, *Some Time in the Sun*, Scribner, New York, 1976, p.30.
13. This was January 1943. Victor S. Navasky, *Naming Names*, Viking, New York, 1980, pp.165–6.
14. Blake to Burnshaw, 9 xii 1942.
15. Blake to Leda Burnshaw (Stanley's third wife), 30 xii 1942.
16. Ibid.
17. Roy Pickard, *The Hollywood Studios*, Frederick Muller, London, 1978, p.370.
18. Otto Friedrich, *City of Nets*, Harper & Row, New York, 1986, p.157.
19. CS's membership card dates from 21 January 1943. Since union membership was part of the MGM contract, it is strange that she joined near the end of her employment. (The card is in Gilbert Stead's archives.)

20. Nancy Lynn Schwartz, *The Hollywood Writers' Wars*, p.191.
21. Salka Viertel, *The Kindness of Strangers*, Holt, Rinehart & Winston, NY, 1969. David King Dunaway, *Huxley in Hollywood*, Bloomsbury, London, 1989.
22. Robert Drewe interview with Christina Stead (1982), *Scripsi*, vol. 4, no. 1, July 1986, p.25.
23. Blake's teaching there, in February 1943, was mentioned in *Clipper*, the magazine of the Hollywood chapter of the League of American Writers. It also made it into Blake's FBI file. Other notable leftists who taught there were Paul Jarrico, Donald Ogden Stewart, John Howard Lawson, and journalist and travel-writer Cedric Belfrage.
24. Blake to Burnshaw, 9 xii 1942.
25. John Howard Lawson was cited for contempt of Congress in November 1947, and sentenced to one year in prison. Blacklisted, he emigrated to Mexico—as did Albert Maltz. He never again worked on films under his own name.
26. Larry Ceplair & Steven Englund, *The Inquisition in Hollywood*, pp.307–8.
27. Otto Friedrich, *City of Nets*, pp.47–52. It is true that perhaps as much as two-thirds of the Party in Hollywood was Jewish (Neal Gabler, *An Empire of their Own*, Crown, New York, 1988, p.331).
28. Ruth McKenney, *Love Story*, Harcourt, Brace, New York, 1950.
29. *Laughing*, p.58.
30. David Caute, *The Great Fear*, Simon & Schuster, New York, 1978.
31. Ruth McKenney, *Love Story*, pp.277–9.
32. Neal Gabler, *An Empire of their Own*, pp.334–5.
33. Otto Friedrich, *City of Nets*, pp.322–3. Lawson's father, Simon Levy, had changed the family name. (Neal Gabler, *An Empire of their Own*, p.332.)
34. *Daily Worker*, 21 June 1943. CS's letter is noted in her FBI file (NY 100–82232).
35. CS interview with Ann Whitehead, (1973), *Australian Literary Studies*, vol. 6, no. 3, May 1974, p.246.
36. Ibid.
37. Conversation with Jessie and Ettore Rella, New York, 12 October 1987.
38. Conversation with Asa Zatz, New York, 14 October 1987. Zatz translated Bruckner's play *Fährten* (Tracks), which Erwin Piscator directed. For Zatz, it was the beginning of a career of translation.
39. CS to Burnshaw, 19 ii 1965. (*SL*)
40. CS to Rella, 31 v 1979. (*SL*)
41. Blake to Burnshaw, 8 xii 1942.
42. Blake's FBI file (NY 100–50990).
43. Blake to CS. Undated. (July 1944.) NLA, Box 16, folder 119.
44. This is how Burnshaw describes the writing process. (Conversation with Burnshaw, 5 June 1988; Burnshaw to me 20 ix 1992.)
45. George E. Sokolsky, 'Who Done It?', *Sun* (New York), 30 December 1944.
46. *Dogs*, p.185.
47. *Dogs* has strong echoes of Shakespeare's play. There is even a country wedding, in which the bridal pair appear from the wood. Two of the characters' names, Lydia and Leander, evoke Hermia and Lysander in *A Midsummer Night's Dream*.
48. Blake to CS. Undated. (July 1944.) The letters referred to are *different* letters. All are undated.
49. Ibid. Undated. (July 1944.)
50. CS to Blake, 5 vii 1944.
51. The model for Victor-Alexander in the novel.
52. Conversation with Asa Zatz, New York, 10 October 1987. Stanley Hooper, who came from an aristocratic, nineteenth-century family, had studied piano at the same time as Aida, whom he had almost married. (Zatz says he was obviously homosexual, but maybe did not know it.) In order to be close to Aida, he acquired a piece of land from the Hunter holding, and planted an exquisite garden there.
53. CS to Blake. Undated. (July 1944.)
54. These are CS's own comments on *Dogs*. (See Geering, 'Christina Stead's Description of Her Books', *Southerly*, no. 4, 1990, pp.421–5.)
55. CS to Aida Kotlarsky. Undated. (Early August 1944.) Don Shaw papers.
56. *Dogs*, p.65.
57. Ibid., p.315.

58. Ibid., p.152.
59. Ibid., p.94.
60. Ibid., p.294.
61. Ibid., p.320.
62. Ibid., p.337.
63. Helen Strauss does not even mention Stead in her jaunty, self-congratulatory memoir *A Talent for Luck*. (Random House, New York, 1979.)
64. Edith Roberts, *Book Week*, 29 October 1944, p.14.
65. CS describes it in an interview with Joan Lidoff (1973), *Christina Stead*, Ungar, New York, 1982, p.196.
66. The jacket was designed by Isidor Steinberg, a commercial artist friend of Stead's. She seems not to have realised how inappropriate it was.
67. Jose Yglesias, 'Marx as Muse', *Nation*, 5 April 1965, p.368.
68. Patrick White to Geoffrey Dutton, 5 ii 1967. Dutton papers, NLA, MS 7285, series 5, folder 188.
69. Jennings Rice, *Weekly Book Review*, 22 October 1944.
70. The review is unsigned, and is unlikely to be Clifton Fadiman this time. (*New Yorker*, 21 October 1944.)
71. Diana Trilling, *Nation*, 28 October 1944.
72. Ruth Page, *New York Times*, 29 October 1944.
73. Katherine Shorey, *Library Journal*, 15 October 1944.
74. *Times Literary Supplement*, 13 October 1945, p.485.
75. The *Listener*, 1 November 1945.
76. Douglas Stewart, review of *Love*, 'The Red Page', *Bulletin*, 13 February 1946. The review was reprinted in D. Stewart, *The Flesh and the Spirit*, A & R, Sydney, 1948.
77. Anonymous review of *Love*, *Daily Telegraph* (Sydney), 13 January 1945, p.13.
78. L. V. Kepert, review of *Love*, *Sydney Morning Herald*, 30 December 1944, p.7. (Anonymous reviewer's name courtesy of Margaret Harris.)
79. CS, 'Workshop in the Novel', NLA, Box 11, folder 84.
80. CS to Thistle Harris, 6 iv 1942. (*SL*)
81. Angela Carter, *Expletives Deleted*, Chatto & Windus, London, 1992.
82. *Love*, p.356.
83. Flaubert, cited in Linda Nochlin, *Realism*, Penguin, Harmondsworth, 1971, p.43.
84. CS to Anderson. Undated. (End of March or early April, 1961.)
85. Ibid., 7 iii 1961.
86. Susan Sheridan, *Christina Stead*, Harvester Wheatsheaf, London, 1988, pp.14, 22.
87. *Laughing*, p.120.
88. *Dogs*, pp.14–15.
89. *Salzburg*, pp.367–8.
90. CS, 'Workshop in the Novel', NLA, Box 11, folder 84.
91. Ibid.
92. Ibid.
93. She lists these books on the subject of women's lives in her 'Workshop in the Novel' notes, ibid.
94. CS interview with Jonah Raskin, 'Christina Stead in Washington Square', *London Magazine*, vol. 9, no. 11, February 1970, pp.70–7.
95. CS referred her students to Stanislavski's book *An Actor Prepares* (1935).
96. CS, 'Workshop in the Novel', NLA, Box 11, folder 84.
97. See Stead's comment in the *Daily Telegraph* (Sydney), 25 October 1947.
98. CS, notes for *Letty*, NLA, Box 2, folder 7.
99. CS interview with Barry Hill, *Sydney Morning Herald*, 17 July 1982, p.33.
100. The friend was Phil Shahn, brother of Ben Shahn, the socialist-realist painter. (Phil had modified the spelling of his name.) The notes, called 'Zany Department', are dated 21 November 1939. (NLA, Box 6, folder 44.)
101. Stead interviewed by Joan Lidoff (1973), p.195.
102. CS to Blake, 14 iv 1944. NLA, Box 16, folders 119–20.
103. Conversation with Burnshaw, 5 June 1988.
104. Conversation with Ruth Hall, 5 October 1987.
105. Ruth Hall is convinced Stead made use of these. (Conversation with Ruth Hall, 5 October 1987.)
106. CS to Blake, May 1942. (Exact date unknown.)

107. Conversations with Nadine Mendelson, New York, 12 October 1987, and 6 July 1988.
108. NLA, Box 6, folder 41.
109. The girl's exact words, translated almost word for word in the novel, are: '*Il faut que tu la lise—il faut que tu connaisse Natasha, qui est la femme la plus femme qu'il existe! Il faut que tu entendes parler la jeunesse dans le livre de Tolstoi, et tu t'arrêteras à chaque phrase avec les larmes aux yeux tellement tout ce que tu entendras sera vrai, sera profond.*'
110. *Letty*, Chapter 30.
111. Jean Saxelby & GW-S, 'Christina Stead' in *Biblionews*, vol. 2, no. 14, December 1949, pp.69–77. See, too, Anita Segerberg, 'A Fiction of Sisters: Christina Stead's *Letty Fox*', *Australian Literary Studies*, vol. 14, no. 1, May 1989.
112. CS to Anderson, 4 v 1944. (Anderson papers.)
113. This was written in 1944, probably May. (Anderson papers.)
114. Anderson to me, 8 vii 1988.
115. Albert Maltz, 'What shall we ask of writers?', *New Masses*, 12 February 1946, pp.19–20.
116. Daniel Aaron, *Writers on the Left*, Oxford University Press, 1961, Galaxy Book, 1973, pp.386–9. It has been speculated that Godfrey Bowles, in *Laughing*, who joins Moffat Byrd with equal ardour in 'straightening out' Emily and Stephen, is modelled on Albert Maltz. Perhaps Maltz attacked McKenney and Bransten, for they were all in Hollywood at the same time. (Letter from a friend to Judith Kegan Gardiner, 24 vi 1987. Courtesy of Judith Kegan Gardiner.)
117. *Laughing*, p.128.
118. *Daily Worker*, 27 May 1945.
119. Irving Howe & Lewis Coser, *The American Communist Party*, Frederick A. Praeger, New York, 1962, p.447.
120. Anderson's unpublished manuscript, 'Cold War Marriage'. (Anderson's papers.)
121. Anderson to me, 7 iv 1991.
122. Announcements in the *New Masses* or the *Daily Worker* give an indication of Blake's demanding political work. He spoke at Camp Beacon in July 1945. He spoke in Boston at a luncheon given by the Joint Anti-Fascist Refugee Committee. He spoke on 'Imperialism in the Cycle of Wars and Revolutions' at the Village Branch of the CPUSA on 11 September 1946.
123. Irving Howe & Lewis Coser, *The American Communist Party*, p.449.
124. CS to Aida Kotlarsky, 14 ix 1946. Don Shaw papers.
125. CS to Anderson, 20 ix 1946. 'If I don't usually say much on the phone it is because our phone is tapped all the time.'
126. CS to Anderson, 7 viii 1945. (Anderson papers.)
127. NLA, Box 6, folder 45.
128. Stead intended to include a story she had heard from Richard Bransten which had greatly amused her, about his friend Bill Dunne, a prominent Labor leader, who had visited Uzbekistan, in the Soviet Union, in the Twenties and was asked to address a meeting of peasants. Though he spoke English and they could not understand a word, they still expected him to talk from sunrise to sundown. He did—in the end saying anything which came into his head, with great animation. ('Jan Kalojan, 4 October 1946', NLA, Box 6, folder 45.)
129. More than two-thirds of the writers in the collection are males.
130. Kol Blount says this in *Poor Men*, pp.61–2.
131. *Modern Women in Love*, Edited by Christina Stead and William Blake, Introduction by Louis Untermeyer, Dryden Press, New York, 1945.
132. CS to FJ, Montreux, 1 ii 1948.
133. CS to Aida Kotlarsky, 16 viii 1946. (Don Shaw papers.)
134. Conversation with Ruth Hall, 5 October 1987.
135. Report dated March 1944, included in Bill Blake's FBI file. (NY 100–50990.)
136. William J. Blake, 'Birobidjan—The Crossroads of Destiny', *Nailebn*, September 1946.
137. Blake to CS. Undated. (Early September 1946)
138. When communist Howard Fast wrote *My Glorious Brothers* in 1948, about Israel's ancient freedom, the Soviets omitted the book from bibliographies of his work. In the United States, Fast was brought up before the Party Secretariat on charges of Jewish bourgeois nationalism. (Howard Fast, *The Naked God*, Frederick A. Praeger, New York, 1957.)
139. CS to Aida Kotlarsky, 16 viii 1946.

140. These were *Lost Haven* by Kylie Tennant, *Cousin from Fiji*, by Norman Lindsay, and *Sun on the Hills* by Margaret Trist. *New York Times Book Review*, 7 April 1946, pp.8, 10.
141. The *Morgen Freiheit* was founded in 1922. It was the largest communist foreign-language newspaper in the States, its circulation sometimes surpassing that of the *Daily Worker*. (Arthur Liebman, *Jews and the Left*, John Wiley & Sons, New York, 1979, p.61.)
142. CS to Mike Gold, 13 vii 1947. (Mike Folsom papers.)
143. CS to Blake, 12 ix 1946. (NLA, Box 16, folders 119–20)
144. *Letty*, p.398.
145. CS to Blake (10 ix 1946): 'I was feeling very low about the dumb Communists and Jacky's letter—wrote a yammering letter to Branstens. They sent me a long gorgeous telegram cheering me up—you will see it. Such darlings.' Despite her fear of libel, Stead gave Nadine Lewin a copy of *Letty*, inscribing it, in September 1946: 'To dear Nadine . . . affectionately.' (Nadine Mendelson papers.)
146. Conversation with Ruth Hall, 5 October 1987.
147. Mary McGrory, *New York Times*, 6 October 1946, p.24.
148. *New Yorker*, 5 October 1946, p.123.
149. Barbara Giles, review of *Letty* in *New Masses*, 10 December 1946, pp.23–4.
150. Harrison Smith, review of *Letty* in *Saturday Review of Literature*, 12 October 1946, p.40.
151. Theo Moody, ' "I'm really a puritan," Christina Stead says', *Daily Telegraph*, 25 October 1946.
152. Stead told FJ several years later that *Letty* sold 21 000 copies in the States alone. This was probably an exaggeration. (CS to FJ, 25 x 1955.)
153. CS to Aida Kotlarsky, 14 ix 1946.
154. Blake (Montreal) to CS, Friday afternoon. Undated. (Probably April 1944.)
155. In order to facilitate his visa application, he arranged for a letter to be sent to him (in French) from Alfred Hurst's Grain Union in Antwerp. The letter states that Blake will be taking over the management of the Montreal branch of the Grain Union, and invites him to Antwerp for a business visit. (Grain Union, 18 iii 1946. Ruth Blake's papers.)
156. Blake to CS, 2 xii 1946.
157. Ibid., 4 xii 1946.
158. Ibid., 2 xii 1946.
159. Ibid.
160. Ibid., 4 xii 1946.
161. CS to Blake, 22 xii 1946.
162. Ibid., 7 xii 1946.
163. Ibid., 19 xii 1946.
164. CS to Mike Gold, 13 vii 1947. (Courtesy Mike Folsom.)
165. CS to Blake, 17 xii 1946.
166. Ibid., 19 xii 1946.
167. Ibid., 20 xii 1946.
168. This detail is taken from the story 'Girl from the Beach', which is based on this farewell scene. (pp.209–210)
169. CS to Blake, 24 xii 1946.
170. *Dogs*, p.323.
171. Ibid.
172. Conversation with Asa Zatz, 27 June 1988.
173. *Dogs*, p.329.

11: From One Perch to Another

1. CS's FBI file No. 100–82232, opened New York, 18 February 1947.
2. Blake to CS, 26 xi 1946. NLA, Box 16, folder 119.
3. This is given in Stead's FBI file as the reason for the investigation.
4. Investigators interminably raked over the same ground: his family background and his political activities in the Thirties and Forties.
5. CS to Mike Gold, London, 24 vii 1947. (Mike Folsom papers, Boston.)
6. David Caute, *The Great Fear*, Simon & Schuster, New York, 1978, p.30.
7. CS to Nadine and Lina Lewin, London, 1 ix 1947. (*SL*)

8. Angela Carter, 'Unhappy Families', *London Review of Books*, 16 September–6 October 1982, p.12. Carter claims that the change of style occurred after *The Man*. In my opinion, it occurred after *Love*.
9. CS to Nettie Palmer, New York, 8 i 1936. (*SL*)
10. CS to Anderson, London, 7 ii 1950.
11. Ibid., 8 vi 1947.
12. Ibid., 9 iii 1963.
13. CS uses the term to describe David Flack in *Tea* (p.80).
14. CS, 'Les Amoureux. (Life of Two Writers)', *Ocean*, p.504.
15. *Tea*, pp.55–6.
16. CS, 'Les Amoureux', p.504. (The maid's comment was: 'Is that a life, typing all day?')
17. CS to Anderson, London, 8 vi 1947.
18. CS to Nettie Palmer, Lausanne, 5 xii 1950. (Palmer papers.) (*SL*)
19. *Tea*, p.19.
20. Ibid., p.31.
21. Ibid., p.32.
22. Ibid., p.33.
23. Ibid., pp.51–2.
24. Ibid., pp.80–1.
25. CS to Gilbert Stead, Montreux, 2 i 1948.
26. CS interviewed by Rodney Wetherell (1980), published in *Australian Literary Studies*, vol. 9, no. 4, October 1980.
27. Blake to FJ, Lausanne, 8 xii 1948. (FJ papers.)
28. Blake told Burnshaw: 'Laski saw some of the book in London and lavished praise on it: I do not value his opinion but his publicity reaction surprised me happily.' (Lausanne, 3 ii 1949.) To Blake, Laski was a Labour man, not a genuine Marxist.
29. CS to FJ, Montreux, 1 ii 1948.
30. CS to Mike Gold, London, 13 vii 1947.
31. Peter Davies married Margaret Ruthven, daughter of Lord Ruthven, in 1932.
32. See Colin Chambers, *The Story of Unity Theatre*, Lawrence & Wishart, London, 1989.
33. Sydney *Sun*, 9 October 1946.
34. Ibid., 6 October 1946.
35. Australian Archives, Canberra, Series A425/1, item 49/1976.
36. Review of *Letty*, *Sydney Morning Herald*, 1 March 1947. (It was signed K. M.—Kenneth 'Seaforth' MacKenzie. Information courtesy Margaret Harris.)
37. Theo Moody, 'They call her book obscene', *Daily Telegraph* (Sydney), 25 October 1946.
38. *For Love Alone* had been translated into Italian as *Tutto accade a chi Vuole* (Baldini & Castoldi, Rome, 1947) and French as *Vent d'amour* (Editions des Deux Rives, Paris, 1948).
39. CS to Anderson, London, 30 viii 1947.
40. CS to Anderson, London, 10 ix 1947.
41. Ibid., 23 ix 1947.
42. CS to Blake, Paris, 29 ix 1947. (NLA, Box 16, folders 119–20.)
43. CS to Mike Gold, Montreux, 3 xi 1947.
44. CS to Anderson, Montreux, 7 x 1947.
45. In 1949, Leo Huberman set up the *Monthly Review* with Paul Sweezy. In 1952 he established the Monthly Review Press, for books which would not otherwise find a publisher in the era of McCarthyism.
46. CS to Kate Stead (undated, June 1951).
47. CS to Anderson, Montreux, 13 xi 1947.
48. Otto Friedrich, *City of Nets*, Harper & Row, New York, pp.332–6.
49. CS to Aida Kotlarsky, undated. (Probably early September 1947). (Don Shaw papers, New York.)
50. CS to Mike Gold, Montreux, 3 xi 1947.
51. Ibid.
52. CS, 'Jan Callowjan', NLA, Box 6, folder 45. 'The Azhdanov Tailors', *Ocean*, pp.115–25.
53. CS to Anderson, Montreux, 20 i 1948.
54. 'Trains', *Ocean*, p.390.
55. CS to Gilbert Stead, London, 12 iv 1949.
56. CS to GW-S, 10 iii 1949.

57. CS to Gilbert Stead, 12 iv 1949.
58. CS to FJ, Montreux, 1 ii 1948. (FJ papers.)
59. CS to Blake, Montreux, 11 iii 1948.
60. *Cotters'* p.231.
61. CS to GW-S, London, 16 vii 1949. Colin Roderick had written a confused review of *Letty* in *Southerly*, no. 1, 1948, pp.55–8. However, he praised *Beauties* in *Southerly* vol. 7, 1946, and Stead's works generally in his *Introduction to Australian Fiction*, A & R, Sydney, 1950.
62. CS to Nettie Palmer, St Germain-en-Laye, 9 v 1951. (*SL*)
63. CS to Pilar Libenson, Bologna, 10 v 1948. (Unsent.) NLA, Box 7, folder 50.
64. CS to FJ, Bologna, 16 v 1948.
65. Blake to FJ, Lausanne, 8 xii 1948.
66. In *Dogs*, Edward Massine feels elated during a huge post-war May Day march in New York (pp.105–9).
67. CS to FJ, Bologna, 16 v 1948.
68. Ibid.
69. It was published in 1950: by Doubleday in New York, and Cassell in London.
70. CS to Anderson, Basle, 7 vii 1948.
71. Ibid., Lausanne, 5 x 1948.
72. Ibid., Lausanne, 15 i 1949.
73. Robert Knittel, 'Unpleasant little group', *New York Times Book Review*, 22 August 1948, p.13.
74. Anonymous review of *Tea*, in *Time*, 13 September 1948, p.39.
75. CS to FJ, Basle, 10 vi 1948.
76. Jerome Stern, review of *The Angel*, New York, Doubleday, 1950; *New York Compass*, 13 July 1950, p.19.
77. 'Bill is going through, saying "You said that fourteen times before" etc. He is really a wonderful help and an angel. All this takes place without my tearing out his hair or mine. Miraculous but true.' (CS to Anderson, Lausanne, 6 xi 1948.)
78. Blake to FJ, Lausanne, 28 x 1948.
79. CS to GW-S, Montreux, 12 xi 1950.
80. Dymphna Cusack angrily raised the issue of overseas royalties in *Meanjin*, vol. 51, no. 4, 1952, pp.406–10. 'Best-sellers don't pay'.
81. CS to GW-S, Lausanne, 10 iii 1949.
82. Blake to Burnshaw, Lausanne, 3 ii 1949.
83. CS to FJ, Lausanne, 28 iii 1949.
84. Blake to CS, Milan, undated. (Early May 1949.) (NLA, Box 16, folder 119.)
85. Conversation with Julie James Bailey, Sydney, 4 April 1988.
86. CS to Gilbert Stead, London, 12 iv 1949.
87. CS to GW-S, London, 3 vi 1949.
88. CS to Anderson, London, 27 viii 1949.
89. Ibid., London, 22 ix 1949.
90. CS to FJ, London, 17 vi 1949.
91. CS to Kate Stead, London, 29 vi 1949.
92. Nellie Cook is 'a strange thing', with a 'beak' and forward-bending backbone and 'thin long legs stepping prudently, gingerly, like a marsh bird'. *Cotters'*, p.13. The real-life description of Anne Dooley (apparently very similar to the fictional portrait) comes from Ruth Hall.
93. In *Cotters'* (pp.239–41), CS describes one of these car trips with 'Tom'. Stead's fictional counterpart is Frida, a fair woman, who ponders him surreptitiously while he drives.
94. CS to Anderson, London, 27 viii 1949.
95. Ruth McKenney & Richard Bransten, *Here's England*, Rupert Hart-Davis, London, 1951.
96. CS to Anderson, London, 22 ix 1949.
97. CS to Gilbert and Sylvia Stead, London, 24 vii 1950.
98. CS to Blake, Newcastle-upon-Tyne, 29 x 1949.
99. Ibid., 2 xi 1949.
100. Ibid., 7 xi 1949.
101. Blake to CS, 2 xi 1949.
102. Blake is thanked for his 'wise and painstaking counsel' in the Preface of the 1951 edition of *Here's England*. Later editions merely mention his name.

103. Kostov's trial tested the Stalinist propaganda machine to the limit for Kostov, in full view of the Western press, retracted the forced 'confession' which formed the basis of the case against him. Kostov was later executed. The so-called 'show trials' were losing credibility.
104. CS to Aida Kotlarsky, London, 29 xii 1949. (Don Shaw papers.)
105. CS to GW-S, London, 8 i 1950.
106. CS to Rodney Pybus, 16 xi 1968. (Unsent—at least in this form.) (*SL*)
107. Rodney Pybus, '*Cotters' England*: In Appreciation', *Stand*, vol. 23, no. 4, 1982, pp.40–7.
108. CS to Anderson, London, 20 i 1950.
109. CS to GW-S, London, 8 i 1950.
110. *Dymphna*. Norman Freehill with Dymphna Cusack, Thomas Nelson, Melbourne, 1975, p.60.
111. CS to Dorothy Green, 14 iii 1976. (NLA, Dorothy Green papers.)
112. CS to Anderson, 6 ii 1951. Unsent. (NLA, Box 7, folder 50.)
113. CS to Aida Kotlarsky, London, 29 xii 1949.
114. CS to FJ, Basle, 10 vi 1948.
115. CS to Anderson, London, 20 i 1950.
116. Ibid., Lausanne, 13 xii 1950.
117. Burnshaw to me, 31 vii 1992.
118. CS to Anderson, Montreux, 11 x 1950.
119. Ibid., Brussels, 25 x 1952.
120. *Laughing*, p.437.
121. CS to Burnshaws, 6 iii 1967. (*SL*)
122. *Laughing*, p.24.
123. Ibid., pp.71–2.
124. CS to Anderson, Montreux, 11 x 1950.
125. Ibid.
126. On 5 October 1965, when Stead was thinking of returning to *Laughing*, which she had put aside, she asked Burnshaw if he would lend her his letters from Richard Bransten. 'I use them, not verbatim, of course; but to get the right feeling for dialogue.' Burnshaw did not send them.
127. Blake to Ruth Blake, Leipzig, 20 iii 1950. (Ruth Hall papers.)
128. Ibid., Montreux, 16 x 1950. (Ruth Hall papers.)
129. Blake to CS, Leipzig, Tuesday. (Undated, March 1950)
130. Ibid., 14 iii 1950. (NLA, Box 16, folder 119.)
131. Blake to Ruth Blake, Montreux, 16 x 1950. (Ruth Hall papers.)
132. CS to Kate Stead, London, 2 vi 1950. (Kate Stead papers.)
133. CS to Nettie Palmer, Lausanne, 5 xii 1950. (*SL*)
134. CS to Anderson, 14 xi 1950.
135. CS to Gilbert Stead, London, 24 vii 1950.
136. CS to Anderson, London, 20 vii 1950.
137. Ibid.
138. Jack Lindsay, *Life Rarely Tells*, Penguin, Harmondsworth, 1982, p.804.
139. CS to Gilbert Stead, London, 24 vii 1950.
140. CS, 'A View of Australian Fiction', *National Times*, 18–23 October 1976.
141. CS to Anderson, Brussels, 21 viii 1950.
142. CS to GW-S, Montreux, 12 xi 1950.
143. CS to Anderson, Montreux, 11 x 1950.
144. CS to GW-S, 12 xi 1950.
145. CS to Anderson, Montreux, 11 x 1950.
146. *The God that Failed*, Hamish Hamilton, London, 1950. The other four ex-communists are Louis Fischer, Arthur Koestler, Ignazio Silone and Stephen Spender.
147. CS to Anderson, Lausanne, 27 xii 1950.
148. Ibid.
149. CS, diary, 'The Travellers' Bed and Breakfast', 7 November 1950. Box 15, folder 111.
150. Diary, 5 December 1950. (NLA, Box 15, folder 111.)
151. Ibid., 16 January 1951.
152. CS to Anderson, Lausanne, 13 xii 1950.
153. Diary, 7 December 1950. (NLA, Box 15, folder 111.)
154. Ibid.

155. Conversation with Bill Ash, Blake's literary executor, London, 24 September 1987.
156. CS to Aida Kotlarsky, St Germain-en-Laye, 21 iii 1951.
157. CS, 'The Captain's House', *Ocean*, p.280.
158. 'The Captain's House' and 'Yac, Yac' are in *Ocean*, presumably written around this time.
159. CS to Aida Kotlarsky, 21 iii 1951. (Don Shaw papers.)
160. Diary, 19 March 1951. (NLA, Box 15, folder 111.)
161. CS to Anderson, St Germain-en-Laye, 16 iv 1951.
162. Ibid.
163. Diary, 17 April 1951.
164. CS to Anderson, St Germain-en-Laye, 16 iv 1951.
165. Diary, 17 April 1951.
166. In 'Girl from the Beach', the girl, Linda, discovers letters to her father from Laura, in which Laura alludes to his women friends. (*Ocean*, p.224) Janet Bloom says this really happened.
167. Conversation with Janet Ladenheim (née Bloom), New Jersey, 17 August 1988.
168. Blake had first met Henry Jordan in Hollywood in 1942.
169. The novella, published for the first time that year, was one of a collection of four in *Puzzleheaded*.
170. Conversation with Mike Bloom, New York, 5 August 1988.
171. Conversation with Janet Ladenheim, 17 August 1988. Though she says that most of the story is 'true', she did not go back to the States and marry the 'boy from the Beach'. She married in 1959.
172. CS to Kate Stead, Brussels, 30 v 1951.
173. CS to GW-S, 25 vi 1951.
174. Conversation with Kate Stead, Sydney, 20 January 1987.
175. CS to Burnshaw, 4 x 1975.
176. Conversation with Kate Stead, 20 January 1987.
177. *The Man*, p.332.
178. 'The Oats Fantasia', NLA, Box 5, folder 31.
179. 'The Lodger in the Bones', NLA, Box 5, folder 34.
180. Ibid.
181. CS to Anderson, Paris, 23 ix 1951.
182. Ibid.

12: Literary Hacks

1. CS to GW-S, Paris, 16 vii 1952.
2. Ibid.
3. CS to Geering, 13 vii 1967. (*SL*)
4. CS to Geering, 23 viii 1978.
5. R. G. Howarth, review of *The Aunt's Story*, *Southerly*, no. 4, 1950, pp.209–10.
6. *Southerly*, no. 2, 1952. It was the first chapter of the short novel she had begun in Lausanne in the late Forties. She was now completing it, but it would not be published until 1973 —under the title *The Little Hotel*.
7. R. G. Howarth, 'Christina Stead', in *Biblionews*, vol. 11, no. 1, January 1958, p.18.
8. CS to Walter Stone (editor of *Biblionews*), 24 iii 1958. (*SL*)
9. CS to GW-S, Paris, 16 vii 1952.
10. Anne Matheson was once personal secretary of E. W. MacAlpine. At this time. Stead thought her 'a splendid woman'. Later, Anne Matheson became one more of Stead's women friends to be denigrated as a 'lesbian'.
11. CS to Anderson, Brussels, 25 x 1952.
12. The divorce certificate for William James Blech and Mollie Grossman is among Ruth Blake's papers.
13. The marriage certificate for William James Blake (otherwise Blech) and Christina Ellen Stead is held by Gilbert Stead in his family archives.
14. *Love*, p.461.
15. CS to FJ, Paris, 18 iv 1952.
16. CS to Anderson, London, 4 xi 1952.
17. Ibid., Paris, 24 iii 1952.
18. Ibid.
19. Ibid., Brussels, 25 x 1952.
20. Ibid., 4 xi 1952.
21. Ibid., 25 x 1952.

22. Included in ASIO file on Christina Stead. Australian Archives, Canberra, A6119 XRI. 231.
23. CS to Nettie Palmer, 5 xii 1950. (*SL*)
24. Ibid., St Germain-en-Laye, 9 May 1951. Arthur Phillips' article, 'The Cultural Cringe', appeared in *Meanjin*, vol. 9, no. 4, 1950. Most leftwing intellectuals thought it an excellent piece.
25. CS quotes Nettie Palmer in a letter to FJ, Paris, 16 vi 1952.
26. Nettie Palmer, *Fourteen Years*, Meanjin Press, Melbourne, 1948.
27. The humiliation of the UNESCO incident is transposed into fiction in *Miss Herbert* (pp.271–5). Bob Standfast (note the irony of the name) tells Miss Herbert that 'it would be easy for a girl like her' to find work in UNESCO. She pays the fare from London to Paris in vain.
28. CS to FJ, 16 vi 1952.
29. CS to Ann and Jack Lindsay, Paris, 10 vii 1952. (Jack Lindsay papers, NLA MS 7168.)
30. The Ronkins lived at No. 45 rue de Flandre, Paris XIX.
31. CS to FJ, 16 vi 1952.
32. Blake to FJ, The Hague, 9 ii 1953.
33. CS to Anderson, Paris, 30 iv 1952. Based on experiences in Europe during their wandering years, Stead's stories were now called *The Traveller's Bed and Breakfast*.
34. Diana Brydon, *Christina Stead*, Macmillan, London, 1987, p.138.
35. *Hotel*, p.179.
36. CS to FJ, 18 iv 1952.
37. After CS's irritation with Nettie Palmer, FJ had written a discreet letter to Clem Christesen suggesting he write to Stead at the Paris address she supplied. (FJ to Christesen, Meanjin Papers, Baillieu Library, University of Melbourne.)
38. *Meanjin*, vol. 11, no. 4, 1952, pp.421–3.
39. Francis Jeanson's review, '*Albert Camus ou l'âme révoltée*', appeared in the May 1952 issue of *Les Temps Modernes*.
40. CS to Clem Christesen, Brussels, 7 ix 1952. (Meanjin Papers.) Five years later she would write: 'A shame they gave the NOBEL PRIZE to Camus, a shadow, a 2-dimensional imitator built up by the great publicist Sartre: but if they don't give it to leftists, the field is getting narrower every day.' (CS to Anderson, Leipzig, 23 x 1957.)
41. Clem Christesen to FJ, 3 vi 1953. (Meanjin Papers.) (He quotes Arthur Levy in his letter to FJ.)
42. Dymphna Cusack, 'Paris Journal', *Meanjin*, vol. 12, no. 2, 1953, pp.201–8.
43. Notes by Bill Pearson, NLA, MS 7570, folder 2.
44. CS to Mrs Howarth, London, 16 i 1952. (Stead papers: Harry Ransom Humanities Research Center, University of Texas at Austin.)
45. CS to FJ, Brussels, 16 xi 1952.
46. See Allan Ashbolt, 'The great literary witch-hunt of 1952', *Australia's First Cold War 1945–1953*, Eds. Ann Curthoys and John Merritt, Sydney, George Allen & Unwin, 1984.
47. *Australia-New Zealand Civil Liberties Society Bulletin*, No. 3, March 1953. Bill Pearson papers, NLA, MS 7570, folder 2.
48. The application and references are in the Australian Archives in Canberra, Series A463/18, Item 58/588.
49. Stead and Blake were 'put off by his political worthlessness'. (CS to FJ, Basle, vi 10 1948.)
50. CS wrote about the maid, Louise, in the non-fictional piece, 'Les Amoureux'. She also mentioned her in letters to FJ (11 x 1952) and Anderson (25 x 1952).
51. CS quotes the publisher in a letter to Anderson, 24 iii 1952.
52. HS, *New Republic*, 7 April 1952.
53. John Barkham, *New York Times*, 13 January 1952, p.4.
54. Rose Feld, *New York Herald Tribune Book Review*, 13 January 1952, p.4.
55. CS to Anderson, Brussels, 25 x 1952.
56. Ruth Hall did not divulge who it was. (Conversation with Ruth Hall, 25 September 1988.)
57. The Pension van Son was at No. 4, Laan Copes-van-Cattenburg, The Hague.
58. One of the many examples is a letter to her brother David Stead begun on 14 January 1961, continued on 31 January and finally finished on 29 March. This letter, like many others, was interrupted when the Blakes moved house.
59. CS to FJ, The Hague, 24 xi 1952.
60. Ibid., 3 vii 1953.

61. See 'Les Amoureux'.
62. CS to Anderson, The Hague, 29 i 1953.
63. 'Les Amoureux'. CS to FJ, The Hague, 3 vii 1953.
64. Ibid., 16 i 1953.
65. CS to Anderson, 17 ii 1953.
66. CS to FJ, The Hague, 20 iii 1953.
67. 'Les Amoureux', p.512.
68. William Blake, *Späte Liebe*, tr. Eva Schumann, Aufbauverlag, Berlin, 1957. An extract from the English original would be published in the leftwing American journal *Mainstream* in July 1960.
69. The manuscript is held by Murray Teigh Bloom, an American friend who visited the Blakes in the early Fifties and was shocked by their circumstances. A great admirer of *The World is Mine*, he tried without success to get it re-issued in paperback. (Conversation with M. T. Bloom, Long Island, 8 July 1988.)
70. Blake to FJ, The Hague, 9 ii 1953.
71. *Daily Worker*, 7 iii 1953.
72. CS to Gilbert Stead, The Hague, 17 iii 1953. (*SL*)
73. CS to Anderson, The Hague, 17 ii 1953.
74. CS to FJ, The Hague, 8 vi 1953.
75. Ibid.
76. Ibid., 3 vii 1953.
77. Ibid., 21 v 1953.
78. CS to Anderson, 25 viii 1953.
79. Interview with Laurence Hall, Châteauneuf-de-Grasse, 5 x 1987.
80. CS to FJ, The Hague, 20 ii 1953. Ruth had also met the MacAlpines in Sydney, and Nettie Palmer in Melbourne.
81. Conversation with Tella Friedmann, Greve-in-Chianti, 29 ix 1988.
82. The same detail recurs in 'The Puzzleheaded Girl', *Puzzleheaded*, pp.56–7.
83. '1954: Days of the Roomers', *Ocean*, pp.404–5.
84. CS to GW-S, 31 xii 1953.
85. Stead uses this expression in *Herbert*, when she describes just such a house (p.204).
86. CS to GW-S, London, 31 xii 1953.
87. CS to FJ, 3 xi 1953.
88. FJ to CS, London, 5 xi 1953.
89. CS to FJ, London, 7 xi 1953.
90. Ibid.
91. Ibid, 11 xi 1953.
92. CS to Anderson, 22 ix 1953.
93. '1954: Days of the Roomers'.
94. There is a rough draft of a letter among Stead's papers. CS to Miss Dowding, *Times Literary Supplement*, undated (on back of letter dated January 1954), NLA, Box 7, folder 49.
95. Geering points out that the *Times Literary Supplement*'s 'treatment of certain of the early Stead novels might most charitably be described as incompetent'. He adds that the *TLS* 'made amends in 1974 (24 May) with an excellent review of *The Little Hotel*'—but this was after 1965, when Stead's reputation had been generally re-appraised. (Geering, 'What is Normal? Two recent novels by Christina Stead', *Southerly*, no. 4, 1978, pp.462–73.)
96. The *Times Literary Supplement* reviews were anonymous, but Professor Margaret Harris has checked the *TLS* accounts. There is no evidence of any reviews by Stead.
97. Peter Davies to A. S. Frère, 12 x 1953. (Courtesy Secker & Warburg files, Octopus Publishing Group. Peter Davies was now publishing under the Heinemann imprint.) Did Peter Davies truly appreciate Stead's greatness? He told friends Shakespear and Parkyn that the 'two best books' he ever published were Frederic Manning's *The Middle Parts of Fortune* and *Scenes and Portraits*. (3 ii 1955, Rare Books and Manuscripts, Mitchell Library, Sydney.)
98. William Blake, *Understanding the Americans*, London, Muller, 1954. A surviving copy is dedicated: 'To my môme—this sorry tidbit, Billo (with love)/King Lud's fog factory.' (Copy held by Rare Books, Fisher Library, University of Sydney.) This was perhaps Ruth Blake's copy: *môme* is colloquial French for 'kid' (child). Bill also did occasional research for Murray Teigh Bloom in New York, whose payment in American dollars was particularly welcome.

99. *Great Stories of the South Sea Islands*, selected with a foreword by Christina Stead, Muller, London, 1955. There are nine stories: the best known authors are Jack London, Robert Louis Stevenson, J. A. Michener, Somerset Maugham, William Hope Hodgson.

100. Fernand Gignon, *Colour of Asia*, Muller, London, 1955.

101. CS to GW-S, London, 31 xii 1953.

102. Blake to Anderson, Broadhurst Gardens, 2 vii 1954.

103. CS to Anderson, Broadhurst Gardens, 15 xii 1954.

104. *Herbert*, p.229.

105. Blake to Anderson, 2 vii 1954.

106. CS, '1954: Days of the Roomers', p.407.

107. David Caute makes the point that being a communist was seen as something to be ashamed of and concealed. This atmosphere, and recourse to the Fifth Amendment, prevented ex-communists from standing up and being counted like 'red-blooded' Americans. (*The Great Fear*, Simon & Schuster, New York, 1978, p.103.)

108. Conversation with Jacques Coe, New York, 19 July 1988.

109. Blake's FBI file. This information (including the affidavits in full) is set out in an Office Memorandum, 24 January 1957.

110. Tella refers to Stead's letters as 'nonsense letters'. She destroyed them, thinking them too trite to be of interest. One letter survives, probably never sent, in which CS writes about Hannah Weinstein's wedding. (16 iv 1958.) (*SL*)

111. Blake to Murray T. Bloom, 23 v 1954. (Murray Bloom papers.)

112. CS to Anderson, Broadhurst Gardens, 28 x 1954.

113. Jean Giltène, *The Candid Killer*, (*Trente ans de frousse*), tr. Christina Stead, Muller, London, 1956.

114. Auguste Piccard, *In Balloon and Bathyscaphe*, (*Au Fond des mers en bathyscaphe*), tr. Christina Stead, Cassell, London, 1956.

115. CS to Anderson, Adelaide Rd, 26 i 1956. (The translation was by Grazia Brambilla Pisoni, published by Baldini & Castoldi, Milan, 1953.)

116. W. Augustiny, *The Road to Lambarene*, tr. William Blake, Muller, London, 1956. CS to Neil Stewart, 21 x 1955. (*SL*)

117. Blake to Murray Teigh Bloom, Primrose Gardens, 12 viii 1955. (Murray Bloom papers.)

118. CS to H. Weinstein, 30 xi 1955. Presumably rough draft. She encloses typescript of 'Four Just Men'. (NLA, Box 4, folder 23.)

119. Randall Jarrell, 'Speaking of Books', *New York Times Book Review*, 24 July 1955, p.2.

120. Elizabeth Hardwick, 'The Novels of Christina Stead', *New Republic*, 1 August 1955, pp.17–19. The article would be reprinted, in 1962, in her book *A View of My Own*, New York, Farrer, Strauss & Cudahy, pp.41–8.

121. Conversation with Tella Friedmann, 29 September 1988.

122. CS to Edith Anderson, London, 28 vi 1957.

123. Conversation with GW-S, Sydney, 16 January 1987.

124. Hortense Calisher, *Encounters*, ed. Kai Erikson, Yale University Press, New Haven, 1989. Calisher met Stead in August or September 1956.

125. Blake to Max Schroeder, 26 xi 1955. (Anderson papers.)

126. CS to Anderson, Adelaide Rd, 3 i 1956.

127. Ibid., 2 xi 1956.

128. Ibid., 14 xi 1956.

129. CS interviewed by Joan Lidoff (1973), *Christina Stead*, Ungar, New York, 1982, p.220.

130. *Herbert*, p.249.

131. Ibid., p.257.

132. The friend was Dorothy Green. (Conversation with Dorothy Green, Canberra, 9 April 1988.)

133. *Herbert*, p.265.

134. Ibid., p.258.

135. Ibid., p.278.

136. Ibid., pp.278–9.

137. Ibid., p.55.

138. In many ways, Stead got Simone de Beauvoir quite wrong. She comments on *The Second Sex*: 'Some of it makes me squeamish because it is presented in this gushing untrained way, yet I think it is a first-rate book in many ways, really feminine and therefore of great value for the feminine viewpoint. She is unfortunately sunk in the

Sartre-Kierkegaard tradition, and has more faith in psychoanalysis than is called for . . . but it is sympathetic and the principal thing is that it is the viewpoint of an intelligent woman.' (CS to Anderson, 3 i 1956.)

139. CS to Anderson, 22 x 1956.
140. There is a close resemblance between Eleanor Herbert in Paris and Lydia, the young woman in 'The Dianas'. In this section of *Herbert* Stead obviously had someone other than FJ in mind.
141. Conversation with DDS, Sydney, 9 January 1987.
142. CS to Anderson, 9 viii 1956.
143. CS to Gilbert Stead, 9 x 1956.
144. Ibid., 27 xii 1956.
145. CS to Anderson, 10 ix 1956.
146. CS to Gilbert Stead, 9 x 1956.
147. They were Beryl and John Collard. It was on their farm, in September 1956, that CS took notes on A. S. Makarenko's *A Book for Parents*, for *Herbert*. (NLA, Box 3, folder 18.)
148. Blake to Murray Teigh Bloom, 9 x 1956. (Murray Bloom papers.)
149. CS to Anderson, Adelaide Road, 14 xi 1956.
150. Humboldt had asked Stead for a story. She sent him an extract from *Cotter's*. He asked for changes, and for greater clarity to be worked into the material. She did not want 'to explain it all away' and asked for the story to be sent back to her.
151. CS to Charles Humboldt, 26 i 1957. (Humboldt papers, Manuscripts and Archives, Yale University.) (*SL*)
152. CS to Anderson, 28 vi 1957.
153. CS to Anderson, 24 iv 1957.
154. CS to Neil Stewart, 22 xii 1957. Rare Books and Manuscripts, Fisher Library, University of Sydney.
155. CS to Anderson, 11 x 1957.
156. William Blake, *Maria Meïnhardt*, tr. Roland Schacht, Aufbau verlag, Berlin, 1952.
157. Blake to Anderson, 15 vii 1957.
158. CS to Anderson, 25 vii 1957.
159. She once told Edith: 'I don't like face to face conversations.' (CS to Anderson, 4 vi 1964.)
160. Blake to Klaus Gysi, director of Aufbau, 22 iv 1959. (Aufbau papers, Berlin, courtesy Anderson.)
161. See Peter Kurth, *American Cassandra. The Life of Dorothy Thompson*, Little, Brown & Co, Boston, 1990. During the Thirties, Hermann Budzislawski had been editor of the Marxist *Neue Weltbühne*. (See David Caute, *The Fellow Travellers*, Yale University Press, New Haven, 1973, p.162.)
162. CS to Anderson, Leipzig, 10 x 1957.
163. Ibid., Hotel Elefant, Weimar, 8 xi 1957.
164. Ibid., 30 x 1957.
165. CS to Charlotte Mayerson, undated. (Probably May 1982.) (Mayerson papers.)
166. CS to Neil Stewart, 22 xii 1957.
167. CS to Anderson, 21 vii 1958.
168. Ibid., 8 xi 1957.
169. Conversation with the Friedmanns, Greve-in-Chianti, 29 September 1988.
170. CS to Neil Stewart, London, 6 iii 1958. (*SL*)
171. CS to Anderson, London, 30 xii 1957.
172. Conversation with the Friedmanns, 29 September 1988.
173. 'Foxwarren Hall' diary, NLA, Box 3, folder 21.
174. The same photograph is mentioned in 'Girl from the Beach', *Puzzleheaded*, pp.223, 246.
175. CS to Anderson, 23 ix 1963.
176. Blake to Klaus Gysi, Aufbau, 12 vi 1958. (Aufbau papers, Berlin, courtesy Anderson.)
177. 'Foxwarren Hall' diary, NLA, Box 3, folder 21.
178. They are in the possession of the Blooms' eldest son, Michael Bloom.
179. CS to Eldon Branda, 22 v 1963. (*SL*)
180. CS to Anderson, 7 iii 1961.

181. The surviving draft is among Stead's papers, NLA, Box 3, folder 19. (One page is written on the back of an episode of *Robin Hood!*)
182. CS to Anderson, Camberley, undated. (March or April 1961.)
183. CS to Kate Stead, 21 vii 1960. 'My handwriting made it quite secret, almost from me. But I have deciphered it.' (*SL*) It is her 'Foxwarren Hall' diary, Box 3, folder 21, Box 4, folder 22.
184. CS to Aida Kotlarsky, 18 vii 1960. (Don Shaw papers.)
185. CS to Anderson, 2 ix 1958.
186. Ibid., 31 vii 1959.
187. Stead may have had the character of Tom Cotter in mind.
188. Conversation with Ring Lardner Jnr, Lorne, Victoria, 23 March 1991.
189. They were produced by Sidney Cole, an English producer. Hannah Fisher was executive producer.
190. Howard Koch, *As Time Goes By*, Harcourt Brace Jovanovich, New York, 1979, p.202.
191. At one stage, Stead did some research for Weinstein on a BBC series, *Women in Love*. The title and the idea came from their anthology. Stead complained that Bill was never paid for the idea and she received a mere 'tip' for her research.
192. Stead papers. 'A Killing', from *Fan Pearl*, NLA, Box 3, folder 19.
193. Pasternak, under great pressure in his own country, eventually rejected the prize.
194. CS to Neil Stewart, 31 i 1959. (*SL*)
195. *Friendship*, May–June 1959.
196. See her reviews in *Friendship* of V. Kaverin's *Two Captains* (June 1957), Ritkheyu's *Stories from Chukotka* (August 1957, pp.12–13), Gorky's *Foma Gordeyev* (March 1958), Valentin Katayev, *The Small Farm in the Steppes* (January 1959).
197. Chris Williams found that in 1957 and 1958 Blake published two reviews in *Friendship* under the name W. Stephen Marlowe, a name he had once used on the *Magazine of Wall Street*. (C. Williams, *Christina Stead*, McPhee Gribble, Melbourne, 1989, p.222.)
198. Blake to Burnshaw, 11 x 1961.
199. Conversation with Tella and Boy Friedmann, Greve-in-Chianti, 29 September 1988.
200. CS to Anderson, 16 i 1965.
201. Ibid., 11 xii 1964.
202. Blake to Murray Bloom, 21 ii 1959.
203. Blake to Burnshaw, 30 vi 1959.
204. Blake to Murray Bloom, 21 ii 1959.
205. CS to Anderson, 18 xi 1959.
206. Blake to Burnshaw, 20 ix 1960. Blake's argument resembles Simone de Beauvoir's in *The Second Sex*: that women had not yet dared contest the human situation—that is, expose its contradictions—because they had hardly begun to assume it. (He had read the book and admired it.)
207. Ibid.
208. Stephen Koch, review of *Herbert*, *Saturday Review*, 7 October 1976, p.50.
209. Thomas Shapcott, review of *Herbert*, *Australian*, 30 April 1977.
210. Blake to Burnshaw, 30 vi 1959.
211. CS to Anderson, 29 x 1959.

13: 'Bill, My True Companion'

1. Blake to Burnshaw, 31 viii 1960.
2. Ibid., 2 xii 1960.
3. Blake to Burnshaws, 17 xii 1960.
4. Conversation with Mike Bloom, New York, 31 July 1988.
5. Conversation with Boyce and Tella Friedmann, Greve-in-Chianti, 29 September 1988. Conversation with Pera Koston, Oxford, 27 October 1988.
6. Among Stead's married female friends, Edith Anderson, Ruth Bakwin, Betty Collard (a leftwing activist who ran a newspaper on Middle Eastern affairs) and Anne Dooley were all supposed to be 'lesbians'.
7. CS to Norman Rosten, 7 viii 1967. NLA, Box 14, folder 109.
8. Anderson to me. Undated letter, 1989.
9. Conversation with Anderson, Berlin, 2 November 1988.

10. CS to Anderson, 10 i 1961.
11. Anderson to me. Undated letter, 1989.
12. CS to Doris and David Stead. The letter was begun on 14 i 1961, continued on 31 i and completed on 29 iii. (Gilbert Stead papers.)
13. Northbrook, Hawley Lane, Hawley, near Camberley, Surrey.
14. CS to DDS and Doris Stead, 14 i 1961.
15. CS to Anderson, 9 iii 1963.
16. CS to Anderson. Undated. (Around the end of March, 1961.)
17. Blake to Burnshaws, 5 iv 1961.
18. Ibid.
19. Conversation with Ruth Hall, Châteauneuf-de-Grasse, 5 x 1987.
20. CS to Anderson, 16 v 1961.
21. Blake had approached Jarrell about it, but the idea was eventually considered too great a financial risk. Blake to Randall Jarrell, 20 iii 1956. (Randall Jarrell papers, Henry W. and Albert A. Berg Collection, Astor, Lenox and Tilden Foundations, New York Public Library.)
22. Stanley Burnshaw, *Robert Frost Himself*, George Braziller, New York, 1986, p. 178.
23. Blake to Burnshaw, 27 viii 1963.
24. CS and Blake to Burnshaw, 13? ix 1963. (Date unclear.)
25. CS to Anderson, 22 iii 1963.
26. CS to Burnshaw, 17 iv 1964.
27. Blake to Burnshaw, 15 x 1962.
28. Ibid., 31 vii 1963.
29. CS to Anderson, 11 xii 1964.
30. Blake to Burnshaws, 4 xii 1962.
31. CS to Maurice Temple Smith, 31 i 1968. (Secker & Warburg papers, University of Reading.)
32. CS to Anderson, 22 iii 1963.
33. Conversation with Boyce and Tella Friedmann, 29 September 1988.
34. Conversation with Philip and Leah Harvey, 20 September 1987. Conversation with Pera Koston, 27 October 1988.
35. Conversation with Philip and Leah Harvey, London, 20 September 1987.
36. Blake to Burnshaw, 28 ix 1962.
37. Ibid., 1 vii 1962.
38. CS to Barbara Baer, 10 i 1974. (Baer papers.)
39. CS to Anderson, 9 iii 1963.
40. Ibid., 11 xii 1964.
41. Ibid., 4 vi 1964.
42. Ibid., 21 vii 1964.
43. Ibid., 11 xii 1964.
44. 'What a delightful comical fellow, full of genial ideas and creative impulses.' (CS to Paul Koston, 15 v 1967.) (*SL*)
45. Conversation with Paul Koston, Brighton, England, 8 November 1988.
46. Conversation with Pera Koston, Oxford, 27 October 1988.
47. Conversation with Paul Koston, 8 November 1988.
48. CS to Paul Koston, 19 xi 1964.
49. CS to Rodney Pybus, 16 xi 1968. (*SL*) 'The Girl from the Beach' was based on Janet Bloom; 'The Dianas' was based loosely on Nadine Lewin (also part model for Jacky in *Letty*).
50. At first Stead thought of calling it *The Dianas*, after another of the stories. She commented that she had read Jules Vallès' 'Les Réfractaires' several times during the writing of the novellas, for he also described the puzzleheaded sort of girl. (CS to Neil Stewart, 2 x 1965.) (*SL*)
51. CS to Burnshaw, 22 vii 1965. (*SL*)
52. CS to Anderson, 27 viii 1963.
53. Stead replied: 'Thank you for letting me use the letters, I thought you would; but it's good of you. I am sorry I can't let you have them too. I thought of various ways; could I type them all out and send you copies? But with YOUR treasury of correspondence, it would be rather an undertaking.' (23 ix 1963.)

54. CS to Anderson, 11 xii 1964.
55. These letters were in Stead's possession at the time of her death.
56. CS to Anderson, 5 i 1965.
57. Ibid., 25 xi 1965.
58. Anderson to me, 3 xi 1988.
59. CS to Anderson, 8 xii 1965. It was their second to last communication. The last was after Bill died. Edith, temporarily in New York, sent Christina a lace handkerchief and condolences. Stead replied on 11 v 1968: 'Thank you for the sweet and delicate thought: that is like you. The handkerchief is delicious. I trust I will be in New York June 5 or so, c/o Burnshaw. [She gives Burnshaw's address.] Are you well? Are you staying in NY, living there I mean? As ever, Christina.'
60. 'More Lives than One', NLA, Box 1, folder 1, and 'Agnes', NLA, Box 5, folder 34.
61. 'Agnes', NLA, Box 5, folder 34.
62. CS to Barbara Baer, 7 x 1972. (Baer papers.)
63. CS to Dorothy Green, 31 iii 1970. (NLA, MS 54678, Box 6.)
64. CS to Burnshaw, 14 ix 1965.
65. Ibid., 18 ix 1965.
66. CS to Paul Koston, 25 i 1965. (Koston papers.)
67. CS to Maurice Temple Smith, 7 xi 1966. (Secker & Warburg papers.)
68. The novel's complex symbolism is influenced by folklore and ballads from north-east England. (CS to Rella, 17 iv 1967.)
69. CS to George Lanning, editor of *Kenyon Review*, 18 v 1965. (Courtesy of Chris Williams.)
70. CS to Burnshaw, 23 ii 1965. (*SL*)
71. CS to Paul Koston, 25 i 1965.
72. CS to Burnshaws, 14 ix 1965. (*SL*)
73. CS to Geering, 13 vii 1967. (*SL*)
74. In Freudian terms, Stead exhibited 'repetition compulsion'—a perpetual recurrence of the same destructive behaviour patterns. (Sigmund Freud, 'Beyond the Pleasure Principle', in *On Metapsychology*, The Pelican Freud Library, vol. 11, Penguin, Harmondsworth, p.292.)
75. CS interview with Ann Whitehead (1973), *Australian Literary Studies*, vol. 6, no. 3, May 1974, p.247.
76. Conversation with Ruth Hall, 6 October 1987.
77. Burnshaw says: 'I told her, "It's your imagination! Chris is crazy about men." But she was sure.' (Conversation with Burnshaw, 5 June 1988.)
78. Conversation with Pera Koston, Oxford, 27 October 1988.
79. CS to GW-S, 13 vi 1972. (GW-S papers.)
80. *Beauties*, pp.69–70.
81. Conversation with Pera Koston, 27 October 1988.
82. 'A Household', written in Basle in 1952, was meant for the collection of short stories called *The Traveller's Bed and Breakfast*, which was never completed. *Southerly*, no. 4, 1962, *Christina Stead Special Issue*.
83. 'UNO 1945'. It appeared in *Southerly* with the sub-heading: 'Chapter One of an unpublished novel *I'm Dying Laughing*'. In the final, posthumously published version of the novel, it is Chapter Four.
84. Geering, 'The Achievement of Christina Stead', *Southerly*, no. 4, 1962, pp.193–212.
85. CS to Eldon Branda, 22 v 1963. (*SL*)
86. Jarrell received $300 for his Introduction.
87. James Burns Singer to Frederick Warburg, 13 iv 1964. (Secker & Warburg papers.)
88. Blake to Murray Bloom, 1 xii 1964.
89. CS to Burnshaw, 15 xii 1964. (*SL*)
90. Ibid., 7 xii 1964. (*SL*)
91. Ibid., 23 ii 1965. (*SL*)
92. CS to Randall Jarrell, 16 iii 1965. (Jarrell papers.)
93. CS to Burnshaw, 23 ii 1965. (*SL*)
94. CS to Randall Jarrell, 8 ix 1965. (Jarrell papers.)
95. Ibid.
96. Peter Taylor and Robert Penn Warren (eds), *Randall Jarrell, 1914–1965*, Farrar, Straus & Giroux, New York, 1967, pp.101–12.
97. CS to Oliver Stallybrass, 19 x 1965. (Secker & Warburg papers.)

98. CS to Mary Jarrell, 15 ix 1966. (Jarrell papers.)
99. (I deduce his question from the answer.) Stead's reply was mysterious: 'How does it feel to be "famous"—My dear Stanley ... to tell you, would be to tell you a big secret, not fit for print.' (CS to Burnshaw, 2 iv 1965.) (*SL*)
100. Harry Bloom to CS, 20 iv 1965. (NLA, Box 15, folder 114.)
101. Cecil Hemley, *Saturday Review*, 10 April 1965, p.44.
102. Christopher Ricks, *New York Review of Books*, 17 June 1965, p.14.
103. Jose Yglesias, *Nation*, 5 April 1965.
104. 'I do like the Jose Yglesias review very much, it is pertinent and canny (leaving out the kind remarks).' (CS to Burnshaw, 2 iv 1965.) 'I have just been proclaimed a "Marxian muse" to everyone's astonishment, my own not least.' (CS to Harry Bloom, 23 iv 1965. (Michael Bloom papers.)
105. Burnshaw to CS, 28 iv 1965. (Burnshaw papers.)
106. Patrick White provided this quote for publicity purposes. A Secker & Warburg in-house memorandum citing White is dated 22 June 1966, from Maurice Temple Smith to Harvey Fothergill. (Secker & Warburg files.)
107. CS to Anne and Harry Bloom, 23 iv 1965.
108. CS to Burnshaws, 10 vi 1965. (*SL*)
109. Burnshaw to CS, July 1965. (Exact date unknown.) (Stanley Burnshaw papers, Harry Ransom Humanities Research Center, University of Texas at Austin.)
110. Oliver Stallybrass' publisher's report on *The Puzzleheaded Girl*, 9 June 1965. (Secker & Warburg files.)
111. CS to Oliver Stallybrass, 22 x 1965. (Secker & Warburg files.)
112. Conversation with Philip and Leah Harvey, London, 20 September 1987.
113. Fred Warburg to Charlotte Mayerson, 17 ii 1966. (Secker & Warburg files.)
114. Oliver Stallybrass to Charlotte Mayerson, 31 xii 1965.
115. Oliver Stallybrass to CS, 30 xii 1965. (Secker & Warburg files.)
116. The title was actually CS's second choice. She told Warburg: 'There is a dancing in a hall of mirrors; and the entire story of this eccentric brother and sister is a dancing, nothing but reflections.' (CS to Frederick Warburg, 22 ii 1966.)
117. CS to Burnshaw, 18 ix 1965.
118. CS to Ruth Hall, 4 vi 1975. (Ruth Hall papers.)
119. Blake to Harry Bloom, 21 ix 1965.
120. CS to Aida Kotlarsky, 8 i 1968.
121. Russell Jacoby writes: 'The *Monthly Review* authors stood largely outside the universities and they wrote for the educated reader ... They are last generation Marxist intellectuals, having more in common with Edmund Wilson and Lewis Mumford than with the university Marxists who follow them.' (Russell Jacoby, *The Last Intellectuals*, Basic Books, New York, 1987, pp.176–9.)
122. CS to Burnshaw, 4 v 1965.
123. Ibid., 26 iv 1965.
124. CS to Aida Kotlarsky, 18 vii 1960.
125. Conversation with Tella and Boyce Friedmann, Greve-in-Chianti, 29 September 1988.
126. Conversation with Philip Harvey, London, 20 September 1987.
127. CS to Burnshaws, 18 v 1965.
128. Ibid., 10 vi 1965.
129. R. J. Scholfield, *Bulletin*, 22 May 1965, pp.29–31.
130. CS to Burnshaw, 9 vii 1965. (*SL*)
131. Conversation with Charlotte Mayerson, New York, 26 July 1988.
132. 'The Puzzleheaded Girl', *Kenyon Review*, vol. 27, no. 3, 1965, pp.399–456.
133. It was published as 'The Huntress' in the *Saturday Evening Post*, 23 October 1965, pp.76–89.
134. Blake to Harry Bloom, 21 ix 1965. (Michael Bloom papers.)
135. Harry Bloom to Blake, 10 viii 1965. (NLA, Box 15, folder 114.)
136. CS to Burnshaw, 9 iv 1966.
137. Ibid.
138. CS to Harry Bloom, 16 ix 1965.
139. Ibid. Philip Harvey remembers Stead upbraiding herself along the lines: 'Why do I write about all these worthless people? Why don't I write about someone positive and worthwhile?' (Conversation with Philip Harvey, 20 September 1987.)

140. Stead wrote, or revised, a number of other stories around this time. She refers to them as 'Eleanor', 'The Painted Ceiling', and 'The Spirit of the Living'. None of them are published.
141. CS to Harry Bloom, 14 xi 1965.
142. Christina Stead, *The Palace with Several Sides: A Sort of Love Story*. First published by Officina Brindabella, Canberra, 1986, ed. R. G. Geering. Reprinted in *Southerly*, no. 2, 1987, pp.115–25.
143. CS to Paul and Pera Koston, 15 iii 1966. (Paul Koston papers.)
144. CS to Burnshaw. Undated. (March or April 1966.)
145. CS to Percia Stead, Surbiton, 25 vi 1966. (*SL*)
146. CS to Burnshaw, 10 xi 1966. (*SL*)
147. Robert Lowell to Burnshaw, 3 x 1964. (Stanley Burnshaw papers.)
148. CS to Burnshaws, 13 vii 1967. (*SL*)
149. Conversation with Norman Rosten, Brooklyn, 15 October 1987.
150. Hortense Calisher, 'Seeking out Christina Stead', *Encounters*, ed. Kai Erikson, Yale University Press, New Haven and London, 1989, p.87–8.
151. CS to Burnshaw. Undated. (March or April 1966.)
152. CS to Judah Waten, Puerto Rico, 2 v 1966. (NLA, Waten papers, MS 4536/2/859.) (*SL*)
153. Conversation with Janet Ladenheim (née Bloom) and Michael Bloom, New Jersey, 17 August 1988. They heard this from their parents.
154. CS to Burnshaw. Undated. (March or April 1966.)
155. Conversation with Michael Bloom, 31 July 1988.
156. Judah Waten had not bothered to check his facts for his article in the *Age* (19 February 1966, p.22). For example, he wrote of Stead: 'When she left Australia quite a while before the second world war she was already well known, indeed famous, as a novelist, regarded by many critics as one of our best.' Waten was plainly more impressed by Jack Lindsay. ('I believe that Australia has never produced a greater man of letters.')
157. CS to Judah Waten, Puerto Rico, 2 v 1966. (*SL*)
158. CS to Burnshaws, 20 xi 1967.
159. CS to Judah Waten, 2 v 1966. (*SL*)
160. CS to Anne and Harry Bloom, 31 v 1966. (Michael Bloom papers.)
161. CS to Burnshaws, 20 xi 1967.
162. CS to Percia Stead, 25 vi 1966. (*SL*)
163. CS to Burnshaw, 6 xii 1966.
164. CS to Burnshaws, 10 xi 1966. (*SL*)
165. Conversation with Burnshaw, New York, 5 June 1988.
166. Burnshaw to CS, 27 ii 1967. (Burnshaw papers.)
167. Cyrilly Abels to Maurice Temple Smith, 30 vii 1968. (Secker & Warburg papers.)
168. Maurice Temple Smith to CS, 11 vii 1968. (Secker & Warburg papers.)
169. Joseph Mathewson, *New York Times Book Review*, 11 September 1966, p.4.
170. CS to Elisabeth Gold, 22 v 1967. (Mike Folsom papers.) Extracts from the letter were published in the *Daily Worker*, 17 June 1967.
171. CS to Paul Koston, 15 v 1967. (*SL*)
172. CS to Aida Kotlarsky, 8 i 1968. (Don Shaw papers.)
173. CS to Burnshaw, 8 i 1968. (*SL*)
174. CS to Aida Kotlarsky, 8 i 1968. (Don Shaw papers.)
175. CS to Paul Koston, 16 x 1967. (Koston papers.)
176. CS to Rellas, 8 i 1968.
177. CS to Aida Kotlarsky, 8 i 1968.
178. Australian currency was decimalised in February 1966: one pound became two dollars. In 1967, a lecturer's salary in Australia ranged from $5400 to $7300.
179. He had vowed to accept no more prizes—though he did accept the Nobel Prize for Literature in 1973.
180. 'The Britannica Australia Awards Constitution'. (Clement Semmler papers.)
181. The Committee members were Vincent Buckley and Professor Sam Goldberg of the University of Melbourne; Geoffrey Dutton, publisher; Professor R. Quentin of the University of New South Wales; Wally Hamilton and Clement Semmler of the Australian Broadcasting Commission.
182. W. S. Hamilton to Clement Semmler, 21 ix 1967. (Clement Semmler papers.)

183. Minutes of Meeting of General Council held in Sydney on 27 October 1969. (Clement Semmler papers.)
184. Clement Semmler to Mr J. Salmon, General Manager, Encyclopaedia Britannica Inc., 13 xi 1967. (Clement Semmler papers.)
185. Stuart Sayers, 'Novelist deprived of $10,000 award', *Age*, 12 December 1967, p.6.
186. *Australian*, 13 December 1967.
187. Letters to editor, *Sydney Morning Herald*, 13 xii 1967, p.2.
188. Lyndon Dadswell, a Sydney sculptor, won the art award that year.
189. CS to Kate Stead, 12 xii 1967. (Catherine Stead papers.)
190. CS to Harry Bloom, 13 xii 1967. (Michael Bloom papers.)
191. Sir Robert Madgwick refers to 'vexed questions, such as the overseas talent drain' in his Preface to *Literary Australia*, eds. Clement Semmler and Derek Whitelock, F. W. Cheshire, Melbourne, 1966.
192. Jean Rhys had been writing in the Thirties, but had only just been 'discovered', at the age of 76, with her recent novel *Wide Sargasso Sea*.
193. Nin Hutton, 'Christina Stead—born to write', *Age*, 17 October 1969.
194. In December 1968, Stead's cousin Elsie Ford (née Butters) sent a heartfelt letter to the *Sydney Morning Herald* explaining that Christina Stead had never been able to afford to make the trip home. ('Before judgement is passed on absent Australians who live and work abroad it surely should be ascertained whether they could, in fact, return here and still be able to support themselves.') (*SMH*, 6 December 1968.)
195. *Sydney Morning Herald*, 30 November 1968.
196. Conversation with Philip Harvey, London, 20 September 1987.
197. Blake to Blooms, 16 xi 1967. (Michael Bloom papers.)
198. CS to Aida Kotlarsky, 8 i 1968.
199. CS to Burnshaw, 8 i 1968. (*SL*)
200. CS to Aida Kotlarsky, 8 i 1968.
201. There are five letters from Stead to Blake in hospital, which Geering did not wish me to peruse, and which are closed until 2001. They apparently begin: 'My darling boy . . .' NLA, Box 16, folders 119–20.
202. CS to Aida Kotlarsky, 8 i 1968.
203. Conversation with Ruth Hall, Châteauneuf-de-Grasse, 5 October 1987.
204. William Ash, 'In Memory of Bill Blake', *Monthly Review*, June 1968, p.62.
205. CS to Kate Stead, 20 i 1968.
206. CS to Aida Kotlarsky, 24 i 1968.
207. CS to Burnshaw, 22 iv 1968.
208. CS to Burnshaws, 10 ii 1968. (*SL*)
209. Ibid.
210. Conversation with Philip Harvey, 20 September 1987.
211. Stead added (showing how concerned she was to be reticent about their personal life): 'Although I try not to gossip on this unlucky subject, I have had to write a good many letters.' (CS to Burnshaw, 1 ii 1968.)
212. CS to Burnshaw, 16 iv 1968. Burnshaw used these words in a poem he wrote about Bill Blake.
213. Conversation with Ruth Hall, 5 October 1987.
214. CS to Aida Kotlarsky, 5 ii 1968. After Blake's death, Stanley Burnshaw sent Stead a poem, 'Friend Across the Ocean', dedicated to Bill, which Stead found deeply moving. It begins:

    I go to my quiet bed, put out the light, prepare to sleep
    And my friend across the ocean lies in his sickbed
    waiting.

    Dying with nothing more to reach for . . .
    The poem is included in Stanley Burnshaw, *In the Terrified Radiance*, George Braziller, New York, 1972, p.54.

14: Hundred Thousand Regrets

1. CS to Hyrell and Judah Waten, 24 xi 1978. (Judah Waten papers, NLA, MS 4536, Box 13, folder marked Correspondence.)
2. CS to Burnshaw, 19 i 1969.
3. CS to Anne and Harry Bloom, 5 ii 1968. (Michael Bloom papers.)

4. Conversation with Philip and Leah Harvey, London, 20 September 1987.
5. CS to Aida Kotlarsky, 5 ii 1968. (Don Shaw papers.)
6. Ibid.
7. CS to Harry Bloom, 5 ii 1968. (Michael Bloom papers.)
8. CS to Burnshaws, 10 ii 1968.
9. CS to Burnshaws, 15 ii 1968.
10. Conversation with Ruth Hall, Châteauneuf-de-Grasse, 5 October 1987.
11. CS to Ruth Hall, 30 iv 1969. (Ruth Hall papers.)
12. William Ash, 'In Memory of Bill Blake', *Monthly Review*, June 1968, pp.62–3.
13. CS to Paul Koston, 16 viii 1968.
14. Conversation with William Ash, London, 24 September 1987. For more about Ash see William Ash, *A Red Square*, Howard Baker, London, 1978.
15. Bill Ash still has the manuscript on imperialism and the guide to Marxism that Blake wrote in the Sixties. Murray Teigh Bloom has the unpublished sequel to *The World is Mine*. The other unpublished manuscripts are in the possession of Ruth Hall.
16. FJ to CS, 13 ii 1968. (NLA, Box 7, folder 50.)
17. CS to Margaret Hanks (née Stead), 19 ii 1968. (Margaret Hanks papers.)
18. CS to Rella, 15 viii 1968.
19. CS to Burnshaws, 18 iii 1971.
20. Peter Smark, 'Christina Stead, discovering that you *can* go home again', *Australian*, 13 June 1969, p.9.
21. Greeba Jamison, 'Profile', *Walkabout*, vol. 36, no. 2, February 1970, p.36.
22. CS to Rella, 21 xi 1970. (*SL*)
23. Christina Stead, Open Letter, *Partisan Review*, XLVI, 1979, pp.271–3.
24. Interview with Joan Lidoff (1973) in *Christina Stead*, Ungar, New York, 1982.
25. Interview with Rodney Wetherell (1980), *Australian Literary Studies*, vol. 9, no. 4, October 1980, p.439.
26. Harry Bloom to CS, 14 ii 1968. (NLA, Box 15, folder 114.)
27. CS to Burnshaw, 30 iv 1968.
28. Ibid., 2 v 1968.
29. Harry Bloom to CS, 29 iv 1968. (NLA, Box 15, folder 114.)
30. CS to Burnshaw, 6 v 1968.
31. In the Thirties, Stead and Asa Zatz were sitting in an open window in the Café Crown on 2nd Avenue, when some passing gypsies took Stead's hand and told her she would live to a ripe old age. She was convinced they knew something. (CS to Anne and Harry Bloom, 11 vii 1972.)
32. CS to Burnshaw, 7 v 1968.
33. Ibid., 15 v 1968.
34. Ibid., 13 v 1968.
35. Stead quoted the line to the Burnshaws, pointing out that it had been said about Jerusalem. (CS to Burnshaw, 1 vii 1968.)
36. Stead and Cyrilly Abels had a large correspondence during the Sixties and Seventies, but Joan Daves, Abels' successor, would not make it available to me.
37. CS to Harveys, 3 ix 1968. (*SL*)
38. CS to Aida Kotlarsky, 10 iii 1969. (Don Shaw papers.)
39. CS to Burnshaw, 10 vii 1968.
40. CS to Burnshaws, 3 viii 1968.
41. Ibid., 24 viii 1968. (*SL*)
42. Conversation with Burnshaw, New York, 5 June 1988.
43. CS to GW-S, 21 ii 1972.
44. Harry Bloom to CS, 21 viii 1968. NLA, Box 15, folder 114.
45. She also commented: 'I have his letters, but he was not a letter-writer; many good writers are poor at it: they put their real life into their writing.' (CS to Rellas, 8 iii 1969.)
46. 'Christina Stead in Washington Square'. Interview by Jonah Raskin, September 1968. *London Magazine*, February 1970, pp.70–7.
47. CS to Burnshaws, 24 viii 1968. (*SL*)
48. Conversation with Charlotte Mayerson, New York, 26 July 1988. 'Serious drinking' is Mayerson's expression.
49. CS to Philip and Leah Harvey, 3 ix 1968. (*SL*)
50. Harry Bloom to CS, 23 vii 1969.
51. CS to Burnshaws, 24 viii 1968.

52. CS to Aida Kotlarsky, 18 iii 1969.
53. CS to Burnshaws, 23 ix 1968. (*SL*)
54. Conversation with Rellas, New York, 12 October 1987.
55. CS to Rellas, 15 xi 1968.
56. Ibid., 22 xi 1968.
57. Harry Bloom to CS, 12 xii 1968.
58. CS to Aida Kotlarsky, 21 vii 1970.
59. CS to Dorothy Green, 4 i 1971. (*SL*)
60. CS to GW-S, 13 vi 1972. (GW-S papers.)
61. Conversation with Paul Koston, Brighton, England, 8 November 1988.
62. CS to Philip Harvey, 26 ii 1969.
63. CS had already contributed a brief statement on Vietnam to *Authors take sides on Vietnam*, eds Cecil Woolf & John Bagguley, Simon & Schuster, New York, 1967. In a letter to the editors dated 5 October 1966, she made the following statement: 'I believe the problems of Vietnam should be solved by the Vietnamese alone. The only other nations that might have any say in the matter, are the signatories to the Geneva Convention. The United States was not a signatory . . . The correct solution, I think, is to have no foreign troops in Vietnam, no military aid, no foreign installations. The S. Vietnamese should be allowed to act in accord with the Geneva Conventions. Their decisions should be arrived at after absolute free speech and discussion of their own problems by the Vietnamese alone.' (New York Public Library, Henry W. and Albert A. Berg Collection, Astor, Lenox & Tilden Foundations.)
64. Conversation with Harveys, London, 20 September 1987.
65. CS to Aida Kotlarsky, 7 v 1969. (Don Shaw papers.)
66. Shirley Cass, Ros Cheney, David Malouf & Michael Wilding (eds), *We took their orders and are dead*, Ure Smith, Sydney, 1971. The book contains essays, fictional extracts and poems by 77 Australian writers and critics.
67. 'Doctor in Vietnam', NLA, Box 4, folder 25.
68. She sent *Meanjin* 'The Woman in the Bed', taken from her still unpublished novelette *The Little Hotel*. (*Meanjin*, vol. 27, no. 4, 1968, pp.430–52.) Her autobiographical piece, 'A Writer's Friends', was published in *Southerly*, no. 3, 1968, pp.163–8.
69. D. K. R. Hodgkin (Registrar of the ANU) to CS, 20 ii 1969. (Creative Arts Fellowships, Christina Stead file 13234, Chancellery, ANU.)
70. 'Christina Stead is coming back', *Canberra Times*, 6 June 1969, p.3.
71. Memorandum from Assistant Registrar (R. J. C. Horan) to Registrar (D. K. R. Hodgkin), 9 June 1969. '. . . I should not like people to think that we offer Creative Arts Fellowships from motives of sour grapes.' (Creative Arts Fellowships, Christina Stead file 13234, Chancellery, ANU.)
72. CS tells D. K. R. Hodgkin, Registrar, ANU, that she said this to a friend in Puerto Rico. CS to Hodgkin, 3 ii 1970. (Creative Arts Fellowships, Stead file 13234, Chancellery, ANU.)
73. CS to Clem Christesen, 17 i 1969. (*SL*)
74. CS to Fred Warburg, 27 iii 1969. (Secker & Warburg papers, University of Reading.)
75. Ibid., 3 iv 1969.
76. CS to Burnshaw, 15 vii 1969. (*SL*)
77. Diane Cole, review of *Laughing*, *New York Times*, 20 September 1987.
78. *Times on Sunday* (Sydney), 19 April 1987.
79. CS to Charlotte Mayerson, 28 v 1969. (Charlotte Mayerson papers.)
80. CS to Paul Koston, 24 vii 1969. (Paul Koston papers.)
81. 'Another View of the Homestead', *Ocean*, p.515.
82. Janet Hawley, 'Author is home—$10,000 poorer but no hard feelings', *Australian*, 1 August 1969, p.3.
83. CS, 'Another View of the Homestead', *Ocean*, p.518.
84. Interview with Rodney Wetherell (1980).
85. CS interview with Giulia Giuffré, 30 April 1982, in *A Writing Life*, Allen & Unwin, Sydney, 1990.
86. Conversation with GW-S, 24 September 1991.
87. CS to Harveys, 11 viii 1969. (*SL*)
88. 'Christina Stead is coming home', *Canberra Times*, 6 June 1969, p.3.
89. NLA, Box 7, folder 49.
90. CS to Harveys, 11 viii 1969. (*SL*)

91. CS to Paul Koston, 9 viii 1969. (*SL*)
92. Stuart Sayers, 'Books you just listen to', *Age*, 23 August 1969, p.10.
93. Anne Matheson, *Australian Women's Weekly*, 23 July 1969, p.7.
94. CS to Burnshaws, 10 xi 1969.
95. CS to Philip Harvey, 21 viii 1969.
96. CS to Burnshaws, 10 xi 1969.
97. Brenda Judge, 'Visit by Australian Novelist Christina Stead', *ANU News*, vol. 4, no. 3, November 1969, p.12.
98. Stead told Dymphna Cusack: 'I saw Florence, but only for a few words at the Fellowship affair . . . and after that we went to dinner and did not return, so I did not say goodbye. It was unintentional.' (24 x 1969.)
99. Conversation with FJ, Melbourne, 8 January 1989.
100. Patrick White to Geoffrey Dutton, 22 ix 1969. (Dutton papers, NLA, MS 7285, Series 5, folder 189.)
101. CS to Harveys, 24 ix 1969.
102. CS to Burnshaw, 26 vii 1973.
103. Ibid., 7 viii 1973.
104. CS to Philip Harvey, 16 x 1969. (*SL*)
105. Conversation with G. W. K. Duncan, 27 February 1987; and conversations with Geering.
106. Enid Wall, née Looke, is the daughter of Florence Butters, sister to Ellen.
107. CS to Philip Harvey, 16 xi 1969. (*SL*)
108. 'Another View of the Homestead', *Ocean*, p.520.
109. CS to Burnshaw, 21 xii 1969.
110. Conversation with Boy and Tella Friedmann, 29 September 1988.
111. Fred Warburg to CS, 3 xii 1969.
112. CS to Fred Warburg, 29 xii 1969.
113. CS to Burnshaw, 8 viii 1973.
114. CS to Rellas, 28 xii 1969.
115. CS to Burnshaw, 15 i 1970.
116. CS to Dorothy Green, 20 i 1970.
117. 'A Waker and Dreamer' was published in *Overland* 53, Spring 1972, and reprinted in *Ocean*.
118. 'An Iced Cake with Cherries', about Bill's mother, was published in *Meanjin*, vol. 29, no. 4, 1970. 'The Azhdanov Tailors', about Henryk Grossmann, was published in *Commentary* 52, vol. 1, July 1971. 'The Milk Run', an episode from Stead's early childhood, was published in the *New Yorker*, 9 December 1972.
119. CS to GW-S, 28 iv 1972.
120. CS to Burnshaw, 23 i 1970. (*SL*)
121. CS to Barbara Baer, 30 viii 1972. (Baer papers.)
122. CS to Doris and David Stead, 10 vii 1972. (*SL*)
123. CS to Philip Harvey, 17 iii 1970. (*SL*)
124. Harry Bloom to CS. Undated. (1970?)
125. Ibid., 18 xi 1969. NLA, Box 15, folder 114.
126. Ibid., 23 xi 1969.
127. CS to Burnshaw, 25 v 1971.
128. CS to Aida Kotlarsky, 21 vii 1970.
129. CS to Geering, 14 i 1974. (*SL*)
130. CS to Anne and Harry Bloom, 16 xi 1970.
131. CS to Burnshaws, 9 xi 1970.
132. CS to Paul Koston, 29 x 1970. (*SL*)
133. CS to Burnshaw, 13 xii 1970.
134. Ibid., 19 x 1971.
135. CS to Rella, 3 viii 1971.
136. Ibid., 12 x 1971.
137. CS to Judah Waten, 14 ix 1971. (NLA MS 4536/2/1755.)
138. CS to Burnshaw, 28 x 1971.
139. 'On the Beach', NLA, Box 4, folder 26.
140. CS to Burnshaw, 28 x 1971.
141. NLA, Box 3, folder 19.
142. 'Street Idyll', *Sydney Morning Herald*, 3 January 1972. It is included in the collection *Ocean*.

143. CS to Rellas, 8 i 1972. (*SL*)
144. CS to Burnshaws, 9 i 1972.
145. CS to GW-S, 16 v 1972. (GW-S papers.)
146. CS to Aida Kotlarsky, 18 vii 1972.
147. CS to GW-S, 13 vi 1972.
148. Peggy and Neil O'Connor also came. She was a GP, he a psychologist, originally from Perth.
149. CS to Burnshaw, 13 xii 1972. (*SL*)
150. Ibid., 18 x 1973.
151. CS to Judah Waten, 12 iii 1973. (*SL*)
152. Ibid.
153. CS to Barbara Baer, 6 i 1973. (Baer papers.)
154. CS to Rellas, 21 xii 1973.
155. CS to GW-S, 5 xii 1972.
156. Conversation with Elizabeth Harrower, Sydney, 13 January 1987.
157. CS to Rellas, 18 vii 1973.
158. CS to Gilbert Stead, 6 v 1972.
159. CS to Aida Kotlarsky, 18 vii 1972.
160. Stead quotes Bloom in a letter to GW-S, 29 ii 1972.
161. CS to Burnshaws, 15 iv 1973.
162. CS to Blooms, 4 viii 1972.
163. See Ron Geering, 'On Virginia Woolf', *Southerly* no. 4, 1990. Geering writes: 'Christina ends up creating a Virginia Woolf as fictional as the life-based characters of *The Man Who Loved Children* or *For Love Alone*.'
164. CS to Burnshaws, 6 ix 1972. (*SL*)
165. Stead's notes on Woolf are in NLA, Box 15, folder 113.
166. CS to Clem Christesen, 1 ix 1972. (*SL*)
167. CS to Burnshaws, 6 ix 1972. (*SL*)
168. Geering points out in his article 'On Virginia Woolf' that this was 'a plain statement of fact, as Leonard had just resigned from the Colonial Office in order to marry her'.
169. CS to Burnshaws, 6 ix 1972. (*SL*)
170. CS to Burnshaw, 13 xii 1972. (*SL*)
171. CS to Emile Capouya, 3 i 1973. This is a draft, but Stead has noted at the top of the letter: 'Sent similar letter 3.1.73.' (NLA, Box 15, folder 113.)
172. CS to GW-S, 28 xii 1972.
173. Notes on Woolf, 'Spectral Presences', NLA, Box 15, folder 113.
174. CS to GW-S, 8 v 1973.
175. CS to Blooms, 25 x 1972. (Michael Bloom papers.)
176. CS to Burnshaw, 16 v 1973. (*SL*)
177. CS to Dorothy Green, 1 viii 1973. (*SL*)
178. Ann Whitehead interview (1973), *Australian Literary Studies*, vol. 6, no. 3, May 1974.
179. CS to GW-S, 20 viii 1973.
180. CS to Burnshaw, 11 i 1974.
181. CS to GW-S, 20 viii 1973.
182. Hiram Haydn to CS, 20 vii 1973. (Emphasis his.) NLA, Box 8, folder 55.
183. CS to Burnshaw, 12 ii 1974. (*SL*)
184. Ibid., 11 i 1974.
185. Ibid., 12 ii 1974. (*SL*)
186. Christina Stead, '"Some deep spell" A view of Stanley Burnshaw', *Agenda* (London), vol. 21, no. 4–vol. 22, no. 1, 1983–4.
187. CS to Aida Kotlarsky, 30 iii 1974.
188. CS to Rella, 20 viii 1974. (*SL*)
189. CS to Burnshaw, 26 x 1974. (*SL*)
190. CS to Rella, 8 x 1974. (*SL*)
191. CS to Ruth Hall, 16 v 1974. (Ruth Hall papers.)
192. CS to Philip Harvey, 16 v 1974.
193. Harvey is quoted by Stead in a letter to Burnshaws, 5 vi 1974. (*SL*)
194. Stanley Burnshaw, *The Refusers*, Horizon Press, New York, 1981.
195. CS to Burnshaw, 31 iv 1974. (Quoted in *SL*, erroneously, as 30 iv 1974.)
196. Harry Bloom to CS, 10 iii 1974. NLA, Box 15, folder 114.
197. CS to Burnshaws, 5 vi 1974. (*SL*)

198. CS to Rella, 8 x 1974. (*SL*)
199. CS to Burnshaws, 26 vi 1974.
200. CS to Aida Kotlarsky, 23 vi 1974.
201. Ibid., 25 vi 1974.
202. CS to Harveys, 20 vii 1974. (*SL*)
203. CS to Burnshaw, 26 x 1974. (*SL*)
204. CS to Aida Kotlarsky, 15 viii 1974.
205. CS to Rella, 8 x 1974. (*SL*)

15: Humping Her Own Bluey

1. CS to Burnshaw, 11 vi 1970.
2. *Laughing*, p.66.
3. CS to Rellas, Hurstville, 10 ix 1974.
4. CS to Burnshaw, 4 iv 1975.
5. CS to Rellas, 29 vi 1977.
6. *Time*, 7 June 1976, p.83.
7. Conversation with Thistle Harris, Sydney, 15 January 1987.
8. 'Another View of the Homestead', *Ocean*, p.515.
9. Ibid.
10. CS to Rella, 17 x 1974. (*SL*)
11. Ibid., 11 xii 1974.
12. CS to Burnshaws, 20 iv 1975.
13. Conversation with Mary Lord, Melbourne, 26 June 1991.
14. CS to Rella, 24 viii 1975.
15. Ibid., 17 x 1974. (*SL*)
16. Future winners included David Campbell, John Blight, Sumner Locke-Elliott, Gwen Harwood, Randolph Stow, Bruce Dawe, Dal Stivens, Bruce Beaver.
17. Patrick White to Marshall Best, Viking Press, quoted in David Marr, *Patrick White. A Life*, Random House, Sydney, 1991, p.707, note 31.
18. CS to Rellas, 17 x 1974. (*SL*)
19. CS to Ruth Hall, 15 viii 1977.
20. Patrick White to Geoffrey Dutton, 5 ii 1967. (Dutton papers, NLA, MS 7285, Series 5, folder 188.)
21. Ibid., 13 i 1975. (Dutton papers, NLA, MS 7285, Series 5, folder 191.)
22. Ibid., 22 ix 1969. (Dutton papers, NLA, MS 7285, Series 5, folder 189.)
23. CS to Rellas, 17 x 1974. (*SL*)
24. CS to Jessie Rella, 15 i 1975.
25. CS to Geering, 5 ix 1969. (Geering papers.)
26. Ibid., 30 ix 1978.
27. CS to Rellas, 5 xi 1976.
28. Ibid., 20 ii 1975. (*SL*)
29. Ibid., 5 xi 1976.
30. CS to W. H. Pearson, 3 ix 1975. NLA, MS 7570.
31. CS to Jessie Rella, 3 xii 1974.
32. Graeme Kinross Smith, 'Christina Stead—A Profile', *Westerly*, no. 1, March 1976.
33. CS to Dorothy Green, 15 xi 1974. (*SL*)
34. CS to Jessie Rella, 15 i 1975.
35. CS to Rellas, 1 i 1975.
36. CS to Burnshaws, 30 vi 1976. (*SL*)
37. CS to Aida Kotlarsky, 21 iii 1975. (Don Shaw papers.)
38. CS to Burnshaws, 20 iv 1975.
39. In February 1976 Hellman sent CS a cheque for $3000 for an option from January 1976. It ran out in January 1977 and Hellman did not renew it.
40. CS to Charlotte Mayerson. Undated. Hurstville, 1976. (Mayerson papers.)
41. CS to Burnshaw, 16 vii 1976.
42. *Herbert*, p.305.
43. CS to Burnshaw, 16 vii 1976.
44. Conversation with Kel Semmens, Kyneton, Victoria, 22 January 1989.
45. CS to DDS, 13 v 1975. (Gilbert Stead papers.)
46. CS to Rella, 24 viii 1975.

47. CS to Burnshaw, 16 vii 1976.
48. CS to Aida Kotlarsky, 3 x 1976.
49. CS to Burnshaw, 7 xii 1976.
50. Conversation with Kel Semmens, 22 January 1989.
51. CS to Rella, 1 x 1975.
52. CS to Burnshaw, 4 x 1975.
53. Conversation with Elizabeth Harrower, Sydney, 13 January 1987.
54. CS to Rellas, 22 x 1975.
55. CS to Dorothy Green, 19 xi 1975. (Green papers, NLA, MS 54678, Box 6.)
56. Conversation with Dorothy Green, Canberra, 9 April 1988.
57. CS to Ruth Hall, 15 viii 1977. (Ruth Hall papers.)
58. CS to Charlotte Mayerson. Undated, 1976.
59. CS to Rellas, 12 iii 1976.
60. CS to Rella, 24 iii 1976.
61. In her novel *Regards to the Czar*, University of Queensland Press, St Lucia, 1988, Margaret Coombs writes about a 'distinguished elderly woman novelist' being entertained to dinner by an aspiring woman writer's father-in-law. (The chapter is called 'A Lesson from the Idol'.) Today, Margaret Coombs stresses that the portrait is 'representation' rather than a 'transparent portrait'. She now finds the picture 'misleading and cruel'. (M. Coombs in telephone conversation with me, 30 September 1991.)
62. CS to H. C. Coombs, Newcastle, 24 vi 1976. H. C. Coombs papers, NLA, MS 802, folder 377.
63. Coombs went to England in 1931 and did a doctorate at the London School of Economics (like W. G. K. Duncan five years earlier). In his autobiography *Trial Balance*, Macmillan, Melbourne, 1981, he writes that the publication in 1936 of J. M. Keynes' *General Theory of Employment, Interest and Money* 'was for me and many of our generation the most seminal intellectual event of our time'. (Duncan had of course been influenced by the less moderate Harold Laski.)
64. H. C. Coombs to CS, 22 xii 1978. (Coombs papers, NLA, MS 802, folder 377.)
65. Graham Williams, 'The greening of "Nugget" Coombs,' *Sydney Morning Herald*, 24 March 1979, pp.2–5.
66. Joseph Glascott, 'Simple lifestyle the aim of Dr. Coombs,' *Sydney Morning Herald*, 25 October 1977, p.6.
67. CS to Rellas, 14 i 1976.
68. CS to Rellas, 11 viii 1976.
69. Don Dunstan to me, 13 ix 1991.
70. NLA, Box 5, folder 37.
71. CS to Philip Harvey, 22 xi 1978.
72. Designed by Harold Desbrowe Annear, one of the pioneers of modern domestic architecture in Victoria.
73. Helen Yglesias, *New York Times Book Review*, 13 June 1976.
74. R. Z. Sheppard, *Time*, 7 June 1976, pp.61–2.
75. Graeme Beaton, 'Our Miss Stead praised as a giant in literature', *The Australian*, 3 June 1976, p.5.
76. Marion McDonald interview with CS, *National Times*, 22–7 November 1976.
77. CS to Rellas, 24 ix 1976.
78. CS, 'A View of Australian fiction', *National Times*, 18–23 October 1976.
79. CS to Dorothy Green, 19 iv 1977. (*SL*)
80. CS quotes this to Burnshaw, 21 vi 1977. (*SL*)
81. CS to Rellas, 27 i 1977. (*SL*)
82. Ibid., 9 i 1977. (*SL*)
83. CS to Dorothy Green, 12 iii 1977. (*SL*)
84. CS to Rellas, 29 vi 1977.
85. Ibid., 5 iv 1977.
86. CS to Michael Costigan, 11 vi 1977. (NLA, Box 7, folder 51.)
87. See the portrait of him by Jack Beasley in *Red Letter Days*, Australasian Book Society Ltd, Sydney, 1979.
88. CS to Rella, 3 v 1977.
89. CS to Burnshaw, 21 vi 1977. (*SL*)
90. CS to Rellas, 14 vi 1977.
91. Ibid., 29 vi 1977.

92. Ibid., 8 vii 1977.
93. Telephone conversation with Clem Christesen, 1 May 1988, and conversation with Clem and Nina Christesen, Eltham, Victoria, 24 June 1991.
94. The previous year Stephen Murray-Smith, editor of *Overland*, had paid Stead's first-class airfare from Sydney to Melbourne as special guest for the *Overland* annual dinner. She had stayed with him and Nita.
95. CS to Rellas, 18 vii 1977.
96. Geoffrey Blainey, then head of the Australia Council, was a guest. Others were painter Fred Williams; Ian Turner, Australian Labour historian; Ray Marginson, Vice-Principal of the University of Melbourne; Ray Ericksen, historian and writer.
97. CS to Geerings, 18 vii 1977. (*SL*)
98. CS to Dorothy Green, 23 ix 1977. (*SL*)
99. CS to DDS, 24 x 1977.
100. CS to Rellas, 13 ix 1977.
101. CS to Rellas, 21 ix 1977.
102. CS to Dorothy Green, 10 ix 1977.
103. CS to H. C. Coombs, Eltham, 14 vii 1977. (Coombs papers, NLA, MS 802, folder 377.)
104. CS to DDS, 24 x 1977.
105. CS to George·Lanning, c/o Joan Daves, New York. Undated. (November or December 1977.) (Lanning papers, courtesy Chris Williams.)
106. CS to DDS, 4 xii 1977. (*SL*).
107. Ibid., 28 xi 1977.
108. CS tells this to Dorothy Green, 4 xii 1977. (*SL*)
109. 'Valiant Knight'. Ibid.
110. Ibid.
111. CS to Elizabeth Harrower, 6 xii 1977. (*SL*)
112. *New York Times Book Review*, 4 December 1977.
113. CS to Rellas, 4 iii 1978.
114. Ibid., 7 ii 1978.
115. CS to Philip Harvey, 15 iii 1978. (*SL*)
116. CS to Rellas, 5 iv 1978. (*SL*)
117. CS to Geering, 2 iv 1978. (*SL*)
118. Ibid.
119. Ibid.
120. CS to Burnshaw, 25 xi 1978.
121. Conversation with Dorothy Green, Canberra, 9 April 1988.
122. Dorothy Green's obituary of CS, *Sydney Morning Herald*, 8 April 1983.
123. CS to H. C. Coombs, 7 vi 1978. (Coombs papers, NLA, MS 802, folder 377.)
124. CS to Ruth Hall, 1 vi 1978.
125. CS to Philip Harvey, 23 v 1978.
126. Philip Harvey to CS, 2 ix 1978. (NLA, MS 4967, Box 15, folder 118.)
127. CS to Norman Rosten, 11 viii 1978. (Rosten correspondence, NLA, MS 4967, Box 14, folder 109.)
128. CS to Ruth Hall, 1 vi 1978.
129. CS to Burnshaw, 14 vi 1978.
130. CS to Rellas, 26 v 1980.
131. CS to Philip Harvey, 22 xi 1978.
132. CS to Burnshaw, 31 viii 1978.
133. 'The Old School' was published in *Southerly*, no. 1, March 1984, posthumously. (Included in *Ocean*.)
134. CS to Philip Harvey, 1 ix 1979. (*SL*)
135. CS to Donald Macdonald, 21 vi 1980. (Macdonald papers.)
136. CS to Rellas, 1 ix 1979.
137. Conversation with Mary Lord, Melbourne, 26 June 1991.
138. CS to Watens, 24 xi 1978. (Waten papers, NLA, MS 4536, Box 13.)
139. David I. Smith, Official Secretary to the Governor General, to CS, 18 xii 1978. (Geering papers.)
140. *Sabba familiare*, tr. Floriana Bossi, Garzanti, Rome, 1978.
141. CS to DDS, 8 xii 1980.
142. The film was eventually not released until 1986; Stephen Wallace wrote the final script.

143. CS to H. C. Coombs, 16 viii 1978. (Coombs papers, NLA, MS 802, folder 377.)
144. Ibid., 31 v 1979.
145. Conversation with Mary Lord, 26 June 1991.
146. CS to Rellas, 30 ix 1979.
147. Ibid., 26 x 1979.
148. Dr R. F. Brissenden, Chairman, to CS, 30 xi 1979. Australia Council, Emeritus Fellowships, Christina Stead file, No. 82/514/003.
149. Stead file 82/514/003. Stead wrote to thank Bob Brissenden on 13 December 1979. She told him (it was not true) that she had never applied for a Guggenheim Fellowship. By the middle of 1982, Stead's fellowship had been increased to $5400.
150. Conversation with Mary Lord, 26 June 1991.
151. CS to Rellas, 18 ii 1980.
152. Ibid., 5 iii 1980.
153. Ibid., 29 i 1980.
154. Ibid.
155. Don Dunstan to me, 13 ix 1991.
156. In retrospect, Dunstan was relieved that Stead did not send a story. He resigned the editorship when he discovered that the management was not paying contributors. (Don Dunstan to me, 13 ix 1991.)
157. Rodney Wetherell interview with Christina Stead, broadcast on ABC Radio Two on 24 February 1980. Published in *Australian Literary Studies*, vol. 9, no. 4, October 1980.
158. CS to Geerings, 9 vi 1980. (*SL*)
159. *Christina Stead*, Australia Council Video Series on Australian Writers, 1980. Producer: Haydn Kernan.
160. CS to H. C. Coombs, 14 v 1980. (Coombs papers, NLA, MS 802, folder 377.)
161. Conversation with Ralph Elliott, Canberra, 19 August 1991.
162. Dobson papers, NLA, MS 4955, folder 43.
163. CS to Ruth Hall, 28 v 1980. (Ruth Hall papers.)
164. CS to Burnshaw, 28 vii 1980. (*SL*)
165. Ibid.
166. Ibid., 5 iii 1981. (*SL*)
167. CS to Philip Harvey, 30 vii 1980. (*SL*)
168. CS to Geering, 21 x 1980.
169. Conversation with H. C. Coombs, Cremorne, Sydney, 8 January 1987.
170. CS to Rellas, 15 vii 1980.
171. CS to Burnshaw, 28 vii 1980. (*SL*)
172. CS to Rellas, 4 viii 1980.
173. Geering to Philip Harvey, 1 ix 1983. (Philip and Leah Harvey correspondence, NLA, MS 4967, Box 15, folder 118.)
174. CS to Rellas, 29 ix 1980.
175. Mark Higgie to me, 1 x 1991.
176. CS interview with Anne Chisholm, *National Times*, 29 March–4 April 1981, pp.32–4.
177. CS to Burnshaw, 5 iii 1981. (*SL*)
178. Conversation with Ralph Elliott, Canberra, 19 August 1991.
179. Conversation with H. C. Coombs, Cremorne, 8 January 1987.
180. CS to Burnshaw, 29 xi 1982. (*SL*)
181. CS to Rellas, undated. (19 v 1982.)
182. CS to Rosemary Dobson, 2 vii 1982. (Dobson papers, NLA, MS 4955, folder 42.) 'Humping the bluey' is Australian slang for carrying one's pack on one's shoulders.
183. CS to Rellas, 19 v 1982. (Second letter that day.)
184. Conversation with Don Shaw, New York, 23 August 1988.
185. CS interview with Barry Hill, *Sydney Morning Herald*, 17 July 1982.
186. Conversation with Dorothy Green, Canberra, 9 April 1988.
187. Elizabeth Harrower to me, 8 x 1991.
188. Ibid.
189. David Marr, *Patrick White*, p.609. Elizabeth Harrower remembers the exchange. She maintains that David Marr's account of the same incident confuses certain details. (Harrower to me, 8 x 1991.)
190. Ibid.
191. Patrick White to DDS, 1 v 1983. (DDS papers.)
192. Cited in interview with Tom Krause, *Australian*, 7 December 1982.

193. The cheque came with a letter from Hellman: 'Dear Christina, This comes to you with the greatest admiration I have ever had for any woman writer, as I have been loudly saying for so many years. It gives me enormous pleasure that you have accepted it from me because I feel that you must have some faith in me for accepting it. From a long way away, if admiration could turn into love, my admiration has.' Lillian Hellman to CS, 11 xi 1982. (Jonathan LaPook papers.)

194. Jonathan LaPook to me, 6 xii 1991.

195. Conversation with Elizabeth Harrower, Sydney, 13 January 1987.

196. CS to Burnshaw, 29 xi 1982. (*SL*)

197. For the Victorian Premier's Literary Award in 1986, three years after her death, a panel of three judges unanimously chose the posthumously published *Ocean of Story*. Premier John Cain rejected the judges' choice, arguing that the Award was meant to encourage living writers. The judges protested: nothing in the guidelines said the awards should go to a living writer. Did he want the awards to be seen as 'government grants rather than prizes based solely on literary merit?'

198. CS to Rosemary Dobson and Alec Bolton, 21 xii 1982. (*SL*)

199. Programme of events, Stead papers, NLA, Box 91, folder 70.

200. CS to Rosemary Dobson and Alec Bolton, 21 xii 1982. (*SL*)

201. Conversation with Heather Stewart, Sydney, 13 July 1987.

202. CS to Rosemary Dobson, 21 xii 1982. Dobson papers, NLA, MS 4955, folder 42.

203. Susan Molloy interview with Christina Stead, *Sydney Morning Herald*, 20 January 1983.

204. Ibid.

205. CS to H. C. Coombs, 7 v 1982. (Coombs papers, NLA, MS 802, folder 377.)

206. Conversation with H. C. Coombs, 8 January 1987.

207. H. C. Coombs to CS, 19 vi 1982. (NLA, Coombs papers, MS 802, folder 377.)

208. *A Christina Stead Reader*, selected by Jean B. Read. Random House, New York, 1978. There was no income, but Mayerson was touched by the gesture.

209. A lump sum of $47 300 went to the ACF at Stead's death. Between March 1983 and December 1990, the ACF received approximately $89 000 from royalties. (I owe this information to George Dalton, Australian Conservation Foundation, Melbourne.)

210. Robert Irving, John Kinstler, Max Dupain, *Fine Houses of Sydney*, Methuen, Sydney, 1982.

211. Conversation with Helena Berenson and Geoff Davis, Sydney, 26 September 1991.

212. Ibid.

213. The probable cause of death was a pulmonary embolism.

214. CS to Blake, 10 vi 1942. (NLA, Box 16, folders 119–20.)

Epilogue

1. These quotations are all from the Preface to *Ocean of Story*.

Bibliography

Works by Christina Stead

Fiction

The following are first publications; the modern editions cited in the end-notes are given last.

The Salzburg Tales. Peter Davies, London, 1934; D. Appleton-Century, New York, 1934; Sun Books, Melbourne, 1966.

Seven Poor Men of Sydney. Peter Davies, London, 1934; D. Appleton-Century, New York, 1934; A & R, Sydney, 1965.

The Beauties and Furies. Peter Davies, London, 1936; D. Appleton-Century, New York, 1936; Virago, London, 1982.

House of All Nations. Simon & Schuster, New York, 1938; Peter Davies, London, 1938; A & R, Sydney, 1974.

The Man Who Loved Children. Simon & Schuster, New York, 1940; Peter Davies, London, 1941; Penguin, Harmondsworth, 1970.

For Love Alone. Harcourt, Brace, New York, 1944; Peter Davies, London, 1945; A & R, Sydney, 1966.

Letty Fox: Her Luck. Harcourt, Brace, New York, 1946; Peter Davies, London, 1947; A & R, Sydney, 1974.

A Little Tea, A Little Chat. Harcourt, Brace, New York, 1948; Virago, London, 1981.

The People with the Dogs. Little, Brown, Boston, 1952; Virago, London, 1981.

Dark Places of the Heart. Holt, Rinehart & Winston, New York, 1966; *Cotters' England*, Secker & Warburg, London, 1967; A & R, Sydney, 1974.

The Puzzleheaded Girl. Holt, Rinehart & Winston, New York, 1967; Secker & Warburg, London, 1968; Virago, London, 1984.

The Little Hotel, A & R, London and Sydney 1973; Holt, Rinehart & Winston, New York, 1975.

Miss Herbert (The Suburban Housewife). Random House, New York, 1976; Virago, London, 1979.

Anthologies and Translations

Modern Women in Love: Sixty Twentieth-Century Masterpieces of Fiction. Edited by Christina Stead and William Blake. Dryden Press, New York, 1945.

Great Stories of the South Sea Islands. Selected with a foreword by Christina Stead. Muller, London, 1955.

Gignon, Fernand. *Colour of Asia.* Muller, London, 1955.

Giltène, Jean. *The Candid Killer.* Muller, London, 1956.

Piccard, Auguste. *In Balloon and Bathyscaphe.* Cassell, London, 1956.

Posthumous Publications

Ocean of Story. The uncollected stories of Christina Stead, edited with an afterword by R. G. Geering. Viking/Penguin, Ringwood, Victoria, 1985.

I'm Dying Laughing: The Humourist. Edited with a preface by R. G. Geering. Virago, London, 1986.

The Palace with Several Sides: A Sort of Love Story. Limited edition, edited by R. G. Geering. Officina Brindabella, Canberra, 1986; repr. in *Southerly,* no. 2, 1987, pp.115–25.

A Web of Friendship. Selected Letters (1928–1973). Edited with preface and annotations by R. G. Geering. A & R, Sydney, 1992.

Talking into the Typewriter. Selected Letters (1973–1983). Edited with preface and annotations by R. G. Geering. A & R, Sydney, 1992.

(Note: Geering's two volumes are referred to henceforth as *Selected Letters* [SL].)

Selected Articles

(This list does not include pieces re-published in *Ocean of Story.*)

'The Writers Take Sides', *Left Review,* vol. 1, no. 2, July 1935, pp.435–63, 469–75.

'America' (1935), *Australian Book Review,* June 1992.

'About Woman's Insight, There Is a Sort of Folklore We Inherit', Contribution to a symposium on 'Women's Intuition', *Vogue* (US) vol. 158, no. 5, 15 September 1971, pp. 61, 130.

'What Goal in Mind?' In Shirley Cass, Ros Cheney, David Malouf and Michael Wilding (eds), *We Took their Orders and Are Dead.* Ure Smith, Sydney, 1971, pp.119–30.

'On the Women's Movement', *Partisan Review,* vol. 46, no. 2, 1979, pp.271–4.

'Some Deep Spell: A View of Stanley Burnshaw', *Agenda* (London) Special Issue on Stanley Burnshaw, vol. 21, no. 4, vol. 22, no. 1, 1983–4.

Selected Interviews

Beston, John. 'An Interview with Christina Stead' (September 1975), *World Literature Written in English,* vol. 15, no. 1, April 1976, pp.87–95.

Chisholm, Anne. *National Times,* 29 March–4 April 1981, pp.32–4.

'Christina Stead', *Wilson Library Bulletin,* vol. 13, no. 4, December 1938, p.234.

'Christina Stead', Australian Writers series, Program Two, Australian Broadcasting Corporation, 23 March 1976. Copyright No. 76/AW/2.

Drewe, Robert. 'Christina Stead' (1982), *Scripsi,* vol. 4, no. 1, July 1986.

Guiffré, Giulia. 'Christina Stead', in *A Writing Life,* Allen & Unwin, Sydney, 1990.

Hill, Barry. 'Christina Stead at 80 says love is her religion', *Sydney Morning Herald,* 17 July 1982, p.33; *Age,* 17 July 1982, p.2.

Keneally, Thomas. 'Conversation Piece', *Vogue Australia,* vol. 21, no. 4, May 1977, pp.91–3.

Kinross Smith, Graeme. 'Christina Stead—A Profile', *Westerly,* no. 1, 1976, pp.67–75.

Lidoff, Joan. 'An Interview with Christina Stead'. Surbiton, England, June, 1973. In Lidoff, *Christina Stead,* Frederick Ungar, New York, 1982, pp.180–220.

Raskin, Jonah, 'Christina Stead in Washington Square', *London Magazine,* vol. 9, no. 2, February 1970, pp.70–7.

Riddell, Elizabeth (interviewer). *Christina Stead* (1980), Australia Council Archival Film Series. Producer: Haydn Kernan.

Wetherell, Rodney, 'Christina Stead: An Interview', *Australian Literary Studies,* vol. 9, no. 4, October 1980, pp.431–48.

Whitehead, Ann, 'Christina Stead: An Interview' (1973), *Australian Literary Studies,* vol. 6, no. 3, May 1974, pp.230–48.

Williamson, Jean, 'Christina Stead Tells of Her Latest Book!', *Australian Women's Weekly,* 9 March 1935.

Manuscript Sources

Christina Stead's manuscripts, diaries and miscellaneous correspondence are held in the Manuscript Collection of the National Library of Australia, Canberra, MS 4967.

Much of Stead's correspondence remains in private collections. The public collections are listed below. (The letters to be found in *Selected Letters*, ed. R. G. Geering, are indicated in the end-notes.)

Correspondence with William Blake, NLA, MS 4967, Box 16, folders 119–20. (Closed until 2001.)

Letters from Harry Bloom (1949–74), NLA, MS 4967, Box 15, folder 114.

Correspondence with Stanley Burnshaw, Stanley Burnshaw papers, Harry Ransom Humanities Research Center, University of Texas at Austin.

Clem Christesen papers, Meanjin Archives, Baillieu Library, University of Melbourne.

H. C. Coombs papers, NLA, MS 802, Box 49, folder 377. (Restricted.)

Rosemary Dobson papers, NLA, MS 4955, folder 43.

Geoffrey Dutton papers, NLA, MS 7285.

Dorothy Green papers, NLA, MS 54678, Box 6. (Closed until 2000.)

Philip and Leah Harvey correspondence, NLA, MS 4967, Box 15, folder 118.

Guy Howarth papers, Harry Ransom Humanities Research Center, University of Texas at Austin.

Charles Humboldt papers, Manuscripts and Archives, Yale University Library.

Randall Jarrell papers, Henry W. and Albert A. Berg Collection, New York Public Library.

Stephen Murray-Smith papers, Overland Collection, La Trobe Library, State Library of Victoria, Box 121, 137.

Palmer papers, NLA, MS 1174.

W. H. Pearson papers, NLA, MS 7570, folder 2.

Ettore and Jessie Rella correspondence, NLA, MS 4967, Box 15, folders 115, 116.

Norman Rosten correspondence, NLA, MS 4967, Box 14, folder 109.

Isidor Schneider papers, Rare Books and Manuscripts, Butler Library, Columbia University.

Neil Stewart papers, Rare Books, Fisher Library, University of Sydney.

Judah Waten papers, NLA, MS 4536, Box 13.

I have also drawn on the following manuscript sources:

ASIO file on Stead, Australian Archives, Series A 6119 XRI, Item 231.

Aufbauverlag papers, Berlin.

Correspondence regarding Australia Council Emeritus Fellowships, Australia Council, Christina Stead file, No. 82/514/003.

Correspondence regarding Creative Arts Fellowships, Australian National University, Chancellery, ANU, Christina Stead file 13234.

Correspondence of Literature Censorship Board, Canberra, regarding *Letty* and *Tea*, Australian Archives, Canberra, Series A425/1, Item 49/1976.

FBI files on William James Blake and Christina Ellen Stead (small file 100–82232), General File No. 100–236179.

R. G. Geering papers, Sydney. Miscellaneous papers not yet lodged with the NLA.

Simon & Schuster collection, Rare Books & Manuscripts, Butler Library, Columbia University.

Stead correspondence to Little, Brown publishers regarding the publication of *Dogs*, Special Collections, Boston University, Massachusetts.

Stead's correspondence with Secker & Warburg, Secker & Warburg files, Archives & Manuscripts, University of Reading.

Stead, 'Uses of the Many-Charactered Novel', Paper delivered at the Third American Writers' Congress, 4 June 1939. League of American Writers papers, Rare Books and Manuscripts, Bancroft Library, University of California.

Stead's 1941 application for a Guggenheim Fellowship, John Simon Guggenheim Memorial Foundation, New York.

Woolf, Cecil and John Bagguley, (eds) *Authors take sides on Vietnam*. Correspondence with Christina Stead, Astor, Lenox and Tilden Foundations, New York Public Library.

Books and Selected Articles on Christina Stead

Arac, Jonathan. 'The Struggle for the Cultural Heritage: Christina Stead refunctions Charles Dickens and Mark Twain', *The New Historicism*, ed. H. Aram Veeser. Routledge, New York & London, 1989, pp.116–31.

Brydon, Diana. *Christina Stead*. Macmillan, London, 1987.

Carter, Angela, 'Unhappy Families', *London Review of Books*, 16 September–6 October 1982, pp.11–13.

—— Introduction to *The Puzzleheaded Girl*. Virago, London, 1984.

Chisholm, Anne. 'Stead', *National Times*, 29 March–4 April 1981, pp.32–3.

Clancy, Laurie. *Christina Stead's 'The Man Who Loved Children' and 'For Love Alone'*. Shillington House, Melbourne, 1981.

Eldershaw, M. Barnard. 'Christina Stead', in *Essays in Australian Fiction*, Melbourne University Press, Melbourne, 1938.

Fagan, Robert. 'Christina Stead', *Partisan Review*, no. 46, 1979, pp.262–70.

Geering, R. G. 'The Achievement of Christina Stead', *Southerly*, no. 4, 1962. Christina Stead Special Issue.

—— *Christina Stead*, Twayne World Author Series, Twayne, New York, 1969; republished A & R, Sydney, 1979.

—— 'What is Normal? Two recent novels by Christina Stead', *Southerly*, no. 4, 1978, pp.462–73.

—— (ed.) 'Christina Stead Special Issue. Unpublished Writings', *Southerly*, no. 1, 1984.

—— 'Christina Stead's description of her books', *Southerly*, no. 4, 1990, pp.421–5.

—— 'The Bank Novel. *House of All Nations*', *Southerly*, no. 4, 1990.

Green, Dorothy. 'Chaos, or a Dancing Star? Christina Stead's *Seven Poor Men of Sydney*', *Meanjin*, vol. 27, no. 2, 1968, pp.150–61.

Hardwick, Elizabeth. 'The Neglected Novels of Christina Stead', *New Republic*, 1 August 1955, pp.17–19. Reprinted in *A View of My Own*, Farrar, Straus & Cudahy, New York, 1962, pp.41–8.

Harris, Margaret, '"To Hell with Conservatories": Christina Stead and the Fiction of William J. Blake', *Meridian*, vol. 8, no. 2, October 1989, pp.161–73.

Higgins [Sheridan], Susan, 'For Love Alone: A Female Odyssey?' *Southerly*, no. 4, 1984, pp.394–413.

Howarth, R. G. 'Christina Stead', *Biblionews*, vol. 11, no. 1, January 1958, p.18.

Jarrell, Randall. 'An Unread Book'. Introduction to *The Man*, Holt, Rinehart & Winston, New York, 1965.

Lidoff, Joan. *Christina Stead*. Ungar, New York, 1982.

Macainsh, N. 'The Art of Compromise: Christina Stead's *For Love Alone*', *Westerly*, vol. 32, no. 4, December 1987, pp. 79–88.

Pybus Rodney, '*Cotters' England*: In appreciation', *Stand*, vol. 23, no. 4, 1982, pp.40–7.

Roderick, Colin, *Introduction to Australian Fiction*, A & R, Sydney, 1950.

Rowley, Hazel. 'A "Wanderer": Christina Stead', *Westerly*, vol. 33, no. 1, March 1988, pp.15–21.

—— 'Christina Stead: The Voyage to Cythera', *Span*, no. 26, April 1988, pp.33–45.

—— 'Christina Stead: Politics and Literature in the Radical Years, 1935–1942', *Meridian*, vol. 8, no. 2, October 1989, pp.149–59.

—— 'How Real is Sam Pollit? "Dramatic Truth" and "Procès-verbal" in *The Man Who Loved Children*', *Contemporary Literature* (Wisconsin), vol. 31, no. 4, Winter 1990, pp.499–511.

Saxelby, Jean & Gwen Walker-Smith. 'Christina Stead', *Biblionews*, vol. 2, no. 14, December 1949, pp.37–43.

Segerberg, Anita. 'A Fiction of Sisters: Christina Stead's *Letty Fox*', *Australian Literary Studies*, vol. 14, no. 1, May 1989.

Sheridan, Susan. *Christina Stead*. Harvester Wheatsheaf, London, 1988.

Twentieth Century Authors. A Biographical Dictionary of Modern Literature, ed. S. J. Kunitz & H. Haycroft, Wilson, New York, 1942.

Who's Who in Australia. Herald and Weekly Times, Melbourne, begun 1922.

Williams, Chris. *Christina Stead. A Life of Letters*. McPhee Gribble, Melbourne, 1989.

Wilson Bulletin for Librarians. 'Christina Stead', vol. 13, no. 4, December 1938, p.234.

Yglesias, Jose, 'Marx as Muse', *Nation* (New York), no. 100, 5 April 1965, pp.363–70.

Picture Credits

VARIOUS PEOPLE HAVE kindly allowed me to use photographs and material from their collections, and I thank them for their generosity.

Gilbert Stead 2, 3, 4, 5, 6, 9, 16, 37; Gwen Walker-Smith 1, 17, 18, 19, 39; David D. Stead 8; Graeme Kinross Smith 7, 41; *High School Chronicle 1919*, Sydney Girls High 10; Thistle Harris 11; Julie James Bailey 12, 13; Duncan papers, courtesy of Hugh Stretton 14, 15; Ron Geering 23, 28, 31, 32, 34, 38; *Daily Mail*, London 20; Stead Papers, National Library of Australia 22, 29; Elisabeth Granich Humeston 21, 24; Stuart Monro, London 25; Edith Anderson 26; *Current Biography* 1942, 27; Australian Archives Canberra 30; Philip Harvey 33; Federal Bureau of Investigation files 35; Michael Bloom 36, 40; Kate Llewellyn 42; Jonathan LaPook 43; John Fairfax & Sons (photo by Gerrit Fokkama) 44.

Acknowledgements

ONE OF THE great pleasures I have had writing this biography has been my interaction with so many interesting and inspiring people, many of whom have given remarkably generously of their time. Throughout the six years that I have been involved in this project, I have had assistance and encouragement from three continents.

The biographical trail has its dramatic ups and downs, excitements and frustrations. Stead's old friends, Edith Anderson, Stanley Burnshaw, Ron Geering, Florence James were all cautious at first, neither encouraging nor discouraging. Later, their generous assistance and encouragement seemed to have no bounds. I cannot express my gratitude enough. In addition, Burnshaw and Geering spent days reading through my final manuscript and giving me the benefit of their critical and stylistic comments.

I am above all indebted to Ron Geering, Stead's literary executor, for his trust in me, and for generously allowing me to see and quote from Stead material otherwise closed until 2001. I thank him for granting me world rights to quote from Stead's unpublished papers and letters held in the National Library of Australia.

Several of Stead's friends and acquaintances, hurt by her behaviour towards them, declined to talk to me. Edith Anderson, traced to an address in East Berlin, at first refused my entreaties. But after more correspondence came the reply, covered with DDR stamps: 'Dear Hazel Rowley, what a temptress you are!' The four days spent perusing letters in her flat were a source of invaluable material and seeded a warm friendship.

I owe special thanks to Gwen Walker-Smith, with her astounding recall and her affectionate insights into the Stead family. And I am indebted to the late Gilbert Stead, who was always encouraging and whose family archives were a rich source of material.

Numerous people gave freely of their time and recollections in interviews with me in Australia, England, France, Germany, Italy and the United States. I sincerely thank the following: William Ash, Barbara Baer, Julie James Bailey, Phyllis Barnett, Cedric Belfrage, Helena Berenson, Jack Bermond, Norman Berry, Geoffrey Blainey, Michael Bloom, Murray Teigh Bloom, Alec Bolton, Phil Brown, Clem and Nina Christesen, Axel Clark, Jacques Coe, H. C. Coombs, Margaret Coombs, Beatrice Davis, Geoff Davis, Rosemary Dobson, W. G. K. Duncan, Don Dunstan, Geoffrey Dutton, Ralph Elliott, Clifton Fadiman, Mike Folsom, Elsie Ford (née Butters), Boyce and Tella Friedmann, Judith Kegan Gardiner, Dorothy Green, Ruth Hall (née Blech), Margaret Hanks (née Stead), Thistle Harris, Elizabeth Harrower, Philip and Leah Harvey, Shirley Hazzard, Mark Higgie, Shirley Hokin, Edward Huberman, Elisabeth Granich Humeston (Gold), Yvonne Kapp, Graeme Kinross Smith, Hortense Kooluris, Richard Kopley, Paul Koston, Pera Koston, Janet Ladenheim (née Bloom), George Lanning, Jonathan LaPook, Ring Lardner Jnr, Pilar Libenson, Mary Lord, Donald and Wendy Macdonald, Margaret Mackie, Harry Magdoff, Tempe Mann (née Datson), Charlotte Mayerson, Nadine Mendelson (née Lewin), Stuart Monro, Nita Murray-Smith, Pauline Nestor, Neil and Peggy O'Connor, Bill Packard, Jenny Palmer, E. F. Patterson, Gerald Pollinger, Betty Lewis Reid, Ettore and Jessie Rella, Elizabeth Riddell, Miriam Risner, Betty Roland, Norman Rosten, Albert Rubin, Kel Semmens, Clement Semmler, Don Shaw, Gunnwor Stallybrass, David D. Stead, Gilbert Stead, Ivy and Kelvin Stead, Kate Stead, Miriam Stern, Heather Stewart, Jean Stone, Hugh and Pat Stretton, Helen Thomson, Pat Waddington (Coontz), Patricia and Donald Walker, Gwen Walker-Smith, Enid Wall, Noel Warry, Michael Wilding, Marguerite Young and Asa Zatz.

For practical help, editorial guidance and stimulating discussions, I am grateful to the following: Louise Adler, Stephen Alomes, Lawrie Brown, David Carter, Art Casciato, Garry Disher, Robin Dizard, Frank Folsom, Terence Greer, Joy Hooton, Kate Jennings,

Paul Judd, Graeme Kinross Smith, Kate Llewellyn, Caroline Lurie, Lilette Maurer, Deidre Missingham, John Murphy, Michèle Nayman, Brenda Niall, Paul and Susan Nulsen, Kevin Sharpe, Susan Sheridan, Jennifer Strauss, Jacques Tempé, Glen Tomasetti, Chris Williams, Louise Yelin and Shane Youl.

My thanks go to Deakin University for an initial travel grant of $2000 for research abroad, funding for several research trips to Sydney and Canberra, six months study leave in 1988, and finally a grant of $15000, enabling me to take a semester in the first half of 1992 to finish the book.

I thank Peter Barclay, Russell Sharp and Bill Clydesdale at Deakin University for copying photographs lent to me over the years.

I am grateful to the Institute for Research on Women and Gender at Columbia University for providing excellent working conditions for my three-month stay in New York in 1988, and to the Humanities Research Centre at the Australian National University for enabling me to enjoy a most productive two months there in January to February 1990.

It was a pleasure to work on Christina Stead's papers in the manuscripts and archives room of the National Library of Australia in Canberra, and I thank Marlene Bonny, Elizabeth Penc, Graeme Powell and Pam Ray for their friendly helpfulness and efficiency.

I thank the Estate of Christina Stead, Harcourt Brace and Co., Henry Holt and Co., Martin Secker & Warburg Ltd, Random House Ltd and Virago Press Ltd for permission to print material from Christina Stead's novels. Angus & Robertson are to be thanked for permission to include material from *Seven Poor Men of Sydney*, *For Love Alone*, *House of All Nations*, *The Salzburg Tales* and *Letty Fox*. I thank Penguin Books Australia for permission to use extracts from *Oceans of Story*.

For their valuable assistance and for permission to quote material from their collections, I thank the following institutions and their librarians: Baillieu Library, University of Melbourne; La Trobe Library, State Library of Victoria; Fisher Library, University of Sydney; Aufbauverlag papers, Berlin; Special Collections, Boston University, Massachusetts; Bancroft Library, University of California; Irene Stevens at the Australia Council; the Australian Archives in Canberra; the Australian Conservation Foundation; the Berg Collection in the New York Public Library; Jean Rose at the Reed Consumer Books Library, Rushden, Northants; Michael Bott for photocopying the Secker & Warburg papers, Archives and Manuscripts, Reading University Library; Bernard Crystal in the Rare Book and Manuscript Library, Butler Library, Columbia University; the Harry Ransom Humanities Research Center, University of

Texas at Austin; the State Archives of New South Wales; the Mitchell Library, Sydney; the Yale University Library, New Haven, Connecticut; the Mugar Memorial Library at Boston University; Jim Fletcher, Historical Research Officer in the Department of Education, New South Wales; Sydney Teachers' College; the John Simon Guggenheim Memorial Foundation; the William Morris Agency, New York; the Federal Bureau of Investigation, US Department of Justice, Washington.

I thank Marian Wood at Henry Holt and Co., New York; Brenda Taylor at Little, Brown & Co., Boston; Bryan Unwin, Deputy Registrar of the Australian National University for access to the Creative Arts Fellowship files; Joan Wood at the Community Library in Hawks Nest; the *New York Times* for placing an advertisement at short notice which resulted in several useful contacts. Margaret Harris, another Stead scholar, has shared her research findings most generously.

I think fondly of the afternoon of 15 February 1986, when I was walking on Phillip Island with Bruce Coram. He convinced me to take on a project that then seemed too difficult. I am indebted to Damien Broderick for encouraging me to dance across the page. And I particularly want to thank Lynn Buchanan, Peter Christoff and Margaret Munro Clark, who read through my manuscript at different stages, and offered comments and suggestions from which I have greatly profited.

I thank my parents, Derrick and Betty Rowley, for their support and encouragement. And I am grateful to Bill and Nettie McGrath for generously allowing me the use of their house in the south of France while I did research for a month in 1988.

Most of all, I feel deep gratitude to Ann Timoney Jenkin, who has read three complete drafts of the book, and seen it—and me— develop and change along the way. She has provided that sustained, concentrated and altruistic editorial assistance that writers rarely find. We discussed biographical strategies; she encouraged me to take off my restrictive academic boots. From another city, she spurred me on in bleak moments and rejoiced in my good fortunes.

Index

Bold type has been used to indicate
entries for photographs.